W9-DHF-207

PROVENCE &
THE FRENCH RIVIERA

Rick Steves & Steve Smith

CONTENTS

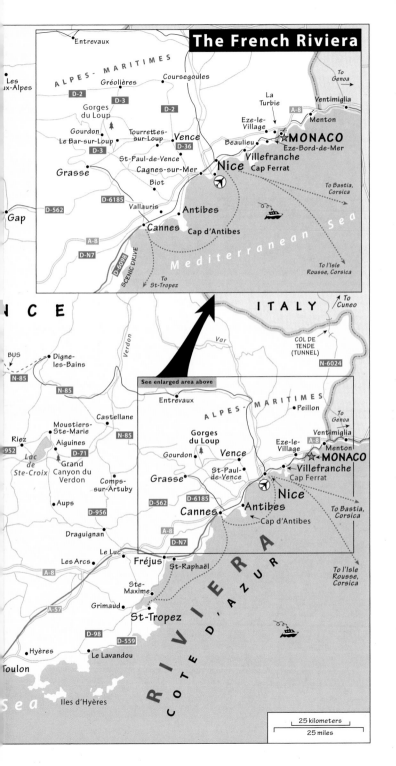

The French Riviera

Enlarged area (top map):

Entrevaux

ALPES - MARITIMES

Les
ux-Alpes

Gréolières
Coursegoules

D-2
D-3
D-2

Gorges
du Loup

La Turbie

To Genoa

Ventimiglia

A-8

Menton

Gourdon
Le Bar-sur-Loup
Tourrettes-sur-Loup
Vence

Eze-le-Village

D-3
D-36

MONACO
Eze-Bord-de-Mer

St-Paul-de-Vence
Cagnes-sur-Mer

Beaulieu

Villefranche

Grasse

Nice

Cap Ferrat

Biot

D-562
D-6185

To Bastia, Corsica

Vallauris

Gap

A-8

Antibes

D-N7

Cannes

Cap d'Antibes

D-6098
SCENIC DRIVE

Mediterranean Sea

To St-Tropez

To l'Isle Rousse, Corsica

N
I
C
E

ITALY

To Cuneo

BUS

Digne-les-Bains

N-85

Verdon

Var

COL DE TENDE (TUNNEL)

N-6024

N-85

See enlarged area above

Entrevaux

ALPES - MARITIMES

Peillon

To Genoa

Moustiers-Ste-Marie
Castellane

N-85

Gorges du Loup

Eze-le-Village

Ventimiglia

A-8

Menton

Riez

Aiguines

D-71

Gourdon

Vence

MONACO

Lac de Ste-Croix

Grand Canyon du Verdon

Comps-sur-Artuby

St-Paul-de-Vence

Villefranche

Cap Ferrat

Grasse

Nice

Aups

D-562

D-6185

Antibes

To Bastia, Corsica

D-956

Cannes

Cap d'Antibes

Draguignan

A-8

D-N7

Le Luc

Fréjus

St-Raphaël

R
I
V
I
E
R
A

Les Arcs

A-8

A-57

Ste-Maxime

C
Ô
T
E

D
'
A
Z
U
R

To l'Isle Rousse, Corsica

Grimaud

St-Tropez

D-98

D-559

Hyères

Le Lavandou

Toulon

Sea

Iles d'Hyères

25 kilometers

25 miles

A sun-dappled café in the Luberon

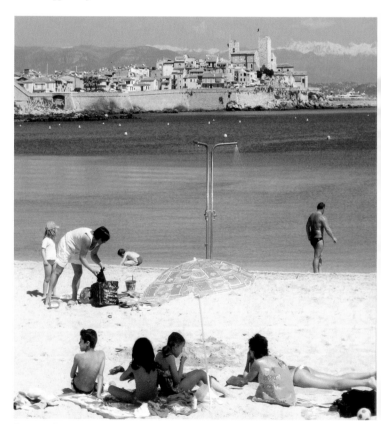

Summer beach scene in Antibes

Nice's old port

Market day in Provence

Roussillon huddling atop its ochre cliffs

Rick Steves

PROVENCE &
THE FRENCH RIVIERA

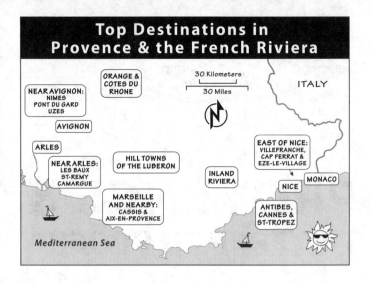

Top Destinations in Provence & the French Riviera

ORANGE & COTES DU RHONE

NEAR AVIGNON: NIMES PONT DU GARD UZES

AVIGNON

ARLES

NEAR ARLES: LES BAUX ST-REMY CAMARGUE

HILL TOWNS OF THE LUBERON

MARSEILLE AND NEARBY: CASSIS & AIX-EN-PROVENCE

INLAND RIVIERA

EAST OF NICE: VILLEFRANCHE, CAP FERRAT & EZE-LE-VILLAGE

NICE

MONACO

ANTIBES, CANNES & ST-TROPEZ

ITALY

30 Kilometers
30 Miles

Mediterranean Sea

INTRODUCTION

Provence and the French Riviera are an intoxicating bouillabaisse of enjoyable cities, warm stone villages, Roman ruins, contemporary art, and breathtaking coastlines steaming with sunshine and stirred by the wind. There's something about the play of light in this region, where natural and man-made beauty mingle to dazzle the senses and nourish the soul. It all adds up to *une magnifique* vacation.

Provence and the Riviera stretch along France's southeast Mediterranean coast from the Camargue (south of Arles) to Monaco, and ramble north along the Rhône Valley into the Alps. The regions combined are about the same size as Massachusetts—you can take a train or drive from one end to the other in just three hours—yet they contain more sightseeing opportunities and let's-live-here villages than anywhere else in France. Marseille and Nice, the country's second- and fifth-largest cities, provide good transportation and an urban perspective to this otherwise laid-back region, where every day feels like Sunday.

In Provence, gnarled sycamores line the roads that twist their way through stone towns and between oceans of vineyards. France's Riviera is about the sea and money—it's populated by a yacht-happy crowd wondering where the next "scene" will be. Provence feels older and more *español* (with paella on menus and bullfights on Sundays), while the Riviera feels downright Italian—with fresh-Parmesan-topped pasta and red-orange, pastel-colored buildings. For every Roman ruin in Provence, there's a modern-art museum in the Riviera. Provence is famous for its wines and wind, while the bikini and ravioli were conceived on the Riviera. You can't go wrong.

This book covers the predictable biggies, from jet-setting beach resorts to famous museums, but it also mixes in a healthy

INTRODUCTION

Provence & the French Riviera

dose of Back Door intimacy. Along with Pont du Gard, Nice, and Avignon, we'll introduce you to our favorite villages and scenic walks. You'll marvel at ancient monuments, take a canoe trip down the meandering Sorgue River, and settle into a shaded café on a made-for-movies square. Claim your favorite beach to call home, and at day's end dive headfirst into a southern France sunset. You'll enjoy tasty-yet-affordable wines while feasting on a healthy cuisine that's heavy on olives, tomatoes, and spices.

This book is selective, including only the most exciting sights and romantic villages. There are *beaucoup de* Provençal hill towns... but we cover only the most intriguing. And though there are scads of beach towns on the Riviera, we recommend our favorite three.

The best is, of course, only our opinion. But after spending more than half of our adult lives writing and lecturing about travel, guiding tours, and gaining an appreciation for all things French, we've developed a sixth sense for what touches the traveler's imagination.

ABOUT THIS BOOK

Rick Steves Provence & the French Riviera is a personal tour guide in your pocket. Better yet, it's actually two tour guides in your pocket: The co-author of this book is Steve Smith. Steve, who has lived in France several times, now travels there annually (as he has since 1986) as a guide, a researcher, a homeowner, and a devout Francophile. He has restored an old farmhouse in Burgundy and today keeps one foot on each side of the Atlantic. Together, Steve and I keep this book up-to-date and accurate (though for simplicity, from this point "we" will shed our respective egos and become "I").

This book is organized by destinations. Each is a mini-vacation on its own, filled with exciting sights, strollable neighborhoods, af-

Provence & the French Riviera Almanac

Official Name: Provence and the French Riviera are part of the Provence-Alpes-Côte-d'Azur (PACA), one of 27 administrative regions of France.

Capital: Marseille is the region's capital city.

Regional Population: Over 4.9 million.

Main Cities: Marseille (851,000), Nice (344,000), Aix-en-Provence (140,000), Avignon (90,000), Antibes (75,000), Cannes (73,000), Arles (52,000), St-Tropez (5,600).

Language: French is the official language. More than 1.5 million people in the south of France speak one of two lesser-known dialects: Occitan, and specifically in the Provence region, Provençal (both dialects are closely related to Catalan, a dialect of Spanish).

Geography: Located in the southeast of France, the Provence-Alpes-Côte-d'Azur region spans over 71 miles of Mediterranean coastline, from Marseille and Toulon in the west, to Monaco and the Italian border in the east, where the Alps stretch to the north.

Climate: The Hautes-Alpes and Rhône-Alpes shield the region from severe weather and give Provence and the Riviera the highest average temperatures in France (a comfortable 72° F in summer, and around 43° F in winter). Locals enjoy more than 300 days of sun per year, but experience more storms (70-110 per year) than other parts of France.

Economy: The Provence-Alpes-Côte-d'Azur region is the third wealthiest in France and annually contributes nearly $158 billion (7%) to France's GDP. Tourism and service industries account for 80 percent of jobs, but the region is also a leading center for agriculture, biotechnology, and microelectronics.

fordable places to stay, and memorable places to eat. The content consists of two obvious parts: Provence and the Riviera (although almost everything covered in this book is officially considered part of the "Provence-Alpes-Côte d'Azur region" by the French government). The Provence half highlights Arles, Nîmes, and Avignon, and their day-trip destinations; the photogenic hill towns of the Côtes du Rhône and Luberon; and the coastal towns of Marseille and Cassis, and nearby Aix-en-Provence. On the high-rolling French Riviera, I cover the waterfront destinations of Nice, Villefranche-sur-Mer, Cap Ferrat, Monaco, Antibes, Cannes, and St-Tropez—plus the best of the inland hill towns and the truly grand Grand Canyon du Verdon.

The introductions to **Provence** and **The French Riviera** acquaint you with the history, cuisine, and wine of the places you'll be visiting, and give practical advice on what to see, how to get

Agriculture: Provence is known for its herbs (such as oregano, thyme, and rosemary), vegetables, and olive oil; and the region produces nearly two-thirds of France's olives. These ingredients, combined with elements of French, Spanish, and Italian cooking, make Provence's cuisine fresh, colorful, and flavorful.

Crafts: In the 17th century, Marseille began manufacturing expen-

sive and colorful printed linens called "Indiennes," inspired by fabrics imported from India. Though most traditional textile factories are closed today, Provence still produces cotton fabrics (scarves, shawls) using original "Indienne" techniques and featuring the local cicada *(cigale)* in their designs.

Tourism: The Provence-Alpes-Côte-d'Azur region welcomes over 34 million tourists every year. Celebrities and wealthy Brits have vacationed on the French Riviera since the 19th century (giving the Promenade des Anglais in Nice its name). Nowadays, the Riviera attracts more than just celebrities: More than 5 million tourists visit every summer, with Nice at the center of the tourist commotion.

Famous Residents: The rich and famous have homes throughout Provence and the Riviera, including actors Brigitte Bardot, Sean Connery, Mel Gibson, Brad Pitt, and Angelina Jolie; musicians Bono, Elton John, Tina Turner, Bill Wyman, and Rod Stewart; and billionaire Bill Gates.

around, and lots more. Don't overlook the valuable tips in these chapters.

In the destination chapters, you'll find these sections:

Planning Your Time suggests a schedule for how to best to use your limited time.

Orientation has specifics on public transportation, helpful hints, local tour options, easy-to-read maps, and tourist information.

Sights describes the top attractions and includes their cost and hours.

Self-Guided Walks help you explore these fascinating towns and places on foot: Avignon, Nîmes, Arles, Marseille, Aix-en-Provence, Les Baux, Isle-sur-la-Sorgue, Roussillon, Monaco, Antibes, Villefranche-sur-Mer, and Cannes. (A few in-depth walks and tours get their own chapters: a stroll along Nice's Promenade des Anglais, a walk through Vieux Nice, and a guided visit to the

INTRODUCTION

Map Legend

⊾ Viewpoint	🚲 Bike Rental/ Bike Route	⟟ Wine Tasting
⬆ Entrance	Ⓣ Taxi Stand	▭ Pedestrian Zone
⊕ Tourist Info	+🚃+ Tram & Stop	▭ Railway
🆆🅲 Restroom	Ⓑ Bus Stop	⋯ Ferry/Boat Route
⛫ Castle	🅿 Parking	✈ Airport
⛪ Church	Ⓡ RER Train	▮▮▮ Stairs
▪ Statue/Point of Interest	Ⓣ Tourist Train	⋅⋅⋅⋅ Walk/Tour Route
⬚ Park	Ⓑ Batobus Stop	− − − Trail
◎ Fountain	Ⓜ Métro Stop	

Use this legend to help you navigate the maps in this book.

Chagall Museum.) I also include **self-guided driving tours,** allowing you to explore the Côtes du Rhône wine road, the Grand Canyon du Verdon, and inland hill towns of the Riviera with the knowledge of a local.

Sleeping describes my favorite hotels, from good-value deals to cushy splurges.

Eating serves up a buffet of options, from inexpensive cafés to fancy restaurants.

Connections outlines your options for traveling to destinations by train and bus, plus route tips for drivers.

The book also includes detailed chapters on these key topics:

Traveling with Children offers general tips and destination-specific advice, like kid-friendly hotels and restaurants. Both co-authors have kids, and we've used our substantial experience traveling with children to improve this book. Our kids have greatly enriched our travels, and we hope the same will be true for you.

Shopping has suggestions for this region's best souvenirs and bargains. My longtime friendships with shopkeepers, local guides, and vintners have contributed greatly to the savvy shopping advice.

France: Past and Present gives you a quick overview of the country.

Practicalities is a traveler's tool kit, with my best tips about money, sightseeing, sleeping, eating, staying connected, and transportation (trains, buses, car rentals, driving, and flights).

The **appendix** has the nuts-and-bolts: useful phone numbers and websites, a holiday and festival list, recommended books and films, a climate chart, a handy packing checklist, and French survival phrases.

Browse through this book, choose your favorite destinations, and link them up. Then have a *très bon voyage!* Traveling like a tem-

Key to This Book

Updates

This book is updated regularly—but once you pin down Provence, it wiggles. For the latest, visit www.ricksteves.com/update. For a valuable list of reports and experiences—good and bad—from fellow travelers, check www.ricksteves.com/feedback.

Abbreviations and Times

I use the following symbols and abbreviations in this book:

Sights are rated:

▲▲▲	Don't miss
▲▲	Try hard to see
▲	Worthwhile if you can make it
No rating	Worth knowing about

Tourist information offices are abbreviated as **TI,** and bathrooms are **WC**s. To categorize accommodations, I use a **Sleep Code** (described on page 66).

Like Europe, this book uses the **24-hour clock.** It's the same through 12:00 noon, then keeps going: 13:00, 14:00, and so on. For anything over 12, subtract 12 and add p.m. (14:00 is 2:00 p.m.).

When giving **opening times,** I include both peak season and off-season hours if they differ. So, if a museum is listed as "May-Oct daily 9:00-16:00," it should be open from 9 a.m. until 4 p.m. from the first day of May until the last day of October (but expect exceptions).

For **transit** or **tour departures,** I first list the frequency, then the duration. So, a train connection listed as "2/hour, 1.5 hours" departs twice each hour and the journey lasts an hour and a half.

porary local, you'll get the absolute most out of every mile, minute, and dollar. As you visit places I know and love, I'm happy that you'll be meeting some of my favorite French people.

Planning

This section will help you get started planning your trip—with advice on trip costs, when to go, and what you should know before you take off.

TRAVEL SMART

Your trip to France is like a complex play—it's easier to follow and really appreciate on a second viewing. While no one does the same trip twice to gain that advantage, reading this book in its entirety before your trip accomplishes much the same thing.

Design an itinerary that enables you to visit sights at the best

INTRODUCTION

The Language Barrier and That French Attitude

You've probably heard that the French are "mean and cold and refuse to speak English." This is an out-of-date preconception left over from the days of Charles de Gaulle—and it's especially incorrect in this region. In these southern lands kissed by the sun and sea, you'll find your hosts more jovial and easygoing (like their Italian neighbors) than in the more serious north. Still, be reasonable in your expectations: Waiters are paid to be efficient, not chatty. And Provençal postal clerks are every bit as speedy, cheery, and multilingual as ours are back home.

The biggest mistake most Americans make when traveling in France is trying to do too much with limited time. This approach is a mistake in the bustling north, and a virtual sin in the laid-back south. Hurried, impatient travelers who miss the subtle pleasures of people-watching from a sun-dappled café often misinterpret French attitudes. By slowing your pace and making an effort to understand French culture by living it, you're far more likely to have a richer experience. With the five weeks of paid vacation and 35-hour work week that many French workers consider as nonnegotiable rights, your hosts can't fathom why anyone would rush through their vacation.

The French take great pride in their customs, clinging to the belief in their own cultural superiority despite the fact that they're no longer a world superpower. Let's face it: It's tough to keep on smiling when you've been crushed by a Big Mac, Mickey Moused by Disney, and drowned in Starbucks coffee. Your hosts are cold only if you decide to see them that way. Polite and formal, the French respect the fine points of culture and tradition. Here, strolling down the street with a big grin on your face and saying

possible times. Note holidays, specifics on sights, and days when sights are closed. To connect the dots smoothly, read the tips in Practicalities on taking trains and buses, or renting a car and driving. Designing a smart trip is a fun, doable, and worthwhile challenge.

Make your itinerary a mix of intense and relaxed stretches. To maximize rootedness, minimize one-night stands. It's worth taking a long drive after dinner (or a train ride with a dinner picnic) to get settled in a town for two nights. Every trip—and every traveler—needs slack time (laundry, picnics, people-watching, and so on). Pace yourself. Assume you will return.

Reread this book as you travel, and visit local tourist information offices (abbreviated as TI in this book). Upon arrival in a new town, lay the groundwork for a smooth departure; confirm the train, bus, or road you'll take when you leave.

Even with the best-planned itinerary, you'll need to be flexhello to strangers is a sign of senility, not friendliness (seriously). They think that Americans, though friendly, are hesitant to pursue more serious friendships. Recognize sincerity and look for kindness. Give them the benefit of the doubt.

Communication difficulties are exaggerated. To hurdle the language barrier, bring a small English/French dictionary, a phrase book (look for mine, which contains a dictionary and menu decoder), a menu reader (if you're a gourmet eater, get the pricey but thorough *A to Z of French Food, a French to English Dictionary of Culinary Terms,* by G. de Temmerman), and a good supply of patience (for a list of survival phrases, see page 543). In transactions, a small notepad and pen minimize misunderstandings about prices; have vendors write the price down.

Though many French people—especially those in the tourist trade, and in big cities—speak English, you'll get better treatment if you learn and use the French pleasantries. If you learn only five phrases, choose these: *bonjour* (good day), *pardon* (pardon me), *s'il vous plaît* (please), *merci* (thank you), and *au revoir* (goodbye). The French value politeness. Begin every encounter with *"Bonjour* (or *S'il vous plaît), madame* or *monsieur"* and end every encounter with *"Au revoir, madame* or *monsieur."*

The French are language perfectionists—they take their language (and other languages) seriously. Often they speak more English than they let on. This isn't a tourist-baiting tactic, but timidity on their part about speaking another language less than fluently. Start any conversation with, *"Bonjour, madame* or *monsieur. Parlez-vous anglais?"* and hope they speak more English than you speak French.

ible. Update your plans as you travel. Though I encourage you to disconnect from life back home and immerse yourself in the French experience, you can get online or call ahead to double-check tourist information, learn the latest on sights (special events, tour schedules, and so on), book tickets and tours, make reservations, reconfirm hotels, and research transportation connections.

Enjoy the friendliness of the French people. Connect with the culture. Learn a new French expression each day and practice it. Cheer for your favorite bowler at a *boules* match, leave no chair unturned in your quest for the best café, find that perfect hill-town view, and make friends with a waiter (it happens). Slow down and be open to unexpected experiences. Ask questions—most locals are eager to point you in their idea of the right direction. Keep a notepad in your pocket for noting directions, organizing your thoughts, and confirming prices. Wear your money belt, learn the currency,

Provence and the French Riviera at a Glance

Destinations are listed in the order they appear in this book.

Provence

▲▲▲**Arles** Once-important Roman outpost, now a bustling town famous for its market days, ancient amphitheater, and as a site that inspired Vincent van Gogh.

▲▲**Near Arles** Several compelling sights: the cliff-topping castle ruins at Les Baux; St-Rémy with Roman ruins and a mental hospital that treated Van Gogh; and the Camargue—a nature lover's refuge, with flamingos, bulls, and white horses.

▲**Avignon** Fourteenth-century residence of the popes, today a youthful city with atmospheric cafés, lively squares and pedestrian areas, and a famous broken bridge.

▲▲▲**Near Avignon** Three worthy destinations, including the stunning Pont du Gard aqueduct; thriving Nîmes, with world-class Roman monuments; and pedestrian-friendly Uzès, a refreshing break from power monuments and busy cities.

▲▲▲**Orange and the Côtes du Rhône** Starring Orange's remarkably intact Roman theater, plus the sunny Côtes du Rhône wine road, cozy villages, and fields of lavender, anchored by charming Vaison-la-Romaine.

▲▲**Hill Towns of the Luberon** Boasting crumbled castles, ocher canyons, and meditative abbeys; the sturdy market town of Isle-

and figure out how to estimate prices in dollars. Those who expect to travel smart, do.

TRIP COSTS

Five components make up your trip costs: airfare, surface transportation, room and board, sightseeing and entertainment, and shopping and miscellany.

Airfare: Nice is the handiest airport for Provence and the Riviera (Marseille is a good second choice). A basic round-trip flight from the US to Nice or Paris can cost, on average, about $1,000-2,000 total, depending on where you fly from and when (cheaper in winter). Smaller budget airlines may provide bargain service from Paris and other European cities to places such as Marseille, Toulouse, Avignon, and Montpellier (see "Flights" on page sur-la-Sorgue; and delightful rock-top villages like Roussillon, Lacoste, and Ménerbes.

▲▲**Marseille and Nearby** Photogenic port of Marseille with a gritty charm; the coastal town of Cassis, home of the *calanques* (Mediterranean fjords); and inland, genteel Aix-en-Provence.

The French Riviera

▲▲▲**Nice** The Riviera's metropolis, with a sun-drenched promenade, a delightful French-Italian old city, and museums dedicated to Chagall and Matisse.

▲▲▲**East of Nice** Small, Italianate beach town of Villefranche-sur-Mer, ritzy but woodsy Cap Ferrat, and little cliff-topping Eze-le-Village—linked by the panoramic roads known as the Three Corniches.

▲▲**Monaco** Tiny independent principality, known for its Grand Prix car race and classy casino.

▲**Antibes, Cannes, and St-Tropez** The Riviera's west: laid-back Antibes, with a medieval old town and Picasso Museum; glamorous Cannes, with sandy beaches and movie stars; and the luxurious port town of St-Tropez.

▲▲**Inland Riviera** Perfectly perched hill towns of Vence and St-Paul-de-Vence (France's most-visited village), the perfume capital of Grasse, and the spectacular Grand Canyon du Verdon.

529 for details). If your trip covers a wide area, consider saving time and money in Europe by flying into one city and out of another—for instance, into Nice and out of Paris.

Surface Transportation: Allow $30 per day per person for public transportation (trains, buses, and taxis). If you'll be renting a car, allow at least $230 per week, not including tolls, gas, and supplemental insurance. If you'll be keeping the car for three weeks or more, look into leasing, which can save you money on insurance and taxes for trips of this length. Car rentals (if four days or longer) and leases are cheapest if arranged from the US.

Rail passes only make sense if you are traveling to regions beyond Provence and the Riviera, as distances are short and point-to-point fares are reasonable. If traveling elsewhere in France or Europe, consider flying, as budget airlines are often cheaper than

Best Two-Week Trip of Provence & the French Riviera by Car

Day   Plan

1   **Fly into Nice.** Settle in at your hotel, then follow my self-guided walk along the Promenade des Anglais. Sleep in or near Nice.

2   **All Day in Nice.** Start the morning with my self-guided walk through Vieux Nice. Take time to smell the *fougasse* and sample *un café*. Spend your afternoon at one or more of Nice's fine museums. Have dinner on the beach. Sleep in or near Nice.

3   **Coastal Route to Monaco.** Take the train or bus to nearby Villefranche-sur-Mer, explore, and have lunch. Consider my recommended seaside walks in Cap Ferrat, or take the one-hour boat cruise from Nice's port. Spend the afternoon or evening in almost neighboring Monaco. Sleep in or near Nice.

4   **Inland Riviera.** Pick up your rental car as early as possible in Nice. Drive north to Vence or Grasse (you choose), then continue on to the Gorges du Verdon and sleep in tiny Aiguines or Moustiers-Ste-Marie.

5   **Drive to Provence.** Continue west into the Luberon and explore the villages of the Provençal heartland—*la Provence profonde*. Stay in or near Roussillon.

6   **Luberon Hill Towns.** Spend your day sampling hill towns in the Luberon. Taste a village market, then drive over the hills to the valley of the Côtes du Rhône. Sleep in or near Vaison-la-Romaine (Mon arrival is ideal because market day is Tue).
From late June to late July, when the lavender blooms, the drive to Vaison-la-Romaine via Sault is a must.

7   **Côtes du Rhône Villages.** Explore Vaison-la-Romaine's upper medieval village and lower Roman city. Set sail along the Côtes du Rhône wine road (following my self-guided driving tour) and visit a winery or wine cooperative. Tour little Crestet and take a walk above Gigondas. Sleep in or near Vaison-la-Romaine.

8   **Orange and Châteauneuf-du-Pape.** Start your day touring the Roman theater in Orange and consider a quick stop in Châteauneuf-du-Pape. Continue south and set up in Avignon. In the afternoon, take my self-guided Avignon

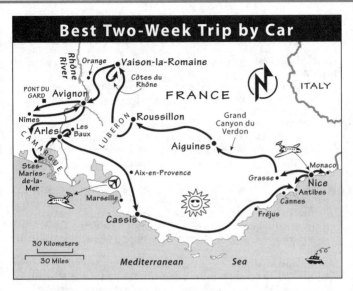

Best Two-Week Trip by Car

walks and enjoy dinner on one of the town's many atmospheric squares. Sleep in Avignon.

9 **Nîmes and Pont du Gard.** Spend the day visiting Nîmes (Roman amphitheater) and Pont du Gard (Nîmes works better first). If the weather's good, bring your swimsuit and float on your back for views of the 2,000-year-old aqueduct. Sleep in Avignon.

10 **The Camargue.** Take a joyride through the Camargue (but if it's summer, when flamingos are scarce and mosquitoes aren't, skip it and visit Les Baux instead). Wind up in Arles (big Saturday morning market). Sleep in Arles.

11 **All Day in and near Arles.** Spend most of your day in Arles. Drive to Les Baux for late afternoon sightseeing and dinner. Sleep in Arles.

12 **Aix-en-Provence or Marseille.** Drive to Cassis, stopping for lunch and a midday visit to Aix-en-Provence or Marseille (Marseille is dicier by car). Set up in Cassis and watch the sun set from the old port while you savor a bouillabaisse dinner. Sleep in Cassis.

13 **All Day in Cassis.** Spend all day in Cassis enjoying *la vie douce*. Take a boat trip or hike to the *calanques*, watch the *pétanque* balls fly, and end your day with a drive up Cap Canaille. Sleep in Cassis.

14 **Fly Away.** Fly out of Marseille today or, if leaving from Nice, drive to Antibes and spend your final day and evening there.

15 **Trip over.**

INTRODUCTION

Best Two-Week Trip of Provence & the French Riviera by Train and Bus

Note that on Sundays, fewer trains run, and buses often disappear.

Day	Plan
1	**Fly into Nice.** Settle in at your hotel, then follow my self-guided walk along the Promenade des Anglais. Sleep in or near Nice.
2	**All Day in Nice**. Start the morning with my self-guided walk through Vieux Nice. Take time to smell the *fougasse* and sample *un café*. Spend your afternoon at one or more of Nice's fine museums. Have dinner on the beach. Sleep in or near Nice.
3	**Coastal Route to Monaco.** Take the train or bus to nearby Villefranche-sur-Mer, explore, and have lunch. Consider my recommended seaside walks in Cap Ferrat, or take the one-hour boat cruise from Nice's port. Spend the afternoon or evening in (almost) neighboring Monaco. Sleep in or near Nice.
4	**Inland Villages.** Take a bus north to Vence and St-Paul-de-Vence. Stop for a stroll and visit the Fondation Maeght and/or Matisse's Chapel of the Rosary. Or link Vence with Grasse by bus (skipping St-Paul-de-Vence to save time). Sleep in Vence or back in Nice.
5	**Isle-sur-la-Sorgue.** Take a train from Nice to Isle-sur-la-Sorgue via Marseille (best to arrive on Sat or Wed and awaken the next morning for market day). Wander and explore the town. Consider a canoe ride down the crystal-clear Sorgue River. Sleep in Isle-sur-la-Sorgue.
6	**Isle-sur-la-Sorgue and Avignon.** Enjoy market day this morning, then take a train to Avignon. Take my self-guided Avignon walks this afternoon and enjoy dinner on one of Avignon's many atmospheric squares. Sleep in Avignon.
7	**Day Trip to Nîmes and Pont du Gard.** Visit Nîmes (Roman amphitheater) in the morning and Pont du Gard in the afternoon. If the weather's good, bring your swimsuit and float on your back for views of the 2,000-year-old aqueduct. Have dinner and sleep back in Avignon.

taking the train. For more on public transportation, car rental, and flights, see "Transportation" in the Practicalities chapter.

Room and Board: You can thrive in Provence and the Riviera on $135 a day per person for room and board. This allows an average of $12 for breakfast, $18 for lunch, $40 for dinner with drinks, and $65 for lodging (based on two people splitting the cost of a $130 double room). Students and tightwads can enjoy Provence and the Riviera for as little as $60 a day ($30 per bed, $30 for meals and snacks).

Sightseeing and Entertainment: Figure about $10 per major

8   **Vaison-la-Romaine.** Take a direct bus to Vaison-la-Romaine (1/day); otherwise, ride a morning train to Orange (frequent departures), then connect to a less frequent bus to Vaison-la-Romaine (market day is Tue, so a Mon arrival is ideal). Set up in Vaison-la-Romaine for two nights. Explore the town's upper medieval village and lower Roman city this afternoon.

9   **Côtes du Rhône Villages.** Get to a wine village near Vaison-la-Romaine. Take a minivan tour of the wine road (see "Tours in Provence" on page 26), bike to Séguret and Gigondas, or hike to Crestet for lunch (taxi back). Sleep in Vaison-la-Romaine.

10   **Orange and Arles.** Take a morning bus back to Orange, visit the Roman theater, then hop a train to Arles (big Sat morning market) and explore the city this afternoon. Check into Arles for the next two nights.

11   **Les Baux and Arles.** Take a minivan tour or a taxi (or, in summer, a bus) to Les Baux and have breakfast with a view. Return to Arles by taxi or bus (minivan tours will probably include other destinations), and spend your afternoon there; or take a taxi from Les Baux to St-Rémy, explore there, then catch a bus back to Arles.

12   **Marseille, then Cassis.** Hop the train to Marseille, check your bags at the station, and take my walking tour of the ancient center. End your day in Cassis and watch the sunset from the old port while you savor a bouillabaisse dinner. Sleep in Cassis.

13   **Cassis.** Spend all day in Cassis enjoying *la vie douce.* Take a boat trip or hike to the *calanques,* then watch the *pétanque* balls fly. Sleep in Cassis.

14   **Fly Away.** Fly out of nearby Marseille or, if leaving from Nice, take a train back to Nice and savor a last night on the Promenade des Anglais. Sleep in Nice.

15   **Trip over.**

sight (Arles' Roman Arena-$9, Nice's Chagall Museum-$9, Avignon's Palace of the Popes-$13), around $6 for minor ones (e.g., climbing church towers), $30 for guided walks, and $40-70 for splurge experiences (such as bullfights or concerts). An overall average of $25 a day works for most people. Don't skimp here. After all, this category is the driving force behind your trip—you came to sightsee, enjoy, and experience this wonderfully French region.

Shopping and Miscellany: Figure $4 per ice-cream cone, café au lait, or soft drink. Shopping can vary in cost from nearly nothing to a small fortune. Good budget travelers find that this category has little to do with assembling a trip full of lifelong memories.

SIGHTSEEING PRIORITIES

So much to see, so little time. How to choose? Depending on the length of your trip, and taking geographic proximity into account, here are my recommended priorities:

6 days:	Arles and day trips to Pont du Gard and Les Baux, a night in a Côtes du Rhône village, and Nice with a day trip to Monaco
9 days, add:	Avignon and Cassis
12 days, add:	Luberon, Grand Canyon du Verdon, and Antibes
14 days, add:	Nîmes, Marseille, Aix-en-Provence, and the Camargue

This includes nearly everything on the map on page 13. If you don't have time to see it all, prioritize according to your interests. The "Provence and the Riviera at a Glance" sidebar can help you decide where to go (page 10). For a day-by-day itinerary of a two-week trip, see this chapter's two recommended routes (by car, and by train and bus).

WHEN TO GO

With more than 300 days of sunshine per year, Provence and the Riviera enjoy France's sunniest weather. Spring and fall are best, with generally comfortable weather—though crowds can be a problem, particularly during holiday weekends and major events (May is worst). April can be damp, and any month can be windy.

Summer means festivals, lavender, steamy weather, long hours at sights, and longer lines of cars along the Riviera. Europeans vacation in July and August, jamming the Riviera, the Gorges du Verdon, and Ardèche (worst from mid-July through mid-Aug), but leaving the rest of this region relatively calm. Though many French businesses close in August, the traveler hardly notices.

September brings the grape harvest, when small wineries are off-limits to taste-seeking travelers (for information on wine tasting, see page 34). Late fall delivers beautiful foliage and a return to tranquility.

Although you can find mild, sunny weather in any season, Provence is famous for its bone-chilling temperatures when the wind blows (see page 171). Winter travel is OK in Nice, Aix-en-Provence, and Avignon, but you'll find smaller cities and villages buttoned up tight. Sights and tourist-information offices keep shorter hours, and some tourist activities (such as English-language castle tours) vanish altogether.

Rick Steves Audio Europe

My **Rick Steves Audio Europe app** makes it easy to download audio content to enhance your trip. It includes my audio tours of many of Europe's top destinations, as well as a far-reaching library of insightful travel interviews from my public radio show with experts from around the globe—including many of the places in this book. The app and all of its content are entirely free. You can download Rick Steves Audio Europe via Apple's App Store, Google Play, or the Amazon Appstore. For more information, see www.ricksteves.com/audioeurope.

Thanks to Provence's temperate climate, fields of flowers greet the traveler much of the year:

May: Wild red poppies *(coquelicots)* sprout.

June: Lavender begins to bloom in the lower hills of Provence, generally during the last week of the month.

July: Lavender is in full swing in Provence, and sunflowers are awakening. If you can find adjacent fields with lavender and sunflowers, celebrate! Cities, towns, and villages everywhere overflow with carefully tended flowers.

August-September: Sunflowers flourish.

October: In the latter half of the month, the countryside glistens with fall colors (most trees are deciduous). Vineyards go for the gold.

KNOW BEFORE YOU GO

Check this list of things to arrange while you're still at home.

You need a **passport**—but no visa or shots—to travel in France. You may be denied entry into certain European countries if your passport is due to expire within three months of your ticketed date of return. Get it renewed if you'll be cutting it close. It can take up to six weeks to get or renew a passport (for more on passports, see www.travel.state.gov). Pack a photocopy of your passport in your luggage in case the original is lost or stolen.

Book rooms well in advance if you'll be traveling during peak season (spring, summer, and September) or any major holidays (see page 534).

Call your **debit- and credit-card companies** to let them know the countries you'll be visiting, to ask about fees, request your PIN code (it will be mailed to you), and more. See page 472 for details.

Do your homework if you want to buy **travel insurance.** Compare the cost of the insurance to the cost of your potential loss.

How Was Your Trip?

Were your travels fun, smooth, and meaningful? If you'd like to share your tips, concerns, and discoveries, please fill out the survey at www.ricksteves.com/feedback. To check out readers' hotel and restaurant reviews—or leave one yourself—visit my travel forum at www.ricksteves.com/travel-forum. I value your feedback. Thanks in advance.

Also, check whether your existing insurance (health, homeowners, or renters) covers you and your possessions overseas. For more tips, see www.ricksteves.com/insurance.

Consider buying a **rail pass** after researching your options. This likely only makes sense if Provence is part of a larger trip (see page 511 and www.ricksteves.com/rail for specifics).

All **high-speed trains** (TGVs) in France require a seat reservation; book as early as possible, as these trains fill fast, and some routes use TGV trains almost exclusively. If you're using a rail pass, book even earlier—there's a tight limit on seat reservations for passholders. Traveling between Marseille and Nice can be tricky (most trains are TGV), so think about reserving that trip ahead. If you're taking an overnight train (especially to international destinations), and you need a *couchette* (overnight bunk) or sleeper—and you *must* leave on a certain day—consider booking it in advance through a US agent (such as www.raileurope.com), even though it may cost more. (For more on train travel, see the Practicalities chapter.)

If you want to hire a **local guide,** reserve ahead by email. Popular guides can get booked up.

If you're bringing a **mobile device,** consider signing up for an international plan for cheaper calls, texts, and data (see page 503). Download any apps you might want to use on the road, such as translators, maps, transit schedules, and **Rick Steves Audio Europe** (see page 17).

If you'll be **traveling with children,** read over the list of pre-trip suggestions on page 445.

Traveling as a Temporary Local

We travel all the way to France to enjoy differences—to become temporary locals. You'll experience frustrations. Certain truths that we find "God-given" or "self-evident," such as cold beer, ice in drinks, bottomless cups of coffee, "the customer is king," and bigger being better, are suddenly not so true. One of the benefits of travel is the eye-opening realization that there are logical, civil, and even better alternatives.

With a history rich in human achievement, France is an understandably proud country. To enjoy its people, you need to celebrate the differences. A willingness to go local ensures that you'll enjoy a full dose of French hospitality.

Europeans generally like Americans. But if there is a negative aspect to the French image of Americans, it's that we are loud, wasteful, ethnocentric, too informal (which can seem disrespectful), and a bit naive.

The French (and Europeans in general) place a high value on speaking quietly in restaurants and on trains. Listen while on the bus or in a restaurant—the place can be packed, but the decibel level is low. Try to adjust your volume accordingly to show respect for the culture.

While the French look bemusedly at some of our Yankee excesses—and worriedly at others—they nearly always afford us individual travelers all the warmth we deserve.

Judging from all the happy feedback I receive from travelers who have used this book, it's safe to assume you'll enjoy a great, affordable vacation—with the finesse of an independent, experienced traveler.

Thanks, and *bon voyage!*

Back Door Travel Philosophy

From *Rick Steves Europe Through the Back Door*

Travel is intensified living—maximum thrills per minute and one of the last great sources of legal adventure. Travel is freedom. It's recess, and we need it.

Experiencing the real Europe requires catching it by surprise, going casual..."Through the Back Door."

Affording travel is a matter of priorities. (Make do with the old car.) You can eat and sleep—simply and safely—anywhere in Europe for $100 a day plus transportation costs. In many ways, spending more money only builds a thicker wall between you and what you traveled so far to see. Europe is a cultural carnival, and time after time, you'll find that its best acts are free and the best seats are the cheap ones.

A tight budget forces you to travel close to the ground, meeting and communicating with the people. Never sacrifice sleep, nutrition, safety, or cleanliness to save money. Simply enjoy the local-style alternatives to expensive hotels and restaurants.

Connecting with people carbonates your experience. Extroverts have more fun. If your trip is low on magic moments, kick yourself and make things happen. If you don't enjoy a place, maybe you don't know enough about it. Seek the truth. Recognize tourist traps. Give a culture the benefit of your open mind. See things as different, but not better or worse. Any culture has plenty to share. When an opportunity presents itself, make it a habit to say "yes."

Of course, travel, like the world, is a series of hills and valleys. Be fanatically positive and militantly optimistic. If something's not to your liking, change your liking.

Travel can make you a happier American, as well as a citizen of the world. Our Earth is home to seven billion equally precious people. It's humbling to travel and find that other people don't have the "American Dream"—they have their own dreams. Europeans like us, but with all due respect, they wouldn't trade passports.

Thoughtful travel engages us with the world. It reminds us what is truly important. By broadening perspectives, travel teaches new ways to measure quality of life.

Globetrotting destroys ethnocentricity, helping us understand and appreciate other cultures. Rather than fear the diversity on this planet, celebrate it. Among your most prized souvenirs will be the strands of different cultures you choose to knit into your own character. The world is a cultural yarn shop, and Back Door travelers are weaving the ultimate tapestry. Join in!

PROVENCE

PROVENCE

"There are treasures to carry away in this land, which has not found a spokesman worthy of the riches it offers."
—Paul Cézanne

This magnificent region is shaped like a giant wedge of quiche. From its sunburned crust, fanning out along the Mediterranean coast from the Camargue to Marseille, it stretches north along the Rhône Valley to Orange. The Romans were here in force and left many ruins—some of the best anywhere. Seven popes, artists such as Vincent van Gogh and Paul Cézanne, and author Peter Mayle all enjoyed their years in Provence. This destination features a splendid recipe of arid climate, oceans of vineyards, dramatic scenery, lively cities, and adorable hill-capping villages.

Explore the ghost town that is ancient Les Baux, and see France's greatest Roman ruins, the Pont du Gard aqueduct and the theater in Orange. Admire the skill of ball-tossing *boules* players in small squares in every Provençal village and city. Spend a few Van Gogh-inspired starry, starry nights in Arles. Youthful but classy Avignon bustles in the shadow of its brooding Palace of the Popes. Stylish and self-confident Aix-en-Provence lies 30 minutes from the sea and feels more Mediterranean. It's a short hop from Arles or Avignon into the splendid scenery and villages of the Côtes du Rhône and Luberon regions. To properly understand southern France, day-trip into gritty Marseille, and if you prefer a Provençal beach fix, find Cassis, just east of Marseille.

CHOOSING A HOME BASE
With limited time, make Arles or Avignon your sightseeing base—particularly if you have no car. Italophiles prefer smaller Arles,

Provence

To Lyon & Burgundy
Ardèche
Ardèches Gorges
Bollène
Rhône
St. Cécile
Rasteau
Sablet
Séguret
Gigondas
Orange
Vacqueyras
Suzette
Beaumes de Venise
Malaucène
Châteauneuf-du-Pape
Grignan
Valréas
Nyons
Buis-les-Baronnies
To Chamonix & Alps
Vaison-la-Romaine
Dentelles de Montmirail
Mont Ventoux
Gard
To Gorges du Tarn
Uzès
PONT DU GARD
Remoulins
Avignon
Isle-sur-la-Sorgue
Gordes
Joucas
Roussillon
Apt
Oppède
Cavaillon
Nîmes
Beaucaire
Tarascon
Durance
Les Baux
St-Rémy
Fontvieille
Alpilles
LUBERON
Lourmarin
Pertuis
Aigues-Mortes
CAMARGUE
Rhône
Petit Rhône
Saintes-Maries-de-la-Mer
Aix-en-Provence
To Gorges du Verdon
Palette
Martigues
Marseille
To Nice & Côte d'Azur
Aubagne
Mediterranean Sea
Les Calanques
Cassis
20 Kilometers
20 Miles
Paris
FRANCE
100 Miles

PROVENCE

while poodles pick urban Avignon. Many enjoy nights in both cit-ies. (With a car, head for St-Rémy or the hill towns.)

Arles has a blue-collar quality; the entire city feels like Van Gogh's bedroom. It also has this region's best-value hotels and is handy to Les Baux, St-Rémy, and the Camargue.

Avignon—double the size of Arles—feels sophisticated, with more nightlife and shopping. Avignon makes a good base for non-drivers thanks to its convenient public-transit options (within an hour, you can reach Pont du Gard, Uzès, Nîmes, and St-Rémy by bus, or Marseille by train; within a half-hour, you can reach Arles, Isle-sur-la-Sorgue, and Aix-en-Provence by train).

Or, for drivers who prefer a smaller-town base, **St-Rémy-de-Provence** is manageable and central. It offers a nice range of hotels with free and easy parking, good restaurants, and a few sights of its own. The towns of **Vaison-la-Romaine** (in the Côtes du Rhône region) and **Roussillon** (in the Luberon) are two good but remote hill-town options.

Aix-en-Provence works well as a base for Provence sights east of Arles and Avignon, with easy access to Marseille, Cassis, and some Luberon villages. About halfway between Arles and Nice, Aix-en-Provence also makes a convenient stopover, and if you're flying in or out of Marseille, Aix has quick access to the airport, making it a convenient first- or last-day stop.

PLANNING YOUR TIME

The bare minimum you should spend in Provence is three days: one day for sightseeing in Arles and Les Baux (Arles is best on Wed or Sat, when it's market day); a day for Pont du Gard and Nîmes; and a full day for Orange and the Côtes du Rhône villages. Add two more days to explore Avignon; Uzès or St-Rémy; and more Provençal villages. Allow an additional two days in Cassis, using one of them for a day trip to Marseille or Aix-en-Provence (or both). Ideally, see the cities—Arles, Nîmes, Avignon, Aix-en-Provence, and Marseille—by train, then rent a car for the countryside.

To measure the pulse of rural Provence, spend at least a few nights in the smaller towns. Provençal villages come to life on market days, but can be quiet on Mondays—when shops are shuttered tight—and are terminally quiet from mid-October to Easter. I've described many towns in the Côtes du Rhône and Luberon. The Côtes du Rhône is ideal for wine connoisseurs and an easy stop for those heading to or from the north. The Luberon was made for hill-town lovers and works well for travelers heading east, toward Aix-en-Provence or the Riviera. Avoid speeding through these areas. Provençal village evenings are what books are written about—spend the night, or two, or...

The small port town of Cassis is a marvelous Mediterranean meander between Provence and the Riviera (and more appealing than most Riviera resorts). It has easy day-trip connections to Marseille and Aix-en-Provence.

Depending on the length of your trip, here are my recommended priorities for Provence:

4 days:	Arles and Les Baux; Pont du Gard and Nîmes; and Orange and Côtes du Rhône villages
5-6 days, add:	Cassis, Marseille, and Aix-en-Provence
7-8 days, add:	Luberon hill towns
9-10 days, add:	Avignon and either St-Rémy or Uzès

HELPFUL HINTS

Resources: Imagine Tours (near Avignon) offers free assistance to travelers. They can work with you to plan your itinerary, book hotels, or help you deal with problems that might arise during your trip (for contact information, see page 28).

Cruise-Ship Sightseeing: Cruise lines that visit Provence call at either Marseille or Toulon (about 40 miles east of Marseille; see page 246). Public-transit options are limited—with a short day, only Marseille, Cassis, and Aix-en-Provence are doable. (It's possible to visit Avignon or Arles from Marseille—but only with a long day in port.) To journey beyond the immediate area and/or connect several sights in one busy day, join a cruise-line excursion, hire a driver or guide (see "Tours in Provence," later), or rent a car. For in-depth coverage, consider my guidebook, *Rick Steves Mediterranean Cruise Ports*.

GETTING AROUND PROVENCE

By Bus or Train: Public transit is good between cities and decent to some towns, but marginal at best to the smaller villages. Frequent trains link Avignon, Arles, and Nîmes (no more than 30 minutes between each). Avignon has good train connections with Orange and adequate service to Isle-sur-la-Sorgue. Marseille is well-connected to all cities in Provence, with frequent service to Cassis (25 minutes) and Aix-en-Provence (45 minutes).

Buses connect many smaller towns, though service can be sporadic. From Arles you can catch a bus to Les Baux (high season only), Stes-Maries-de-la-Mer (in the Camargue), or St-Rémy. From Avignon, you can bus to Pont du Gard, St-Rémy, Uzès, Isle-sur-la-Sorgue (also by train), and to some Côtes du Rhône villages. St-Rémy, Isle-sur-la-Sorgue, and Uzès are the most accessible and interesting small towns. Vaison-la-Romaine—my favorite town—is a manageable bus ride from Orange (with fast and frequent train connections to Avignon). A visit here works well with a tour of Orange's Roman Theater.

While a tour of the villages of the Côtes du Rhône or Luberon is best on your own by car, a variety of minivan tours and basic bus excursions are available. (TIs in Arles and Avignon also have information on bus excursions to regional sights that are hard to reach *sans* car; see "Tours in Provence," later.)

By Car: The region is made to order for a car, though travel time between some sights will surprise you—thanks, in part, to narrow roads and endless roundabouts (for example, figure an hour from Les Baux to Pont du Gard, and two hours from Arles to Vaison-la-Romaine). Michelin map #527 (1:275,000 scale) covers this book perfectly. Michelin maps #332 (Luberon and Côtes du Rhône) and #340 (Arles area) are also worth considering. I've described key sights and a variety of full-day drives deep into the countryside. Be wary of thieves: Park only in well-monitored spaces and leave nothing valuable in your car.

Avignon (pop. 110,000) is a headache for drivers. Arles (pop. 52,000) is easier but still challenging. Les Baux and St-Rémy work well from Arles or Avignon (or vice versa). Nîmes and Pont du Gard are a short hop west of Avignon. The town of Orange ties in tidily with a trip to the Côtes du Rhône villages and with destinations farther north. If you're heading north from Provence, consider a half-day detour through the spectacular Ardèche Gorges (see page 186). The Luberon villages are about halfway between Arles or Avignon and Aix-en-Provence (little Lourmarin works as a base for day trips to Aix-en-Provence). And if you're continuing on to the Riviera, let yourself be lured into the Grand Canyon du Verdon detour (see the Inland Riviera chapter). Most drivers will prefer exploring congested Marseille on foot—take the train from Cassis or Aix-en-Provence (both towns have parking at their train stations with frequent trains and buses to the center of Marseille).

By Bike: Wind, heat, and hilly terrain make this region a challenge to bike. If you're determined, I list bike rental options in most cities (including electric bikes). Try Telecycles, which will deliver your bike to your hotel (tel. 04 90 92 83 15 or 06 11 64 04 69, www.telecycles-location.com).

TOURS IN PROVENCE

Towns with a lot of tourism generally have English-speaking guides available for private hire (about €130 for a 3-hour guided walk). It's also possible to take half-day or full-day excursions to most of the sights in Provence. TIs have wads of brochures on day trips and can help you make a reservation. Excursions are best from Avignon, where most tours can pick you up at your hotel, the TI, or at either of the city's train stations. Here are several good options to consider:

Tours with a Wine Focus
Wine Safari

Dutchman Mike Rijken runs a one-man show, taking travelers through the region he adopted more than 20 years ago. His English is fluent, and though his focus is on wine and wine villages, Mike knows the region thoroughly and is a good teacher of its history (€75/half-day, €130/day, priced per person, group size varies from 2 to 6; pickups possible in Arles, Avignon, Lyon, Marseille, or Aix-en-Provence; tel. 04 90 35 59 21, mobile 06 19 29 50 81, www.winesafari.net, mikeswinesafari@orange.fr).

Le Vin à la Bouche

Celine Viany, a wine *sommelier* and charming tour guide, is an easy-to-be-with expert on her region and its chief product (from €75/half-day per person, from €90/day for up to 6 people, tel. 04

Top 10 Provençal Towns and Villages

1. **Roussillon,** a beautiful hill town sitting atop a huge ochre deposit, giving it a red-rock appeal, popular with American tourists; see page 200.
2. **Uzès,** a chic town with manicured pedestrian streets, popular with European tourists; see page 143.
3. **Joucas,** an adorable little village where flowers and stones are lovingly maintained, a magnet for artists; see page 208.
4. **Brantes,** a spectacularly situated cliff village literally at the end of the road, with few tourists; see page 186.
5. **Vaison-la-Romaine,** a bustling midsize town that spans both sides of a river and has Roman ruins, popular with tourists; see page 160.
6. **Lourmarin,** a lovely upscale village, busy during the day but quiet at night; see page 223.
7. **Crestet,** an overlooked village with a sensational hilltop location and one commercial enterprise; see page 175.
8. **Séguret,** a linear hillside village with memorable views, many day-trippers, but few overnighters; see page 173.
9. **Gigondas,** a world-famous wine village with a nice balance of commercial activity and quiet; see page 181.
10. **Nyons,** an overlooked midsize town with a few pedestrian streets, famous for its olive oil and ideal climate; see page 185.

PROVENCE

90 46 90 80, mobile 06 76 59 56 30, www.levinalabouche.com, contact@degustation-levinalabouche.com).

Avignon Wine Tour
For a playful and distinctly French perspective on wines of the Côtes du Rhône region, contact François Marcou, who runs his tours with passion and energy (€110/person for all-day wine tours that include 4 tastings, €80/person for half-day tours, €350 for private groups, less in winter, mobile 06 28 05 33 84, www.avignon-wine-tour.com, avignon.wine.tour@modulonet.fr).

Wine Uncovered
Passionate Englishman Olivier Hickman takes small groups on focused tours of selected wineries in Châteauneuf-du-Pape and in the villages near Vaison-la-Romaine. Olivier knows his subject matter inside and out. His in-depth tastings include a half-day tour of two or three wineries (€35-70/person for half-day to full-day tours, prices subject to minimum tour fees, mobile 06 75 10 10 01, www.wine-uncovered.com, olivier.hickman@orange.fr).

Tours du Rhône

American Doug Graves, who owns a small wine *domaine* in the Côtes du Rhône, runs custom tours of Châteauneuf-du-Pape, the villages of the Côtes du Rhône, and the Luberon Valley (€125/day per person for up to 4 people, mobile 06 37 16 04 56, www.toursdurhone.com, doug@masdelalionne.com).

Winery Plus Tours

This company offers small group tours centered on wine and food with a good dose of history and local culture. Experienced guide, chef, and wine connoisseur Joe McLean's tours focus on the wines of Uzès, Châteauneuf-du-Pape, and the Côtes du Rhône (ask about his cooking classes). Pick-ups are possible in Uzès, Avignon, and Arles (per person: €60/half-day, €100/-day; tel. 06 73 08 23 97, www.promo-vinum.com/gb/winetours, info@promo-vinum.com).

Provence & Wine

Romain Gouvernet is a young and sincere wine guide concentrating on the Côtes du Rhône (per person: €95/half-day, €140/day; tel. 06 86 49 56 76, www.provenceandwine.com, provenceandwine@gmail.com).

Cultural/Historical Tours
Imagine Tours

This organization focuses on cultural excursions, offering personalized tours that allow visitors to discover the "true heart of Provence and Occitania." The itineraries are adapted to your interests, and the guides will meet you at your hotel or the departure point of your choice (€190/half-day, €315/day, prices for up to 4 people starting from near Avignon or Arles, mobile 06 89 22 19 87, www.imagine-tours.net, imagine.tours@gmail.com). They can also help plan your itinerary, book hotel rooms, or address other travel issues.

Local Guide

Catherine d'Antuono is a smart, capable guide for Aix-en-Provence and other areas. She runs a small company with four guides leading private tours who can guide as far west as Pont du Gard and as far east as St-Tropez (€450/day for 2 people, add €15/person after that up to 8 maximum, mobile 06 17 94 69 61, tour.designer@provence-travel.com).

Discover Provence

Sarah Pernet—who was born in England but has lived in Aix-en-Provence for 15 years—works with a small team to offer enjoyable excursions within and from her adopted city, from walking tours in Aix to truffle-hunting in rural Provence (€120/half-day, €180/day, prices per person for up to 6 people, tel. 06 16 86 40 24, www.discover-provence.net, discoverprovence@hotmail.com).

Basic Transportation-only Tours
Visit Provence
This company runs day tours from Avignon, Arles, Marseille, and in Aix-en-Provence. Tours from Avignon run year-round and cover a great variety of destinations; tours from other cities run April through September only and are more limited in scope. While the tours provide introductory commentary, there's no guiding at the actual sights. They use eight-seat, air-conditioned minivans (about €60-80/half-day, €100-120/day). Ask about their cheaper big-bus excursions, or consider hiring a van and driver for your private use (plan on €220/half-day, €490/day, tel. 04 90 14 70 00, www. provence-reservation.com).

HOW ABOUT THEM ROMANS?
Provence is littered with Roman ruins. Many scholars claim the best-preserved ancient Roman buildings are not in Italy, but in France. These ancient stones will compose an important part of your sightseeing agenda in this region, so it's worth learning about how they came to be.

Classical Rome endured from about 500 b.c. through a.d. 500—spending about 500 years growing, 200 years peaking, and 300 years declining. Julius Caesar conquered Gaul—which included Provence—during the Gallic Wars (58-51 b.c.), then crossed the Rubicon River in 49 b.c. to incite civil war within the Roman Republic. He erected a temple to Jupiter on the future site of Paris' Notre-Dame Cathedral.

The concept of one-man rule lived on with his grandnephew, Octavian (whom he had also adopted as his son). Octavian killed Brutus, eliminated his rivals (Mark Antony and Cleopatra), and united Rome's warring factions. He took the title "Augustus" and became the first in a line of emperors who would control Rome for the next 500 years—ruling like a king, with the backing of the army and the rubber-stamp approval of the Senate. Rome morphed from a Republic into an Empire: a collection of many diverse territories ruled by a single man.

Augustus' reign marked the start of 200 years of peace, prosperity, and expansion known as the *Pax Romana*. At its peak (c. a.d. 117), the Roman Empire had 54 million people and stretched from Scotland in the north to Egypt in the south, as far west as Spain and as far east as modern-day Iraq. To the northeast, Rome was bounded by the Rhine and Danube Rivers. On Roman maps, the Mediterranean was labeled *Mare Nostrum* ("Our Sea"). At its peak, "Rome" didn't just refer to the city, but to the entire civilized Western world.

The Romans were successful not only because they were good

PROVENCE

Top 10 Roman Sights in Provence

1. Pont du Gard aqueduct and its museum
2. Roman Theater in Orange
3. Maison Carrée in Nîmes
4. Ancient History Museum in Arles
5. Arena in Nîmes
6. Arena in Arles
7. Roman city of Glanum (in St-Rémy)
8. Ruined aqueduct near Fontvieille
9. Roman city of Vaison-la-Romaine
10. Julien Bridge (near Roussillon)

soldiers, but also because they were smart administrators and busi-nessmen. People in conquered territories knew they had joined the winning team and that political stability would replace barbarian invasions. Trade thrived. Conquered peoples were welcomed into the fold of prosperity, linked by roads, education, common laws and gods, and the Latin language.

Provence, with its strategic location, benefited greatly from Rome's global economy and grew to become an important part of its worldwide empire. After Julius Caesar conquered Gaul, Emperor Augustus set out to Romanize it, building and renovating cities in the image of Rome. Most cities had a theater (some had several), baths, and aqueducts; the most important cities had sports arenas. The Romans also erected an elaborate infrastructure of roads, post offices, schools (teaching in Latin), police stations, and water-supply systems.

With a standard language and currency, Roman merchants were able to trade wine, salt, and olive oil for foreign goods. The empire invested heavily in cities that were strategically important for trade. For example, the Roman-built city of Arles was a crucial link in the trade route from Italy to Spain, so they built a bridge across the Rhône River and fortified the town.

A typical Roman city (such as Nîmes, Arles, Orange, or Vai-son-la-Romaine) was a garrison town, laid out on a grid plan with two main roads: one running north-south (the *cardus*), the other east-west (the *decumanus*). Approaching the city on your chariot, you'd pass by the cemetery, which was located outside of town for hygienic reasons. You'd enter the main gate and speed past ware-houses and apartment houses to the town square (forum). Facing the square were the most important temples, dedicated to the patron gods of the city. Nearby, you'd find bathhouses; like today's fitness clubs, these served the almost sacred dedication to personal vigor. Also close by were businesses that catered to the citizens' needs: the marketplace, bakeries, banks, and brothels.

Aqueducts brought fresh water for drinking, filling the baths, and delighting the citizens with bubbling fountains. Men flocked to the stadiums in Arles and Nîmes to bet on gladiator games; eager couples attended elaborate plays at theaters in Orange, Arles, and Vaison-la-Romaine. Marketplaces brimmed with exotic fruits, vegetables, and animals from the far reaches of the empire. Some cities in Provence were more urban 2,000 years ago than they are today. For instance, Roman Arles had a population of 100,000—double today's size. Think about that when you visit.

In these cities, you'll see many rounded arches. These were constructed by piling two stacks of heavy stone blocks, connecting them with an arch (supported with wooden scaffolding), then inserting an inverted keystone where the stacks met. *Voilà!* The heavy stones were able to support not only themselves, but also a great deal of weight above the arch. The Romans didn't invent the rounded arch, but they exploited it better than their predecessors, stacking arches to build arenas and theaters, stringing them side by side for aqueducts, stretching out their legs to create barrel-vaulted ceilings, and building freestanding "triumphal" arches to celebrate conquering generals.

When it came to construction, the Romans' magic building ingredient was concrete. A mixture of volcanic ash, lime, water, and small rocks, concrete—easier to work than stone, longer-lasting than wood—served as flooring, roofing, filler, glue, and support. Builders would start with a foundation of brick, then fill it in with poured concrete. They would then cover important structures, such as basilicas, in sheets of expensive marble (held on with nails), or decorate floors and walls with mosaics—proving just how talented the Romans were at turning the functional into art.

PROVENCE'S CUISINE SCENE

Provence has been called France's "garden market," featuring farmfresh food (vegetables, fruit, and meats) prepared in a simple way, and meant to be savored with family and friends. Grilled foods are common, as are dishes derived from lengthy simmering—in part a reflection of long days spent in the fields. Colorful and lively,

Provençal cuisine hammers the senses with an extravagant use (by French standards) of garlic, olive oil, and herbs. Order anything *à la provençale,* and you'll be rewarded with aromatic food heightened by rich and pungent sauces. Thanks to the proximity of the Riviera, many seafood dishes show up on Provençal menus (see "The Riviera's Cuisine Scene" on page 286).

Unlike other French regional cuisines, the food of Provence is inviting for nibblers. Appetizers (hors d'oeuvres) often consist of bowls of olives (try the plump, full-flavored black *tanche* or the green, buttery *picholine*), as well as plates of fresh vegetables served with lusty sauces ready for dipping. These same sauces adorn dishes of hard-boiled eggs, fish, or meat. Look for tapenade, a paste of pureed olives, capers, anchovies, herbs, and sometimes tuna. True anchovy-lovers dig into *anchoïade* (a spread of garlic, anchovy, and parsley) or *bagna cauda* (a warm sauce of anchovies and melted butter or olive oil).

Aioli—a rich, garlicky mayonnaise spread over vegetables, potatoes, fish, or whatever—is another Provençal favorite. In the summertime, entire village festivals celebrate this sauce. Watch for signs announcing *aioli monstre* ("monster aioli") and, for a few euros, dive into a deeply French eating experience.

Despite the heat, soup is a favorite in Provence. *Soupe au pistou* is a thin yet flavorful vegetable soup with a sauce (called *pistou*) of basil, garlic, and cheese—pesto minus the pine nuts. Or try *soupe à l'ail* (garlic soup, called *aigo bouido* in the Provençal dialect). For details on seafood soups, see page 286.

Provençal main courses venerate fresh vegetables and meats. (Eat seafood on the Riviera and meat in Provence.) Ratatouille is a mixture of Provençal vegetables (eggplant, zucchini, onions, and peppers are the usual suspects) in a thick, herb-flavored tomato sauce. It's readily found in charcuteries and often served at room temperature, making it the perfect picnic food. Ratatouille veggies also show up on their own, stuffed and served in spicy sauces. Look for *aubergines* (eggplants), *tomates* (tomatoes), *poivrons* (sweet peppers), and *courgettes* (zucchini—especially *fleurs de courgettes,* stuffed and batter-fried zucchini flowers). *Tians* are gratin-like vegetable dishes named for the deep terra-cotta dish in which they are cooked and served. *Artichauts à la barigoule* are stuffed artichokes flavored with garlic, ham, and herbs (*barigoule* is from the Provençal word for thyme, *farigoule*). Also look for *riz de Camargue*—the reddish, chewy, nutty-tasting rice that has taken over the Camargue area, a marshy region that is otherwise useless for agriculture.

The famous herbs of Provence influence food long before it's cooked. The locally renowned lambs of the *garrigue* (shrub-covered hills), as well as rabbits and other small edible beasts in Provence, dine on wild herbs and spicy shrubs—preseasoning their delicate meat. Regional specialties include lamb (*agneau,* most often leg of lamb, *gigot d'agneau*), grilled and served no-frills, or the delicious *lapin à la provençale*—rabbit served with garlic, mustard, tomatoes, and herbs in white wine. Locals have a curious passion for quail *(caille).* These tiny, bony birds are often grilled and served with any variety of sauces, including those sweetened with Provençal cherries or honey and lavender. *Daube,* named for the traditional cooking vessel *daubière,* is generally beef simmered in wine with spices and herbs—and perhaps a touch of orange zest—until it is spoon-tender; it's then served with noodles or the local rice. *Taureau* (bull's meat), usually raised in the marshy Camargue, melts in your mouth.

By American standards, the French undercook meats: *bleu* (bluh) is virtually raw (just flame-kissed); *saignant* (seh-nyahn) is close to raw; *à point* (ah pwahn)—their version of "medium"—is rare; and *bien cuit* (bee-yehn kwee, "well cooked") is medium. (Because French cows are raised on grass rather than corn, the beef is leaner than in the US, so limiting the cooking time keeps the meat tender.)

There are a few dishes to avoid: *Pieds et paquets* is a scary dish of sheep's feet and tripe (no amount of Provençal sauce can hide this flavor). *Tourte de blettes* is a confused "pie" made with Swiss chard; both savory and sweet, it can't decide whether it should be a first course or dessert (it shows up as both).

Eat goat cheese *(fromage de chèvre)* in Provence. Look for *banon de banon* or *banon à la feuille* (dipped in *eau-de-vie* to kill bad mold, then wrapped in a chestnut leaf), spicy *picodon* (the name means "spicy" in the old language), or the fresh, creamy *brousse du Rove* (often served mixed with cream and sugar for dessert). On Provençal cheese platters, you'll find small rounds of bite-size chèvres, each flavored with a different herb or spice—and some even rolled in chopped garlic.

Desserts tend to be light and fruit-filled, or traditionally French. Treat yourself to fresh tarts made with seasonal fruit, regional Cavaillon melons (cantaloupes, served cut in half with a trickle of the sweet Rhône wine Beaumes de Venise), and ice cream or sorbet sweetened with honey and flavored with various herbs such as lavender, thyme, or rosemary. Don't miss the region's delicious cherries and apricots, which are often turned into jams and candied fruits.

Provence also produces some of France's great wines at relatively reasonable prices (€5-10/bottle on average). Look for wines

from Gigondas, Rasteau, Cairanne, Beaumes-de-Venise, Vacqueyras, and Châteauneuf-du-Pape. For the cheapest but still tasty
wines, look for labels showing Côtes du Rhône Villages or Côtes
de Provence. If you like rosé, you'll be in heaven here. Rosés from
Tavel are considered among the best in Provence. For reds, splurge
for Châteauneuf-du-Pape or Gigondas, and for a fine aperitif wine
or a dessert wine, try the Muscat from Beaumes-de-Venise.

Remember, restaurants serve only during lunch (12:00-14:00)
and dinner (19:00-21:00, later in bigger cities), but some cafés serve
food throughout the day.

For details on dining in France's restaurants, cafés, and brasseries, getting takeout, and assembling a picnic—as well as a rundown of French cuisine—see the "Eating" section in the Practicalities chapter (page 487).

WINES OF PROVENCE

The American wine-tasting experience (I'm thinking Napa Valley)
is generally informal, chatty, and entrepreneurial (logo-adorned
baseball caps and golf shirts). Although Provençal vintners are welcoming and more easygoing than in other parts of France, it's still a
serious, wine-focused experience. Your hosts are not there to make
small talk, and they're likely to be "all business." Still, Provence's
shorts-and-T-shirt climate and abundance of hearty, reasonably
priced wines make for an enjoyable experience, particularly if you're
patient and willing to learn. See the "French Wine-Tasting 101"
sidebar (page 36) for the basics.

Provence saw the first grapes planted in France, in about 600
B.C., by the Greeks. Romans built on what the Greeks started, real-
izing 2,000 years ago that Provence had an ideal climate for producing wine: mild winters and long, warm summers (but not too
hot—thanks to the cooling winds). This sun-baked, wine-happy
region offers Americans a chance to sample wines blended from
several grapes—resulting in flavors unlike anything we get at home
(yes, we have good cabernet sauvignons, merlots, and pinot noirs,
but Rhône wines are new to many of us).

In France, wine production is strictly controlled by the government to preserve the overall quality. This ensures that vintners
use specified grapes that grow best in that region and follow certain grape-growing procedures. The *Appellation d'Origine Controlée*
(AOC) label found on many bottles is the government's seal of approval, indicating that a wine has met various requirements. The
type and percentages of grapes used, vinification methods, and
taste are all controlled and verified.

Provençal vintners can blend wines using a maximum of 13
different types of grapes (five white and eight red)—unique in
France. Only in Châteauneuf-du-Pape are all 13 grapes used; most

vintners blend four or five types of grapes. (In Burgundy and Alsace, only one grape variety is used for each wine—so pinot noir, chardonnay, Riesling, Tokay, and pinot gris are each 100 percent from that grape.) This blending allows Provençal winemakers great range in personalizing their wine. The most prevalent types of red grapes are Grenache, Mourvèdre, Syrah, Carignan, and Cinsault. The white grapes include Grenache-Blanc, Roussanne, Marsanne, Bourboulenc, and Clairette.

There are three primary growing areas in Provence: Côtes du Rhône, Côtes de Provence, and Côteaux d'Aix-en-Provence. A few wines are also made along the Provençal Mediterranean coast. All regions produce rich, fruity reds and dry, fresh rosés. Only about five percent of wine produced here is white (the best of which comes from Cassis and Châteauneuf-du-Pape). Most Provençal whites are light, tart, with plenty of citrus and minerals, and work best as a pre-dinner drink or in a *kir*.

In Provence, I often drink rosé instead of white. French rosé is often crisp and fruity, a perfect match to the hot days and Mediterranean cuisine. Rosé wines are made from red grapes. After the grapes are crushed, their clear juice is left in contact with their dark-red skins just long enough to produce the pinkish color (no more than 24 hours). Rosés from Tavel (20 minutes north and west of Avignon) are the darkest in color and best-known outside of Provence, but you'll find many good producers at affordable prices in other areas as well. If you're unaccustomed to drinking rosés, try one here.

Here's some terminology to help you decipher what you'll see on bottles:

appellation: area in which a wine's grapes are grown
bouquet: bouquet (the fragrance when first opened)
cave: cellar (or wine shop)
cépage: grape variety (Syrah, Chardonnay, etc.)
côte, côteaux: hillside or slope
domaine: wine estate
étiquette: label
fût, tonneau: wine barrel
grand vin: excellent wine
millésimé: wine from a given year
mis en bouteille au château/à la domaine: estate-bottled (bottled where it was made)
vin de table: table wine (can be a blend of several wines)
vin du pays: wine from a given area (a step up from vin de table)

Côtes du Rhône Wines

The Côtes du Rhône, which follows the Rhône River from just south of Lyon to near Avignon, is the king of Provençal wines. Our

PROVENCE

French Wine-Tasting 101

France is peppered with wineries and wine-tasting opportunities. For some visitors, trying to make sense of the vast range of French wines can be overwhelming, particularly when faced with a no-nonsense winemaker or sommelier. Take a deep breath, do your best to follow my guidance, and don't linger where you don't feel welcome.

Visit several private wineries or stop by a *cave cooperative* or a *caveau*—an excellent opportunity to taste wines from a number of local vintners in a single, less intimidating setting. (Throughout this book, I've tried to identify which vineyards are most accepting of wine novices.) You'll have a better experience if you call ahead to a winery to let them know you're coming—even if they are open all day, it's good form to announce your visit (ask your hotelier for help). Avoid visiting places be-

tween noon and 14:00—many wineries are closed then, and those that aren't are staffed by people who would rather be at lunch.

Winemakers are happy to work with you...especially if they can figure out what you want. When you enter a winery, it helps to know what you like (drier or sweeter, lighter or full-bodied, fruity or more tannic, and so on). The people serving you may know those words in English, but you're wise to learn the key words in French (see the "French Wine Lingo" section later).

French wines usually have a lower alcohol level than American or Australian wines. Whereas many Americans like a big, full-bodied wine, most French prefer subtler flavors. They judge a wine by how well it pairs with a meal—and a big, oaky wine would overwhelm most French cuisine. The French enjoy sampling younger wines and divining how they will taste in a few years, allowing them to buy bottles at cheaper prices and stash them in their cellars. Americans want it now—for today's picnic.

Remember that the vintner is hoping you'll buy a bottle or two. If you don't buy, you may be asked to pay a small fee for the tasting. They understand that North Americans can't take much wine with them, but they do hope you'll look for their wines in the US. Some of the places I list will ship your purchase home—ask.

focus is on the southern section, roughly from Vaison-la-Romaine to Avignon (though wine-lovers should also try the big, complex reds found in the northern Rhône wines of St-Joseph, Crozes-Hermitage, and Cornas, as well as the tasty whites of Condrieu). The wines of the southern Rhône are consistently good, sometimes exceptional, and usually inexpensive. The reds are full-bodied, rosés

French Wine Lingo
Here are some phrases to get you started when wine-tasting:

Hello, sir/madam.
Bonjour, monsieur/madame.
(bohn-zhoor, muhs-yur/mah-dahm)

We would like to taste a few wines.
Nous voudrions déguster quelques vins.
(noo voo-dree-ohn day-goo-stay kehl-kuh van)

We would like a wine that is _____ and _____ .
Nous voudrions un vin _____ et _____ .
(noo voo-dree-ohn uhn van ay)

Fill in the blanks with your favorites from this list:

English	French
wine	*vin* (van)
red	*rouge* (roozh)
white	*blanc* (blahn)
rosé	*rosé* (roh-zay)
light	*léger* (lay-zhay)
full-bodied	*robuste* (roh-bewst)
fruity	*fruité* (frwee-tay)
sweet	*doux* (doo)
tannic	*tannique* (tah-neek)
fine	*fin, avec finesse* (fan, ah-vehk fee-nehs)
ready to drink (mature)	*prêt à boire* (preh tah bwar)
not ready to drink	*fermé* fair-may
oaky	*goût du fût de la chêne* (goo duh foo duh lah sheh-nuh)
from old vines	*de vieille vignes* (duh vee-yay-ee veen-yah)
sparkling	*pétillant* (pay-tee-yahn)

are dry and fruity, and whites are dry and fragrant. For more on this wine region, including a self-guided driving tour of the area's villages and vintners, see the Côtes du Rhône chapter.

Many subareas of the southern Côtes du Rhône are recognized for producing outstandingly good wines, and have been awarded their own *appellations* (like Châteauneuf-du-Pape, Gigondas, Beaumes-de-Venise, Côtes de Ventoux, Tavel, and Côtes du Luberon). Wines often are named for the villages that produce them. The "Côtes du Rhône Villages" appellation is less prestigious, covering 20 villages on the eastern side of the Côtes du Rhône, including Séguret, Sablet, Rasteau, and Cairanne. Strict guidelines govern the production of these wines (called *appellation controllé*).

Here's a summary of what you might find on a Côtes du Rhône *carte des vins* (wine list):

Châteauneuf-du-Pape: Almost all wines from this famous village are reds (often blends; the most dominant grapes are Grenache, Mourvèdre, and Syrah). These wines have a velvety quality and can be spicy, with flavors of licorice and prunes. A few delicious whites are made here and worth sampling. Châteauneuf-du-Pape red wines merit lengthy aging. Considered among the best producers are Château de Beaucastel, Le Vieux Télégraphe, Clos des Papes, and Château la Nerthe. It's a breeze to find their wines in North America. It's also worth seeking out lesser-known names and smaller wineries (many of which are listed in this book).

Gigondas: These wines have many of the same qualities as Châteauneuf-du-Pape, but are lesser known and usually cheaper. Gigondas red wines are spicy, meaty, and can be pretty tannic. Again, aging is necessary to bring out the full qualities of the wine. Look for Domaine du Terme, Château de Montmirail, Domaine de Cassan, or Domaine de Coyeux for good quality.

Beaumes-de-Venise: While reds from this village are rich and flavorful, Beaumes-de-Venise is most famous for its Muscat—a sweet, fragrant wine usually served as an aperitif or with dessert. It often has flavors of apricots and peaches, and it should be consumed within two years of bottling. Try Domaine de Coyeux, Domaine de Durban, and Château Redortier.

Rasteau: This village sits across the valley from Gigondas and shares many of its qualities—at lower prices. Rasteau makes fine rosés, robust (at times "rough") and fruity reds, and a naturally sweet wine (Vin Doux Naturel). Their Côtes du Rhône Villages can be excellent. The cooperative in Rasteau is good, as are the wines from Domaine des Girasols.

Sablet: This village lies down in the valley below Gigondas and makes decent, fruity, and inexpensive reds and rosés.

Tavel: The queen of French rosés is 20 minutes north and west of Avignon, close to Pont du Gard. Tavel produces a rosé that is dry, crisp, higher in alcohol, darker, and more full-bodied than other rosés from the region. Look for any rosé from Tavel.

The Rules of *Boules*

The game of *boules*—also called *pétanque*—is the horseshoes of France. Invented here in the early 1900s, it's a social yet serious sport, and endlessly entertaining to watch—even more so if you understand the rules.

The game is played with heavy metal balls and a small wooden target ball called a *cochonnet* (piglet). Whoever gets

his *boule* closest to the *cochonnet* is awarded points. Teams commonly have specialist players: a *pointeur* and a *tireur*. The *pointeur*'s goal is to lob his balls as close to the target as he can. The *tireur*'s job is to blast away opponents' *boules*.

In teams of two, each player gets three *boules*. The starting team traces a small circle in the dirt (in which players must stand when launching their *boules*), and tosses the *cochonnet* about 30 feet to establish the target. The *boule* must be thrown underhand, and can be rolled, launched sky-high, or rocketed at its target. The first *pointeur* shoots, then the opposing *pointeur* shoots until his *boule* gets closer. Once the second team lands a *boule* near the *cochonnet*, the first team goes again. If the other team's *boule* is very near the *cochonnet*, the *tireur* will likely attempt to knock it away.

Once all *boules* have been launched, the tally is taken. The team with a *boule* closest to the *cochonnet* wins the round, and they receive a point for each *boule* closer to the target than their opponents' nearest *boule*. The first team to get to 13 points wins. A regulation *boules* filed is 10 feet by 43 feet, but the game is played everywhere—just scratch a throwing circle in the sand, toss the *cochonnet,* and you're off.

Côtes de Provence Wines

The lesser-known vineyards of the Côtes de Provence run east from Aix-en-Provence almost to St-Tropez. Typical grapes are Cinsault, Mourvèdre, Grenache, Carignan, and a little cabernet sauvignon and Syrah. The wines are commonly full-bodied and fruity, and are meant to be drunk when they're young. They cost less than Côtes du Rhônes and have similar characteristics. But the region is most famous for its "big" rosés that can be served with meat and garlic dishes (rosé accounts for 60 percent of production).

For one-stop shopping, make it a point to find the superb **La Maison des Vins Côtes de Provence** on RN-7 in Les Arcs-sur-Argens (a few minutes north of the A-8 autoroute, about halfway between Aix-en-Provence and Nice). This English-speaking wine shop and tasting center represents hundreds of producers, selling bottles at vineyard prices and offering good tastings (tel. 04 94 99 50 20, www.maison-des-vins.fr).

Côteaux d'Aix-en-Provence Wines

This large wine region, between Les Baux and Aix-en-Provence, produces some interesting reds, whites, and rosés. Commonly used grapes are the same as in Côtes de Provence, though several producers (mainly around Les Baux) use a higher concentration of cabernet sauvignon, which helps distinguish their wines. The vintners around Les Baux produce some exceptionally good wines, and many of their vineyards are organic. Try Domaine d'Eole or Domaine Gourgonnier. The tiny wine-producing area of Palette houses only three wineries, all of which make exceptional rosés; one (Château Simone) also makes a delicious white wine. The Côtes de Provence-Sainte-Victoire wineries, with their beautiful views of Mont Ste-Victoire (famously painted by Cézanne), produce some excellent rosés.

Provençal Mediterranean Wines

Barely east of Marseille, Cassis and Bandol sit side by side, overlooking the Mediterranean. Though very close together, they are designated as separate wine-growing areas because of the distinctive nature of their wines. Cassis is one of France's smallest wine regions and is known for its strong, fresh, and very dry whites (made with the Marsanne grape)—arguably the best white wine in Provence. Bandol is known for its luscious, velvety reds. This wine, aged in old oak and made primarily from the Mourvèdre grape, is one of your author's favorites.

ARLES

By helping Julius Caesar defeat his archrival Gnaeus Pompey at Marseille, Arles (pronounced "arl") earned the imperial nod and was made an important port city. With the first bridge over the Rhône River, Arles was a key stop on the Roman road from Italy to Spain, the Via Domitia. After reigning as the seat of an important archbishop and as a trading center for centuries, the city became a sleepy backwater of little importance in the 1700s. Vincent van Gogh settled here in the late 1800s, but left only a chunk of his ear (now long gone). American bombers destroyed much of Arles

in World War II as the townsfolk hid out in its underground Roman galleries. But today Arles thrives again, with its evocative Roman ruins, an eclectic assortment of museums, made-for-ice-cream pedestrian zones, and squares that play hide-and-seek with visitors.

Workaday Arles is not a wealthy city, and compared to its neighbors Avignon and Nimes, it feels unpolished and even a little dirty. But to me, that's part of its charm.

PLANNING YOUR TIME

Start at the Ancient History Museum (at the edge of town, closed Tue; see page 60) for a helpful overview—drivers should try to do this museum on their way into Arles—then dive into the city-center sights, linked by my Arles City Walk. For cost-efficient sightseeing, get the Liberty Passport, which covers the ancient monuments and the Ancient History Museum (see "Helpful Hints").

Orientation to Arles

Arles faces the Mediterranean, turning its back on Paris. And though the town is built along the Rhône, it largely ignores the river. Landmarks hide in Arles' medieval tangle of narrow, winding streets. Hotels have good, free city maps, and helpful street-corner signs point you toward sights and hotels. Speeding cars enjoy Arles' medieval lanes, turning sidewalks into tightropes and pedestrians into leaping targets.

TOURIST INFORMATION

The TI is on the ring road Boulevard des Lices, at Esplanade Charles de Gaulle (April-Sept daily 9:00-18:45; Oct-March Mon-Sat 9:00-16:45, Sun 10:00-13:00; tel. 04 90 18 41 20, www.arlestourisme. com). While there, take advantage of free Wi-Fi, pick up the city map and bus schedules, and request English information on nearby destinations such as the Camargue. Ask about walking tours and "bullgames" in Arles and nearby towns (Provence's more humane version of bullfights—see page 64). The TI sells the worthwhile Liberty Passport (see "Helpful Hints," later).

ARRIVAL IN ARLES

By Train: The train station is on the river, a 10-minute walk from the town center. There's no baggage storage at the station, but you can walk 10 minutes to stow it at Hôtel Régence (see "Helpful Hints," later).

To reach the town center or Ancient History Museum from the train station, wait for the free **Envia minibus** at the glass shelter facing away from the station (cross the street and veer left, 2/hour Mon-Sat 7:00-19:00, none Sun). The bus makes a counterclockwise loop around Arles, stopping near most of my recommended hotels (see map on page 68 for stops). **Taxis** usually wait in front of the station (if there's not a taxi waiting, call 04 90 96 52 76 or the posted telephone numbers, or ask the info desk staff to call for you). Taxi rates are fixed—allow about €11 to any of my recommended hotels.

By Bus: The bus station is next to the train station; follow the directions above to reach the sights.

By Car: Most hotels have metered parking nearby (free Mon-Sat 12:00-14:00 & 19:00-9:00, and all day Sun; some meters limited to 2.5 hours). For most hotels, first follow signs to *Centre-Ville*, then *Gare SNCF* (train station). You'll come to a big roundabout (Place Lamartine) with a Monoprix department store to the right. You can park along the city wall (except on Tue night when tow trucks clear things out for the Wed market); the hotels I list are no more than a 15-minute walk from here. Fearless drivers can plunge into the narrow streets between the two stumpy towers via Rue de la Calade, and follow signs to their hotel. Theft is a problem—leave nothing in your car, and trust your hotelier's advice on where to park.

If you can't find parking near your hotel, Parking des Lices (Arles' only parking garage), near the TI on Boulevard des Lices, is a good fallback (€2.50/hour, €18/24 hours).

HELPFUL HINTS

Sightseeing Tips: Arles has a smart ticket-and-hours plan for its sightseeing. Ancient monuments, such as the Roman Arena and Classical Theater, all have the **same hours** (daily May-Sept 9:00-19:00, April and Oct 9:00-18:00, Nov-March 10:00-17:00). A good-value €11 combo-ticket—the **Liberty Passport** (Le Passeport Liberté)—covers any four monuments, the Ancient History Museum, and the Réattu Museum (but not the Fondation Van Gogh gallery). Buy the pass at the TI or any included sight.

> While only the Ancient History Museum is essential to enter, the pass makes the city fun to explore, as you can pop into nearly everything, even for just a couple of minutes. The moral: Buy the pass and see more.

Market Days: The big markets are on Wednesdays and Saturdays. For details, see page 452.

Crowds: An international photo event jams hotels the second weekend of July. The let-'er-rip, twice-yearly Féria draws crowds over Easter and in mid-September (described on page 65).

Internet Access: The TI has free Wi-Fi. An Internet café is near Place Voltaire at 31 Rue Augustin Tardieu.

Baggage Storage and Bike Rental: The recommended **Hôtel Régence** will store your bags for €3 (daily 7:30-22:00 mid-March-mid-Nov, closed in winter, 5 Rue Marius Jouveau). They also rent bikes (€7/half-day, €15/day, reserve ahead for electric bikes, one-way rentals within Provence possible, same hours as baggage storage). From Arles you can ride to Les Baux (25 miles round-trip). It's a darn steep climb going into Les Baux, so consider busing up there (regional buses have bike racks) and gliding back. Those in great shape can consider biking into the Camargue (40 miles round-trip, forget it in the wind).

Laundry: A launderette is at 12 Rue Portagnel (daily 7:00-21:30, you can stay later to finish if you're already inside). Another is nearby on Rue du 4 Septembre.

Car Rental: Avis is at the train station (tel. 04 90 96 82 42); **Europcar** and **Hertz** are downtown (Europcar is at 61 Avenue

ARLES

Arles

Arles Walk

1. The Yellow House (Easel)
2. Starry Night over the Rhône (Easel)
3. Rue de la Cavalerie
4. Old Town
5. Arena (Easel) & Roman Arena
6. Alpilles Mountains View
7. Jardin d'Eté (Easel)
8. Classical Theater
9. Republic Square
10. Cryptoporticos
11. St. Trophime Church
12. Rue de la République

13. Espace Van Gogh (Easel)
14. Fondation Van Gogh
15. Daycare and Bullfight Bar on Rue du Docteur Fanton
16. Place du Forum & Café at Night (Easel)

Other

17. Baggage Storage & Bike Rental
18. Launderette (2)
19. Internet Access
20. Avis Car Rental
21. To Europcar Car Rental
22. Hertz Car Rental

RUE DES CAPUCINS

RUE DE LA VERRIÈRE

RUE ROBESPIERRE

RUE CAMARGUE

TRINQUETAILLE

QUAI ST. PIERRE

Rhône

TRINQUETAILLE BRIDGE

PROMENADE

QUAI MARX DORMOY

R. DE LA TOUR DU FABRE

R. DR. FANTON

R. TRUCHET

14

15

LIBERTE

® Envia Bus Stops

RUE A. FRANCE

R. JOUVENE

ARLATEN FOLK MUSEUM
(REOPENS IN 2018)

QUAI DE LA ROQUETTE

R. DES PORCELETS

RUE DE LA RÉPUBLIQUE

RUE GAMBETTA

13

12

Place Paul Doumier

RUE DE LA ROQUETTE

RUE DE CHARTROUSE

RUE JEAN GRANAUD

ESPACE VAN GOGH

R. PRES. WILSON

RUE CROIX ROUGE

LA ROQUETTE

RUE MOLIERE

RUE MOLIERE

To Ancient History Museum

Place Genive

RUE FLEURY PRUDHON

To Nîmes via A-84

RUE RAILLON

BLVD. G CLEMENCEAU

RUE PARMENTIER

To Ancient History Museum

ARLES

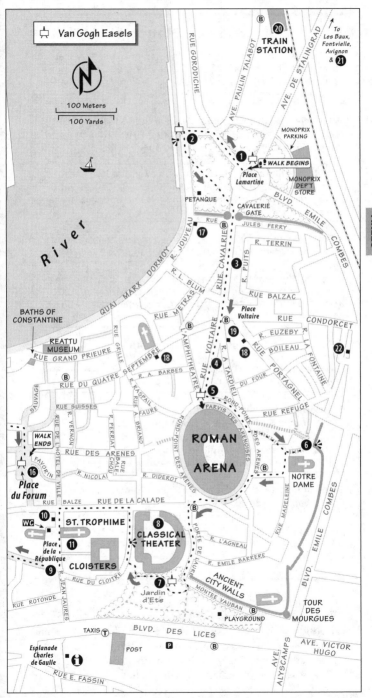

Van Gogh Easels

N

100 Meters
100 Yards

River

TRAIN STATION ⑳

To Les Baux, Fontvielle, Avignon & ㉑

MONOPRIX PARKING

① WALK BEGINS

Place Lamartine

MONOPRIX DEP'T STORE

BLVD. EMILE COMBES

②

PETANQUE

CAVALERIE GATE

JULES FERRY

RUE CAVALERIE

⑰

R. TERRIN

R. PUITS

③

RUE BALZAC

QUAI MARX DORMOY

RUE JOUVEAU

RUE METRAS

R. L. BLUM

Place Voltaire

RUE CONDORCET

⑲

R. EUZEBY

RUE BOILEAU

R. A. TARDIEU

RUE DU FOUR

LA FONTAINE

㉒

BATHS OF CONSTANTINE

REATTU MUSEUM

RUE GRAND PRIEURE

RUE GRILLE

L'AMPHITHEATRE

⑱

RUE DU QUATRE SEPTEMBRE

⑱

④

RUE PORTAGNEL

RUE REFUGE

Ⓑ

RUE SUISSES

R. R. A. BARBES

R. KASPAIL

R. FAURE

R. BRIAND

ROND-POINT DES ARENES

PARVIS DES ARENES

⑤

ROND-POINT DES ARENES

WALK ENDS

RUE DE L'HOTEL DE VILLE

RUE DES ARENES

R. PERRIAT

R. CHIOU

R. NICOLAI

R. DIDEROT

ROMAN ARENA

NOTRE DAME

⑥

RUE MADELEINE

BLVD. EMILE COMBES

⑯

Place du Forum

RUE BALZE

RUE DE LA CALADE

WC ⑩

ST. TROPHIME

CLASSICAL THEATER

⑧

R. L'AGNEAU

PORTE DE LAURE

R. EMILE BARRERE

ANCIENT CITY WALLS

Place de la République

⑪

CLOISTERS

RUE DU CLOITRE

⑨

RUE ROTONDE

R. JEAN JAURES

Jardin d'Ete

⑦

MONTEE VAUBAN

PLAYGROUND

TOUR DES MOURGES

Esplanade Charles de Gaulle

TAXIS Ⓣ

POST

P

Ⓑ

BLVD. DES LICES

AVE. VICTOR HUGO

AVE. ALYSCAMPS

RUE E. FASSIN

Arles at a Glance

▲▲**Roman Arena** This big amphitheater, once used by gladiators, today hosts summer "bullgames" and occasional bullfights. **Hours:** Daily May-Sept 9:00-19:00, April and Oct 9:00-18:00, Nov-March 10:00-17:00. See page 51.

▲▲**Ancient History Museum** Filled with models and sculptures, this museum takes you back to Arles' Roman days. **Hours:** Wed-Mon 10:00-18:00, closed Tue. See page 60.

▲▲**St. Trophime Church** Church with exquisite Romanesque entrance. **Hours:** Church—daily April-Sept 9:00-12:00 & 14:00-18:30, until 17:00 Oct-March; cloisters—same hours as Arena. See page 54.

▲**Forum Square** Lively, café-crammed square that was once the Roman forum. **Hours:** Always open. See page 57.

▲**Réattu Museum** Decent, mostly modern art collection in a fine 15th-century mansion. **Hours:** March-Oct Tue-Sun 10:00-18:00, Nov-Feb Tue-Sun 10:00-17:00, closed Mon year-round. See page 64.

▲**Fondation Van Gogh** Small gallery with works by major contemporary artists paying homage to Van Gogh. **Hours:** Generally daily 11:00-19:00, likely closed Mon off-season. See page 57.

Cryptoporticos Underground support structure for Roman forum. **Hours:** Same as Arena. See page 54.

Classical Theater Ruined Roman theater, recently restored and still used for events. **Hours:** Same as Arena. See page 52.

Baths of Constantine Remains of Arles' Roman public baths. **Hours:** Same as Arena. See page 63.

La Roquette District Arles' little-visited western fringe, with cafés, bakeries, and bistros. **Hours:** Always open. See page 63.

de Stalingrad, tel. 04 90 93 23 24; Hertz is closer to Place Voltaire at 10 Boulevard Emile Combes, tel. 04 90 96 75 23).

Local Guides: Charming **Agnes Barrier,** who knows Arles and nearby sights intimately, enjoys her work. Her tours cover Van Gogh and Roman history (€130/3 hours, mobile 06 11 23 03 73, agnes.barrier@hotmail.fr). **Alice Vallat** offers a variety of scheduled visits of Arles' key sights (€15/person for 1.5-hour group tour, €130 for 3-hour private tour, tel. 06 74 01 22 54, www.guidearles.com, alice.vallat@voila.fr).

English Book Exchange: A small exchange is available at the recommended **Soleileis** ice-cream shop.

Public Pools: Arles has three pools (indoor and outdoor). Ask at the TI or your hotel.

Boules: The local "*boul*ing alley" is by the river on Place Lamartine. After their afternoon naps, the old boys congregate here for a game of *pétanque* (see page 39 for more on this popular local pastime).

Frank Gehry Tower: The buzz in Arles is the 180-foot-tall Gehry-designed aluminum tower rising in a rundown neighborhood southeast of the center. Slated for completion in 2018, the project promises to revitalize that zone with galleries and apartments.

GETTING AROUND ARLES

In this flat city, everything's within **walking** distance. Only the Ancient History Museum requires a healthy walk. The elevated riverside promenade provides Rhône views and a direct route to the Ancient History Museum (to the southwest) and the train station (to the northeast). Keep your head up for *Starry Night* memories, but eyes down for doggie droppings.

Arles' **taxis** charge a set fee of about €11, but nothing except the Ancient History Museum is worth a taxi ride. To call a cab, dial 04 90 96 52 76 or 04 90 96 90 03.

The free **Envia minibus** circles the town, useful for access to the train station, hotels, and the Ancient History Museum (see map on page 68, 2/hour, Mon-Sat 7:00-19:00, none Sun).

Arles City Walk

The joy of Arles is how its compact core mixes ancient sights, Van Gogh memories, and a raw and real contemporary scene that can be delightfully covered on foot. All of the dimensions of the city come together in this self-guided walk. While workable in the evening, taking this walk during business hours allows you to pop into the sights and shops that give the city its unique character.

Much of the walk focuses on the story of Van Gogh in Arles. We'll also visit ancient sites including the Roman Arena, Classical Theater, Cryptoporticos, and the cloisters at St. Trophime Church (all covered by the Liberty Passport—described earlier, under "Helpful Hints"), along with some of Arles' most characteristic streets and squares. For context, visit the Ancient History Museum

ARLES

before taking this walk (see "Sights in Arles," later). To trace the route of this walk, see the map on page 44.

BACKGROUND

The life and artistic times of Dutch artist **Vincent van Gogh** form a big part of Arles' draw, and the city does a fine job of highlighting its Van Gogh connection: Throughout town, about a dozen steel-and-concrete "easels," with photos of the final paintings and the actual view of that painting's subject, provide then-and-now comparisons.

In the dead of winter in 1888, 35-year-old Van Gogh left big-city Paris for Provence, hoping to jump-start his floundering career and social life. He was as inspired as he was lonely. Coming from the gray skies and flat lands of the north, Vincent was bowled over by everything Provençal—the sun, bright colors, rugged landscape, and raw people. For the next two years he painted furiously, cranking out a masterpiece every few days.

Only a few of the 200-plus paintings that Van Gogh did in the south can be found today in the city that so moved him (you can see a few at the Fondation Van Gogh gallery, which we'll visit on this stroll). But here you can walk the same streets he knew and see the places he painted.

• *Start at the north gate of the city, just outside the medieval wall in Place Lamartine (100 yards in front of the medieval gate, with the big Monoprix store across the street to the right, just beyond the roundabout). A four-foot-tall metal panel (or "easel") shows Van Gogh's painting.*

❶ *The Yellow House* Easel

Vincent arrived in Arles on February 20, 1888, to a foot of snow. He rented a small house on the north side of Place Lamartine.

The house was destroyed in 1944 by an errant bridge-seeking bomb, but the four-story building behind it—where you see the brasserie—still stands (find it in the painting). The house had four rooms, including a small studio and the cramped trapezoid-shaped bedroom made famous in paintings. It was painted yellow inside and out, and Vincent named it..."The Yellow House." In the distance, the painting shows the same bridges you see today, as well as a steam train—which was a rather recent invention in France, allowing people like Vincent to travel greater distances and be jarred by new experiences. (Today's TGV system continues that trend.)

Freezing Arles was buttoned up tight when Vincent arrived, so he was forced to work inside, where he painted still lifes and self-portraits—anything to keep his brush moving. In late March, spring finally arrived. In those days, a short walk from Place Lamartine led to open fields. Donning his straw hat, Vincent set up his easel outdoors and painted quickly, capturing what he saw and felt—the blossoming fruit trees, gnarled olive trees, peasants sowing and reaping, jagged peaks, and windblown fields, all lit by a brilliant sun that drove him to use ever-brighter paints.

ARLES

• *Walk directly to the river. You'll pass a monument in honor of two WWII American pilots killed in action during the liberation of Arles (erected in 2002 as a post-9/11 sign of solidarity with Americans), a post celebrating Arles' many sister cities (left), and a big concrete high school (right).*

At the river, find the easel in the wall where ramps lead down. The Roman bridge stood here (look for a few stones directly across), and just upstream are the remains of a modern bridge bombed by the Allies in World War II. This is the busier-than-ever cruise port, which brings crowds into the city throughout the season. Looking downstream, notice the new embankment constructed in recent years. Now, turn your attention to the...

❷ *Starry Night over the Rhône* Easel

One night, Vincent set up shop along the river and painted the stars boiling above the city skyline. Vincent looked to the night sky

for the divine and was the first to paint outside after dark, adapting his straw hat to hold candles (which must have blown the minds of locals back then). As his paintings progressed, the stars became larger and more animated (like Vincent himself). The lone couple in the painting pops up again and again in his work. Experts say that Vincent was desperate for a close relationship with another being...someone to stroll the riverbank with under a star-filled sky. (Note: This painting is not the *Starry Night* you're thinking of—that one was painted later in St-Rémy; described on page 88.)

To his sister Wilhelmina, Vincent wrote, "At present I absolutely want to paint a starry sky. It often seems to me that night is still more richly colored than the day; having hues of the most intense violets, blues, and greens. If only you pay attention to it, you will see that certain stars are lemon-yellow, others pink or a green, blue, and forget-me-not brilliance." Vincent painted this scene on his last night in Arles. If you're taking this walk in the daytime, come back at night to match his painting with today's scene.

• *With your back to the river, angle right through the small park of syca-more trees, where the old boys gather for* pétanque *(a favorite French pastime). Observe the action. If you're inclined (and charming), you may be invited to give it a try. Continue into town through the park (past a WC) and through the stumpy 14th-century stone towers where the city gates once stood.*

❸ Rue de la Cavalerie

Van Gogh walked into town the same way. Arles' 19th-century red light district was just east of Rue de la Cavalerie, and the far-from-home Dutchman spent many lonely nights in its bars and brothels. The street still has a certain edgy local color. Belly up to the bar in the down-and-dirty café at Hôtel de Paris for a taste. It's a friendly watering hole with fun paintings of football and bull fighting.

• *Continuing uphill, you'll come to an ornately decorated fountain from 1887: two columns with a mosaic celebrating the high culture of Provence (she's the winged woman who obviously loves music and reading).*

Stay left and keep walking uphill to Place Voltaire, a center of this working-class neighborhood (you'll see the local Communist Party head-quarters across on the left). Arles is famously red; its communist mayor is in his third term and quite popular.

❹ Old Town

You've left the bombed-out part of town and entered the old town, with buildings predating World War II. The stony white arches of the ancient Roman Arena ahead mark your destination. As you hike up Rue Voltaire, notice the shutters, which contribute to Arles' character. The old town is strictly preserved: These traditional shut-ters come in a variety of styles but cannot be changed.

• *Keep straight up Rue Voltaire, climb to the Roman Arena, and find the* Arena *easel at the top of the stairs, to the right.*

❺ *Arena* Easel

All summer long, fueled by sun and alcohol, Vincent painted the town. He loved the bullfights in the arena and sketched the color-ful surge of the crowds, spending more time studying the people than watching the bullfights (notice how the bull is barely visible). Vincent had little interest in Arles' antiquity—it was people and nature that fascinated him.

• *Now, let's visit the actual...*

Roman Arena (Amphithéâtre)

This well-preserved arena is worth ▲▲ and is still in use today. Nearly 2,000 years ago, gladiators fought wild animals here to the

delight of 20,000 screaming fans. Now local daredevils still fight wild animals here—"bullgame" posters around the arena advertise upcoming spectacles (see page 64).

Cost and Hours: €8 combo-ticket with Classical Theater, covered by Liberty Passport—see "Helpful Hints," earlier; open daily May-Sept 9:00-19:00, April and Oct 9:00-18:00, Nov-March 10:00-17:00, Rond-point des Arènes, tel. 04 90 49 36 86, www.arenes-arles.com.

Visiting the Arena: After passing the ticket kiosk, find the helpful English information display that describes the arena's history and renovation, then take a seat in the upper deck. In Roman times, games were free (sponsored by city bigwigs), and fans were seated by social class. More than 30 rows of stone bleachers extended all the way to the top of those vacant arches that circle the arena. All arches were numbered to help distracted fans find their seats. The many passageways you'll see (called vomitoires) allowed for rapid dispersal after the games—fights would break out among frenzied fans if they couldn't leave quickly. During medieval times and until the early 1800s, the arches were bricked up and the stadium became a fortified town—with 200 humble homes crammed within its circular defenses. Parts of three of the medieval towers survive (the one above the ticket booth is open and rewards those who climb it with terrific views).

For more on Roman amphitheaters, see the description of Nîmes' Arena on page 130.

• Leaving the arena, walk clockwise around its perimeter, marveling at the ancient stonework. A quarter of the way around, go up the cute stepped lane (Rue Renan, next to Volubilis Restaurant). Take three steps and turn around to study the arena. The big stones are Roman. Notice the little medieval stones—more like rubble—filling two upper-level archways. These serve as a reminder of how the arena encircled a jumble of makeshift houses through the Middle Ages. You can even see roof lines and beam holes where the Roman structure provided a solid foundation to lean on.

Hike up the pretty lane and continue past the stark and stony church to the highest point in Arles. Take in the view.

❻ Alpilles Mountains View

This view pretty much matches what Vincent, an avid walker, would have seen. Imagine him hauling his easel into those fields under intense sun, leaning against a ferocious wind, struggling to keep his hat on. He trekked into the pastoral countryside many times during his stay in Arles, just to paint the farm workers. Vincent venerated but didn't deify peasants. Wanting to accurately show their lives and their struggles, he reproached Renoir and Monet for glorifying them in their works.

Vincent carried his easel as far as the medieval Abbey of Montmajour, that bulky structure three miles straight ahead on the hill. The St. Paul Hospital, where he was eventually treated in St-Rémy, is on the other side of the Alpilles mountains, several miles beyond Montmajour.

• *Continue circling the Roman Arena. At the high point, turn left and walk out Rue de Porte de Laure. (You'll pass the Classical Theater on your right, which we'll see later.) After a couple of blocks, just after the street turns left, go right, down the curved staircase into the park. At bottom of the stairs take the second right (through the gate and into the park) and find the...*

❼ Jardin d'Eté Easel

Vincent spent many a sunny day painting the leafy Jardin d'Eté. In another letter to his sister, Vincent wrote, "I don't know whether you can understand that one may make a poem by arranging colors...In a similar manner, the bizarre lines, purposely selected and multiplied, meandering all through the picture may not present a literal image of the garden, but they may present it to our minds as if in a dream."

• *Hike uphill through the park toward the three-story surviving tower of the ancient Roman Theater. On the right in the grass is a monument that reads "to 1.5 million Armenian victims of the 1915 Genocide." (French law makes it a crime to deny the Ottoman Empire's genocide of Armenians, causing tension with today's Turkey.) At the ancient tower, follow the white metal fence to the left along "the garden of stone"—a collection of ancient carved bits of a once grand Roman theater. Go up four steps and around to the right for a fine view of the...*

❽ Classical Theater (Théâtre Antique)

This first-century B.C. Roman theater once seated 10,000...just like the theater in nearby Orange. But unlike Orange, here in Arles there was no hillside to provide structural support. Instead, this elegant, three-level structure had 27 buttress arches radiating out behind the seats. From the outside, it looked much like the adjacent arena. (For more on Roman theaters, read about the theater in Orange; see page 152).

Cost and Hours: €8 combo-ticket with Roman Arena, covered by Liberty Passport, same hours as Arena.

Visiting the Theater: Start with the 10-minute video outside, which provides helpful background information and images that make it easier to put the scattered stones back in place (crouch in front to make out the small English subtitles). A large information panel nearby on the grass adds more context.

Walk into the theater and pull up a stone seat in a center aisle. Imagine that for 500 years, ancient Romans gathered here for entertainment. The original structure was much higher, with 33 rows of seats covering three levels to accommodate demand. During the Middle Ages, the old theater became a convenient town quarry—much of St. Trophime Church was built from theater rubble. Precious little of the original theater survives—though it still is used for events, with seating for 2,000 spectators.

Two lonely Corinthian columns are all that remain of a three-story stage wall that once featured more than 100 columns and statues painted in vibrant colors. Actors with main roles entered through the central arch, over which a grandiose statue of Caesar Augustus stood (it's now on display at the Ancient History Museum). Bit players entered through side arches. The orchestra section is defined by a semicircular pattern in the stone in front of you. Stepping up onto the left side of the stage, look down to the slender channel that allowed the brilliant-red curtain to disappear below, like magic. The stage, which was built of wood, was about 160 feet across and 20 feet deep. The actors' changing rooms are backstage, down the steps.

• *From the theater, walk downhill on Rue de la Calade. Take the first left into a big square.*

❾ Republic Square (Place de la République)

This square used to be called "Place Royale"...until the French Revolution. The obelisk was the former centerpiece of Arles' Roman Circus (outside of town). The lions at its base are the symbol of the city, whose slogan is (roughly) "the gentle lion." Observe the age-old scene: tourists, peasants, shoppers, pilgrims, children, and street musicians. The City Hall (Hôtel de Ville) has a French Baroque facade, built in the same generation as Versailles. Where there's a City Hall, there's always a free WC (if you win the Revolution, you can pee for free at the mayor's home). Notice the flags: The yellow-and-red of Provence is the same as the yellow-and-red of Catalunya, its linguistic cousin in Spain.

• *Today's City Hall sits upon an ancient city center. Inside you'll find the entrance to an ancient cryptoportico (foundation).*

⑩ Cryptoporticos (Cryptoportiques)

This dark, drippy underworld of Roman arches was constructed to support the upper half of Forum Square. Two thousand years ago, most of this gallery of arches was at or above street level; modern Arles has buried about 20 feet of its history over the millennia. Through the tiny windows high up you would have seen the sandals of Romans on their way to the forum. Other than dark arches and broken bits of forum littering the dirt floor, there's not much down here beyond ancient memories (€3.50, covered by Liberty Passport, same hours as Arena).

• *The highlight of Place de la République is St. Trophime Church. Enjoy its exquisitely carved facade.*

⑪ St. Trophime Church

Named after a third-century bishop of Arles, this church, worth ▲▲, sports the finest Romanesque main entrance I've seen anywhere. The Romanesque and Gothic interior—with tapestries, relics, and a rare painting from the French Revolution when this was a "Temple of Reason"—is worth a visit.

Cost and Hours: Free, daily 9:00-12:00 & 14:00-18:30, until 17:00 Oct-March.

Exterior: Like a Roman triumphal arch, the church **facade** trumpets the promise of Judgment Day. The tympanum (the semicircular area above the door) is filled with Christian symbolism. Christ sits in majesty, surrounded by symbols of the four evangelists: Matthew (the winged man), Mark (the winged lion), Luke (the ox), and John (the eagle). The 12 apostles are lined up below Jesus. It's Judgment Day...some are saved and others aren't. Notice the condemned (on the right)—a chain gang doing a sad bunny-hop over the fires of hell. For them, the tune trumpeted by the three angels above Christ is not a happy one. Below the chain gang, St. Stephen is being stoned to death, with his soul leaving through his mouth and instantly being welcomed by angels. Study the exquisite detail. In an illiterate medieval world, long before the vivid images of our Technicolor time, this was colorfully painted, like a neon billboard over the town square. It's full of meaning, and a medieval pilgrim understood it all.

Interior: Just inside the door on the right, a chart locates the interior highlights and helps explain the carvings you just saw on the tympanum. The tall 12th-century Romanesque nave is decorated by a set of tapestries (typical in the Middle Ages) showing scenes from the life of Mary (17th century, from the French town of Aubusson). Circle the church counterclockwise.

Stop into the brightly lit **Chapel of Baptism** to view a statue of St. John Paul II under the window. Facing the window, look to the right wall where you'll see a faded painting from 1789. The French Revolution secularized the country and made churches "Temples of Reason." The painting of a triangle with a sunburst is the only example of church decor I've seen from this age.

Amble around the ambulatory toward the **Gothic apse.** Choose which chapel you need or want: If you have the plague or cholera, visit the chapel devoted to St. Roch—notice the testimonial plaques of gratitude on the wall. Some spaces are still available...if you hurry.

Two-thirds of the way around, find the **relic chapel** behind the ornate wrought iron gate, with its fine golden boxes that hold long-venerated bones of obscure saints. These relics generated lots of money for the church from pilgrims through the ages. Pop in a coin to share some light. The next chapel houses the skull of St. Anthony of the Desert.

Several chapels down, look for the early-Christian **sarcophagi** from Roman Arles (dated about A.D. 300). One sarcophagus shows Moses and the Israelites crossing the Red Sea. You'll see Christians wearing togas and praying like evangelicals do today—hands raised. The heads were likely lopped off during the French Revolution.

This church is a stop on the ancient pilgrimage route to Santiago de Compostela in northwest Spain. For 800 years pilgrims on their way to Santiago have paused here...and they still do today. Notice the modern-day pilgrimages advertised on the far right near the church's entry.

• *To reach the adjacent peaceful cloister, leave the church, turn left, then left again through a courtyard.*

St. Trophime Cloisters

Worth seeing if you have the Liberty Passport (otherwise €4, same hours as Arena), the cloisters' many small columns were scavenged from the ancient Roman theater. Enjoy the sculpted capitals, the rounded Romanesque arches (12th century), and the pointed Gothic ones (14th century). The pretty vaulted hall exhibits 17th-century tapestries showing scenes from the First Crusade to the Holy Land. There's an instructive video at the base of the stairs. On the second floor, you'll walk along an angled rooftop designed to catch rainwater—notice the slanted gutter that channeled the water into a cistern and the heavy roof slabs covering the tapestry hall below.

• *From Place de la République, exit on the far corner (opposite the church and kitty-corner from where you entered, to stroll a delightful pedestrian street.*

ARLES

⓬ Rue de la République

Rue da la République is Arles' primary shopping street. Walk downhill, enjoying the scene and popping into shops that catch your interest.

At the start is **Soulier Bakery.** Inside you'll be tempted by *fougasse* (bread studded with herbs, olives, and bacon bits), *sablés Provençal* (cookies made with honey and almonds), *tarte lavande* (a sweet almond lavender tart), and big crispy meringues (the egg-white-and-sugary answer to cotton candy—a cheap favorite of local kids). A few doors down is **Restaurant L'Atelier** (with two prized Michelin stars), **L'Occitane en Provence** (local perfumes), **Puyri-card Chocolate** (with enticing €1 treats and *calisson*, a sweet/bit-ter almond delight), as well as local design and antique shops. The fragile spiral columns on the right (just before the tourist-pleasing Lavender Boutique on the corner) show what 400 years of weather can do to decorative stonework.

• *Take the first left onto Rue Président Wilson. Just after the butcher shop (Chez Mère Grand, with local pork-and-bull sausages hanging above a counter filled with precooked dishes to take home and heat up), turn right to find the **Hôtel Dieu**, a hospital made famous by one of its patients: Vincent van Gogh.*

⓭ Espace Van Gogh Easel

In December 1888, shortly after his fa-mous ear-cutting incident (see *Café at Night* easel, described later), Vincent was admitted into the local hospital—today's Espace Van Gogh cultural center (the Espace is free, but only the courtyard is open to the public). It surrounds a flowery courtyard that the artist loved and paint-ed, when he was being treated for blood loss, hallucinations, and severe depression that left him bedridden for a month. The citizens of Arles circu-lated a petition demanding that the mad Dutchman be kept under medical supervision. Félix Rey, Vincent's kind doctor, worked out

 a compromise: The artist could leave during the day so that he could continue painting, but he had to sleep at the hospi-tal at night. Look through the postcards sold in the courtyard and find a painting of Vincent's ward showing nuns attending to patients in a gray hall *(Ward of Arles Hospital).*

• *Return to Rue de la République. Take a left and continue two blocks downhill. Take the second right up Rue Tour de Fabre and follow signs to* Fondation Van Gogh. *After a few steps, you'll pass* **La Main Qui Pense** *(The Hand That Thinks) pottery shop and workshop, where Cécile Cayrol is busy creating and teaching. A couple blocks farther at the* no right turn *sign, turn right onto Rue du Docteur Fanton. On your immediate right is the...*

❹ Fondation Van Gogh

This art foundation, worth ▲, delivers a refreshing stop for modern-art lovers and Van Gogh fans, with two temporary exhibits per year in which contemporary artists pay homage to Vincent through thought-provoking interpretations of his works. You'll also see at least one original work by Van Gogh (painted during his time in the region). The gift shop has a variety of souvenirs, prints, and postcards.

Cost and Hours: €9, daily 11:00-19:00 except closed between exhibits and likely Mon off-season—check website for current hours, audioguide-€3, Hôtel Leautaud de Donines, 35 Rue du Docteur Fanton, tel. 04 90 49 94 04, www.fondation-vincentvangogh-arles.org.

• *Continue down Rue du Docteur Fanton toward the river.*

❺ Rue du Docteur Fanton

A string of recommended restaurants is on the left. On the right is the **Crèche Municipale.** Open workdays, this is a free government-funded daycare where parents can drop off their infants up to two years old. The notion: No worker should face financial hardship in order to receive quality childcare. At the next corner is the recommended **Soleileis,** Arles' top ice cream shop.

At the strawberry-and-vanilla ice cream cone, turn right and step into **Bar El Paseo** at 4 Rue des Thermes. The main museum-like room is absolutely full of bull—including the mounted heads of three big ones who died in the local arena and a big black-and-white photo of Arles' arena packed to capacity. Senora Leal—whose family is famous for its bullfighters—has wallpapered the place with photos and bullfighting memorabilia, and serves good Spanish Rioja wine and sangria.

• *A few steps further is...*

❻ Forum Square (Place du Forum)

Named for the Roman forum that once stood here, Forum Square, worth ▲, was the political and religious center of Roman Arles. Still lively, this café-crammed square is a local watering hole and popular for a *pastis* (anise-based aperitif). The bistros on the square can put together a passable salad or *plat du jour*—and when you sprinkle on the ambience, that's €14 well spent.

At the corner of Grand Hôtel Nord-Pinus (a favorite of Pablo Picasso), a plaque shows how the Romans built a foundation of galleries to make the main square level in order to compensate for Arles' slope down to the river. The two columns are all that survive from the upper story of the entry to the forum. Steps leading to the entrance are buried—the Roman street level was about 20 feet below you.

The statue on the square is of **Frédéric Mistral** (1830-1914). This popular poet, who wrote in the local dialect rather than in French, was a champion of Provençal culture. After receiving the Nobel Prize in Literature in 1904, Mistral used his prize money to preserve and display the folk identity of Provence. He founded a regional folk museum (the Arlaten Folk Museum, closed until 2018) at a time when France was rapidly centralizing and regions like Provence were losing their unique identities. (The local mistral wind—literally "master"—has nothing to do with his name.)

• *Nearby, facing the brightly painted yellow café, find your final Van Gogh easel.*

Café at Night Easel

In October 1888, lonely Vincent—who dreamed of making Arles a magnet for fellow artists—persuaded his friend Paul Gauguin to come. He decorated Gauguin's room with several humble canvases of sunflowers (now some of the world's priciest paintings), knowing that Gauguin had admired a similar painting he'd done in Paris. Their plan was for Gauguin to be the "dean" of a new art school in Arles, and Vincent its instructor-in-chief. At first, the two got along well. They spent days side by side, rendering the same subjects in their two distinct styles. At night they hit the bars and brothels. Van Gogh's well-known *Café at Night* captures the glow of an absinthe buzz at Café la Nuit on Place du Forum.

After two months together, the two artists clashed over art and personality differences (Vincent was a slob around the house, whereas Gauguin was meticulous). The night of December 23, they were drinking absinthe at the café when Vincent suddenly went ballistic. He threw his glass at Gauguin. Gauguin left. Walking through Place Victor Hugo, Gauguin heard footsteps behind him and turned to see Vincent coming at him, brandishing a razor. Gauguin quickly fled town. The local paper reported what happened next: "At 11:30 p.m., Vincent van Gogh, painter from Holland, appeared at the brothel at no. 1, asked for Rachel, and gave her his cut-off earlobe, saying, 'Treasure this precious object.' Then he vanished." He woke up the next morning at home with his head wrapped in a bloody towel and his earlobe missing. Was Vincent emulating a successful matador, whose prize is cutting off the bull's ear?

The **bright-yellow café**—called Café la Nuit—was the subject of one of Vincent van Gogh's most famous works in Arles. Although his painting showed the café in a brilliant yellow from the glow of gas lamps, the facade was bare limestone, just like the other cafés on this square. The café is now a tourist trap that its current owners painted to match Van Gogh's version...and to cash in on the Vincent-crazed hordes who pay too much to eat or drink here.

In spring 1889, the bipolar genius (a modern diagnosis) checked himself into the St. Paul Monastery and Hospital in St-Rémy-de-Provence (see page 86). He spent a year there, thriving in the care of nurturing doctors and nuns. Painting was part of his therapy, so they gave him a studio to work in, and he produced more than 100 paintings. Alcohol-free and institutionalized, he did some of his wildest work. With thick, swirling brushstrokes and surreal colors, he made his placid surroundings throb with restless energy. Today, at the hospital in St-Rémy, you can see a replica of his room and his studio, plus many scenes he painted in situ like these in Arles—the courtyard, the plane trees, the view out the upstairs window of nearby fields, and the rugged Alpilles mountains.

Eventually, Vincent's torment became unbearable. In the spring of 1890, he left Provence to be cared for by a sympathetic doctor in Auvers-sur-Oise, just north of Paris. On July 27, he wandered into a field and shot himself. He died two days later.

• *With this walk, you have seen the best of Arles. The colorful Roquette District and the charming Réattu Museum are each a short walk away (both described later). But I'd rather enjoy a drink on the Place du Forum and savor the joy of experiencing the essence of Provence.*

Sights in Arles

The Ancient History Museum provides valuable background on Arles' Roman history: Visit it first, before delving into the rest of the city's sights (drivers should stop on the way into town). For a deeper understanding, read "How About Them Romans?" on page 29. Many of Arles' city-center sights are covered on my self-guided walk, earlier.

A Day in the Life of an Arles Citizen in the Roman Era

Ancient Rome has often been compared to America...without cars or electricity, but with slaves to make up for it. Rome's wealth made a lifestyle possible that was the envy of the known world. Let's look at a typical well-to-do Arles citizen and his family in the era of Roman rule over the course of a day.

In the morning, Nebulus reviews the finances of the country farm with his caretaker/accountant/slave. He's interrupted by a "client," one of many poorer people dependent upon him for favors. The client, a shoemaker, wants permission from the government to open a new shop. He asks Nebulus to cut through the red tape. Nebulus promises to consult a lawyer friend in the basilica, or legal building.

Hungry, Nebulus stops at Burger Emp to grab a typical fast-food lunch. Most city dwellers don't cook in their cramped, wooden apartments because of the fire hazard. After a siesta, he walks to the baths for a workout and a little business networking. He discusses plans for donating money to build a new aqueduct for the city.

The children, Raucous and Ubiquitous, say good-bye to the pet dog and head off to school in the Forum. Nothing funny happens on the way. At school, it's down to business. They learn the basic three Rs. When they get older, they'll study literature, Greek, and public speaking. (The saving grace of this dreary education is that they don't have to take Latin.)

Work done, Nebulus heads for the stadium. The public is

ON THE OUTSKIRTS
▲▲Ancient History Museum
(Musée de l'Arles et de la Provence Antiques)

Begin your town visit here, for Roman Arles 101. Located on the site of the Roman chariot racecourse (the arc of which is built into the parking lot), this air-conditioned, all-on-one-floor museum is just west of central Arles along the river. Models and original sculptures re-create the Roman city, making workaday life and culture easier to imagine. Sadly, this excellent museum describes most of its treasures only in French.

Cost and Hours: €8, covered by Liberty Passport—see "Helpful Hints," earlier; open Wed-Mon 10:00-18:00, closed Tue; Presqu'île du Cirque Romain, tel. 04 13 31 51 03, www.arles-antique.cg13.fr.

crazy about the chariot races. There are 12 per day, 240 days a year. Four teams dominate the competition (Reds, Whites, Blues, and Greens), and Nebulus has always been a die-hard Blue.

Back home, Nebulus' wife, Vapid, tends to the household affairs. She pauses in the bedroom to offer a prayer to her personal goddess for good weather for tonight. Meanwhile, the servants clean the house and send clothing to the laundry. A typical outfit is a simple woolen tunic: two pieces of cloth, front and back, sewn together at the sides. But tonight they'll dress up for a dinner party. She'll wear silk, with a wreath of flowers, and Nebulus will wear his best toga, a 20-foot-long white cloth. It's heavy and hard to put on, but it's all the rage. Nebulus dons his phallic-shaped necklace, which serves as an amulet against the evil eye and as a symbol of good luck in health, business, and bed.

At the dinner party, Vapid marvels over the chef's creation: ham soaked with honey, pasted in flour and baked. The guests toast each other with clay goblets bearing inscriptions like "Fill me up," and "Love me, baby!" Reclining on a couch, waited on by slaves, Nebulus orders a bowl of larks' tongues and a roast pig stuffed with live birds, then washes it down with wine. He calls for a feather, vomits, and starts all over. He catches the eye of a dark-skinned slave dancer from Egypt, and he takes her to the bedroom just down the hall...

...Or so went the stories. In fact, the legendary Roman orgy was just that—legendary. Romans advocated moderation and fidelity. Stuffiness and business sense were the rule. The family unit was considered sacred. If anything, the decadence of Roman life was confined to the upper classes in the later years of the empire.

Getting There: Drivers will see signs for the museum as you enter the city. Without a car, to reach the museum from the city center, take the free **Envia minibus** (stops at the train station and along Rue du 4 Septembre, then along the river—see map on page 44; 2/hour Mon-Sat, none Sun). If you're coming **on foot** from the city center (a 20-minute walk), turn left at the river and take the scruffy riverside path under two bridges to the big, modern

blue building (or better, consider strolling through Arles' enjoyable La Roquette neighborhood, described later). As you approach the museum, you'll pass the verdant Hortus Garden—designed to recall the Roman circus and chariot racecourse that were located here. A **taxi** ride costs €11 (museum can call a taxi for your return).

Visiting the Museum: The permanent collection is housed in a large hall flooded with natural light. You'll tour it counterclockwise: models of the ancient city and its major landmarks, the Roman boat (with a fine video in a tiny theater at the end of the hall), statues, mosaics, and sarcophagi. Read what English you can find, but—as much of the exhibit is in French only—here's a rundown on what you'll see.

A wall **map** of the region during the Roman era greets visitors and shows the geographic importance of Arles: Three important Roman trade routes—vias Domitia, Grippa, and Aurelia—all converged on or near Arles.

After a small exhibit on pre-Roman Arles you'll come to fascinating **models** of the Roman city and the impressive Roman

structures in (and near) Arles. These breathe life into the buildings as they looked 2,000 years ago. Start with the model of Roman Arles and ponder the city's splendor over 2,000 years ago when Arles' population was double that of today. Find the forum—it's still the center of town, though only two columns survive (the smaller section of the forum is where today's Place du Forum is built). Look at the space Romans devoted to their arena and huge racecourse—a reminder that a passion for sports is not unique to modern civilizations (the museum you're in is at the far end of the racecourse). The model also illustrates how little Arles' core has changed over two millennia, with its houses still clustered around the city center, and warehouses still located on the opposite side of the river.

At the museum's center stands the original **statue** of Julius Caesar, which once graced Arles' ancient theater stage wall. From there find individual models of the major buildings shown in the city model: the elaborately elegant forum; the floating wooden bridge that gave Arles a strategic advantage (over the widest, and therefore slowest, part of the river); the theater (with its magnificent stage wall); the arena (with its movable stadium cover to shelter spectators from sun or rain); and the hydraulic mill of Barbegal (with its 16 waterwheels powered by water cascading down a hillside).

Don't miss the large model of the **chariot racecourse.** Part of the original racecourse was just outside the windows, and though long gone, it likely resembled Rome's Circus Maximus.

A new wing (to the right) is dedicated to the museum's newest and most exciting exhibit: a **Gallo-Roman vessel** and much of its cargo. This almost-100-foot-long Roman barge was hauled out of the Rhône in 2010, along with some 280 amphorae and 3,000 ceramic artifacts. It was typical of flat-bottomed barges used to shuttle goods between Arles and ports along the Mediterranean (vessels were manually towed upriver). It sank with about 30 tons of quarried stone on board. At the end of the room, a good 30-minute video (French only) illustrates how the barge was removed from the river.

Continuing your counterclockwise circle of the museum, you'll see displays of pottery, jewelry, metal, and glass artifacts, as well as well-crafted mosaic floors that illustrate how Roman Arles was a city of art and culture. The many **statues** are all original, except for the greatest—the *Venus of Arles,* which Louis XIV took a liking to and had moved to Versailles. It's now in the Louvre—and, as locals say, "When it's in Paris...bye-bye."

The final section is dedicated to expertly carved pagan and early-Christian **sarcophagi** (from the second to fifth century A.D.). These would have lined the Via Aurelia outside the town wall. In the early days of the Church, Jesus was often portrayed beardless and as the good shepherd, with a lamb over his shoulder.

MORE SIGHTS IN ARLES
La Roquette District
To escape the tourist beat in Arles, take a detour into Arles' little-visited western fringe. Find Rue de la Roquette near the Trinqu-etaille Bridge and stroll several blocks into pleasing Place Paul Doumier, where you'll find a lively assortment of cafés, bakeries, and inexpensive bistros with nary a tourist in sight (see map on page 44). Continue along Rue de la Roquette and turn right on charming Rue Croix Rouge to reach the river. Those walking to or from the Ancient History Museum can use this appealing stroll as a shortcut.

Baths of Constantine (Thermes de Constantin)
These partly intact Roman baths were built in the early fourth century when Emperor Constantine declared Arles an imperial residence. Roman cities such as Arles had several public baths like this, fed by aqueducts and used as much for exercising, networking, and chatting with friends as for bathing. These baths were located near the Rhône River for easy water disposal. You can get a pretty good look at the baths through the fence. If you enter you'll walk elevated metal corridors at the original floor level. Imagine the elaborate engineering: the hypocaust system for heating the floor and big tubs with various temperatures—hot, tepid, and cold—next to a sauna and steam room heated by slave-stoked, wood-burning ovens.

Cost and Hours: €3, covered by Liberty Passport, same hours as Roman Arena—daily May-Sept 9:00-19:00, April and Oct 9:00-18:00, Nov-March 10:00-17:00.

▲Réattu Museum (Musée Réattu)

Housed in the former Grand Priory of the Knights of Malta, this modern-art collection, while always changing, is a stimulating and well-lit mix of new and old. Picasso loved Arles and came here regularly for the bullfights. At the end of his life in 1973, he gave the city a series of his paintings, some of which are always on display here. The permanent collection usually includes a series of works by homegrown Neoclassical artist Jacques Réattu.

Cost and Hours: €8, covered by Liberty Passport, March-Oct Tue-Sun 10:00-18:00, Nov-Feb until 17:00, closed Mon year-round, 10 Rue du Grand Prieuré, tel. 04 90 49 37 58, www.museereattu.arles.fr.

Experiences in Arles

▲▲Markets

On Wednesday and Saturday mornings, Arles' ring road erupts into an open-air festival of fish, flowers, produce...and everything Provençal. The main event is on Saturday, with vendors jamming the ring road from Boulevard Emile Combes to the east, along Boulevard des Lices near the TI (the heart of the market), and continuing down Boulevard Georges Clemenceau to the west. Wednesday's market runs only along Boulevard Emile Combes, between Place Lamartine and Avenue Victor Hugo; the segment nearest Place Lamartine is all about food, and the upper half features clothing, tablecloths, purses, and so on. On the first Wednesday of the month, a flea market doubles the size of the usual Wednesday market along Boulevard des Lices near the main TI. Both markets are open until about 12:30. Dive in: Buy some flowers for your hotelier, try the olives, sample some wine, swat a pickpocket, and speak some Arabic.

Part of the market has a North African feel, thanks to the many Algerians and Moroccans who live in Arles. As with immigrants in any rich country, they came to do the lowly city jobs that locals didn't want, and now they mostly do the region's labor-intensive agricultural jobs (picking olives, harvesting fruit, and working in local greenhouses; see sidebar on page 229).

▲▲Bullgames *(Courses Camarguaises)*

Provençal "bullgames" are held in Arles and in neighboring towns. Those in Arles occupy the same seats that fans have used for nearly 2,000 years, and deliver the city's most memorable experience—the *courses camarguaises* in the ancient arena. The nonviolent bullgames are more sporting than bloody bullfights (though traditional Spanish-style bullfights still take place on occasion). The bulls of Arles (who, locals insist, "die of old age") are promoted in posters even more boldly than their human foes. In the bullgame, a ribbon *(cocarde)* is laced between the bull's horns. The *razeteur,* with a special hook, has 15 minutes to snare the ribbon. Local businessmen encourage a *razeteur* (dressed in white, with a red cummerbund) by shouting out how much money they'll pay for the *cocarde*. If the bull pulls a good stunt, the band plays the famous "Toreador" song from *Carmen*. The following day, newspapers report on the games, including how many *Carmens* the bull earned.

ARLES

Three classes of bullgames—determined by the experience of the *razeteurs*—are advertised in posters: The *course de protection* is for rookies. The *trophée de l'Avenir* comes with more experience. And the *trophée des As* features top professionals. During Easter *(Féria du Pâques)* and the fall rice-harvest festival *(Féria du Riz),* the arena hosts traditional Spanish bullfights (look for *corrida*) with outfits, swords, spikes, and the whole gory shebang. (Nearby villages stage *courses camarguaises* in small wooden bullrings nearly every weekend; TIs have the latest schedule.)

Cost and Hours: Arles' bullgame tickets usually run €7-20; bullfights are pricier (€36-100). Schedules for bullgames vary (usually July-Aug on Wed and Fri)—ask at the TI or check online at www.arenes-arles.com.

Easter and Fall Fairs (Féria du Pâques and Féria du Riz)

For 150 years, Arles has thrown citywide parties to celebrate the arrival of spring and fall. During the four days that each event lasts, more than 500,000 people pile into Arles for bullfights, street concerts, piles of paella, and parties (*Feria du Pâques* is Fri-Mon of Easter weekend, and *Feria du Riz* is Fri-Mon on the second weekend of Sept). The Easter event kicks off the bullfighting season, while the September event celebrates the land and traditions of Arles. Only during these fairs are bulls killed in the bullfights and only during these events does Arles feel overrun.

Sleeping in Arles

Hotels are a great value here—many are air-conditioned, though few have elevators. The Calendal, Musée, and Régence hotels offer exceptional value.

$$$ Hôtel le Calendal*** is a thoughtfully managed place

ARLES

Sleep Code

Abbreviations   **(€1 = about $1.10, country code: 33)**
S=Single, **D**=Double/Twin, **T**=Triple, **Q**=Quad, **b**=bathroom,
*=French hotel rating (0-5 stars)
Price Rankings
  $$$ **Higher Priced**—Most rooms €90 or more
   $$ **Moderately Priced**—Most rooms €65-90
    $ **Lower Priced**—Most rooms €65 or less
Unless otherwise noted, credit cards are accepted, breakfast
is not included, free Wi-Fi and/or a guest computer are gener-
ally available, and English is spoken. Prices change; verify cur-
rent rates online or by email. For the best prices, always book
directly with the hotel.

---

ideally located between the Roman Arena and Classical Theater.
The hotel opens to the street with airy lounges and a lovely palm-
shaded courtyard, providing an enjoyable refuge. They serve an
elaborate €12 buffet breakfast and offer lunch in the courtyard
or at their café/sandwich bar (daily 8:00-19:00). The rooms sport
Provençal decor and come in random shapes and sizes (standard
Db-€119, larger or balcony Db-€139-159, Tb/family-€199, air-
con, reserve ahead for parking-€8/day, just above arena at 5 Rue
Porte de Laure, tel. 04 90 96 11 89, www.lecalendal.com, contact@
lecalendal.com). They also run the nearby, budget Hostel La Maison du Pelerin, described later.

$$ Hôtel du Musée** is a quiet, affordable manor-home hide-
away tucked deep in Arles (if driving, ask for access code to street
barrier so you can drop off your bags). This delightful place comes
with 28 wood-floored rooms, a flowery courtyard, and comfortable
lounges. Lighthearted Claude and English-speaking Laurence are
good hosts (Sb-€65, Db-€70-90, Tb-€95-100, Qb-€130, buffet
breakfast-€8.50, no elevator, garage parking-€10/day, follow signs
to *Réattu Museum* to 11 Rue du Grand Prieuré, tel. 04 90 93 88 88,
www.hoteldumusee.com, contact@hoteldumusee.com).

$$ Hôtel de la Muette**, run by Brigitte and Alain, is located
in a quiet corner of Arles. Rooms come with stone walls, tiled floors,
and pebble showers (Db-€81, Tb-€95, family room-€100, direct
booking discount for Rick Steves readers, buffet breakfast-€9, no
elevator, private garage-€10/day, 15 Rue des Suisses, tel. 04 90 96
15 39, www.hotel-muette.com, hotel.muette@wanadoo.fr).

$ Hôtel Régence**, a top budget deal, has a riverfront location,
comfortable Provençal rooms, safe parking, and near the train station (Db-€60-75, Tb-€90-105, Qb-€100-120, choose river-view
or quieter courtyard rooms, good buffet breakfast-€6, no elevator
but only two floors, garage parking-€7/day; from Place Lamartine,

turn right after passing between towers to reach 5 Rue Marius Jouveau; tel. 04 90 96 39 85, www.hotel-regence.com, contact@hotel-regence.com). Gentle Valérie and Eric speak English.

$$ Hôtel Acacias**, just off Place Lamartine and inside the old city walls, is a modern hotel with small yet inviting and comfortable rooms (standard Sb-€60, Db-€60-75, Tb-€75-90, breakfast-€8, air-con, 2 Rue de la Cavalerie, tel. 04 90 96 37 88, www.hotel-acacias.com, contact@hotel-acacias.com).

$ Hôtel Voltaire rents 12 small, spartan rooms with ceiling fans and nifty balconies overlooking a colorful, working-class square. A block below the arena, the rooms have rough edges but are really cheap. "Mr." Ferran loves the States, and hopes you'll add to his license plate or postcard collection (D-€32, Ds-€37, Db-€42, no air-con, no elevator, Wi-Fi in restaurant only, 1 Place Voltaire, tel. 04 90 96 49 18, levoltaire13@aol.com).

$ Hostel La Maison du Pelerin offers good dorm rooms with three to six beds per room. It's a great value for pilgrims, backpackers, and those on a shoestring, with a shared kitchen and homey living area. Check in next door at the recommended Hôtel le Calendal (they own the place, €25/person, sheets included but not towels, shared baths, just above the Roman Arena at 26 Place Pomme, tel. 06 99 71 11 89, www.arles-pelerins.fr).

NEAR ARLES

Many drivers, particularly those with families, prefer staying outside Arles in the peaceful countryside, with easy access to the area's sights. (See also "Sleeping in and near Les Baux," on page 82.)

$$$ Mas du Petit Grava is a vintage Provençal farmhouse 15 tree-lined minutes east of Arles. Here California refugees Jim and Ike offer an enthusiastic welcome and rent four large and well-cared-for rooms with tubs, tiles, and Van Gogh themes (Jim is an expert on Vincent's life and art). Their lovely garden surrounds a swimming pool (Db-€110-130, includes fine breakfast, no air-con, tel. 04 90 98 35 66, www.masdupetitgrava.net, masdupetitgrava@masdupetitgrava.net). From Arles, drive east on D-453 toward St-Martin de Crau (1.5 miles), then turn left on route St. Hippolyte to the right of the large white-and-blue building.

$$$ Mas Petit Fourchon is a grand farmhouse with spacious rooms on a sprawling property a few minutes from Arles. There's acres of room to roam and a big pool (Db-€115-135, includes breakfast, no air-con, 1070 Chemin de Nadal in the Fourchon suburb, tel. 04 90 96 16 35, www.petitfourchon.com, info@petitfourchon.com).

$$ Domaine de Laforest, located a few minutes below Fontvieille, near the aqueduct of Barbegal, is a 320-acre spread engulfed

ARLES

Arles Hotels & Restaurants

1. Hôtel/Rest. le Calendal & Hostel La Maison du Pelerin
2. Hôtel du Musée
3. Hôtel de la Muette
4. Hôtel Régence
5. Hôtel Acacias
6. Hôtel/Rest. Voltaire
7. To Mas du Petit Grava & Mas Petit Fourchon
8. To Domaine de Laforest
9. La Taverne du Forum
10. La Piazza des Thermes
11. Cafés de la Major
12. La Cuisine de Comptoir
13. Fad'Ola
14. Rue du Dr. Fanton Eateries
15. Le Criquet Restaurant
16. Delicate and Saine Wine Bar
17. L'Atelier & A Côté Restaurants
18. Soleileis Ice Cream

CHEMIN VERRERIE

RUE GEORGES GUYNEMER

RUE DES CAPUCINS

RUE ROBESPIERRE

RUE DE LA VERRERIE

RUE

TRINQUETAILLE

RUE CAMARGUE

RUE ST. PIERRE

QUAI ST. PIERRE

R. A. BENOIT

Rhône

TRINQUETAILLE BRIDGE

QUAI MARX DORMOY

R. DE LA TOUR DU FABRE

R. TRUCHET

R. DR. FANTON

14

FONDATION VAN GOGH

12

LIBERTE

Ⓑ Envia Bus Stops

RUE A. FRANCE

R. JOUVENE

ARLATEN FOLK MUSEUM (REOPENS IN 2018)

QUAI DE LA ROQUETTE

R. DES PORCELETS

Place Paul Doumier

RUE DE LA REPUBLIQUE

ESPACE VAN GOGH

RUE CROIX ROUGE

RUE DE LA ROQUETTE

RUE DE CHARTROUSE

RUE JEAN GRANAUD

RUE GAMBETTA

RUE PRES. WILSON

To Ancient History Museum

LA ROQUETTE

RUE MOLIERE

Place Genive

RUE FLEURY PRUDHON

RUE MOLIERE

To Nîmes via A-84

RUE RAILLON

To Ancient History Museum

BLVD. G. CLEMENCEAU

RUE PARMENTIER

ARLES

N

100 Meters
100 Yards

River

TRAIN & BUS STATION Ⓑ

To Les Baux, Fontvielle, Avignon & ⑧

RUE GORODICHE

AVE. PAULIN TALBOT

AVE. DE STALINGRAD

MONOPRIX PARKING

MONOPRIX DEP'T STORE

Place Lamartine Ⓑ

PETANQUE

CAVALERIE GATE

BLVD. EMILE COMBES Ⓑ

RUE JULES FERRY

④ ⑤

RUE CAVALERIE

R. TERRIN

R. PUITS

QUAI MARX DORMOY

R. JOUVEAU

R. L. BLUM

RUE METRAS

RUE BALZAC

⑥ Place Voltaire

RUE CONDORCET

BATHS OF CONSTANTINE

REATTU MUSEUM

RUE GRAND PRIEURE

② Ⓑ

RUE DE QUATRE SEPTEMBRE

RUE GRILLE

L'AMPHITHEATRE

RUE DU QUATRE SEPTEMBRE

R. R. A. BARBES

INTERNET CAFE

RUE VOLTAIRE

RUE EUZEBY

R. BOILEAU

LA FONTAINE

RUE PORTAGNEL

A. TARDIEU

DU FOUR

⑩

SAUVAGE

⑪

RUE SUISSES

R. RASPAIL

R. A. BRIAND

R. FAURE

RUE REFUGE

③

R. VERNON

R. PERRIAT

R. CHOU

ROND-POINT DES ARENES

PARVIS DES ARENES

⑱ ⑬

RUE DE L'HOTEL DE VILLE

RUE DES ARENES

ROMAN ARENA

NOTRE DAME

FAVORIN

R. NICOLAI

R. DIDEROT

ROND-POINT DES ARENES

RUE MADELINE

⑨ Place du Forum

R. BALZE

RUE DE LA CALADE

⑯

①

BLVD. EMILE COMBES

WC

ST. TROPHIME

CLASSICAL THEATER

PORTE DE LAURE

R. L'AGNEAU

⑮

Ⓑ

Place de la République

CLOISTERS

R. EMILE BARRERE

ANCIENT CITY WALLS

R. JEAN JAURES

RUE DU CLOITRE

MONTEE VAUBAN

TOUR DES MOURGUES

⑰

RUE ROTONDE

Jardin d'Ete

PLAYGROUND

TAXIS Ⓣ

BLVD. DES LICES

AVE. VICTOR HUGO

Esplanade Charles de Gaulle ❶

POST

Ⓟ

Ⓑ

AVE. ALYSCAMPS

To ⑦

by vineyards, rice fields, and swaying trees. The sweet owners (Sylvie and mama Mariette) rent eight two-bedroom apartments with great weekly rates, rentable for fewer days when available (€310, €400, or €850 per week, air-con, washing machines, pool, big lawn, swings, 1000 Route de l'Aqueduc Romain, tel. 04 90 54 70 25, www.domaine-laforest.com, contact@domaine-laforest.com).

Eating in Arles

You can dine well in Arles on a modest budget (most of my listings have *menus* for under €25). Sunday is a quiet night for restaurants, though eateries on Place du Forum are open. For groceries, consider the big, Monoprix supermarket/department store on Place Lamartine (Mon-Sat 8:30-20:00, closed Sun).

PLACE DU FORUM NEIGHBORHOOD

Great atmosphere and mediocre food at fair prices await on Place du Forum. Avoid the garish yellow Café la Nuit. Other cafés on the square deliver acceptable quality and terrific ambience. For serious cuisine, wander away from the square.

On and near Place du Forum

Before dinner on the main square, consider one of the most local rituals you can enjoy in Arles: enjoying a *pastis*. This anise-based aperitif is served straight with ice, along with a carafe of water—dilute to taste.

La Taverne du Forum is my choice for a fun and inexpensive meal on Place du Forum—with a good selection of salads, pizzas, and *plats* for €12 or so. Their tables are the best on the square, it's family friendly, and the servers are fun to clown around with (13 Place du Forum, no indoor seating, tel. 04 90 96 08 80).

La Piazza des Thermes, an inviting eatery a few blocks north of Place du Forum, serves good pizza and pasta for €10-15 and has comfortable indoor and outdoor seating (daily except closed Sun lunch, 6 Rue du Sauvage, tel. 04 90 49 60 64).

Cafés de la Major is *the* place to go to recharge with some serious coffee or tea (Tue-Sat 8:30-19:00, closed Sun-Mon, 7 bis Rue Réattu, tel. 04 90 96 14 15).

La Cuisine de Comptoir offers light dinners of *tartine*—a cross between pizza and bruschetta, served with soup or salad for €11—and offers a fun array of pizza-style *tartine* toppings from which to choose. This Provençal answer to a pizzeria—run by Alexandre and Vincent—has mostly indoor seating (closed Sun, just off the lower end of Place du Forum at 10 Rue de la Liberté, tel. 04 90 96 86 28).

Fad'Ola is a colorful hole-in-the-wall serving fresh and simple dishes and sandwiches just off Place du Forum. Canadian expat Cindy offers a good €12 deal: sandwich, greens, and a drink (daily 12:00-17:00, July-Aug until 23:00, Nov-March until 15:00, 46 Rue des Arènes, tel. 04 90 49 70 73).

On Rue du Docteur Fanton

Rue du Docteur Fanton, a block below the Forum, is lined by four good restaurants. Each has its own character and serves enticing *menus* for around €14 at lunch and €20-30 for dinner. Come here to peruse your options side by side. You can't go wrong—all offer good value and have appealing indoor and outdoor seating. And, for your dessert pleasure, the town's best ice cream place is just across the street.

Les Filles du 16 is a warm, affordable place to enjoy a fresh salad (€11), or a fine two- or three-course dinner (€21-27). The choices are limited, so check the selection before sitting down. The *taureau* (bull's meat) in a tasty sauce is a good choice (closed Sat-Sun, 16 Rue du Docteur Fanton, tel. 04 90 93 77 36).

Au Brin de Thym, a few doors down, offers a blend of traditional French and Provençal cuisine in an intimate setting with rickety little Bohemian-chic tables. Arrive early for an outdoor table (€14 lunch *menus,* €31 at dinner, €20 *plats;* closed Tue, 22 Rue du Docteur Fanton, tel. 04 90 97 85 18).

Le Plaza buzzes with happy diners and is run by a young couple (Stéphane cooks while Graziela serves). It features delicious Provençal cuisine at good prices (€23 *menus,* closed Wed Oct-March, 28 Rue du Docteur Fanton, tel. 04 90 96 33 15).

Le Galoubet is a popular local spot, blending a warm interior, traditional French cuisine, and service with a smile, thanks to owner Frank. It's the most expensive of the places I list on this street and the least flexible, serving a €32 *menu* only. If it's cold, a roaring fire keeps you toasty (closed Sun-Mon, great fries and desserts, 18 Rue du Docteur Fanton, tel. 04 90 93 18 11).

And for Dessert: Soleileis has Arles' best ice cream, made with organic milk, fresh fruit, all-natural ingredients, and creative flavors that fit the season. There's also a shelf of English books for exchange (daily 14:00-18:30, closed in winter, a block off the Forum at 9 Rue du Docteur Fanton, run by Marijtje).

NEAR THE ROMAN ARENA

Several little restaurants overlook the Roman Arena, offering a stony and ancient backdrop for your dinner.

Le Criquet, a sweet little place two blocks above the arena, serves Provençal classics with joy at good prices. If you're really hungry, try the €25 *bourride*—a creamy fish soup thickened with aioli and garlic and stuffed with mussels, clams, calamari, and more (good €24-28 *menus,* indoor and outdoor dining, 21 Rue Porte de Laure, tel. 04 90 96 80 51).

Delicate and Saine Wine Bar has no real kitchen, but Julie Moreau manages to dish up enticing €5-10 gourmet *plats,* matched with a nice list of wine by the glass and huge arena views (30 Rond-Point des Arènes, tel. 06 82 44 88 74).

Hôtel le Calendal, just around the corner from the arena without the view, serves light seasonal food in its lovely courtyard or at the café (delicious little €2.50 sandwiches, daily 8:00-19:00, see hotel listing, earlier, for location).

Hôtel Voltaire, on a characteristic square away from most tourists, serves simple three-course lunches and dinners at honest prices (€14 *menus;* hearty *plats* and filling salads for €11—try the *salade fermière, salade Latine,* or, if tapenade is your thing, the filling *assiette Provençale;* closed Sun evening, on Place Voltaire below the arena).

A GASTRONOMIC DINING EXPERIENCE

One of France's most recognized chefs, Jean-Luc Rabanel, runs two very different places 50 yards from Place de la République (at 7 Rue des Carmes). They sit side by side, both offering indoor and terrace seating.

L'Atelier, a destination restaurant with two Michelin stars, attracts people from great distances to happily pay €125 for dinner and €65 for lunch. There is no menu, just a parade of delicious taste sensations served in artsy dishes. Don't plan on a quick dinner, and don't come for a traditional setting: Everything is enthusiastically contemporary. You'll probably see or hear the famous chef with his long salt-and-pepper hair and deep voice (closed Mon-Tue, book ahead, friendly servers will hold your hand through this palate-widening experience, tel. 04 90 91 07 69, www.rabanel.com).

A Côté, next door, offers a smart wine bar/bistro ambience and top-quality cuisine for much less money. Here you can sample the famous chef's talents with the €31 three-course *menu* (limited selection of wines by the glass, open daily, tel. 04 90 47 61 13, www.bistro-acote.com).

Arles Connections

BY TRAIN

Note that some trains in and out of Arles require a reservation. These include connections with Nice to the east and Bordeaux to the west (including intermediary stops). Ask at the station.

Compare train and bus schedules: For some nearby destinations the bus may be the better choice, and it's usually cheaper.

From Arles by Train to: Paris (11/day, 2 direct TGVs—4

hours, 9 more with transfer in Avignon—5 hours), **Avignon Cen-tre-Ville** (roughly hourly, 20 minutes), **Nîmes** (9/day, 30 minutes), **Orange** (4/day direct, 35 minutes, more with transfer in Avignon), **Aix-en-Provence Centre-Ville** (10/day, 2 hours, transfer in Marseille, train may separate midway—be sure your section is going to Aix-en-Provence), **Marseille** (11/day, 1 hour), **Cassis** (7/day, 2 hours), **Carcassonne** (4/day direct, 2.5 hours, more with transfer in Narbonne, direct trains may require reservations), **Beaune** (10/day, 5 hours), **Nice** (11/day, 4 hours, most require transfer in Marseille), **Barcelona** (3/day, 4.5 hours, transfer in Nîmes), **Italy** (3/day, transfer in Marseille and Nice; from Arles, it's 5 hours to Ventimiglia on the border, 8 hours to Milan, 9 hours to Cinque Terre, 11 hours to Florence, and 13 hours to Venice or Rome).

BY BUS

Arles' bus station is next to its train station. All buses to regional destinations depart from here and most cost only €1.50. Get schedules at the TI or from the bus company (tel. 08 10 00 13 26, www.lepilote.com).

From Arles Train Station to Avignon TGV Station: The direct SNCF bus is easier than the train (€9, 8/day, 1 hour, included with rail pass). You can also take the train from Arles to Avignon's Centre-Ville Station, then catch the *navette* (shuttle bus) to the TGV Station (2-block walk, see page 98).

From Arles by Bus to Les Baux and St-Rémy: Bus #57 connects Arles to St-Rémy-de-Provence via Les Baux (6/day daily July-Aug, Sat-Sun only in May-June and Sept, none Oct-April; 35 minutes to Les Baux, 50 minutes to St-Rémy, then runs to Avignon). Bus #54 also goes to St-Rémy but not via Les Baux (5/day Mon-Fri, 3/day Sat, none on Sun, 1 hour). For other ways to reach Les Baux and St-Rémy, see page 76.

By Bus to Other Destinations: Nîmes (8/day Mon-Sat, 3/day Sun, 1 hour), **Aix-en-Provence** (faster than trains, 5/day Mon-Sat, 2/day Sun, 1.5 hours), **Fontvieille** (6/day, 10 minutes), **Camargue/Stes-Maries-de-la-Mer** (bus #20, 6/day Mon-Sat, 3/day Sun, 1 hour).

NEAR ARLES

Les Baux • St-Rémy-de-Provence • The Camargue

The diverse terrain around Arles harbors many worthwhile and easy day trips. The medieval ghost town of Les Baux haunts the eerie Alpilles mountains, while chic and compact St-Rémy-de-Provence awaits just over the hills, offering Roman ruins and memories of Vincent van Gogh. For an entirely different experience, the flat Camargue knocks on Arles' southern door with sandy beaches, saltwater lakes, rice paddies, flamingos, wild horses, and wild black bulls.

PLANNING YOUR TIME

Because public transportation in this area is sparse, these sights are most convenient by car, taxi, or minivan tour. For a memorable one-day road trip from Arles or Avignon, spend the morning in Les Baux (before the crowds), have lunch in St-Rémy and explore its sights, then finish at the Roman aqueduct of Barbegal. Nondrivers can do the same day trip (without the aqueduct) by bus and taxi. If you have more time or are a nature or bird-watching buff, head for the Camargue. A good market pops up on Friday mornings in little Eyguières (near Les Baux and St-Rémy).

Near Arles

Les Baux

The hilltop town of Les Baux crowns the rugged Alpilles (ahl-pee) mountains, evoking a tumultuous medieval history. Here, you can imagine the struggles of a strong community that lived a rough-and-tumble life—thankful more for their top-notch fortifications than for their dramatic views. It's mobbed with tourists most of the day, but Les Baux rewards those who arrive by 9:00 or after 17:30. (Although the hilltop citadel's entry closes at the end of the day, once you're inside, you're welcome to live out your medieval fantasies all night long, even with a picnic.) Sunsets are dramatic, the castle is brilliantly illuminated after dark, and nights in Les Baux are pin-drop peaceful. (If you like what you see here, but want a more off-the-beaten-path experience, head for the Luberon and find Fort de Buoux—see page 221).

GETTING TO LES BAUX

By Car: Les Baux is a 20-minute drive from Arles: Follow signs for *Avignon*, then *Les Baux*. Drivers can combine Les Baux with St-Rémy (15 minutes away) and the ruined Roman aqueduct of Barbegal.

By Bus: From Arles, Cartreize **bus #57** runs to Les Baux (daily July-Aug, in May-June and Sept Sat-Sun only, none Oct-April, 6/day, 35 minutes; via Abbey of Montmajour, Fontvieille, and Le Paradou; destination: St-Rémy, timetables at www.lepilote.com).

St-Rémy, about seven miles north of Les Baux, is a workable transit point for those home-basing in Avignon: Ride Cartreize bus #57 from Avignon to St-Rémy (6/day, 45 minutes); you can continue to Les Baux on the same bus daily in July-August and on weekends in May-June and September (none Oct-April, timetables at www.lepilote.com). Otherwise, continue to Les Baux by taxi (next).

By Taxi: If buses aren't running to Les Baux, you can taxi there from St-Rémy, then take another taxi to return to St-Rémy or to your home base. Figure €30 for a taxi one-way to Les Baux from Arles, €55 from Avignon, and €20 from St-Rémy (mobile 06 80 27 60 92).

By Minivan Tour: The best option for many is a minivan tour, which can be both efficient and economical (easiest from Avignon; see page 26).

Orientation to Les Baux

Les Baux is actually two visits in one: castle ruins perched on an almost lunar landscape, and a medieval town below. Savor the castle, then tour—or blitz—the lower streets on your way out. While the town, which lives entirely off tourism, is packed with shops, cafés, and tourist knickknacks, the castle above stays manageable because crowds are dispersed over a big area. The lower town's polished-stone gauntlet of boutiques is a Provençal dream come true for shoppers.

TOURIST INFORMATION

The TI is immediately on the left as you enter the village (April-Oct Mon-Fri 9:00-18:00, Sat-Sun 10:00-17:30; off-season Mon-

Sat 9:30-17:00, closed Sun). The TI has free Wi-Fi and can call a cab for you.

ARRIVAL IN LES BAUX

Drivers pay €5 to park near the village (behind the barrier), or €4 to park several blocks below (you'll pass the parking lot on your way in; the ticket is good for the day). Pay at the machine just below the town entry (next to the WC and bakery) before you return to your car—you'll need the validated ticket to exit the lot. You can park for free at the Carrières de Lumières (described later) and walk along the road to Les Baux (be careful—the road is narrow, with blind curves).

After parking, walk up the cobbled street into town, where you're greeted first by the TI. From here the main drag leads directly to the castle—just keep going uphill (a 10-minute walk).

Sights in Les Baux

▲▲▲THE CASTLE RUINS (CHATEAU DES BAUX)

The sun-bleached ruins of the stone fortress of Les Baux are carved into, out of, and on top of a rock 650 feet above the valley floor.

Many of the ancient walls of this striking castle still stand as a testament to the proud past of this once-feisty village.

Cost and Hours: €8, €10 if there's "entertainment" (described next), €15 combo-ticket with Carrières de Lumières (described later), includes excellent audioguide available up to one hour before closing, daily Easter-June and Sept 9:00-19:15, July-Aug 9:00-20:15, March and Oct 9:30-18:30, Nov-Feb 10:00-17:00, www.chateau-baux-provence.com. If you're inside the castle when the entry closes, you can stay as long as you like.

Entertainment: Every day from April through September, the castle presents medieval pageantry, tournaments, demonstrations of catapults and crossbows, and jousting matches. Pick up a schedule as you enter (or check online).

Picnicking: While no food or drink is sold inside the castle grounds, you're welcome to bring your own and use one of several picnic tables (the best view table is at the edge near the siege weaponry). Sunset dinner picnics are memorable.

Background: Imagine the importance of this citadel in the Middle Ages, when the Lords of Baux were notorious warriors (who could trace their lineage back to one of the "three kings" of

Les Baux

1 Le Mas d'Aigret Hôtel
2 Hostellerie de la Reine Jeanne
3 To Maussane Hotels & Rest.
4 To Le Mazet des Alpilles B&B

D-27

To Views,
Carrières de Lumières
& St-Rémy
via most scenic route

100 Meters

100 Yards

To St-Rémy,
Maussane,
Le Paradou & 3

1

D-27A

RUE PORTE MAGE

PORTE
MAGE

WC

2

1

DONJON

MUSEUM OF
SANTONS

Place
St-Louis
Jou

Uphill!

CASTLE
RUINS

GRAND RUE

LOWER

MANVILLE
MANSION
CITY HALL

CITADEL

EYGUIERES
GATE

TOWN

YVES BRAYER
MUSEUM

NEUVE

RENAISSANCE
WINDOW

FOURS

CHATEAU

CHAPEL OF
PENITENTS

ST.
VINCENT

WC

R. L'ORME

TICKETS &
ENTRY TO
CASTLE RUINS

Cemetery

TRENCAT

ST. BLAISE
CHAPEL

Cliffs

Cliffs

To Arles,
Fontvielle
& 4

CHARLOUN-RIEU
MONUMENT

NEAR ARLES

Christmas-carol fame, Balthazar). In the 11th century, Les Baux was a powerhouse in southern France, controlling about 80 towns. The Lords of Baux fought the counts of Barcelona for control of Provence...and eventually lost. But while in power, these guys were mean. One ruler enjoyed forcing unransomed prisoners to jump off his castle walls.

In 1426, Les Baux was incorporated into Provence and France. Not accustomed to subservience, Les Baux struggled with the French king, who responded by destroying the fortress in 1483. Later, Les Baux regained some importance and emerged as a center of Protestantism. Arguing with Rome was a high-stakes game in the 17th century, and Les Baux's association with the Huguenots brought destruction again in 1632 when Cardinal Richelieu (under King Louis XIII) demolished the castle. Louis rubbed salt in the wound by billing Les Baux's residents for his demolition expenses. The once-powerful town of 4,000 was forever crushed.

Visiting the Castle: Buy your ticket in the old olive mill and inspect the models of Les Baux before its 17th-century destruction.

Note the time and location for any scheduled medieval entertainment and pick up your audioguide. The audioguide follows posted numbers all around the rocky spur. As you wander, key in the number for any of the 30 narrated stops that interest you.

As you walk on the windblown spur (*baux* in French), you'll pass kid-thrilling medieval siege weaponry (go ahead, try the battering ram). Good displays in English help reconstruct the place. Imagine 4,000 people living up here. Notice the water-catchment system (a slanted field that caught rainwater and drained it into cisterns—necessary during a siege) and find the reservoir cut into the rock below the castle's highest point. Look for post holes throughout the stone walls that reveal where beams once supported floors.

For the most sensational views, climb to the blustery top of the citadel. Hang on. The mistral wind just might blow you away.

The St. Blaise chapel across from the entry/exit runs videos with Provençal themes (plays continuously; just images and music, no words).

▲LOWER TOWN

After your castle visit, you can shop and eat your way back through the lower town. Or, escape some of the crowds by visiting these minor but worthwhile sights as you descend. I've linked the sights with walking directions.

• *Follow the main drag about 100 yards through the town and look for the flags marking...*

Manville Mansion City Hall

The 15th-century City Hall offers art exhibits under its cool vaults. It occasionally flies the red-and-white flag of Monaco amid several others, a reminder that the Grimaldi family (longtime rulers of the tiny principality of Monaco) owned Les Baux until the French Revolution (1789). In fact, in 1982, Princess Grace Kelly and her royal husband, Prince Rainier Grimaldi, came to Les Baux to receive the key to the city.

Exit left and walk uphill 20 steps to the empty 1571 **Renaissance window frame.** This beautiful stone frame stands as a reminder of this town's Protestant history. This was probably a place of Huguenot worship—the words carved into the lintel, *Post tenebras lux,* were a popular Calvinist slogan: "After the shadow comes the light."

• *Continue walking uphill, and turn right on Rue des Fours to find the...*

Yves Brayer Museum (Musée Yves Brayer)

This enjoyable museum lets you peruse three floors of paintings (Van Gogh-like Expressionism) by Yves Brayer (1907-1990), who spent his final years here in Les Baux. Like Van Gogh, Brayer was inspired by all that surrounded him, and by his travels through Morocco, Spain, and the rest of the Mediterranean world. Pick up the descriptive English sheet at the entry.

Cost and Hours: €5, daily April-Sept 10:00-12:30 & 14:00-18:30, shorter hours and closed Tue Oct-Dec and March, closed Jan-Feb, tel. 04 90 54 36 99, www.yvesbrayer.com.

• *Next door is...*

St. Vincent Church

This 12th-century Romanesque church was built short and wide to fit the terrain. The center chapel on the right (partially carved out of the rock) houses the town's traditional Provençal processional chariot. Each Christmas Eve, a ram pulled this cart—holding a lamb, symbolizing Jesus, and surrounded by candles—through town to the church.

• *As you leave the church, WCs are to the left (dug into the stone wall) and up the stairs. Directly in front of the church is a vast view, making clear the strategic value of this rocky bluff's natural fortifications. A few steps away is the...*

Chapel of Penitents

Inside, notice the Nativity scene painted by Yves Brayer, illustrating the local legend that says Jesus was born in Les Baux.

• *As you leave the church, turn left and find the old town "laundry"—*

with a pig-snout faucet and 14th-century stone washing surface designed for short women.

Continue past the Yves Brayer Museum again, branch off to the left, and walk 100 yards down steep Rue de la Calade, passing a café with wonderful views, the town's fortified wall, and one of its two gates. Before long, you'll run into the...

Museum of Santons

This free and fun "museum" displays a collection of *santons* ("little saints"), popular folk figurines that decorate local Christmas mangers. Notice how the Nativity scene "proves" once again that Jesus was born in Les Baux. These painted clay dolls show off local dress and traditions (with good English descriptions).

NEAR LES BAUX

▲Carrières de Lumières (Quarries of Light)

A 10-minute walk from Les Baux, this colossal quarry-cave with immense vertical walls offers a mesmerizing sound-and-slide experience. Enter a darkened world filled with floor-to-ceiling images and booming music. Wander through a complex of cathedral-like aisles, transepts, and choirs (no seating provided) as you experience the spectacle. There's no storyline to follow, but information panels by the café give some background. The show lasts 40 minutes and runs continuously. If you'd like an intermission, you can exit the "show" into a part of the quarry that opens to the sky and take a break at the café before re-entering. Dress warmly, as the cave is cool.

Cost and Hours: €11, €16 combo-ticket with Les Baux castle ruins, daily April-Sept 9:30-19:30, March and Oct-Dec 10:00-18:00, closed Jan-Feb, tel. 04 90 54 47 37, www.carrieres-lumieres.com.

Les Baux Views and St-Rémy Loop Trip

A half-mile beyond Les Baux, D-27 (toward Maillane) leads to dramatic views of the hill town. There are pullouts with great vistas, and cavernous caves in former limestone quarries dating back to the Middle Ages. (The limestone is easy to cut, but gets hard and nicely polished when exposed to the weather.) In 1821, the rocks and soil of this area were found to contain an important mineral for making aluminum. It was named after the town: bauxite.

For sensational views over Les Baux, continue up D-27 to the top, turn right on the paved road (at the red *Alt.110* sign), and go 100 yards. You'll see walking trails nearby (ask at TIs for info on hikes in the Alpilles; Les Baux to St-Rémy is a 2.5-hour hike).

D-27 continues to St-Rémy, allowing for a handy loop trip (to complete the loop, return from St-Rémy to Les Baux via D-5). For details, see "Getting to St-Rémy" on page 85.

BETWEEN LES BAUX AND ARLES
Abbey of Montmajour

This brooding hulk of a ruin, just a few minutes' drive from Arles toward Les Baux, was once a thriving abbey and a convenient papal retreat (c. A.D. 950). Today, the vacant abbey church is a massive example of Romanesque architecture that comes with great views from its tower. Film buffs will appreciate this sight as the setting for *The Lion in Winter*, where Eleanor of Aquitaine (played by Katharine Hepburn) battled with her husband, Henry II (Peter O'Toole). For more on abbeys, see the sidebar on page 212.

The surrounding fields were a favorite of Van Gogh, who walked here from Arles to paint his famous wheat fields.

Cost and Hours: €8; closed Mon; tel. 04 90 54 64 17.

▲Roman Aqueduct of Barbegal

To be all alone with evocative Roman ruins, drivers can take a quick detour to the crumbled arches of ancient Arles' principal aqueduct.

The aqueduct *(L'Aqueduc Romain)* is a few minutes south of Fontvieille on the D-82 (well signed off the D-17 to Arles). Park at the dirt pullout (just after the *Los Pozos Blancos* sign, where the ruins of the aqueduct cross the road).

From the parking area, follow the dirt path through the olive grove and along the aqueduct ruins for 200 yards. Approaching the bluff with the grand view, you'll see that the water canal is split into two troughs: One takes a 90-degree right turn and heads for Arles; the other goes straight to the bluff and over, where it once sent water cascading down to power eight grinding mills. Romans grew wheat on the vast fields you see from here, then brought it down to the mega-watermill of Barbegal. Historians figure that this mill produced enough flour each day to feed 12,000 hungry Romans. If you saw the model of this eight-tiered mill in Arles' Ancient History Museum, the milling is easy to visualize—making a visit here quite an exciting experience.

Returning to your car, find the broken bit of aqueduct—it's positioned like a children's playground slide—and take a look at the waterproofing mortar that lined all Roman aqueducts.

Sleeping in and near Les Baux

IN LES BAUX

$$$ Le Mas d'Aigret*** is a 10-minute walk east of Les Baux on the road to St-Rémy (D-27). From this refuge, you can stare up at the castle walls rising beyond the heated swimming pool, or enjoy valley views from the groomed

---

Sleep Code

Abbreviations   **1=about $1.10, country code: 33)**
S=Single, **D**=Double/Twin, **T**=Triple, **Q**=Quad, **b**=bathroom,
*=French hotel rating (0-5 stars)
Price Rankings
 $$$ Higher Priced—Most rooms €100 or more
  $$ Moderately Priced—Most rooms €70-100
    $ Lower Priced—Most rooms €70 or less
Unless otherwise noted, credit cards are accepted, breakfast
is not included, free Wi-Fi and/or a guest computer is gener-
ally available, and English is spoken. Prices change; verify cur-
rent rates online or by email. For the best prices, always book
directly with the hotel.

---

terraces. The rooms are simple and slightly worn (viewless Db-
€125-148, larger Db with balcony and view-€160, Tb/Qb-€220-
255, two cool troglodyte Db rooms-€225, breakfast-€14, convenient half-pension dinner and breakfast option-add €46/person,
air-con, rooms have some daytime road noise, tel. 04 90 54 20 00,
www.masdaigret.com, contact@masdaigret.com, Dutch Marieke
and French Eric are wonderful hosts).

$ Hostellerie de la Reine Jeanne** is just inside the gate to
Les Baux, across from the TI. It's warmly run by Marc and English-speaking Gaelle, who rent a handful of good-value, tastefully
decorated rooms above their busy restaurant (standard Db-€56, Db
with view deck-€70, Tb-€80, cavernous family suite-€100, air-con
in some rooms, for view deck ask for *chambre avec terrasse,* tel. 04
90 54 32 06, www.la-reinejeanne.com, marc.braglia@wanadoo.fr).

IN MAUSSANE

The untouristed village of Maussane lies a few minutes' drive south
of Les Baux (15 minutes from Arles). It has a few hotels, a handful of restaurants, and a smattering of shops that revolve around
its inviting café-lined square. If St-Rémy feels overrun, sleep here.
There's also a small TI (tel. 04 90 54 33 60, www.maussane.com).
These two accommodations are worth considering.

$$ Hôtel les Magnanarelles**, in the center of Maussane,
gives solid two-star value in its 18 tastefully designed rooms above
a handsome restaurant and swimming pool (Db-€78-85, extra per-
son-€17, breakfast-€8, ask for room off the street, no air-con, 104
Avenue de la Vallée des Baux, tel. 04 90 54 30 25, www.logishotels.
com, hotel.magnanarelles@wanadoo.fr).

$$ Le Mas de l'Esparou *chambres d'hôte* is welcoming and
kid-friendly, with four simple-yet-spacious rooms, a big swimming
pool, table tennis, swings, and distant views of Les Baux. Jacque-

line loves her job, and her lack of English only makes her more animated. She dislikes email though, so you'll have to call (Db-€80, Tb/Qb-€125-150, includes breakfast, cash only, no air-con, between Les Baux and Maussane on D-5, look for white sign with green lettering, close to the *gendarmerie,* tel. 04 90 54 41 32).

IN LE PARADOU
$ Le Mazet des Alpilles is a small home with three tidy, air-conditioned rooms around a lovely garden, located just outside the sleepy village of Le Paradou, five minutes south of Les Baux (Db-€70, ask for largest room, includes breakfast, cash only, child's bed available, drive into Le Paradou and look for signs, Route de Brunelly, tel. 04 90 54 45 89, or 06 12 14 93 06, www.alpilles.com/mazet.htm, lemazet@wanadoo.fr).

Eating in and near Les Baux

You'll find quiet cafés with views as you follow my walking directions through the **lower town.**

The recommended **Hostellerie de la Reine Jeanne** offers friendly service and good-value meals indoors or out (€15 salads and plates, open daily).

You'll also find several worthwhile places in Maussane, a short hop south of Les Baux. **Place de la Fontaine,** the town's central square, makes a good stop for café fare (several good choices). **Pizza Brun** has tasty wood-fired pizza to take out or eat in, with fun seating indoors and out (closed Mon-Tue, 1 Rue Edouard Foscalina; with your back to Place de la Fontaine, walk to the right for about 10 minutes and look for colored tables in an alleyway; tel. 04 90 54 40 73).

St-Rémy-de-Provence

Sophisticated and sassy, St-Rémy (sahn ray-mee) gave birth to Nostradamus and cared for a distraught artist. Today, it caters to shoppers and Van Gogh fans. A few minutes from the town center, you can visit the once-thriving Roman city called Glanum and the psychiatric ward where Vincent van Gogh was sent after lopping off his earlobe. Best of all is the chance to elbow your way through St-Rémy's raucous Wednesday market (until 12:30). A ring road hems in a pedestrian-friendly center that's fully loaded with fine foods, beauticians, art galleries, and the latest Provençal fashions.

Almost-too-popular St-Rémy offers good hotel options and makes a fine base for day trips to Arles, Avignon, Les Baux, and the Luberon.

GETTING TO ST-REMY-DE-PROVENCE

By Car: From Les Baux, St-Rémy is a spectacular 15-minute drive over the hills and through the woods. Roads D-5 and D-27 each

provide scenic routes between these towns, making a loop drive between them worthwhile. The most scenic approach is on D-27; from Les Baux, take the road toward Maillane that passes the Carrière des Lumières. Take advantage of the many good pullouts and get out of your car for the view.

Parking in St-Rémy is tricky; it's easiest at the TI lot (free Mon-Sat 12:30-14:30 and all day Sun). Parking on Place Charles de Gaulle is always free, but farther from the center (leave the ring road on Avenue Frédéric Mistral).

By Bus: It's one hour from Arles via **bus #54** (5/day Mon-Fri, 3/day Sat, none on Sun) or **bus #57** (6/day, daily July-Aug, Sat-Sun only in May-June and Sept, none Oct-April) and 45 minutes from Avignon via bus #57 (10/day Mon-Sat, 6/day Sun). If arriving in St-Rémy by bus, get off on the ring road at the République stop and continue uphill. The TI is a block up Avenue Durand Maillane (to the right).

By Taxi: From Les Baux, allow €20 one-way; from Avignon, count on €40 (mobile 06 80 27 60 92 or 06 09 52 71 54). St-Rémy's four taxis park on Place de la République, next to the bus stop, but it's best to have the TI call for you.

By Bike: Sun-e-Bike rents electric bikes in St-Rémy (€38/day, 16 Boulevard Marceau, tel. 04 32 62 08 39, www.sun-e-bike.com).

Orientation to St-Rémy-de-Provence

From St-Rémy's circular center, it's a 15-minute walk along a busy road with no sidewalk to Glanum and the St. Paul Monastery (Van Gogh's psychiatric hospital).

TOURIST INFORMATION

The TI is two blocks toward Les Baux from the ring road (Mon-Sat 9:00-12:30 & 14:00-18:30, Sun 10:00-12:30; free Wi-Fi, tel. 04 90 92 05 22, www.saintremy-de-provence.com). Pick up a town map, bus schedules, and a map tracing Van Gogh's favorite painting lo-

NEAR ARLES

cations with in situ copies of the painted scenes (*Starry Night* panel is just outside the TI). Hikers can buy the good trail map (the hike to Les Baux is about 10 miles and 5 hours). The TI runs English "In the Footsteps of Van Gogh" walking tours (€8, 1.5 hours; departs TI at 10:00—usually Tue and Thu-Sat; also gives occasional afternoon town tours, 6-person minimum, call ahead to confirm).

Each year during the last week of September, St-Rémy celebrates *les fêtes votives*, a tradition in the Camargue region honoring the town's patron saint. The carnival-like festivities include bullfights, parades, and *boules* competitions.

Sights in St-Rémy-de-Provence

St-Rémy's key sights—the ruins at Glanum and the hospital where Vincent van Gogh was treated—lie an unappealing 15-minute walk south of the TI. If you're driving, you can park for free at the St. Paul Monastery (coming from Les Baux, it's the first right after passing Glanum) and walk a few minutes on a footpath to Glanum from there (or pay €3 to park at the Glanum site; leave nothing of value in your car).

▲St. Paul Monastery and Hospital
(Le Monastère St. Paul de Mausole)

The still-functioning psychiatric hospital (Clinique St. Paul) that treated Vincent van Gogh from 1889 to 1890 is a popular pilgrimage for Van Gogh fans. Here you'll enter Vincent's temporarily peaceful world: a small chapel, intimate cloisters, a re-creation of his room, and a small lavender field with several large displays featuring copies of his paintings. Inside, read the thoughtful English explanations about Vincent's tortured life. Amazingly, in his 53 weeks here he completed 143 paintings and more than 100 drawings (none of which remains anywhere nearby today). The contrast between the utter simplicity of his room (and his life) and the multimillion-dollar value of his paintings today is jarring.

"I wanted you to know that I think I've done well to come here, first, in seeing the reality of life for the diverse mad or crazy people in this menagerie, I'm losing the vague dread, the fear of the thing. And little by little I can consider my madness as being an illness like any other. And the change of surroundings is doing me good, I imagine. The idea of the duty to work comes back to me a lot."
—Vincent van Gogh's letter to brother Theo, May 9, 1889

In the spring of 1890, Vincent left St-Rémy and traveled to Auvers-sur-Oise near Paris to enter the care of Dr. Paul Gachet, whom he hoped could help stabilize his mental condition. Gachet

St-Rémy Area

To Maillane ↑

↑ To Isle-sur-la-Sorgue & Avignon

AVE. ALBERT SCHWEITZER

AVE. F. MISTRAL

D-99

AVE. MAL DE LATTRE

To A-7 Freeway, Cavaillon & Luberon via D-99 →

D-571

D-99

■ POOL

D-5

(See detail)

Most scenic route to Les Baux & Arles ←

AVE. ALBERT GLEIZES   AVE. LOUIS

MISTRAL

RING ROAD

OLD TOWN

D-99A

POST ■

AVE. DE LA LIBERATION

AVE. JEAN MOULIN

BUS & TAXI STOP ■

AVE. DURAND MAILLANE

AVE. PASTEUR

CHEMIN DE LA COMBETTE

AVE. DU SOUVENIR FRANÇAIS

❷

❹ ■

■ ❺

F. BARONCELLI

CH. LA CROIX DES VERTUS

CHEMIN GAULOIS

❶

AVE. ANTOINE DE LA SALLE

AVE. VINCENT VAN GOGH

300 Meters

300 Yards

❼

❸ ■

❻ ■

"LES ANTIQUES" ROMAN ■ ARCH & TOWER

■ **ST. PAUL MONASTERY**

P *Free*

P *Pay*

To Les Baux & Arles ↓

D-5

■ **GLANUM RUINS**

---

❶ Le Mas des Carassins Hôtel & Restaurant

❷ Mas des Tourterelles Chambres

❸ Hôtel Villa Glanum

❹ Hôtel du Soleil

❺ Le Castelet des Alpilles

❻ Chez Laure Restaurant

❼ "Footsteps of Van Gogh" Path

NEAR ARLES

---

advised the artist to throw himself into his work as a remedy for his illness, which he did—Vincent spent the last 70 days of his life knocking out a painting a day. On July 27, 1890, Vincent wandered into the famous Auvers wheat field and shot himself, dying of his injuries two days later.

In and around the complex, you'll see copies of Vincent's

works—some located right where he painted them. The TI has a map with a list of the reproductions and where to find them. Stand among flame-like cypress trees, gaze over the distant skyline of St-Rémy, and realize you're in the midst of Van Gogh's most famous work, *The Starry Night*.

For more on Vincent van Gogh's time in this region, see the Arles chapter.

Cost and Hours: €5, daily April-Sept 9:30-19:00, Oct-March 10:15-17:00, tel. 04 90 92 77 00.

▲Glanum Ruins

These crumbling stones are the foundations of a Roman market town, located at the crossroads of two ancient trade routes between Italy and Spain. A heavy Roman arch and tower stand across the road from the site as proud reminders of the town's glory days. These lonely monuments marked the entry to Glanum 2,000 years ago. The plump triumphal arch, now missing its upper level, was designed to impress visitors with scenes of Rome's power—and by association, Glanum's prestige.

The three-level tower was built as a mausoleum by one of Glanum's most distinguished families. The battle scene relief on the lowest level is dripping with intensity: The Romans were not just good builders, but skilled artists as well.

Cost and Hours: €7.50, under age 18-free, daily April-Sept 9:30-18:30, Oct-March 10:00-17:00, parking-€3/day, tel. 04 90 92 23 79.

Lunch: La Taverne Romaine, just past Glanum's entry, serves café fare and an "authentic" Roman meal with good seating in the site (May-Sept only, same hours as site).

Visiting the Ruins: The free English handout, exhibits in the entry, and information panels scattered about the site all help to provide context to the ruins you'll see. Serious students of ancient Rome will want to spring for the well-done *Itineraries* book (€7).

While the ruins are, well...ruined, their setting at the base of the rocky Alpilles is splendid. It's also unshaded and can be very hot (making it easier to enjoy early or late).

The Roman site was founded in 27 B.C. and occupied for about 30 years. About 2,500 people lived in Glanum at its zenith (the Roman city was about seven times bigger than the ruins you see today). And though this was an important town, with grand villas, temples, a basilica, a forum, a wooden dam, and aqueducts, it was not important enough to justify an arena or a theater (such as those in Arles, Nîmes, and Orange). Locals had to charter buses to reach events in those cities.

Stroll up Glanum's main street and see remains of a market hall, a forum, thermal baths, reservoirs, and more. The view from the belvedere justifies the effort. These ruins highlight the range and prosperity of the Roman Empire. Taken together with other Roman monuments in Provence, they paint a more complete picture of Roman life. For more on Roman history, see page 29.

Sleeping in St-Rémy-de-Provence

Unless otherwise noted, the following hotels have easy parking, free Wi-Fi, and air-conditioning.

$$$ Le Mas des Carassins*, a 15-minute walk from the center, is well-run by Michel and Pierre. Luxury is affordable here, with two generously sized pools, ample outdoor lounging spaces, and top comfort. The 22 rooms are split between the more traditional main building and the newer annex, with larger rooms and more modern decor (standard Db-€150, superior Db-€200, deluxe Db with terrace-€225, includes American-style breakfast, table tennis, look for signs 200 yards toward Les Baux from TI, 1 Chemin Gaulois, tel. 04 90 92 15 48, www.masdescarassins.com, info@masdescarassins.com).

$$$ Mas des Tourterelles Chambres, a Provençal farmhouse in a pleasant neighborhood, is a 10-minute walk from the town center. It has six sharp rooms and an apartment, pool, and small garden with outdoor picnic facilities including a fridge, glasses, and plates (Db-€125, 2-night minimum, includes breakfast, air-con in top-floor rooms—others don't need it, 21 Chemin de la Combette, tel. 09 54 64 83 30 or 06 15 87 24 55, www.masdestourterelles.com, contact@masdestourterelles.com). Turn right at the top of Place de la République onto Chemin de la Combette; after 400 yards look for the brown sign down a lane on the left (past the speed bumps).

$$$ Hôtel Villa Glanum* is a big spread on the main road (some traffic noise) facing the St. Paul Monastery and Glanum ruins. It's a 15-minute walk from the town center, with smallish but tasteful rooms, a restaurant/café, and ample garden areas. The rooms in the main building are larger, but I prefer the smaller *bastide* rooms with private terraces around the pretty pool (*bastide* Db-€100-130 depending on size; main building Db-€120, Tb-€140; cheaper off-season, 46 Avenue Van Gogh, tel. 04 90 92 03 59, www.villaglanum.com, contact@villaglanum.com).

$$$ Hôtel du Soleil, a quick walk from St-Rémy's center, is a sharp hotel, with fresh white stone and beige decor throughout. Its spotless rooms cluster around a courtyard and pool (standard Db-€100-110, bigger Db-€120-130, Tb-€165-180, 5 rooms have

NEAR ARLES

Food Lovers' Guide to St-Rémy

Wednesday is market day in St-Rémy, but you don't have to fast until then. Foodies will appreciate these shops clustered around the ring road in St-Rémy, near the turnoff to Les Baux.

L'Epicerie Calanquet, in the same family for five generations, is where locals buy olive oil. The shop lets you sample products (daily, in the town center at 8 Rue de la Commune).

Le Petit Duc offers a remarkable introduction to traditional cookies (closed Sun-Mon, 7 Boulevard Victor Hugo, tel. 04 90 92 08 31).

Just one whiff from **Joel Durand Chocolates** will lure chocoholics inside. Ask for a sample and learn the letter-coded system. The lavender is surprisingly good (daily, a few doors down from Le Petit Duc at 3 Boulevard Victor Hugo, tel. 04 90 92 38 25).

---

small terraces, 2-room apartment-€140-165, easy parking, a block above the TI at 35 Avenue Pasteur, tel. 04 90 92 00 63, www.hotelsoleil.com, info@hotelsoleil.com).

$$ Le Castelet des Alpilles*** is Old World, but the location is good, the terrace is big, and the pool is refreshing. Most rooms are big and airy, and some have views of the Alpilles (Db-€98, Db with view balcony-€120, 6 Place Mireille, tel. 04 90 92 07 21, www.castelet-alpilles.com, hotel.castel.alpilles@wanadoo.fr).

Eating in St-Rémy-de-Provence

The town is packed with restaurants, each trying to outdo the other. Join the evening strollers and compare.

Le Mas des Carassins is a special experience. One *menu* (€36) is prepared each night and served in an intimate setting inside or out. Review their website to see what's cooking before booking a table (see listing under "Sleeping in St-Rémy," earlier).

L'Estagnol, a small splurge, serves fine Provençal cuisine on a terrific outdoor terrace or in their modern, classy interior (€30 *menus,* closed Mon, where the ring road meets the road to Les Baux at 18 Boulevard Victor Hugo, tel. 04 90 92 05 95).

Crêperie Lou Planet, on pleasant Place Favier, is cheap and peaceful, with outdoor seating in summer, tasty crêpes, good salads, and inexpensive, fine house wine. Owner Jean has been here for more than 30 years and still hasn't changed the menu

Restaurants in St-Rémy's Old Town

1. L'Estagnol
2. Crêperie Lou Planet
3. Bar-Tabac des Alpilles
4. Café de la Place
5. L'Epicerie du Calanquet
6. Le Petit Duc
7. Joel Durand Chocolates
8. Bike Rental

NEAR ARLES

(daily April-Sept 12:00-22:00, behind Hôtel de Ville at Place Favier, next to Musée des Alpilles).

Bar-Tabac des Alpilles, a favorite among locals, sits on the ring road. It offers a great salad selection and good standard café fare, including pasta dishes for €10 (open daily for lunch and dinner, 21 Boulevard Victor Hugo, tel. 04 90 92 0 17).

Café de la Place, on Place de la République behind the parking lot, is a hit with the young, local crowd. With funky decor, a huge *terrasse,* and free Wi-Fi, it's good for a meal or just a drink (*plats*-€18-24, salads-€14-16, open daily, tel. 04 90 92 02 13).

Chez Laure is a simple, local, and relaxed outdoor restaurant. It's located a mile from St-Rémy in a park-like setting with toys available for kids (salads, €13 *plats,* €18-24 lunch *menu,* €20-24 dinner *menu,* closed Mon, Sun evening concerts run June-Aug and range from jazz to area folk music, on Ave. Antoine de la Salle/Route du Lac, tel. 04 90 92 51 99). To find the restaurant, look for signs between the Glanum ruins and the TI.

The Camargue

The Camargue region, occupying the vast delta of the Rhône River, is one of Europe's most important wetlands. This marshy area exists where the Rhône splits into two branches (big and little), just before it flows into the Mediterranean. Over the millennia, a steady flow of sediment has been deposited at the mouth of the rivers—thoroughly land-locking villages that once faced the sea.

Since World War II, farmers have converted large northern tracts of the Camargue to rice fields, making the delta a major producer of France's rice. Salt is the other key industry in the Camargue: You can see vast salt marshes and evaporation beds around the town of Salin de Giraud. Because the salt marshes were long considered useless, the land has remained relatively untouched, leaving it a popular nature destination today.

Today the Camargue Regional Nature Park is a protected and "wild" area, where pink flamingos, wild bulls, nasty boars, nastier mosquitoes (in every season but winter—come prepared), and the famous white horses wander freely through lagoons and tall grass. For more on these animals, see the sidebar.

The Camargue's subtle wetlands beauty makes it a worthwhile joyride for naturalists. The Everglades-like scenery is a birder's paradise, and occasional bulls and wild horses add to the enjoyment. But for avid city sightseers, this can feel like a big swamp—interesting to drive through, but where's the excitement? The best time to visit is in spring, when the flamingos are out in full force;

The Wildlife of the Camargue

In this nature reserve, amusing flamingos and countless other bird species flourish—attracting birdwatchers from all over the world. Once an endangered species, the flamingos flock here because of all that salt—which is why they come to the Camargue rather than to, say, the sandy beaches of the Riviera. Ten thousand flamingos leave here each fall, heading to warmer climates, and then return in March to pink up the Camargue (a visit here in the spring reaps big, pink rewards). To see a formation of these long, clumsy-looking birds in flight is an experience you won't soon forget.

The black bulls are raised for bullfights (by local cowboys called *gardians*) and eventually end up on plates in Arles' restaurants (you may have met one already). The *gardians*, who have patrolled the Camargue on local horses for centuries, give the area a Wild West aura. The region's unique small horses—born brown or black, later turning light gray or white—are one of the oldest breeds in the world, and may have existed in the area since prehistoric times.

With the continual loss of wetlands throughout the world, it's critical that places like this remain preserved and that we understand their significance.

NEAR ARLES

the worst time to visit is in summer, when birds are fewest and the mosquitoes are most abundant. For helpful information on the Camargue, check www.kustgids.nl/camargue-en.

If you have children, a picnic on the long sandy beach at Plage d'Arles may be just what the doctor ordered. Also called Plage de Piemanço, this public beach is six miles (10 kilometers) after Salin de Giraud (see map on page 75). Bring everything you might need, as there are no vendors.

GETTING TO THE CAMARGUE

There are several ways aside from a car to experience the Camargue: horseback, mountain bikes, and jeep safaris. All three options are available in Stes-Maries-de-la-Mer, and jeep safaris are also offered from Arles (ask at TI). Hiking is not good in the Camargue, as there are few decent trails. The best biking is across the Digue (dike) to Phare de la Gacholle.

By Scenic Drive: There are two primary driving routes from Arles through the Camargue: to Stes-Maries-de-la-Mer, and toward Salin de Giraud.

My favorite route is toward **Salin de Giraud** (see map on page 75): Leave Arles toward Stes-Maries-de-la-Mer and find the D-570. Skip the D-36 turnoff to Salin de Giraud (you'll return along this route). After about 3.5 miles (6 kilometers), consider a stop at the **Camarguais Museum** (described later). Next, continue along D-570, then turn left on D-37 and follow it as it skirts the Etang de Vaccarès lagoon. The lagoon is off-limits, but this area has views and good opportunities to get out of the car and smell the marshes (look for viewing stands, but any dirt turnoff works). Turn right off D-37 onto the tiny road at Villeneuve, following signs for C-134 to La Capelière and La Fiélouse.

Make time for a stop at **La Capelière** (headquarters for Camargue sightseers), where you can pick up a good map, ask the eager staff questions, and enjoy a small exhibit (handheld English explanations) and one-mile walking trail with some English information on the Camargue (modest trail fee, daily 9:00-13:00 & 14:00-18:00). Birders can look at the register to see what birds have been spotted recently (observations in English are in red), and enthusiasts can buy the €5 Camargue booklet, *Fiches Camargue,* in English.

The best part of this drive (particularly in spring) is the next stretch to and around **La Digue de la Mer,** about six scenic miles past La Capelière. At La Digue de la Mer, get out of your car and walk to experience the best of the Camargue. This is a critical reproduction area for flamingos (about 13,000 couples produce 5,000 offspring annually)—seeing them in flight is a memorable experience. If you rented a mountain bike, now would be the right time to use it: It's about eight bumpy but engaging miles between water and sand dunes to Stes-Maries-de-la-Mer.

By Bus: Buses serve the Camargue (stopping at Camarguais Museum and Stes-Maries-de-la-Mer) from Arles' bus or train station (bus #20, 6/day Mon-Sat, 3/day Sun, 1 hour, tel. 08 10 00 13 26, www.lepilote.com).

Sights and Towns in the Camargue

Camarguais Museum (Musée Camarguais)

Located in a traditional Camargue barn on the road to Stes-Maries-de-la-Mer, this well-designed folk museum does a good job of describing the natural features and cultural traditions of the Camargue. The costumes, tools, and helpful exhibits come with some English explanations (look for handouts and small screens). A two-mile nature trail, picnic tables, and a WC round out the amenities.

Cost and Hours: €5; April-Sept daily 9:00-18:00, Oct-March Wed-Mon 10:00-17:00, closed Tue; 8 miles from Arles on D-570 toward Stes-Maries-de-la-Mer, at Mas du Pont de Rousty farmhouse; tel. 04 90 97 10 82, www.parc-camargue.fr/musee.html.

Stes-Maries-de-la-Mer

At the western end of the Camargue lies this whitewashed, Span-ish-feeling seafront town with acres of flamingos, bulls, and horses at its doorstep. From the bus stop, walk to the church (10 min-utes) to get oriented. The place is so popular that it's best avoided on weekends and during holidays. It's a French Coney Island—a trinket-selling, perennially windy place.

The town is also famous as a mecca for the Roma (Gypsies). Every May, Roma from all over Europe pile in their caravans and migrate to Stes-Maries-de-la-Mer to venerate the town's statue of Saint Sarah. Legend has it that Mary Magdalene made landfall here in a boat with no oars after an epic journey across the Medi-terranean from Egypt. Fleeing persecution for practicing the new and unpopular Christian faith, she was accompanied by two other "Stes-Maries": Mary Jacobe, the mother of the apostle James, and Mary Salome, the mother of the apostles James and John. Also in the boat was "Black Sarah," an Egyptian servant. Sarah collected alms for the poor; over time, her request for handouts became asso-ciated with the Roma people, who embrace her as their patron saint (the name Gypsy comes from the label Europeans gave those who came across from Egypt—*Gyptians*). Today's impressive spectacle to honor Sarah is like a sprawling flea market spilling out from the town for two weeks.

Tourist Information: Stes-Maries-de-la-Mer's TI is located along its waterfront promenade (daily April-Sept 9:00-19:00, until 20:00 in summer, Oct-March 10:00-17:00, 5 Avenue Van Gogh, tel. 04 90 97 82 55, www.saintesmaries.com).

Sights and Activities: Outside of May, the town of Stes-Maries-de-la-Mer has little to offer except its beachfront prom-enade, bullring, and towering five-belled fortified church. The **church** interior is worth a look for its unusual decorations and arti-facts, including the statue of Saint Sarah (free, small fee to climb to roof for Camargue and sea views). Avoid the women with flowers and the assertive palm readers, who often cluster near the church.

Most tourists come to take a horse, a jeep, or a bike into the Camargue—and there's no lack of outfits ready to take you for a ride. The TIs in Arles and Stes-Maries-de-la-Mer have long lists. Rental bikes (for the ride out to La Digue de la Mer) and advice on the best routes are available at Le Vélo Saintois (€18/day, 19 Rue de la République in Stes-Maries-de-la-Mer, tel. 04 90 97 74 56, www.levelosaintois.camargue.fr). Jerry Perkins offers Jeep excur-sions at Nature et Découverte (2-hour trips from €40, on Route d'Aigues-Mortes near Stes-Maries-de-la-Mer, tel. 06 12 44 64 74, www.visite-camargue.com). Les Cabanes de Cacharel gives horseback tours (about €20, plan on at least 2 hours, Route de

Cacharel near Stes-Maries-de-la-Mer, tel. 04 90 97 84 10, www.cabanesdecacharel.com, info@camargueacheval.com).

Aigues-Mortes

This strange walled city, on the western edge of the Camargue (20 miles from Nîmes), was built by Louis IX as a jumping-off point for his Crusades to the Holy Land. Although Aigues-Mortes was a strategically situated royal port city, it was actually never near the sea—ships reached it via canals that were dug through an immense lagoon. Today its tall towers and thick fortifications seem oddly out of place, surrounded by nothing but salt marshes and flamingos. The name "Aigues-Mortes" means "Dead Waters," which says it all. Skip it unless you need more souvenirs and crowded streets, although drivers going between Nîmes and Arles can detour to Aigues-Mortes for a quick-and-easy taste of the Camargue. Aigues-Mortes and Nîmes are linked by buses (6/day, 50 minutes) and trains (6/day, 45 minutes).

AVIGNON

Famous for its nursery rhyme, medieval bridge, and brooding Palace of the Popes, contemporary Avignon (ah-veen-yohn) bustles and prospers behind its mighty walls. For nearly 100 years (1309-1403) Avignon was the capital of Christendom, home to seven popes. (And, for a difficult period after that—during the Great Schism when there were two competing popes—Avignon was "the other Rome.") During this time, it grew from a quiet village into a thriving city. Today, with its large student population and fashionable shops, Avignon is an intriguing blend of medieval history, youthful energy, and urban sophistication. Street performers entertain the international throngs who fill Avignon's ubiquitous cafés and trendy boutiques. And each July the city goes crazy during its huge theater festival (with about 2,000 performances, big crowds, higher prices, and hotels booked up long in advance). Clean, lively, and popular with tourists, Avignon is more impressive for its outdoor ambience than for its museums and monuments.

Orientation to Avignon

Cours Jean Jaurès, which turns into Rue de la République, runs straight from the Centre-Ville train station to Place de l'Horloge and the Palace of the Popes, splitting Avignon in two. The larger eastern half is where the action is. Climb to the Jardin du Rochers des Doms for the town's best view, tour the pope's immense palace, lose yourself in Avignon's back streets (following my "Discovering Avignon's Back Streets" self-guided walk), and find a shady square to call home.

TOURIST INFORMATION

The TI is helpful, with lots of information about the city and the region (April-Oct Mon-Sat 9:00-18:00, Sun 10:00-17:00, daily until 19:00 in July; Nov-March Mon-Fri 9:00-18:00, Sat 9:00-17:00, Sun 10:00-12:00; free Wi-Fi, between the train station and the old town at 41 Cours Jean Jaurès, tel. 04 32 74 32 74, www. avignon-tourisme.com).

At the TI, pick up the free **Avignon Passion Pass** (for up to 5 family members). Get it stamped at your first sight to receive discounts at the others (e.g., €2 off at the Palace of the Popes and €3 off at the Petit Palais). The pass comes with the Avignon "Passion" map and guide, which includes several good (but tricky-to-follow) walking tours. The TI also has bike maps for good rides in the area, including the Ile de la Barthelasse.

ARRIVAL IN AVIGNON
By Train

Avignon has two train stations: Centre-Ville and TGV (linked to downtown by shuttle trains). While most TGV trains serve only the TGV Station, some also stop at Centre-Ville—verify your station in advance.

The **Centre-Ville Station** *(Gare Avignon Centre-Ville)* gets all non-TGV trains (and a few TGV trains). To reach the town center, cross the busy street in front of the station and walk through the city walls onto Cours Jean Jaurès. The TI is three blocks down, at #41.

The **TGV Station** *(Gare TGV)*, on the outskirts of town, has a summer-only TI (short hours), but no baggage storage. Car rental, buses, and taxis are outside the north exit *(sortie nord)*. To reach the city center, take the **shuttle train** from platform A or B to Centre-Ville Station (€1.60, 2/hour, 5 minutes, buy ticket from machine on platform or at desk in main hall). A **taxi** ride between the TGV station and downtown Avignon costs about €15.

If you're connecting from the Avignon TGV Station to other points, you'll find **buses** to Arles' Centre-Ville train station at the second bus shelter (€9, 9/day, 1 hour, included with rail pass, schedule posted on shelter and available at info booths inside TGV Station). If you're **driving** a rental car directly to Arles, St-Rémy-de-Provence, Les Baux, or the Luberon, leave the station following signs to *Avignon Sud*, then *La Rocade*. You'll soon see exits to Arles (best for St-Rémy and Les Baux) and Cavaillon (for Luberon villages).

AVIGNON

By Bus

The efficient bus station *(gare routière)* is 100 yards to the right as you leave the Centre-Ville train station, beyond and below Hôtel Ibis (info desk open Mon-Fri 8:00-19:30, Sat 10:00-12:30 & 13:30-18:00, closed Sun, tel. 04 90 82 07 35).

By Car

Drivers entering Avignon follow *Centre-Ville* and *Gare SNCF* (train station) signs. You'll find central pay lots (about €12/half-day, €20/24 hours) in the garage next to the Centre-Ville train station and at the Parking Jean Jaurès under the ramparts across from the station (enter the old city through the Porte St-Michel gate). Hotels have advice for overnight parking, and some offer parking deals.

Two free parking lots have complimentary shuttle buses to the center except on Sunday (follow *P Gratuit* signs): **Parking de l'Ile Piot** is across Daladier Bridge (Pont Daladier) on Ile de la Barthelasse, with shuttles to Place Crillon; **Parking des Italiens** is along the river east of the Palace of the Popes, with shuttles to Place Carnot (allow 30 minutes to walk from either to the center). Street parking is free in the *bleu* zones 12:00-14:00 and 19:00-9:00. It's €2 for about three hours 9:00-12:00 and 14:00-19:00. (Hint: If you put €2 in the meter anytime between 19:00 and 9:00, you're good until 14:00.)

No matter where you park, leave nothing of value in your car.

HELPFUL HINTS

Book Ahead for July: During the July theater festival, rooms are sparse—reserve very early, or stay in Arles or St-Rémy.

Local Help: David at **Imagine Tours,** a nonprofit group whose goal is to promote this region, can help with hotel emergencies or tickets to special events (mobile 06 89 22 19 87, www.imagine-tours.net, imagine.tours@gmail.com). If you don't get an answer, leave a message.

Wi-Fi: The TI has free Wi-Fi, as does the park next door (one hour/day only). Many bigger cafés provide free Wi-Fi to anyone who buys a drink.

English Bookstore: Try **Camili Books & Tea,** a second-hand bookshop with a refreshing courtyard and hot drinks (Tue-Sat 12:00-19:00, closed Sun-Mon, free Wi-Fi, 155 Rue Carreterie, in Avignon's northeast corner).

Laundry: At **La Blanchisseuse,** you can drop off your laundry and pick it up the same day for about €12 a load (daily 7:00-21:00, a few blocks west of main TI at 24 Rue Lanterne, tel. 04 90 85 58 80). The launderette at 66 Place des Corps-Saints, where

AVIGNON

Avignon

SHUTTLE BOAT

VIEW WALK

Ile de la Barthelasse

ST. BENEZET BRIDGE

PORTE DU ROCHER

BLVD. DE LA

Jardin du Rochers des Doms

N.D. DES DOMS

PALACE OF THE POPES

PORTE DU RHONE

PETIT PALAIS MUSEUM

N-580

To P (de l'Île Piot) Villeneuve & Tower of Philip the Fair

Rhône River

PONT E. DALADIER

Palace Square

R. REMPART DU RHONE

R. RUE GRANDE FUSTERIE

RUE BALANCE

R. ST. ETIENNE

PORTE DE L'OULLE

Place Crillon

RUE

RUE VERNET

"DISCOVERING BACK STREETS" WALK BEGINS

HOTEL LA MIRANDE

PEYROLLERIE

ST. PIERRE

Place Carnot

SYNA-GOGUE

"WELCOME TO AVIGNON" WALK BEGINS

Place de l'Horloge

RUE FAVART

R. MARCHANDS

ALLEE DE L'OULLE

BLVD. DE L'OULLE

RUE REMPART DE L'OULLE

RUE JOSEPH

R. ST. AGRICOL

R. PETITE FUST.

ST.

R. RACINE

RUE LA BOUQUERIE

RUE BANCASSE

RUE GALANTE

RUE ROUGE

R. VIEUX SEXTIER

PATRICK MALLARD PASTRIES

To TGV Train Station

RUE VICTOR HUGO

RUE D'ANNANELLE

CALVET MUSEUM

RUE VERNET

RUE DE LA REPUBLIQUE

Place St. Didier

R. ROI

OLD CITY WALLS

R. REMPART ST-DOMINIQUE

RUE VELOUTERIE

RUE JOSEPH VERNET

RUE SAINT-CHARLES

MUSEE LAPIDAIRE

FONDATION ANGLADON-DUBRUJEAUD

BLVD. RASPAIL

R. H. FABRE

PORTE ST. ROCH

RUE REMPART SAINT-ROCH

RUE PERDIGUIER

R. DE LA BOURSE

Place des Corps-Saints

RUE SAINT-MICHEL

RUE

To Nimes via A-9

BLVD. SAINT-ROCH

POST

TGV Shuttle & Bus #11

COURS JEAN JAURÈS

Place de la Republique

Jean Jaurès

PORTE ST. MICHEL

PORTE ST. CHARLES

PORTE DE LA REPUBLIQUE

AVE. DE 7EME GENIE

AVE. EISENHOWER

CENTRE-VILLE TRAIN STATION

BUS STATION

AVE. MONCLAR

AVE. SAINT-RUF

200 Meters

200 Yards

AVIGNON

AVIGNON

① Best Views &
Stairs to Tower
② More Views
③ Camili Books & Tea
④ Launderettes (2)
⑤ Carrefour City
Grocery
⑥ Monoprix
⑦ Bike Rental
⑧ Tourist Train

Rue Agricol Perdiguier ends, has English instructions and is handy to most hotels (daily 7:00-20:00).

Grocery Store: Carrefour City is central and has long hours (Mon-Sat 7:00-22:00, Sun 9:00-12:00, 2 blocks from TI, toward Place de l'Horloge on Rue de la République). **Monoprix** is also on Rue de la République, at #24, a block from the TI.

Bike Rental: Rent pedal and electric bikes and scooters near the train station at **Provence Bike** (April-Oct 9:00-18:30, 7 Avenue St. Ruf, tel. 04 90 27 92 61, www.provence-bike.com). You'll enjoy riding on the Ile de la Barthelasse (the TI has bike maps), but biking is better in and around Isle-sur-la-Sorgue (described in the Hill Towns of the Luberon chapter) and Vaison-la-Romaine (consider taking a bike on the train to Bédarrides, biking from there to Châteauneuf-du-Pape and on to Orange, then taking it on the train back to Avignon; see the Orange and the Côtes du Rhône chapter).

Car Rental: The TGV Station has counters for all the big companies; only Avis is at the Centre-Ville Station.

Shuttle Boat: A free shuttle boat, the *Navette Fluviale,* plies back and forth across the river (as it did in the days when the town had no functioning bridge) from near St. Bénezet Bridge (3/hour, daily April-June and Sept 10:00-12:30 & 14:00-18:00, July-Aug 11:00-21:00; Oct-March weekends and Wed afternoons only). It drops you on the peaceful Ile de la Barthelasse, with its recommended riverside restaurant, grassy walks, and bike rides with terrific city views. If you stay on the island for dinner, check the schedule for the last return boat—or be prepared for a taxi ride or a pleasant 25-minute walk back to town.

Tourist Train: The little train leaves regularly from in front of the Palace of the Popes and offers a decent overview of the city, including the Jardin du Rochers des Doms and St. Bénezet Bridge (€7, 2/hour, 40 minutes, English commentary, mid-March-mid-Oct daily 10:00-18:00, until 19:00 July-Aug).

Commanding City Views: For great views of Avignon and the river, walk or drive across Daladier Bridge, or ferry across the Rhône on the *Navette Fluviale* (described above). I'd take the boat across the river, walk the view path to Daladier Bridge, and then cross back over the bridge (45-minute walk). You can enjoy other impressive vistas from the top of the Jardin du Rochers des Doms, from the tower in the Palace of the Popes, from the end of the famous,

Festival d'Avignon

Avignon hosts a massive theater festival for three weeks each July with more than 1,500 official performances and countless events in the streets. Every possible venue is in action as the event creates a Mardi Gras-like atmosphere. Contemporary theater groups come from throughout Europe. While many performances book up well in advance, many more are available the same day (tickets generally €15-20). The festival is indoors, but venues overflow onto the streets. Organizers need 20 different locations to hold all of the performances, from actual theater spaces to small chapels to the inner courtyard of the Palace of the Popes, which seats 800. There's also a "fringe festival," called Avignon-Off, which adds another 100 venues and countless performances, as well as a children's theater festival, with storytellers, dance, musicals, and marionettes. During the festival, the entire city is a stage, with mimes, fire-breathers, singers, and musicians filling the streets. Most performances are in French, but many are in English, and many dance performances don't require language at all (www.festival-avignon.com and www.avignonleoff.com).

broken St. Bénezet Bridge, and from the entrance to Fort St. André, across the river in Villeneuve-lès-Avignon.

Private Guide: Isabelle Magny is a good local guide for the city and region (€160/half-day, €330/full-day, no car, tel. 06 11 82 17 92, magnyisab@numericable.fr).

Food Tour: The **Avignon Gourmet Walking Tour** is a wonderful experience if you like to eat. Charming and passionate Aurelie meets small groups daily (except Sun and Mon) at the TI at 9:15 for a well-designed 3-hour, 8-stop walk. Her tour is filled with information and tastes of top-quality local foods and drinks, and finishes in the market hall (€55/person, 2-8 people per group, tel. 06 35 32 08 96, www.avignongourmetours.com). Book in advance on her website.

Guided Excursions from Avignon: Several minivan tour companies based in Avignon offer transportation to destinations described in this book, including Pont du Gard, the Luberon, and the Camargue (see "Tours in Provence" on page 26).

Avignon at a Glance

▲▲**Scenic Squares** Numerous hide-and-seek squares ideal for postcard-writing and people-watching—pick your favorite: Place des Corps-Saints, Place St. Pierre, Place des Châtaignes (adjacent to Place St. Pierre), Place Crillon, Place St. Didier (near the recommended Caveau du Théâtre restaurant), and the big Place Pie (see map on page 100). **Hours:** Always open.

▲▲**Palace of the Popes** Fourteenth-century Gothic palace built by the popes who made Avignon their home. **Hours:** Daily March-June and Sept-Oct 9:00-19:00, July-Aug 9:00-20:00, Nov-Feb 9:30-17:45. See page 108.

▲**Jardin du Rochers des Doms** Park and ramparts at the hilltop where Avignon was first settled, with great views of the Rhône River Valley and the famous broken bridge. **Hours:** Daily April-May and Sept 7:30-20:00, June-Aug 7:30-21:00, Oct-March 7:30-18:00. See page 107.

▲**St. Bénezet Bridge** The "Pont d'Avignon" of nursery-rhyme fame, once connecting the pope's territory to France. **Hours:** Daily March-June and Sept-Oct 9:00-19:00, July-Aug 9:00-20:00, Nov-Feb 9:30-17:45. See page 107.

▲**Tower of Philip the Fair** Massive tower across St. Bénezet Bridge, featuring the best view over Avignon and the Rhône basin. **Hours:** Tue-Sun May-Oct 10:00-12:30 & 14:00-18:00, Feb-April 14:00-17:00, closed Nov-Jan and Mon year-round. See page 113.

Petit Palais Museum "Little palace" displaying the Church's collection of medieval Italian painting and sculpture. **Hours:** Wed-Mon 10:00-13:00 & 14:00-18:00, closed Tue. See page 106.

Fondation Angladon-Dubrujeaud Museum with a small but enjoyable Post-Impressionist collection, including art by Cézanne, Van Gogh, Daumier, Degas, and Picasso. **Hours:** Tue-Sun 13:00-18:00, closed Mon. See page 113.

Calvet Museum Fine-arts museum with a good collection and English audioguide. **Hours:** Wed-Mon 10:00-13:00 & 14:00-18:00, closed Tue. See page 113.

Avignon Walks

For a fine overview of the city, combine the following two self-guided walks. "Welcome to Avignon" covers the major sights, while "Discovering Avignon's Back Streets" leads you along the lanes less taken, delving beyond the surface of this historic city.

▲▲WELCOME TO AVIGNON WALK

• *Start your tour where the Romans did, on Place de l'Horloge, in front of City Hall (Hôtel de Ville).*

Place de l'Horloge

In ancient Roman times this was the forum, and in medieval times it was the market square. The square is named for the clock tower (now hiding behind the more recently built City Hall) which, in its day, was a humanist statement. In medieval France, the only bells in town rang from the church tower to indicate not the hours but the calls to prayer. With the dawn of the modern age, secular clock towers like this rang out the hours as people organized their lives.

Taking humanism a step further, the City Hall (Hôtel de Ville), built after the French Revolution, obstructed the view of the old clock tower while celebrating a new era. The slogan "liberty, equality, and brotherhood" is a reminder that the people supersede the king and the church. And today, judging from the square's jammed cafés and restaurants, it's the people who do rule.

The square's present popularity arrived with the trains in 1854. Facing City Hall, look left down the main drag, Rue de la République. When the trains came to Avignon, proud city fathers wanted a direct, impressive way to link the new station to the heart of the city—so they plowed over homes to create Rue de la République and widened Place de l'Horloge. This main drag's Parisian feel is intentional—it was built not in the Provençal manner, but in the Haussmann style that is so dominant in Paris (characterized by broad, straight boulevards lined with stately buildings). Today, this Champs-Elysées of Avignon is lined with department stores and banks.

• *Walk slightly uphill past the neo-Renaissance facade of the theater and the carousel (public WCs behind). Look back to see the late Gothic bell tower. Then veer right at the Hôtel des Palais des Papes and continue into...*

Palace Square (Place du Palais)

Pull up a concrete stump just past the café. Nicknamed *bites* (slang for penis), these effectively keep cars from double-parking in areas designed for people. Many of the metal ones slide up and down by remote control to let privileged cars come and go.

Now take in the scene. This grand square is lined with the Palace of the Popes, the Petit Palais, and the cathedral. In the 1300s the entire headquarters of the Roman Catholic Church was moved to Avignon. The Church bought Avignon and gave it a complete makeover. Along with clearing out vast spaces like this square and building a three-acre palace, the Church erected more than three miles of protective wall (with 39 towers), "appropriate" housing for cardinals (read: mansions), and residences for its entire bureaucracy. The city was Europe's largest construction zone. Avignon's population grew from 6,000 to 25,000 in short order. (Today, 13,000 people live within the walls.) The limits of pre-papal Avignon are outlined on your city map: Rues Joseph Vernet, Henri Fabre, des Lices, and Philonarde all follow the route of the city's earlier defensive wall (about half the diameter of today's wall).

The imposing facade behind you, across the square from the Palace of the Popes' main entry, was "the papal mint," which served as the finance department for the Holy See. The Petit Palais (Little Palace) seals the uphill end of the square and was built for a cardinal; today it houses medieval paintings (museum described later).

Avignon's 12th-century Romanesque cathedral, just to the left of the Palace of the Popes, has been the seat of the local bishop for more than a thousand years. Predating the Church's purchase of Avignon by 200 years, its simplicity reflects Avignon's modest, pre-papal population. The gilded Mary was added in 1854, when the Vatican established the doctrine of her Immaculate Conception.

• *You can visit the massive* **Palace of the Popes** *(described on page 108) now, but it works better to visit that palace at the end of this walk, then continue directly to the "Discovering Avignon's Back Streets" walk, described later.*

Now is a good time to take in the…

Petit Palais Museum (Musée du Petit Palais)

This former cardinal's palace now displays the Church's collection of (mostly) art. The information is only in French, but a visit here before going to the Palace of the Popes helps furnish and populate that otherwise barren building. You'll see bits of statues and tombs—an inventory of the destruction of exquisite Church art that was wrought by the French Revolution (which tackled established French society with Taliban-esque fervor). Then comes many rooms filled with religious Italian paintings, organized in chronological order from early Gothic to late Renaissance.

Cost and Hours: €6, Wed-Mon 10:00-13:00 & 14:00-18:00, closed Tue, at north end of Palace Square, tel. 04 90 86 44 58.

• *From Palace Square, head up to the cathedral (enjoy the viewpoint overlooking the square), fill your water bottle just outside the gate, ponder the war memorial (World War I and World War II, as well as Algeria*

1954-1962), then side-trip 20 yards to the left to pause at a memorial to the 300 Jews deported from here to concentration camps by the Nazis. Now zig-zag up the ramps to the top of a rocky hill where Avignon was first settled. Atop the hill is an inviting café and pond in a park—the Jardin du Rocher des Domes. At the far side is a viewpoint high above the river from where you can see Avignon's beloved broken bridge.

▲Jardin du Rocher des Doms

Enjoy the view from this bluff. On a clear day, the tallest peak you see, with its white limestone cap, is Mont Ventoux ("Windy

Mountain"). Below and just to the right, you'll spot free passenger ferries shuttling across the river, and—tucked amidst the trees on the far side of the river—a fun, recommended restaurant, Le Bercail, a local favorite. The island in the river is the Ile de la Barthelasse, a lush nature preserve where Avignon can breathe. To the left in the distance, is the TGV rail bridge.

The Rhône River marked the border of Vatican territory in medieval times. Fort St. André (across the river on the hill) was across the border, in the kingdom of France. The fort was built in 1360, shortly after the pope moved to Avignon, to counter the papal incursion into this part of Europe. Avignon's famous bridge was a key border crossing, with towers on either end—one was French, and the other was the pope's. The French one, across the river, is the Tower of Philip the Fair (described later, under "More Sights in Avignon").

Cost and Hours: Free, park gates open daily April-May and Sept 7:30-20:00, June-Aug 7:30-21:00, Oct-March 7:30-18:00.

• *Take the walkway down to the left and find the stairs (closed at dusk) leading down to the tower. You'll catch glimpses of the...*

Ramparts

The only bit of the rampart you can walk on is accessed from St. Bénezet Bridge (pay to enter—see next). Just after the papacy took control of Avignon, the walls were extended to take in the convents and monasteries that had been outside the city. What you see today was partially restored in the 19th century.

• *When you come out of the tower on street level, exit out of the walls, then turn left along the wall to the old bridge. Pass under the bridge to find its entrance shortly after.*

▲St. Bénezet Bridge (Pont St. Bénezet)

This bridge, whose construction and location were inspired by a shepherd's religious vision, is the "Pont d'Avignon" of nursery-rhyme fame. The ditty (which you've probably been humming all day) dates back to the 15th century: *Sur le Pont d'Avignon, on y danse, on y danse, sur le Pont d'Avignon, on y danse tous en rond* ("On the bridge of Avignon, we will dance, we will dance, on the bridge of Avignon, we will dance all in a circle").

And the bridge was a big deal even outside of its kiddie-tune fame. Built between 1171 and 1185, it was strategic—one of only three bridges crossing the mighty Rhône in the Middle Ages, important to pilgrims, merchants, and armies. It was damaged several times by floods and subsequently rebuilt. In 1668 most of it was knocked out for the last time by a disastrous icy flood. The townsfolk decided not to rebuild this time, and for more than a century, Avignon had no bridge across the Rhône. While only four arches survive today, the original bridge was huge: Imagine a 22-arch, 3,000-foot-long bridge extending from Vatican territory across the island to the lonely Tower of Philip the Fair, which marked the beginning of France (see displays of the bridge's original length).

Cost and Hours: €5, includes audioguide, €13.50 combo-ticket includes Palace of the Popes, same hours as Palace of the Popes, tel. 04 90 27 51 16.

Visiting the Bridge: The ticket booth is housed in what was a medieval hospital for the poor (funded by bridge tolls). Admission includes a small room that displays a 3-D reconstruction of the bridge and your only chance to walk a bit of the ramparts (enter both from the tower). A Romanesque chapel on the bridge is dedicated to St. Bénezet. Though there's not much to see on the bridge, the audioguide included with your ticket tells a good enough story. It's also fun to be in the breezy middle of the river with a sweeping city view.

• *To get to the Palace of the Popes from here, leave via the riverfront exit, turn left, then turn left again back into the walls. Walk to the end of the short street, then turn right following signs to* Palais des Papes. *Next, look for brown signs leading left under the passageway, then stay the course up the narrow steps to Palace Square.*

▲▲Palace of the Popes (Palais des Papes)

In 1309 a French pope was elected (Pope Clément V). His Holiness decided that dangerous Italy was no place for a pope, so he moved the whole operation to Avignon for a secure rule under a supportive

French king. The Catholic Church literally bought Avignon (then a two-bit town), and popes resided here until 1403. Meanwhile, Italians demanded a Roman pope, so from 1378 on, there were twin popes—one in Rome and one in Avignon—causing a schism in the Catholic Church that wasn't fully resolved until 1417.

Cost and Hours: €11, €13.50 combo-ticket includes St. Bénezet Bridge, daily March-June and Sept-Oct 9:00-19:00, July-Aug 9:00-20:00, Nov-Feb 9:30-17:45, last entry one hour before closing; thorough and essential audioguide-€2; tel. 04 90 27 50 00, www.palais-des-papes.com.

Visiting the Palace: Visitors follow a one-way route. A big room near the start functions as "the museum," with artifacts (such as cool 14th-century arrowheads) and a good intro video.

The palace was built stark and strong, before the popes knew how long they'd be staying (and before the affluence and fanciness of the Renaissance and Baroque ages). This was the most fortified palace of the time (remember, the pope left Rome to be more secure). With 10-foot-thick walls, it was a symbol of power. There are huge ceremonial rooms (rarely used) and more intimate living quarters. The bedroom comes with the original wall paintings, a decorated wooden ceiling, and a fine tiled floor. And there's one big "chapel" (twice the size of the adjacent cathedral) which, while simple, is majestic in its pure French Gothic lines.

This largest surviving Gothic palace in Europe was built to accommodate 500 people as the administrative center of the Holy See and home of the pope. Seven popes ruled from here, making this the center of Christianity for nearly 100 years. The last pope checked out in 1403, but the Church owned Avignon until the French Revolution in 1791. During this interim period, the palace still housed Church authorities. Avignon residents, many of whom had come from Rome, spoke Italian for a century after the pope left, making the town a cultural oddity within France.

The palace is pretty empty today—nothing portable survived both the pope's return to Rome and the French Revolution. In fact, Revolutionary leaders (who called the building "the Bastille of the South") decreed that it be demolished but lacked the money to carry out the destruction. With the Napoleonic age, the palace found a practical use, housing about 1800 troops. It remained a barracks until 1906.

You can climb the tower (Tour de la Gâche) for grand views. The artillery room is now a gift shop channeling all visitors on a full tour of knick-knacks for sale.

AVIGNON

• *You'll exit at the rear of the palace, where my next walk, "Discovering Avignon's Back Streets," begins. Or, to return to Palace Square, make two rights after exiting the palace.*

▲▲DISCOVERING AVIGNON'S BACK STREETS

Use the map in this chapter or the TI map to navigate this easy, level, 30-minute walk. We'll begin in the small square (Place de la Mirande) behind the Palace of the Popes. If you've toured the palace, this is where you exit. Otherwise, from the front of the palace, follow the narrow, cobbled Rue de la Peyrolerie—carved out of the rock—around the palace on the right side as you face it.

• *Our walk begins at the...*

Hôtel La Mirande: Located on the square, Avignon's finest hotel welcomes visitors. Find the atrium lounge and consider a coffee break amid the understated luxury (€15 afternoon tea served daily 15:00-18:00, includes a generous selection of pastries).

• *Turn left out of the hotel and left again on Rue de la Peyrolerie ("Coppersmiths Street"), then take your first right on Rue des Ciseaux d'Or ("Street of the Golden Scissors"). On the small square ahead you'll find the...*

Church of St. Pierre: The original walnut doors were carved in 1551, when tales of New World discoveries raced across Europe. (Notice the Indian headdress, top center of left-side door.) The fine Annunciation (eye level on right-side door) shows Gabriel giving Mary the exciting news in impressive Renaissance 3-D. The five niches are empty except for one mismatched Mary and Child filling the center niche. (The original was ransacked by the Revolution.) Now take 10 steps back from the door and look way up. The tiny statue breaking the skyline of the church is the pagan god Bacchus, with oodles of grapes. What's he doing sitting atop a Christian church? No one knows. The church's interior holds a beautiful Baroque altar.

• *Facing the church door, turn left and pass the recommended* L'Epicerie *restaurant, then follow the alley, which was covered and turned into a tunnel during the town's population boom. It leads into...*

Place des Châtaignes: The cloister of St. Pierre is named for the chestnut *(châtaigne)* trees that once stood here (now replaced by plane trees). The practical atheists of the French Revolution destroyed the cloister, leaving only faint traces of the arches along the church side of the square.

• *Continue around the church and cross the busy street. At the start of little Rue des Fourbisseurs find the classy...*

15th-Century Building: With its original beamed eaves showing, this is a rare vestige from the Middle Ages. Notice how this building widens the higher it gets. A medieval loophole based taxes on ground-floor square footage—everything above was tax-free. Walking down Rue des Fourbisseurs ("Street of the Animal Furriers"), notice how the top floors almost touch. Fire was a constant danger in the Middle Ages, as flames leapt easily from one home to the next. In fact, the lookout guard's primary responsibility was watching for fires, not the enemy.

• *Walk down Rue des Fourbisseurs past lots of shops and turn left onto the traffic-free Rue du Vieux Sextier ("Street of the Old Balance," for weighing items); another left under the first arch leads in 10 yards to one of France's oldest synagogues.*

Synagogue: Jews first arrived in Avignon with the Diaspora (exile after the Romans destroyed their great temple) in the first century. Avignon's Jews were nicknamed "the Pope's Jews" because of the protection that the Church offered to Jews expelled from France. Although the original synagogue dates from the 1220s, in the mid-19th century it was completely rebuilt in a Neoclassical Greek-temple style by a non-Jewish architect. This is the only synagogue under a rotunda that you'll see anywhere. It's an intimate, classy place—where a community of 200 local Jews worships—dressed with white colonnades and walnut furnishings. To enter the synagogue, you'll have to email in advance of your visit (free, closed Sat-Sun, 2 Place Jerusalem, tel. 04 90 85 21 24, rabinacia@hotmail.fr).

• *Retrace your steps to Rue du Vieux Sextier and turn left. A few steps down the street (on the right) is Patrick Mallard—the most venerable pastry shop in town. It's one of two shops authorized to sell Avignon's one-of-a-kind, thistle-shaped candy called* papalines d'Avignon *(dark chocolate wrapped in pink-hued chocolate and filled with a liquor made from local plants).*

Continue down Rue du Vieux Sextier to the big square (across the busy street) and find the big, boxy market building with the hydroponic garden growing out its front wall.

Market (Les Halles): In 1970, the town's open-air market was replaced by this modern one. The market's jungle-like hy-

droponic green wall reflects the changes of seasons and helps mitigate its otherwise stark exterior (Tue-Sun until 13:00, closed Mon). Step inside for a sensual experience of organic breads, olives, and festival-of-mold cheeses. Cheap cafés, bars, and good cheese shops are mostly on the right—the stinky fish stalls are on the left. This is an absolutely wonderful place for lunch (doors close weekdays at 13:30, Sat-Sun at 14:00)—especially if you'd fancy a big plate of mixed seafood with a glass of white wine (see "Eating in Avignon," later).

• *Walk through the market and exit out the back door, turn left on Rue de la Bonneterie ("Street of Hosiery"), and track the street for five minutes to the plane trees, where it becomes...*

Rue des Teinturiers: This "Street of the Dyers" is a tie-dyed, tree- and stream-lined lane, home to earthy cafés and galleries. This was the cloth industry's dyeing and textile center in the 1800s. The stream is a branch of the Sorgue River. Those stylish Provençal fabrics and patterns you see for sale everywhere were first made here, after a pattern imported from India.

About three small bridges down, you'll pass the Grey Penitents chapel on the right. The upper facade shows the GPs, who dressed up in robes and pointy hoods to do their anonymous good deeds back in the 13th century. (While the American KKK dresses in hoods to hide their hateful racism, these hoods symbolized how all are equal in God's eyes.) As you stroll on, you'll see the work of amateur sculptors, who have carved whimsical car barriers out of limestone. Fun restaurants on this atmospheric street are recommended later, under "Eating in Avignon."

• *Farther down Rue des Teinturiers, you'll come to the...*

Waterwheel: Standing here, imagine the Sorgue River—which hits the mighty Rhône in Avignon—being broken into several canals in order to turn 23 such wheels. Starting in about 1800, waterwheels powered the town's industries. The little cogwheel above the big one could be shoved into place, kicking another machine into gear behind the wall. (For more on the Sorgue River and its waterwheels, see my self-guided walk of Isle-sur-la-Sorgue on page 192.)

• *To return to the center of town, double back on Rue des Teinturiers and turn left on Rue des Lices, which traces the first medieval wall. (A lice is the no-man's-land along a protective wall.) After a long block you'll pass a striking four-story building that was a home for the poor in the 1600s, an army barracks in the 1800s, a fine-arts school in the 1900s, and is a deluxe condominium today (much of this neighborhood is going high-class residential). Eventually you'll return to Rue de la République, Avignon's main drag.*

More Sights in Avignon

Most of Avignon's top sights are covered earlier by my self-guided walks. With more time, consider these options.

Fondation Angladon-Dubrujeaud

Visiting this museum is like being invited into the elegant home of a rich and passionate art collector. It mixes a small but enjoyable collection of art from Post-Impressionists to Cubists (including Paul Cézanne, Vincent van Gogh, Edgar Degas, and Pablo Picasso), with re-created art studios and furnishings from many periods. It's a quiet place with a few superb paintings.

Cost and Hours: €6.50, Tue-Sun 13:00-18:00, closed Mon, 5 Rue Laboureur, tel. 04 90 82 29 03, www.angladon.com.

Calvet Museum (Musée Calvet)

This fine-arts museum, ignored by most, impressively displays a collection highlighting French Baroque works and Northern masters such as Hieronymus Bosch and Pieter Bruegel. You'll find a few gems upstairs: a painting each by Manet, Sisley, Géricault, and David. On the ground floor is a room dedicated to more modern artists, with works by Soutine, Bonnard, and Vlamnick.

Cost and Hours: €6, includes audioguide, Wed-Mon 10:00-13:00 & 14:00-18:00, closed Tue, in the western half of town at 65 Rue Joseph Vernet, tel. 04 90 86 33 84, www.musee-calvet.org.

Nearby: The museum's antiquities collection, **Le Musée Lapidaire,** is hosted in a church a few blocks away at 27 Rue de la République (€2, €7 combo-ticket with Calvet Museum; same hours except open Tue and closed Mon, tel. 04 90 85 75 38, www.musee-lapidaire.org).

NEAR AVIGNON

▲Tower of Philip the Fair (Tour Philippe-le-Bel)

Built to protect access to St. Bénezet Bridge in 1307, this hulking tower, located in nearby Villeneuve-lès-Avignon, offers a terrific view over Avignon and the Rhône basin. It's best late in the day.

Cost and Hours: €2.40; Tue-Sun May-Oct 10:00-12:30 & 14:00-18:00, Feb-April 14:00-17:00, closed Nov-Jan and Mon year-round.

Getting There: To reach the tower from Avignon, drive five minutes (cross Daladier Bridge, follow signs to *Villeneuve-lès-Avignon*), or take bus #5 (2/hour, catch bus in front of post office on Cours Président Kennedy across from train station—see map on page 100).

Sleeping in Avignon

Hotel values are better in Arles, though I've found some pretty good deals in Avignon. Avignon is crazy during its July festival (see sidebar on page 103), when you must book long ahead and pay inflated prices. Drivers should ask about parking discounts through hotels.

NEAR CENTRE-VILLE STATION

These listings are a five-to-ten-minute walk from the Centre-Ville train station.

$$$ Hôtel Bristol*** is a big, professionally run place on the main drag, offering predictable "American" comforts at fair rates. Enjoy spacious public spaces, large rooms with neutral tones, and a generous buffet breakfast (standard Db-€120, bigger Db-€145, Tb/Qb-€175, breakfast-€13, parking-€13/day, 44 Cours Jean Jaurès, tel. 04 90 16 48 48, www.bristol-hotel-avignon.com, contact@bristol-avignon.com).

$$$ Hôtel Ibis Centre Gare*** offers predictable comfort and generous public spaces near the central train and bus stations (Db-€95-105, 42 Boulevard St. Roch, tel. 04 90 85 38 38, www.ibishotel.com, h0944@accor.com).

$$ Hôtel Colbert** is on a quiet lane, with a dozen spacious rooms gathered on four floors around a skinny spiral staircase (no elevator). Patrice decorates each room as if it was his own with a colorful (occasionally erotic) flair. There are warm public spaces and a sweet little patio (Sb-€74, small Db-€82, bigger Db-€100, some tight bathrooms, no triples, rooms off the patio can be musty, closed Nov-mid-March, 7 Rue Agricol Perdiguier, tel. 04 90 86 20 20, www.lecolbert-hotel.com, contact@avignon-hotel-colbert.com).

$$ Hôtel le Splendid**, run by young and eager Agnes and Fabrice, rents 16 bright and spotless rooms with tight baths at fair rates (Db-€90, no elevator, 17 Rue Agricol Perdiguier, tel. 04 90 86 14 46, www.avignon-splendid-hotel.com, splendidavignon@gmail.com).

$$ Hôtel Boquier**, run by engaging managers Madame Sendra and husband Pascal, has 12 quiet, good-value, and homey rooms under wood beams in a central location (small Db-€79, bigger Db-€88, Tb-€90, Qb-€105, buffet breakfast-€9, steep and narrow stairways to some rooms, no elevator, parking-€12/day, near the TI at 6 Rue du Portail Boquier, tel. 04 90 82 34 43, www.hotel-boquier.com, contact@hotel-boquier.com).

$ Hôtel Innova/Cardabella* is a shy little place with 11 cute and modest rooms at good rates (D-€43, Db-€55-63, extra person-€7, breakfast-€5, no air-con, no elevator, no Wi-Fi, 100 Rue Joseph Vernet, tel. 04 90 82 54 10, www.hotel-cardabella.fr, hotel.cardabella@gmail.com).

Sleep Code

Abbreviations   **(€1=about $1.10, country code: 33)**
S=Single, **D**=Double/Twin, **T**=Triple, **Q**=Quad, **b**=bathroom,
*=French hotel rating (0-5 stars)
Price Rankings
   $$$ **Higher Priced**—Most rooms €90 or more
     $$ **Moderately Priced**—Most rooms €65-90
       $ **Lower Priced**—Most rooms €65 or less
Unless otherwise noted, credit cards are accepted, English is spoken, there's an elevator and air-conditioning, and free Wi-Fi and/or a guest computer is available. Prices change; verify current rates online or by email. For the best prices, always book directly with the hotel.

IN THE CENTER, NEAR PLACE DE L'HORLOGE

$$$ Hôtel d'Europe*****, with Avignon's most prestigious address, lets peasants sleep royally without losing their shirts—but only if they land one of the 13 reasonable *"classique"* rooms. Enter through a shady courtyard, linger in the lounges, and savor every comfort. The hotel is located on the handsome Place Crillon, near the river (standard *"classique"* Db-€230, large Db-€390-€590, view suites-€1,100, breakfast-€22, garage parking-€20/day, near Daladier Bridge at 12 Place Crillon, tel. 04 90 14 76 76, www.heurope. com, reservations@heurope.com). The hotel's fine restaurant is described in "Eating in Avignon," later.

$$$ Hôtel de l'Horloge**** is as central as it gets—on Place de l'Horloge. It offers 66 unimaginative but comfortable rooms at fair rates, some with terraces and views of the city and the Palace of the Popes (standard Db-€140-170, bigger Db with terrace-€180-225, elaborate €18 buffet breakfast served until 11:00, 1 Rue Félicien David, tel. 04 90 16 42 00, www.hotel-avignon-horloge.com, hotel.horloge@hotels-ocre-azur.com).

$$$ Hôtel Mercure Palais des Papes****, about a block from the Palace of the Popes, has an ugly exterior but 89 big, smartly designed rooms, many with small balconies (standard Db-€175, large Db-€200, breakfast-€16, about half the rooms have views over Place de l'Horloge, check for deals on website, 1 Rue Jean Vilar, tel. 04 90 80 93 00, www.mercure.com, h1952@accor.com).

$$$ Hôtel Pont d'Avignon****, just inside the walls near St. Bénezet Bridge, is part of the same chain as Hôtel Mercure Palais des Papes, with the same prices for its 87 rooms. There's an airy atrium breakfast room and small garden terrace (direct access to a garage makes parking easier than at the other Mercure hotel, parking deals, on Rue Ferruce, tel. 04 90 80 93 93, www.mercure.com, h0549@accor.com).

AVIGNON

Avignon Hotels & Restaurants

AVIGNON

AVIGNON

1 Hôtel Bristol
2 Hôtel Ibis Centre Gare
3 Hôtel Colbert
4 Hôtel le Splendid
5 Hôtel Boquier
6 Hôtel Innova/Cardabella
7 Hôtel d'Europe & La Vieille Fontaine Restaurant
8 Hôtel de l'Horloge
9 Hôtel Mercure Palais des Papes
10 Hôtel Pont d'Avignon
11 Autour du Petit Paradis Apts.
12 Aux Augustins Apartments
13 Hôtel Médiéval
14 Hôtel Mignon
15 Auberge Bagatelle (Hostel)
16 To Jardin de Bacchus B&B
17 L'Essentiel Restaurant
18 Restaurant Numéro 75
19 L'Agape & Place des Corps-Saints Eateries
20 L'Epicerie Restaurant
21 Le Fou de Fafa Restaurant
22 La Vache à Carreaux Rest.
23 Le Zinzolin Restaurant
24 La Cave des Pas Sages Wine Bar
25 Le Bercail Restaurant
26 L'Epice and Love Restaurant
27 Place des Châtaignes Eateries
28 Restaurant Françoise
29 Les Halles Market
30 Hôtel La Mirande (Aft. Tea)
31 Groceries (2)

$$$ **Autour du Petit Paradis Apartments** and **Aux Augustins,** run by Sabine and Patrick, offers 22 contemporary, well-furnished apartments spread over two locations conveniently located in the city center (€550-850/week, Db-€180 with 3-night minimum, 5 Rue Noël Biret and 16 Rue Carreterie, tel. 04 90 81 00 42, www.autourdupetitparadis.com, contact@autourdupetitparadis.com).

$$ **Hôtel Médiéval****, burrowed deep a few blocks from the Church of St. Pierre, was built as a cardinal's home. This stone mansion's grand staircase leads to 35 comfortable, pastel rooms (Sb-€65, Db-€75-102, Tb-€120, no elevator, 5 blocks east of Place de l'Horloge, behind Church of St. Pierre at 15 Rue Petite Saunerie, tel. 04 90 86 11 06, www.hotelmedieval.com, hotel.medieval@wanadoo.fr, run by helpful Régis).

$$ **Hôtel Mignon*** is a good-enough, one-star place with fair comfort, air-conditioning, drab halls, and tiny bathrooms (Sb-€60, Db-€70-75, Tb-€87, Qb-€100, 12 Rue Joseph Vernet, tel. 04 90 82 17 30, www.hotel-mignon.com, reservation@hotel-mignon.fr).

ON THE OUTSKIRTS OF TOWN

$ **Auberge Bagatelle** offers dirt-cheap beds in two buildings—a budget hotel and a youth hostel—and has a young and lively vibe, café, grocery store, launderette, great views of Avignon, and campers for neighbors (Db-€68, D with private shower but toilet down the hall-€48, Tb-€97, Qb-€100, dorm bed-€18, breakfast-€5, across Daladier Bridge on Ile de la Barthelasse, bus #5 from main post office, tel. 04 90 86 30 39, www.campingbagatelle.fr, auberge.bagatelle@wanadoo.fr).

NEAR AVIGNON

$$$ At **Jardin de Bacchus,** a 15-minute drive northwest of Avignon by car and convenient to Pont du Gard, enthusiastic and English-speaking Christine and Erik offer two double rooms in their village home overlooking the famous rosé vineyards of Tavel (Db-€100-120, includes breakfast, fine €30 dinner if arranged in advance, swimming pool, great patio, possible bike rentals). They also offer apartments for two or four people (4-night minimum in off-season, one-week minimum in summer, tel. 04 66 90 28 62 or 06 74 41 77 94, www.jardindebacchus.fr, jardindebacchus@gmail.com). By car, it's just off the A-9 autoroute (exit 22); by bus, it's a 30-minute ride from Avignon (www.edgard-transport.fr).

AVIGNON

Eating in Avignon

Avignon offers a good range of restaurants and settings, from lively squares to atmospheric streets. Skip the overpriced, underwhelming restaurants on Place de l'Horloge and find a more intimate location for your dinner. Avignon is riddled with delightful squares and back streets lined with little restaurants eager to feed you. If you need to dine before 19:00, find **Restaurant Françoise** on Place Pie (described later). At the finer places, reservations are generally smart (especially on weekends); your hotel can call for you.

FINE DINING WORTH THE SPLURGE

L'Essentiel is where in-the-know locals go for a fine meal at reasonable prices. The setting is classy-contemporary inside, the back terrace is romantic, the wine list is extensive, the cuisine is classic French, and gentle owner Dominique makes timid diners feel at ease (inside and outdoor seating, €31-45 *menus,* closed Sun-Mon, 2 Rue Petite Fusterie, tel. 04 90 85 87 12, www.restaurantlessentiel. com).

La Vieille Fontaine, just inside the gates of Hôtel d'Europe, earned a Michelin star for its gourmet traditional cuisine served in an elegant dining room and on a spacious courtyard terrace. Do your best to dress up for this place (€68 *menu,* €48 lunch *menu,* near Daladier Bridge at 12 Place Crillon, tel. 04 90 14 76 76, www. heurope.com).

Restaurant Numéro 75 is worth the walk. It fills the Pernod mansion (of *pastis* liquor fame) with a romantic, chandeliered, Old World dining hall that extends to a leafy, gravelly courtyard. They serve delightful lunch salads, fish is a forte, and the French cuisine is beautifully presented (€32 lunch *menu,* dinner *menus:* €29 two-course and €37 three-course, Mon-Sat 12:00-14:00 & 19:45-22:00, closed Sun, 75 Rue Guillaume Puy, tel. 04 90 27 16 00, www.numero75.com).

L'Agape shares an atmospheric square with cafés and cheaper places. Here, discerning diners can eat well while enjoying great outdoor ambience (*menus* from €31, closed Sun-Mon, 21 Place des Corps-Saints, tel. 04 90 85 04 06).

DINING WELL IN THE OLD CENTER ON A MODERATE BUDGET

L'Epicerie sits alone under green awnings on the romantic Place St-Pierre square and is ideal for dinner outside (or in the small but cozy interior). The cuisine is as delicious as the setting (€10 starters, €24 *plats*, daily, 10 Place St-Pierre, tel. 04 90 82 74 22).

Le Fou de Fafa's is a warm place with ample space between its 12 tables and a menu of delicious cuisine at good prices. Delightful Antonia serves while her husband cooks (inside dining only, book ahead or arrive early, €24-30 *menus*, Tue-Sat from 18:30, closed Sun-Mon, 17 Rue des Trois Faucons, tel. 04 32 76 35 13).

La Vache à Carreaux venerates cheese and wine while offering a range of choices from its big chalkboard. It's a young, lively place, with colorful décor, easygoing service (thanks to owner Jean-Charles) and a reasonable wine list (€12 starters, €12-16 *plats*, €5 wines by the glass, daily, just off atmospheric Place des Châtaignes at 14 Rue de la Peyrolerie, tel. 04 90 80 09 05).

BOHEMIAN CHIC, CANALSIDE ON RUE DES TEINTURIERS

Rue des Teinturiers' fun concentration of midrange, popular-with-the-locals eateries justifies the long walk. It's a trendy, youthful area, spiffed up but with little hint of tourism. You'll find wine bars, North African places, vegetarian diners, and live music at rickety metal tables under shady trees along the canal. I'd walk the street's entire length to find the best ambience before making a choice. (Note that the finer Restaurant Numéro 75, listed earlier, is just around the corner.)

Le Zinzolin is a bohemian bistro serving international cuisine to a younger crowd at fair prices with a few vegetarian options. The atmosphere is good inside and out (€14 meal-size salads, €15 *plats*, €5 desserts, closed Mon evening and Sun, 22 Rue des Teinturiers, tel. 04 90 82 41 55).

La Cave des Pas Sages, a characteristic wine bar, is a fun place to start your evening (even if you're not eating in the area). Linger with the locals over a cheap glass of regional wine or beer. Choose from the blackboard by the bar that lists all the open bottles, then join the gang outside by the canal (Mon-Sat 10:00-24:00, closed Sun, no food in evening, across from waterwheel at 41 Rue des Teinturiers).

LOCAL FAVORITE ACROSS THE RHONE

Le Bercail offers a fun opportunity to get out of town (barely) and take in *le fresh air* with a terrific riverfront view of Avignon, all while enjoying big portions of Provençal cooking (*menus* from €28, daily April-Oct, serves late, reservations recommended, tel.

AVIGNON

04 90 82 20 22). Take the free shuttle boat (located near St. Bénezet Bridge) to the Ile de la Barthelasse, turn right, and walk five
minutes. As the boat usually stops running at about 18:00 (except
in July-Aug, when it runs until 21:00), you can either taxi back or
walk 25 minutes along the pleasant riverside path and over Daladier Bridge.

GOOD BUDGET PLACES IN THE CENTER

L'Epice and Love (pronounced "lay peace and love") is a tiny,
flower-child-like restaurant with a few colorfully decorated tables
(inside only). Friendly, English-speaking owner Marie stokes the
conviviality and her selection changes weekly: tasty meat, fish, and
vegetarian dishes, some with a North African touch, all served at
good prices (€16-20 *menus,* closed Sun, 30 Rue des Lices, tel. 04
90 82 45 96).

Place des Châtaignes: This square offers cheap meals and a fun
commotion of tables. The **Crêperie du Cloître** makes cheap, mediocre dinner crêpes and salads but has the best seating on the square
(daily). **La Pause Gourmande** bakery/deli is tops on the square for
lunch (great *fougasse,* quiche with salad or *plats* for €10, lunch only,
closed Sun).

Place des Corps-Saints: This welcoming square offers the best
feeling of a neighborhood dining, drinking, and simply living outdoors together. It's my choice for outdoor dining in Avignon, with
several eateries in all price ranges sharing the same great setting
under big plane trees. Survey the square before deciding. With
tables crammed into every nook and cranny, there's standard café
fare, Italian options, and finer dining choices. **Bistrot à Tartines**
serves big slices of toast smothered in a variety of toppings, and
has tasty desserts (€7 *tartines* and salads, daily, tel. 04 90 85 58 70).
Zeste is a friendly, modern deli offering fresh soups, pasta salads,
wraps, smoothies, and more (lunch only, closed Sun, tel. 09 51 49
05 62).

Place Pie: Avignon's youth make their home on this big square
filled with cafés. Just off the square, **Restaurant Françoise** is a fine
deli-café, where fresh-baked tarts—savory and sweet—and a variety of salads and soups make a healthful meal, and vegetarian
options are plentiful. Order at the counter and eat inside or out
(€5-8 salads, €10 entrees, Wi-Fi, Mon-Sat 8:00-19:00, closed Sun,
a block off Place Pie at 6 Rue Général Leclerc, tel. 04 32 76 24 77).

The Farmers' Market: Les Halles (described in the "Discovering Avignon's Back Streets" walk, closed Mon) has a handful
of wonderfully characteristic and cheap places serving locals the
freshest of food surrounded by all that market fun. You'll need to
be done by 13:30 (14:00 on weekends), as that's when they lock the
place up. For **seafood** the shops in either far corner can't be beat.

They'll assemble you the plate of your dreams at a painless price (e.g., a big assortment for two on ice for €18) and pour you a glass of local white wine...and you're set. While the prices at both these places are about the same, one spot feels like a little restaurant and the other a picnic at the marina.

Avignon Connections

BY TRAIN

Remember, there are two train stations in Avignon: the suburban TGV Station and the Centre-Ville Station in the city center (€1.60 shuttle trains connect the stations, buy ticket from machine on platforms or at a counter, 2/hour, 5 minutes). TGV trains usually serve the TGV Station only, though a few depart from Centre-Ville Station (check your ticket). The TGV Station has almost all the car rental agencies; only Avis is at Centre-Ville Station. Some cities are served by slower local trains from Centre-Ville Station as well as by faster TGV trains from the TGV Station; I've listed the most convenient stations for each trip.

From Avignon's Centre-Ville Station to: Arles (roughly hourly, 20 minutes, less frequent in the afternoon), Orange (15/day, 20 minutes), Nîmes (12/day, 60 minutes), Isle-sur-la-Sorgue (10/day on weekdays, 5/day on weekends, 30 minutes), Lyon (10/day, 2 hours, also from TGV Station in 70 minutes—see below), Carcassonne (8/day, 7 with transfer in Narbonne or Nîmes, 3 hours), Barcelona (2/day, 5.75 hours with changes in Nîmes and Figueres-Vilafant; more frequent but slower, with a change in Cerbère).

From Avignon's TGV Station to: Nice (10/day, most by TGV, 4 hours, many require transfer in Marseille), Marseille (10/day, 35 minutes), Cassis (7/day, transfer in Marseille, 1.5 hours), Aix-en-Provence TGV (12/day, 25 minutes), Lyon (12/day, 70 minutes, also from Centre-Ville Station—see above), Paris' Gare de Lyon (10/day direct, 2.5 hours; more connections with transfer, 3-4 hours), Paris' Charles de Gaulle airport (7/day, 3.25 hours).

BY BUS

The bus station (gare routière) is just past and below Hôtel Ibis, to the right as you exit the train station. Nearly all buses leave from this station (a few leave from the ring road outside the station—ask, buy tickets on bus, small bills only). Service is reduced or nonexistent on Sundays and holidays. Check your departure time beforehand, and make sure to verify your destination with the driver.

From Avignon to Pont du Gard: Buses go to this famous Roman aqueduct (3/day, 50 minutes, departs from bus station). For a more worthwhile day trip, see my suggested train/bus excursion that combines Nîmes and Pont du Gard (see "Planning Your Time," next chapter).

By Bus to Other Regional Destinations: Arles (8/day, 1 hour, leaves from TGV Station); Nîmes: 12/day, 1 hour), **Aix-en-Provence** (6/day Mon-Sat, 3/day Sun, 75 minutes, faster and easier than train), **Uzès** (3-5/day, 60-80 minutes, stops at Pont du Gard); **St-Rémy-de-Provence** (Cartreize #57 bus, 10/day Mon-Sat, 6/day Sun, 45 minutes); **Orange** (Mon-Sat hourly, 5/day Sun, 1 hour—take the train instead); **Isle-sur-la-Sorgue** (6-8/day Mon-Sat, 3-4/day Sun, 45 minutes, stall #13, some leave from ring road). For the **Côtes du Rhône** area, the bus runs to **Vaison-la-Romaine, Nyons, Sablet,** and **Séguret** (3-6/day during the school year—*période scolaire*, 3/day otherwise; 1/day from TGV Station; 1.5 hours, all buses pass through Orange—faster to take train to Orange, and transfer to bus there; 1-hour express bus runs to Vaison-la-Romaine from Avignon once per day). For the **Luberon** area—including **Lourmarin, Roussillon,** and **Gordes**—take the bus to Cavaillon, then take bus #8 toward Pertuis for Lourmarin (3/day) or bus #15 for Gordes/Roussillon (only 1/day); you must reserve a day ahead for buses from Cavaillon (tel. 04 90 74 20 21).

AVIGNON

NEAR AVIGNON

Nîmes • Pont du Gard • Uzès

Although Avignon lacks Roman monuments of its own, some of Europe's greatest Roman sights are an easy, breezy day trip away. (To get the most out of these sights, read "How About Them Romans?" on page 29 before you visit.) The Pont du Gard aqueduct is a magnificent structure to experience, as is the city it served 2,000 years ago, Nîmes, which wraps a handful of intriguing Roman monuments together in a mellow, bigger-city package. The pedestrian-friendly town of Uzès, between Nîmes and Pont du Gard, offers a refreshing break from power monuments and busy cities. Combining these three sights makes a memorable (if busy) day trip into the Languedoc-Roussillon region. Traveling by car, you'll drive scenic roads between Uzès and Nîmes that show off the rugged *garrigue* landscape that this area is famous for.

PLANNING YOUR TIME

Consider getting away from the tourists and spending the night in classy Nîmes or cozy Uzès; both beat Avignon for quick and easy access to Pont du Gard. If you're on a tighter schedule, this region's sights are easy to cover as day trips from Avignon, even without a car. Avignon to Pont du Gard is a 30-minute drive; it's 45 minutes to Uzès, and 45 minutes to Nîmes. Car-less day-trippers from Avignon have these options:

Minivan Tour: An army of companies run day trips from Avignon to Pont du Gard, Uzès, and other popular destinations. Ask for a list at Avignon's TI, and see page 26 (Winery Plus Tours is based near Uzès).

Bus, Train, and/or Taxi: With as few as three buses a day connecting Avignon with Pont du Gard and Uzès, plan carefully—particularly off-season when weekend service all but vanishes. Check schedules at Avignon's bus station (see page 122), at a TI,

Near Avignon

Note: In some cases regular train lines and TGV lines share the same track

10 Kilometers
10 Miles

To Lyon
A-7
D94
D-976
Vaison-la-Romaine
D-977
Orange
Malaucène
Rhône
TGV High-Speed Line
D-938
A-7
D-950
D-17
Châteauneuf-du-Pape
Carpentras
Uzès
PONT DU GARD
D-981
A-9
D-938
D-979
D-100
Avignon
TGV STN
Isle-sur-la-Sorgue
Roussillon
Nîmes
A-9
D-986
N-570
D-100
Cavaillon
Apt
A-54
D-99
St-Rémy
A-7
LUBERON
D-6113
GLANUM
Petit Rhône
Les Baux
Rhône
Arles
To Marseille

Distance By Bus/Train From Avignon

Orange: 20 min by train; 60 min by bus

Isle-sur-la-Sorgue: 30 min by train; 45 min by bus

Nîmes: 30 min by train; 60 min by bus

Uzès: 60–80 min by bus only

Pont du Gard: 45 min by bus only

Arles: 20 min by train; 60 min by bus

St-Rémy-de-Provence: 45 min by bus only;
    Les Baux is 20 min more by bus.

Vaison-la-Romaine: 60–90 min by bus;
    faster via train to Orange, then bus.

or at www.edgard-transport.fr (tel. 08 10 33 42 73). Arrive at bus stops at least five minutes early, pay the driver (coins or small bills), and verify your stop and direction with the driver.

Buses (€2) take around 45 minutes from Avignon or Nîmes to Pont du Gard; almost hourly trains (€10) take 30 minutes to connect Avignon and Nîmes. Allow €60 and 30 minutes for a one-way taxi ride from Avignon or Nîmes to Pont du Gard.

Here are three day-trip plans to consider. Double-check all departure times before you set out. The first buses usually depart Avignon for Pont du Gard at about 8:45 and 11:40.

Day Trip to Pont du Gard Only: Take a morning bus from Avignon's bus station to Pont du Gard, tour the site, then hop on an afternoon bus back to Avignon. For more flexibility, catch a cab from Avignon, then ride the bus back.

Day Trip to Pont du Gard and Nîmes: Take a morning bus from Avignon to Pont du Gard, tour the site, then take an early-afternoon bus to Nîmes for more sightseeing. Return by train to Avignon.

Day Trip to Pont du Gard and Uzès: Take a morning bus from Avignon to Pont du Gard, tour the site, then catch a midday bus to Uzès and stroll the town. Catch the late-afternoon bus back to Avignon.

Nîmes

Most travelers make time in their schedules for Arles and Avignon, but ignore Nîmes. Arles and Avignon may have more touristic appeal, but Nîmes—which feels richer and surer of itself—is refreshingly lacking in overnight tourists. This thriving town of classy shops and serious businesses is studded with world-class Roman monuments and laced with traffic-free lanes. (And if you've visited the magnificent Pont du Gard, you gotta be curious where all that water went.)

Since the Middle Ages, Nîmes has exported a famous fabric: The word "denim" actually comes from here (*de Nîmes* = "from Nîmes"). Denim caught on in the United States in the 1800s, when a Bavarian immigrant, Levi Strauss, popularized its use in the American West.

Today, Nîmes is officially in the Languedoc-Roussillon region (for administrative purposes), yet historically the town has been a key player in the evolution of Provence. Only 30 minutes by train from Arles or Avignon, and three hours from Paris on the TGV, Nîmes is easy to reach. The city keeps its clean and tranquil old center a secret for its well-heeled residents. (Locals admit they don't need the tourism money as much as other Provençal towns.) While most visitors understandably prefer sleeping in Arles or Avignon, a night here provides a good escape from tourist crowds and a truer taste of a Provençal city.

Orientation to Nîmes

Nîmes ("neem") has no river or natural landmark to navigate by, so it's easy to become disoriented. For a quick visit, limit yourself to the manageable triangle within the ring of roads formed by boulevards Victor Hugo, Amiral Courbet, and Gambetta.

The town's landmarks are connected by 10-minute walks: It's 10 minutes from the train station to the arena, 10 minutes from the arena to the Roman temple of Maison Carrée, and 10 minutes from

Maison Carrée to either the Castellum or the Fountain Garden. Apart from seeing this handful of ancient monuments, appreciate the city's traffic-free old center—a delight for browsing, strolling, sipping coffee, and people-watching.

TOURIST INFORMATION

The TI, across the street and a half-block up from Maison Carrée, is a 20-minute walk from the train station (Mon-Sat 8:30-19:00, Sun 10:00-18:00, 6 Rue Auguste, tel. 04 66 58 38 00, www.ot-nimes.fr). Pick up the *Discovering Nîmes* pamphlet, which includes a map with a description of the city's sights and museums, and a worthwhile old-town walk. You can also rent an audioguide for a walking tour of Old Nîmes (€8, €10/2 people).

ARRIVAL IN NIMES

By Train and Bus: Trains and buses use the same station (handy if you're combining Pont du Gard with Nîmes). There's no baggage storage. Confirm return schedules before leaving the station (beware of gaps in train service to Arles).

The bus station and bus information office are out the rear of the train station. Find the bright yellow *Edgard* office banners a block straight out the station's back door (Mon-Fri 8:00-12:00 & 14:00-18:00, Sat 8:00-12:00, closed Sun, www.edgard-transport.fr). If departing from Nîmes by bus, arrive early to double check schedules and ask in the office which stall your bus leaves from (usually between 8 and 14; the shelters are to the right out the rear exit of the train station). Route numbers posted on buses may not correspond to paper timetables—confirm your destination with the driver. Buy your ticket from the driver (about €2 one-way to Pont du Gard, bring small bills or coins).

The arena is a pleasant 10-minute walk out the front of the train station (see map on page 128). Head up the pedestrian parkway, go left at the big plaza, curve right, and you'll see the arena (to find its entrance, walk counterclockwise around it). The Maison Carrée and TI are an enjoyable stroll from the arena through Nîmes' traffic-free old town.

By Car: Follow signs for *Centre-Ville* and *TI,* then *Arènes Parking,* and pay to park underneath the arena. (It's a huge garage; make a note of where you parked.) If the garage is full, Parking des Feuchères is nearby (behind the train station), and Parking Maison Carrée is close to the TI (around €9/4 hours; not all pay machines accept bills so come with coins).

HELPFUL HINTS

Summer Thursdays: The "Jeudi de Nîmes" (Thursdays of Nîmes) tradition turns the entire old center of town into a festival of

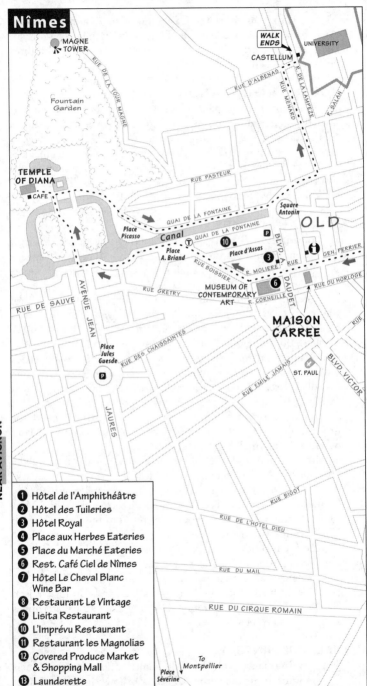

Nîmes

NEAR AVIGNON

1. Hôtel de l'Amphithéâtre
2. Hôtel des Tuileries
3. Hôtel Royal
4. Place aux Herbes Eateries
5. Place du Marché Eateries
6. Rest. Café Ciel de Nîmes
7. Hôtel Le Cheval Blanc Wine Bar
8. Restaurant Le Vintage
9. Lisita Restaurant
10. L'Imprévu Restaurant
11. Restaurant les Magnolias
12. Covered Produce Market & Shopping Mall
13. Launderette

N

200 Meters
200 Yards

RUE CLERISSEAU

To Uzès & Pont du Gard

ST. CHARLES

POST

BLVD. GAMBETTA

R. CORCONNE

RUE DU

BAT-D'ARGENT

RUE DES LOMBARDS

RUE NATIONALE

R. CORC.

RUE F. VIEILLE

RUE DES ORANGERS

Place du Château

ST. BAUDILE

RUE DE BEAUCAIRE

RUE GUIZOT

LES HALLES

12 P

RUE CREMIEUX

RUE ST. CASTOR

11 Place des Esclafidous

R. CURATERIE

COURBET

Place G. Péri

RUE D'ESPAGNE

Place Robert

RUE VINCENT FAITA

To Beaucaire & Tarascon

CLOCK TOWER

Place de l'Horloge

Place aux Herbes **4**

L'HUILERIE EPICERIE

RUE X MARCH

CATHEDRAL

RUE CHAPITRE

MUSEUM OF OLD NIMES

RUE POISE

RUE DOKEE

ARCHAEOLOGICAL MUSEUM

GRAND RUE

BLVD. AMIRAL

MADELEINE

RUE DE L'ASPIC

8

RUE TRESORERIE

RUE DES GREFFES

13

TOWN

RUE PRESQUE

R. BROQ.

R. D'ARENE

5

Place du Marché

1

9

RUE DE LA VIOLETTE

Square de la Couronne

RUE NOTRE DAME

2

STE. PERPETUE

RUE MONJARDIN

HUGO

BLVD.

DES ARENES

BLVD. DE LA LIBERATION

Esplanade-Charles-de-Gaulle

WALK BEGINS

ARENA

Place des Arènes

7

P Arènes

RUE BRICONNET

POST

AVENUE FEUCHERES

RUE DE LA REPUBLIQUE

RUE DE LA CITE FOULC

MUSEE DES BEAUX-ARTS

RUE GUILLEMETTE

RUE DE GENERAC

BLVD. SERGENT TRIAIRE

TRAIN STATION

BUS INFO OFFICE

BUS STN.

BOISSY D'ANGLAIS

To Arles

BLVD. NATOIRE

NEAR AVIGNON

shops, street music, and liveliness on Thursday nights in July and August from 18:00 until late.

Laundry: A launderette is near many of my recommended hotels at 1 Rue des Fourbisseurs (daily 7:00-21:00).

Taxi: Call 04 66 29 40 11 for a cab. It costs about €60 for a ride to Pont du Gard.

Car Rental: Near the station, you'll find **Avis** (tel. 04 66 29 66 36), **Europcar** (tel. 04 66 29 07 94), and **Hertz** (tel. 04 66 76 25 91).

Local Guide: Sylvie Pagnard is a delightful guide whose walking tours are top quality. She also does regional tours (€145/3 hours, €360/8 hours, a little extra if she drives her car, tel. 04 66 20 33 14, mobile 06 03 21 37 33, sylviepagnard@gmail.com).

View Café: Ride the glass elevator to the recommended, top-floor Restaurant Café Ciel de Nîmes at the Museum of Contemporary Art for a great view over the ancient Maison Carrée and a quiet break.

Nîmes Walk

I've described Nîmes' best sights below in a logical order for a good daylong visit, linked by walking directions starting from the arena (near the train station, with easy underground parking). Many of the sights I mention are free; the major exception is the arena.

▲▲Arena (Amphithéâtre)

Nîmes' arena dates from about A.D. 100 and is more than 425 feet in diameter and 65 feet tall. Considered the best-preserved arena

of the Roman world, it's a fine example of Roman engineering...and propaganda. In the spirit of "give them bread and circuses," it was free. The agenda was to create a populace that was thoroughly Roman—enjoying the same activities and entertainment, all thinking as one (not unlike Americans' nationwide obsession with the same reality-TV shows). The 24,000 seats could be filled and emptied in minutes (through 60 passageways called *vomitoires*).

Cost and Hours: €9.50, includes great audioguide; daily June 9:00-19:00, July and Aug 9:00-20:00, March-April and Sept-Oct 9:00-18:00, Nov-Feb 9:00-17:00. Buy the €11 combo-ticket if you plan to visit the Maison Carrée. Tel. 04 66 21 82 56, www.arenes-nimes.com.

Visiting the Arena: Pick up the included audioguide (or pay extra for the fancy tablet tour). You'll find helpful English information panels as you tour the arena, which combine with the excellent audioguide to give a thorough and enjoyable history lesson. Don't miss the panels describing the different types of gladiators.

Climb to the very **top.** It's a rare opportunity to enjoy the view from a surviving high point—the nosebleed seats—of a Roman arena. An amphitheater is literally a double theater: two theaters facing each other, designed so that twice the people could view a *Dirty Harry* spectacle—without the acoustics provided by the back wall of a theater stage. (You may think of this as a "colosseum," but that's not a generic term. Rome's Colosseum was a one-of-a-kind arena—named for a colossal statue of Nero that stood nearby.)

The **floor** where the action took place was the *arena* (literally, "sand," which absorbed the blood, as in bullfights today). The arena's floor, which covered passages and storage areas underneath, came with the famous elevator for surprise appearances of wild animals. (While Rome could afford exotic beasts from the tropics, places like Nîmes made do with snarling local beasts...bulls, wild boars, and lots of bears.) The standard fight was as real as professional wrestling is today—mostly just crowd-pleasing. Thumbs down and kill the guy? Maybe in Rome, but only rarely (if ever) here.

After Rome fell, and stability was replaced by Dark Age chaos, a huge structure like this was put to good use—bricked up and made a fortress (just like the Roman Arena in Arles). In the 13th century, after this region was incorporated into France, the arena became a gated community housing about 700 people—with streets, plumbing, and even gardens on the top level. Only in 1809 did Napoleon decide to scrape away the dwellings and make this a historic monument, thus letting the ancient grandeur of Roman France shine.

Two **multimedia exhibits** on the arena's ground floor are each well covered by the audioguide (see numbers before entering). *Couleurs des Corridas* (V104) shows the thrilling Camargue bull games in action, as well as a serious Spanish-style bullfight. And the *Quartier des Gladiateurs* (gladiators' locker room, at V106) brings bullfighting and gladiating to life in a kid-friendly way. Since 1850, Nîmes' arena has been a venue for spectacles, including Spanish-style bullfights and rock concerts featuring musical gladiators like Sting and Santana.

• *From the arena, enter Nîmes' "protected sector"—the Old City.*

▲▲Old City

Those coming to Nîmes only for its famous Roman sights are unexpectedly enchanted by its carefully preserved old center. Here, you can study how elements from the medieval and Renaissance times artfully survive in the buildings: Shop interiors incorporate

NEAR AVIGNON

Roman Nîmes

Born a Celtic city (about 500 B.C.), Nîmes joined the Roman Empire in the first century B.C. Because it had a privileged status within the Roman Empire, Nîmes was never really considered part of the conquered barbarian world. It rated highly enough to merit one of the longest protective walls in the Roman world and to have a 30-mile-long aqueduct (Pont du Gard) built to serve its growing population.

Today, the physical remains of Roman Nîmes testify to its former importance. The city's emblem—a crocodile tied to a palm tree—is a reminder that Nîmes was a favorite retirement home for Roman officers who had conquered Egypt. (The crocodile is Egypt, and the palm tree symbolizes victory.) All over town, little bronze croc-palm medallions shine on the sidewalks. In the City Hall, 400-year-old statues of crocodiles actually swing from the top of a monumental staircase (worth a look).

medieval brick with stone arches; windows expose Gothic finery; and Renaissance staircases grace peaceful courtyards.

• *With your back to the arena's ticket office, angle right to follow Rue des Arènes one block into...*

Place du Marché

With an inviting café ambience, including a wispy palm-tree-and-crocodile fountain (Nîmes' emblem in Roman times—see sidebar), this fine square is ideal for lunch or a coffee break. Facing the fountain, the recommended **Le Courtois Café/Pâtisserie** is the class act of the square—check out its old-time interior. Marie Manuelle can explain how it's been in her family since 1892. If you have a sweet tooth, let the sweet women here serve you the house specialty, a chocolate-dipped *nélusko;* it's like a cross between a cake and a cookie, and the oldest recipe of the house. Or try a Nîmes specialty, *caladon*—literally "cobble," like on the street—a hard honey-and-almond cookie.

• *Leave the square, passing the croc on your right (on Rue des Broquiers), then turn left on Rue de l'Aspic, the town's primary shopping spine. Follow Rue de l'Aspic straight past lots of shops several blocks to Place de l'Horloge (with its free-standing bell tower of the city government), the center of the old town. From here pedestrian-friendly streets fan out in all directions, including directly to Maison Carrée. We'll take unsigned Rue de la Madeleine, the first street to the right as you enter Place de l'Horloge, to the...*

▲Place aux Herbes

This inviting square is the site of Nîmes' oldest market. At the center of the old town, it's a good hub for a bit of sightseeing and café lounging (see "Eating in Nîmes," later). The next three sights are on or within a block of this square.

Nîmes Cathedral: While its Romanesque facade survives from the 12th century, the cathedral's interior—gutted over centuries of dynastic squabbles, Reformation, and Revolution—is unremarkable Neo-Romanesque, mostly from the 19th century.

Museum of Old Nîmes: Taking a left as you leave the cathedral leads you to this humble museum, inhabiting a 17th-century bishop's palace. You'll get a sense of how the bishop lived; see a room of fine, carved hutches; and learn the story of indigo, 19th-century denimwear, and early Levi's (free, no English, Tue-Sun 10:00-18:00, closed Mon, tel. 04 66 76 73 70).

Old-Time Spice Shop: L'Huilerie Epicerie is a charming time warp displaying spices and herbs, oils, and candy (Tue-Sun 9:00-12:00 & 15:00-19:00, closed Mon; 50 yards from the church, down the small lane by Le Petit Moka café, at 10 Rue des Marchands). To revel in more of Nîmes' medieval atmosphere, find the nearby Passage du Vieux Nîmes.

• *With your back to the church door, leave the square at the far right corner and go one block down Rue des Halles. Cross Rue Général Perrier and enter the big, modern black-and-green market hall.*

Covered Produce Market

Les Halles Centre Commerciale looks black and ugly on the outside, but inside its ground floor is a thriving, colorful market, well worth exploring (Tue-Sun until 13:00, closed Mon). Within the market, **Halles Auberge** is a cheap and characteristic lunch-only spot. If it's hot, and/or you need to shop, escalate a floor up to the air-conditioned mall.

• *Leaving the market, take a right on Rue Général Perrier, and walk several blocks to the...*

▲▲▲Maison Carrée

This stunning temple rivals Rome's Pantheon as the most complete and splendid building that survives from the Roman Em-

pire. Admire the original columns and Corinthian capitals. The temple survived in part because it's been in constant use for the last thousand years—as a church, a City Hall, a private stable, an archive during the Revolution, a people's art gallery after the Revolution (like Paris' Louvre), and finally as the monument you visit today. It's a textbook example of a pseudoperipteral temple (surrounded by columns, half of which support the roof over a porch, and half of which merely decorate the rest of the building) and a "six-column temple" (a standard proportion—if it's six columns wide, it must be eleven columns deep).

The lettering across the front is long gone, but the tiny surviving "nail holes" presented archaeologists with a fun challenge: Assuming each letter would leave a particular series of nail holes as evidence, derive the words. Archaeologists agree: This temple was built to honor Caius and Lucius, the sons of Emperor Augustus. And from this information, they date the temple to the year A.D. 4.

Maison Carrée ("Square House"—named before they had a word for "rectangle") was the centerpiece of a fancy plaza surrounded by a U-shaped commercial, political, and religious forum. This marked the core of Roman Nîmes. As was the case in all Roman temples, only the priest went inside. Worshippers gathered for religious rituals at the foot of the steps. Climb the steps as a priest would—starting and ending with your right foot...*dexter* (from the Latin for "right") rather than *sinister* ("left"). Put your right foot forward for good karma.

Inside, the "Nemausus—The Birth of Nîmes" **movie** tells the story of Nîmes...it's like watching a cheesy TV dramatization (€6, every 30 minutes, daily 10:00-19:00, soundtrack in Latin and French with English subtitles).

Nearby: The modern building facing the temple is Nîmes' **Carrée d'Art** ("Square of Art"), designed by British architect Lord Norman Foster. It's home to the city's Museum of Contemporary Art (Tue-Sun 10:00-18:00, closed Mon, WCs, recommended view café). Nîmes' TI is across the street and a few steps up from Maison Carrée.

• Next, walk down Rue Molière with the Museum of Contemporary Art on your left. Dogleg right until you hit the tree-lined canal, then follow the canal left until you reach the...

▲Fountain Garden (Jardin de la Fontaine)

Centuries before the Romans arrived in Nîmes, the Spring of Nemo was here (named, like the town itself, for a Celtic god). When the Romans built a shrine to Emperor Augustus around the spring, rather than bulldoze the Nemo temple, they built alongside it and welcomed Nemo into their own pantheon (as was their more-gods-the-merrier tradition). Today, the spring remains, though the temple is gone.

Cost and Hours: Free to enter, open daily April-mid-Sept 7:30-22:00, mid-Sept-March 7:30-18:30.

Visiting the Garden: Walk into the center of the Fountain Garden and look into the canal. In the early 1700s, Nîmes needed a reliable source of water for its textile industry—to power its mills and provide water for the indigo dyes for the fabric *serge de Nîmes* (denim). In about 1735, the city began a project to route a canal through the city and discovered a Roman temple. The city eventually agreed to fund a grander project that resulted in what you see today: a lavish Versailles-type park, complete with an ornate network of canals and boulevards. It was finished just 50 years after the construction of Versailles, and to the French, this place has a special significance: These were the first grand gardens not meant for a king, but for the public. The industrial canals built then still wind throughout the city.

• *Hiding behind trees in the back-left corner of Fountain Garden, find the...*

▲Temple of Diana

This first-century "temple," which modern archaeologists now believe was more likely a Roman library, has long been considered one of the best examples of ancient stonework. Its roof—a round Roman barrel vault laced together with still-visible metal pegs (find the panel with a drawing of the temple before entering)—survived until it was hit by a blast in the 1500s, during the Catholic-Protestant Wars of Religion.

Cost and Hours: Free to enter; same hours as Fountain Garden, above.

Visiting the Temple: At first glance, all the graffiti seems odd. But it's actually part of the temple's story. For centuries, France had a highly esteemed guild of stone-, metal-, and woodworkers called the Compagnons, founded by Gothic-church builders in the Middle Ages. As part of their ritualistic training, these craftsmen would visit many buildings—including the great structures of antiquity (such as this one)—for inspiration. Walk through the side aisle for a close look at the razor-accurate stonework and the 17th-, 18th-, and 19th-century signatures of the Compagnon craftsmen inspired by this building. Notice how their signatures match their era—no-nonsense "Enlightened" chiseling of the 18th century gives way to ornate script in the Romantic 19th century.

Skip the hike up to Tour Magne (at the top of the gardens), which has two remaining levels of a Roman tower; the view is worth neither the sweat nor the €3 entry fee. Instead, consider a coffee break or snack at the park's café, located next to the Temple of Diana.

• *The next sight is a 10-minute walk away. Angle back across the park, turning left at the canal (Quai de la Fontaine). Halfway to the end, notice one of the trees that line the canal is actually a carving of a diving nymph (Nemausa) with her legs gracefully fluttering up in the sky. After the little waterfall at the busy road, continue straight another block. Just after the tiny park, turn left onto tiny Rue Ménard. Follow it uphill for three blocks, then head right on Rue d'Albenas, following the sign that leads to the...*

▲Castellum

This small excavation site, sitting next to the street, is free and always open. It shows a modest-looking water distribution tank that was the grand finale of the 30-mile-long Pont du Gard aqueduct.

Discovered in the 1850s, this is one of only two known Roman distribution tanks (the other is in Pompeii). The water needs of Roman Nîmes grew beyond the capacity of its local springs. Imagine the jubilation on the day (in A.D. 50) that this system was finally operational. Suddenly, the town had an abundance of water—for basic needs as well as for cool extras like public fountains.

Notice the square hole marking the end of the aqueduct, a pool, a lower water channel, and the water-distribution holes. The lower channel, which runs under you, served top-priority needs, providing water via stone and lead pipes to the public wells that graced neighborhood squares. The higher holes—which got wet only when the supply was plentiful—routed water to the homes of the wealthy, to public baths, and to nonessential fountains. (For more on this impressive example of Roman engineering, see the "Pont du Gard" section, later.)

Sleeping in Nîmes

$$$ Hôtel de l'Amphithéâtre*** is ideally located on a pedestrian street a spear's toss from the arena. Run by gracious Ghislaine and Marcus, this is a top Nîmes value, with quiet, spacious, and sharp rooms at good rates (Sb-€72, Db-€94, Tb-€110, no elevator, 4 Rue des Arènes, tel. 04 66 67 28 51, www.hoteldelamphitheatre.com, contact@hoteldelamphitheatre.com).

$$ Hôtel des Tuileries** is a sure value, with helpful English hosts (Andrew and Caryn) and a central location 10 minutes on foot from the train station. Rooms are large and modern, and most have balconies (Sb/Db-€75-90, 22 Rue de Roussy, tel. 04 66 21 31 15, www.hoteldestuileries.com, les-tuileries@wanadoo.fr).

$$ Hôtel Royal*** rents comfortable, good-enough rooms at two- and three-star prices and makes a sleepable fallback if other hotels are full. It's an artsy place well-located on a main street near Maison Carrée (Db-€70-130, cheaper rooms are smaller and lack air-con, breakfast-€14, 1 Place d'Assas, tel. 04 66 58 28 27, www.royalhotel-nimes.com, contact@royalhotel-nimes.com).

Sleep Code

Abbreviations   **(€1=about $1.10, country code: 33)**
S=Single, **D**=Double/Twin, **T**=Triple, **Q**=Quad, **b**=bathroom,
*=French hotel rating (0-5 stars)
Price Rankings
  $$$ **Higher Priced**—Most rooms €85 or more
    $$ **Moderately Priced**—Most rooms €60-85
     $ **Lower Priced**—Most rooms €60 or less
Unless otherwise noted, credit cards are accepted, English
is spoken, there's air-conditioning and an elevator, and free
Wi-Fi and/or a guest computer is available. Prices change;
verify current rates online or by email. Book directly with the
hotel for best rates.

Eating in Nîmes

FOR LUNCH

Enjoy the elegance of Nîmes by eating lunch on one of its charming
squares. Most of these cafés serve lunch but close for dinner.

Place aux Herbes: This square, beautifully situated in the shadow of the cathedral, boasts several popular bistros where you can
lunch for €10. All places on this square close daily at 19:00 and all
day on Sundays.

Place du Marché: A block from the arena, this square is home
to several worthwhile eateries. **Le Courtois Café/Pâtisserie,** with
a fine *salade Nîmoise* (local pâté, anchovies, and *brandade*-€12) and
trademark desserts (described under my self-guided walk—see
page 132) makes a good choice (daily May-Oct 8:00-24:00; Nov-
April 8:00-19:30, closed Wed; tel. 04 66 67 20 09).

Overlooking the Maison Carrée: **Restaurant Café Ciel de
Nîmes** fills a terrace atop the city's Norman Foster-designed contemporary art gallery, offering great views of the Roman temple
(€12-16 *plats du jour*, €15 salads, Tue-Sun 10:00-18:00, closed
Mon, Place de la Maison Carrée, tel. 04 66 36 71 70). Facing the
temple, you'll see the terrace atop the modern building on your
right. The elevator is to the right upon entering the glassy building.

FOR DINNER

Many places close on Sunday and Monday.

At the wine bar **Hôtel Le Cheval Blanc,** diners can start,
end, or spend their entire evening. It's a cozy place serving good
wine, appetizers, and full meals (€16 *plats*, closed Sun, 1 Place des
Arènes, tel. 04 66 76 19 59).

Restaurant Le Vintage, a cool and contemporary wine bar/
bistro, offers local cuisine and wines with an easygoing ambience

inside or outside on a sweet little terrace (€27 *menus*, €16 *plats*, reasonable wine prices, closed Sun-Mon, a few blocks up Rue Fresque from Place du Marché at 7 Rue de Bernis, tel. 04 66 21 04 45, www.restaurant-levintage-nimes.com).

Lisita, a dressy place a few steps from the arena, serves serious French cuisine, and has a smart interior and terrific exterior seating. The chef refused a Michelin star to keep the prices affordable—that's amazing (€30 *menus*, €18 *plats*, daily June-Sept, otherwise closed Sun-Mon, 2 Boulevard des Arènes, tel. 04 66 67 29 15, www.lelisita.com).

L'Imprévu is a modern bistro serving traditional cuisine on a breezy square. It's a popular place with locals, and has fine terrace seating and a well-appointed interior (€21-28 *menus,* closed Tue-Wed, 6 Place d'Assas, tel. 04 66 38 99 59).

Place des Esclafidous: Four colorful restaurants serving a variety of cuisines ring this cute little square with outdoor tables. The square is two blocks behind the cathedral: Find the post office on Rue Crémieux and walk behind it. At **Restaurant les Magnolias,** meals are tasty, with a big variety of Mediterranean specialties. Plus, it's open on weekends (€20-25 *menus,* €12 big salads, closed Tue, tel. 04 66 21 64 01).

Nîmes Connections

Trains and buses depart from the same station in Nîmes (see "Arrival in Nîmes," earlier).

From Nîmes by Train to: Arles (9/day, 30 minutes, beware of gaps in the afternoon), **Avignon** (12/day, 30 minutes), **Aigues-Mortes** in the Camargue (6/day, 45 minutes), **Carcassonne** (8/day, 2.5 hours, transfer in Narbonne), **Paris** (10/day, 3 hours).

By Bus to: Uzès (#B21 or #E52, 7/day Mon-Fri, 3/day Sat, 2/day Sun, 40 minutes), **Pont du Gard** (#E21, 6/day Mon-Fri, 4/day Sat, 2/day Sun, no buses on weekends Nov-April, 40 minutes), **Aigues-Mortes** in the Camargue (6/day, 50 minutes), **Arles** (8/day Mon-Sat, 3/day Sun, 1 hour).

Pont du Gard

Throughout the ancient world, aqueducts were like flags of stone that heralded the greatness of Rome. A visit to this sight still works to proclaim the wonders of that age. This impressively preserved Roman aqueduct was built in about 19 B.C., and while most of it is on or below the ground, at Pont du Gard it spans a canyon on a massive bridge over the Gardon River—one of the most remarkable

Pont du Gard

TRAIL ALONG CANAL

PONT DU GARD

CANAL TUNNEL

Wow!

To Canal Ruins

Garrigue Natural Area

P *Rive Droite* DON'T PARK HERE

To Remoulins & Nîmes

Gardon River

B *To/From Avignon & Nîmes (Summer Only)*

MUSEUM COMPLEX
CINEMA, LUDO (KIDS' SPACE), INFO, SHOP, WC & RESTAURANT

P *Rive Gauche* PARK HERE

To Avignon & Nîmes **B**

D-981

B *From Avignon & Nîmes*

ROUNDABOUT

D-981

To Uzès

To Remoulins, Nîmes, Avignon, Arles & A-9 Freeway

Not to scale:
Roundabout to Museum is a 10-minute walk
Museum to Pont du Gard is a 5-minute walk

surviving Roman ruins anywhere. The 30-mile aqueduct supported a small canal that, by dropping one inch for every 350 feet, supplied nine million gallons of water per day (about 100 gallons per second) to Nîmes—one of ancient Europe's largest cities. Allow about four or five hours for visiting Pont du Gard (including transportation time from Avignon).

GETTING TO PONT DU GARD

The famous aqueduct is between Remoulins and Vers-Pont du Gard on D-981, 17 miles from Nîmes and 13 miles from Avignon.

By Car: Pont du Gard is a 30-minute drive due west of Avignon (follow N-100 from Avignon, tracking signs to *Nîmes* and *Remoulins,* then *Pont du Gard* and *Rive Gauche*), and 45 minutes northwest of Arles (via Tarascon on D-6113). If going to Arles from Pont du Gard, follow signs to *Nîmes* (not *Avignon*), then D-6113, or A-54 (autoroute) to Arles.

By Bus: Buses run to Pont du Gard (on the Rive Gauche side) from Avignon (3/day, 50 minutes), Nîmes, and Uzès. Combining Pont du Gard with Nîmes and/or Uzès makes a good day-trip excursion from Avignon.

Buses stop at the traffic roundabout 400 yards from the

NEAR AVIGNON

museum (stop name: Rond Point Pont du Gard; see Pont du Gard map). In July and August, however, buses usually drive into the Pont du Gard site and stop at the parking lot's ticket booth. If leaving by bus, make sure you're waiting on the correct side of the traffic circle (stops have schedules posted), and wave your hand to signal the bus to stop for you—otherwise, it may drive on by. Buy your ticket when you get on and verify your destination with the driver.

By Taxi: From Avignon, it's about €60 for a taxi to Pont du Gard (tel. 04 90 82 20 20). If you're staying in Avignon and only want to see Pont du Gard (and not Nîmes or Uzès), consider splurging on a taxi to the aqueduct in the morning, then take the early-afternoon bus back.

ORIENTATION TO PONT DU GARD

There are two riversides to Pont du Gard: the Left Bank (Rive Gauche) and Right Bank (Rive Droite). Park on the Rive Gauche, where you'll find the museums, ticket booth, TI, ATM, cafeteria, WCs, and shops—all built into a modern plaza. You'll see the aqueduct in two parts: first the fine museum complex, then the actual river gorge spanned by the ancient bridge.

Cost: €18 per car (regardless of number of passengers). (The €23 annual pass lets you come back for the evening lights without paying double.) Those arriving on foot, by bus, or by bike pay €7 per person. This gives you access to the aqueduct, museum, film, and outdoor *garrigue* nature area.

Hours: Museum—daily May-Sept 9:00-19:00, until 20:00 in July and Aug, until 17:00 Oct-April, closed two weeks in Jan; aqueduct and parking lot—daily until 24:00. The aqueduct is illuminated on summer evenings (mid-June-mid-Sept 22:00-24:00).

Information: Tel. 04 66 37 59 99, www.pontdugard.fr.

Pont du Gard After Hours: During summer months, the site is open until midnight so people can hike, enjoy a picnic or the riverside restaurant, and watch the music-and-light show projected on the monument. The parking lot is staffed and guarded until 24:00, and after the museum closes you'll pay only €10 per carload to enter. If you don't care to see the museum, seeing Pont du Gard in the evening is dramatic (and cheap). The music-and-light show is projected from the north, so those in the picnic area and at the restaurant enjoy a good view.

Hiking Tour Across Pont Du Gard: In July and August, six tours a day go through the water channel at the top of the aqueduct (€4, pay guide directly, includes 10-minute intro and 20-minute hike, commentary in French and English, generally starting at the bottom of the hour from 10:30—check times posted at the museum and entry). No reservations are taken; you just wait at the metal gate on top of the bridge on the side opposite the museum. The first 33 people get in. If you do this tour, notice the massive calcium buildup lining the channel from more than 400 years of flowing water.

Canoe Rental: Floating under Pont du Gard by canoe is an unforgettable experience. Collias Canoes will pick you up at Pont du Gard (or elsewhere, if prearranged) and shuttle you to the town of Collias. You'll float down the river to the nearby town of Remoulins, where they'll pick you up and take you back to Pont du Gard (€21/person, €12/child under 12, usually 2 hours, though you can take as long as you like, reserve the day before in July-Aug, tel. 04 66 22 85 54).

Plan Ahead for Swimming and Hiking: Pont du Gard is perhaps best enjoyed on your back and in the water—bring along a swimsuit and flip-flops for the rocks. (Note that local guides warn that the bridge can create whirlpools and be dangerous to swim under.) The best Pont du Gard viewpoints are up steep hills with uneven footing—bring good shoes, too.

SIGHTS AT PONT DU GARD
▲Museum
In this state-of-the-art museum (well-presented in English), you'll enter to the sound of water and understand the critical role fresh water played in the Roman "art of living." You'll see copies of lead pipes, faucets, and siphons; walk through a mock rock quarry; and learn how they moved those huge rocks into place and how those massive arches were made. A wooden model shows how Roman engineers determined the proper slope. While actual artifacts from the aqueduct are few, the exhibit shows the immensity of the undertaking as well as the payoff. Imagine the jubilation when this extravagant supply of water finally tumbled into Nîmes. A relaxing highlight is the scenic video of a helicopter ride along the entire 30-mile course of the structure, from its start at Uzès all the way to the Castellum in Nîmes.

Other Activities
Several additional attractions are designed to give the sight more meaning (but for most visitors, the museum is sufficient). A 15-minute film plays in the same building as the museum on a loop. The nearby kids' museum, called *Ludo*, offers a scratch-and-sniff teaching experience (in English) of various aspects of Roman life and the importance of water. The extensive outdoor *garrigue* natural area, closer to the aqueduct, features historic crops and landscapes of the Mediterranean.

NEAR AVIGNON

▲▲▲Viewing the Aqueduct

A park-like path leads to the aqueduct. Until a few years ago, this was an actual road—adjacent to the aqueduct—that had spanned the river since 1743. Before you cross the bridge, walk to the riverside viewpoint: Pass under the bridge and aqueduct and hike about 300 feet along the riverbank to the concrete steps leading down to a grand view of the world's second-highest standing Roman structure. (Rome's Colosseum is only 6 feet taller.)

This was the biggest bridge in the whole 30-mile-long aqueduct. The arches are twice the width of standard aqueducts, and the main arch is the largest the Romans ever built—80 feet across (the width of the river). The bridge is about 160 feet high and was originally about 1,200 feet long.

Though the distance from the source (in Uzès, on the museum side of the site) to Nîmes was only 12 miles as the eagle flew, engineers chose the most economical route, winding and zigzagging 30 miles. The water made the trip in 24 hours with a drop of only 40 feet. Ninety percent of the aqueduct is on or under the ground, but a few river canyons like this required bridges. A stone lid hides a four-foot-wide, six-foot-tall chamber lined with waterproof mortar that carried the stream for more than 400 years. For 150 years, this system provided Nîmes with good drinking water. Expert as the Romans were, they miscalculated the backup caused by a downstream corner, and had to add the thin extra layer you can see just under the lid to make the channel deeper.

The bridge and the river below provide great fun for holiday-goers. While parents suntan on rocks, kids splash into the gorge from under the aqueduct. For the most refreshing view, float flat on your back underneath the structure (but beware of whirlpools, which can be dangerous).

The appearance of the entire gorge changed in 2002, when a huge flood flushed lots of greenery downstream. Those floodwaters put Roman provisions to the test. Notice the triangular-shaped buttresses at the lower level—designed to split and divert the force of any flood *around* the feet of the arches rather than *into* them. The 2002 floodwaters reached the top of those buttresses. Anxious park rangers winced at the sounds of trees crashing onto the ancient stones...but the arches stood strong.

The stones that jut out—giving the aqueduct a rough, unfinished appearance—supported the original scaffolding. The protuberances were left, rather than cut off, in anticipation of future repair needs. The lips under the arches supported wooden templates that allowed the stones in the round arches to rest on something until the all-important keystone was dropped into place. Each stone weighs from two to six tons. The structure stands with no mortar (except at the very top, where the water flowed)—taking full advantage of the innovative Roman arch, made strong by gravity.

Hike over the bridge for a closer look and the best views. Steps lead up a high trail (marked *view point/panorama*) to a superb vista

(go right at the top; best views are soon after the trail starts descending). You'll also see where the aqueduct meets a rock tunnel, which was built in the 1800s to try to reuse the aqueduct to provide water to Nîmes (it failed). Notice how the aqueduct curves left before the tunnel.

Back on the museum side, steps lead up to the Rive Gauche side of the aqueduct, where you can follow the canal path along a trail (marked with red-and-white horizontal lines) to find some remains of the Roman canal. You'll soon reach an-

other *panorama* with more great views of the aqueduct. Hikers can continue along the path, following the red-and-white markings that lead through a forest, after which you'll come across more remains of the canal (much of which are covered by vegetation). There's not much left to see because of medieval cannibalization—frugal builders couldn't resist the precut stones as they constructed area churches. The path continues for about 15 miles, but there's little reason to go farther.

Uzès

Located near the source of the spring that fed the Pont du Gard aqueduct, this intriguing, less-trampled town is officially in Languedoc-Roussillon, not Provence. Uzès (oo-zehs) feels like it must have been important once—and it was, as a bishopric from the fifth century until 1789. Today Uzès offers a refreshing small-town break from serious sightseeing. If you sleep here, try to arrive on a Tuesday or Friday night to enjoy the next morning's market.

GETTING TO UZES

Uzès is a short hop west of Pont du Gard. It's well-served by **bus** from Nîmes (Edgard buses #E52 and #B21, 7/day Mon-Fri, 3/day Sat, 2/day Sun, 40 minutes, €1.50), but less so from Avignon (Edgard bus #A15, direction Pont St-Esprit, 3-5/day, 60-80 minutes, stops near Pont du Gard, €1.50). Check www.edgard-transport.fr or call 08 10 33 42 73 for schedules. The bus stop for Uzès is labeled "Esplanade."

By **car**, Uzès is 15 minutes from Pont du Gard and 45 minutes from Nîmes and Avignon. Drivers will circle the old town on the busy ring road. The TI and one hotel that I list are on this ring road.

Orientation to Uzès

The **TI** sits at the top of the ring road on Place Albert I. Pick up the brief self-guided tour brochure in English (June-Sept Mon-Fri 9:00-18:00, Sat-Sun 10:00-13:00 & 14:00-17:00; shorter hours and closed Sun Oct-May; tel. 04 66 22 68 88, www.uzes-tourisme.com).

Sights in Uzès

Strolling the Town

The traffic-free, tastefully restored town itself is the sight. It's best seen slowly on foot, with a lingering coffee break in its arcaded and mellow main square, **Place aux Herbes** (not so mellow during the colorful Wed morning market and even bigger all-day Sat market).

In spite of all those bishops, there are no important sights to visit in Uzès. You can follow the TI's self-guided walking tour, but skip their sad audioguide tour and avoid the dull, overpriced Palace of the Duché de Uzès. The town's trendy boutiques are as numerous as its English-speaking visitors, which give the place an upscale, international feel. The unusual circular tower called Tour Fenestrelle is all that remains of a 12th-century cathedral.

Medieval Garden

Even if you're not a plant enthusiast, pop into the Medieval Garden, a "living herbarium" with plants thought to have curative qualities. The garden is at the foot of the King's and Bishop's towers. The entrance fee includes a little shot of lemongrass tea lovingly delivered by the volunteers who care for this sight (€5, April-Sept daily 14:00-18:00, plus 10:30-12:30 on Sat-Sun and daily in July-Aug; Oct daily 14:00-17:00; closed Nov-March, English handout and some information posted, tel. 04 66 22 38 21).

NEAR UZES

The **Musée du Bonbon** candy museum, a mile and a half below Uzès on the road to Avignon and Pont du Gard, explains the history and manufacturing process of Haribo (of Gummi Bears fame). It's interactive and makes a worthwhile detour for the kids (adults-€7, kids ages 5-15-€5, kids under 5 free, July-Aug daily 10:00-19:00, shorter hours and closed Mon Sept-June, last entry one hour before closing, tel. 04 66 22 74 39, www.museeharibo.fr).

To taste wines near Uzès, consider a stop at **La Gramière winery,** run by a delightful American couple (Amy Lillard and Matthew Kling) who are making a splash with their excellent wines just a hop, skip, and a jump from Pont du Gard (Place de la Fontaine Vers Pont du Gard, tel. 06 89 38 08 29, www.lagramiere.com).

Sleeping in Uzès

Hotels in Uzès mirror the upscale flavor of the town. Pale-green signs direct drivers to hotels from the ring road.

$$$ La Maison d'Uzès**,** in the heart of the old town, is filled with modern luxury and nestled in the charm of a beautifully restored 17th-century building. In this boutique hotel, you'll find sumptuous lounges, a gastronomic restaurant, a spa complete with a waterfall Roman bath, and nine well-designed rooms (Db-€280-360, bigger "deluxe" Db-€380-600, elevator serves half of the rooms, 18 Rue du Docteur Blanchard, tel. 04 66 20 07 00, www.lamaisonduzes.fr).

$$$ L'Hostellerie Provençale,** a charming place with nine plush rooms, is just off the ring road, a few blocks after the TI. Breakfast and dinner can be served on their splendid rooftop terrace or downstairs in the cozy restaurant (standard Db-€125, pricey breakfast-€17 on terrace, garage parking-€15/day, restaurant closed Sun, 1 Rue de la Grande Bourgade, tel. 04 66 22 11 06, www. hostellerieprovencale.com, contact@hostellerieprovencale.com).

Eating in Uzès

When the weather cooperates, it's hard to resist meals on Place aux Herbes, which is lined with appealing café options.

Resto Burger serves gourmet Charolais burgers and good salads, each for about €14. It has good wines by the glass. Beware: Only Americans eat their burgers with their hands—the French use a knife and fork (creative options including kids' and vegetarian *menus,* daily 12:00-22:00 except closed Mon-Tue Nov-March, 19 Place aux Herbes, tel. 04 66 20 21 03).

Le Zanelli Italian, dishing up pizzas and more, is located on the most prized, tucked-away terrace in the center of Uzès. Leave

Place aux Herbes through the passage left of Resto Burger (allow €8-18, daily July-Aug, otherwise closed Tue-Wed, Place Nicolas Froment, tel. 04 66 03 01 93).

To dine well indoors or high above the town on their roof-top terrace, find **La Parenthèse** restaurant (four-course dinner *menus* from €36, closed Sun) in the recommended L'Hostellerie Provençale.

ORANGE AND THE COTES DU RHONE

*Orange • Châteauneuf-du-Pape •
Vaison-la-Romaine • Best of the
Côtes du Rhône Villages • More
Côtes du Rhône Drives*

The sunny Côtes du Rhône wine road—one of France's most en-gaging—starts at Avignon's doorstep and winds north along a mountainous landscape carpeted with vines, studded with warm stone villages, and presided over by the Vesuvius-like Mont Ven-toux. The wines of the Côtes du Rhône (grown on the *côtes*, or hillsides, of the Rhône River Valley) are easy on the palate and on your budget. But this hospitable place offers more than wine—its hill-capping villages inspire travel posters, its Roman ruins add a historical perspective, and the locals are, well, welcoming...and often as excited about their region as you are. Yes, you'll have good opportunities for enjoyable wine-tasting, but there is also a soul to this area...if you take the time to look and listen.

Located 30 minutes north of Avignon, the ancient town of Orange has vineyards on its outskirts. But it's because of its well-preserved Roman Theater that Orange gets (and deserves) atten-tion.

PLANNING YOUR TIME

Vaison-la-Romaine is the handy hub of this region, offering limited bus connections with Avignon and Orange, bike rental, and a mini Pompeii in the town center. Nearby, you can visit the impressive Roman Theater in Orange, drive to the top of Mont Ventoux, fol-low my self-guided driving tour of Côtes du Rhône villages and wineries, or pedal along small lanes to nearby towns for a breath of fresh air. The vineyards' centerpiece, the Dentelles de Montmirail mountains, are laced with a variety of trails ideal for hikers.

To explore this area, allow two nights for a decent dabble. Drivers should head for the hills (read this chapter's self-guided driving tour before deciding where to stay). Those without wheels

The Côtes du Rhône Area

To Lyon

Grignan

D-541

D-86

Rhône

A-7

D-71

D-59

N-7

To
Vallon-Pont-d'Arc
& Balazuc

D-94

Bollène

Ardèche
Gorges

St-Martin

D-290

D-901

Ardèche

D-8

Sainte-Cécile-
les-Vignes

Pont-
St-Esprit

D-994

Cairrane

D-8

D-86

N-7

D-976

Bagnols-sur-Ceze

A-7

Orange

D-977

A-9

D-68

Rhône

D-907

Paris

FRANCE

100 Miles

D-976

D-17

Châteauneuf-
du-Pape

D-17

D-6086

A9

To
Pont du
Gard

A7

To
Avignon

D-942

find that Vaison-la-Romaine and Orange make the only practical home bases (or, maybe better, consider a minivan tour for this area).

GETTING AROUND THE COTES DU RHONE

By Car: Pick up Michelin maps #332 or #527 to navigate your way around the Côtes du Rhône. (Landmarks like the Dentelles de Montmirail and Mont Ventoux make it easy to get your bearings.) I've described my favorite driving route on page 172.

For a scenic spin, connect the Côtes du Rhône with the **Luberon** (next chapter) via Mont Ventoux between mid-April and mid-November—check with the TI beforehand to make sure the summit is open (follow signs to *Malaucène*, then to *Mont Ventoux*,

allowing 2 hours to Roussillon). This route is one of the most spectacular in Provence. But if the summit is closed (in bad weather
years, the reopening can be delayed through May), skip the long,
underwhelming alternative route through Bédoin. Instead, zip to
the Luberon by taking the autoroute via Orange and Cavaillon.
A third, more direct route takes you through the traffic-snarled,
difficult-to-navigate city of Carpentras, which is better avoided.
Get advice from your hotelier.

By Bus: Lieutaud buses run to Vaison-la-Romaine from Orange and Avignon (3-6/day, 45 minutes from Orange, 1.5 hours
from Avignon) and connect several wine villages with Vaison-la-
Romaine and Nyons to the north. From Avignon, an express bus

goes direct to Vaison-la-Romaine daily (1/day, 1 hour.) Another bus line runs from Vaison-la-Romaine to Carpentras, serving Crestet, Malaucène, and Le Barroux (3/day Mon-Sat, none on Sun, tel. 04 90 36 05 22, www.cars-lieutaud.fr/provence/en/regular-lines). Both routes provide scenic rides through this area.

By Train: Trains get you as far as Orange (from Avignon: 15/day, 20 minutes).

By Minivan Tour: There's no shortage of people willing to take you for a ride through this marvelous region—so buyer beware. For my recommendations on wine-focused tours, more general tours, and private guides, see "Tours in Provence" on page 26.

COTES DU RHONE MARKET DAYS

Monday: Bédoin (intimate market, between Vaison-la-Romaine and Mont Ventoux)

Tuesday: Vaison-la-Romaine (great market with produce and antiques/flea market)

Wednesday: Malaucène (good and less-touristy market with produce and antiques/flea market, near Vaison-la-Romaine), Buis-les-Barronies (on recommended loop drive north into the Drôme Provençale), and Sault (handy if you're driving to the Luberon area)

Thursday: Orange (produce and local goods), Nyons (great market with produce and antiques/flea market), and Vacqueyras

Friday: Châteauneuf-du-Pape (small market) and Carpentras (big market)

Saturday: Sainte-Cécile-les-Vignes, near Vaison-la-Romaine

Orange

COTES DU RHONE

Orange, called *Arausio* in Roman times, is notable for its Roman arch and grand Roman Theater. Orange was a thriving city in ancient times—strategically situated on the Via Agrippa, connecting the important Roman cities of Lyon and Arles. It was actually founded as a comfortable place for Roman army officers to enjoy their retirement. Even in Roman times, professional military men retired with time for a second career. Did the emperor want thousands of well-trained, relatively young guys hanging around Rome? No way. What to do? "How about a nice place in the south of France...?"

Today's Orange (oh-rahnzh) is a busy, workaday city with a gritty charm that reminds me of Arles. Leafy café-lined squares, a handful of traffic-free streets, a sensational Hôtel de Ville (City Hall), and that theater all give the town some serious street appeal.

For some, Orange works well as a base, with its quick access to the Côtes du Rhône wine villages by car (slower but OK by bus) and quick rail access to Avignon (which even drivers should consider).

Orientation to Orange

TOURIST INFORMATION

The unnecessary TI is located next to the fountain and parking area at 5 Cours Aristide Briand (April-Sept Mon-Sat 9:00-18:30, Sun 9:00-13:00 & 14:00-18:30; shorter hours and closed Sun off-season; tel. 04 90 34 70 88, www.otorange.fr). Another TI is across from the theater entrance (summer only, same hours).

Market Day: Thursday is market day, and it's a big deal here, with all the town's streets and squares crammed with produce and local goods for sale. I like this market because it focuses on locals' needs and not touristy knick-knacks.

ARRIVAL IN ORANGE

By Train: Orange's train station is a level 15-minute walk from the Roman Theater (or an €8 taxi ride, mobile 06 09 51 32 25). The recommended Hôtel de Provence, across from the station, will keep your bags for no charge, though it's polite to buy a drink from the café (see "Sleeping and Eating in Orange," later). To walk into town from the train station, head straight out of the station (down Avenue Frédéric Mistral), merge left onto Orange's main shopping street (Rue de la République), then turn left on Rue Caristie; you'll run into the Roman Theater's massive stage wall.

By Bus: Lieutaud buses stop at the train station (Gare SNCF) and at Place Pourtoules, two blocks from the Roman Theater (walk to the hill and turn right to reach the theater, bus station tel. 04 90 34 15 59, www.cars-lieutaud.fr/provence/en/regular-lines).

By Car: Follow *Centre-Ville* signs, then *Théâtre Antique* signs, and park as close to the Roman Theater's huge wall as possible—the easiest option is labeled *Parking Office du Tourisme* (by the fountain and the TI). Those coming from the autoroute will land here by following *Centre-Ville* signs; others should follow *Centre-Ville* signs, then *Office du Tourisme* signs, to find this parking lot. To reach the theater, walk to the hill and turn left. If you're arriving on a Thursday morning (market day), you'll encounter lots of traffic and scarce parking; it's better to park on the road leading to the train station (15-minute walk to the theater).

CÔTES DU RHONE

Sights in Orange

▲▲▲Roman Theater (Théâtre Antique)

Orange's ancient theater is the best-preserved in existence, and the only one in Europe with its acoustic wall still standing. (Two others in Asia Minor also survive.)

Cost and Hours: €10, drops to €9 one hour before closing; ticket includes film, multimedia show, good audioguide (not available if you arrive within an hour of closing), and entry to the small museum across the street; daily April-Sept 9:00-18:00 except June-Aug until 19:00; Oct and March 9:30-17:30; Nov-Feb 9:30-16:30; closing times can change for evening performances or rehearsals, tel. 04 90 51 17 60, www.theatre-antique.com.

Cheap Trick: Vagabonds wanting a partial-but-free view of the theater can see it from the bluff high above in the Parc de la Colline St-Eutrope. Find the *escalier est* (east staircase) off Rue Pourtoules and start climbing—it's several hundred steps to the top. At the sign for *Promenade Botanique,* keep left, and at the next fork, follow the stairs up to the right. When you see the playground, head to the right to find the view. Benches and grassy areas make this a good picnic spot (but no WCs), and you can scamper about for views of the theater from different angles.

Museum: Pop into the museum across the street (Musée d'Art et d'Histoire, included with ticket, free audioguide) for a quick spin to see a few theater details and a rare marble grid, ordered by Emperor Vespasian in 79 A.D., which was used as the official property-ownership registry—each square represented a 120-acre plot of land.

Eating: The café in the theater, La Grotte d'Auguste, has reasonably priced snacks and lunches plus views (closed Sun year-round, closed Mon off-season, tel. 04 90 60 22 54). A shaded, café-filled square, Place de la République, is two blocks from the theater up Rue Ségond Weber.

❍ Self-Guided Tour: After you enter (to the right of the actual theater), you'll see a huge dig—the site of the Temple to the Cult of the Emperor (English explanations posted). *Arausio* is the Roman name for the town.

Look for signs to a worthwhile film and fun multimedia show that run continuously. The 15-minute **film** gives a good historical account of the theater and its uses since the Romans packed up and left (near the ticket office, English subtitles). *The Ghosts of the Theatre* **multimedia show** covers four different periods of performance history (including rock concerts) and is located inside a hall in the theater, one floor up.

Enter the theater, then climb the steep stairs to find a seat high up to appreciate the acoustics (eavesdrop on people by the stage).

CÔTES DU RHÔNE

Contemplate the idea that 2,000 years ago, Orange residents enjoyed grand spectacles with high-tech sound and lighting effects—such as simulated thunder, lightning, and rain.

A grandiose **Caesar** overlooks everything, reminding attendees of who's in charge. If it seems like you've seen this statue before, you probably have. Countless sculptures identical to this one were mass-produced in Rome and shipped throughout the empire to grace buildings like this theater for propaganda purposes. To save money on shipping and handling, only the heads of these statues were changed with each new ruler. The permanent body wears a breast-plate emblazoned with the imperial grif-fon (body of a lion, head and wings of an eagle) that only the emperor could wear. When a new emperor came to power, new heads were made in Rome and shipped off throughout the empire to replace the pop-off heads on all these statues. (Imagine Barack Obama's head on George W. Bush's body—on second thought...)

Archaeologists believe that a puny, vanquished Celt was included at the knee of the emperor, touching his ruler's robe respectfully—a show of humble subservience to the emperor. It's interesting to consider how an effective propaganda machine can con the masses into being impressed by their leader.

The horn has blown. It's time to find your **seat:** row 2, number 30. Sitting down, you're comforted by the "EQ GIII" carved into the seat (*Equitas Gradus* #3...three rows for the Equestrian order). You're not comforted by the hard limestone bench (thinking it'll probably last 2,000 years). The theater is filled with 10,000 people. Thankfully, you mix only with your class, the nouveau riche—merchants, tradesmen, and city big shots. The people seated above you are the working class, and way up in the "chicken roost" section is the scum of the earth—slaves, beggars, prostitutes, and youth hostellers. Scanning the orchestra section (where the super-rich sit on real chairs), you notice the town dignitaries hosting some visiting VIPs.

OK, time to worship. They're parading a bust of the emperor from its sacred home in the adjacent temple around the **stage.** Next is the ritual animal sacrifice called *la pompa* (so fancy, future generations will use that word for anything full of such...pomp). Finally, you settle in for an all-day series of spectacles and dramatic entertainment. All eyes are on the big stage door in the middle—where the Angelina Jolies and Brad Pitts of the day will appear. (Lesser actors come out of the side doors.)

The play is good, but many come for the halftime shows—jugglers, acrobats, and striptease dancers. In Roman times, the theater was a festival of immorality. An ancient writer commented, "The vanquished take their revenge on us by giving us their vices through the theater."

With an audience of 10,000 and no amplification, **acoustics** were critical. A roof made of linen (called the velarium) originally covered the stage, somewhat like the glass-and-iron roof you see today (installed to protect the stage wall). The original was designed not to protect the stage from the weather, but to project the voices of the actors into the crowd. For further help, actors wore masks with leather caricature mouths that functioned as megaphones. The theater's side walls originally rose as high as the stage wall and supported a retractable roof that gave the audience some protection from the sun or rain. After leaving the theater, look up to the stage wall from the outside and notice the supports for poles that held the velarium in place, like the masts and sails of a ship.

The Roman Theater was all part of the "give them bread and circuses" approach to winning the support of the masses (not unlike today's philosophy of "give them tax cuts and *American Idol*"). The spectacle grew from 65 days of games per year when the theater was first built (and when Rome was at its height) to about 180 days each year by the time Rome finally fell.

In the fourth century (under Christian emperor Constantine), the church forced many theaters to close their doors. Later, during the barbarian invasions, the stage wall became a protective wall and the theater became a secure residence for many. Amazingly, people squatted here until the 19th century. You can still see traces of some buildings within the theater.

▲Roman "Arc de Triomphe"
This just-cleaned, 60-foot-tall arch is in the center of a big traffic circle, a level 15-minute walk from the theater due north of the city center. Technically the only real Roman arches of triumph are in Rome's Forum, built to commemorate various emperors' victories. But this arch was the model for those in Rome, preceding both the famous arches of Septimius Severus and Constantine. The great Roman arch of Orange is actually a municipal arch erected in about A.D. 19 to commemorate a general named Germanicus, who protected the town. The facade is covered with reliefs of military exploits, including naval battles and Romans beating up on barbarians and those nasty Gauls.

Hôtel de Ville
Orange owns Provence's most beautiful City Hall, worth the short detour to appreciate it (in the heart of the old town on Place Georges Clemenceau).

Sleeping and Eating in Orange

Sleeping: **$$ Hôtel de Provence****, at the train station, is air-conditioned, quiet, comfortable, and affordable. Gentle Monsieur Motte runs this traditional place with grace (Db-€65-85, Tb-€75-110, family rooms €90-110, breakfast-€9, small rooftop pool, café,

COTES DU RHONE

Sleep Code

Abbreviations   **(€1=about $1.10, country code: 33)**
S=Single, **D**=Double/Twin, **T**=Triple, **Q**=Quad, **b**=bathroom, *=French hotel rating (0-5 stars)
Price Rankings
  $$$ **Higher Priced**—Most rooms €85 or more
    $$ **Moderately Priced**—Most rooms €55-85
     $ **Lower Priced**—Most rooms €55 or less
Unless otherwise noted, breakfast is not included, hotel staff speak basic English, and credit cards are accepted. Free Wi-Fi and/or a guest computer is generally available. Prices can change without notice; verify the hotel's current rates online or by email. For the best prices, always book directly with the hotel.

parking-€5/day, 60 Avenue Frédéric Mistral, tel. 04 90 34 00 23, www.hotelprovence-orange.com, hoteldeprovence84@orange.fr).

$$ Hôtel Logis Le Glacier****, across from the TI, is run by English-speaking and affable Philippe. It's a good value, with easy parking, a small bar in a comfortable lobby, and well-designed rooms (Db-€70-96, bigger Db-€98-130, elevator, air-con, a few parking spaces, 46 Cours Aristide Briand, tel. 04 90 34 02 01, www.le-glacier.com, info@le-glacier.com).

Eating: For lunch or dinner, Orange has several inviting squares with ample choices in all price ranges. I like dining across from the theater. **V Café** works well, with a large terrace and €12 *tartines* and *plats* (daily, 2 Place des Frères Mounet, tel. 04 90 66 32 14). For a more refined meal, **Au Petit Patio** delivers elegant dining and fine cuisine (€27-37 *menus,* closed Wed-Thu and Sun, 58 Cours Aristide Briand, tel. 04 90 29 69 27).

Orange Connections

From Orange by Train to: Avignon (15/day, 20 minutes), **Arles** (4/day direct, 35 minutes, more frequent with transfer in Avignon), **Lyon** (16/day, 2 hours).

    By Bus to: Châteauneuf-du-Pape (2/day, none Sun, 30 minutes), **Vaison-la-Romaine** (3-6/day, 45 minutes), **Avignon** (Mon-Sat hourly, 5/day Sun, 1 hour—take the train instead). Buses to Vaison-la-Romaine and other wine villages depart from the train station and from Place Pourtoules (turn right out of the Roman Theater, and right again onto Rue Pourtoules). Bus #4 to Vaison-la-Romaine leaves from across the street and to the right of the main shelter/stop (see map on page 153).

Near Orange: Châteauneuf-du-Pape

This most famous of the Côtes du Rhône wine villages is busy with tourists eager to sample its famous product and stroll its climbing lanes. While I prefer the less-famous wine villages farther north (described later, under "The Best of the Côtes du Rhône Villages"), this welcoming, wine-drenched town makes an easy day trip from Avignon and works well with a visit to nearby Orange.

Châteauneuf-du-Pape means "New Castle of the Pope," named for the pope's summer retreat—now a ruin capping the beautiful-to-see but little-to-do hill town (more interesting during the Friday market). Wine-loving popes planted the first vines here in the 1300s. The pope's crest is embossed on all bottles of this deservedly famous wine.

Approaching from Avignon, signs announce, *"Here start the vineyards of Châteauneuf-du-Pape."* Pull over and stroll into a vineyard with a view of the hill town. Notice the rocky soil—perfect for making a good wine grape. Those stones retain the sun's heat (plentiful here) and force the vines to struggle, resulting in a lean grape—lousy for eating, but ideal for producing big wines (see "Côtes du Rhône Wines" on page 35). Eight different grapes are blended to make the local specialty, which has been strictly controlled for 80 years. Grenache dominates the blend, accounting for about 75 percent of the grapes grown. Syrah and Mourvèdre are the other two most-used grapes, each contributing about 10 percent to the final blend. The most interesting white wines in Provence are also made here (a blend of up to five grapes), but the reds are what attract most visitors. Most reds show their full flavor five years after bottling. For more information on the area's wines, look for the Wine Museum (described later) at the start of the village as you come from Avignon.

Orientation to Châteauneuf-du-Pape

To visit Châteauneuf-du-Pape you can take a bus from Avignon or Orange (no buses on Sun) or drive. If you're coming by car, park below the town. Follow *Château* signs up the hill to the main square, Place du Portail. The helpful TI on Place du Portail has a long list of wineries that you can visit and good documentation on the area (July-Sept Mon-Sat 9:30-18:00, closed Sun; Oct-June

CÔTES DU RHÔNE

Mon-Sat 9:30-12:30 & 14:00-18:00, closed Wed and Sun; tel. 04 90 83 71 08). Appealing streets fan out from here, most with cellars selling the famous wine.

Sights in Châteauneuf-du-Pape

Wine Museum (Musée du Vin)

Located at the Brotte Winery, this museum provides useful background for your Côtes du Rhône exploration. After a brief look at the basics of grape-growing, the winemaking process, and the work of a *vigneron* (audioguides are essential for the high-tech displays), enjoy a tasting. You'll need to tell them what you want; see "French Wine-Tasting 101" on page 36. English-speaking Thomas is ready to help you make your choices. For a clear contrast, taste a "ready-to-drink" wine (*prêt à boire;* preh tah bwar), then a wine from "old vines" (*vieille vignes;* vee-yay-ee veen-yuh).

Cost and Hours: Free, daily April-Oct 9:00-13:00 & 14:00-19:00, Nov-March 9:00-12:00 & 14:00-18:00, on Avenue Pierre de Luxembourg, at start of village if coming from Avignon, tel. 04 90 83 59 44, www.brotte.com.

Wine Tasting

The town offers many places to taste wine, including these four cellars.

Near the TI: These two cellars are central. With your back to the TI, walk on the level road to the right to find Daniele Brunel's **The Best Vintage Cave,** a top place to sample Châteauneuf-du-Pape wines. Speaking fluent English and offering wines from 25 different producers (including her own), charismatic Daniele provides a good introduction to area wines. The youngest member of the famous Brunel wine family, Daniele represents a new generation of winemakers who combine traditional values and modern techniques. She can arrange shipping back to the States—expensive but you're spared the VAT tax (daily March-Oct 10:30-12:30 & 13:30-18:30, shorter hours Nov-Dec, closed Jan-Feb, near Place du Portail at 7 Rue de la République, tel. 04 90 83 31 75, www.thebestvintage.fr). A basic WC is next door.

Continuing along this street and up the staircase (then turn left), you'll find **Vinadéa Maison des Vins,** where you can taste and buy more than 200 kinds of Châteauneuf-du-Pape appellation wines from 90 different producers. Marie speaks English (daily June-Sept 10:00-13:00 & 14:00-18:30, shorter hours off-season, 8 Rue Maréchal Foch, tel. 04 90 83 70 69, www.vinadea.com).

Uphill from Place du Portail: These two cellars are best suited for serious tasters.

Les Caves St. Charles offers tastings inside a 13th-century cellar, surrounded by barrels and *beaucoup* ambience. Helpful Guy

Brémond answers all your questions in superb English (May-Oct Mon-Sat 10:00-19:00, closed Sun, near the church at 10 Rue des Papes, tel. 04 90 39 13 85, www.cave-saint-charles.com).

You can huff and puff (or drive) to the fancy restaurant **Cave du Verger des Papes,** where tastings include a look at underground ruins from Roman times (free, best to call ahead, rotating selection of 3-4 wines, Mon-Sat July-Aug 10:00-19:00, closed Sun; Sept-June shorter hours and closed Mon; 2 Rue Montée du Château, tel. 04 90 83 58 08, www.caveduverger.com).

NEAR CHATEAUNEUF-DU-PAPE
Mas de Lionne

Lying on the fringe of Châteauneuf-du-Pape, Mas de Lionne winery is where American Doug Graves is following his retirement dream. Doug bought this small vineyard in 2008 and has been living and working it nonstop since. He does just about everything by himself, but still has time to greet travelers and explain how his wines are made. Because his vineyard is across a tiny road from the officially designated Châteauneuf-du-Pape area, he can't label his wine with this prestigious name. Instead, his wines are designated Côtes du Rhône, even though they share much in common with Châteauneuf-du-Pape (notice the rocky soil). Doug makes a light rosé and velvety red wines using 100 percent Grenache grapes (unusual in this area, where typically several grapes are blended). His interesting story and ability to explain winemaking to Anglophones make this a worthwhile stop for aficionados.

Hours: Tue-Sat 14:00-18:00, closed Sun-Mon; find the town of Sorgues and look for *Mas de Lionne* signs off N-7, pass the first house with the small *Mas de Lionne* sign—the winery is 100 yards up the road at 948 Chemin de la Lionne, mobile 06 37 16 04 56, www.masdelalionne.com.

Sleeping and Eating in Châteauneuf-du-Pape

To bed down in Châteauneuf-du-Pape, try the traditional **$$ Hôtel-Restaurant La Garbure,** ideally located one door up the (mostly) pedestrian street from the TI (Db-€76-92, classy **restaurant** with *menus* from €28-32, 3 Rue Joseph Ducos, tel. 04 90 83 75 08, www.la-garbure.com).

You'll find several appealing eateries around Place du Portail on Rue Joseph Ducos. **Le Pistou** serves salads and *menus* from €13 (closed Sun evening and all day Mon, #15, tel. 04 90 83 71 75). **La Maisouneta,** at #7, is good for fresh pasta dishes (*menus* from €15, closed Tue evenings and all day Wed, tel. 04 90 32 55 03).

It's well worth the time and energy to follow signs up the hill to **Le Verger des Papes,** a fine restaurant where you can feast both on the terrace views and on their traditional and sophisticated cuisine (€20 lunch *menu,* €31 dinner *menu;* closed all day Mon, closed Tue and Sun evenings; reservations smart, 4 Rue Montée du Château—drivers can follow *Château* signs and park at the top to skip the climb, tel. 04 90 83 50 40, www.vergerdespapes.com).

Picnics: Try one of the **three cafés** that surround the TI, which can all make their sandwiches to go, or find the small grocery, **Le Cigalou,** halfway up Rue Joseph Ducos (Mon 15:30-19:30, Tue-Fri 8:00-12:30 & 15:30-19:30, Sat-Sun hours vary).

Côtes du Rhône

The Côtes du Rhône region features classic Provençal scenery, characteristic villages, cozy wineries, fields of fragrant lavender, and excellent good-value restaurants. If you're sleeping in this area, Vaison-la-Romaine is a handy home base. Delve into the region's highlights by following my self-guided driving tour. With more time, dig deeper into the Côtes du Rhône with a drive up Mont Ventoux, a spin around the Drôme Provençale, or a visit to the Ardèche Gorges.

Vaison-la-Romaine

With quick access to vineyards, villages, and Mont Ventoux, this lively little town of 6,000 makes a good base for exploring the Côtes du Rhône region by car, by bike, or on foot. You get two villages for the price of one: Vaison-la-Romaine's "modern" lower city has Roman ruins, a lone pedestrian street, and a lively main square—café-lined Place Montfort. The car-free medieval hill town looms above, with meandering cobbled lanes, art galleries and cafés, and a ruined castle with a fine view from its base. (Vaison-la-Romaine is also a good place to have your hair done, since there are more than 20 hairdressers in this small town.)

Orientation to Vaison-la-Romaine

The city is split in two by the Ouvèze River. The Roman Bridge connects the more modern lower town (Ville-Basse) with the hill-capping medieval upper town (Ville-Haute).

TOURIST INFORMATION

The superb TI is in the lower city, between the two Roman ruin sites, at Place du Chanoine Sautel (June-Aug Mon-Fri 9:00-18:45, Sat-Sun 9:00-12:30 & 14:00-18:45; Sept-May Mon-Sat 9:30-12:00 & 14:00-17:45, Sun 9:30-12:00—except closed Sun mid-Oct-March; tel. 04 90 36 02 11, www.vaison-ventoux-tourisme.com). Say *bonjour* to *charmante* and ever-so-patient Valerie, use the free Wi-Fi, ask about festivals and other events, and pick up information on walks and bike rides. The big wall map shows hiking trails in the area.

ARRIVAL IN VAISON-LA-ROMAINE

By Bus: The unmarked bus stop to Orange and Avignon is in front of the Cave la Romaine winery (by the driveway closer to the roundabout). Buses from Orange or Avignon drop you across the street (3-6/day, 45 minutes from Orange, 1.5 hours from Avignon, best from Orange and just €3; 1/day express from Avignon, 1 hour). Tell the driver you want the stop for the *Office de Tourisme*. When you get off the bus, walk five minutes down Avenue Général de Gaulle to reach the TI and recommended hotels.

By Car: Follow signs to *Centre-Ville*, then *Office de Tourisme;* parking is free across from the TI—most parking is free in Vaison-la-Romaine as well.

HELPFUL HINTS

Market Day: Sleep in Vaison-la-Romaine on Monday night, and you'll wake to an amazing Tuesday market. But be warned: Mondays are quiet during the day, as many shops close (but sights are open). If you spend a Monday night, avoid parking at market sites and where signs indicate *Stationnement Interdit le Mardi*, or you won't find your car where you left it—ask your hotelier where you can park.

Internet Access: The **TI** and **Café Universal,** on atmospheric Place Montfort, offer free Wi-Fi. **Vaison 2 Mils** has computers and printers (51 Cours Taulignan, closed Mon, tel. 04 90 36 23 24).

Vaison-la-Romaine

1 Hôtel/Rest. le Beffroi
2 L'Evêché Chambres
3 Hôtel la Fête en Provence
4 Hôtel Burrhus & Brasserie de l'Annexe
5 Les Tilleuls d'Elisée
6 La Belle Etoile Restaurant
7 Crêperie & Pizzeria
8 Le Comptoir des Voconces Restaurant & Supermarket
9 O'Natur'elles Restaurant
10 La Bartavelle Restaurant
11 Le Brin d'Olivier Restaurant
12 La Lyriste Restaurant
13 Internet Access (2)
14 Launderette
15 Vélo-Vaison Bike Rental
16 Bus to Avignon/Orange
17 Bus from Avignon/Orange

CÔTES DU RHÔNE

Laundry: The self-service **Laverie la Lavandière** is on Cours Taulignan, near Avenue Victor Hugo (figure about €10, daily 8:00-22:00, English instructions). The friendly owners, who work next door at the dry cleaners, will do your laundry—for around €20—while you sightsee (dry cleaners open Mon-Fri 9:00-12:00 & 15:00-19:00, Sat 9:00-12:00, closed Sun).

Supermarket: A handy **Casino** is on Place Montfort in the thick of the cafés (Mon-Sat 7:30-13:00 & 15:30-19:30, Sun 9:00-13:00).

Bike Rental: The TI has a list. **Location Vélo-Vaison** is most central, near the "new bridge" (160 Avenue René Cassin, tel. 06 13 41 11 53). **Vélo Speed,** less than a mile from the center on Route de Nyons, rents top-end bikes (Alain speaks some English and has good suggestions for routes to avoid the busy roads; tel. 04 90 28 17 84). For help with bike rental and biking plans, contact John and Monique at the recommended **L'Ecole Buissonnière Chambres** (see listing later, under "Sleeping in Vaison-la-Romaine").

Taxi: Call 04 90 36 00 04 or 04 90 46 89 42.

Car Rental: You can rent cars by the day, though they must be returned to Vaison-la-Romaine; ask at the TI for locations.

Local Guide: Let sincere and knowledgeable **Anna-Marie Melard** bring the Roman ruins to life for you (tel. 04 90 36 50 48). Scottish by birth and an attorney by profession, **Janet Henderson** offers in-depth historic walks of Vaison-la-Romaine (€30/person, minimum 3 people or €80, allow 2 hours, janet.henderson@wandoo.fr, www.provencehistorytours.com).

Cooking Classes: Charming **Barbara Schuerenberg** offers reasonably priced cooking classes from her view home in Vaison-la-Romaine, where you'll pick herbs from the garden to use in the recipes (€80, cash only, includes lunch, 4-person maximum, tel. 04 90 35 68 43, www.cuisinedeprovence.com, cuisinedeprovence@gmail.com).

Sights in Vaison-la-Romaine

Roman Ruins

Ancient Vaison-la-Romaine had a treaty that gave it a preferred "federated" relationship with Rome (rather than simply being a colony). This, along with a healthy farming economy (olives and vineyards), made it a most prosperous place...as a close look at its sprawling ruins demonstrates. About 6,000 people called Vaison-la-Romaine home 2,000 years ago. When the barbarians arrived,

the Romans were forced out, and the townspeople fled into the hills (see the sidebar on page 176). The town has only recently reached the same population it had during its Roman era.

Cost and Hours: €8; daily April-May 9:30-18:00, June-Sept 9:30-18:30, shorter hours off-season, closed Jan-Feb; video-

guide–€3 or download free app to
your mobile device, tel. 04 90 36 50
48, www.vaison-la-romaine.com.

Visiting the Ruins: Vaison-la-
Romaine's Roman ruins are split by
a modern road into two sites: Puymin and La Villasse. Each is well-
presented, thanks to the videoguide
and occasional English information
panels, offering a good look at life during the Roman Empire.
The Roman town extended all the way from here to the river, and
its main square (forum) still lies under today's main square, Place
Montfort. What you can see is only a small fraction of the Roman
town's extent—most is still buried under today's city. For helpful
background about Roman civilization, read "How About Them
Romans" on page 29.

Visit **Puymin** first. Nearest the entry are the scant but impressive ruins of a sprawling mansion. Find the faint remains of a
colorful frescoed wall. Climb the hill to the good little **museum**
(pick up your videoguide here; exhibits also explained in English
loaner booklet). Be sure to see the **3-D film** that takes you inside
the home of a wealthy Vaison resident and explores daily life some
2,000 years ago. Behind the museum is a still well-used, 6,000-seat
theater, with just enough seats for the whole town (of yesterday and
today).

Back across the modern road in **La Villasse,** you'll explore a
"street of shops" and the foundations of more houses. You'll also see
a few wells, used before Vaison's two aqueducts were built.

Lower Town (Ville-Basse)

Vaison-la-Romaine's modern town centers on café-friendly Place
Montfort. Tables grab the north side of the square, conveniently
sheltered from the prevailing mistral wind while enjoying the generous shade of the ubiquitous plane *(platane)* trees. The trees are
cut way back each year to form a leafy canopy (see sidebar on page
267).

A 10-minute walk below Place Montfort, the stout **Notre-
Dame de Nazareth Cathedral** is a good example of Provençal
Romanesque architecture and dates from the 11th century, with
an evocative cloister and fine stone carvings (free, daily June-Sept
9:30-18:00, shorter hours off-season, closed Oct-March). The pedestrian-only Grand Rue is a lively shopping street leading to the
small river gorge and the Roman Bridge.

Roman Bridge

The Romans cut this sturdy, no-nonsense vault into the canyon
rock 2,000 years ago, and it has survived ever since. Find the

COTES DU RHONE

information panel at the new-town end of the bridge. Until the 20th century, this was the only way to cross the Ouvèze River. See the stone plaque *(Septembre 22-92...)* on the wall to the left as you approach the bridge, showing the high-water mark of the record flood that killed 30 people. The flood swept the modern top of this bridge—and several other modern bridges—downstream, but couldn't budge the 55-foot Roman arch.

Upper Town (Ville-Haute)

Although there's nothing of particular importance to see in the fortified medieval old town atop the hill, the cobbled lanes and enchanting fountains make you want to break out a sketchpad. Vaison-la-Romaine was ruled by a prince-bishop starting in the fourth century. He came under attack by the Count of Toulouse in the 12th century. Anticipating a struggle, the prince-bishop abandoned the lower town and built a castle on this rocky outcrop (about 1195). Over time, the townspeople followed, vacating the lower town and building their homes at the base of the château behind the upper town's fortified wall.

To reach the upper town, hike up from the Roman Bridge (passing memorials for both world wars) through the medieval gate, under the lone tower crowned by an 18th-century wrought-iron bell cage. Look for occasional English information plaques as you meander. The château is closed, but a steep, uneven trail to its base rewards hikers with a sweeping view.

▲▲Market Day

In the 16th century, the pope gave Vaison-la-Romaine market-town status. Each Tuesday morning since then, the town has hosted a farmers' market. Today merchants turn the entire place into a festival of produce and Provençal products. This market is one of France's best, but it can challenge claustrophobes. Be warned that parking is a real headache unless you arrive early (see "Helpful Hints," earlier; for tips on enjoying market day, see the Shopping chapter).

Wine Tasting

Cave la Romaine, a five-minute walk up Avenue Général de Gaulle from the TI, offers a big variety of good-value wines from nearby villages in a pleasant, well-organized tasting room (free tastes,

Mon-Sat 9:00-18:30 but closes for lunch, Sun 9:00-12:00, Avenue St-Quenin, tel. 04 90 36 55 90, www.cave-la-romaine.com).

▲Hiking

The TI has information on hikes into the hills above Vaison-la-Romaine, and sells a printed guide to local hikes.

It's about 1.25 hours to the quiet hill town of Crestet, though views begin immediately. To find this trail, drive or walk on the road past the upper town (with the rock base and castle on your left), continue on Chemin des Fontaines (blue signs), and stay the course as far as you like (follow yellow Crestet signs). Cars are not allowed on the road after about a mile.

To find the five-mile trail to Séguret (allow 2 hours), take the same road above Vaison-la-Romaine and look for a yellow sign to the right. For either hike, consider going on foot one way and taking a taxi back.

Biking

If the air's calm, the five-mile ride to cute little Villedieu (with the recommended La Maison Bleue restaurant) is a delight. Options for renting an electric bike make this an easier outing (see "Helpful Hints," earlier). The bike route is signed along small roads; you'll find signs from Vaison-la-Romaine to Villedieu at the roundabout past Cave La Romaine, and then turn right on the D-51 (see map on page 162). With a bit more energy, you can pedal beyond Villedieu on the lovely road to Mirabel (from Villedieu, follow signs to *Nyons*). Make a detour to Pigeon (to avoid that busy section of road between Mirabel and Vaison), then rejoin the busy D-938 to reach Vaison (figure about 18 miles total). Alternatively, get a good map and connect the following villages for an enjoyable 11-mile loop ride: Vaison-la-Romaine, St-Romain-en-Viennois, Puyméras (with the recommended La Girocedre restaurant), Faucon, and St-Marcellin-lès-Vaison. The TI and bike shops have good information on mountain-biking trails.

Sleeping in Vaison-la-Romaine

Hotels in Vaison-la-Romaine are a good value and are split between the upper medieval village (with all the steps) and the lower main town (with all the services). Those in the upper town (Ville-Haute) are quieter, cozier, cooler, and give you the feeling of sleeping in a hill town (some come with views), with all the services of a real town just steps away. But they require a 10-minute walk to the town center and Roman ruins. If staying at one of the first three places, follow signs to *Cité Médiévale* and park just outside the upper village entry (driving into the Cité Médiévale itself is a challenge, with tiny lanes and nearly impossible parking).

If you have a car, think about staying in one of the Côtes du Rhône villages near Vaison-la-Romaine. I've listed a few nearby places here; for more suggestions see the "Côtes du Rhône Wine Road Driving Tour," later.

IN THE UPPER TOWN

$$$ Hôtel le Beffroi*** hides deep in the upper town, just above a demonstrative bell tower (you'll hear what I mean). It offers 16th-century red-tile-and-wood-beamed-cozy lodgings with nary a level surface. The rooms—split between two buildings a few doors apart—are Old World comfy, and some have views. You'll also find antique-filled public spaces, a garden with view tables (light meals available in the summer), a small pool with more views, and animated Nathalie at the reception (standard Db-€100-130, superior Db-€165, Tb-€190, several good family rooms, Rue de l'Evêché, tel. 04 90 36 04 71, www.le-beffroi.com, info@le-beffroi.com). The hotel's **restaurant** offers *menus* from €29 (closed for lunch weekdays and all day Tue).

$$$ L'Evêché Chambres, almost next door to Hôtel le Beffroi in the upper town (look for the ivy), is a five-room melt-in-your-chair B&B. The owners (the Verdiers) have an exquisite sense of interior design and are passionate about books, making this place feel like a cross between a library and an art gallery (Sb-€78-85, standard Db-€85-95, Db suite-€120-145, the *solanum* suite is worth every euro, Tb-€120-145, Rue de l'Evêché, tel. 04 90 36 13 46, http://eveche.free.fr, eveche@aol.com).

$$$ Hôtel la Fête en Provence, conveniently located for drivers at the entry to the medieval upper town, works in a pinch. Rooms are located around a courtyard—with noise from the restaurant in summer—but there's an outdoor pool and Jacuzzi next door (Db-€90-120, Cité Médiévale, tel. 04 90 36 36 43, www.hotellafete-provence.com, fete-en-provence@wanadoo.fr). Their apartments (€230) sleep up to six people, and come with kitchenettes and sitting areas.

IN THE LOWER TOWN

$$ Hôtel Burrhus** is part art gallery, part simple, funky hotel—and the best value in the lower town. It's a central, laid-back, go-with-the-flow place, with a broad terrace over the raucous Place Montfort (the double-paned windows are effective, but for maximum quiet, request a back room). Its floor plan will confound even the ablest navigator, but the jukebox works in the lobby (Db-€73-78, larger Db-€87-97, Qb apartment-€140, extra bed-€15, breakfast-€9, air-con, 1 Place Montfort, tel. 04 90 36 00 11, www.burrhus.com, info@burrhus.com).

$$ Les Tilleuls d'Elisée is a terrific *chambre d'hôte* in a big stone, blue-shuttered home near the Notre-Dame de Nazareth Cathedral, a few minutes' walk below the TI. Enthusiastic Anne and Laurent Viau run this traditional, five-room place with grace and offer great rates (Db-€78, air-con, €7 wine-tasting lessons, 1 Avenue Jules Mazen, tel. 04 90 35 63 04, www.vaisonchambres.info, anne.viau@vaisonchambres.info).

NEAR VAISON-LA-ROMAINE

$$$ **La Madelène Chambres** is a few miles off the road between Vaison-la-Romaine and Malaucène. This smartly restored ancient farmhouse comes with pleasant English owners (Jude and Philip) and complete isolation. The place has meditative terraces, a view pool, and five very comfortable and spacious rooms (Db-€125-155, includes breakfast, a few bikes available for guests, Route d'Entrechaux 84340, Malaucène, tel. 06 75 78 84 97, www.bighouseinprovence.com). Ask about their wine-tasting packages (€1,900/couple for 3-night stay with visits to several wineries, www.rhonewineholidays.com).

$$ **L'Ecole Buissonnière Chambres** is run by an engaging Anglo-French team, John and Monique, who share their peace and quiet 10 minutes north of Vaison-la-Romaine. This creatively restored farmhouse has three character-filled, half-timbered rooms and comfy public spaces. Getting to know John, who has lived all over the south of France, is worth the price of the room. The outdoor kitchen allows guests to picnic in high fashion in the tranquil garden (Db-€68-77, Tb-€85-95, Qb-€99-107, includes breakfast, cash only; between Villedieu and Buisson on D-75—leave Vaison following signs to *Villedieu*, then follow D-51 toward Buisson and turn left onto D-75; tel. 04 90 28 95 19, www.buissonniere-provence.com, ecole.buissonniere@wanadoo.fr).

Eating in Vaison-la-Romaine

Vaison-la-Romaine offers a handful of terrific dining experiences—arrive by 19:30 in summer or reserve ahead, particularly on weekends. And while you can eat very well on a moderate budget in Vaison, it's well worth venturing to nearby Côtes du Rhône villages to eat. I've listed three nearby places; for recommendations farther afield see the "Côtes du Rhône Wine Road Driving Tour," later. Wherever you dine, begin with a fresh glass of Muscat from the nearby village of Beaumes-de-Venise.

IN THE UPPER TOWN

The recommended **Hôtel le Beffroi's** garden is just right for a light dinner in the summer (*menus* from €29, closed at lunch weekdays, and all day Tue).

La Belle Etoile is where locals go for simple, fresh, and good-value meals. Outside tables come with views over the lower town (open irregular days April-Sept, closes when they run out of food; it's the first place you pass when coming from the lower town, tel. 04 90 37 31 45).

You'll also find a simple *crêperie* and a **pizzeria** on the main street leading up to the old town. Both have decks with views over the river, plastic chairs, and cheap food (good for families).

DINING ON PLACE MONFORT

Come here for lighter café fare and to observe the daily flow of life in Vaison-la-Romaine. Dine here only if you enjoy sitting outside.

Reliable **Brasserie l'Annexe** has €12 meals (open daily), and **Le Comptoir des Voconces** is the happening hangout with a pub-like ambience. **O'Natur'elles** is ideal for vegetarians; the all-organic dishes can be served with or without meat. Locals love this place, though service can be slow. It's small, so reservations are smart (€16-20 *plats*, closed Tue evening, tel. 04 90 65 81 67).

ELSEWHERE IN THE LOWER TOWN

La Bartavelle, run by friendly Berenger, is a good place to savor traditional French cuisine, with a tourist-friendly mix-and-match choice of local options. Her €30 *menu* gets you four courses; the €23 *menu* gives you access to all the top-end main-course selections and dessert (closed Mon, Fri at lunch, and off-season on Sun; small terrace outside, air-con, 12 Place de Sus Auze, tel. 04 90 36 02 16).

Le Brin d'Olivier is the most romantic place I list, with soft lighting, hushed conversations, earth tones, and a semi-gastronomic range of food that celebrates Provence (€31 and €45 three-course *menus*, closed Wed except July-Aug, off-season also closed Tue and Sun evenings, 4 Rue du Ventoux, tel. 04 90 65 51 43, www.restaurant-lebrindolivier.com, owner Patrick speaks a little English).

La Lyriste, named for the loudest "singing" *cigale* (cicada), puts cuisine above decor. Marie serves what hubby Benoît cooks. Both are shy, yet proud of their restaurant. There's a fine *menu* for €22 with choices that are inventive and *très delectable*. Let Marie suggest your wine from the very reasonably priced list (closed Mon, vegetarian options, indoor and outdoor seating, 45 Cours Taulignan, tel. 04 90 36 04 67).

NEAR VAISON-LA-ROMAINE

La Girocedre, easiest for drivers, is an enchanting place to eat lunch or dinner if the weather's nice. Just three picturesque miles north of Vaison-la-Romaine in the village of Puyméras, this eatery offers a complete country-Provençal package: outdoor tables in a lush garden, warm interior decor, and real Provençal cuisine (€17 lunch *menu*, €29 dinner *menu*, closed all day Mon and for lunch Tue, off-season closed all day Tue, reservations smart; take road into Puyméras, then turn right toward Mirabel and park across the road from the fountain; tel. 04 90 46 50 67, www.legirocedre.fr).

La Maison Bleue, about four miles north of Vaison-la-Romaine on Villedieu's delightful little square, serves pizzas and salads with great outdoor ambience. Skip it if the weather forces you inside (March-Oct Thu-Sun open for lunch and dinner, closed Mon-Wed except July-Aug closed Mon only, tel. 04 90 28 97 02).

Auberge d'Anaïs, at the end of a dirt road 10 minutes from Vaison-la-Romaine, is another find—and a true Provençal experience. Outdoor tables gather under cheery lights with views and reliable cuisine. Ask for a table *sur la terrasse* (€13 weekday lunch *menu*, good three-course dinner *menus* from €20, closed Sun evening and Mon, tel. 04 90 36 20 06). Heading east of Vaison-la-Romaine, follow signs to *Carpentras*, then *St. Marcellin*. Signs will guide you from there.

Vaison-la-Romaine Connections

The most central **bus stop** is a few blocks up Avenue Général de Gaulle from the TI at the main winery, Cave la Romaine.

From Vaison-la-Romaine by Bus to: Avignon (3-6/day, local buses pass through Orange, 1.5 hours; also direct express 1/day, 1 hour), **Orange** (3-6/day, 45 minutes), **Nyons** (3-5/day, 45 minutes), **Crestet** (lower village below Crestet, 2/day, 5 minutes), **Carpentras** (2/day, 45 minutes).

The Best of the Côtes du Rhône Villages

Officially, the Côtes du Rhône vineyards follow the Rhône River from just south of Lyon to Avignon. Our focus is the southern section of the Côtes du Rhône, centering on the small area between Châteauneuf-du-Pape and Vaison-la-Romaine. This area is best toured by car or bike. My self-guided driving tour starts in the village of Séguret, then returns to Vaison-la-Romaine and winds clockwise around the Dentelles de Montmirail, visiting the mountaintop village of Crestet, adorable little Suzette, and the renowned wine villages of Beaumes-de-Venise and Gigondas. I've listed several wineries *(domaines)* along the way. Before you go, study up with "French Wine-Tasting 101" on page 36. Even if wine isn't your thing, don't miss this scenic drive. Theft is a problem in this beautiful area—leave absolutely nothing in your car.

Le Mistral

Provence lives with its vicious mistral winds, which blow 30-60 miles per hour, about 100 days out of the year. Locals say it blows in multiples of threes: three, six, or nine days in a row. The mistral clears people off the streets and turns lively cities into ghost towns. You'll likely spend a few hours or days taking refuge. The winds are strongest between noon and 15:00.

When the mistral blows, it's everywhere, and you can't escape. Author Peter Mayle said it could blow the ears off a donkey (I'd include the tail). According to the natives, it ruins crops, shutters, and roofs (look for stones holding tiles in place on many homes). They'll also tell you that this pernicious wind has driven many people crazy (including young Vincent van Gogh). A weak version of the wind is called a mistralet.

The mistral starts above the Alps and Massif Central mountains and gathers steam as it heads south, gaining momentum as it screams over the Rhône Valley (which acts like a funnel between the Alps and the Cévennes mountains) before exhausting itself when it hits the Mediterranean. And though this wind rattles shutters everywhere in the Riviera and Provence, it's strongest over the Rhône Valley...so Avignon, Arles, and the Côtes du Rhône villages bear its brunt. While wiping the dust from your eyes, remember the good news: The mistral brings clear skies.

PLANNING YOUR TIME

Although seeing the Côtes du Rhône is possible as a day trip by car from Arles or Avignon, you'll have a more enjoyable and intimate experience if you sleep in one of the villages (my favorite accommodations are listed under "Sleeping in Vaison-la-Romaine" on page 166).

With a car, the best one-day plan is to take the driving tour described below (allow an entire day for the 80-mile round-trip from Avignon). Try to get the first two stops done before lunch (most wineries are closed 12:00-14:00; call ahead if possible), then complete the loop in the afternoon. Some wineries are closed on Sundays, holidays, and during the harvest (mid-Sept). This route is picnic-friendly, but there are few shops along the way—stock up before you leave.

GETTING AROUND THE
COTES DU RHONE VILLAGES

This area is clearly easiest if you have four wheels. Without a car, it's tougher, but a representative sampling is doable by **bike** (for ideas, see "Biking" on page 166) or by **bus** (3-6 buses/day from Avignon and Orange stop at several Côtes du Rhône villages; consider tak-

COTES DU RHONE

ing the bus one-way, then returning by taxi). For less effort and more expense, several of the local guides and minivan tour companies I list are happy to follow this route (see "Tours in Provence" on page 26).

Côtes du Rhône Wine Road Driving Tour

This self-guided driving tour introduces you to the characteristic best of the Côtes du Rhône wine road. While circling the rugged Dentelles de Montmirail mountain peaks, you'll experience all that's unique about this region: its natural beauty, glowing limestone villages, inviting wineries, and rolling hills of vineyards. As you drive, notice how some vineyards grow at angles—they're planted this way to compensate for the strong effect of the mistral wind. One hundred million years ago, the Mediterranean Sea extended this far north, leaving behind a sandy soil base for today's farmers (the wine town of Sablet's name comes from the French word *sable*, meaning sand).

This trip provides a crash course in Rhône Valley wine, an excuse to meet the locals who make the stuff, and breathtaking scenery—especially late in the day, when the famous Provençal sunlight causes colors to absolutely pop. This region is not only about wine; you'll pass orchards of apricots, figs, cherries, and table grapes as well.

Remember that the wineries you'll visit are serious about their wines—and they hope that you'll take them seriously, too. At private wineries, tastings are not happy-go-lucky chances to knock back a few glasses and buy a T-shirt with the property's label on it. Show genuine interest in the wines, and buy some if you enjoy your tastes.

Drivers can enjoy a wealth of country-Provençal hotel and dining opportunities in rustic settings within 15 minutes of Vaison-la-Romaine. They offer a great opportunity for drivers who want to experience rural France and get better values. All restaurants listed have some outdoor seating and should be considered for lunch or dinner.

SEGURET TO CRESTET, SUZETTE, GIGONDAS, AND BACK

Our tour starts a bit south of Vaison-la-Romaine in little Séguret. By bike, or for a more scenic drive from Vaison-la-Romaine, cross to the Cité Médiévale side of the river, then follow D-977 signs downriver to Séguret. A hiking trail from above Vaison-la-Romaine's castle leads to Séguret in 8.5 miles (see page 166).

COTES DU RHONE

Côtes du Rhône Driving Tour

1 Séguret
2 Domaine de Mourchon Winery
3 Crestet
4 Col de la Chaîne Mountain Pass
5 Suzette
6 Domaine de Coyeux Winery
7 Gigondas

❶ Séguret

Blending into the hillside with a smattering of shops, two cafés, made-to-stroll lanes, and a natural spring, this hamlet is understandably popular. Séguret makes for a good coffee or ice cream stop.

Séguret's name comes from the Latin word *securitas* (meaning "security"). The bulky entry arch came with a massive gate, which drilled in the message of the village's name. In the Middle Ages, Séguret was patrolled 24/7—they never took their *securitas* for granted. Walk through the arch. To appreciate how the homes' outer walls provided security in those days, drop down the first passage on your right (near the fountain). These exit passages, or *poternes,* were needed in periods of peace to allow the town to expand below.

Find Séguret's open washbasin *(lavoir),* a hotbed of social activity and gossip over the ages. The basins behind the fountain (now planted) were reserved for washing animals (which outnumbered residents in the Middle Ages); the larger ones (on the left) were for laundry only. Public washbasins like this were used right up until World War II. Farther on, take a left at the fork. The community bread oven *(four banal)* was used for festivals and celebrations. Rue Calade leads up to the unusual 12th-century St. Denis church for views (the circular village you see below is Sablet). This rock-sculpted church is usually closed, but it's worth a look from the outside. High above, a castle once protected Séguret, but all that's left today is a tower that you can barely make out (trails provide access).

At Christmas, this entire village transforms itself into one big crèche scene—a Provençal tradition that has long since died out in other villages. Make your way down to the main drag and a café, and return to parking along Rue des Poternes.

Sleeping and Eating in Séguret: **$$$ Domaine de Cabasse***** is a lovely spread flanked by vineyards at the foot of Séguret (with a walking path to the village). Winemaking is their primary business—free tastings are offered every evening at 18:30 from April through September. Most of the 23 rooms have contemporary decor, air-conditioning, and nice views; some have balconies. Four Old World rooms have view terraces but no air-conditioning (traditional Db-€135, renovated Db-€162-180, elevator, big pool, on D-23 between Sablet and Séguret, entry gate opens automatically... and slowly, tel. 04 90 46 91 12, www.cabasse.fr, hotel@cabasse.fr). The **restaurant** offers fine, though limited, €28-41 dinner *menus.*

• *Signs near Séguret's parking will lead you up, up, and away to our next stop, Domaine de Mourchon.*

❷ Domaine de Mourchon Winery

This high-flying winery blends state-of-the-art technology with traditional winemaking methods (a shiny ring of stainless-steel vats holds grapes grown on land plowed by horses). The wines are winning the respect of international critics, yet the (Scottish) owners seem eager to help anyone understand Rhône Valley wines. Language is not an issue here, nor is

COTES DU RHONE

a lack of stunning views. Free and informative English tours of the vineyards are usually offered (wines-€8-33/bottle; winery open Mon-Sat 9:00-18:00, Sun by appointment only; from Easter-Sept, call to verify; tel. 04 90 46 70 30, www.domainedemourchon.com).

• *Next, return to Vaison-la-Romaine and follow signs toward Carpentras/Malaucène. After passing through "lower" Crestet, look for signs leading up to* Le Village *and use the Parking Visiteurs lot at its entry.*

❸ Crestet

This village—founded after the fall of the Roman Empire, when people banded together in high places like this for protection from marauding barbarians—followed the usual hill-town evolution (see sidebar on page 176). The outer walls of the village did double duty as ramparts and house walls. The castle above (from about A.D. 850) provided a final safe haven when the village was attacked.

The Bishop of Vaison-la-Romaine was the first occupant, lending little Crestet a certain prestige. With about 500 residents in 1200, Crestet was a big deal in this region, reaching its zenith in the mid-1500s, when 660 people called it home. Crestet's gradual decline started when the bishop moved to Vaison-la-Romaine in the 1600s, though the population remained fairly stable until World War II. Today, about 35 people live within the walls year-round (about 55 during the summer boom).

Wander the peaceful lanes and appreciate the amount of work it took to put these stones in place. Notice the elaborate water channels. Crestet was served by 18 cisterns in the Middle Ages. The peaceful (usually closed) church has a beautiful stained-glass window behind the altar. Imagine hundreds of people living here and animals roaming everywhere. Get to the top of town.

Eating in Crestet: The village's only business, the recommended café-restaurant **Le Panoramic** at the top of town, has an upstairs terrace with a view that justifies the name...even if the food is mediocre. It serves average salads, crêpes, and *plats* at what must be Provence's greatest view tables (€15 *plats du jour,* April-Nov daily 10:30-22:00, closed in bad weather and Dec-March, tel. 04 90 28 76 42). Drivers should pass by the first parking lot in Crestet and keep climbing to park at Place du Château. The restaurant is well-signed at the top of the village.

• *Signs from the top of the village lead to the footpath to Vaison-La-Romaine. The trail leaves from Chemin de la Verrière at the very top of the village (by the intersection with the road from below). Look for the brown sign, which indicates that it's 8 kilometers (about 5 miles) to Vaison-la-Romaine, and—in a few steps—turn right, following the yellow sign that shows it's 5.1 kilometers (3 miles) to Vaison-la-Romaine (via Chemin des Fontaines).*

Drivers should carry on and reconnect with the road below, fol-

The Life of a Hill Town in Provence

Heat-seeking northerners have made Provence's hill towns prosperous and worldly. But before the 1960s, few wanted to live in these sun-drenched, rock-top settings. Like lost ships in search of safe harbor, the people of long ago took refuge here only out of necessity.

When the Romans settled Provence (125 B.C.), they brought stability to the warring locals, and hill-towners descended en masse to the Roman cities (such as Arles, Orange, Nîmes, and Vaison-la-Romaine). There they enjoyed theaters, fresh water from aqueducts, and commercial goods brought via the Roman road that stretched from Spain to Italy (passing along the northern edge of the Luberon).

When Rome fell (A.D. 476), barbarians swept in to rape and pillage, forcing locals back up into the hills, where they'd stay for almost 1,000 years. These "Dark Ages" were when many of the villages we see today were established. Most grew up around castles, since peasants depended on their lord for security. The hill-towners gathered stones from nearby fields and built their homes side by side to form a defensive wall, terracing the hillsides to maximize the scarce arable land. They would gather inside heavy-stone Romanesque churches to pray for salvation. Medieval life was not easy behind those walls—there were barbarians, plagues, crop failures, droughts, thieves, wars, and the everyday battle with gravity.

As the Renaissance approached, and Provence came under the protection of an increasingly centralized French nation, barbarian invasions dwindled. Just when the hill-towners thought the coast was clear to relocate below, France's religious wars (1500s) chased them back up. As Protestants and Catholics duked it out, hilltop villages prospered, welcoming refugees. Little Séguret (pop. 100 today) had almost 1,000 residents; the village of Mérindol (near Avignon) sprouted from nowhere; and Fort de Buoux (near Apt, nothing but ruins today—see page 221) was an impregnable fortress. The turmoil of the Revolution (1789) continued to make the above-the-fray hill towns desirable.

Over the next century, hill towns slept peacefully as the rest of France modernized. Most of the hill towns you'll visit housed between 200 and 600 people and were self-sufficient, producing

lowing signs to Malaucène. *As you near Malaucène, look for the huge* boules *courts separated by logs (on your left). (For a sleeping recommendation near Malaucène, see page 166). Entering Malaucène, turn right on D-90 (direction: Suzette) just before the gas station. After a few minutes you'll approach a pass. Look for signs on the left to Col de la Chaîne (Chain Pass). From this point on, the scenery gets better fast.*

just what was needed (farmers, lawyers, and telemarketers were at equilibrium). Many town fountains and communal washrooms date from this time. Animals were everywhere, outnumbering humans four to one.

But 20th-century life down below required fewer stairs—and was closer to the convenience of trains, planes, and automobiles. So after World War I, down the hill-towners moved. To build in the flatlands, they pillaged the hill towns' stones, roof tiles—you name it, they took it—leaving those villages in ruin. By mid-century, most of these lovely villages became virtual ghost towns (in 1965, Crestet had but 15 residents—less than a third of its current population).

In recent years, hill towns have bounced back. Lavender production took off, and the government launched irrigation projects. But most of all, real estate boomed as Parisians, northern Europeans, and (to a lesser extent) North Americans discovered the rustic charm of hill-town life. They invested huge sums—far more than most locals could afford—to turn ancient stone structures into modern vacation homes (in many cases, buying several houses and combining them into one). Today's hill towns survive in part thanks to these outsiders' deep pockets.

Today, many villages have organizations to preserve their traditions and buildings (such as Les Amis de Séguret, or "Friends of Séguret"). Made up of older residents, groups like these raise money, sponsor festivals and dances, and even write collective histories of their villages. Many fear that younger folks won't have the motivation to carry on this tradition.

But hope springs eternal, as there may be a movement of locals back to these villages. Some northerners are finding hill-town life less romantic as their knee replacements fail. Meanwhile, the popularity of organic produce is making it financially viable for hill-town farmers with smaller plots to pursue their healthy dreams of living off the land. Finally, the Internet age has allowed some hill-towners to live in remote villages and telecommute, rather than move into bigger cities. Could the cycle be restarting? Armed with laptops, smartphones, and tablets, will hill-towners once again prosper when the next wave of barbarians comes?

❹ Col de la Chaîne Mountain Pass

Get out of your car at the pass (elevation: about 1,500 feet) and enjoy the breezy views. Wander about. The peaks in the distance—thrusting up like the back of a stegosaurus or a bad haircut (you decide)—are the Dentelles de Montmirail, a small range running just nine miles basically north to south and reaching 2,400 feet in elevation. This region's land is constantly shifting. Those rocky tops were the result of a gradual uplifting of the land, then were

Cicadas (*Cigales*)

In the countryside, listen for *les cigales*. They sing in the heat and are famous for announcing the arrival of summer. (Locals say their song also marks the coming of the tourists...and more money.) People here love these ugly, long-winged bugs, an integral part of Provençal life. You'll see souvenir cicadas made out of every material possible. If you look closely—they are well-camouflaged—you can find live specimens on tree trunks and branches. Cicadas live for about two years, all but the last two weeks of which are spent quietly underground as larvae. But when they go public, their chirping begins with each sunrise and goes nonstop until sunset.

blown bald by the angry mistral wind. Below, pine and oak trees mix with the shrub Scotch broom, which blooms brilliant yellow in May and June. You may see rich yellow-to-reddish patches of land—the result of deposits of ochre located deep below. The village below the peaks is Suzette (you'll be there soon). The yellow-signed hiking-only trail leads to the castle-topped village of Le Barroux (3.5 miles, mostly downhill).

The scene is gorgeous and surprisingly undeveloped. You can thank the lack of water for the absence of more homes or farms in this area. Water is everything in this parched region, and if you don't have ready access to it, you can't build or cultivate the land. (Some farmers have drilled as far as 1,300 feet down to try to find water.) With no water at hand, farmers here lie awake at night worrying about fire. Hot summers, dry pines, and windy days make a scary recipe for fast-traveling fires.

Now turn around and face Mont Ventoux. Are there clouds on the horizon? You're looking into the eyes of the Alps (behind Ventoux), and those "foothills" help keep Provence sunny.

• *Time to push on. You'll pass yellow trail signs along this drive. (The Dentelles provide fertile ground for walking trails.) With the medieval castle of Le Barroux topping the horizon in the distance (off to the left), drive on to little...*

❺ Suzette

Tiny Suzette floats on its hilltop, with a small 12th-century chapel, one café, a handful of residents, and the gaggle of houses where they live. Park in Suzette's lot, below, then find the big orientation board above the lot (Rome is 620 kilometers—385 miles—away). Look out to the broad shoulders of Mont Ventoux. At 6,000 feet, it always seems to have some clouds hanging around. If it's clear, the top looks like it's snow-covered; if you drive up there, you'll see it's actually white stone (see the Mont Ventoux drive on page

COTES DU RHONE

The Phoenicians' Wine-Growing Almanac

Phoenicians brought about five grape varieties with them to southern Europe approximately 3,000 years ago. Today there

are more than 2,000 different grape varieties in the world, of which 150 are in France and 14 are in the Côtes du Rhône.

But some things have changed very little over the past three millennia: Today's Provençal farmers tend their grapes following much the same rhythm as did their Phoenician forerunners.

After a quiet winter, the plants begin waking up in March, pushing out new growth. By about mid-May, the plants are growing at a very fast pace, requiring farmers to do their first pruning of the year. Often working by hand, they pull off sucker plants and prune back new shoots, focusing the plant's energy on four to five main stalks.

Over the next three months, the farmers plow the soil, encouraging moisture to reach the plants. Every few weeks they spray for mildew (not a big problem in this dry area).

Next comes the harvest. Its precise date is dictated by how much sun and warmth the vines absorbed through the spring and summer: The hotter and drier the weather, the earlier the harvest.

In France, the grape harvest starts in the south and rolls north, ending about six weeks later in the country's northernmost vineyards, in Champagne. During the harvest, grapes are picked from the vines—either by hand or by machine—then separated from their stems. Pressing comes 2-3 weeks later, and the winemaking process is under way.

In the fall, farmers are busy watching and tweaking their wines. By December it's time for heavy pruning, when the plants are cut way back for the winter hibernation. Farmers spend the winter months catching up on maintenance, reading...and sleeping.

183). If it's very cloudy, the mountain takes on a dark, foreboding appearance.

Look to the village. A sign asks you to *Respectez son Calme* (respect its peace). Suzette's homes once lived in the shadow of an imposing castle, destroyed during the religious wars of the mid-1500s. Good picnic tables lie just past Suzette on our route. Back across the road from the orientation table is a tasting room for

Château Redortier wines (unreliable hours, English brochure and well-explained wine list provided).

Sleeping and Eating in and near Suzette: **Les Coquelicots,** a tiny eatery surrounded by vines and views in minuscule Suzette, is a sweet spot. The food is good and the setting is memorable (May-Sept usually closed Tue evening and all day Wed, Oct-April open weekends only, tel. 04 90 65 06 94).

$$ La Ferme Dégoutaud is a splendidly situated, roomy, and utterly isolated *chambre d'hôte* about halfway between Malaucène and Suzette (well-signed, a mile down a dirt road). Animated Véronique (speaks minimal English, her son Thibault more) rents three country-cozy rooms with many thoughtful touches, a view pool, table tennis, picnic-perfect tables, and a barbecue at your disposal (Db-€75, Tb-€85, Qb-€95, includes breakfast, apartments available by the week, a 20-minute drive from Vaison-la-Romaine, tel. 04 90 62 99 29, www.degoutaud.fr, le.degoutaud@wanadoo.fr).

Côté Vignes, off a short dirt road between Suzette and Beaumes-de-Venise, is a lighthearted wood-fired-everything place with outdoor tables flanked by fun interior dining. Young English-speaking Corinne runs the restaurant with enthusiasm; try the Camembert cheese flambé with lettuce, potatoes, and ham (€10 salads and good pizza, *menus* from €20-32, closed Wed year-round, Oct-Nov and April also closed Mon-Tue evenings, closed Dec-March, tel. 04 90 65 07 16).

• *Continue from Suzette in the direction of Beaumes-de-Venise. You'll drop down into the lush little village of La Fare. Here, joyriders can take a 20-minute detour into the mountains by taking a sharp right on entering the village, following* Dentelles de Montmirail *signs. The* **Domaine de Cassan winery** *(tastings possible, Mon–Sat 10:00–12:00 & 14:00–18:00, closed Sun, tel. 04 90 62 96 12) lies near the end of the road that also leads to the Col du Cayron hiking trail (to the village of Gigondas). Your partner could drop you off and meet you in Gigondas (it's a 1.5-hour walk over the pass).*

But La Fare's best wine-tasting opportunity is back on our route just after leaving the village, at...

❻ Domaine de Coyeux Winery

A private road winds up and up to this impossibly beautiful setting, with the best views of the Dentelles I've found. Olive trees frame the final approach, and *Le Caveau* signs lead to a modern tasting room (you may need to ring the buzzer). The owners and staff (mainly Marion) are sincere and take your interest in their wines seriously—skip it if you only want a quick taste or are not interested in buying. These wines have earned their excellent reputation, and are now available in the US. Let Marion guide you and make recommendations for the tasting (wines—€8-16/bottle; winery generally open daily 10:00-12:00 & 14:00-18:00, except closed Sun off-season and no midday closure July-Aug; tel. 04 90 12 42 42, domainedecoyeux.com/en, some English spoken).

• *Drive on toward Beaumes-de-Venise. You'll soon pass the recommended* **Côté Vignes** *(see above), a good stopping place for lunch or dinner.*

Next, navigate through Beaumes-de-Venise, following signs for Vacqueyras. *At a big roundabout, you'll pass Beaumes-de-Venise's massive* cave coopérative, *which represents many growers in this area (big selection, but too slick for my taste). Continue following signs for* Vacqueyras *(a famous wine village with a Thursday market and another* cave coopérative*), and then signs for* Gigondas *and* Vaison par la route touristique. *As you enter Gigondas, follow signs to the TI and park on or near the tree-shaded square.*

❼ Gigondas

This town produces some of the region's best reds and is ideally situated for hiking, mountain-biking, and driving into the mountains. The **TI** has Wi-Fi, lists of wineries and *chambres d'hôte*, rental bikes, and tips for good hikes or drives (Mon-Sat 10:00-12:30 & 14:00-18:00, closed Sun, Place du Portail, tel. 04 90 65 85 46, www.gigondas-dm.fr). The €2.50 *Chemins et Sentiers du Massif des Dentelles* hiking map is helpful, though not critical, because routes are well-signed. Take

a short walk through the village lanes above the TI—the church is an easy destination with good views over the heart of the Côtes du Rhône vineyards.

You'll find several good tasting opportunities on the main square. **Le Caveau de Gigondas** is the best, where Sandra and

Barbara await your visit in a handsome tasting room with a large and free selection of tiny bottles for sampling, filled directly from the barrel (daily 10:00-12:00 & 14:00-18:30, close to the TI on the main town square, tel. 04 90 65 82 29, www.caveaudugigondas.com). Here you can compare wines from 75 private

Lavender

Whether or not you travel to Provence during the late-June and July lavender blossom, you'll see and smell examples of this particularly local product every- where—in shops, on tables in restaurants, and in your hotel room. And if you come during lavender season, you'll experience one of Europe's great color events, where rich fields of purple lavender meet equally rich yellow fields of sunflowers. While lavender season is hot, you'll find the best fields in the cooler hills, because the flowers thrive at higher altitudes. The flowers are harvested in full bloom (beginning in mid-July), then distilled to extract the oils for making soaps and perfume.

And though lavender seems like an indigenous part of the Provence scene, it wasn't cultivated here until about 1920, when it was imported by the local perfume-makers. Because lavender is not native to Provence, growing it successfully requires great care. Three kinds of lavender are grown in Provence: true lavender (traditionally used by perfume-makers), spike lavender, and lavandin (a cloned hybrid of the first two). Today, a majority of Provence lavender fields are lavandin—which is also mass-produced at factories, a trend that is threatening to put true lavender growers out of business.

Some of the best lavender fields bloom near Vaison-la-Romaine. Lavender blooms later the higher you go; the ones described here are listed from lowest to highest elevations. For an impressive display, drive north of Vaison-la-Romaine and ramble the tiny road between Valréas and Vinsobres (D-190 and D-46). You'll see more beautiful fields along D-538 between Nyons and Dieulefit, and still more if you climb Mont Ventoux to Sault (described on page 183).

COTES DU RHONE

producers in an intimate, low-key surrounding. The provided list of wines is helpful. A self-imposed gag rule (intended to keep staff from favoring the production of a single winery in this co-op showcase) makes it hard to get a strong recommendation here, so it's best to know what you want (see "French Wine-Tasting 101" on page 36).

Sleeping and Eating in and near Gigondas: The shaded red tables of **Du Verre à l'Assiette** ("From Glass to Plate") entice lunchtime eaters (also good interior ambience, €16-26 *menus*, open for lunch daily except Wed, open for dinner Fri-Sat nights, located diagonally across from TI, Place du Village, tel. 04 90 12 36 64).

$$$ Hôtel les Florets**, with tastefully designed rooms, is a half-mile above Gigondas, buried in the foothills of the Dentelles de Montmirail. It comes with an excellent restaurant, a vast terrace with views, and hiking trails into the mountains (standard Db-€120-145, superior Db-€150-180, several good family rooms, annex rooms by pool have front patios, breakfast-€16, tel. 04 90 65 85 01, www.hotel-lesflorets.com, accueil@hotel-lesflorets.com).

The **restaurant** at Hôtel les Florets is a traditional, family-run place that's well worth it—particularly if you dine on the magnificent terrace. Dinners are a blend of classic French cuisine and Provençal accents, served with class by English-speaking Thierry. The weighty wine list is literally encyclopedic (*menus* from €37, closed Wed except to hotel guests, service can be slow).

• *From Gigondas, follow signs to the circular wine village of Sablet—with generally inexpensive yet tasty wines (the TI and wine coopérative share a space in the town center)—then past Séguret and back to Vaison-la-Romaine, where our tour ends.*

If you haven't had your fill, consider adding on some...

VILLAGES NORTH OF THE COTES DU RHONE

Cairanne, toward Orange from Vaison-la-Romaine, is a pleasant village producing fine wines with one of the largest and most respected wine *coopératives* in this region. The **Cave de Cairanne,** officially known as the **Maison Camille Cayran,** has been making wine for more than 80 years with grapes from more than 100 different farmers. Start with the free, museum-esque "sensory trail," which explores the five senses through interactive displays in English and French and prepares you to taste their large range of wines (free, daily wine tasting 9:00-18:00 but closes at lunchtime, museum closes at 17:30, lots of English spoken, on Route de Bollene on the outskirts of town on D-8—you can't miss the signs, tel. 04 90 65 98 15, www.maisoncamillecayran.com).

Consider a meal afterward at the nearby wine-bar/restaurant **Le Tourne au Verre** (€16 three-course lunch *menu*, €14-23 *plats*, closed Mon and Sun evenings, Route de Sainte-Cécile, tel. 04 90 30 72 18, www.letourneauverre.com).

More Côtes du Rhône Drives

For further explorations of the Côtes du Rhône region, consider these suggestions: a scenic mountaintop, an off-the-beaten-path countryside ramble, and an impressive gorge.

▲MONT VENTOUX AND LAVENDER

The drive to Mont Ventoux is worth ▲▲▲ if the summit is open (see later) and skies are crystal-clear, or in any weather between late

COTES DU RHONE

June and the end of July, when the lavender blooms. It also provides a scenic connection between the Côtes du Rhône villages and the Luberon. Allow an hour to drive to the top of this 6,000-foot mountain, where you'll be greeted by cool temperatures, crowds of visitors, and acres of white stones. Most days you'll see any number of cyclists braving the long, grueling ascent, made famous by its annual inclusion in the Tour de France.

Mont Ventoux is Provence's rooftop, referred to as the "Giant of Provence" or "the Bald Mountain," with astonishing Pyrenees-to-Alps views when it's really clear (it usually isn't). But even under hazy skies, it's an interesting place. The top combines a barren and surreal lunar landscape with souvenirs, bikers, and hikers. All that chalky mess you see was once the bottom of a sea. Miles of poles stuck in the rock identify the route (the top is usually snowbound mid-Nov to April, sometimes May). **Le Vendran** restaurant (near the old observatory and Air Force control tower) offers snacks and meals with commanding views. An orientation board is available on the opposite side of the mountaintop.

Between Mont Ventoux and the Luberon, you'll duck into and out of several climate zones and remarkably diverse landscapes. The scene alternates between limestone canyons, lush meadows, and wildflowers. Forty-five minutes east of Mont Ventoux (about 16 miles), lavender fields forever surround the rock-top village of **Sault** (pronounced "soh"), which produces 40 percent of France's lavender essence.

Sault, a welcoming town in any season, goes unnoticed by most hurried travelers. It's a slow-down-and-smell-the-lavender kind of place, with a sociable "mountain market" on Wednesdays.

There's no reason to sleep in Sault, but it's a fine place for lunch or *un café*. **La Promenade** café has simple salads and grilled meats with territorial valley views (daily mid-April-mid-Sept, closed Sun off-season, tel. 04 90 64 13 29). Or enjoy the same views with a picnic in the adjacent, tree-lined area, the "promenade."

Getting to Mont Ventoux: Two roads lead to the peak of Mont Ventoux, both of which have small ski stations at 4,600 feet (about 4 miles from the top); Mont Serein station is on the north and Chalet Reynard station is on the south. The mountain pass between these stations (Col de Mont Ventoux), including the summit, is closed annually due to snow and ice from mid-November to mid-April (sometimes later for the north road). Confirm that the pass is open before you leave.

To reach Mont Ventoux from Vaison-la-Romaine, drive to Malaucène (15 minutes), then wind up D-974 for 45 minutes to the top. Another option is to drive around the base of the Mont, over the Col de la Madeleine (follow signs from Maulaucène) and through the quaint village of Bédoin (good Monday market); from there D-974 leads to the south road and offers a much longer, but perhaps prettier route to the top. If continuing to Sault (a worthwhile detour when the lavender blooms) or on to the Luberon (worthwhile anytime—see next chapter), follow signs to *Sault,* then *Gordes.* The *Les Routes de la Lavande* brochure suggests driving and walking routes in the area (available online at www.routeslavande.com).

DROME PROVENCALE LOOP DRIVE

This meander north into the Drôme Provençale is overkill for many, as the scenery is only subtly different than what you'll see closer to your hotel. But if you haven't had your fill of pretty vistas, this drive is away from popular tourist areas and combines rugged scenery with overlooked towns and villages (see map on page 148). I'd only do it on Thursdays, when it's market day in Nyons, or on Wednesdays, when it's market day in Buis-les-Barronies. Allow most of a day for this up-and-down, curve-filled drive, particularly if the market in Nyons is on. Or you can just do Nyons and call it a day.

From Vaison-la-Romaine, drive to **Nyons,** an attractive mid-size town set along a river and against the hills. Here you'll find a Roman bridge with views, an olive mill, a lavender distillery, a handful of walking streets, and an arcaded square—all with few tourists. Nyons is famous for its rollicking Thursday market (until 12:30) and for producing France's best olives, which you can taste at its well-organized *coopérative* (daily 9:00-12:30 & 14:00-19:00, closes at 18:00 on Sun, interesting museum about olives, on Place Olivier de Serres, tel. 04 75 26 95 00).

From Nyons, head for the hills following signs to *Gap* on D-94, then follow signs to *Ste-Jalles* on D-64. Little Ste-Jalles hovers above the road, with a pretty Romanesque church (usually closed), two cafés (Café de Lavande overhangs the river, providing a fine backdrop for a drink, lunch, or a snack), and a small winery making crisp whites and easy reds (Domaine de Rieu Frais, daily 10:00-12:00 & 14:00-18:00, closed Sun in winter, tel. 04 75 27 31 54, www.domaine-du-rieu-frais.com, jean-yves.liotaud@wanadoo. fr, best to call ahead and let them know you're coming).

From Ste-Jalles, cross the bridge following D-108 and *Buis-les-Barronnies* signs, and start your ascent over the rocky mountains. Prepare for miles of curves, territorial views, and no guardrails. Drop down (er, drive down) and meet the Ouvèze river, then follow it into bustling **Buis-les-Barronnies** (with all the services, including a slew of cafés and an attractive old town to stroll). Buis-les-Barronnies is the linden tree capital of France and hosts an earthy outdoor market on Wednesdays with produce and crafts.

From Buis-les-Barronnies, continue south on D-5, then turn left toward Eygaliers on D-72. Follow this slow, serpentine road along the back side of Mont Ventoux and go all the way to the jewel of this trip: **Brantes,** one of Provence's most spectacularly located villages. Stop here for some fresh air and a look at the local pottery.

Finally, follow signs back to Vaison-la-Romaine along the faster, less curvy D-40. A few minutes before Vaison-la-Romaine, you'll pass through pleasing little Entrechaux.

▲ARDECHE GORGES (GORGES DE L'ARDECHE)

These gorges, which wow visitors with abrupt chalky-white cliffs, follow the Ardèche River through immense canyons and thick forests. To reach the gorges from Vaison-la-Romaine, drive west 1.5 hours, passing through Bollène and Pont Saint-Esprit to **Vallon-Pont-d'Arc** (the tourist hub of the Ardèche Gorges). From Vallon-Pont-d'Arc, you can canoe along the peaceful river through some of the canyon's most spectacular scenery and under the rock arch of Pont d'Arc (half-day, all-day, and 2-day trips possible; less appealing in summer, when the river is crowded and water levels are low), and learn about hiking trails that get you above it all (**TI** tel. 04 75 88 04 01, www.vallon-pont-darc.com).

The Ardèche region is a hot destination, thanks to the 2015 opening of a replica of one of France's largest and most impressive prehistoric caves, the **Chauvet Pont-d'Arc,** just outside the village of Vallon-Pont-d'Arc. Not discovered until 1994, the cave holds the oldest and best preserved man-made images anywhere (some date back over 36,000 years). The original cave is closed to the public, but the full-scale replica reproduces its art and artifacts, using cutting-edge techniques to create the same feeling that seeing the original cave inspires (for details on how to visit, see http://en.cavernedupontdarc.fr, http://lacavernedupontdarc.org/en/, or call 04 75 37 17 68).

If continuing north toward Lyon, connect Privas and Aubenas, then head back on the autoroute. Endearing little **Balazuc**— a village north of the gorges, with narrow lanes, flowers, views, and a smattering of cafés and shops—makes a great stop.

COTES DU RHONE

HILL TOWNS OF THE LUBERON

France's Answer to Italy's Tuscany

Just 30 miles east of Avignon, the Luberon region hides some of France's most captivating hill towns and sensuous landscapes. Those intrigued by Peter Mayle's best-selling *A Year in Provence* love joyriding through the region, connecting I-could-live-here villages, crumbled castles, and meditative abbeys. Mayle's book, which marked its 25th anniversary in 2015, describes the ruddy local culture from an Englishman's perspective as he buys a stone farmhouse, fixes it up, and adopts the region as his new home. *A Year in Provence* is a great read while you're here—or, better, get it as an audiobook and listen while you drive.

The Luberon terrain in general (much of which is a French regional natural park) is as enticing as its villages. Gnarled vineyards and wind-sculpted trees separate tidy stone structures from abandoned buildings—little more than rock piles—that challenge city slickers to fix them up. Mountains of limestone bend along vast ridges, while colorful hot-air balloons survey the scene from above. The wind is an integral part of life here. The infamous mistral wind, finishing its long ride in from Siberia, hits like a hammer (see the sidebar on page 171).

PLANNING YOUR TIME

There are no obligatory museums, monuments, or vineyards in the Luberon. Treat this area like a vacation from your vacation. Downshift your engine. Brake for views, and lose your car to take a walk. Get on a first-name basis with a village.

To enjoy the ambience of the Luberon, you'll want at least one night and a car (only Isle-sur-la-Sorgue—and, to a lesser extent, Lourmarin—are accessible by train or bus). Allow a half-day for Isle-sur-la-Sorgue if it's market day (less time if not). Add more

Luberon

To Carpentras — D-938
To Mont Ventoux
Murs ❻
ABBEY DE SENANQUE
To Avignon — D-901
D-31
Isle-sur-la-Sorgue
Fontaine-de-Vaucluse
D-102
❺
Joucas
D-31
D-901
Gordes
D-2
BORIES ■
Lagnes
St-Pantaléon
D-900
❶
❶
Coustellet
❶❹ D-103
A-7
D-938
Goult
5 Kilometers
Cavaillon
D-2
D-3
Oppède-le-Vieux ❾
5 Miles
D-973
Ménerbes
Lacoste
A-7
ABBEY ST. HILAIRE
To St-Rémy & Les Baux — D-99
To Aix & Marseille
To Aix & Marseille

❶ Sous l'Olivier Chambres
❷ Le Mas d'Estonge Chambres
❸ Hôtel les Sables d'Ocre
❹ Le Clos des Cigales Chambres
❺ Hostellerie des Commandeurs
❻ Le Mas du Loriot Hôtel
❼ Hotel le Clos du Buis
❽ Mas del Sol Chambres

time if you want to paddle the Sorgue River or pedal between villages. You'll also want at least a full day for the Luberon villages.

For the ultimate Luberon experience, drivers should base themselves in or near Roussillon. To lose the tourists, set up in Oppède-le Vieux, St-Saturnin-lès-Apt, or Buoux.

If you lack wheels or prefer streams to hills and like a little more action, stay in Isle-sur-la-Sorgue, located within striking distance of Avignon and on the edge of the Luberon. Adequate train service from Avignon and Marseille, and some bus service, connects Isle-sur-la-Sorgue with the real world. Level terrain, quiet, tree-lined roads, and nearby villages make Isle-sur-la-Sorgue good for biking.

The village of Lourmarin works as a southern base for visiting Luberon sights, as well as Aix-en-Provence, Cassis, and Marseille. Determined travelers can take a bus from Avignon or Aix-en-Provence to reach Lourmarin.

GETTING AROUND THE LUBERON

By Car: Luberon roads are scenic and narrow. With no major landmarks, it's easy to get lost in this area—and you will get lost—but getting lost is the point. Consider buying the Michelin map #332 or #527 to navigate, and look for a copy of the free *Carte Touristique du Pays d'Apt* at local TIs.

LUBERON

To Mont Ventoux

D-943
St-Saturnin-lès-Apt
11
D-2
10
Rustrel
2
D-943
D-227
Roussillon
LE COLORADO PROVENCAL
D-33
4 **3**
D-4
D-22
D-209
Viens
Apt
D-190
To Grand Canyon du Verdon →
Le Chêne
St-Martin
D-900
JULIEN BRIDGE
Saignon
D-900
13
D-943
Buoux
8 **7**
12
Bonnieux
Fort de Buoux
D-943
LUBERON
Lourmarin

Paris
FRANCE
100 Miles

9 Petit Café & Chambres		**12** L'Auberge des Seguins
10 Mas Perréal Chambres & Moulin à Huile Jullien		**13** Château de la Canorgue Winery
11 Hôtel des Voyageurs		**14** Moulin Saint Augustin Shop

If connecting this region with the **Côtes du Rhône,** avoid driving through Carpentras (terrible traffic, confusing signage). If you're in a hurry, use the autoroute between Cavaillon and Orange. If time is not an issue, drive via Mont Ventoux—one of Provence's most spectacular routes (see end of previous chapter).

By Bus: Isle-sur-la-Sorgue is connected with Avignon's town center by the Raoux-TransVaucluse bus line #6 (€2 one-way, 6-8/day Mon-Sat, 3-4/day Sun, 45 minutes, central stop near post office in Isle-sur-la-Sorgue, ask for schedule at TI or download French-only schedule from www.voyages-raoux.fr/lignes/index.php). Buses link Lourmarin with Avignon (3/day, 1.5 hours, transfer in Cavaillon) and Aix-en-Provence (3/day, 1.25 hours, transfer in Pertuis, www.pacamobilite.fr), making it a workable village stop between these cities. Without a car or minivan tour, skip the more famous hill towns of the Luberon.

By Train: Trains get you to Isle-sur-la-Sorgue (station called "L'Isle-Fontaine de Vaucluse") from Avignon (10/day on weekdays, 5/day on weekends, 30 minutes) or from Marseille (8/day, 1.5 hours). If you're day-tripping by train, check return times before leaving the station.

By Minivan Tour: I list several minivan tour companies and private guides who can guide you through this marvelous region (see "Tours in Provence" on page 26).

LUBERON

By Taxi: Contact **Luberon Taxi** (based in Maubec off D-3, mobile 06 08 49 40 57, www.luberontaxi.com, contact@ luberontaxi.com).

By Bike: Hardy bikers can ride from Isle-sur-la-Sorgue to Gordes, then to Roussillon, connecting other villages in a full-day loop ride (30 miles round-trip to Roussillon and back, with lots of hills). Several appealing villages are closer to Isle-sur-la-Sorgue (see page 197). **Vélo Services** can help you plan a route and will deliver a rental bike anywhere in the Luberon (see "Isle-sur-la-Sorgue—Helpful Hints," later). **Sun-e-Bike,** based in Bonnieux and St-Rémy-de-Provence, rents electric bikes and has a network of partners with spare batteries scattered across the Luberon, extending the range of your e-bike trip. They can also arrange bike tours and shuttle your bags between hotels (1 Avenue Clovis Hugues in Bonnieux, tel. 04 90 74 09 96, www.location-velo-provence.com).

LUBERON AREA MARKET DAYS

Monday: Cavaillon (produce and antiques/flea market)
Tuesday: Gordes, St-Saturnin-lès-Apt, and Lacoste (all small)
Wednesday: Sault (produce and antiques/
   flea market)

Thursday: Roussillon (cute) and Isle-sur-la-Sorgue (good, but smaller than its Sunday market)
Friday: Lourmarin (very good) and Bonnieux (pretty good)
Saturday: Apt (huge produce and antiques/flea market)
Sunday: Isle-sur-la-Sorgue (granddaddy of them all, produce and antiques/flea market) and Coustellet (very good and less touristy)

Isle-sur-la-Sorgue

This sturdy market town—literally, "Island on the Sorgue River"—sits within a split in its crisp, happy little river. It's a workaday town that feels refreshingly real after so many adorable villages. It also makes a good base for exploring the Luberon (15 minutes by car, doable by hardy bikers) and Avignon (30 minutes by car or train) and can work for exploring the Côtes du Rhône by car (allow an hour to Vaison-la-Romaine).

After the arid cities and villages elsewhere in Provence, the presence of water at every turn is a welcome change. In Isle-sur-la-Sorgue—called the "Venice of Provence"—the Sorgue River's extraordinarily clear and shallow flow divides like cells, producing water, water everywhere. The river has long nourished the region's economy. The fresh spring water of the Sorgue's many branches has provided ample fish, irrigation for crops, and power for local industries for centuries. Today, antique shops power the town's economy—every other shop seems to sell some kind of antique.

Orientation to Isle-sur-la-Sorgue

Although Isle-sur-la-Sorgue is renowned for its market days (Sun and Thu), it's an otherwise pleasantly average town with no important sights and a steady trickle of tourism. It's lively on weekends, calm most weeknights, and dead on Mondays. The town revolves around its river, the church square, and two pedestrian-only streets, Rue de la République and Rue Carnot.

Tourist Information: The TI has information on hiking, biking itineraries, and a line on rooms in private homes, all of which are outside town (April-Sept Mon-Sat 9:00-12:30 & 14:30-18:00, Sun 9:00-12:30, Oct-March Mon-Sat 9:00-12:30 & 14:00-17:30, Sun 9:00-12:30; Wi-Fi, in town center next to church, tel. 04 90 38 04 78, www.oti-delasorgue.fr).

ARRIVAL IN ISLE-SUR-LA-SORGUE

By Car: Traffic is a mess and parking is a headache on market days (all day Sun and Thu mornings). Circle the ring road and look for parking signs. There are several lots just west of the roundabout at Le Bassin (see map on page 194). You'll also pass freestyle parking on roads leaving the city. Don't leave anything visible in your car.

By Train: Remember that the train station is called "L'Isle-Fontaine de Vaucluse." To reach my recommended hotels, walk straight out of the station and turn right on the ring road.

By Bus: The bus from Avignon drops you near the post office (PTT, ask driver for "*luh pay-tay-tay*"), a block from the recommended Hôtel les Névons.

HELPFUL HINTS

Shop Hours: The antique shops this town is famous for are open Friday afternoon to Monday only.

Laundry: A *laverie automatique* is in the town center, just off **Rue de la République** on Impasse de l'Hôtel de Palerme (open 24/7). Another, perhaps easier for drivers, is at the **Centre**

Commercial Super U supermarket (daily 9:00-19:00, on the ring road at the roundabout, Cours Fernande Peyre).

Supermarket: A well-stocked **Utile** market is on the main ring road, near the Peugeot Car shop and the train station (Mon-Sat 8:30-20:00, Sun 8:30-13:00). A smaller, more central **Casino** market is on pedestrian Rue de la République (Tue-Sun 7:30-12:30 & 15:30-19:30, closed Mon).

Bike Rental: Vélo Services, run by helpful David Bollack, is at 3 Rue Docteur Tallet, but he can deliver bikes just about anywhere and help plan your trip. He has dozens of free downloadable maps and route ideas in English (€15-30/day depending on bike, also has electric bikes; daily, mobile 06 38 14 49 50, http://veloservices.jimdo.com). **Luberon Biking,** in the nearby village of Velleron, can also deliver bikes (daily, tel. 04 90 90 14 62, www.luberon-biking.fr).

Taxi: Try **Luberon Taxi** (tel. 04 90 76 70 08, mobile 06 08 49 40 57, www.luberontaxi.com).

Public WC: A WC is in the parking lot between the post office (PTT) and the Hôtel les Névons.

Hiking: The TI has good information on area hikes; most trails are accessible by short drives, and you can use a taxi to get there.

Isle-sur-la-Sorgue Walk

The town has crystal-clear water babbling under pedestrian bridges stuffed with flower boxes, and its old-time carousel is always spinning. For this self-guided wander (shown on the map on page 194), navigate by the town's splintered streams and nine mossy waterwheels, which, while still turning, power only memories of the town's wool and silk industries.

• *Start your tour at the church next to the TI—where all streets seem to converge—and make forays into the town from there. Go first to the church.*

Notre-Dame des Anges: This 12th-century church has a festive Baroque interior and feels too big for today's town. Walk in. The curls and swirls and gilded statues date from an era that was all about Louis XIV, the Sun King. This is propagandist architecture, designed to wow the faithful into compliance. (It was made possible thanks to profits generated from the town's river-powered industries.) When you enter a church like this, the heavens should open up and assure you that whoever built it had celestial connections (daily 10:00-12:00 & 15:15-17:00, Mass on Sun at 10:30).

Outside the church, notice the buildings' faded facades around you, recalling their previous lives (*fabrique de chaussures* was a shoemaker; *meubles* means furniture; *3 étages d'exposition* means 3 showroom floors). Admire Fauque Beyret's antique facade. Isle-sur-la-Sorgue retains a connection to its past uncommon in this renovation-happy region.

• *For a reality check, head into the town's historic (though less polished) side. Wander down Rue Danton, the narrow street to the right of the* meubles *sign, to lose the crowds. Keep going until you see an Irish pub and find...*

Three Waterwheels: These big, forgotten waterwheels have been in business here since the 1200s, when they were first used

for grinding flour. Paper, textile, silk, and woolen mills would later find their power from this river. At its peak, Isle-sur-la-Sorgue had 70 waterwheels; in the 1800s, the town competed with Avignon as Provence's cloth-dyeing and textile center. Those stylish Provençal fabrics and patterns you see for sale everywhere were made possible by this river.

• *Double back to the church, turn left under the arcade, then find the small stream just past the TI. Breakaway streams like this run under the town like subways run under Paris. Take a right on the first street after the stream; it leads under a long arch (along Rue J. J. Rousseau). Look up for more faded facades (*bains, douches, *and* chambres meublées *means baths, showers, and furnished rooms). Follow this straight, and veer slightly right at Place F. Buisson onto Place Rose Goudard (likely crowded with parked cars), and walk to the main river. Then turn left and walk along the many café terraces until you come to...*

Le Bassin: Literally translated as a "pond," this is where the Sorgue River crashes into the town and separates into many branches. Track as many branches as you can see (Frank Provost hides a big one), and then find the round lookout point for the best perspective (carefully placed lights make this a beautiful sight after dark). Fishing was the town's main industry until the waterwheels took over. In the 1300s, local fishermen provided the pope with his fresh-fish quota. They trapped them in nets and speared them while standing on skinny, flat-bottomed boats. Several streets are named after the fish they caught—including Rue de l'Aiguille ("Eel Street") and Rue des Ecrevisses ("Crayfish Street").

The sound of the rushing water reminds us of the power that rivers can generate. With its source (a spring) a mere five miles away, the Sorgue River never floods and has a constant flow and temperature in all seasons. Despite its exposed (flat) location, Isle-sur-la-Sorgue prospered in the Middle Ages, thanks to the natural protection this river provided. Walls with big moats once ran along the river, but they were destroyed during the French Revolution.

• *Cross the busy roundabout, and walk to the neon orange* **Delices**

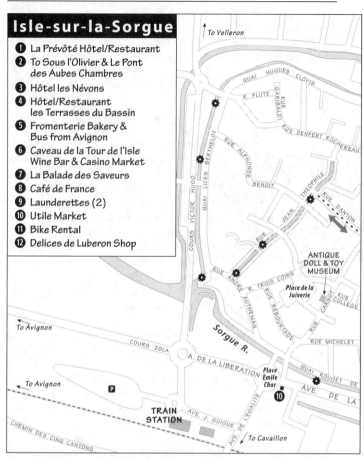

Isle-sur-la-Sorgue

1. La Prévôté Hôtel/Restaurant
2. To Sous l'Olivier & Le Pont des Aubes Chambres
3. Hôtel les Névons
4. Hôtel/Restaurant les Terrasses du Bassin
5. Fromenterie Bakery & Bus from Avignon
6. Caveau de la Tour de l'Isle Wine Bar & Casino Market
7. La Balade des Saveurs
8. Café de France
9. Launderettes (2)
10. Utile Market
11. Bike Rental
12. Delices de Luberon Shop

de Luberon store. *Find the small tasting table with 12 scrumptious tapenades. Walk behind the store to find the river and take a refreshing...*

Riverfront Stroll: Follow the main river upstream, along the bike/pedestrian lane, as far as you like. The little road meanders about a mile, following the serene course of the river, past waterfront homes and beneath swaying trees. It ends at the Hôtel le Pescador and a riverfront café. The wide and shallow Partage des Eaux, where the water divides before entering Isle-sur-la-Sorgue, is perfect for a cool swim on a hot day.

Activities and Sights in Isle-sur-la-Sorgue

▲▲Market Days

The town erupts into a carnival-like market frenzy each Sunday and Thursday, with hardy crafts and local produce. The Sunday market is astounding and famous for its antiques; the Thursday market is more intimate and focused more on produce than antiques (see market tips in the Shopping chapter). Find a table across from the church at the Café de France and enjoy the scene.

Antique Toy and Doll Museum
(Musée du Jouet et de la Poupée Ancienne)

The town's lone sight is a fun and funky toy museum with more than 300 dolls displayed in three small rooms. Most dolls date from 1880 to 1930.

Cost and Hours: €3.50, kids-€1.50; July-Sept daily 11:00-18:00; May-June daily 14:00-18:00; shorter hours and closed Mon off-season; call ahead to confirm opening times, at 26 Rue Carnot down a short alley, www.poupeesdelisle.com.

LUBERON

NEAR ISLE-SUR-LA-SORGUE
Fontaine-de-Vaucluse

You'll read and hear a lot about this overrun village, impressively located at the source of the Sorgue River, where the medieval Italian poet Petrarch mourned for his love, Laura. The river seems to magically appear from nowhere (the actual source is a murky, green waterhole) and flows through the town past a lineup of cafés, souvenir shops, and wall-to-river tourists. The setting is beautiful—with cliffs jutting to the sky and a ruined castle above—but the trip is worth it only if the spring is flowing. *Sans* flowing spring, this is the most overrated sight in France. Ask your hotelier if the spring is active, and arrive early or late to avoid crowds. It's a good bike ride here from Isle-sur-la-Sorgue (about four miles).

Arriving by car, you'll pay to park (€4), and then walk about 20 minutes along the sparkling river to *la source* (the spring), located in a cave at the base of the cliff. (It's an uphill hike for the last part.) The spring itself is the very definition of anticlimactic, unless it's surging. At those times, it's among the most prolific water producers in the world, with a depth no one has yet been able to determine.

The path to the spring is lined with distractions. The only stops worth your time are the riverfront cafés and restaurants—**Philip's** offers the best seats—and the **Moulin à Papier,** a reproduction of a 17th-century paper mill. Here you'll see the value of harnessing the river's power. In the mill, a 22-foot-diameter paddle wheel turns five times a minute, driving hammers that pound paper for up to 36 hours (free, daily 9:00-19:00). As you watch the hammers pound away, imagine Isle-sur-la-Sorgue's waterwheels and the industries they once powered. The shop inside sells paper in every size.

Canoe Trips on the Sorgue

A better way to travel to Fontaine-de-Vaucluse is to canoe down the river. If you're *really* on vacation, take this five-mile, two-hour trip. The guide escorts small groups in canoes (or you can go it alone), starting in Fontaine-de-Vaucluse and ending in Isle-sur-la-Sorgue; you'll return to Fontaine-de-Vaucluse by shuttle bus (call for departure times; ask about shuttle service from Isle-sur-la-Sorgue). The company, **Kayaks Verts,** is a family operation (late April-mid-Oct, €18/person, tel. 04 90 20 35 44, www.canoe-france.com/en/sorgue). To combine bike and boat, ask about shuttling your rental bikes back to Isle-sur-la-Sorgue while you float from Fontaine-de-Vaucluse (see suggested bike route below).

Biking

Isle-sur-la-Sorgue is ideally situated for short biking forays into the mostly level terrain. Pick up a biking itinerary at the TI, or consult with David at Vélo Services (see "Helpful Hints," earlier). These towns make easy biking destinations from Isle-sur-la-Sorgue: **Velleron** (5 flat miles north, a tiny version of Isle-sur-la-Sorgue with waterwheels, fountains, and an evening farmers' market Mon-Sat 18:00-20:00); **Lagnes** (3 miles east, a pretty and well-restored hill town with views from its ruined château); and **Fontaine-de-Vaucluse** (5 gently uphill miles northeast, described earlier). Allow 30 miles and many hills for the round-trip ride to Roussillon.

Sleeping in and near Isle-sur-la-Sorgue

Pickings are slim for good sleeps in Isle-sur-la-Sorgue, though the few I've listed provide solid values.

$$$ La Prévôté*** has the town's highest-priced digs. Its five meticulously decorated rooms—located above a classy restaurant—are adorned in earth tones, with high ceilings, a few exposed beams, and carefully selected furnishings. Séverine manages the hotel while chef-hubby Jean-Marie controls the kitchen (standard Db-€150, larger Db-€180, suite Db-€225, includes breakfast, cheaper for longer stays, limited times for check-in and check-out, no elevator, rooftop deck with Jacuzzi, no parking, one block from the church at 4 Rue J. J. Rousseau, tel. 04 90 38 57 29, www.la-prevote.fr, contact@la-prevote.fr).

$$$ Sous l'Olivier is 10 minutes from Isle-sur-la-Sorgue, off D-900 near Petit Palais. Here big Julien, quiet Carole, and sons Hugo and Clovis adopt you into their sprawling old stone farmhouse, with grass to burn, a big pool, yards of chairs and lounges, and views to the Luberon range. The six rooms are big but lack air-conditioning. Dinner is a family affair, worth every euro (Db-€110-140, Tb-€150-190, three apartments available, dinner-€34,

---

Sleep Code

| **Abbreviations** | (€1=about $1.10, country code: 33) |

S=Single, **D**=Double/Twin, **T**=Triple, **Q**=Quad, **b**=bathroom, *=French hotel rating (0-5 stars)

Price Rankings

$$$ **Higher Priced**—Most rooms €95 or more
$$ **Moderately Priced**—Most rooms €60-95
$ **Lower Priced**—Most rooms €60 or less

Unless otherwise noted, credit cards are accepted, English is spoken, breakfast and city tax are not included, and Wi-Fi is free. Prices change; verify current rates online or by email. For the best prices, always book directly with the hotel.

LUBERON

cash only, tel. 04 90 20 33 90, www.chambresdhotesprovence.com, souslolivier@orange.fr). Heading east on D-900, go 200 yards past the sign to *Mas du Jonquier*.

$$ Le Pont des Aubes Chambres has two huggable rooms in an old green-shuttered farmhouse right on the river a mile from town. Borrow a bike or a canoe. From here you can cross a tiny bridge and walk 15 minutes along the river into Isle-sur-la-Sorgue. Charming Martine speaks English, while husband Patrice speaks smiles (Db-€95, 1-room apartments-€500-600/week, cash only, a mile from town toward Apt, next to Pain d'Antan Boulangerie at 189 Route d'Apt, tel. 04 90 38 13 75, www.lepontdesaubes.com).

$$ Hôtel les Névons**, two blocks from the center (behind the post office), is concrete motel-modern outside, but has well-priced, comfortable rooms within and a roof deck with a small pool (standard Db-€75, Db with balcony-€85, big Db with terrace-€110, Tb-€130, Qb-€150, breakfast-€9, air-con, elevator, easy and safe parking, 205 Chemin des Névons, push and hold the gate button a bit on entry, tel. 04 90 20 72 00, www.hotel-les-nevons.com, info@hotel-les-nevons.com).

$$ Hôtel les Terrasses du Bassin's friendly owners Corinne and Gilles rent nine good-value rooms over a pleasant restaurant right on Le Bassin. Several rooms look out over the river, most have a little traffic noise, and a few have queen-size beds (Db-€63-90, Tb-€105, air-con, 2 Avenue Charles de Gaulle, tel. 04 90 38 03 16, www.lesterrassesdubassin.com, corinne@lesterrassesdubassin.com).

Eating in Isle-sur-la-Sorgue

Cheap and mediocre restaurants are a dime a dozen in Isle-sur-la-Sorgue. You'll see several brasseries on the river, good for views and basic café fare. The restaurants I list offer good values, but none of them is really "cheap." Dining on the river is a unique experience in this arid land, and shopping for the perfect table is half the fun. To assemble a riverside picnic, try the **Fromenterie bakery,** and head to **Rue de la République,** which has bakeries, butchers, a *traiteur* (deli), cheesemongers, a wine shop, and a supermarket.

Begin your dinner with a glass of wine (€3-5) at the cozy wine and cheese cellar **Caveau de la Tour de l'Isle.** Or for a light meal, order a selection of cheeses (€10-18, great to share) with your wine and call it good (a few tables outside or find the bar hiding in the rear behind the cheese counter and wine shop; Tue-Sun 9:30-12:30 & 15:30-20:00, closed Mon and Wed except in July-Aug; 12 Rue de la République, tel. 04 90 20 70 25).

Les Terrasses du Bassin is a sure riverside option with a brasserie-like feel, reasonable prices, and tasty choices. Come for a full meal or just a *plat,* and eat on the river if you can (€13-17 lunch salads and starters, €20 dinner *plats,* €22-26 dinner *menus,* closed Wed year-round and Tue off-season, 2 Avenue Charles de Gaulle, tel. 04 90 38 03 16, www.lesterrassesdubassin.com).

La Balade des Saveurs is a refreshing change from the many run-of-the-mill riverfront places. Here, Sophie and Benjamin deliver fresh, Provençal cuisine at riverside tables or in their elegantly sky-lit interior at fair prices. The asparagus soup with egg is a winning twist on a French classic (€27-38 three-course *menus,* daily, 3 Quai Jean Juarès, tel. 04 90 95 27 85, www.balade-des-saveurs.com).

La Prévôté is the place in town to do it up. Its lovely dining room is country-classy but not stuffy. A stream runs under the restaurant, visible through glass windows (€41-75 *menus,* closed Mon-Wed, on narrow street that runs along left side of church as you face it, 4 Rue J. J. Rousseau, tel. 04 90 38 57 29, www.la-prevote.fr).

The **Fromenterie** bakery next to the post office (PTT) sells decadent quiche, monster sandwiches, prepared salads, desserts, wine and other drinks, and even plastic cutlery and cups—in other words, everything you need to picnic (daily until 19:30, 19 Avenue des Quatre Otages).

The Heart of the Luberon

A 15-minute drive east of Isle-sur-la-Sorgue brings you to this protected area, where canyons and ridgelines rule, and land developers take a back seat. Still-proud hill towns guard access to winsome valleys, while carefully managed vineyards (producing inexpensive wines) play hopscotch with cherry groves, lavender fields, and cypress trees.

Twenty-some years ago, Peter Mayle's *A Year in Provence* nudged tourism in this area into overdrive. A visit to Mayle's quintessential Provence includes many of the popular villages and sights described in this chapter. While the hill towns can be seen as subtly different variations on the same theme, each has a distinct character. Look for differences: the color of shutters, the pattern of stones, the way flowers are planted, or the number of tourist boutiques. Every village has something to offer—it's up to you to discover and celebrate it.

Stay in or near Roussillon. By village standards, Roussillon is always lively, and it struggles to manage its popularity. When restaurant hunting, read descriptions of the villages in this chapter—many good finds are embedded in the countryside. For aerial views high above this charmed land, consider a hot-air balloon trip.

LUBERON

PLANNING YOUR TIME

With a car and one full day, I'd linger in Roussillon in the morning, visit the Julien Bridge, then have lunch nearby in Lacoste or Bonnieux. After lunch, continue the joyride via Ménerbes to Oppède-le-Vieux, then return through Coustellet and Gordes. With a second full day, I'd start by climbing the Fort de Buoux, then lunch nearby. After lunch, continue to Saignon and Viens, then loop back via Le Colorado Provençal and St-Saturnin-lès-Apt.

I've described sights at each stop, but you'll need to be selective—you can't (and don't need to) see them all. Read through your options and choose the ones that appeal most. Slow down and get to know a few places well, rather than dashing between every stop you can cram in. The best sight is the dreamy landscape between the villages.

Roussillon

With all the trendy charm of Santa Fe on a hilltop, photogenic Roussillon requires serious camera and café time. Roussillon has been a protected village since 1943 and has benefited from a complete absence of modern development. An enormous deposit of ochre, which gives the earth and its buildings that distinctive reddish color, provided this village with its economic base until shortly after World War II. This place is popular; it's best to visit early or late in the day.

Orientation to Roussillon

Roussillon sits atop Mont Rouge ("Red Mountain") at about 1,000 feet above sea level, and requires some uphill walking to reach. Exposed ochre cliffs form the village's southern limit.

TOURIST INFORMATION

The little TI is in the center, across from the Chez David restaurant. Hotel hunters can leaf through their binders describing area hotels and *chambres d'hôte*. Walkers should get info on trails from Roussillon to nearby villages (TI hours are unreliable, usually Mon-Sat April-Oct 9:30-12:30 & 14:00-18:00, Nov-March 14:00-17:30, closed Sun year-round, Place de la Poste, tel. 04 90 05 60 25, otroussillon.pagesperso-orange.fr).

Roussillon

1. Le Clos de la Glycine Hôtel & Chez David Restaurant
2. Hôtel Rêves d'Ocres
3. To Madame Cherel Chambres, Le Clos des Cigales Chambres & Hôtel les Sables d'Ocre
4. To Le Mas d'Estonge Chambres
5. La Grappe de Raisin Rest.
6. Le Comptoir des Arts Rest.
7. Le Bistrot de Roussillon, Café Couleur & Le Castrum Rest.
8. Croqu'la Vie Bookshop & Internet
9. Orientation Table, View & Start of Walk

ARRIVAL IN ROUSSILLON

Parking lots are available at every entry to the village (free if you're staying overnight and have arranged it with your hotel). **Parking des Ocres** (also called "P2") is the large lot on the hill toward the ochre cliffs. Day-trippers should head straight here, as spots are more available and the view of Roussillon is striking. Leave nothing of value visible in your car.

Parking Sablons is near the recommended Hôtel Rêves

d'Ocres. **Parking Pasquier** is closest to the village center, but has only 16 spots and a three-hour limit (avoid overnight parking here before market days).

HELPFUL HINTS

An **ATM** is next to the TI. Free **Wi-Fi** and a modest selection of English books are available at the delightful **Croqu'la Vie** bookshop on the main square (daily 10:00-18:00, later July-Sept, Place de la Mairie, tel. 04 90 71 55 72). Public **WCs** are uphill toward the ochre cliffs.

Roussillon Walk

This quick self-guided walk will take you through Roussillon's village to its ochre cliffs.
• *To begin the walk, climb from any parking lot to the village center, cross the adorable square, and then pass under the bell tower and the church). Continue past the church to the summit of...*

▲The Village

Find the orientation table and the **viewpoint,** often complete with a howling mistral wind. During the Middle Ages, a castle occupied this space on the top of the appropriately named Red Mountain (Mont Rouge), and watched over the village below. Though nothing remains of the castle today, the strategic advantage of this site is clear. Count how many villages you can identify, and then notice how little sprawl there is in the valley below. Because the Luberon has been declared a natural reserve (Parc Naturel Régional du Luberon), development is strictly controlled.

Stroll back to the **church.** Duck into the pretty 11th-century Church of St. Michel, and appreciate the natural air-conditioning and the well-worn center aisle. The white interior tells you that the stone came from elsewhere, and the WWI memorial plaque over the side door suggests a village devastated by the war (more than 40 people from little Roussillon died).

On leaving the church, look across the way to the derelict building, a reminder of Roussillon's humble roots. After World War II, when the demand for ochre faded, this was a dusty, desolate village with zero tourist appeal. Adding to the town's economic woes, many residents fled for an easier life below, with fewer steps and modern conveniences. Abandoned buildings like this

LUBERON

presented a serious problem (common throughout France)...until tourists discovered Roussillon, and folks began reinvesting in the village. This building is still looking for a buyer. Detour behind the building to the left down a small lane to find the Chemin de Ronde, with terrific views of the Luberon and Gordes from atop the medieval walls.

• *Return to the church and continue down to the village.*

Notice the clamped-iron beams that shore up old walls. Examine the different hues of yellow and orange. These lime-finished exteriors, called *chaux* (literally, "limes"), need to be redone about every 10 years. Locals choose their exact color...but in this town of ochre, it's never white. The church tower that you walk under once marked the entrance to the fortified town. Just before dropping down to the square, turn right and find the gigantic 150-year-old grapevine that decorates Restaurant la Treille. This is what you get when you don't prune.

Linger over *un café,* or—if it's later in the day—*un pastis,* in what must be the most picturesque village square in Provence

(Place de la Mairie). Watch the stream of shoppers. Is anyone playing *boules* at the opposite end? You could paint the entire town without ever leaving the red-and-orange corner of your palette. Many do. While Roussillon receives its share of daytrippers, mornings and evenings are romantically peaceful on this square. The Croqu'la Vie bookshop on the square's corner deserves a visit (see page 202).

• *With the cafés on your right, drop downhill past the lineup of shops and turn right past the TI to find the parking lot just beyond. Animals grazed here for centuries. It was later turned into a school playground.*

When tourists outnumbered students, it became a parking lot. Walk past the parking lot and head left uphill, hugging the cliffs to find the...

▲▲Ochre Cliffs Trail (Le Sentier des Ocres)

Roussillon was Europe's capital for ochre production until World War II. A stroll to the south end of town, beyond the upper parking lot, shows you why: Roussillon sits on the world's largest known ochre deposit. A radiant orange path leads around the richly colored, Bryce Canyon-like cliffs.

LUBERON

Ochre is made of iron oxide and clay. When combined with sand, it creates the yellowish-red pigments you see in these buildings. Although ochre is also produced in the US and Italy, the quality of France's ochre is considered *le best*.

The value of Roussillon's ochre cliffs was known even in Roman times. Once excavated, the clay ochre was rinsed with water to separate it from sand, then bricks of the stuff were dried and baked for deeper hues. The procedure for extracting the ochre did not change much over 2,000 years, until ochre mining became industrialized in the late 1700s. Used primarily for wallpaper and linoleum, ochre use reached its zenith just before World War II. (After that, cheaper substitutes took over.)

Cost and Hours: €2.50, €7.50 combo-ticket with Ochre Conservatory—described next; March-April and Oct 10:00-17:00, May-June and Sept 9:30-18:30, July-Aug 9:00-19:30, shorter hours off-season, closed Jan. Beware: Light-colored clothing (especially shoes) and orange powder don't mix.

Sights near Roussillon

▲Ochre Conservatory
(Conservatoire des Ocres et de la Couleur)

For a good introduction to the history and uses of ochre, visit this intriguing reconstructed ochre factory. Grab a pamphlet to follow the well-done self-guided tour, which shows how ochre is converted from an ore to a pigment (allow 45 minutes). Your visit ends with a great bookshop and a chance to try your hand at ochre painting.

Cost and Hours: €6.50, €7.50 combo-ticket with ochre cliffs, daily 9:00-18:00 but closed for lunch, July-Aug until 19:00, about a half-mile below Roussillon toward Apt on D-104, tel. 04 90 05 66 69, www.okhra.com.

Domaine de Tara

Just below Roussillon, on the road to Joucas, this welcoming winery has been making excellent wines for about 15 years. Pascale runs the tasting room, and her husband makes wines to please every palate: red, white, rosé, sparkling, and sweet. Pop into the barrel room where they occasionally exhibit local artists' work. They don't mind if you picnic on the property afterward.

Cost and Hours: Prices vary by wine, daily April-Oct 10:00-19:30, Nov-March and Wed until 18:00, tel. 04 90 05 74 87, www.domainedetara.com.

Hot-Air Balloon Flight

Ply the calm morning air above the Luberon in a hot-air balloon. The **Montgolfières-Luberon** outfit offers a flight that includes a picnic and champagne (€230, around 1 hour in balloon, allow 3 hours total, maximum 4 passengers, reserve a few days ahead, mobile 06 03 54 10 92, www.montgolfiere-luberon.com).

Goult

Bigger than its sister hill towns, this surprisingly quiet village seems content to be away from the tourist path. Explore the small lanes and wander up the hill to the panoramic view and windmill. Notice how many of the historic buildings are built right on top of thick rock strata. Consider having a nice meal in one of Goult's many good restaurants—where you won't have to compete with tourists for a table. **Aux Fines Herbes** is ideally situated just off the main square, and its food is affordable and tasty (*menus* from €29, closed all day Wed, closed Sat for lunch, Rue de la République, tel. 04 32 50 23 54). Trendier **La Bartavelle** is *the* place in town to dine, but is darn popular (book a table a week in advance, *menus* from €44, closed Tue-Wed, Rue du Cheval Blanc, tel. 04 90 72 33 72).

Sleeping in Roussillon

The TI posts a list of hotels and *chambres d'hôte*. Parking is free if you sleep in Roussillon; pre-arrange with your hotelier. The village offers three acceptable-value accommodations—conveniently, one for each price range.

$$$ Le Clos de la Glycine*** delivers Roussillon's plushest accommodations with nine lovely rooms located dead-center in the village (Db-€135-176, big Db-€190, loft suite with deck and view-€280, off-season deals, breakfast-€14, air-con, located at the recommended refined restaurant Chez David—they prefer you pay for half-pension, across from the TI on Place de la Poste, tel. 04 90 05 60 13, www.luberon-hotel.com, contact@luberon-hotel.fr).

$$ Hôtel Rêves d'Ocres** is well-located and provides a fair two-star value. Rooms are tastefully decorated, though the bathrooms could use updating. Eight smaller rooms under the roof have low ceilings and small terraces; I prefer the larger rooms on the second floor (Db without balcony-€85, Db with balcony-€90, Tb-€115, Qb-€140, meek air-con, Route de Gordes, tel. 04 90 05 60 50, www.hotel-revesdocres.com, hotelrevesdocres@wanadoo.fr). Coming from Gordes and Joucas, it's the first building you pass in Roussillon.

$ Madame Cherel rents bare-bones rooms with firm beds and a shared view terrace at fair rates (S-€41, D-€51, discounts for longer stays, cash only, includes basic breakfast, access to kitchenette, often closed in off-season, 3 blocks from upper parking lot, between Casino store and school, La Burlière, tel. 04 90 05 71 71, mulhanc@hotmail.com). Chatty and sincere Cherel speaks English and is a wealth of regional travel tips—spend some time here getting to know a woman who is *vraiment provençale*.

NEAR ROUSSILLON

These listings are for drivers only. The last two are most easily found by turning north off D-900 at the *Roussillon/Les Huguets* sign (the second turnoff to Roussillon coming from Avignon). Joucas and St-Saturnin-lès-Apt (both described later) also have good beds near Roussillon.

$$$ At Le Mas d'Estonge, charming Christiane and Robert ("call me Bob") welcome you into their little Provençal paradise in a small neighborhood 10 minutes from Roussillon. Their four well-furnished and comfy rooms share a sweet patio, a common kitchen, and a pool (Db-€90-135, suites-€165-190, 10 minutes from Roussillon on D-227, tel. 04 90 05 63 13, www.destonge. com, destonge@gmail.com).

$$$ Hôtel les Sables d'Ocre** offers 22 meticulously maintained, motel-esque rooms, a big pool, the greenest grass around, air-conditioning, and fair rates (four simple Sb/Db-€98-108, spring for the *"supérieur"* Db with garden balcony-€98-128, Db with private terrace-€98-148, half-pension available-€42/person, a half-mile from Roussillon toward Apt at intersection of D-108 and D-104, tel. 04 90 05 55 55, www.sablesdocre.com, sablesdocre@ orange.fr).

$$ Le Clos des Cigales is a good refuge run by friendly Philippe and his wife, Brigitte. Of their five blue-shuttered, stylish bungalows, two are doubles and three are two-room suites with tiny kitchenettes; all have private patios facing a big pool. When you arrive, you'll understand the name—the cacophony from the *cigales* (cicadas) is deafening (Db-€80-95, Tb/Qb suite-€100-125, includes breakfast, table tennis, hammock, 5 minutes from Roussillon toward Goult on D-104, tel. 04 90 05 73 72, www. leclosdescigales.com, philippe.lherbeil@wanadoo.fr).

Eating in Roussillon

Choose ambience over cuisine if dining in Roussillon, and enjoy any of the eateries on the main square. It's a festive place, where children twirl while parents dine, and dogs and cats look longingly for leftovers. Restaurants change with the mistral here—what's good one year disappoints the next. Consider my suggestions and go with what looks best (or look over my recommendations in other Luberon villages, like Goult, just a few minutes away by car). Look also at the hotels listed in Joucas (see "Sleeping and Eating in Joucas," later)—all offer quality cuisine at fair prices, just a few minutes' drive from Roussillon.

Luberon Restaurants Worth the Trip

Many of the restaurants in the countryside near Roussillon are worth a detour. Use the list below as a quick reference, then flip to the full descriptions of those that sound most appealing. All are within a 20-minute drive from Roussillon. Remember that Isle-sur-la-Sorgue is a manageable 30-minute drive from Roussillon.

For Dinner
Chez David, in Roussillon, offers cuisine as terrific as its views (daily; see below).

Hôtel des Voyageurs, in St-Saturnin-lès-Apt, is a local favorite (page 218).

L'Auberge de la Loube is the ultimate country/Provençal experience. Located in Buoux, it makes for a long after-dinner drive, so many prefer it for lunch (page 222).

Roussillon's village square offers a selection of reasonably priced places all sharing the same great atmosphere (open daily).

Aux Fines Herbes and **La Bartavalle,** both in overlooked Goult, offer fresh and fairly priced food (page 205).

Best Places to Lunch
Chez David, L'Auberge de la Loube, and Le Bistrot de Roussillon—listed for dinner, above—are also top lunch stops. Here are others to consider:

Le Terrail, in Bonnieux, serves good-enough cuisine on an outside terrace with stunning vistas (page 214).

Bar/Restaurant de France, in Lacoste, is an easygoing eatery with sensational view tables (page 215).

Le Petit Jardin Café, in remote Viens, offers an unpretentious lunch or dinner stop, with cozy interior tables and a garden terrace (page 220).

On Place de la Poste: **Chez David,** at the recommended hotel Le Clos de la Glycine (described earlier), is a good place to splurge. You can enjoy a fine meal on the terrace or from an interior window table with point-blank views over the ochre cliffs. The Provençal cuisine is as fabulous as the scenery (€33-53 *menus,* daily, Place de la Poste, tel. 04 90 05 60 13).

La Grappe de Raisin is a top choice, with a fine selection of salads and a house specialty of a simple but tasty plate of vegetables and fish served with aioli (€16.50 aioli plate, closed Wed except July-Aug, next to TI, tel. 04 90 71 38 06).

Le Comptoir des Arts offers fair prices and a fine view. Try the aioli platter smothered with veggies and fish, or the Provençal burger topped with ratatouille (Place du Pasquier, tel. 04 90 74 11 92).

LUBERON

On Place de la Mairie: These places on this atmospheric square offer similar ambience and value. At least one should be open.

Le Bistrot de Roussillon offers decent salads and *plats* for the right price. There's a breezy terrace in back and a comfy interior (€16 for a filling salad and dessert, €13-18 *plats,* daily, tel. 04 90 05 74 45). Or try **Café Couleur** and **Le Castrum,** which flank Le Bistrot de Roussillon.

Joucas

This understated, quiet, and largely overlooked village slumbers below the Gordes buzz. Vertical stone lanes with carefully arranged flowers and well-restored homes play host to aspiring Claude Monets and a smattering of locals. There's not much to do or see here, except eat, sleep, and just be. Joucas has one tiny grocery, a view café, one pharmacy, a good kids' play area, and one good-value accommodation option. Sleep here for a central location and utter silence. For views, walk past the little

fountain in the center and up the steep lanes as high as you want.

Several **hiking** trails leave from Joucas. Gordes and Roussillon are each three miles away, uphill. The three-mile hike up to the attractive village of Murs (which has several cafés/restaurants) is more scenic, though it's easier in the other direction (yellow signs point the way from the top of the village). You don't have to go far to enjoy the natural beauty on this trail.

Sleeping and Eating
in and near Joucas

$$ Hostellerie des Commandeurs** has simple, good-value rooms in the center of lovely little Joucas. It's kid-friendly, with a big pool and a sports field/play area next door. Ask for a south-facing room *(coté sud)* for the best views. All rooms have showers and air-conditioning (Db-€70-105, extra bed-€16, breakfast-€9.50, mini fridges, above park at village entrance, hotel open March-Oct, tel. 04 90 05 78 01, www.lescommandeurs.com, hostellerie@lescommandeurs.com). The traditional **restaurant** offers Provençal cuisine at fair prices (three-course *menus* from €23, succulent lamb, memorable crème brûlée with lavender, restaurant closed Wed). Village kids like to hang out around the bar's pool table.

Near Joucas: **$$$ Le Mas du Loriot,** a 10-minute drive up from town, is another worthwhile value. Here, the owners have carved the ideal escape out of an olive grove, with ten soothing rooms, private terraces, a generous pool, and home-cooked dinners—all at fair prices and with a view to remember (Db with view and terrace-€130-160, Db *sans* view and smaller terrace-€130, fine dinners available if you book ahead, on D-102 between Joucas and Murs, tel. 04 90 72 62 62, www.masduloriot.com).

More Luberon Towns

Le Luberon is packed with appealing villages and beautiful scenery, but it has only a handful of must-see sights. I've grouped them by area to make your sightseeing planning easier (see the Luberon map at the beginning of this chapter). The D-900 highway cuts the Luberon in half like an arrow. The more popular and visited section lies above D-900 (with Roussillon and Gordes), while the villages to the south seem a bit less trampled.

The busiest sights are in and near Gordes; I've listed those first, to encourage you to avoid afternoon crowds. Beyond that, you're free to connect the stops however you please. Rambling the Luberon's spaghetti network of small roads is a joy, and getting lost comes with the territory—go with it. None of the sights listed below is a must-see, but all are close to each other. Pick up a good map (Michelin maps #332 and #527 work for me).

Gordes

The Luberon's most impressively situated hill town is worth a quick stop to admire its setting. As you approach Gordes, make a hard

right at the striking viewpoint. Get out and consider this: In the 1960s Gordes was a virtual ghost town of derelict buildings where locals led simple lives and had few ambitions. Then came the theater festival in Avignon, bringing directors who wanted to re-create perfect Provençal villages on film. Parisians, Swiss, Brits, and a few Americans followed, willing to pay any price for their place in the Provençal sun.

Today Gordes is renovated top to bottom and filled with people who live in a world without calluses. Many Parisian big-shots and moneyed foreigners invested heavily, restoring dream homes and putting property values and café prices out of sight for locals.

LUBERON

Between the village's natural beauty and the boutiques that followed the money, expect gridlock and parking headaches in high season (arrive early and pay €4 to park a 10- to 15-minute walk from the village). Beyond its stunning views, the village has little of interest except for its Tuesday market (until 13:00) and its 11th-century castle, which houses contemporary art exhibits.

NEAR GORDES

The first two sights—the Abbey Notre-Dame de Sénanque and the Village des Bories—are both well-marked from Gordes.

Abbey Notre-Dame de Sénanque

This still-functioning and beautifully situated Cistercian abbey was built in 1148 as a back-to-basics reaction to the excesses of Benedictine abbeys. The Cistercians

strove to be separate from the world and to recapture the simplicity, solitude, and poverty of the early Church. To succeed required industrious self-sufficiency—a skill these monks excelled at. Their movement spread and colonized Europe with a new form of Christianity. By 1200 there were more than 500 such monasteries and abbeys in Europe.

Cost and Hours: €8, with or without the French-only tour (mandatory Feb-Oct after 11:00), reservations strongly recommended, call or check website for tour times (tel. 04 90 72 05 72, www.senanque.fr). You can also attend Mass (Mon-Sat at 11:45, Sun at 10:00, check website or call to confirm).

Dress Code: Appropriate clothing is required for entry—shoulders and knees must be covered.

Tours: Those arriving just when the abbey opens find a peaceful place they can tour on their own (good English handout). Those arriving after 11:00 must visit the abbey on a 50-minute, French-only tour (English booklet with translations available).

Visting the Abbey: The abbey is best appreciated from the outside, and is worth the trip for its splendid and remote setting alone. Come first thing, or linger later and stop at a pullout for a bird's-eye view as you descend, then wander the abbey's perimeter. The abbey church (Eglise Abbatiale) is always open (except during Mass, but you're welcome to attend) and highlights the utter simplicity sought by these monks. In late June through much of July, the five hectares of lavender fields that surround the abbey make for breathtaking pictures and draw loads of visitors.

The tour covers Sénanque's church, the small cloisters, the refectory, and a *chauffoir,* a small heated room where monks could copy books year-round. The interior, which doesn't measure up to the abbey's spectacular setting, is a let-down—skip the tour and just wander the grounds.

A small monastic community still resides here. For more on monasteries, see the sidebar.

Leaving the Abbey: If your next destination is near Roussillon, Bonnieux, or Apt, leave the abbey opposite the way you arrived, following signs to *Gordes,* then *Roussillon,* then follow *Murs* and *Joucas*...and enjoy the ride.

Village des Bories

A twisting, mile-long, stone-bordered dirt road sets the mood for this mildly entertaining open-air museum of stone huts *(bories).* The vertical stones you see on the walls as you approach the site were used as counterweights to keep these mortar-free walls intact. The "village" you tour is made up of dry-laid stone structures, proving that there has always been more stone than wood in this rugged region. Stone villages like this predated the Romans—some say by 2,000 years. This one was inhabited for 200 years (from about 1600 to 1800). *Bories* can still be seen in fields throughout the Luberon; most are now used to store tools or hay.

The Village des Bories is composed of five "hamlets." Start with the short film (English subtitles), then duck into several homes and see animal pens, a community oven, and more (identified in English). Study the "beehive" stone-laying method and imagine the time it took to construct. The villagers had no scaffolds or support arches—just hammers and patience.

Cost and Hours: €7, buy €4 booklet of English translations to learn more, daily June-Sept 9:00-20:00, Oct-May 9:00-17:30, tel. 04 90 72 03 48.

Olive Oil Mills with Tastings

The following two places give quick and free tastings with basic explanations, but are only really worth the time if you pass them en route to something else.

Moulin à Huile Jullien is a small, family operation making *"bio"* (organic) oils using modern equipment. Chantal speaks some English, and the hand-drawn signs do a good job of explaining the machinery (April-June 10:00-12:00 & 14:00-18:00, July-Aug 10:00-12:00 & 15:00-19:00, shorter hours and closed Sun off-season, near recommended Mas Perréal—a half-mile downhill from St-Saturnin-lès-Apt, on Route d'Apt, tel. 04 90 75 56 24, www.moulin-huile-jullien.com).

Moulin Saint Augustin, originally a 16th-century flour mill, on the busy D-900 just east of Coustellet, is a property with centu-

LUBERON

Medieval Monasteries

France is littered with medieval monasteries, and Provence is no exception. Most have virtually no furnishings (they never had many), which leaves the visitor with little to reconstruct what life must have been like in these cold stone buildings a thousand years ago. A little history can help breathe life into these important yet underappreciated monuments.

After the fall of the Roman Empire, monasteries arose as refuges of peace and order in a chaotic world. While the pope got rich and famous playing power politics, monasteries worked to keep the focus on simplicity and poverty. Throughout the Middle Ages, monasteries were mediators between Man and God. In these peacefully remote abbeys, Europe's best minds struggled with the interpretation of God's words. Every sentence needed to be understood and applied. Answers later debated in universities were once contemplated in monasteries.

St. Benedict established the Middle Ages' most influential monastic order (Benedictine) in Monte Cassino, Italy, in A.D. 529. He scheduled a rigorous program of monastic duties that combined manual labor with intellectual tasks. His movement spread north and took firm root in France, where the abbey of Cluny (Burgundy) eventually controlled more than 2,000 dependent abbeys and vied with the pope for control of the Church.

Benedictine abbeys grew dot-com rich, and with wealth came excess (king-size beds and Wi-Fi). Monks lost sight of their purpose and became soft and corrupt. In the late 1100s, the determined and charismatic St. Bernard rallied the Cistercian order by

ries of history, but you can only enter the shop. English-speaking Laure explains the qualities of the native olive varieties—yes, just like grapes, there are specific olive varieties that fare better locally (July-Aug Mon-Sat 10:00-19:00, off-season Mon-Sat 9:00-12:00 & 14:00-18:00, closed Sun year-round, 2800 Route d'Apt, tel. 04 90 72 43 66, www.moulin-saintaugustin.fr).

St. Pantaléon

This postage-stamp-sized village feels lost in the valley below Gordes. It comes with an adorable 12th-century Romanesque church that has a remarkable necropolis around back, with tombs—many in the distinct shape of a human body—carved right out of the rock on which the church was built. It's a peaceful, moving site. To visit the interior of the church, you'll need the key: Cross the street to the Mas des Arts guesthouse—where you see the tagoing back to the original rule of St. Benedict. Cistercian abbeys thrived as centers of religious thought and exploration from the 13th through the 15th centuries.

Cistercian abbots ran their abbeys like little kingdoms, doling out punishment and food to the monks, and tools to peasant farmers. Abbeys were occupied by two groups: the favored monks from aristocratic families (such as St. Bernard) and a larger group of lay brothers from peasant stock, who were given the heaviest labor and could join only the Sunday services.

Monks' days were broken into three activities: prayer, reading holy texts, and labor. Monks lived in silence and poverty, with few amenities—meat was forbidden, as was cable TV. In summer, they ate two daily meals—in winter, just one. Monks slept together in a single room on threadbare mats covering solid-rock floors.

With their focus on work and discipline, Cistercian abbeys became leaders of the medieval industrial revolution. Among the few literate people in Europe, monks were keepers of technological knowledge—about clocks, waterwheels, accounting, foundries, gristmills, textiles, and agricultural techniques. Abbeys became economic engines that helped drive France out of its Middle Aged funk.

As France (and Europe) slowly got its act together in the late Middle Ages, cities re-emerged as places to trade and thrive. Abbeys gradually lost their relevance in a brave new humanist world. Universities became the new center of intellectual development. Kings took over abbot selection, further degrading the abbeys' power, and Gutenberg's movable type made monks obsolete. The French Revolution closed the book on abbatial life, with troops occupying and destroying many abbeys. The still-functioning Abbey Notre-Dame de Sénanque, near Gordes, is a rare survivor.

bles outside—owned by two likeable artists (who have a gallery in Roussillon) and ask for the key (*clé*, pronounced "clay"); you're on your own in the church. If they aren't home, try the café downhill, Le Chauvre Sourit, which also has a key and makes a nice spot to stop for a cheap drink (free Wi-Fi; open daily).

Villages and Sights South of Roussillon

These villages and sights below Roussillon and D-900 feel less visited than places north of this busy road. You'll need a good half-day to visit them all (see the map on page 188 to get oriented). They work well in the order described below, with lunch in Bonnieux or Lacoste (for recommendations, see sidebar on page 207). The first sight is situated south of Roussillon, where D-108 crosses D-900.

LUBERON

Julien Bridge (Pont Julien)

This delicate, three-arched bridge, named for Julius Caesar, survives as a testimony to Roman engineers—and to the importance of this rural area 2,000 years ago. It's the only surviving bridge on what was the main road from northern Italy to Provence—the primary route used by Roman armies. The 215-foot-long Roman bridge was under construction from 27 B.C. to A.D. 14. Mortar had not yet been invented, so (as with Pont du Gard) the stones were carefully set in place. Amazingly, the bridge survives today, having outlived Roman march-

es, hundreds of floods, and decades of automobile traffic. A new bridge finally rerouted traffic from this beautiful structure in 2005.

Walk below the bridge. Notice how thin the layer of stone seems between the arch tops and the road. Those open niches weren't for statues, but instead allowed water to pass through when the river ran high. (At its current trickle, that's hard to fathom.) Walk under an arch and examine the pockmarks in the side—medieval thieves in search of free bronze stole the clamps.

Château de la Canorgue Winery

Well-signed halfway between the Julien Bridge and Bonnieux, this is a pretty winery; the film *A Good Year,* with Russell Crowe and French actress Marion Cotillard, was filmed here in 2006. A welcoming tasting room offers the full range of wines—from Viognier and Chardonnay whites to rosés and rich reds—with owner-in-waiting and winemaker Nathalie greeting guests on weekdays. For a good contrast in reds, compare the *Vendanges de Nathalie* with the *vin du pays.* Château de la Canorgue was one of the first wineries in the area to make organic wines, and they have reasonable prices.

Cost and Hours: Average bottle costs €10, Mon-Sat 9:00-19:00 except closed for lunch Sat, closed Sun, tel. 04 90 75 81 01.

Bonnieux

Spectacular from a distance, this town disappoints me up close. It lacks a pedestrian center, though the Friday-morning market briefly creates one. The main reason to visit here is to enjoy the views from a well-positioned restaurant.

Sleeping in and near Bonnieux: **$$$ Hôtel le Clos du Buis***** is an eight-room delight in Bonnieux's center, run by eager-to-please Lydia and Pierre. Their veranda allows fine views over the Luberon (Db-€138-165, includes breakfast, less off-season, pool, free parking, guest kitchen, in the middle of town on Rue Victor

Hugo, tel. 04 90 75 88 48, www.leclosdubuis.fr, le-clos-du-buis@ wanadoo.fr).

The country-elegant *chambre d'hôte* **$$$ Mas del Sol,** between Bonnieux and Lacoste, is perfect for connoisseurs of the Luberon. Young Lucine and Richard Massol rent five bright, spacious rooms that come with views, vines, olives, and a big breakfast. The setting is unbeatable, and the stylish pool and gardens will calm your nerves (Db-€120-180, lower prices are for longer stays and off-season, guest fridge for family picnics, loaner bikes, tel. 04 90 75 94 80, www.mas-del-sol.com, contact@mas-del-sol.com). From D-900, take the D-36 turnoff to Bonnieux and look for *Mas del Sol* signs after about three kilometers (two miles).

Eating in Bonnieux: **Le Terrail** is a local hangout serving up enjoyable cuisine with a sensational view terrace (€13 lunch *plats,* try the aioli, dinner *menus* from €26, open daily, Place Gambetta, tel. 04 90 75 93 73).

Lacoste

Little Lacoste slumbers across the valley from Bonnieux in the shadow of its looming castle. Climb through this photogenic village of arches and stone paths, passing American art students (from the Savannah College of Art and Design) showing their work. Support an American artist, learn about the art, and then keep climbing and climbing to the ruined castle base. The view of Bonnieux from the base of Lacoste's castle is as good as it gets.

The Marquis de Sade (1740-1814) lived in this **castle** for more than 30 years. Author of dirty novels, he was notorious for hosting orgies behind these walls, and for kidnapping peasants for scandalous purposes. He was eventually arrested and imprisoned for 30 years, and thanks to him, we have a word to describe his favorite hobby—sadism. Today, fashion designer Pierre Cardin lives in the lower part of the castle, having spent a fortune shoring up the protective walls and sponsoring a high-priced summer opera series. Some locals are critical of Cardin, claiming that he is buying up the town to create his own "faux-Provence." Could "Cardism" be next?

Eating in Lacoste: If it's time for lunch, find the **Bar/Restaurant de France**'s outdoor tables overlooking Bonnieux and savor the view (€10-13 omelets and *plats,* daily, lunch only off-season, tel. 04 90 75 82 25). A small *épicerie* near the church has just enough fixings to make a picnic.

Abbey St. Hilaire

A dirt road off D-103 between Lacoste and Ménerbes leads down to this long-forgotten and pint-size abbey. There's not much to see here—it's more about the experience. The tranquility and isolation sought by monks 800 years ago are still palpable in the simple

LUBERON

church and modest cloisters. Once a Cistercian outpost for the bigger abbey at Sénanque, Abbey St. Hilaire is now owned by Carmelite Friars. The lone stone bench in front is picnic-ready, and a rugged WC is cut into the rock (across the courtyard). For a pleasing loop walk, start at the abbey and cross over the D-3 road to a path running along the base of the Luberon range (details available at the abbey). Leave nothing valuable in your car at this remote site.

Ménerbes

Ménerbes, (in)famous as the village that drew author Peter Mayle's attention to this region, has an upscale but welcoming feel in its small center. Wine bars, cafés, and a smattering of galleries gather where key lanes intersect. To explore the old town, walk to both ends of the linear rock that extends from the commercial area.

At the east end of Rue Corneille you'll pass the **citadel,** built in 1584 (after the Protestants of Ménerbes were defeated in the religious wars of 1577)—and never tested. The citadel is privately owned today, but from the outside you can still enjoy the impressive facade, which spans the width of the rock. Nearby, the ancient stone prison tower is also worth a peek.

At the village's very western end, find the heavy Romanesque church (closed and under renovation) and **graveyard** (good views in all directions). You're face-to-face with the Grand Luberon ridge. Notice the quarry carved into its side, where the stone for this village came from.

On the way back, foodies can duck into the snazzy **Maison de la Truffe et du Vin,** which offers "truffle discovery workshops" (Place de l'Horloge, tel. 04 90 72 38 37, www.vin-truffe-luberon. com), a little *jardin à la française* (more great views), and a cute tasting room serving Luberon wines. All 180 of the Luberon's wines are sold here for the same price you'd pay at the winery. Their small restaurant serves a *truffe d'été menu* (summer truffle, available June-Sept), best enjoyed in the garden's lovely setting (Sun-Fri 12:30-14:00 & 19:30-21:00 except closed Sun eve, closed Sat).

The **Corkscrew Museum** (Musée du Tire-Bouchon) is actually part of the **Domaine de la Citadelle** winery, a half-mile below Ménerbes. It is worth a stop if you're a corkscrew enthusiast or want to taste their very good wines. They have 1,200 corkscrews on display in glass cases and a well-stocked gift shop (€4 for the "museum," includes tasting, daily 10:00-12:00 & 14:00-19:00, shorter hours and closed Sun off-season, tel. 04 90 72 41 58).

▲Oppède-le-Vieux

This windy barnacle of a town clings with all its might to its hillside. There are a handful of businesses and a dusty little square at the base of a short, ankle-twisting climb to a pretty little church and ruined castle. This off-the-beaten-path fixer-upper of a village was completely abandoned in 1910, and today has a ghost town-like feel (it once housed 200 people). The inhabited village below has a rugged character and shows little inclination for boutiques and smart hotels. It's ideal for those looking to perish in Provence.

Sights in Oppède-le-Vieux: Plan your ascent to the **castle.** It's 20 minutes straight up—the Luberon views justify the effort.

(After making this walk, you'll understand why locals abandoned it for more level terrain.) Small information panels provide a worthwhile background in English as you climb, and the upgraded paving and floodlighting will enhance your appreciation of the lovely setting. Walk under the central arch of the building across from Le Petit Café and climb. After walking under the arch, look back to notice the handsome building it supports. At the fork, you can go either way (though the path to the right is easier). Find the little church terrace. From here, tiled rooftops paint a delightful picture with the grand panorama; the flat plain of the Rhône delta is visible off to the left.

The colorful **Notre-Dame d'Alidon church** (1588) is generally open 9:30-18:30 (depending on availability of village volunteers, who are eager to answer questions). There's been a church on this site for 1,000 years. Pick up the English text and imagine having to climb this distance at least every Sunday—for your entire life. Notice the pride locals have for their church: You'll see new gold-leaf accents and other efforts to spruce up the long-abandoned building. The steps to chapels on the right were necessary, thanks to the church's hillside setting.

Unfortunately, what remains of the castle is now off-limits—it's too dangerous. But the views are worth the climb.

Eating and Sleeping in Oppède-le-Vieux: Once you're back down, consider a meal with views of the castle ruins at **Petit Café,** where all-business Laurent is in charge (€22-28 lunch *menus,* €35 dinner *menus,* closed Wed and mid-Dec-Feb). **$$ Petit Café** also offers simple but comfy rooms, all with nice views (Db-€75-85, big Db-€95, extra bed-€15, includes breakfast, air-con, indoor Jacuzzi and sauna-€15, rooftop terrace, tel. 04 90 76 74 01, www.lepetitcafe.fr).

LUBERON

Getting There: To find Oppède-le-Vieux from D-900, follow signs to *Oppède* and *Oppède le Village,* then *Oppède-le-Vieux,* and drive toward le Petit Luberon massif. You'll follow a long, one-way loop and be forced to park a few hundred yards from the village (unless you're sleeping there), for which you'll get to pay €3. From the lot follow signs to *Vieux Village* up a confusing set of switchbacks—the long walk is worth it.

Villages and Sights East of Roussillon

Provence is busy with tourists, but there are still plenty of less-discovered places to explore. The area east of Roussillon, deep in the heart of Provence *(la Provence profonde),* feels quieter and less touristed. Come here to get a sense of how most villages were before they became "destinations." Here are the key sights in the order that you'll pass them coming from Roussillon or Joucas. Allow a full day to complete this loop. If all you have is a half-day, head straight for Fort de Buoux (see map on page 188).

St-Saturnin-lès-Apt

Most tourists pass by this pleasant town (with a lively Tuesday market) on their way to more famous destinations. I couldn't find a souvenir shop. Ditch your car below the main entry to the town (just below the old city) and walk up the main drag past the Hôtel Saint Hubert (Rue de la République). You'll come to a striking church that's a fine example of Provençal Romanesque, with a tall, rounded spire (the interior is often closed). From here, find the ramp with *Le Château* signs and climb. The ruined "château" grows right out of the rock, making it difficult to tell the man-made from the natural. Go left as you enter and hike as high as the sun allows with no shade—faded green dots guide you up. It's a scamperer's paradise, with views that

rank among the best village-top vistas I've found in Provence. Find your way through the small opening to the little dam. On the opposite side of the reservoir is a shaded picnic table. The small chapel at the very top is only open on Sunday mornings in summer, but at any time you can take the path to the right of the chapel back down the hill to the village, where you'll see a lovely medieval gate.

Sleeping and Eating in or near St-Saturnin-lès-Apt: For a warm welcome, stay at **$$$ Mas Perréal** just outside St-Saturninlès-Apt. American Kevin and his Parisian wife, Elisabeth, left no stone unturned as they restored their lovely farmhouse. Elisabeth teaches French—that's how Kevin met her—and still gives lessons (book in advance). This place features sumptuous rooms (each with its own terrace), a pool, 360-degree views (they own the vineyards and orchards around you), elaborate American-size breakfasts, and no language barrier (Db-€130-140, includes big breakfast; apartments-€140-150 but breakfast extra; tel. 04 90 75 46 31, www.masperreal.com, elisabeth-kevin@masperreal.com). Mas Perréal is off D-943, between St-Saturnin-lès-Apt and D-900. Coming from D-900, turn left at Moulin à Huile Jullien (the olive oil mill listed earlier), continue three-quarters of a mile, cross one "major" road, and have faith until you see the signs—it will be on your right.

$$ Hôtel des Voyageurs*, with amiable owners Nadine and Alain (who speak no English), is a time warp that has survived many Provençal trends with-out changing its look or prod-uct. The basic accommodations gather around uneven floors and a frumpy upstairs terrace that only an artist could love (modest but nice Db-€60-68, big Db-€75, tel. 04 90 75 42 08, http://voyageursenprovence.

fr, hotel.rest.voyageur@orange.fr). The Old World restaurant, with vintage floor tiles, serves traditional cuisine that locals adore (*menus* from €25). Both the hotel and the restaurant are closed all day Wednesday and Thursday until 18:00. It's at the base of the old village—look for signs.

Le Colorado Provençal

This park has ochre cliffs similar to Roussillon's, but they're spread over a larger area, with well-signed trails. If hiking through soft,

orange sand and Bryce Canyon-like rocks strikes your fancy, make time for Le Colorado Provençal.

For the best walk, cross the little footbridge to follow either the Cheminée de Fée ("Fairy Chimney") or the Sahara trail. Trails are color-coded and easy to follow. The Sahara offers a wider spectrum of colors and pro-vides views of the chimney formations. Forgo light-colored clothing and allow about 40 minutes to walk this trail. Signs remind you to remain on the trails and not climb the cliffs.

Cost and Hours: Park is free and always open; located a half-

LUBERON

mile below Rustrel off D-22, between Apt and Gignac—follow signs toward the village of *Rustrel,* the gateway to Le Colorado Provençal. A large, clearly marked parking lot on D-22 has snack stands and WCs (small fee to park—or park along the main road for free). Parking attendants are available from about 9:00 until 17:00 or 18:00.

Viens

Located about 15 minutes uphill and east of Le Colorado Provençal (turn right when leaving Colorado), this village is where Luberon

locals go to get away. With a setting like this, it's surprising that modest Viens is not more developed. The panoramas are higher and more vast than around Roussillon (with some lavender fields), and the vegetation is more raw. Walk the streets of the old town (bigger than it first appears) and visit the few shops scattered about. Uphill, find the courtyard of the old château, then walk to the end of the village and relax at a picnic table to enjoy the grand view. This is how Gordes must have looked before it became chic.

Eating in Viens: **Le Petit Jardin Café,** just below the town's only phone booth, fits perfectly in this unpretentious town where tourists are viewed as curiosities. Come for a drink and rub shoulders with locals (notice the photos on the walls); or, better, have a meal. Dine in the small traditional interior or outside on a garden terrace (€15 weekday *menu du jour,* more elaborate €27 weekend *menu,* lunch served 12:00-14:30, closed Tue eve and all day Wed, tel. 04 90 75 20 05). A small **grocery store** (closed Sun afternoon and Mon) and a **bakery** (closed Mon) are a few blocks past the café, toward St. Martin de Castillon.

To reach the next village (Saignon), follow signs to *St. Martin de Castillon,* then turn right on D-900 toward Apt.

Saignon

Sitting high atop a rock spur, this village looks down onto Apt, a city of only 11,500—which from here looks like a megalopolis after all these tiny villages. You can peek into the too-big-for-this-village Romanesque church (Notre-Dame de la Pitié) and admire its wood doors and tympanum, then follow *Le Rocher* signs through the village up to the "ship's prow." If you need to see it all, climb to the Le Rocher Bellevue for grand views over lavender fields (about three stories of stairs to the top). There are a handful of cafés and a grocery store in the linear village's center. Parking is best just above the town (hike or drive farther above town for sensational views over Saignon).

Buoux

Buoux (pronounced "by-oox"), a way-off-the-beaten-path village, is home to two memorable restaurants and Provence's without-a-doubt best ruined castle. A trip to this far-flung corner rewards with rocky canyons, acres of lavender, and few tourists. Start early and climb to the castle before the heat rises, then have a long, well-earned lunch nearby. If you liked Les Baux but weren't so fond of the crowds and don't need an audioguide, you'll love it here.

Buoux is south of Apt on D-113 between Saignon and Lourmarin. Ambitious travelers can combine a visit to Buoux with Lourmarin and Bonnieux.

Sights in Buoux

▲▲Fort de Buoux

The remains of this remote ridgetop castle are a playground for energetic lovers of crumbled ruins and grand views. You need good

legs and stable shoes to navigate the steep, uneven footing.

Cost and Hours: €4, open from sunrise to sunset, closed in bad weather when it's slippery and dangerous, tel. 04 90 74 25 75.

Getting There: The fort is 10 minutes by car from the village of Buoux. To reach the fort from Apt and the north, drive through Buoux on D-113, pass the recommended L'Auberge de la Loube, drop down, and be on the lookout for small signs to *Fort de Buoux* (and *L'Auberge des Seguins*). Slow down and expect sharp turns. If coming from the south, follow signs to *Apt*, then *L'Auberge des Seguins* and *Fort de Buoux*. You can use one of several dirt parking areas; you'll find the closest lot after passing two others. Once parked, walk through the green gate and then about 15 minutes up a dirt road to the foot of the fort.

Visiting the Fort: Floating like a cloud above the valleys below, the fort is easy to miss—it blends with the limestone rock cliffs that dominate the landscape. The long, rocky outcrop has been inhabited since prehistoric times. In the Middle Ages, it was home to hundreds of residents and a powerful castle that controlled a vast area. Like Les Baux, the fort was destroyed in the 1500s during the wars of religion (it was a Protestant base) and again in the 1600s by a paranoid King Louis XIII (see sidebar on page 176).

Madame la Caretaker, Henriette, lives with her husband in the flowery house where you buy your ticket. (If you want to make her day, bring down any trash you find on the site, as she and her husband maintain the grounds themselves). Get the English map and start climbing. The map suggests a one-way route through the rocky ruins. You'll start with what's left of the village, then scramble around rock piles along the long outcrop to the castle remains, once home to hundreds of residents. You'll also climb around the remains of homes, a church, cisterns, and medieval storage silos.

The unforgettable highlight of this castle is a three-story stone spiral staircase, which would never in a million years be open to the public in the US. Cut into the cliffs, it leads back down to the base. At #36, near the grain silos (the many holes in the ground), walk under the archway and follow the faded white arrows as you leave the ruins (you'll walk uphill at first). The staircase is steep and has no handrails and big steps, so be very careful—or return the way you came. Allow one hour round-trip for this hike.

Sleeping in Buoux

$ L'Auberge des Seguins is a stone's throw from the parking area for the fort and draws a hiking crowd. It's a lush, if modest, Shangri-la kind of place at the end of the valley, with confident young Amélie (and hound Jules) in charge. The rambling old farm is completely isolated and purposefully unmanicured—guests are encouraged to enjoy the natural beauty. The 27 rooms are monk-like simple, clean, and squirreled about the place: Some require a dirt path to reach, some are built into the rocky cliff, and most could use some work. Kids love it (there's also a big pool, but it's not heated). This place is a good value for unpicky types (Db-€58, half-pension with dinner-€68/person, €42/person if you sleep in the cool 20-bed dorm room; coming from Fort de Buoux, take your first possible right, which turns into a dirt road; tel. 04 90 74 16 37, www.aubergedesseguins.com, aubergedesseguins@gmail.com). See also "Eating in Buoux," next.

Eating in Buoux

L'Auberge de la Loube ("Inn of the Wolf") is up the road from the fort in Buoux village and delivers the ultimate in Provençal country-coziness. Plan to stay awhile and enjoy the good cuisine and setting (indoors or out), and the eccentric owner Monsieur Leporati, who loves to sing while cooking. You'll understand why it was one of Peter Mayle's favorites—order the Provençal hors

LUBERON

d'oeuvres for a true taste of the region. Call a day ahead to secure a table (allow €24 for lunch—more on Sun, €33 for dinner, cash only, reasonable wine list, closed Sun eve and all day Mon and Thu, tel. 04 90 74 19 58).

L'Auberge des Seguins (described earlier) has an OK restaurant and a small café with bar food and snacks. The choices are limited, but the produce is usually fresh (€10-15 lunch options, €25 dinner *menu*, indoor and outdoor seating, closed weekdays for lunch).

Lourmarin

The southernmost Luberon village of Lourmarin has a good Friday market, a beautiful Renaissance château on its fringe, and an en-

chanting town center. Lourmarin sits on a level plane and feels strangely peaceful and happy, away from the more-visited villages in the heart of the Luberon. This self-assured and lovely town accommodates a healthy tourist demand without feeling overrun. It's the best Luberon village to enjoy in the winter when other, better-known towns rattle about with few residents and little commercial activity.

Existentialist writer Albert Camus *(The Stranger)* lived in Lourmarin in the 1950s and is buried here, lending it a certain fame that persists today. Author Peter Mayle moved here not so long ago, adding to the village's cachet...and now you're here, too. Lourmarin makes a good base for touring the southern Luberon, Aix-en-Provence, and even Marseille and maybe Cassis. From here you can tour big cities, beaches, and castles, returning every night to the comfort of your village.

Getting There: Three buses per day link Lourmarin to Avignon (1.5 hours) and to Aix-en-Provence (1.25 hours, bus to Pertuis leaves 3/day, transfer there to bus bound for Aix-en-Provence, 2/hour).

Orientation to Lourmarin

The **TI** is located on Place Henri Barthélémy (Mon-Sat 10:00-12:30 & 15:00-18:00, closed Sun, tel. 04 90 68 10 77, www.lourmarin.com). Free public WCs are located to the right as you exit the TI, halfway down the stairs on the left. Lourmarin has experienced a rash of break-ins at its parking lots. Park centrally, and leave nothing of value visible in your car.

Sights in Lourmarin

Château de Lourmarin

This Renaissance château looks across a grassy meadow at the village. It's more impressive from outside than within; you'll visit a few well-furnished rooms, an intriguing kitchen and exterior galleries, and a slick double spiral staircase in stone.

Cost and Hours: €6.50, daily June-Aug 10:00-18:00, shorter hours off-season, weekends only in Jan, decent English handout and posted explanations, tel. 04 90 68 15 23, www.chateau-de-lourmarin.com.

Market Day

Little Lourmarin erupts into a market frenzy every Friday until 13:00. Sleep here Thursday night and awake to the commotion, arrive early, or prepare for a good walk from your car.

Sleeping in Lourmarin

Try to sleep here on a Thursday, so you can be here for Friday's market. The good-value Villa St. Louis and Les Chambres de la Cordière are near each other at the very eastern end of the town center.

$$$ At Les Olivettes, Americans Joseph and Elizabeth DeLiso rent five apartments just a five-minute walk from the village center. The apartments are well-furnished and very comfortable, with kitchens, living rooms, DVD players, and guest computers. Some units have stunning views of the village. They are rentable by the week or half-week in the off-season (1-bedroom unit-€450/3 nights, 2-bedroom unit-€842/3 nights, ask for Rick Steves rate, guest washer and dryer, Avenue Henri Bosco, tel. 04 90 68 03 52, www.olivettes.com, lourmarin@olivettes.com). As it's tricky to find this place even with a GPS, ask for directions when you make a reservation.

$$ Villa St. Louis is a splendid place. It's a cross between a museum, a grand old manor home, and a garage sale. The fun and slightly eccentric owner, Madame Bernadette, adds charm to a house packed with character. The dreamy backyard is ideal for a siesta (hammock provided) and picnics. The rooms are like Grandma's, and there's a common room with a fridge (Db-€65-80, includes breakfast, cash only, secure parking, loaner bikes, 35 Rue de Henri Savournin, tel. 04 90 68 39 18, www.villasaintlouis.com, villasaintlouis@wanadoo.fr).

LUBERON

$$ Les Chambres de la Cordière is a cool getaway. Charm-
ing owner Françoise's goal is to make you feel at home. Six cozy
rooms are tucked into one of the village's oldest buildings (c. 1582),
with a tiny courtyard and welcoming cats (Db-€65-75, Tb-€85,
Qb-€100, 4 rooms come with mini kitchens—the 3 *gîtes* with full
kitchens are usually rented only by the week for about €450, cash
only, some rooms have air-con, one room with Jacuzzi, Rue Albert
Camus, tel. 04 90 68 03 32, mobile 06 81 02 8 04, www.cordiere.
com, cordiereluberon@aol.com).

Eating in Lourmarin

All roads seem to converge on the postcard-perfect intersection near
La Maison Café, where you can enjoy a light meal or snack inside
or outside on their perched ter-
race (closed Mon-Tue, Rue du
Galinier, tel. 04 90 09 54 01).
The first two listings are within
a block of this intersection; the
last is deeper into the old town.
   Restaurant l'Antiquaire,
with stylish decor, is *the* place
to eat well in Lourmarin (€32
menus, €40 bouillabaisse—must

order ahead, closed at lunch Mon-Tue and off-season all day Sun,
only indoor seating but has air-con, a block up from La Maison
Café on 9 Rue du Grand Pré, tel. 04 90 68 17 29, http://restaurant-
antiquaire.com).
   At **La Récré** owner Jean-Louis and his bright smile have been
welcoming guests for more than 30 years. You'll find an inviting
terrace and regional cuisine with vegetarian options (€16-20 *plats,*
€28-35 *menus,* closed Wed except in summer, next to TI on Avenue
Philippe de Girard, tel. 04 90 68 23 73, la-recre-lourmarin.com).
   Café l'Ormeau, on Place l'Ormeau, has reliable café fare and
is near my two in-town B&Bs. Its interior courtyard is a calm re-
treat in the middle of the village bustle (€12-15 salads and *tartines,*
€15-19 *plats,* daily, tel. 04 90 68 02 11).

MARSEILLE & NEARBY

Marseille • Cassis •
Aix-en-Provence

In the rush to get between Avignon and the Riviera, most travelers zip through the eastern fringe of Provence. That's a shame, as this is a land of compelling cities with a strikingly beautiful coastline, all in a tight package. I cover three different-as-night-and-day places, each worth a visit. Marseille is an untouristy, semi-seedy-but-vibrant port city. The nearby coastal village of Cassis offers the perfect antidote to the big city. And just inland, polished Aix-en-Provence is the fancy yin to Marseille's working-class yang, with beautiful people to match its lovely architecture. Aix-en-Provence makes a good and easy first- or last-day stop for those using Marseille's airport.

For good regional guides who specialize in this area, see page 26.

Marseille

Marseille (mar-say) is both the Naples and the Barcelona of France. Big and gritty, it has all the color and pitfalls that come with being a seaport. It's a place with a distinct culture, a proud spirit, and a populace determined to clean up its act. Historic buildings have been renovated, cultural centers opened, daringly modern buildings erected, a sleek new tram rolled out, and the once rough-and-tumble harbor has blossomed into an inviting and fun-loving pedestrian zone. Much of this urban renewal was done in

Marseille & Nearby

To Luberon, Grand Canyon du Verdon & Nice

A-51

A-7   A-8   To Luberon

D-7N

Mont Ste-Victoire

To Arles & Avignon

D-543

Aix-en-Provence

AIX-EN-PROVENCE TGV STN.

Marseille-Provence

Etang de Berre

A-51

D-9

To Nice

A-7

A-8

To Camargue & Arles

A-55

A-52

L'Estaque

A-55

D-560

Marseille

D-4

A-52

FRIOUL ISLANDS

A-50   A-501

CHATEAU D'IF

CASSIS TRAIN STN.

Aubagne

D-559

5 Kilometers

5 Miles

LES CALANQUES   **Cassis**

Paris FRANCE

Cap Canaille

LA ROUTE DES CRETES

La Ciotat

A-50

To Toulon

100 Miles

Mediterranean Sea

preparation for the city's year-long stint as the European Capital of Culture in 2013, which attracted more than 10 million visitors and cost over €3 billion. Marseille is on the move.

France's oldest (600 B.C.) and second biggest city (and Europe's third largest port) owns a history that goes back to ancient Greek times. Marseille is a world apart from France's other leading cities. Rather than offering blockbuster sights, it's a bustling, well-lived-in city with happy-go-lucky residents providing its ambience.

Marseille is Europe's gateway to Africa, with nearly two million people a year riding its ferries—most shuttling between it and Tunisia and Algeria. More than 25 percent of the city's population consists of immigrants from North Africa. In certain quarters you'll hear more Arabic than French. (This infuriates anti-immigrant French people who are certain that the rest of "their" country is destined to follow suit).

Most tourists leave Marseille off their itinerary, as it doesn't fit their idea of the French Riviera or of Provence. But it would be a shame to come to the south of France and not experience the region's leading city and namesake of the French national anthem. By train, it's made-to-order for a convenient day-trip from Aix-en-

Provence (30 minutes away by train), or even from Paris—just a three-hour trip by TGV.

PLANNING YOUR TIME

For a stimulating four-hour tour of Marseille, take my self-guided "Marseille City Walk." You'll head from the train station down La Canebière, dip into the North African market, wander around the old town (Le Panier) as you climb to the La Charité Museum, find the cathedral, and survey the Euroméditerranée (Euromed) development, then return to the port and take the shuttle ferry across to the new town. Finally, take a bus, tourist train, or taxi up to Notre-Dame de la Garde before returning to the station.

Orientation to Marseille

Marseille is big, with 860,000 people, so keep it simple and focus on the area immediately around the Old Port (Vieux Port). A main boulevard (La Canebière) meets the colorful Old Port. The Panier district is the old town, blanketing a hill that tumbles down to the port. The harborside is a lively, broad promenade lined with inviting eateries, amusements, and a morning fish market. Everything described here (except Notre-Dame de la Garde) is within a 30-minute walk of the train station.

TOURIST INFORMATION

The main TI is two blocks up from the Old Port on La Canebière (Mon-Sat 9:00-19:00, Sun 10:00-17:00, free Wi-Fi, 11 La Canebière, toll tel. 08 26 50 05 00—€0.15/minute, www.marseille-tourisme.com). In summer, satellite offices open at the St. Charles train station (see next) and in a kiosk at the cruise port. Pick up the good city map, the flier with a self-guided walk through the old town, and information on museums and the weekly walking tours.

ARRIVAL IN MARSEILLE
By Train

St. Charles Station (Gare St. Charles) is busy, modern, and user-friendly. Many services are along track A, including WCs, a grocery store, and baggage storage (daily). In summer you should find a TI sharing space with the train information office op-

Vive la Différence

Marseille is one of Europe's greatest cultural melting pots. An important trading center since ancient times, Marseille has long been defined by the waves of immigrant peoples who have called this beautiful setting home. Accessible by land and sea to North Africa, Spain, Italy, and Greece, Marseille once attracted Phoenicians, Greeks, and Romans. Today, Marseille houses France's largest concentration of immigrants: 200,000 of its 860,000 residents are Muslim; 80,000 are Jewish (Marseille has had a large Jewish population since the Jews were expelled from Spain in 1492); 80,000 are Armenian Orthodox (escaping Ottoman injustices); and there are 70,000 Comorans (from a group of islands in the Indian Ocean).

There's a spirit of cooperation among Marseille's immigrants, who understand that what benefits one group helps them all. While anti-Semitic and anti-government riots have disrupted other parts of France in recent years (Paris in particular), gritty Marseille has remained relatively quiet. Unlike in Paris, immigrants in Marseille live in the city center, not the suburbs, so they are more visible and harder to ignore. And though unemployment is high among immigrants, it is not as high as in Parisian suburbs. The commercial port, a thriving high-tech industry, and tourism (mostly from cruise ships) fuel Marseille's economy. The city also has invested mightily in jobs programs and city-center renovation projects that have benefited its lower-income residents.

Marseille engenders a strong sense of identity apart from France (and the French language) that unites this city's diverse population. Locals see themselves as *Marseillais* (marsay-ay) first, and as French second (or third, after their native country). Locals' fierce pride is manifested in their passion for Olympique de Marseille, the city's soccer team. Since 1899 *Marseillais* have lived and died with the fate of their team. (A few years ago, I was here the day that 30,000 *Marseillais* fans were boarding trains to Paris for the France finals.) Olympique de Marseille has made a point of creating a team that looks like the city by recruiting players from North African countries (Zinédine Zidane is the most famous example). The strategy seems to have worked—Marseille has won the French Cup more than any other team in France.

Immigrant populations are booming in cities throughout Europe, challenging local governments to accommodate them. Many would do well to study Marseille.

MARSEILLE

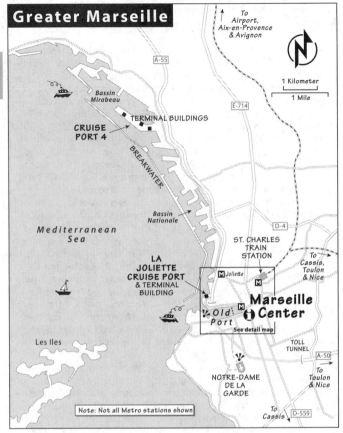

Greater Marseille

To Airport, Aix-en-Provence & Avignon

A-55

E-714

1 Kilometer

1 Mile

Bassin Mirabeau

TERMINAL BUILDINGS

CRUISE PORT 4

BREAKWATER

Bassin Nationale

D-4

ST. CHARLES TRAIN STATION

Mediterranean Sea

LA JOLIETTE CRUISE PORT & TERMINAL BUILDING

Joliette

To Cassis, Toulon & Nice

Old Port

Marseille Center

See detail map

Les Iles

TOLL TUNNEL

A-50

NOTRE-DAME DE LA GARDE

To Toulon & Nice

To Cassis

D-559

Note: Not all Metro stations shown

posite track F (open Mon-Fri only). If you exit the station at track A to Square Narvik, you'll see Hôtel Ibis on your left (with car rental behind it); access to the old city by foot is to the right. With your back to the tracks, you'll find shops, lots of food options, and the bus station and its ticket office (with airport buses and more) to the far right, past track N.

Getting from the Train Station to the Old Port: To reach the Old Port, you can walk, take the Métro, or catch a taxi. On **foot** it's a 15-minute downhill gauntlet along grimy streets. Leave the station through the exit at track A (past the big departure board), veer right, and admire the view from atop the stairs (Toto, we're not in Cassis anymore). That's Notre-Dame de la Garde overlooking the city. Walk down the stairs and straight on Boulevard d'Athènes, which becomes Boulevard Dugommier. When you come to the trams, turn right onto the grand boulevard, La Canebière. This leads to the main TI and the Old Port.

By **Métro** it's an easy subterranean trip from the train station to the Old Port: Go down the escalator opposite track E and then take a longer escalator to your left. Buy a ticket from the machines or ticket window (closed 12:40-13:40). Your €1.50 ticket is good for one hour of travel on Métro; buses and all-day passes cost €5 (www.rtm.fr). Take blue line 1 (direction: La Fourragère) two stops to Vieux Port (Old Port). Following *Sortie* signs, then *la Canebière* exit signs, you'll pop out within sight of the TI. To return to the station from here, take blue line 1 (direction: La Rose) two stops and get off at Gare St. Charles.

Taxis are out the front doors opposite track E. Allow €15 to the port and €20 to Notre-Dame de la Garde—though train station cabbies may refuse these short trips (tel. 04 91 02 20 20). Taxis elsewhere will take you on shorter rides.

By Car

Even drivers who are comfortable in big, crazy cities will be frustrated in Marseille. Traffic is always bad here. If coming from the east (Cassis and other Riviera destinations), opt for autoroute A-50, which leads to Marseille's 1.5-mile-long tunnel (toll about €4)—avoiding much of the city's traffic-ridden center streets—and pops you out under Fort St. Nicolas at the Old Port. After you leave the autoroute from any direction, signs to *Vieux Port, Centre-Ville*, and *Office du Tourisme* take you to the Old Port. At the port, follow the blue *P* signs to the underground *Parking Charles de Gaulle-Canebière* lot. Locals claim pay lots are patrolled and safe, but I wouldn't leave anything visible in the car.

By Plane

Marseille's airport (Aéroport Marseille-Provence), about 16 miles north of the city center, is small and easy to navigate (tel. 08 20 81 14 14, www.marseille.aeroport.fr). Frequent buses run to Marseille's St. Charles train station (€9, 3/hour, 25 minutes) and to Aix-en-Provence (stops at Aix-en-Provence's TGV station or bus station, 2/hour, 35 minutes, www.navetteaixtgvaeroport.com). A taxi to downtown Marseille takes 30 minutes and costs €60 (€75 if it's really early, late, or Sun). A five-minute shuttle bus trip connects the airport to the nearby Vitrolles Aéroport train station, which is handy for its direct service to cities west of Marseille, including Arles, Avignon, and Nîmes. (You can also take a train from this station into Marseille, but the bus described above is easier and more frequent.) For destinations east of Marseille (such as Cassis, Nice, or Italy), take the bus to Marseille's St. Charles Station and connect by train from there. If you need to sleep near the airport, consider the recommended Holiday Inn Express.

By Cruise Ship

For information on arriving in Marseille by cruise ship, see page 246.

HELPFUL HINTS

Pickpockets: As in any big city, thieves thrive in crowds and target tourists. Wear your money belt, and assume any commotion is a smokescreen for theft. Marseille (while nowhere near as dangerous as many American cities) is the most dangerous city in France. Use a little extra caution and don't venture into sketchy areas after dark.

Save on Bus Tickets: The same tickets work on buses and the Métro, but cost €1.50 at a Métro station and €1.90 on the bus.

Bike Cabs: In summer, look for bicycle cabs that will zip you up and down the Old Port for a tip.

Taxi to Cassis or Aix-en-Provence: A taxi from Marseille to Cassis or Aix-en-Provence runs about €65.

Car Rental: All the major companies are represented at St. Charles Station (see "Arrival in Marseille," earlier).

Local Guide: Pascale Benguigui is a smart and colorful guide for Marseille, Aix-en-Provence, St-Tropez, and anything in between (€156/half-day, €248/day, tel. 06 20 80 07 51, macpas@club-internet.fr).

Soccer Matches: *Le football* is to Marseille what American football is to Green Bay: Frenzied fans go crazy, and star worship is fickle. One of France's best-ever soccer players was raised here: Zinédine Zidane (notorious for his head-butt of an Italian opponent during the 2006 World Cup Final). If you're here during soccer season (end of July to mid-May), consider getting tickets to a match (every other Sat, from €30, sold at the TI). To get to the soccer stadium (Stade Vélodrome), take the Métro's red line 2 (direction: Ste. Marguerite-Dromel) to Rond-Point du Prado.

Tours in Marseille

Le Petit Train

These little tourist trains take two routes through town. Unfortunately, the trains depart only from the far northwest corner of the Old Port (a 15-minute walk from the TI) and have skimpy recorded information. The better Notre-Dame de la Garde route (#1) saves you the 30-minute climb to the basilica's fantastic view and runs along a nice section of Marseille's coastline (€8; allow 80 minutes for round-trip, including 20-30 minutes to visit the church; runs daily, about every 20 minutes 10:00-18:00, less frequent Nov-March; tel. 04 91 25 24 69, www. petit-train-marseille.com). The Vieux Marseille route (#2) toots you through the Panier district—best done on foot (€7, 65 minutes including one 30-minute stop, April-Oct only).

Bus Tours

Two companies run pricey big-bus tours. **L'Open Tour**'s double-decker buses with open seating up top offer a 13-stop, hop-on, hop-off route that is very similar to Le Petit Train's routes. Buses depart from near the Petit Train stop and run only every 45 minutes, leaving you too long at most stops, and there's a 1.5-hour gap in service at lunch (€19, 70 minutes round-trip). Alternatively, red **City Tour** buses take a longer route in a two-hour round-trip (€17, 4/day June-Sept, 2-3/day Oct-May, departs from near the TI).

Marseille City Walk

This self-guided walk strings together the main sights in the areas surrounding the Old Port (Vieux Port). I've listed the sights in roughly the order you'll come to them as you amble along La Canebière to the Old Port, from where you'll loop through the Panier district and ultimately wind up across the harbor in the new town (see the map on page 236). This route takes about four hours and is ideal for day-trippers arriving by train. (See directions for walking from the train station to the Old Port under "Arrival in Marseille, By Train" on page 228.)

• *Start at the corner of La Canebière and Boulevard Dugommier (at the Noailles Métro stop), a five-minute walk from the train station.*

Boulevard La Canebière

The Boulevard La Canebière (pronounced "can-ah' bee-air")—with its classy tramway—is the celebrated main drag of Marseille.

While strolling this stubby thoroughfare, you feel surrounded by a teeming, diverse city. Two blocks before the harbor, you'll find two museums, the TI, and a stylish shopping district. The boulevard dead-ends at the Old Port. La Canebière's name comes from the same root as cannabis—not the smoking kind but the rope-making kind. Marseille was long the French kingdom's main naval base, and hemp was a vital ingredient in the rope used by the fleet.

Marseille at a Glance

▲▲**Notre-Dame de la Garde** Marseille's landmark sight: a huge Romanesque-Byzantine basilica, towering above everything, with panoramic views. **Hours:** Daily April-Sept 7:00-20:00, until 19:00 Oct-March. See page 242.

▲▲**Panier District** Marseille's answer to Paris' Montmartre, this charming tangle of lanes in the oldest part of town draws photographers and poets. **Hours:** Always walkable. See page 239.

▲**North African Market** Taste of North Africa in downtown Marseille. **Hours:** Open long hours except Sun. See page 234.

▲**Old Port (Vieux Port)** Economic heart of town, featuring lots of boats and a fish market, protected by two impressive fortresses. **Hours:** Port—always open; fish market—nearly daily until 13:00. See page 238.

▲**La Charité Museum** Housed in a beautiful building with Celtic, Greek, Roman, and Egyptian artifacts. **Hours:** Tue-Sun June-Sept 11:00-18:00, Oct-May 10:00-17:00, closed Mon year-round. See page 239.

• *For a taste of Africa, walk from the Noailles Métro stop a block down La Canebière to Rue Papère, and side-trip left another block to the old tram station (with another entrance to the Noailles Métro stop) and the colorful North African market filling the Place du Marché.*

▲North African Market

Marseille's huge Moroccan, Algerian, and Tunisian populations give the city a special spice. Wander downhill the length of the Place du Marché. Suddenly you're immersed in an exotic and fragrant little medina filled with commotion—and no one's speaking French. The market thrives daily except Sunday with fresh and very cheap produce. Labels show the price as well as the origin: *Moroc, Provence, Côte d'Ivoire,* and so on.

Explore a bit. Linger over a coffee at an outside table at **Café Prinder** (cheap coffee/drinks)—listen to and watch the kaleidoscope of cultures. Next, venture left on Rue Longue des Capucins. Stop by **Soleil d'Egypte** and try a *bourek* wrap (potato and ground round), a *pastilla* wrap (chicken, almonds, onions, and egg), or the crêpe-like *mahjouba* (so nice when hot out of the oven). You'll see the kitchen behind the counter. There's €3 paella to go next door.

At the next corner, Rue d'Aubagne, take a right and stop in for tea or a dessert (Tunisian pastries) at **La Carthage** bakery. In

Chamber of Commerce Building and Marine Museum Grandiose building with small exhibit on the city's maritime history. **Hours:** Daily 10:00-18:00. See page 235.

Cathédrale de la Nouvelle Major Massive striped cathedral with floor and wall mosaics. **Hours:** Tue-Sun 10:00-19:00, closed Mon. See page 240.

Euroméditerranée (Euromed) Culture District The trio of modern cultural centers—Musée Regards de Provence, Villa Méditerranée, and the Museum of European and Mediterranean Civilizations—have impressive architecture but are otherwise of little interest. **Hours:** Always viewable. See page 241.

Château d'If Island with fortress-turned-prison, featured in Alexandre Dumas' *Count of Monte Cristo.* **Hours:** Boats usually depart hourly 9:00-17:00; last departure to visit château is 15:15. See page 243.

this inviting four-table spot you can crank up the music and be in Tunisia. A "Tunisian Plate" is lunch for €5. You could assemble an assortment of baklava-like sweets and have it with mint tea for a sticky memory.

• *Continue downhill to the big street, Cours St. Louis. The grand triumphal arch you see far to the right celebrates the Revolution and French Republic. Head toward the arch and cross to the north side of La Canebière, then turn left and continue downhill toward the Old Port. Two blocks before you hit the water, on the right side (just after the TI), you can't miss the grandiose building.*

Chamber of Commerce (Le Palais de la Bourse) and Marine Museum

Step inside and take in the grand 1860s interior (free, daily 10:00-18:00). A relief on the ceiling shows great moments in Marseille's history. The grand hall is circled by a United Nations of plaques, reminding locals that their economy is based on trade from around the world.

The small ground-floor exhibit on the city's maritime history (€2, to the right as you enter) starts with a portrait of Emperor Napoleon III, who called for the building's construction, and his wife.

MARSEILLE

Marseille

To Cruise Port 4

Place de la Joliette

M Joliette

JETTY

QUAI DE LA JOLIETTE

BLVD. DES DAMES

AVE. ROBERT SCHUMAN

RUE DE LA

Bassin de la Grande Joliette

CATHEDRALE DE LA NOUVELLE MAJOR

R. DU PETIT PUITS

LA CHARITÉ MUSEUM ⑫

RUE PANIER

R.D. BELLES ECUELLES

LA JOLIETTE CRUISE PORT

QUAI DE LA TOURETTE

RUE DES REPENTIES

RUE DU REFUGE

R.D. MUETTES

R.D. MOULIN

LE PANIER

INTER-CONTINENTAL HOTEL

RUE MERY

MUSEE REGARDS DE PROVENCE

RUE JEAN GALLAND

R.D. POURIER

ALTERNATE ROUTE

MONTEE DES ACCOULES

AVE. VAUDOYER

ESPLANADE DE LA TOURETTE

RUE DE LA PRISON

VILLA MEDITERRANEE

RUE ST-LAURENT

RUE

R. CAISSERIE

CITY HALL

RUE DE

MuCEM MUSEUM

ST. LAURENT

LA LOGE

Ⓑ #60

Ⓑ QUAI DU PORT

SKY-BRIDGES

Place de la Tourette

AVE. ST-JEAN

RUE DE ⑦ Ⓑ ⑥

#60 Ⓑ

#60 & Open Bus Tour

Ⓑ #60

Med. Sea

FORT ST. JEAN

WWII MEMORIAL

Ⓑ #60 Ⓣ

Petit Train Stop

Ⓑ #60

CHATEAU

Old Port

Jardin du Pharo

QUAI DE RIVE NEUVE

⑨

BLVD. CHARLES LIVON

TOLL TUNNEL TO A-50

Bassin de Carénage

RUE NEUVE STE. CATHERINE

FORT ST. NICOLAS

RUE ROBERT

RUE SAINTE

BLVD. DE LA CORDERIE

RUE D'ENDOUME

AVE. DE LA CORSE

To Notre-Dame de la Garde

1. Hôtel la Résidence du Vieux-Port
2. Mercure Grand Hôtel Beauvau & Hôtel Carré
3. Hôtels Bellevue & Hermes
4. Hôtel Ibis Marseille Gare St. Charles
5. Hôtel Relax
6. Le Souk Restaurant
7. Les Galinettes Chez Madie Rest.
8. Toinou les Fruits de Mer Seafood Cafeteria
9. Nul Part Ailleurs
10. La Cantine
11. Restaurant Strip
12. La Charité Museum Café
13. North African Markets

It then traces the growth of the city through charts of its harbor, and other rooms display models of big ships over the centuries.

Behind the Chamber of Commerce is a fancy Galeries Lafayette shopping center with a handy food court just inside the entrance; and just beyond the shopping center is the **Marseille History Museum,** with artifacts from Caesar to Louis XIV (€5, Tue-Sun 10:00-18:00, closed Mon).

• *Continue down the main boulevard, cross the busy street to the Old Port, and stop at the copper plaque in the pavement about 30 feet from the water.*

▲Old Port (Vieux Port)

This plaque marks a very central point. In fact, the monument at your feet reads: "On this spot in 600 B.C. Greek sailors landed and founded Marseille from where Western civilization rose."

Protected by two impressive fortresses at its mouth, Marseille's Old Port has long been the economic heart of town. The citadels were built in the 17th century under Louis XIV, supposedly to protect the city. But locals figured the forts were actually designed to keep an eye on Marseille—a city that was essentially autonomous until 1660—and challenge Marseille to thoroughly incorporate into the growing and ever more centralized kingdom of France.

Today, the serious shipping is away from the center, and the Old Port is the happy domain of pleasure craft. The fish market along Quai des Belges—where you're standing—splashes and wiggles nearly every morning. The stalls are gone by 13:00.

Looking out to sea from here, the Panier district (the old town) rises to your right. The harborfront below Le Panier was destroyed in 1943 by the Nazis, who didn't want a tangled refuge for resistance fighters so close to the harbor. It's now filled with modern condos and trendy restaurants. City Hall (see the flags) is in the middle on the harborfront.

Take a spin tour to the right. Farther along is the Jesuit church San Ferreol, a Gothic building with a Neo-Baroque facade slapped on in the 19th century. Spinning past the grand boulevard, La Canebière, you come to le Ombrière ("the shade-giver"), a modern mirror-ceilinged roof on the waterfront that provides both shade and lots of photo fun (it was designed by Norman Foster for the 2013 European Capital of Culture festivities). Behind that to the left is a neighborhood of prostitutes and strip clubs and an area considered unsafe late at night. Capping the hill beyond the mirror is the Notre-Dame de la Garde basilica. And farther to the right is the new town and the Arsenal Quarter, with lots of fun restaurants and bars—the liveliest place in town after dark.

• *Walk around the port with the water on your left. Pass the departure point for tour boats. After a couple of hundred yards you'll reach the small dock (labeled* La Ligne du Ferry Boat*) for the ferry that crosses the port (free, every 10 minutes, generally 8:00-17:00). You'll be back here soon. But for now, turn around and find City Hall.*

▲▲Panier District (Old Town)

The ornate **City Hall** (Hôtel de Ville) stands across from the ferry dock. Its bust of Louis XIV overlooks the harbor. Behind that rises the Panier district. Until the mid-19th century, Marseille was just this hill-capping old town and its fortified port. Today, that historic and tangled hilltop is the best place to find the town's soul. It's a 15-minute or so hike to our next stop, La Charité Museum. But take your time. The city keeps the rent cheap here, so you'll find lots of artists and artisans working and lots of creative little commercial ventures.

• *From City Hall, walk up the broad stairway to the gate of the 18th-century Hôtel Dieu (formerly a hospital, now an Intercontinental Luxury Hotel). Turn left here and explore, following the brown signs up— and up some more—to la Vieille Charité.*

▲La Charité Museum (Centre de la Vieille Charité)

Now a museum, this was once a poorhouse. In 1674 the French king decided that all the poor people on the streets were bad news.

He built a huge triple-arcaded home to take in a thousand needy subjects. In 1940 the famous architect Le Corbusier declared it a shame that such a fine building was so underappreciated. Today, the striking building— renovated and beautiful in its arcaded simplicity—is used as a collection of art galleries surrounding a Pantheon-esque church. You can stroll around the courtyard for free. (Good WCs are in the far-left corner.)

The pediment of the church features the figure of Charity taking care of orphans (as the state did with this building). She's flanked by pelicans (symbolic of charity, for the way they were said to pick flesh from their own bosom to feed their hungry chicks, according to medieval legend). The ground floor outside the church houses temporary exhibits. On the upper levels of the complex you'll find rooms with interesting collections of Celtic (c. 300 B.C.), Greek, and Roman artifacts from this region. There's also a good

Egyptian collection, along with masks from Africa and the South Pacific.

Cost and Hours: €3-6 depending on exhibits, Tue-Sun June-Sept 11:00-18:00, Oct-May 10:00-17:00, closed Mon year-round, idyllic café/bar, tel. 04 91 14 58 80.

• *From La Charité, cross the small cobbled square (with several inviting places for a bite to eat or drink), turn right midway across the square on Rue du Petit Puits, and walk to the end, where you'll run into a charming square with Le Bar des 13 Coins. Have a drink at this eclectic little bar—the inspiration for the main setting of France's most famous soap opera,* Plus Belle La Vie. *(Pétanque players enjoy the little shop opposite, with the best balls for sale and a small court for testing them.) Then descend the stairs behind the bar, go left, and take your first right to find...*

Cathédrale de la Nouvelle Major

Bam. This huge, striped cathedral seems lost out here, away from the action and above the nondescript port. The Neo-Byzantine cathedral was built in the late 1800s to replace the old cathedral that the city had outgrown. It's more impressive from the outside, but worth a quick peek inside for its mosaics (free, Tue-Sun 10:00-19:00, closed Mon).

• *Outside the cathedral, enjoy the view from the terrace. Marseille's modern port sprawls off to the right.*

The Great Maritime Port of Marseille (GPMM)

The economy of Marseille is driven by its modern commercial ports, which extend 30 miles west from here (a nearby canal links Marseille inland via the Rhône River, adding to the port's importance). Over 100 million tons of freight pass through this port each year (60 percent of which is petroleum), making this one of Europe's top three ports. Container traffic is significant but is hampered by crippling strikes, for which the left-leaning city is famous. By contrast, cruise-ship tourism brings more than a million passengers to Marseille each year. And each year two million ferry passengers shuttle between here and Corsica, Sardinia, Algeria, and Tunisia. You're looking at Europe's gateway to Africa.

• *You now have a choice of two ways to return to the Old Port: Either hike down from the cathedral and through the vast new Euromed harbor development (described next) or view it from above as you walk up the tree-lined Esplanade de la Tourette. The Euromed complex contains three of Marseille's newest sights.*

Euroméditerranée Culture District

As Europe's Capital of Culture in 2013, Marseille gained several important cultural centers, including these impressive buildings standing side-by-side on the harbor. Euromed was a grand scheme with a big, politically correct vision to revitalize the old immigration port while tying together the great (and contentious) cultures of the Mediterranean. While the architecture is visually striking, the venues themselves host temporary exhibits that are generally of little interest to tourists.

The **Musée Regards de Provence** is in the building where immigrants were inspected and their clothing was disinfected (www. museeregardsdeprovence.com). The **Villa Méditerranée** hosts events focused on inspiring peace, brotherhood, and understanding between Mediterranean cultures. Its building, with a cantilevered top floor, was designed by Milanese architect Stefano Boeri (www.villa-mediterranee.org). And the **Musée des Civilisations de l'Europe et de la Méditerranée** (MUCEM) has a tiny permanent collection about Mediterranean cultures and hosts more special exhibits. From its rooftop (free access), which has a fine café/restaurant, you can cross the skybridge to Fortress St. Jean (www. mucem.org), which contains more exhibition space.

• *If you've explored Euromed and are coming from Fortress St. Jean, take the skybridge leading to Place de la Tourette. Otherwise, if you're coming from the cathedral, continue walking up Esplanade de la Tourette. From either direction, a fabulous view awaits you at the...*

Place de la Tourette View Terrace

Voilà! This is one of the best views of Marseille, with Notre-Dame de la Garde presiding above, and twin forts below protecting the entrance to the Old Port. The ugly, boxy building marked "Memorial" at the base of the fort (below and to your right) is a memorial to those lost during the Nazi occupation of the city in World War II. The small church to your left is the Church of St. Laurent, which once served as a parish church for sailors and fishermen—notice the lighthouse-like tower.

• *Continue down the steps back to the Old Port. From the bottom of the steps you have a couple of options for getting to the new town: Hop on **bus #60** (stop is across the street and a few steps left, €1.90, direc-*

tion: Notre-Dame de la Garde) and in 20 minutes you'll circle around the harbor to the new town (you can also ride this bus up to the Notre-Dame de la Garde basilica). Or, take a 10-minute walk halfway along the promenade (Quai du Port) to City Hall, where you'll see the fun little **ferry boat** *that shuttles locals across the harbor to the new town (free, every 10 minutes, generally 8:00-17:00).*

New Town

Arriving in the new town aboard the ferry, you'll find popular bars and brasseries in front of the ferry dock and to the left toward the top of the harbor. These are good for a quick meal or a memorable drink. Wander in along Place aux Huiles, make your way left, and find a smart pedestrian zone crammed with cafés and restaurants.

• *You could end your walk here, but be sure to take a trip up to Notre-Dame de la Garde, described next, or consider the boat excursions described later.*

▲▲Notre-Dame de la Garde

Crowning Marseille's highest point, 500 feet above the harbor, is the city's landmark sight. This massive Neo-Romanesque/Neo-Byzantine basilica, built in the 1850s dur-ing the reign of Napoleon III, is a radiant collection of domes, gold, and mosaics. The monumental statue of Mary and the Baby Jesus towers above everything (Jesus' wrist alone is 42 inches around, and the statue weighs 9 tons). And though people come here mostly for the commanding city view, the interior (with its countless ex-voto messages of thanks to Mary) is unforgettable. This hilltop has served as a lookout, as well as a place of worship, since ancient times. Climb to the highest lookout for an orientation table and the best views. The islands straight ahead are the Iles du Frioul, including the island of If—where the Count of Monte Cristo spent time (reachable by a boat excursion).

Cost and Hours: Free, daily April-Sept 7:00-20:00, until 19:00 Oct-March, last entry 45 minutes before closing, cafeteria and WCs are just below the view terrace.

Getting There: To reach the church, you can hike 30 minutes straight up from the harbor, catch a taxi (about €10), hop bus #60, or ride the tourist train—all stop on the harborfront near City Hall (see map on page 236).

Boat Excursions from Marseille

Boats depart from either corner (northeast and southeast) of the top of the Old Port to these destinations—look for the ticket kiosks. Get the latest schedules and info on route options at the TI.

Château d'If and Islands of Frioul (Iles du Frioul)

When King François I visited Marseille in the 16th century, he realized the potential strategic importance of a fort on the uninhabited island of If (one of the Islands of Frioul), just outside the harbor. His château was finished in 1531. The impregnable fortress, which never saw battle, became a prison—handy for locking up Protestants during the Counter-Reformation. Among its illustrious inmates was José Faria, a spiritualist priest who was the idol of Paris and whom Alexandre Dumas immortalized in *The Count of Monte Cristo*. Since 1890 the château has been open to the public, but the required two-hour stay at this French Alcatraz will leave you sensitive to the count's predicament (€6 entry). I'd bypass this prison.

The Island of Frioul (Iles du Frioul), which offer a nature break from the big city with a few hiking paths and cafés, is another

15 minutes away (the next stop after Château d'If). For most people, this is a better place to get off and stretch your legs.

Cost and Hours: €10.50 round-trip for one island, €16 for both, boats usually depart daily and at least hourly 9:00-17:00, last departure to visit château is 15:15, 20-minute trip to château, one-hour round-trip if you don't get off the boat, tel. 04 96 11 03 50, www.frioul-if-express.com. Boats depart from the northeast and southeast corners of the Old Port.

Calanques Cruises

For those who won't get to Cassis, **Croisières Marseille Calanques** offers day trips to the dramatic fjord-like inlets known as *calanques*, east of Marseille (€24/2.5 hours, €30/3.5 hours, tel. 04 91 58 50 58, www.croisieres-marseille-calanques.com). Boats depart from the northeast and southeast corners of the Old Port. To read up on *calanques*, see page 253.

Short and Scenic Cruise to Point Rouge

To appreciate Marseille's remarkable setting, take a round-trip cruise on the *navette* boat south to the Point Rouge neighborhood

(€5 each way, departs on the hour from the southeast corner of the Old Port, about 25 minutes each way).

Sleeping in Marseille

Stay in Marseille only if you want a true urban experience. The scene is more mellow 20 minutes away in Cassis (see page 255).

$$$ Hôtel la Résidence du Vieux-Port****, pricey, slightly faded, but superbly located on the Old Port, offers retro-modern rooms done in primary colors. Most rooms face the port. Many have balconies with fine views, and are worth the extra euros (standard Db-€180-221, view Db with deck-€250-400, look for deals on website, 18 Quai du Port, tel. 04 91 91 91 22, www.hotel-residence-marseille.com, info@hrvpm.com).

$$$ Mercure Grand Hôtel Beauvau**** overlooks the harbor and lets you buy away the gritty reality outside your door with business-class comfort (Db-€190-270, Db with port view-€270-420, rates frequently reduced, 4 Rue Beauvau, tel. 04 91 54 91 00, www.accorhotels.com, h1293@accor.com).

$$$ Hôtel Bellevue sits right on the port and comes with tasteful rooms above a small (view) restaurant/café. All rooms have port views and loaner iPads (Db-€125-180, no elevator, 34 Quai du Port, tel. 04 96 17 05 40, www.hotelbellevuemarseille.com, info@bellevuemarseille.com).

$$$ Hôtel Carré**, a block off the port, has a mod lobby and offers modern comfort at fair rates (Db-€118-150, all rooms have showers, 6 Rue Beauvau, tel. 04 91 33 02 33, www.hvpm.fr, carre@hvpm.fr).

$$ Hôtel Ibis Marseille Gare St. Charles**, with 170 rooms, is a worthwhile value because it's right at the train station—left as you exit—and has all the services, including a restaurant, café, and bar (Db-€105-140, €15 less on weekends, extra bed-€10, breakfast-€10, parking-€14/day, look for deals on website, Square Narvik, tel. 04 91 95 62 09, www.ibishotel.com, h1390@accor.com).

$$ Hôtel Hermes**, barely off the port, houses 29 bright, smallish, but well-maintained rooms. The rooftop terrace delivers smashing views over the port (standard Db-€95-105, view Db with deck-€130, behind Hôtel Bellevue at 2 Rue Bonneterie, tel. 04 96 11 63 63, www.hotelmarseille.com, hotel.hermes@orange.fr).

$ Hôtel Relax* is run by sweet Houria (pronounced "oo-ree-ah," which means "Liberty" in Arabic—she's Algerian) and her husband, Ali. Despite its location in a neighborhood of topless bars and prostitutes, it's quiet and homey. Half of the simple rooms overlook a square—worth requesting, as the back-side rooms can be gloomy (back-side Db-€62, Db on square-€67, no triples or quads, rooms have tight bathrooms with showers, air-con, no elevator, just

---

Sleep Code

Abbreviations   **(€1=about $1.10, country code: 33)**
S=Single, **D**=Double/Twin, **T**=Triple, **Q**=Quad, **b**=bathroom,
*=French hotel rating (0-5 stars)
Price Rankings
 $$$ **Higher Priced**—Most rooms €115 or more
  $$ **Moderately Priced**—Most rooms €70-115
   $ **Lower Priced**—Most rooms €70 or less
Unless otherwise noted, credit cards are accepted, English
is spoken, there's an elevator and air-conditioning, and free
Wi-Fi and/or a guest computer is available. Prices change;
verify current rates online or by email. For the best prices, al-
ways book directly with the hotel.

---

2 blocks off harbor on Place de l'Opéra at 4 Rue Corneille, tel. 04
91 33 15 87, www.hotelrelax.fr, hotelrelax@free.fr).

Near the Airport: **$$ Holiday Inn Express** has easy train con-
nections to Marseille and is handy for those catching an early flight
(Db-€90-150; Impasse Pythagore, Z.I. de Couperigne, 13127 Vi-
trolles; tel. 04 42 15 09 30, www.holidayinn.com).

Eating in Marseille

For lunch I'd be adventurous, eating in the North African market
area or up in the Panier district (around La Charité). Note the eat-
ing options mentioned in my "Marseille City Walk," earlier, for
either zone. Much more forgettable and certainly stress-free is the
food court in Galeries Lafayette shopping center behind the TI
and Chamber of Commerce Building (also mentioned in the walk).

For dinner, I've listed five choices: Moroccan, fancy fish, caf-
eteria fish, fun and basic on the harbor, and elegant in the touristy
restaurant zone.

Le Souk Moroccan Restaurant is a quality and authentic-
feeling place facing the harbor under the old town (€20 couscous
and tagine dishes, €29 three-course *menu*, vegetarian options,
closed Mon, 100 Quai du Port, tel. 04 91 91 29 29).

Les Galinettes Chez Madie is good for bouillabaisse (the
local fish stew specialty) also on the harbor under the old town
(€35/person for bouillabaisse, €25 *menu*, €17 lunch *menu*, closed
Sun, 138 Quai du Port, tel. 04 91 90 40 87).

Toinou les Fruits de Mer Seafood Cafeteria is a fun and easy
way to enjoy fresh seafood without going broke. You join the caf-
eteria line to pick up side dishes, sauces, dessert and drinks and fill
out a checklist to "compose" the seafood plate of your dreams from
their menu. You can survey the catch in the icy bins outside before

choosing (daily 10:00-22:00, a block uphill from TI on corner with La Canebière at 3 Cours St. Louis, tel. 04 91 33 14 94).

Nul Part Ailleurs, overlooking the harbor on the new town side (near the little ferry dock), is a Corsican-run eatery with a fun and accessible menu offering pizza, salads, daily plates, and a passion for steak tartar. Their *tarte-tatin* (apple pie) is big enough to split and understandably popular. It's located just beyond the tourist zone, with great seating inside and out (€14 pizza and salads, €14-20 plats, 18 Quai de Rive Neuve, tel. 04 91 33 58 95).

La Cantine, on the Cours Honoré d'Estiene d'Orves square at #27, is surrounded by tourist joints and the Hard Rock Café, yet maintains its dignity. It's an intimate place—cozy inside and pleasant outside—that serves nicely presented Provençal dishes (€27 menus, €18 plats, daily, tel. 04 91 33 37 08).

The Restaurant Strip: Rue Saint-Saëns and Place aux Huiles are lined with restaurants and littered with sandwich boards listing mostly similar menus. While extremely touristy, the prices are reasonable and an enticing variety of cuisines is offered. It's a melting pot of international eateries, with choices ranging from giant salads and fresh seafood to crêpes, Vietnamese dishes, Belgian waffles, and Buffalo wings. You may enjoy surveying this scene before sitting down to eat.

Marseille Connections

BY TRAIN AND BUS
Marseille is well-served by TGV and local trains, and is the hub for many smaller stations in eastern Provence.

From Marseille by Train to: Cassis (2/hour, 25 minutes, bus is better—see below), **Aix-en-Provence Centre-Ville** (2/hour, 45 minutes), **Antibes** (16/day, 2.5 hours), **Nice** (18/day, 2.5 hours), **Arles** (11/day, 1.5 hours), **Avignon TGV** (10/day, 35 minutes), **Paris** (hourly, 3.25 hours), **Isle-sur-la-Sorgue** (8/day, 1.5 hours), and **London** (just 6 hours by TGV and Eurostar).

From Marseille's Train Station by Bus to: Marseille Airport (3/hour, 25 minutes), **Aix-en-Provence** (4/hour, 30-50 minutes).

From Marseille's Castellane Métro Stop by Bus to: Cassis (better than train, 6/day Mon-Sat, 4/day Sun, 40 minutes, TI has schedule—beware of afternoon gaps in service). The stop in Cassis is labeled *Gendarmerie* (on Avenue du 11 Novembre), from which it's a five-minute walk to the port.

BY CRUISE SHIP
If your cruise visits Provence, you'll arrive either at Marseille or at Toulon, about 40 miles east of Marseille.

Arrival at Marseille: The Marseille Provence Cruise Terminal (MPCT) sprawls beneath a bluff west of downtown. Cruise ships tuck themselves in between cargo vessels at the main port (Porte 4), which has several *postes* (piers).

Most cruise lines offer a convenient **shuttle bus** that takes you to downtown Marseille's Old Port in 15-20 minutes (skip the complicated public-transportation trip—it's worth springing for the shuttle). From the Old Port, you can walk to many of the sights in town or head up to the **train station** (20-minute walk or take Métro to St. Charles stop) to connect to outlying destinations, such as Aix-en-Provence or Cassis (see train connections, earlier).

Taxis meet arriving cruise ships, but rates are high (€15-20 to Old Port, Notre-Dame de la Garde, or train station; one-way to Aix-en-Provence-€55; all-day round-trip to Arles/Avignon area, including several stops-€175-220). Try to agree on a fixed rate up front, or make sure the meter is set to the correct rate.

Arrival at Toulon: Though the city of Toulon has a cruise terminal, most of the big cruise lines actually dock at La Seyne-sur-Mer, across the harbor from Toulon. From there you can take the cruise-line shuttle bus or a public ferry into Toulon, then connect to a train for Marseille (1 hour) or Cassis (30 minutes).

Cassis

Hunkered below impossibly high cliffs, Cassis (kah-see) is an unpretentious port town that gives travelers a sunny break from their busy vacation. Two hours away from the fray of the Côte d'Azur, Cassis is a prettier, poor man's St-Tropez. Outdoor cafés line the small port on three sides, where boaters polish their teak as they chat up café clients. Cassis is popular with the French and close enough to Marseille to be busy on weekends and all summer. Come to Cassis to dine portside, swim in the glimmering-clear water, and explore its rocky *calanques* (inlets).

Orientation to Cassis

The Massif du Puget mountain hovers over little Cassis, with hills spilling down to the port. Cap Canaille cliff rises from the southeast, and the famous *calanques* inlets hide along the coast northwest of town. Hotels, restaurants, and boats line the attractive little port.

TOURIST INFORMATION

The TI is in the modern building in the middle of the port among the boats. They have free Wi-Fi, good maps for sale, and the latest on *calanques* conditions (May-Sept Mon-Sat 9:00-18:30, until

19:00 July-Aug, Sun 9:30-12:30 & 15:00-18:00; Oct-April Mon-Sat 9:30-12:30 & 14:00-18:00, Sun 10:00-12:30, Quai des Moulins, toll tel. 08 92 39 01 03-€0.34/minute, www.ot-cassis.com, info@ot-cassis.com). If you're going to Marseille, pick up a map here.

ARRIVAL IN CASSIS

By Train: Cassis' hills forced the train station to be built two miles away, and those last two miles can be a challenge. It's a small station with no baggage storage and limited hours (Mon-Sun 8:45-12:15 & 13:45-17:25). If you need to buy tickets when the station is closed, use the machines (coins only).

A **taxi** into town costs €12 with baggage and is well worth the expense unless a Marcouline bus is soon to arrive (see below). If there's no taxi waiting, call 04 42 01 78 96. Otherwise, it's a 50-minute walk into town (turn left out of the station and follow signs).

Marcouline **buses** link the station with the town center (€1, about hourly, schedule posted at all stops) but allow extra time—bus schedules in southern France are approximate. Call the TI in advance to get the schedule and plan your arrival accordingly—and be ready to take a taxi. The bus drops you at the Casino stop in Cassis: From here, turn right on Rue de l'Arène and walk downhill five minutes to reach the port.

By Bus: Regional buses (including those from Marseille) run limited hours (check with the TI before taking one). The bus stop is a five-minute walk from the port on Avenue du 11 Novembre (stop is labeled *Gendarmerie*).

By Car: There are two exits from the autoroute for Cassis; the second (coming from Aix-en-Provence, exit #8) saves you 10 minutes, provides easy access to La Route des Crêtes (described later, under "Experiences Near Cassis"), and offers memorable views. The hills above Cassis can make it difficult to navigate. Hotels are signed, though the blue signs can be tricky to follow. Hotel parking is minimal (carefully read each hotel's listing in this book as some have more parking than others).

No matter where you park, leave nothing of value in your car. Outside of summer, drivers arriving by 10:00 usually can find curbside parking (about €1/hour, free 18:00-9:00); latecomers will likely need to park in one of the well-marked pay lots above the port (Parking de la Viguerie is closest but often full, and their *Abonnés* entrance is for locals only). Parking Daudet, up the road from Parking de la Viguerie, usually has better availability, as does Parking La Madie up the road from the Casino bus stop. Another option nearby is Parking des Mimosas, which has a 400-car capacity.

If you're driving here on weekends, holidays, during school

vacation periods (April-June and Sept-Oct), or any day in July and August, Cassis can be packed. Check the closer lots described above first. If need be, take advantage of the free parking at les Gorguettes, high above the town (well-signed), and use the *navettes* shuttle-bus service into town (€1.50 round-trip, hourly July-Aug daily until 24:00, April-June weekends and holidays 9:00-20:00, www.ot-cassis.com/fr/la-navette-port-miou.html). A second *navette* bypasses the town center with stops at Plage du Bestouan (with two of my recommended hotels) and goes straight to Calanque de Port-Miou, saving you a 30-minute walk (stop marked Presqu'ile, same schedule as above). To find the hiking trail from the Presqu'ile stop, exit the bus to the right and when you see the *calanque* water, swing right again to walk around to the other side where you'll find the beginning of the path.

HELPFUL HINTS

Market Days: The market fills the streets around Hôtel de Ville on Wednesdays and Fridays until 12:30.

Beaches: Cassis' beaches are pebbly. The big beach behind the TI is sandier than others. You can rent a mattress with a towel (about €15/day) and pedal boats (about €8/30 minutes). Underwater springs just off the Cassis shore make the water clean, clear, and a bit cooler than at other beaches.

Internet Access: The TI offers 30 minutes of free Wi-Fi, and **K6 Pressing** (see "Laundry," below) has several computers.

Grocery Store: The **Casino** market is next door to Hôtel le Liautaud (daily 8:00-12:30 & 15:30-19:30). There's also a **Spar** market just past Hôtel Laurence on Rue de l'Arène.

Laundry: A self-service *laverie automatique* is at 9 Rue Victor Autheman (daily 6:30-21:30). **K6 Pressing,** just up from the post office at 34 Rue de l'Arène, has computers to use while you get your wash done (Tue-Sat 8:30-13:00 & 14:30-19:00, closed Sun-Mon, tel. 04 42 01 10 36).

Wine Tasting: Le Chai Cassidain is a wine bar with a good selection of regional wines offered by the glass (€5, healthy pours) or by the bottle, with nibbles. Cassis *blanc* and rosé wines are always available (daily 10:00-13:00 & 15:00-22:00, often later, closed Mon in winter, 4 blocks from port at 6 Rue Séverin Icard, tel. 04 42 01 99 80).

Taxi: Call 04 42 01 78 96 or find the main taxi stand across from Hôtel Cassitel by the *boules* court.

Tourist Train: The little white *train touristique,* with commentary in French and English, will take you on a worthwhile 45-minute circuit out to the peninsula on the Port-Miou *calanque* and back (€7, April-Nov, usually at :15 after the hour 11:00-18:00).

MARSEILLE

Cassis

1. Best Western Hôtel la Rade
2. Hôtel le Golfe
3. Hôtel/Restaurant le Clos des Arômes
4. Hôtel de France Maguy
5. Hôtel Cassitel
6. Hôtel Laurence
7. Mahogany Hôtel de la Plage & Le Jardin d'Emile Hôtel
8. Le Château de Cassis
9. El Sol, L'Oustau de la Mar, Bar Canaille & Chez César Rests.
10. Le 8 et Demi Café & Grand Marnier Crêpes
11. Le Calendal Restaurant
12. Le Grand Large Restaurant
13. Bada Restaurant
14. La Girondole Restaurant
15. Le Chai Cassidain Wine Bar
16. Casino Grocery
17. Spar Market
18. Open-Air Market
19. To La Ferme Blanche Wine-Tasting
20. To Bus Stop for Marseille
21. To Clos Ste. Magdeleine Wine-Tasting
22. Launderettes (2)
23. Motorboat Rental & WC
24. Pedal Boat Rental
25. Kayak Rental

AVE. DE VERDUN

AVE. JEAN JAURÈS

AVE. DES DARDANELLES

AVE. DE

RUE ST. CLAIR

RUE DU JEUNE ANA-

QUAI

AVE. DE L'AMIRAL GANTEAUME

QUAI BARTH.

PROMENADE ARISTIDE

AVE. DE L'AMIRAL GANTEAUME

P

Plage du Bestouan

AVE. DES CALANQUES

To Calanque de Port-Miou

To Calanques

Mediterranean

MARSEILLE

Catch it next to the TI—where you can buy tickets; it's cash only on the train.

Cassis Visual Tour from the Port

Find a friendly bench in front of Hôtel le Golfe—or enjoy a drink at their café—and read this quick town intro.

Cassis was born more than 2,500 years ago (on the hill with the castle ruins, across the harbor). Ligurians, Phoenicians, maybe Greeks, certainly Romans, and plenty of barbarians all found this spot to their liking. Parts of the castle date from the eighth century, and the **fortress walls** were constructed in the 13th century to defend against seaborne barbarian raids. The Michelin family sold the fortress to investors who turned it into a luxury five-suite *chambre d'hôtes*, where celebrities often hole up looking for peace and quiet (see "Sleeping in Cassis," later).

In the 18th century life became more secure, and people moved their homes back to the waterfront. Since then, Cassis has made its living through fishing, quarrying its famous white stone, and producing well-respected white wines—which, conveniently, pair well with the local seafood dishes, and *bien sûr*, with tourists like us.

With improvements in transportation following the end of World War II, tourism rose gradually in Cassis, though crowds are still sparse by Riviera standards. While foreigners overwhelm nearby resorts, Cassis is popular mostly with the French and still feels unspoiled. The town's protected status limits the height of the buildings along the waterfront. Cassis' port is home to some nice boats...but they're dinghies compared with those in the glitzier harbors farther east.

The big cliff towering above the castle hill is **Cap Canaille.** Europe's highest maritime cliff, it was sculpted by receding glaciers (wrap your brain around that concept), and today drops 1,200 feet straight down. You can—and should—drive or taxi along the top for staggering views (see "Above Cassis: La Route des Crêtes," later). Return to this bench at sunset, when the Cap glows a deep red.

The rocky shore off to the right looks as if it were cut away just for sunbathers. But Cassis was once an important **quarry,** and stones were sliced right out of this beach for easy transport to ships. Locals say that the Statue of Liberty's base sits on this rock (hmmm). Cassis stone remains highly valued throughout the world...but yesterday's quarrymen have been replaced by today's sunbathers.

Experiences near Cassis

▲▲▲The *Calanques*

Until you see these exotic Mediterranean fjords—with their translucent blue water, tiny intimate beaches, and stark cliffs plunging into the sea or forming rocky prom-
ontories—it's hard to understand
what all the excitement is about.

Calanques (kah-lahnks) are
narrow, steep-sided valleys partially
flooded by the sea, surrounded by
rugged white cliffs usually made
of limestone (quarries along the *calanques* have provided building stone
for centuries). The word comes from
the Corsican word *calanca,* meaning
"inlet"—the island of Corsica also has *calanques.* These inlets began
as underwater valleys carved by the seaward flow of water at river
mouths, and were later gouged deeper by glaciers. About 12,000
years ago, when the climate warmed and glaciers retreated at the
end of the last Ice Age, the sea level rose partway up the steep rocky
sides of the *calanques.* Today the cliffs harbor a unique habitat that
includes rare plants and nesting sites for unusual raptors.

The most famous inlets are in the Massif des Calanques, which
runs along a 13-mile stretch of the coast from Marseille to Cassis.
This area and part of the surrounding region became a national
park in 2012.

You can hike, or cruise by boat or kayak, to many *calanques.*
Bring water, sunscreen, and anything else you need for the day, as
there's nary a baguette for sale. Don't dawdle—to limit crowds and
because of fire hazards, the most popular *calanques* can be closed
to visitors from 11:00 on in high season (mid-June–mid-Sept) and
on weekends. When they are "closed," the only way to see the *calanques* is by boat or kayak. The TI can give you plenty of advice.

Cruising the *Calanques*: Several boats offer trips of various
lengths (3 *calanques*-€16, 2/hour, 45 minutes; 5 *calanques*-€19,
6/day, 1 hour; 8-9 *calanques*-€22-27, 2-6/day, 1.5 hours, www.
calanquesdecassis.com). The three-*calanques* tour is the most popular. Tickets are sold (and boats depart) from a small booth on the
port opposite the Hôtel Lieutaud. *Prochain départ* means "next departure." Boats vary in size (some seat up to 100).

Hiking to the *Calanques*: Plan ahead. From June to September, many of the *calanques* are closed in certain weather conditions

due to the high risk of brush fires. For information, check with the TI or call toll tel. 08 11 20 13 13; wait 30 seconds for English instructions. Conditions and closures are announced starting at 18:00 the day before.

Drivers can save 30 minutes of hiking by driving to Calanque de Port-Miou and paying €8 to park (described below). Anyone can take the *navette* shuttle bus directly from les Gorguettes parking lot to Port-Miou; it runs on weekends (April-June), holidays, and during July and August (see "Arrival by Car," earlier, for hours).

The trail lacing together *calanques* Port-Miou, Port-Pin, and d'En-Vau will warm a hiker's heart. Views are glorious, and the trail is manageable if you have decent shoes (though shade is minimal).

For most, the best *calanque* by foot is **Calanque Port-Pin,** about an hour from Cassis (30 minutes after the linear, boat-lined Calanque Port-Miou, which also works as a destination if time is short). Calanque Port-Pin is intimate and well-forested, with a small beach.

The most spectacular *calanque* is **Calanque d'En-Vau,** but it's a two-hour hike one-way from Cassis with a steep descent to the beach at the end. In summer (mid-June-mid-Sept), access is strictly controlled, and this *calanque* is closed by 11:00.

The TI's free map of Cassis gives a general idea of the *calanques* trail, and they sell a more detailed IGN *calanques* map for €9.50. Most people don't need a map for a basic hike. Start along the road behind Hôtel le Golfe and walk past Plage du Bestouan, then look for hiker signs to *Port-Miou* or *Presqu'ile* (pay attention to your route for an easier return). You'll climb up, then drop down residential streets, eventually landing at the foot of Calanque de Port-Miou, where the dirt trail begins. Follow signs to *Calanques Port-Pin* and *d'En-Vau,* walking 500 yards along a wide trail and passing through an old quarry.

You're now on the *GR (Grande Randonnée)* trail, indicated by red, white, and green markers painted on rocks, trees, and other landmarks. Follow those markers as they lead uphill (great views at top), then connect to a rough stone trail leading down to Calanque Port-Pin (nice beach, good scampering). The trail continues from here back up and on to Calanque d'En-Vau. *Bonne route!*

Other Ways to Reach the *Calanques:* From about mid-April to mid-October, you can rent a **kayak** in Cassis—or in nearby Port-Miou, which is closer to the *calanques.* In Cassis, try Club Sports Loisirs Nautiques on Place Montmorin, behind the merry-go-round (one-seater-€30/4 hours, two-seater-€45/4 hours, tel. 04 42 01 80 01, csln.cassis@gmail.com). In Port-Miou, call mobile 06 75 70 00 73. The TI has brochures for more kayak companies. You can also take a **kayak tour** (€35/half-day, €55/day, €35/sunset tour, reservations smart, mobile 06 12 95 20 12, www.provencekayakmer. fr). If the hiking trails are closed, this is the only way you'll be able to get to those *calanque* beaches.

You can rent a small **motorboat** without a special boating license (€105/morning, €150/day, €700 deposit; at Loca'Bato office, a few steps away from Hôtel le Golfe; mobile 06 43 88 19 07). Another option is JCF Boat Services, located behind the TI toward the lighthouse (about €100/morning, €200/day, mobile 06 75 74 25 81, www.jcfboat.com, contact@jcf-boat-services.com).

▲▲Above Cassis: La Route des Crêtes

If you have a car, or spring for a taxi (€30 for a 30-minute trip, 4 people per taxi), consider this remarkable drive. Ride straight up to the top of Cap Canaille and toward the next town, La Ciotat. It's a twisty road, providing access to numbingly high views over Cassis and the Mediterranean. From Cassis, follow signs to *La Ciotat/ Toulon,* then *La Route des Crêtes.* The towns just east of Cassis (La Ciotat, Bandol, etc.) do not merit a detour. This road is occasionally closed (because of strong winds or the high risk of brush fires June-Sept), though you can usually get partway up—before investing time and money in this trip, check at the TI.

Wine Tasting in the Hills Behind Cassis

The following places offer good opportunities to taste the famous (mostly white) Cassis wine with the folks who make it (remember, if it's a *free* tasting, it's polite to buy a bottle).

The most reputable winery, and easiest to reach without a car, is the **Clos Ste. Magdeleine.** English tours of the vineyard and cellar are offered Monday-Saturday usually at 11:00 and 16:00, finishing with a tasting (€10, 45 minutes, tel. 04 42 01 70 28; confirm times in advance and book with the TI).

La Ferme Blanche offers tastings (but no tours) in a small shop on a busy road, right on D-559 above town. English-speaking Jeromine likes to explain what makes Cassis wine so special (daily 9:00-12:00 & 14:00-19:00, tel. 04 42 01 00 74).

Sleeping in Cassis

Cassis hotels are laid-back places with less polish but lower rates than those on the Riviera (rooms average about €95). Some close from November to March, but those that stay open offer good discounts. All are busy on weekends and in summer, when many can come with late-night noise (though most hotels have effective double-paned windows). Book early for sea views. A few offer parking spots that you can reserve when booking your room. None of the places I list has an elevator. Consider skipping your hotel breakfast and head to the port for café au lait with a view.

NEAR THE PORT OR IN TOWN

$$$ **Best Western Hôtel la Rade*****, a 10-minute walk uphill from the port, has good views from its lovely poolside deck and welcoming lounge. The two "standard" rooms are tiny; pay the extra €20 for a "classique," but skip the "comfort" rooms which promise balconies and views of the pines, but actually look onto a street (standard Db-€120, classique Db-€140, comfort Db-€200, suites-€280, extra bed-€15, parking-€16/day, Route des Calanques, 1 Avenue de Dardanelles, tel. 04 42 01 02 97, www.hotel-cassis.com, larade@hotel-cassis.com).

$$ **Hôtel le Golfe****, over an easygoing (but not late-night) café, has good rates, so-so beds, and the best views of the port. Half of its basic and slightly worn rooms come with port views and small balconies—these are worth booking ahead. Sleep elsewhere if you can't get a view (Sb/Db without view-€95, Sb/Db with view and some noise-€115, Tb-€115-130, Qb-€130-150, dim lighting, 3 parking spaces-€8/day, nearby garage-€10/day, 3 Place Grand Carnot, tel. 04 42 01 00 21, www.legolfe-cassis.fr, contact@legolfe-cassis.fr).

$$ **Hôtel le Clos des Arômes**** is a simple, quiet retreat. This place has appealing ambience with generous public spaces. *Très provençal*, it has a big courtyard terrace and a good restaurant. The rooms have old furnishings, poor lighting, church-bell noise (rooms on the front are quieter), and no air-con (some have ceiling fans), but the place works in spite of these things (Db-€79, bigger Db-€89-99, parking-€14/day, near Parking la Viguerie at 10 Rue Abbé Paul Mouton, tel. 04 42 01 71 84, www.leclosdesaromes.fr, closdesaromes@orange.fr). It's best to book by phone.

$$ **Hôtel de France Maguy**** is a good 10-room place for drivers on a budget (plenty of parking) or those without wheels (friendly owner Franck will pick you up at the station if you book ahead). It's a few blocks up from the port, so it's fairly quiet. Rooms are small and well-maintained. More expensive rooms are slightly larger, have tiny balconies, and come with mini-fridges (Db-€95-130, Tb/Qb-€140-150, includes breakfast and parking—April-Sept only, above the Casino on Avenue du Revestel, tel. 04 42 01 72 21, www.hoteldefrancemaguy.com, hoteldefrancemaguy@gmail.com).

$$ **Hôtel Cassitel****, located on the harbor over a lively café (noisy on weekends), has comfortable rooms and double-paned windows that block out most portside noise. In some rooms the shower and sink are open to the room (standard Db-€75-85, large Db-€95-105, Tb-€105, Qb-€135, parking garage-€12/day, Place Clemenceau, tel. 04 42 01 83 44, www.hotel-cassis.com, cassitel@hotel-cassis.com).

$ **Hôtel Laurence**** offers good budget beds in small but relatively clean rooms (ashtrays by the beds). Back rooms are quieter and some have views of the château. You must call a few days ahead to confirm your reservation (Db-€55-70, Db with balcony-€80-90, Db with view terrace-€90-100, closed in winter, 2 blocks off the port beyond Hôtel Cassitel at 8 Rue de l'Arène, no parking—drop bags in load zone and head to La Madie lot, tel. 04 42 01 88 78, www.cassis-hotel-laurence.com, contact@cassis-hotel-laurence.com, friendly staff—animated Nadia runs reception).

ON PLAGE DU BESTOUAN
The next two hotels are a 10-minute walk from the port on the next beach west, Plage du Bestouan. Easy parking makes them good for drivers.

$$$ Mahogany Hôtel de la Plage*** faces the beach with a concrete exterior and mod interior, generous public spaces, a bar/restaurant facing the sea, and 30 well-conceived, quite comfortable, and mostly spacious rooms at acceptable rates (same price for Db with modern decor, deck, and sea view as for bigger suite-like Db with Provençal decor but no view-€165-185, Db suite with view-€220-280, includes breakfast, air-con, parking-€20/day—reserve ahead, tel. 04 42 01 05 70, www.hotelmahogany.com, info@hotelmahogany.com).

$$$ Le Jardin d'Emile** is a villa-hotel located below the Mahogany Hôtel de la Plage. It's a charming little refuge with rich colors inside and out, plush rooms, and a green garden. Five of the seven rooms have decks, and three have sea views (Db-€130-160, extra bed-€30, air-con, free and secure parking, tel. 04 42 01 80 55, www.lejardindemile.fr, info@lejardindemile.fr).

HIGH ABOVE THE PORT
$$$ Le Château de Cassis, privately owned and closed to the public for many years, recently opened its doors to visitors, renting five luxurious suites as *chambres d'hôtes*. Celebrities are often in residence, so access is strictly forbidden unless you have a reservation (suites-€350-700, spacious pool, gardens, views galore, all the amenities you can imagine, book well in advance, tel. 04 42 01 63 20, www.chateaudecassis.com, contact@chateaudecassis.com).

Eating in Cassis

Peruse the lineup of tempting restaurants along the port, window-shop the recommended places below, and then decide for yourself (all have good interior and exterior seating). You can have a ham-and-cheese crêpe or go all-out for bouillabaisse with the same great view. Arrive by 19:30 for the view tables. Picnickers can enjoy a beggars' banquet at the benches at Hôtel le Golfe or on the beach, or discover your own quiet places along the lanes away from the port (small grocery stores open until 19:30). Local wines are terrific: red from Bandol and whites/rosés from Cassis.

DINING PORTSIDE

The first four places are ideally situated side by side, allowing diners to comparison shop.

El Sol is sharp and popular with discerning diners (*menus*-€21-30, closed Mon-Tue off-season, 20 Quai des Baux, tel. 04 42 01 76 10).

L'Oustau de la Mar has a loyal following and fair prices (*menu*-€25, closed Thu, 20 Quai des Baux, tel. 04 42 01 78 22).

Bar Canaille specializes in fresh seafood platters, oysters, and other shellfish (open daily in summer, closed Wed off-season, 22 Quai des Baux, tel. 04 42 01 72 36).

Chez César was most popular with locals on my last visit, with good prices and selection (€28 *marmite de pêcheur*—a poor man's bouillabaisse, €14 *plats, menus* from €24, closed Sun-Mon, 21 Quai des Baux, tel. 04 42 01 75 47).

Le 8 et Demi serves crêpes, pizza, salads, and ice cream on plastic tables with front-and-center portside views (closed Thu off-season, 8 Quai des Baux, tel. 04 42 01 94 63).

The **Grand Marnier crêpe stand** cooks delicious dessert crêpes to go for €3—the Grand Marnier crêpe rules. This is ideal for strollers (next to Le 8 et Demi, daily April-Sept 15:00-23:30).

DINING AWAY FROM THE PORT

Le Clos des Arômes, listed earlier under "Sleeping in Cassis," is the place to come for a refined, candlelit dinner. Dine on a lovely enclosed terrace (€26 *menu,* daily, tel. 04 42 01 71 84).

Le Calendal serves up *menus* that feature local dishes in a warm, charming, and cozy setting. Don't be surprised if the chef visits your table (indoor or terrace seating available). If you want bouillabaisse, you must order it a day ahead of time (€33 *menu,* closed Sun for lunch and all day Mon, 3 Rue Brémond, tel. 04 42 01 17 70).

Le Grand Large is indeed large and owns the scenic beachfront next to the TI. Come here for a quiet drink before dinner, or to dine seaside rather than portside (€30 *menu* with good choices, open daily, Plage de Cassis, tel. 04 42 01 81 00).

Bada is a trendy beachfront place behind the TI, serving breakfast with the sounds of crashing waves, and €16 salads (daily, dinner June-Sept only, Promenade Aristide Briand, tel. 04 42 83 70 09).

La Girondole is an easy place for families, with cheap pizza, pasta, and salads. It's a block off the port (closed Tue year-round and Mon off-season, 1 Rue Thérèse Rastit, tel. 04 42 01 13 39, takeaway tel. 04 86 33 54 33).

Cassis Connections

Cassis' train station is two miles from the port. Shuttle buses meet some trains on weekdays, and taxis are reasonable (for details, see "Arrival in Cassis," earlier). All destinations below require a transfer in Marseille.

From Cassis by Train to: Marseille (2/hour, 25 minutes), **Aix-en-Provence Centre-Ville** (hourly, 1.5 hours, transfer in Marseille), **Arles** (7/day, 2 hours), **Avignon TGV** (7/day, with transfer in Marseille, 1.5 hours), **Nice** (hourly, 3 hours, transfer in Marseille or Toulon), **Paris** (7/day, 4 hours).

From Cassis by Bus to: Marseille (6/day Mon-Sat, 4/day Sun, 40 minutes, easier than train, TI has schedule—beware of afternoon gaps in service). Buses run from the stop labeled *Gendarmerie* on Avenue du 11 Novembre (a 5-minute walk from the port) to Marseille's Castellane Métro stop.

Aix-en-Provence

Aix-en-Provence is famous for its outdoor markets and handsome pedestrian lanes, as well as its cultivated residents and their abil-

ity to embrace the good life. Nowhere else in France is *l'art de vivre* (the art of living) so stylishly displayed. It was that way when the French king made the town his administrative capital of Provence, and it's that way today. For a tourist, Aix-en-Provence (the "Aix" is pronounced "X") is happily free of any obligatory turnstiles. And there's not a single ancient site to see. It's just a wealthy town filled with 140,000 people—most of whom, it seems, know how to live well and look good. Aix-en-Provence's 40,000 well-dressed students (many from other countries) give the city a year-round youthful energy, and its numerous squares, lined with cafés and fine shops, allow everyone a comfortable place to pose.

Orientation to Aix-en-Provence

With no "must-see" sights, Aix works well as a day trip, and is best on days when the most markets thrive (Tue, Thu, and Sat). The city can be seen in a 1.5-hour stroll from the TI or train station, though connoisseurs of southern French culture will want more time to savor it. Aix makes a handy base for day-tripping to Marseille, Cassis, and southern villages of the Luberon (such as Lourmarin).

Cours Mirabeau (the grand central boulevard) divides the stately, quiet Mazarin Quarter from the lively old town (where the action is). In the old town, picturesque squares are connected by fine pedestrian shopping lanes, many of which lead to the cathedral. Right-angle intersections define the Mazarin Quarter but are rare in the old town—expect to get turned around regularly.

TOURIST INFORMATION

The TI, France's grandest, is located at La Rotonde traffic circle. Use the free Wi-Fi and get the walking-tour brochure *In the Footsteps of Cézanne,* with the best city-center map and a good overview of excursions in the area. The TI also has maps covering areas beyond old Aix (Mon-Sat 8:30-19:00, Sun 10:00-13:00 & 14:00-18:00, longer hours in summer, shorter hours in winter, 300 Avenue Giuseppe Verdi, tel. 04 42 16 11 61, www.aixenprovencetourism.com).

English-language **walking tours** (shown on monitors in the TI) of the old town are offered at 10:00 on Tuesdays; Cézanne walking tours leave at 10:00 on Thursdays and Saturdays (€9, two hours, depart from the TI).

Daily **excursions** into the countryside—Luberon villages, Pont du Gard, Les Baux, wineries, Mt. Ste. Victoire, and more—are also available from the TI (figure per-person costs of €60-80/half-day and €120-140/day).

ARRIVAL IN AIX-EN-PROVENCE

By Train: Aix-en-Provence has two train stations: Centre-Ville, near the city center, and the faraway TGV station. Neither has baggage storage.

Arrival at the Centre-Ville Station: It's a breezy 10-minute stroll to the TI and pedestrian area. Cross the boulevard in front of the station and walk up Avenue Victor Hugo; turn left at the first intersection (you're still on Victor Hugo). At the large fountain (La Rotonde), turn left and go about a quarter of the way around the fountain to find the TI.

Arrival at Aix-en-Provence TGV Station: Shuttle buses *(navettes)* connect the distant TGV station with Aix-en-Provence's city-center bus station, described next (€4, 4/hour, 15 minutes).

From the tracks, follow signs for *Navette-Direction Aix-en-Provence* to the end of the hall and downstairs (buses leave from an underpass below the tracks).

By Bus: Aix-en-Provence's bus station *(gare routière)* is on Avenue de l'Europe near its intersection with Avenue des Belges (tel. 08 21 20 22 03). From the bus station, it's a 10-minute walk to the town center and the TI. Head slightly uphill to the flowery round-about, turn left on Avenue des Belges, and walk to the splashing fountain (La Rotonde, the big traffic circle by the TI).

By Plane: Buses link Marseille's airport with the bus station in Aix-en-Provence (2/hour, 30 minutes, www.navetteaixtgvaeroport.com).

By Car: The city is well-signed (yellow for hotels, green for parking). First, follow signs to *Centre-Ville,* then the yellow signs to find your hotel (GPS is handy). If your hotel has parking, use it. Otherwise, once you've spotted your hotel sign, follow green signs to park in the first pay lot you see (I've noted the closest parking to each hotel under "Sleeping in Aix-en-Provence," later). Day-trippers should look for the La Rotonde parking area (near the TI) or park in any pay lot near the old city—allow €16/day.

HELPFUL HINTS

Markets: Aix-en-Provence bubbles over with photogenic open-air morning markets in several of its squares: **Richelme** (produce daily, my favorite), **Palace of Justice** (produce and flea market Tue, Thu, and Sat), **L'Hôtel de Ville** (flower market Tue, Thu, and Sat; book market first Sun of each month), and along **Cours Mirabeau** (textiles and crafts, Tue and Thu morning). Most pack up at 13:00, except the book market, which runs all day. Saturday market days are the biggest. It's well worth planning your visit for a market day, as these markets are the sightseeing highlights of the town.

Shopping: Signs at fancy bakeries advertise *calissons d'Aix,* the city's famous homemade candy. It's made with almond paste—kind of like a marzipan cake—and makes a pleasing souvenir. You may want to pick up a pair of especially **dark sunglasses** (to be more discreet when appreciating the beautiful people of Aix-en-Provence). There's an upscale, glassy **Apple Store** next to the TI at La Rotonde.

Internet Access: The TI has free Wi-Fi.

Services: Public WCs, as they're not stylish, are rare in Aix. Take advantage of WCs in restaurants, museums, or at other stops you make.

MARSEILLE

Aix-en-Provence

200 Meters
200 Yards

To Atelier Cezanne

AVE. PASTEUR

AVE. JEAN JAURES

TOWER

THERMES SEXTIUS

RUE DU BON PASTEUR

RUE DE LA MOLLE

Jardin de Vendôme

R. MÉRINDOL

OLD

4

To Avignon via A-7

RUE CELONY

Forum des Cardeurs

9

R. DES CORDELIERS

RUE D'ENT.

Place des Tanneurs

COURS SEXTIUS

RUE LISSE DES CORDELIERS

R. DE LA COUR

To Luberon & **25**

ST. JEAN BAPTISTE

13

26

RUE DES BERNADINES

BLVD. DE LA RÉPUBLIQUE

AVE. BONAPARTE

RUE VICTOR LEYDET

Place J. d'Arc

Electric Minibus

La Rotonde

B

AVE. MAX JUVENAL

To Marseille via A-51

POST LAPIERRE

26

WALK BEGINS

RUE GONTARD

AVE. DES BELGES

RUE G. DESPLACES

AVE. DE L'EUROPE

BUS STATION
& TGV SHUTTLE BUS

To Marseille, Cassis & TGV Station

TRAIN STATION

1 Hôtel Cézanne
2 To Chambre d'Hôte Pavillon de la Torse
3 Hôtel Saint Christophe
4 L'Epicerie Chambres
5 Hôtel Cardinal
6 Hôtel des Quatre Dauphins
7 Hôtel le Concorde
8 Bistrot des Philosophes & Le Papagayo Café
9 L'Epicurien Restaurant
10 Restaurant Incontournable
11 L'Epicerie Restaurant
12 Chez Mitch Restaurant
13 Chez Charlotte Restaurant
14 La Pizza
15 La Fromagerie du Passage
16 Les Deux Garçons Restaurant
17 Le Grillon Restaurant
18 La Brocherie Restaurant
19 Boulangerie La Varenne
20 O'Shannon's Pub
21 Pub O'Sullivan
22 Brûlerie Richelme
23 Book In Bar Bookshop
24 Monoprix (Groceries)
25 Car Rentals (3)
26 Launderettes (3)

AVE. JULES ISAAC

BLVD. A. BRIAND

BLVD. FRANCOIS ET EMILE ZOLA

WALK ENDS

ST. SAUVEUR

RUE MARIE CURIE

Place des Martyrs

R. G. DE SAPORTA

RUE F. BERT

COURS ST. LOUIS

RUE MIGNET

RUE BOULEGON

❽

⓫

❿

Hôtel de Ville Square

MADELEINE CHURCH

R. GRANET

CITY HALL

POST

❷❷ Richelme Square

RUE F. GAUT

❷❶

RUE M. FOCH

R. LAURENT FAUCHIER

BRUNET CHOC.

TOWN

Palace of Justice Square

RUE PORTALIS

BLVD CARNOT

PALACE OF JUSTICE

Place de Verdun

RUE MANUEL

RUE E. DAVID

Place Miollis

RUE AUDE

PASSAGE AGARD

❶❺

❶❾

RUE CLEM.

RUE FABROT

RUE DE L'OPERA

❶❷

ST. ESPRIT

R. TANNEURS

RUE ESPARIAT

R. NAZARETH

Place d'Albertas

❶❼

❶❻

Place Forbin

RUE MARECHAL JOFFRE

❶❹

RUE COURT.

❷❹

RUE D'ITALIE

❷❶

COURS MIRABEAU

RUE CABASSOL

MAISON BECHARD

RUE MAZARINE

ARBAUD MUSEUM

RUE F. MISTRAL

RUE FERNAND DOL

❺

❶❽ ❷❻

ST. JEAN DE MALTE

AVE. V. HUGO

RUE LAROQUE

RUE GOYRAND

❷❸

MAZARIN

RUE CARDINALE

Place des 4 Dauphins

❻

RUE 4 SEPTEMBRE

GRANET MUSEUM

To ❷

❸

AVE. VICTOR HUGO

AVE. MALHERBE

QUARTER

❼

COURS GAMBETTA

❶

BLVD. DU ROI RENE

To Cassis via A-8

AVE. V. HUGO

❷❺

AVE. ANATOLE FRANCE

❷❺

Parc Jourdan

English Bookstore: Located on the quiet side of Aix-en-Provence, the atmospheric **Book in Bar** has a good collection of adult and children's books, and a good selection of tourist guides (Cassis, Arles, Avignon, and so on) and an inviting cafe (Mon-Sat 9:00-19:00, closed Sun, 4 Rue Joseph Cabassol, where it crosses Rue Goyrand, tel. 04 42 26 60 07).

Laundry: Launderettes are scattered throughout the city. **Ecolav'**, with free Wi-Fi, is just behind the TI on Square Narvik at 3 Rue Lapierre (daily 7:00-21:00). Others are at 11 Rue des Bernardines and at 3 Rue Fernand Dol (both daily 8:00-19:00).

Supermarket: Monoprix, on Cours Mirabeau, two long blocks up from La Rotonde, has a grocery store in the basement (Mon-Sat 8:30-21:30, closed Sun), but you'll find small ones all over the city.

Taxi: Call 04 42 27 71 11. A taxi from your Aix-en-Provence hotel to Marseille costs about €65 and to Cassis about €90.

Car Rental: Avis and **Hertz** are at the Centre-Ville train station (43 Avenue Victor Hugo, tel. 04 42 27 91 32), and **Europcar** is near La Rotonde (55 Boulevard de la République, toll tel. 08 25 89 69 76). All major companies have offices at the TGV station.

Tours in Aix-en-Provence

Local Guides

Pascale Benguigui is a good choice for this area (also recommended earlier for Marseille; see listing on page 232). Also consider **Catherine d'Antuono** and Sarah Pernet, who runs **Discover Provence Tours** (both listed on page 28).

Electric Minibus Joyride

For a mere €0.50, take a joyride through the winding lanes of the old town center on a *Diabline*—a six-seater electric-powered minibus. It leaves every 10 minutes from the La Rotonde fountain, opposite the TI (Mon-Sat 8:30-19:30, none on Sun, 40 minutes round-trip). You can also wave one down anywhere and hop on. There are three routes (A, B, and C); ask the driver for a map when you board. Line A gives you the best overview of the city and runs a route similar to the self-guided walk described later. It also gets you near Cézanne's studio. Designed with local seniors in mind, the minibus provides a fun (and less glamorous) slice-of-life experience in Aix-en-Provence.

Petit Train

Rest your feet and discover Aix-en-Provence's historic center on a 50-minute tour on the little train, while listening to English com-

Aix-en-Provence History

Aix-en-Provence was founded in about 120 B.C. as a Roman military camp on the site of a thermal hot spring (in France, "Aix" refers to a city built over a hot spring). The Romans' mission: to defend the Greek merchants of Marseille against the local Celts.

Strategically situated Aix-en-Provence was the first Roman base outside Italy—the first foreign holding of what would become a vast empire. (The region's name—Provence—comes from its status as the first Roman province.) But Rome eventually fell, and the barbarians destroyed Aix-en-Provence in the fourth century. Through the Dark Ages, Aix-en-Provence's Roman buildings were nibbled to nothing by people needing their pre-cut stones. No buildings from Roman Aix-en-Provence survive.

Aix-en-Provence was of no importance through the Middle Ages. Because the area was once owned by Barcelona, Provence has the same colors as Catalunya: gold and red. In 1481 the Count of Provence died. He was hairless (according to my guide). Without a hair, Provence was gobbled up by France. When Aix-en-Provence was made the district's administrative center, noble French families moved in, kicking off the city's beautiful age (belle époque). They built about 200 *hôtels particuliers* (private mansions)—many of which survive today—giving Aix-en-Provence its classy look. As you wander around the town, look up, peek in, and notice the stately architecture with its grandiose extra touches.

Aix-en-Provence thrived thanks to its aristocratic population. But when the Revolution made being rich dicey, Aix-en-Provence's aristocracy and clergy fled. Aix-en-Provence entered the next stage of its history as the "Sleeping Beauty city." Later in the 19th century, the town woke up and resumed its pretentious ways. In Aix-en-Provence, the custom of rich people being bobbed along in sedan chairs survived longer than anywhere else in France. After the Revolution, you couldn't have servants do it—but you could hire pallbearers in their off-hours to give you a lift. If being ostentatious ever became the norm...it happened in Aix-en-Provence.

mentary (€7, departs from La Rotonde fountain). Ask about the longer tours that cover Cézanne's steps.

Aix-en-Provence Walk

I've listed these streets, squares, and sights in the order of a handy, lazy orientation stroll. This self-guided walk is highlighted on the map on page 262.

• *Start on Cours Mirabeau at La Rotonde, near the statues on either side of the street, and face...*

La Rotonde

In the 1600s, the roads from Paris and Marseille met just outside the Aix-en-Provence town wall at a huge roundabout called La

Rotonde. From here locals enjoyed a sweeping view of open countryside before entering the town. As time passed, growing Aix-en-Provence needed space more than fortifications. The wall was destroyed and replaced by a grand boulevard (Cours Mirabeau). A modern grid-plan town, the Mazarin Quarter (to the right as you look up Cours Mirabeau), arose across the boulevard from the medieval town (on the left). In 1860, to give residents water and shade, the town graced La Rotonde with a fountain and a grand boulevard lined with trees. The three figures on top of the fountain represent Justice, Agriculture, and Fine Arts. *Voilà:* The modern core of Aix-en-Provence was created. The Apple store facing La Rotonde is another feather in Aix's style cap.

• *Saunter slowly up the right side of Cours Mirabeau.*

Cours Mirabeau

This "Champs-Elysées of Provence" divides the higgledy-piggledy old town (left) and the stately Mazarin Quarter (right). Designed

for the rich and famous to strut their fancy stuff, Cours Mirabeau survives much as it was: a single lane for traffic and an extravagant pedestrian promenade, shaded by plane trees (see sidebar), cafés on the sunny side, and lined by 17th- and 18th-century mansions for the aristocracy. Rich folks lived on the right side (in the Mazarin Quarter); common folk

MARSEILLE

Plane Trees

Stately old plane trees line boulevards such as Cours Mirabeau in Aix-en-Provence and provide canopies of shade for roads and town squares all over southern France. These trees are a part of the local scene.

The plane tree is a hybrid of the Asian and American sycamores—created accidentally in a 16th-century Oxford botanical garden. The result was the perfect city tree: fast-growing, resistant to Industrial Age pollution, and hearty (it can survive with little water and lousy soil). The plane tree was imported to southern France in the 19th century to replace traditional elm trees. Napoleon planted them along roads to give his soldiers shade for their long marches. Plane trees were used to leaf up grand boulevards as towns throughout France—including Aix-en-Provence—built their Champs-Elysées wannabes. Sadly, a modern disease is taking its toll and many trees are dying.

lived on the left side (in the old town). Cross-streets were gated to keep everyone in their place. Which side are you sleeping on?

The street follows a plan based on fours: 440 meters long, 44 meters wide, plane trees (originally elms) 4 meters apart, and decorated by 4 fountains. The "mossy fountains," overgrown by 200 years of neglect, trickle with water from the thermal spa that gave Aix its first name (and make steamy sights on cold winter days).

Cours Mirabeau was designed for showing off. Today, it remains a place for *tendance* (trendiness)—or even *hyper-tendance*. If French culture seems pretentious, you feel that such pretense was born right here. Show your stuff and strut the broad sidewalk. As you stroll up the boulevard, stop in front of Aix's oldest and most venerated *patisserie*, **Maison Béchard** (on the right side at 12 Cours Mirabeau) and get a whiff coming from the vent under the entry. They are famous for the candy called *calisson*. Like many local treats, these come with a history. The venerable delicacy of almond, melon, and orange rind draped in icing, whose name means "hug" in French, was concocted for a royal wedding here in the 14th century.

For a glimpse of the finest surviving mansion in the Mazarin Quarter (described below), take a side-trip from the next fountain one block right down Rue Joseph Cabassol to #3 (peek through the gate). The 17th-century Hôtel Caumont hosts the **Caumont Centre d'Art** (overpriced for most at €11). While it has two permanent rooms offering a feel for aristocratic luxury in the age of Louis XIV, its main attractions are its fine special exhibits, elegant café, and formal garden. Cézanne fans will enjoy the 30-minute movie about the artist in the center's theater—check showtimes as you enter (May-Sept daily 10:00-19:00, off-season until 18:00).

• *Keep strutting up Cours Mirabeau. From the mossy fountain at Rue du 4 Septembre, turn right onto Aix-en-Provence's quiet side, the pleasing little Place des Quatre Dauphins. This marks the center of the...*

Mazarin Quarter (Quartier Mazarin)

Built in a grid plan during the reign of King Louis XIV, the Mazarin Quarter remains a peaceful, elegant residential neighborhood—although each of its mansions now houses several families rather than just one. Study the quarter's Baroque and Neoclassical architecture (from the 17th and 18th centuries). The square's Fountain of the Four Dolphins, inspired by Bernini's fountains in Rome, dates from an age when Italian culture set the Baroque standard across Europe. Appreciate how calm this half of the city feels.

Wander left up Rue Cardinale to a 12th-century church facing a handsome square. St. Jean-de-Malte was built when this area was outside the town wall—500 years before the advent of the Mazarin Quarter. The adjacent **Musée Granet** features Aix's homegrown artists (including several "lesser" paintings by Cézanne). The museum is most popular for its selection of post-Impressionist works, including some by Picasso, Van Gogh, and Braque. Check its website to learn about current exhibits, or ask at the TI (open June-Sept Tue-Sun 10:00-19:00, Oct-May Tue-Sun 12:00-18:00, closed Mon year-round, www.museegranet-aixenprovence.fr).

Walk behind the church (on the left) to the left-hand corner where a sweet mosaic of the Fountain of the Four Dolphins Square gives a fun glimpse of the sedan-chair elegance of this quarter back in its heyday.

• *Turn left on Rue d'Italie, lined by edible temptations. Pause and appreciate the stately architecture mixed with the patina of age. Walk along Rue d'Italie to Place Forbin, and go left to the top of Cours Mirabeau, which is marked by a statue. This is René d'Anjou, the last count of Provence, during whose rule this region joined France (c. 1450). He was nicknamed "Bon Vivant" for his cultured lifestyle and taste for the good life. Stroll down the right side of the street to #53, and spot the venerable...*

Les Deux Garçons

This café, once frequented by Paul Cézanne, remains *the* hangout on the boulevard. Peek inside at its classic old interior. The Cézanne family hat shop was next door (#55). Cézanne's dad parlayed that successful business into a bank, then into greater wealth, setting up his son to be free to enjoy his artistic pursuits.

• *From here we'll enter the lively old town, where pedestrian streets are filled with fine food stores and boutiques, and romantic street musicians. This is the place in Aix-en-Provence for shopping.*

Leave Cours Mirabeau at #55, through the tiny Passage Agard (notice the gate that was locked at night to keep the rich safe from the poor). It leads to a square dominated by the **Palace of Justice,** *which hosts a bustling flea market (Tue, Thu, and Sat mornings, with bric-a-brac at the near end and produce at the far end). If the market is on, explore it. Otherwise, head left along the first street you crossed as you came into the square, Rue Marius Reinaud, which hosts the top designer shops in town. Pause several blocks down when you hear the gurgling of water at the peaceful courtyard square called...*

Place d'Albertas

This sweet little square was created by the guy who lived across the street. He hated the medieval mess of buildings facing his man-

sion, so he drew up a harmonious facade with a fountain, and had his ideal vision built to mask the ugly neighborhood. The long-overdue restoration of this once run-down square hit a snag. Since only two-thirds of the property owners agreed to help fund the work, one-third remains undone.

With your back to the fountain, find the large wooden door on the building across the street. Take a look at the names on the door buzzers—the Albertas family still lives here.

• *Turn right on Rue Aude, the main street of medieval Aix-en-Provence (which turns into Rue du Maréchal Foch). Notice the side streets, with their traffic-barrier stumps that lower during delivery hours. Turn right at Rue Laurent Fauchier, and detour down a few steps for what the French call a little "window licking"...*

Brunet Chocolatier and *Macarons*

In this shop (closed Sun-Mon) you'll find *macarons,* those wonderful confections made of luscious buttercreams sandwiched between two cloud-like almond meringue cookies. While popular throughout France, they are the rage in Aix. You'll find them in every flavor imaginable. Try the caramel with salted butter, pistachio, or blackcurrant violet.

• *Return to the big street and continue uphill to...*

Richelme Square (Place Richelme)

This inviting square hosts a lively market, as it has since the 1300s (daily 8:00-13:00). It's the perfect Provençal scene—lovely buildings, plane trees, and farmers selling local produce. The goat-cheese merchants here add life to the market. The cafés at the end of the square are ideal for savoring the market ambience: Pause for a drink at one or get a fresh-baked snack at Boulangerie La Varenne. To experience the best coffee in Aix (or, perhaps a chocolate frappe), go local at Brûlerie Richelme.

• *One block uphill is the stately...*

L'Hôtel de Ville Square (Place de l'Hôtel de Ville)

This square is anchored by a Roman column. Stand with your back to the column and face the Hôtel de Ville. The center niche of

this 17th-century City Hall once featured a bust of Louis XIV. But since the Revolution, Marianne (the Lady of the Republic) has taken his place. As throughout Europe, the three flags represent the region (Provence), country (France), and the European Union. Provence's flag carries the red and yellow of Catalunya (the proud and semi-autonomous region around Barcelona in Spain) because the counts of Provence originated there. Aix-en-Provence's coat of arms over the doorway combines the Catalan flag and the French fleur-de-lis.

The 18th-century building on your left was once the town's corn exchange (today it's a post office). Its exuberant pediment features figures representing the two rivers of Provence: old man Rhône and madame Durance. While the Durance River floods frequently (here depicted overflowing its frame), it also brings fertility to the fields (hence the cornucopia).

Back toward Hôtel de Ville, the 16th-century bell tower was built in part with stones scavenged from ancient Roman buildings—notice the lighter stones at the tower's base. The niche above the arch also once displayed the bust of the king. Since the Revolution, it has housed a funerary urn that symbolically honors all who gave their lives for French liberty. Walk under the arch to see a small plaque honoring the American 3rd Division that liberated the town in 1944 (with the participation of French troops; Aix-en-Provence got through World War II relatively unscathed).

History aside, the square is a delight for its vintage French storefronts and colorful morning markets, such as the flower mar-

Paul Cézanne in Aix-en-Provence

Post-Impressionist artist Paul Cézanne (1839-1906) loved Aix-en-Provence. He studied law at the university (opposite the cathedral), and produced most of his paintings in and around Aix-en-Provence—even though at the time this conservative town was disinclined to understand him or his art. Today the city fathers milk anything remotely related to his years here. While there's almost no actual art by Cezanne in Aix, fans of the artist will want to pick up the *In the Footsteps of Cézanne* self-guided-tour flier at the TI, and follow the bronze pavement markers around town.

Atelier Cézanne, the artist's last studio, has been preserved as it was when he died and is open to the public. It's a 30-minute walk from the TI, or you can get there on electric minibus A (see "Tours in Provence," earlier). Although there is no art here, his tools and personal belongings make it worthwhile for enthusiasts.

Cost and Hours: €6, daily July-Aug 10:00-18:00, April-June and Sept 10:00-12:00 & 14:00-18:00, Oct-March until 17:00, English-language tours usually at 17:00—must book through TI, 2 miles from TI at 9 Avenue Cézanne, tel. 04 42 16 10 91, www.atelier-cezanne.com.

ket (Tue, Thu, and Sat). On non-market days and each afternoon, café tables replace the market stalls.

• *Stroll under the bell tower and up Rue Gaston de Saporta to the...*

Cathedral of the Holy Savior (Saint-Sauveur)

This church was built atop the Roman forum—likely on the site of a pagan temple. As the cathedral grew with the city, its interior became a parade of architectural styles. The many-faceted interior is at once confusing and fascinating, with three distinct sections: Standing at the entrance, you face the Romanesque section; to the left are the Gothic and then the Baroque sections (daily 8:00-12:00 & 14:00-18:00).

Visiting the Cathedral: In the **Romanesque section** (to the right as you enter) step down and into a different age. Find the baptistery, surrounded by ancient columns with original fourth-century capitals below a Renaissance cupola. Its early Christian (fourth-century) Roman font seems dug into the floor. But 1,600 years ago, the floor was lower. The baptistery was located outside the church until the 14th century, when the church was expanded to encompass the baptistery. The font is big enough for immersion, which was the baptismal style in Roman times.

Farther down is the door to the 12th-century cloister, with its delicate carved capitals (French-only tours on the half-hour except 12:00-14:00). After passing a side chapel, find the closet-sized architectural footprint of the original Christian chapel from the Roman era (like the baptistery, it's several feet below today's floor level). This too would have been outside the current church walls until the 14th century.

In the **Gothic section,** two organs flank the nave: One works, but the other is a prop, added for looks...an appropriately symmetrical Neoclassical touch, as was the style in the 18th century (notice the lack of depth in one of them).

• *Your tour is over. Walking back through town, marvel at a place filled with people who seem to be living life very, very well.*

Sleeping in Aix-en-Provence

Hotel rooms, starting at about €75, are surprisingly reasonable in this highbrow city. Reserve ahead, particularly on weekends. Hotel stars have less meaning here. The best values are on the quiet side of Cours Mirabeau in the Mazarin Quarter.

$$$ Hôtel Cézanne********, a block up from the Centre-Ville train station, delivers professional service with a smile. The lobby and 55 spacious rooms are modern and surround a generous patio (Db-€265, deluxe Db-€375, free parking—must book ahead, 40 Avenue Victor Hugo, tel. 04 42 91 11 11, www.hotelaix.com, hotelcezanne@hotelaix.com). Charming chef Christiane serves a daily gourmet brunch for €20 (try the truffle omelet and the French toast).

$$$ Chambre d'Hôte Pavillon de la Torse is an upscale B&B in a park-like setting. In this urban retreat you'll enjoy big rooms, manicured gardens, and a swimming pool (Db-€160-200, €20 less Nov and March; 2-night minimum, includes breakfast, easy parking, 20-30-minute walk south of the old city at 69 Cours Gambetta, tel. 09 50 58 49 96, www.latorse.com, contact@latorse.com).

$$$ Hôtel Saint Christophe******, a business-class hotel just off La Rotonde, offers acceptable rates though the accommodations play second fiddle to a bustling brasserie. It has 67 well-equipped rooms, some with small terraces (smaller Db-€118, larger Db-€150, mezzanine sleeps up to 4-€210, parking garage-€14/day, 2 Avenue

Victor Hugo, tel. 04 42 26 01 24, www.hotel-saintchristophe.com, saintchristophe@francemarket.com).

$$ L'Epicerie Chambres is an unusual bed-and-breakfast. The reception is a nostalgic general store, and the five rooms above it are tastefully designed and spacious (Db-€115-150, Tb suite-€180, includes breakfast, limited check-in hours, a block off Forum des Cardeurs at 12 Rue du Cancel, mobile 06 08 85 38 68, www. unechambreenville.eu).

$$ Hôtel Cardinal** is a top value in Aix-en-Provence's quiet and classy Mazarin Quarter. It's a creaky old mansion that literally shakes when people walk, with tilting floors, old-time bathrooms, and spacious, 19th-century elegance under chandeliers in each room. The paintings hanging in public spaces were done by the owner Nathalie's papa (Sb-€69, Db-€79, cavernous Db suite in nearby annex-€117, closest parking is Mignet, 24 Rue Cardinale, tel. 04 42 38 32 30, www.hotel-cardinal-aix.com, hotel.cardinal@wanadoo.fr).

$$ Hôtel des Quatre Dauphins** is a simple and sweet Old World place in the quiet quarter with soft rooms and modern bathrooms, and good rates (Db-€75-90, bigger Db-€105, Tb-€105-120, no elevator, three floors, closest parking is Carnot, 54 Rue Roux Alphéran, tel. 04 42 38 16 19, www.lesquatredauphins.fr, lesquatredauphins@wanadoo.fr).

$$ Hôtel le Concorde** sits on the busy ring road, but most of its rooms gather around a quiet, convivial courtyard. Choose between rooms in the main building or the motel-esque rooms on the courtyard (Db-€84, *grand confort* Db-€95-100, thin walls, parking-€10/day, 68 Boulevard du Roi René, tel. 04 42 26 03 95, www. hotel-aixenprovence-concorde.com, contact@hotel-leconcorde.fr).

Eating in Aix-en-Provence

In Aix-en-Provence, you can dine on bustling squares, along a grand boulevard, or on atmospheric side streets. Cours Mirabeau is good for desserts and drinks, as are many of the outdoor places lining leafy squares. While I like to sleep in a quiet neighborhood, I love the commotion of table-lined squares and the romance of a

tangled old town. These recommendations offer plenty of variety. *Bon appétit!*

IN THE OLD TOWN
On Forum des Cardeurs: This traffic-free esplanade is Aix's grandiose living room—a festival of restaurants in all sizes and shapes. It is the high-energy place to be if you want to party with

dinner under the sky—and dining is available on Sunday, too, when most other places are closed. Come early or reserve ahead on good-weather weekends. Otherwise, window-shop the selection from top to bottom, then decide. Here are my three favorite places on the square:

Bistrot des Philosophes, at the top of the square at #20, is a fun place serving good quality Mediterranean dishes to happy locals. It has a cool terrace ambience and the best inside seating on the square (€20-25 filling *plats,* open daily, tel. 04 42 21 64 35).

Le Papagayo, a couple of doors down from Philosophes, feels like a beach resort at chow time. It's an energetic scene with booths and tables anchored around a center island. They offer a good selection of salads, daily specials, and trendy burgers (big €14 salads, €20 *plats,* open daily, tel. 04 42 23 98 35).

L'Epicurien (at #13) serves creative, top-quality Provençal cuisine. Dining outside is better than in the restaurant's tiny interior (€24 *plats,* *menus* €35-52, open daily for lunch and Wed-Sat for dinner, book ahead, tel. 06 89 33 49 83).

On Romantic Place des Ormeaux: Two good restaurants occupy this intimate square, with tables crowding a soothing fountain. This is the candle-lit, romantic-square alternative to the more boisterous Forum des Cardeurs. The outdoor seating for both of these places is more charming than the indoor seating.

Restaurant Incontournable, serving carefully prepared, classic French cuisine with modern twists, is worth booking ahead (€15 lunches, €20 dinner salads and *plats,* €32 three-course *menus,* closed Sun-Mon, 14 Rue Montigny, tel. 09 80 32 86 32).

L'Epicerie Restaurant seems less popular but delivers beautifully presented plates. It's a good fallback if Incontournable is full (closed Sun, Place des 3 Ormeaux, tel. 04 42 57 45 91).

Other Favorites Buried in the Old Town: **Chez Mitch** is a dressier choice for a classic French dinner (no lunch) with modern flair. Enjoy the seasonal well-presented dishes, excellent wine list, and top-notch service that Mitch assures. Book ahead for weekends (€30-50 *menus,* closed Sun, 26 Rue des Tanneurs, tel. 04 42 26 63 08, www.mitchrestaurant.com).

Chez Charlotte is Aix's low-key diner, where locals go for solid food at a good price served by Laurent and Nathalie in a fun back garden. While they have indoor seating, I'd only dine in the garden (€17 three-course *menus* only, open from 20:00, closed Sun-Mon, 32 Rue des Bernardines, tel. 04 42 26 77 56).

La Pizza has been baking pizzas for the neighborhood since 1952. It's a family-friendly place with fine outdoor seating on a pedestrian lane and a jovial interior (€18 pizzas, *tartines,* and hearty salads, closed Wed, 3 Rue Aude).

La Fromagerie du Passage is a creative delight for anyone who's hungry and likes French cheese. Study their menu and ask for help—there's a world of fun options. I like the €19 five-cheeses-bread-and-salad deal—go right up to the cheese counter and pick what looks good (daily 12:00-15:00 & 18:00-23:00, lots of wine served in small tasting portions, big charcuterie plates, off 55 Cours Mirabeau in the Passage Agard, tel. 04 42 22 90 00). They have great seating on three floors. The top-floor terrace is a find.

ALONG COURS MIRABEAU

If you're interested in a delicious view more than delicious food, eat with style on Cours Mirabeau.

Les Deux Garçons has long been the place to see and be seen: a vintage brasserie with door-to-door waiters in aprons, a lovely interior, and well-positioned outdoor tables with properly placed silverware on white tablecloths. It's busy at lunch but quiet for dinner (€20-30 *plats*, three-course *menus* from €27, good steak tartare, open daily, 53 Cours Mirabeau, tel. 04 42 26 00 51).

Le Grillon is a younger, more boisterous choice for dinner on Cours Mirabeau (white tablecloths, €20 *plats*, €17-34 *menus*). Its bar is a hit with locals for the prime seating: front and center on the boulevard's strolling fashion show (open daily for lunch and dinner, corner of Rue Clémenceau and Cours Mirabeau, tel. 04 42 27 58 81).

IN THE MAZARIN QUARTER

La Brocherie dishes up French rather than Provençal cuisine. Its stone-rustic, indoors-only ambience is best for cooler days. This family-owned bistro highlights food from the farm (it's about beef). Dig into the hearty self-service salad buffet (all you can eat, €12) and meats grilled over a wood fire. The €22 *menu* includes the salad bar (closed Sun, indoor seating only, 5 Rue Fernand Dol, tel. 04 42 38 33 21).

LE LATE-NIGHT

Aix is the only French city I know of with a 24/7 bakery, **Boulangerie La Varenne.** They have two branches: on Place Richelme and at the top of Cours Mirabeau (across from #6 Rue la Tournefort). Their chocolate-chip cookies are a rare treat.

Bar Hopping: For the young—and young at heart—the best action centers on Rue de la Verrerie. **O'Shannon's Pub** (#30) makes a great starting point for your evening out, as does **Pub O'Sullivan,** near La Rotonde, next to Hôtel de France on Place des Augustins.

Aix-en-Provence Connections

Remember, Aix-en-Provence has both a TGV station and a Centre-Ville train station (see "Arrival in Aix-en-Provence," earlier). In some cases, destinations are served from both stations; I've listed the station with the best connection. And for some destinations, the bus is a faster option than the train (these are noted below).

From Aix-en-Provence's Center to the TGV Station by Bus or Car: Buses from Aix-en-Provence to the TGV station depart from the bus station (on Avenue de l'Europe, near intersection with Avenue des Belges, tel. 08 21 20 22 03). To find the TGV by car from Aix-en-Provence, get on the A-51 autoroute toward *Marseille*, get off at the first exit (Les Milles), and follow signs for another 10 minutes. There's a small kiosk café in front of the TGV station with sandwiches, drinks, and such.

From Aix-en-Provence's Centre-Ville Station by Train to: **Marseille** (2/hour, 45 minutes), **Cassis** (hourly, 1.5 hours, transfer in Marseille), **Arles** (10/day, 2 hours, transfer in Marseille; train may separate midway—be sure you're in section going to Arles).

From Aix-en-Provence's TGV Station by Train to: **Avignon TGV** (12/day, 25 minutes), **Nice** (10/day, 2-3 hours, usually change in Marseille), **Paris** (14/day, 3 hours, may require transfer in Lyon).

From Aix-en-Provence by Bus to: **Marseille** (4/hour, 35 minutes), **Marseille's airport** (2/hour, 35 minutes), **Avignon** (6/day Mon-Sat, 3/day Sun, 75 minutes, faster and easier than train), **Arles** (faster than trains, 5/day Mon-Sat, 2/day Sun, 1.5 hours), **Lourmarin** (1.25 hours, 3/day, may require transfer in Pertuis), **Nice** (4/day, 2 hours, cheaper and quicker option than taking the train). All regional buses depart from the bus station on Avenue de l'Europe. Several companies operate buses from this station (www.info-ler.fr).

THE FRENCH RIVIERA

THE FRENCH RIVIERA

La Côte d'Azur

A hundred years ago, celebrities from London to Moscow flocked to the French Riviera to socialize, gamble, and escape the dreary weather at home. Today, budget vacationers and heat-seeking Europeans fill belle-époque resorts at France's most sought-after fun-in-the-sun destination.

The region got its nickname from turn-of-the-20th-century vacationing Brits, who simply extended the Italian Riviera west to France to include Nice. Today, the Riviera label stretches even farther westward, running from the Italian border to St-Tropez. To the French, this summer fun zone is known for the dazzling azure color of the sea along this coast: La Côte d'Azur. All my French Riviera destinations are on the sea, except for a few hill towns and the Gorges du Verdon.

This sunny sliver of land has been inhabited for more than 3,000 years. Ligurians were first, then Greeks, then Romans—who, as usual, had the greatest impact. After the fall of Rome, Nice became an important city in the Kingdom of Provence (along with Marseille and Arles). In the 14th century Nice's leaders voted to join the duke of Savoy's mountainous kingdom (also including several regions of northern Italy), which would later evolve into the Kingdom of Sardinia. It was not until 1860 that Nice (and Savoy) became a part of France—the result of a plebiscite. (The "vote" was made possible because the King of Sardinia had to trade the region to France as a quid pro quo for Napoleon III's support of Italian states that wanted to break away from Austria to create modern Italy).

Nice has world-class museums, a splendid beachfront promenade, a seductive old town, and all the drawbacks of a major city (traffic, crime, pollution, and so on). The day-trip possibilities are easy and exciting: Monaco offers a royal welcome and a

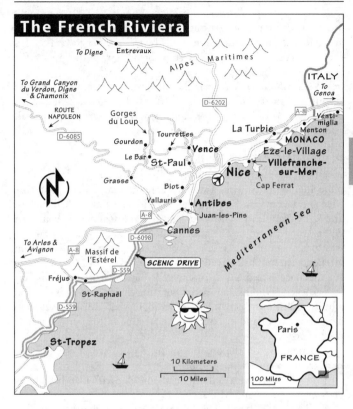

The French Riviera

To Digne • Entrevaux
Alpes   Maritimes
ITALY
To Genoa
ROUTE NAPOLEON
To Grand Canyon du Verdon, Digne & Chamonix
D-6202
A-8
Venti-miglia
Gorges du Loup
La Turbie • Menton
D-6085
Gourdon
Tourrettes
• Vence
MONACO
Eze-le-Village
Le Bar
St-Paul •
• Villefranche-sur-Mer
Grasse
• Nice
Biot •
Cap Ferrat
Vallauris •
• Antibes
A-8
• Juan-les-Pins
To Arles & Avignon
D-6098
Cannes
A-8
Massif de l'Estérel
SCENIC DRIVE
Mediterranean Sea
D-559
Fréjus •
St-Raphaël
D-559
St-Tropez
10 Kilometers
10 Miles
Paris •
FRANCE
100 Miles

FRENCH RIVIERA

fairy-tale past; Antibes has a thriving port and silky sand beaches; and image-conscious Cannes is the Riviera's self-appointed queen, with an elegant veneer hiding...very little. Yacht-happy St-Tropez swims alone an hour west. The Riviera's overlooked interior transports travelers to a world apart, with cliff-hanging villages, steep canyons, and alpine scenery—a refreshing alternative to the beach scene.

CHOOSING A HOME BASE

My favorite home bases are Nice, Antibes, and Villefranche-sur-Mer.

Nice is the region's capital and France's fifth-largest city. With convenient train and bus connections to most regional sights, this is the most practical base for train travelers. Urban Nice also has museums, a beach scene that rocks, the best selection of hotels in all price ranges, and good nightlife options. A car is a headache in Nice.

Nearby **Antibes** is smaller, with a bustling center, a lively night scene, great sandy beaches, grand vistas, good walking trails, and a Picasso museum. Antibes has frequent train service to Nice and Monaco, and quick connections by train or car to Grasse. It's the most convenient overnight stop for drivers, with light traffic and easy hotel parking.

Villefranche-sur-Mer is the romantic's choice, with a serene setting and small-town warmth. It has sand-pebble beaches; quick public transportation to Nice, Monaco, and Cap Ferrat; and a small selection of hotels in most price ranges.

PLANNING YOUR TIME

Ideally, allow a day and a half for Nice itself, an afternoon to explore inland hill towns, a day for Italianesque Villefranche-sur-Mer and lovely Cap Ferrat, a day for Monaco and the Corniches, and—if time allows—a day for Antibes and Cannes. If you must do St-Tropez, visit it while traveling to or from destinations farther west (such as Cassis, Aix-en-Provence, and Arles) and avoid it on weekend afternoons, as well as all summer.

Monaco is radiant at night, and Antibes works well by day (good beaches and hiking) and night (fine choice of restaurants and a lively after-hours scene). Hill-town-loving naturalists should add a night or two inland to explore the charming hill-capping hamlets near Vence.

Depending on the amount of time you have in the Riviera, here are my recommended priorities:

3 days:	Nice, Villefranche-sur-Mer with Cap Ferrat, and Monaco
5 days, add:	Antibes and maybe Cannes, and hill towns near Vence
7 days, add:	Grand Canyon du Verdon and/or just slow down

HELPFUL HINTS

Medical Help: Riviera Medical Services has a list of English-speaking physicians all along the Riviera. They can help you make an appointment or call an ambulance (tel. 04 93 26 12 70, www.rivieramedical.com).

Closed Days: Mondays and Tuesdays can frustrate market lovers and museumgoers. Closed on Monday: Nice's Modern and Contemporary Art Museum, Fine Arts Museum, and Cours Saleya produce and flower market; Antibes' Picasso Museum and market hall (Sept-May). Closed on Tuesday: the Chagall, Matisse, Masséna, and Archaeological museums in Nice; the Renoir Museum in Cagnes-sur-Mer. On Fridays Matisse's Chapel of the Rosary in Vence is closed.

Events: The Riviera is famous for staging major events. Unless you're actually taking part in the festivities, these occasions give you only room shortages and traffic jams. Here are the three biggies: **Nice Carnival** (two weeks in mid-late-Feb, www.nicecarnaval.com), **Cannes Film Festival** (12 days in mid-May, www.festival-cannes.com), and the **Grand Prix of Monaco** (4 days in late May, www.acm.mc). To accommodate the busy schedules of the rich and famous (and really mess up a lot of normal people), the film festival and car race often overlap.

Local Guides with Cars: These two energetic and delightful women have comfortable minibuses and enjoy taking couples and small groups anywhere in the region: **Sylvie Di Cristo** (€600/day, €350/half-day for up to 8 people, mobile 06 09 88 83 83, www.frenchrivieraguides.net, dicristosylvie@gmail.com) and **Ingrid Schmucker** (€490/day for 4 people or €550/day for 5-7 people, €180/half-day or €285/day if you don't need transportation, tel. 06 14 83 03 33, www.kultours.fr, info@kultours.fr). Their websites explain their programs well. The TI and most hotels have information on more economical shared minivan excursions from Nice (roughly €50-70/person per half-day, €80-120/person per day).

Local Guide Without Car: For a guided tour of Nice or the region using public transit or your own car, consider **Pascale Rucker,** an art-loving guide who teaches with the joy and wonder of a flower child (€160/half-day, €260/day, tel. 06 16 24 29 52, pascalerucker@gmail.com).

Foodie Tours: For food and wine walking tours and cooking classes offered in Nice, see page 296.

Cruise-Ship Sightseeing: The French Riviera is a popular cruise destination. Arriving ships are divided about evenly between Nice, Villefranche-sur-Mer, and Monaco (for arrival help, see the "Connections" section at the end of each of those chapters). Because these three ports line up conveniently along a 10-mile stretch of coast—easily connected by train or bus—from any of them, you'll have the Riviera by the tail. Hiring a local guide helps make the most of your limited time in port (listed earlier). For in-depth coverage, consider my guidebook, *Rick Steves Mediterranean Cruise Ports.*

GETTING AROUND THE RIVIERA

If taking the train or bus, have coins handy. Ticket machines don't take US credit cards or euro bills, smaller train stations may be unstaffed, and bus drivers can't make change for large bills.

By Public Transportation: Trains and buses do a good job of connecting places along the coast, with bonus views along many routes. Buses also provide reasonable service to some inland hill

FRENCH RIVIERA

Public Transportation in the French Riviera

From \ To	Cannes	Antibes	Nice
Cannes	N/A	**Train:** 2/hr, 15 min **Bus:** #200, 2-4/hr, 35 min	**Train:** 2/hr, 30 min **Bus:** #200, 2-4/hr, 2 hrs
Antibes	**Train:** 2/hr, 15 min **Bus:** #200, 2-4/hr, 35 min	N/A	**Train:** 2/hr, 20 min **Bus:** #200, 2-4/hr, 1.5 hrs
Nice	**Train:** 2/hr, 30 min **Bus:** #200, 2-4/hr, 2 hrs	**Train:** 2/hr, 20 min **Bus:** #200, 2-4/hr, 1.5 hrs	N/A
Villefranche-sur-Mer	**Train:** 2/hr, 50 min	**Train:** 2/hr, 40 min	**Train:** 2/hr, 10 min **Bus:** #100, 3-4/hr, 20 min; also #81, 2-3/hr, 20 min
Cap Ferrat	**Train:** Bus #81 to Beaulieu-sur-Mer (2-3/hr, 10 min), then train to Cannes (2/hr, 1 hr)	**Train:** Bus #81 to Beaulieu-sur-Mer (2-3/hr, 10 min), then train (2/hr, 40 min) **Bus:** #81 to Nice (2-3/hr, 30 min), then #200 (2-4/hr, 1.5 hrs)	**Bus:** #81, 2-3/hr, 30 min
Eze-le-Village	**Bus/Train:** Bus #83 to Eze-Bord-de-Mer (8/day, 15 min), then train (2/hr, 1 hr)	**Bus/Train:** Bus #83 to Eze-Bord-de-Mer (8/day, 15 min), then train (2/hr, 45 min)	**Bus/Train:** Bus #83 to Eze-Bord-de-Mer (8/day, 15 min), then train (2/hr, 15 min) **Bus:** #82/#112, 8-16/day, 40 min
Monaco	**Train:** 2/hr, 70 min	**Train:** 2/hr, 50 min	**Train:** 2/hr, 20 min **Bus:** #100, 3-4/hr, 45 min

Note: Bus frequencies are given for Monday-Saturday (Sunday often has limited or no bus service).

Villefranche-sur-Mer	Cap Ferrat	Eze-le-Village	Monaco
Train: 2/hr, 50 min	**Train:** 2/hr, 1 hr to Beaulieu-sur-Mer, then bus #81 (2-3/hr, 10 min)	**Train:** 2/hr, 1 hr to Eze-Bord-de-Mer, then bus #83 (8/day, 15 min)	**Train:** 2/hr, 70 min
Train: 2/hr, 40 min	**Train:** 2/hr, 40 min to Beaulieu-sur-Mer, then bus #81 (2-3/hr, 10 min) **Bus:** #200 to Nice (2-4/hr, 1.5 hrs), then #81 (2-3/hr, 30 min)	**Train:** 2/hr, 45 min to Eze-Bord-de-Mer, then bus #83 (8/day, 15 min)	**Train:** 2/hr, 50 min
Train: 2/hr, 10 min **Bus:** #100, 3-4/hr, 20 min; also #81, 2-3/hr, 20 min	**Bus:** #81, 2-3/hr, 30 min	**Train:** 2/hr, 15 min to Eze-Bord-de-Mer, then bus #83 (8/day, 15 min) **Bus:** #82/#112, 8-16/day, 40 min	**Train:** 2/hr, 20 min **Bus:** #100, 3-4/hr, 45 min
N/A	**Bus:** #81, 2-3/hr, 20 min	**Train:** 2/hr, 5 min to Eze-Bord-de-Mer, then bus # (8/day, 15 min) **Bus:** #100 to Eze-Bord-de-Mer, then transfer to #83; also #82/#112 from upper Villefranche	**Train:** 2/hr, 10 min **Bus:** #100, 3-4/hr, 25 min
Bus: #81, 2-3/hr, 20 min	N/A	**Bus:** #100 to Eze-Bord-de-Mer (3-4/hr, 30 min), then bus #83 (8/day, 15 min)	**Bus:** #100, 3-4/hr, 20 min
Bus/Train: Bus #83 to Eze-Bord-de-Mer (8/day, 15 min), then train (2/hr, 5 min) **Bus:** #83 to Eze-Bord-de-Mer, then transfer to #100; also #82/#112 to upper Villefranche	**Bus:** #83 to Eze-Bord-de-Mer (8/day, 15 min), then bus #100 (3-4/hr, 30 min)	N/A	**Bus:** #112, 6/day, 20 min
Train: 2/hr, 10 min **Bus:** #100, 3-4/hr, 25 min	**Bus:** #100, 3-4/hr, 20 min	**Bus:** #112, 6/day, 20 min	N/A

towns, and are typically less expensive and more convenient. Trains are generally faster and more expensive.

Buses are an amazing deal in the Riviera. Any one-way bus or tram ride costs €1.50 (€10 for 10 tickets) whether you're riding just within Nice or to Villefranche-sur-Mer, Monaco, or Antibes. The €1.50 ticket is good for 74 minutes of travel in one direction anywhere within the bus system except for airport buses.

Buy your bus ticket from the driver or from machines at stops, and validate your ticket in the machine on board. Your ticket allows transfers between the buses of the Lignes d'Azur (the region's main bus company, www.lignesdazur.com) and the TAM (Transports Alpes-Maritimes); if you board a TAM bus and need a transfer, ask for *un ticket correspondance*. A €5 all-day ticket is good on Nice's city buses, tramway, and selected buses serving nearby destinations (such as Villefranche, Cap Ferrat, and Eze-le-Village). The general rule of thumb: If the bus number has one or two digits, it's covered with the all-day ticket; with three digits it's not.

The **train** is more expensive but much faster (Nice to Monaco by train is about €4, versus €1.50 by bus), and there's no quicker way to move about the Riviera (http://en.voyages-sncf.com). Speedy trains link the Riviera's beachfront destinations—Cannes, Antibes, Nice, Villefranche-sur-Mer, Monaco, Menton, and the inland perfume town of Grasse. Never board a train without a ticket or valid pass—fare inspectors accept no excuses. The minimum fine: €70.

Nice makes the most convenient base for day trips, though public transport also works well from Riviera towns such as Antibes and Villefranche-sur-Mer. Details are provided under each destination's "Connections" section. For a scenic inland train ride, take the narrow-gauge train into the Alps (see page 305).

For an overview of the most useful Riviera train and bus connections, see the "Public Transportation in the French Riviera" chart on the previous page. The bus frequencies given are for Monday-Saturday (Sunday often has limited or no bus service)—confirm connections and last train/bus times locally.

By Car: This is France's most challenging region to drive in. Beautifully distracting vistas (natural and human), loads of Sunday-driver tourists, and every hour being lush-hour in the summer make for a dangerous combination. Parking can be exasperating. Bring lots of coins and patience.

The Riviera is awash with scenic roads. To sample some of the Riviera's best scenery, connect Provence and the Riviera by driv-

FRENCH RIVIERA

Top Art Sights of the Riviera

These are listed in order of importance.
Chagall Museum (Nice)
Fondation Maeght (St-Paul-de-Vence)
Picasso Museum (Antibes)
Matisse Museum (Nice)
Museum of the Annonciade (St-Tropez)
Chapel of the Rosary (Vence)
Modern and Contemporary Art Museum (Nice)
Renoir Museum (Cagnes-sur-Mer)
Fine Arts Museum (Nice)

ing the splendid coastal road between Cannes and Fréjus (D-6098 from Cannes/D-559 from Fréjus). Once in the Riviera, the most scenic and thrilling road trip is along the three coastal roads—called "corniches"—between Nice and Monaco (see page 360). Farther inland, take my recommended inland hill-towns drive (on page 422). Farther yet, explore the Grand Canyon du Verdon, with breathtaking gorges and alpine scenery. But for basic sightseeing between Monaco and Cannes, I'd park the car and use trains and buses.

By Boat: Trans Côte d'Azur offers boat service from Nice to Monaco or to St-Tropez seasonally, as well as between Cannes and St-Tropez (tel. 04 92 98 71 30, www.trans-cote-azur.com). For details, see "Getting Around the Riviera from Nice" (page 294).

THE RIVIERA'S ART SCENE

The list of artists who have painted the Riviera reads like a Who's Who of 20th-century art. Pierre-Auguste Renoir, Henri Matisse,

Marc Chagall, Georges Braque, Raoul Dufy, Fernand Léger, and Pablo Picasso all lived and worked here—and raved about the region's wonderful light. Their simple, semi-abstract, and—most importantly—colorful works reflect the pleasurable atmosphere of the Riviera. You'll experience the same landscapes they painted in this bright, sun-drenched region, punctuated with views of the "azure sea." Try to imagine the Riviera with a fraction of the people and development you see today.

But the artists were mostly drawn to the uncomplicated lifestyle of fishermen and farmers that has reigned here since time began. As the artists grew older, they retired in the sun, turned their backs on modern art's "isms," and painted with the wide-eyed wonder of children, using bright primary colors, basic outlines, and simple subjects.

A collection of modern- and contemporary-art museums (many described in this book) dot the Riviera, allowing art lovers to appreciate these masters' works while immersed in the same sun and culture that inspired them. Many of the museums were designed to blend pieces with the surrounding views, gardens, and fountains, thus highlighting that modern art is not only stimulating, but sometimes simply beautiful.

Entire books have been written about the modern-art galleries of the Riviera. If you're a fan, do some studying before your visit to be sure you know about that far-out museum of your dreams. If you've never enjoyed modern art, the two best places to give it a try here are the Fondation Maeght in St-Paul-de-Vence and the Chagall Museum in Nice.

THE RIVIERA'S CUISINE SCENE

The Riviera adds an Italian-Mediterranean flair to the food of Provence. While many of the same dishes served in Provence are available throughout the Riviera (see "Provence's Cuisine Scene" on page 31), there are differences, especially if you look for anything Italian or from the sea. The proximity to the water and historic ties to Italy are clear in this region's dishes.

Memorable restaurants that showcase the Riviera's cuisine are more difficult to find than in neighboring Provence. Because most visitors come more for the sun than the food, and because the clientele is predominantly international, many restaurants aim for the middle and are hard to tell apart. When dining on the Riviera, I expect views and ambience more than top-quality cuisine.

La salade niçoise is where most Riviera meals start. A true specialty from Nice, this salad has many versions. While you'll find green beans, rice, and corn in some, the classic version is a base of green salad with boiled potatoes, tomatoes, anchovies, olives, hard-boiled eggs, and lots of tuna. This is my go-to salad for a tasty, healthy, cheap (€12), and fast lunch. I like to spend a couple of extra euros and eat it in an elegant place with a nice ambience and view.

For lunch on the go, look for a *pan bagnat* (like a *salade niçoise* stuffed into a hollowed-out soft roll). Other tasty bread treats include *pissaladière* (bread dough topped with onions, olives, and anchovies), *fougasse* (a spindly, lace-like bread sometimes flavored with nuts, herbs, olives, or ham), and *socca* (a thin chickpea crêpe, seasoned with pepper and olive oil and often served in a paper cone by street vendors).

Invented in Nice, ravioli and potato gnocchi can be found on menus everywhere (ravioli can be stuffed with a variety of fillings, but it's best with seafood). Thin-crust pizza and *pâtes fraîches* (fresh pasta) are generally a good value throughout the Riviera.

Bouillabaisse is the Riviera's most famous dish; you'll find it in any seafront village or city. It's a spicy fish stew based on recipes handed down from sailors in Marseille. It must contain at least four types of fresh fish, though most have five to twelve kinds. A true bouillabaisse never has shellfish. The fish—cooked in a tomato-based stock and flavored with saffron (and sometimes anise and orange)—is separated from the stock before serving. The cook then heightens the flavor of the stock by adding toasted croutons and a dollop of *rouille* sauce (a thickened reddish mayonnaise heady with garlic and spicy peppers). This dish often requires a minimum order of two and can cost up to €40-60 per person.

Those on a budget can enjoy other seafood soups and stews. Far less pricey than bouillabaisse and worth trying is the local *soupe de poisson* (fish soup). It's a creamy soup flavored like bouillabaisse, with anise and orange, and served with croutons and *rouille* sauce (but has no chunks of fish). For a less colorful but still tasty soup, look for *bourride,* a creamy fish concoction thickened with an aioli sauce instead of the red *rouille; or baudroie,* a fishy soup cooked with vegetables and garlic.

The Riviera specializes in all sorts of fish and shellfish. Options include *fruits de mer,* or platters of seafood (including tiny shellfish, from which you get the edible part only by sucking really hard), herb-infused mussels, stuffed sardines, squid (slowly simmered with tomatoes and herbs), and tuna *(thon).* The popular *loup flambé au fenouil* is grilled sea bass, flavored with fennel and torched with *pastis* prior to serving.

Cheese and dessert dishes of the Riviera are indistinguishable from those in Provence (see page 31 for suggestions). For details on dining in France's restaurants, cafés, and brasseries, getting takeout, and assembling a picnic—as well as a rundown of French cuisine—see the "Eating" section in the Practicalities chapter (page 488).

WINES OF THE RIVIERA

Do as everyone else does: Drink wines from Provence. Bandol (red) and Cassis (white) are popular and from a region nearly on the Riviera. The only wines made in the Riviera are Bellet rosé and white, the latter often found in fish-shaped bottles. For more on Provençal wines, see page 36.

FRENCH RIVIERA

NICE

Nice (sounds like "niece"), with its spectacular Alps-to-Mediterranean surroundings, is the big-city highlight of the Riviera. Its traffic-free old town mixes Italian and French flavors to create a spicy Mediterranean dressing, while its big squares, broad seaside walkways, and long beaches invite lounging and people-watching. Nice may be nice, but it's hot and jammed in July and August—reserve ahead and get a room with air-conditioning. Everything you'll want to see in Nice is either within walking distance, or a short bike, bus, or tram ride away.

Orientation to Nice

The main points of interest lie between the beach and the train tracks (about 15 blocks apart). The city revolves around its grand

Place Masséna, where pedestrian-friendly Avenue Jean Médecin meets Vieux (Old) Nice and the Albert I parkway (with quick access to the beaches). It's a 20-minute walk (or about €12 by taxi) from the train station to the beach, and a 20-minute stroll along the promenade from the fancy Hôtel Negresco to the heart of Vieux Nice.

A 10-minute ride on the smooth-as-silk tram through the center of the city connects the train station, Place Masséna, Vieux Nice, and the port (from nearby Place Garibaldi). Work is underway on a new tram line (much of it underground) that will parallel the Promenade des Anglais (scheduled for completion in 2018).

TOURIST INFORMATION

Nice has several helpful TIs (tel. 08 92 70 74 07, www.nicetourisme. com), including branches at the **airport** (daily 9:00-18:00, April-Sept until 20:00), the **train station** (summer, daily 8:00-20:00, rest of year Mon-Sat 9:00-19:00, Sun 10:00-17:00), at 5 **Promenade des Anglais** (daily 9:00-18:00, July-Aug until 20:00), and on the north side of **Place Masséna** (May-mid-Sept only, daily 10:00-17:00). Pick up a free Nice map (the back side gives a focused view of the city's core area) and ask for day-trip information (including maps of Monaco or Antibes, details on boat excursions, and bus schedules).

ARRIVAL IN NICE

By Train: All trains stop at Nice's main station, called Nice-Ville (you don't want the suburban Nice Riquier Station). With your back to the tracks, car rentals are to the right, and airport bus #99 stops in front. The TI is straight out the main doors. There is no baggage storage at the station.

Nice's single tram line zips you to the center in a few minutes (left as you leave the station, departs every few minutes, direction: Hôpital Pasteur; for details, see "Getting Around Nice" on page 293). To walk to the beach, Promenade des Anglais, or many of my recommended hotels, cross Avenue Thiers in front of the station, go down the steps by Hôtel Interlaken, and continue down Avenue Durante.

By Bus: See "Getting Around the Riviera from Nice" on page 294 for stop information.

By Car: To reach the city center on the autoroute from the west, take the first Nice exit (for the airport—called *Côte d'Azur, Central*) and follow signs for *Nice Centre* and *Promenade des Anglais*. Rush hour will slow your progress (Mon-Fri 8:00-9:30 & 17:00-19:30), as Promenade des Anglais grinds to a halt. Hoteliers know where to park (allow €18-30/day; some hotels offer deals but space is limited—book ahead). The parking garage at the Nice Etoile shopping center on Avenue Jean Médecin is near many recommended hotels (ticket booth on third floor, about €26/day, 18:00-8:00). Other centrally located garages have similar rates. All on-street parking is metered (9:00-18:00) but usually free Sunday.

You can avoid driving in the center—and park for free during the day (no overnight parking)—by ditching your car at a parking lot at a remote tram or bus stop. Look for blue-on-white *Parcazur* signs (find locations at www.lignesdazur.com), and ride the bus or tram into town (10/hour, 15 minutes, must buy round-trip tram or bus ticket and keep it with you because you'll need it later to exit the parking lot; for details on riding the tram, see "Getting

NICE

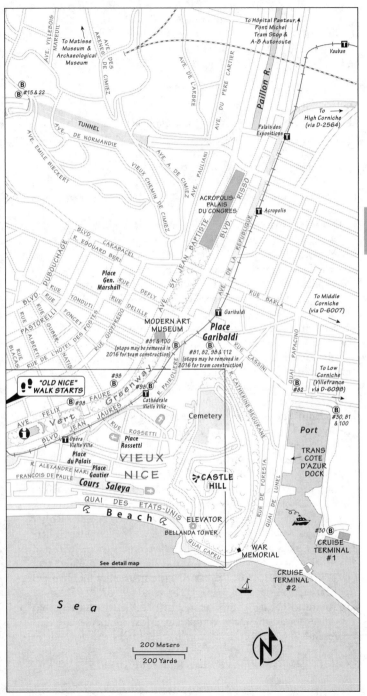

To Hôpital Pasteur,
Pont Michel
Tram Stop &
A-8 Autoroute

Vauban

To Matisse
Museum &
Archaeological
Museum

Paillon R.

To
High Corniche
(via D-2564)

B #15 & 22

TUNNEL

AVE. DE NORMANDIE

Palais des
Expositions

ACROPOLIS-
PALAIS
DU CONGRES

Acropolis

To Middle
Corniche
(via D-6007)

Place
Gen. Marshall

MODERN ART
MUSEUM

Place
Garibaldi

Garibaldi

#81 & 100
(stops may be removed in
2016 for tram construction)

#81, 82, 98 & 112
(stops may be removed in
2016 for tram construction)

To Low
Corniche
(Villefranche
via D-6098)

B #82

#98

"OLD NICE"
WALK STARTS

B #98

#98 B

B #98

Cathédrale
Vieille Ville

Cemetery

B #30, 81
& 100

Port

Opéra
Vieille Ville

Place
Rossetti

VIEUX

TRANS
COTE
D'AZUR
DOCK

Place
du Palais

Place
Gautier

NICE

Cours Saleya

CASTLE
HILL

QUAI DES ETATS-UNIS

Beach

ELEVATOR

BELLANDA TOWER

#30

CRUISE
TERMINAL
#1

QUAI CAPEU

WAR
MEMORIAL

See detail map

CRUISE
TERMINAL
#2

S e a

200 Meters

200 Yards

N

Around Nice," later). As lots are unguarded, don't leave anything in your car.

By Plane or Cruise Ship: For information on Nice's airport and cruise-ship port, see "Nice Connections," at the end of this chapter.

HELPFUL HINTS

Theft Alert: Nice has its share of pickpockets (especially at the train station, on the tram, and trolling the beach). Stick to main streets in Vieux Nice after dark.

Medical Help: Riviera Medical Services has a list of English-speaking physicians. They can help you make an appointment or call an ambulance (tel. 04 93 26 12 70, www.rivieramedical. com).

Sightseeing Tips: The Cours Saleya produce and flower market is closed Monday, and the Chagall and Matisse museums are closed Tuesday.

Internet Access and Wi-Fi: The city offers free Wi-Fi in La Coulée Verte parkway, Place Masséna, Place Garibaldi, and along the Cours Saleya in Old Nice (network: Spot Wifi Nice). All of the hotels I list have free Wi-Fi.

Grocery Store: Small grocery shops are easy to find. The big **Monoprix** on Avenue Jean Médecin and Rue Biscarra has it all (open daily, see map on page 400).

Boutique Shopping: The chic streets where Rue Alphonse Karr meets Rue de la Liberté and then Rue de Paradis are known as the "Golden Square." If you need pricey stuff, shop here.

SNCF Boutique: A French rail ticket office is a half-block west of Avenue Jean Médecin at 2 Rue de la Liberté (Mon-Fri 10:00-17:50, closed Sat-Sun).

Renting a Bike (and Other Wheels): Bike-rental shops are a breeze to find in Nice, and several companies offer bike tours of the city. Bikes *(vélos)* can be taken on trains. **Holiday Bikes** has multiple locations, including one across from the train station, and they have electric bikes (www.loca-bike.fr). **Roller Station** is well-situated near the sea and rents bikes, roller-blades, skateboards, and Razor-style scooters (bikes-€5/hour, €10/half-day, €15/day, leave ID as deposit, open daily, next to yellow awnings of Pailin's Asian restaurant at 49 Quai des Etats-Unis—see map on page 314, tel. 04 93 62 99 05).

Car Rental: Renting a car is easiest at Nice's airport, which has offices for all the major companies. Most companies are represented at Nice's train station and near the southwest side of Albert I Park.

English Radio: Tune in to Riviera-Radio at FM 106.5.

Views: For panoramic views, climb Castle Hill (see page 304), or take a one-hour boat trip (page 295).

Beach Tips: To make life tolerable on the rocks, swimmers should buy a pair of the cheap plastic beach shoes sold at many shops. **Go Sport** at #13 on Place Masséna is a good bet (open daily, see map on page 312). Locals don't swim in July and August, as the warming sea brings swarms of stinging jellyfish. Ask before you dip.

Updates to This Book: For the latest, see www.ricksteves.com/update.

GETTING AROUND NICE
By Public Transportation

Although you can walk to most attractions, smart travelers make good use of the buses and tram.

Tickets: Both buses and trams are covered by the same €1.50 single-ride ticket, or you can pay €10 for a 10-ride ticket that can be shared (each use good for 74 minutes in one direction, including transfers between bus and tram). The €5 all-day pass is valid on city buses and trams, as well as buses to some nearby destinations (but not airport buses). You must validate your ticket on every trip. Buy single tickets from the bus driver or from the ticket machines on tram platforms (coins only—press the button twice at the end to get your ticket). Passes and 10-ride tickets are also available from machines at tram stops. Info: www.lignesdazur.com.

Buses: The bus is handy for reaching the Chagall and Matisse museums and the Russian Cathedral (for specifics, see museum listings under "Sights in Nice"). Validate your ticket in the machine—watch locals to learn how. Route diagrams in the buses identify each stop.

Trams: Nice has a single modern and efficient L-shaped tram line. Trams run every few minutes along Avenue Jean Médecin and Boulevard Jean Jaurès, and con-

nect the main train station with Place Masséna and Old Nice (Opéra stop), the port (Place Garibaldi stop), and buses east along the coast (Vauban stop). Trams also stop near the Chemins de Fer de Provence train station (Libération stop)—the departure point for the scenic narrow-gauge rail journey (see page 305).

Boarding the tram in the direction of Hôpital Pasteur takes you toward the beach and Vieux Nice (direction: Henri Sappia goes the other way). Validate your ticket on the tram (http://tramway.nice.fr).

By Taxi

While pricey, cabs can be useful for getting to Nice's less-central sights (figure €8 for shortest ride, €15 from Promenade des Anglais to the Chagall Museum). Cabbies normally pick up only at taxi stands *(tête de station)*, or you can call 04 93 13 78 78.

GETTING AROUND THE RIVIERA FROM NICE
By Train and Bus

Nice is perfectly situated for exploring the Riviera by public transport. Monaco, Eze-le-Village, Villefranche-sur-Mer, Antibes, Vence, and St-Paul-de-Vence are all within about a one-hour bus or train ride. With a little planning, you can link key destinations in an all-day circuit. For example: Nice, Monaco, and Eze-le-Village or La Turbie, then loop back to Nice (see page 295 for details). For a summary of train and bus connections, see the "Public Transportation in the French Riviera" sidebar on page 282; see also "Nice Connections" at the end of this chapter.

Trains serving Nice arrive at and depart from Nice-Ville Station. To connect to regional destinations, use the following east- and westbound buses (see maps on pages 308 and 312 for stop locations; www.lignesdazur.com).

Eastbound Buses: Due to work on the new tram system, buses to Villefranche-sur-Mer and Monaco may stop only on the port in 2016 (closest tram stop to the port is Garibaldi). Ask at the TI if a closer bus stop is available. Buses to Eze-le-Village and La Turbie leave from the Vauban tram stop. Use the tram to reach any of these eastbound buses (free transfer to all of these destinations, except Monaco).

Westbound Buses: To St-Paul-de-Vence, Vence, Cannes, and Antibes, use the Albert I/Verdun stop on Avenue de Verdun, a 10-minute walk along the parkway west of Place Masséna.

By Boat

In summer, Trans Côte d'Azur offers scenic trips several days a week from Nice to Monaco and Nice to St-Tropez. Boats leave in the morning and return in the evening, giving you all day to explore your destination. Drinks and WCs are available on board.

Boats to **Monaco** depart at 9:30 and 16:00, and return at 11:00 and 18:00 (€39 round-trip, €32 if you don't get off in Monaco, 45 minutes each way, June-Sept Tue, Thu, and Sat only).

Boats to **St-Tropez** depart at 9:00 and return at 19:00 (€66 round-trip, 2.5 hours each way; early-July-Aug daily; late May-early-July and Sept Tue, Thu, and Sat-Sun only).

Reservations are required for both boats, and tickets for St-Tropez should be booked in advance (tel. 04 92 00 42 30, www.trans-cote-azur.com). The boats leave from Nice's port, Bassin des

Amiraux, just below Castle Hill—look for the ticket booth *(billet-erie)* on Quai de Lunel (see map on page 290). The same company also runs one-hour round-trip cruises along the coast to Cap Ferrat (see listing under "Tours in Nice," next).

Tours in Nice

ON WHEELS
Hop-On, Hop-Off Bus
Le Grand Tour Bus provides a 14-stop, hop-on, hop-off service on an open-deck bus with headphone commentary. The route includes the Promenade des Anglais, the old port, Cap de Nice, and the Chagall and Matisse museums (€23/1-day pass, €26/2-day pass, buy tickets on bus, 2/hour, daily 10:00-19:00, 1.5-hour loop, main stop near where Promenade des Anglais and Quai des Etats-Unis meet—across from the Plage Beau Rivage lounge, tel. 04 92 29 17 00, www.nicelegrandtour.com). While not an economical way to get to the Chagall and Matisse museums, it can be a good value if you're looking for a city overview.

Tourist Train
For €8, you can spend 45 embarrassing minutes on the tourist train tooting along the promenade, through the old city, and up to Castle Hill (2/hour, daily 10:00-18:00 or 19:00, recorded English commentary, meet train near Le Grand Tour Bus stop on Quai des Etats-Unis, tel. 02 99 88 47 07).

BY BOAT
▲Trans Côte d'Azur Cruise
To see Nice from the water, hop this one-hour tour run by Trans Côte d'Azur. You'll cruise in a comfortable yacht-size vessel to Cap Ferrat and past Villefranche-sur-Mer, then return to Nice with a final lap along Promenade des Anglais.

Guides play Robin Leach (in French and English), pointing out mansions owned by famous people, including Elton John, Sean Connery, and Microsoft co-founder Paul Allen (€18; April-Oct Tue-Sun 2/day, usually at 11:00 and 15:00, no boats Mon or in off-season; verify schedule, arrive 30 minutes early to get best seats; for directions to the dock and contact information, see "Getting Around the Riviera from Nice—By Boat," earlier).

ON FOOT
Local Guides and Walking Tours
If interested in hiring a local guide for Nice and other regional destinations, see page 281 for suggestions.

The TI on Promenade des Anglais organizes weekly walking

NICE

NICE

Nice at a Glance

▲▲▲**Promenade des Anglais** Nice's four-mile sun-struck seafront promenade. **Hours:** Always open. See page 297.

▲▲▲**Chagall Museum** The world's largest collection of Marc Chagall's work, popular even with people who don't like modern art. **Hours:** May-Oct Wed-Mon 10:00-18:00, Nov-April Wed-Mon 10:00-17:00, closed Tue year-round. See page 298.

▲▲**Vieux Nice** Charming old city offering enjoyable atmosphere and a look at Nice's French-Italian cultural blend. **Hours:** Always open. See page 298.

▲**Matisse Museum** Modest collection of Henri Matisse's paintings, sketches, and paper cutouts. **Hours:** Wed-Mon 10:00-18:00, closed Tue. See page 298.

▲**Russian Cathedral** Finest Orthodox church outside Russia (closed for renovation through much of 2016). **Hours:** Tue-Sat 9:00-12:00 & 14:00-19:00, Sun 9:00-12:00, closed Mon. See page 303.

▲**Castle Hill** Site of an ancient fort boasting great views. **Hours:** Park closes at 20:00 in summer, earlier off-season. See page 304.

Modern and Contemporary Art Museum Ultramodern museum with enjoyable collection from the 1960s and '70s, including Warhol and Lichtenstein. **Hours:** Tue-Sun 10:00-18:00, closed Mon. See page 302.

Fine Arts Museum Lush villa shows off impressive paintings by Monet, Sisley, Bonnard, and Raoul Dufy. **Hours:** Tue-Sun 10:00-18:00, closed Mon. See page 302.

Masséna Museum Lavish beachfront mansion houses museum of city history, including exhibits of Napoleonic paraphernalia and images of Nice over the years. **Hours:** Wed-Mon 10:00-18:00, closed Tue. See page 302.

tours of Vieux Nice in French and English (€12, May-Oct only, usually Sat morning at 9:30, 2.5 hours, reservations necessary, depart from TI, tel. 08 92 70 74 07). They also have evening art walks on Fridays at 19:00.

Food Tours and Cooking Classes
Charming Canadian Francophile Rosa Jackson, a food journalist, Cordon Bleu-trained cook, and longtime resident of France, runs

Les Petits Farcis, which offers a variety of food-and-wine-oriented walking tours in Nice (visit the market, five tasting stops, €80-120/person). She also teaches popular cooking classes in Vieux Nice, which include a morning shopping trip to the market on Cours Saleya and an afternoon session cooking (€195/person, mobile 06 81 67 41 22, www.petitsfarcis.com).

Nadia Farmer combines food and wine with history in her walking tours of Nice (€65/person for 3 hours, includes tastings, tel. 07 62 90 11 50, www.nicefoodandwinetours.com).

Sights in Nice

WALKS AND BEACHES
▲▲▲Promenade des Anglais and Beach

Enjoying Nice's four-mile seafront promenade on foot or by bike is an essential Riviera experience. From the days when wealthy Eng-

lish tourists filled the grand seaside hotels, this stretch has always been *the* place to be in Nice.

To rev up the pace of your promenade saunter, rent a bike and glide along the coast in either or both directions (about 30 minutes each way; for rental info see page 292). Both of the following paths start along Promenade des Anglais.

The path to the **west** stops just before the airport at perhaps the most scenic *boules* courts in France. Pause here to watch the old-timers while away the afternoon tossing shiny metal balls (for more on this game, see page 39). If you take the path heading **east,** you'll round the hill—passing a scenic promontory and the town's memorial to both world wars—to the harbor of Nice, with a chance to survey some fancy yachts. Walk or pedal around the harbor and follow the coast past the Corsica ferry terminal (you'll need to carry your bike up a flight of steps). From there the path leads to an appealing tree-lined residential district.

For most, the attraction is the **beach.** Settle in on the smooth

rocks. While beaches are free to the public (by law), you can get more comfortable by renting a lounge chair or mattress (*chaise longue* or *transat*-about €15, umbrella-€5, towel-€4). Have lunch in your bathing suit (€14 salads and pizzas in bars and restaurants all along the beach). Or, for a peaceful café au lait on the Mediterranean, stop here first thing in the morning before the crowds hit. *Plage Publique* signs explain the 10 beach no-nos (translated into English).

📖 See the Promenade des Anglais Walk chapter.

▲▲Wandering Vieux Nice (Old Nice)

Offering an intriguing look at Nice's melding of French and Italian cultures, the old city is a fine place to linger. Enjoy its narrow lanes, bustling market squares, and colorful people.

📖 See the Old Nice Walk chapter.

MUSEUMS

Most museums listed here charge €10 (and most are not worth it). The Chagall Museum is €8 (well worth it). The €20, seven-day Nice Museum Ticket includes all museums except the Chagall (not worth it for most).

The first two museums (Chagall and Matisse) are a long walk northeast of Nice's city center. Because they're in the same direction and served by the same bus line (#15 Mon-Sat, #22 Sun), try to visit them on the same trip. From Place Masséna, the Chagall Museum is a 10-minute bus ride, and the Matisse Museum is a few stops beyond that.

▲▲▲Chagall Museum (Musée National Marc Chagall)

Inspired by the Old Testament, his Jewish/Russian heritage, and the ethereal light of the Riviera, Marc Chagall custom-painted works for this building, which he considered a "House of Brother-hood." The museum—the best Chagall sight in Europe—is a can't-miss treat for Chagall fans, and a hit even for people who usually don't like modern art.

Cost and Hours: €8, €1-2 more with special exhibits, includes audioguide, May-Oct Wed-Mon 10:00-18:00, Nov-April Wed-Mon 10:00-17:00, closed Tue year-round, Avenue Docteur Ménard, tel. 04 93 53 87 20, http://en.musees-nationaux-alpesmaritimes.fr.

📖 See the Chagall Museum Tour chapter.

▲Matisse Museum (Musée Matisse)

This small and neglected little museum, which fills an old mansion in a park surrounded by scant Roman ruins, contains a sampling of works from the various periods of Henri Matisse's artistic career. The museum offers an introduction to the artist's many styles and materials, both shaped by Mediterranean light and by fellow Côte d'Azur artists Picasso and Renoir.

NICE

Cost and Hours: €10, Wed-Mon 10:00-18:00, closed Tue, 164 Avenue des Arènes de Cimiez, tel. 04 93 81 08 08, www.musee-matisse-nice.org.

Getting There: Take a cab (€15 from Promenade des Anglais). Alternatively, hop bus #15 Mon-Sat or #22 on Sun (6/hour, 15 minutes, board from east end of Galeries Lafayette department store, near Masséna tram stop, on Rue Sacha Guitry—see map on page 312; from train station catch #17). Get off at the Arènes-Matisse bus stop (look for the crumbling Roman arena), then walk 50 yards into the park to find the pink villa.

Background: Henri Matisse, the master of leaving things out, could suggest a woman's body with a single curvy line—letting the viewer's mind fill in the rest. Ignoring traditional 3-D perspective, he expressed his passion for life through simplified but recognizable scenes in which dark outlines and saturated, bright blocks of color create an overall decorative pattern.

Matisse understood how colors and shapes affect us emotionally. He could create either shocking, clashing works (early Fauvism) or geometrical, balanced, harmonious ones (later cutouts). Whereas other modern artists reveled in purely abstract design, Matisse (almost) always kept the subject matter at least vaguely recognizable. He used unreal colors and distorted lines not just to portray what an object looks like, but to express its inner nature (even inanimate objects). Meditating on his paintings helps you connect with life—or so Matisse hoped.

As you tour the museum, look for Matisse's favorite motifs—including fruit, flowers, wallpaper, and sunny rooms—often with a window opening onto a sunny landscape. Another favorite subject is the *odalisque* (harem concubine), usually shown sprawled in a seductive pose and with a simplified, masklike face. You'll also see a few souvenirs from his travels, which influenced much of his work.

Visiting the Museum: Rooms on the entry level usually house paintings from Matisse's formative years as a student (1890s). Notice how quickly his work evolves: from dark still lifes *(nature mortes)*, to colorful Impressionist scenes, to more abstract works, all in the matter of a few years. A beige banner describes his "Découverte de la Lumière" (discovery of light), which the Riviera (and his various travels to sun-soaked places like Corsica, Collioure, and Tahiti) brought to his art.

Other rooms on this floor highlight Matisse's fascination with dance and the female body. You'll see pencil and charcoal drawings, and a handful of bronze busts; he was fascinated by sculpture. *The Acrobat*—painted only two years before Matisse's death—shows the artist at his minimalist best. A room devoted to two 25-foot-long watery cutouts for an uncompleted pool project *(La Piscine)* for the city of Nice shows his abiding love of deep blue.

NICE

Henri Matisse (1869-1954)

Here's an outline of Henri Matisse's busy life:

1880s and 1890s—At age 20, Matisse, a budding lawyer, is struck down with appendicitis. Bedridden for a year, he turns to painting as a healing escape from pain and boredom. After recovering, he studies art in Paris and produces dark-colored, realistic still lifes and landscapes. His work is exhibited at the Salons of 1896 and 1897.

1897-1905—Influenced by the Impressionists, he experiments with sunnier scenes and brighter colors. He travels to southern France, including Collioure (on the coast near Spain), and seeks still more light-filled scenes to paint. His experiments are influenced by Vincent van Gogh's bright, surrealistic colors and thick outlines, and by Paul Gauguin's primitive visions of a Tahitian paradise. From Paul Cézanne, he learns how to simplify objects into their basic geometric shapes. He also experiments (like Cézanne) with creating the illusion of 3-D not by traditional means, but by using contrasting colors for the foreground and background.

1905—Back in Paris, Matisse and his colleagues (André Derain and Maurice de Vlaminck) shock the art world with an exhibition of their experimental paintings. The thick outlines, simple forms, flattened perspective, and—most of all—bright, clashing, unrealistic colors seem to be the work of "wild animals" (fauves). Fauvism is hot, and Matisse is instantly famous. (Though notorious as a "wild animal," Matisse himself was a gentle, introspective man.)

1906-1910—After just a year, Fauvism is out, and African masks are in. This "primitive" art form inspires Matisse to simplify and distort his figures further, making them less realistic but more expressive.

1910-1917—Matisse creates his masterpiece paintings. Cubism is the rage, pioneered by Matisse's friend and rival for the World's Best Painter award, Pablo Picasso. Matisse dabbles in Cubism, simplifying forms, emphasizing outline, and muting his colors. But

---

The floor above features sketches and models of Matisse's famous Chapel of the Rosary in nearby Vence (see page 427) and related religious works. On the same floor, you may find paper cutouts from his *Jazz* or *Dance* series, more bronze sculptures, various personal objects, and linen embroideries inspired by his travels to Polynesia.

The bookshop, WCs, and additional temporary exhibits are in the basement level. The wall-hanging near the bookshop—Matisse's colorful paper cutout *Flowers and Fruits*—shouts, "Riviera!"

ultimately it proves to be too austere and analytical for his deeply sensory nature. The Cubist style is most evident in his sculpture.

1920s—Burned out from years of intense experimentation, Matisse moves to Nice (spending winters there from 1917, settling permanently in 1921). Luxuriating under the bright sun, he's reborn, and he paints colorful, sensual, highly decorative works. Harem concubines lounging in their sunny, flowery apartments epitomize the lush life.

1930s—A visit to Tahiti inspires more scenes of life as a sunny paradise. Matisse experiments with bolder lines, swirling arabesques, and decorative patterns.

1940s—Duodenal cancer (in 1941) requires Matisse to undergo two operations and confines him to a wheelchair for the rest of his life. Working at an easel becomes a struggle for him, and he largely stops painting in 1941. But as World War II ends, Matisse emerges with renewed energy. Now in his 70s, he explores a new medium: paper cutouts pasted onto a watercolored surface (découpage on gouache-prepared surface). The technique plays to his strengths—the cutouts are essentially blocks of bright color (mostly blue) with a strong outline. Scissors in hand, Matisse says, "I draw straight into the color." (His doctor advises him to wear dark glasses to protect his weak eyes against the bright colors he chooses.) In 1947, Matisse's book *Jazz* is published, featuring the artist's joyful cutouts of simple figures. Like jazz music, the book is a celebration of artistic spontaneity. And like music in general, Matisse's works balance different tones and colors to create a mood.

1947-1951—Matisse's nurse becomes a Dominican nun in Vence. To thank her for her care, he spends his later years designing a chapel there. He oversees every aspect of the Chapel of the Rosary (Chapelle du Rosaire) at Vence, from the stained glass to the altar to the colors of the priest's robe (see page 427). Though Matisse is not a strong Christian, the church exudes his spirit of celebrating life and sums up his work.

1954—Matisse dies.

NICE

Leaving the Museum: Turn left from the museum into the park, exiting at the Archaeological Museum. The bus stop across the street is for bus #17, which goes to the train station, and #20, which heads to the port. For buses #15 and #22 (frequent service to downtown and the Chagall Museum), turn right passing the stop above, walk to the small roundabout, and find the shelter (facing downhill).

Modern and Contemporary Art Museum (Musée d'Art Moderne et d'Art Contemporain)

This ultramodern museum features an explosively colorful, far-out, yet manageable collection focused on American and European-American artists from the 1960s and 1970s (Pop Art and New Realism styles are highlighted; see page 285 for an overview of modern art on the Riviera). The exhibits cover three floors and include a few works by Andy Warhol, Roy Lichtenstein, and Jean Tinguely, and images of Christo's famous wrappings. You'll find rooms dedicated to Robert Indiana, Yves Klein, and Niki de Saint Phalle. The temporary exhibits can be as appealing to modern-art lovers as the permanent collection: Check the museum website for what's playing. Don't leave without exploring the views from the rooftop terrace.

Cost and Hours: €10, Tue-Sun 10:00-18:00, closed Mon, near Vieux Nice on Promenade des Arts, tel. 04 93 62 61 62, www.mamac-nice.org.

Fine Arts Museum (Musée des Beaux-Arts)

Housed in a sumptuous Riviera villa with lovely gardens, this museum holds 6,000 artworks from the 17th to 20th centuries. Start on the first floor and work your way up to enjoy paintings by Monet, Sisley, Bonnard, and Raoul Dufy, as well as a few sculptures by Rodin and Carpeaux.

Cost and Hours: €10, Tue-Sun 10:00-18:00, closed Mon; inconveniently located at the western end of Nice, take bus #12 from train station to Rosa Bonheur stop and walk to 3 Avenue des Baumettes; tel. 04 92 15 28 28, www.musee-beaux-arts-nice.org.

Archaeological Museum (Musée Archéologique)

This museum displays various objects from the Romans' occupation of this region. It's convenient—just below the Matisse Museum—but has little of interest to anyone but ancient Rome aficionados (and has limited information in English). You also get access to the Roman bath ruins...which are, sadly, overgrown with weeds.

Cost and Hours: €10, Wed-Mon 10:00-18:00, closed Tue, near Matisse Museum at 160 Avenue des Arènes de Cimiez, tel. 04 93 81 59 57.

Masséna Museum (Musée Masséna)

Like Nice's main square, this museum was named in honor of Jean-André Masséna (born in Antibes), a highly regarded commander during France's Revolutionary and Napoleonic wars. The beach-front mansion is worth a look for its lavish decor and lovely gardens alone (no English labels in museum, but a €3 booklet in English is available).

Cost and Hours: €10 but free to enter gardens, Wed-Mon

10:00-18:00, closed Tue, 35 Promenade des Anglais, tel. 04 93 91 19 10.

Visiting the Museum: There are three levels. The elaborate reception rooms on the ground floor host occasional exhibits and give the best feeling for aristocratic Nice from 1860, when it joined France, until World War I (find Masséna's portrait to the right).

The first floor up, offering a folk-museum-like look at Nice through the years, deserves most of your time. Moving counter-clockwise around the floor, you'll find Napoleonic paraphernalia, Josephine's impressive cape and tiara, and Napoleon's vest. Next, you'll find bric-a-brac of the aristocracy and antique posters promoting vacations in Nice—look for the model and photos of the long-gone La Jetée Promenade and its casino, Nice's first. You'll see paintings of some of the Russian and British nobility who appreciated Nice's climate, and images of the city before the Promenade des Anglais was built and the town's river was covered over by Place Masséna. You'll also find paintings honoring Italian patriot and Nice favorite Giuseppe Garibaldi. The top floor is a painting gallery with temporary exhibits.

OTHER SIGHTS IN NICE
▲Russian Cathedral (Cathédrale Russe)

Nice's Russian Orthodox church—claimed by some to be the finest outside Russia—is worth a visit (but is closed until late 2016). Five hundred rich Russian families wintered in Nice in the late 19th

century, and they needed a worthy Orthodox house of worship. Czar Nicholas I's widow provided the land and Czar Nicholas II gave this church to the Russian community in 1912. (A few years later, Russian comrades who *didn't* winter on the Riviera assassinated him.) Here in the land of olives and anchovies, these proud onion domes seem odd. But, I imagine, so did those old Russians.

Cost and Hours: Free; when it reopens, likely Tue-Sat 9:00-12:00 & 14:00-19:00, Sun 9:00-12:00, closed Mon; chanted services Sat at 17:30 or 18:00, Sun at 10:00; no tourist visits during services, no shorts allowed, 17 Boulevard du Tzarewitch, tel. 04 93 96 88 02, www.cathedrale-russe-nice.ru/fr.

Getting There: It's a 10-minute walk from the train station. Head west on Avenue Thiers, turn right on Avenue Gambetta, then look for signs. Or take any bus heading west from the station on Avenue Thiers and get off at Avenue Gambetta.

Visiting the Cathedral: Pick up an English info sheet on your way in. The one-room interior is filled with icons and candles, and traditional Russian music adds to the ambience. The wall of icons (iconostasis) divides the spiritual realm from the temporal world of the worshippers. Only the priest can walk between the two worlds, by using the "Royal Door."

Take a close look at items lining the front (starting in the left corner). The angel with red boots and wings—the protector of the Romanov family—stands over a symbolic tomb of Christ. The tall black hammered-copper cross commemorates the massacre of Nicholas II and his family in 1918. Notice the Jesus icon to the right of the Royal Door. According to a priest here, as worshippers meditate, staring deep into the eyes of Jesus, they enter a lake where they find their souls. Surrounded by incense, chanting, and your entire community...it could happen. Farther to the right, the icon of the Virgin and Child is decorated with semiprecious stones from the Ural Mountains. Artists worked a triangle into each iconic face—symbolic of the Trinity.

Nearby: The park around the church stays open at lunch and makes a fine setting for picnics.

▲Castle Hill (Colline du Château)

This hill—in an otherwise flat city center—offers sensational views over Nice, the port (to the east, created for trade and military use in the 15th century), the foothills of the Alps, and the Mediterranean. The views are best early, at sunset, or whenever the weather's clear.

Nice was founded on this hill. Its residents were crammed onto the hilltop until the 12th century, as it was too risky to live in the flatlands below. Today you'll find a playground, a café, and a cemetery—but no castle—on Castle Hill.

Cost and Hours: Park is free and closes at 20:00 in summer, earlier off-season.

Getting There: You can get to the top by foot, by elevator (free, daily 10:00-19:00, until 20:00 in summer, next to beachfront Hôtel Suisse), or by pricey tourist train (see page 295).

ᗕ See the Promenade des Anglais Walk chapter for a pleasant stroll that ends near Castle Hill.

Leaving Castle Hill: After enjoying the views and hilltop fun, you can walk via the cemetery directly down into Vieux Nice (just follow the signs), descend to the beach (via the elevator or a stepped lane next to it), or hike down the back side to Nice's port (departure point for boat trips and buses to Monaco and Ville-franche-sur-Mer).

EXCURSION FROM NICE
Narrow-Gauge Train into the Alps
(Chemins de Fer de Provence)

Leave the tourists behind and take the scenic train-bus-train combination that runs between Nice and Digne through can-

yons, along whitewater rivers, and through tempting villages (4/day, departs Nice from Chemins de Fer de Provence Station, two blocks from the Libération tram stop, 4 Rue Alfred Binet, tel. 04 97 03 80 80, www.trainprovence.com).

An appealing stop on the scenic railway is little **Entrevaux,** a good destination that feels forgotten and still stuck in its medieval shell (€24 round-trip, 1.5 scenic hours from Nice). Cross the bridge, meet someone friendly, and consider the steep hike up to the citadel (€3, TI tel. 04 93 05 45 73). Sisteron's Romanesque church and the view from the citadel above make this town worth a visit.

Nightlife in Nice

While you should choose your neighborhoods with caution, the city is a delight after dark. Promenade des Anglais, Cours Saleya, the old town, and Rue Masséna are all safe and worth an evening walk. Nice's bars play host to a happening late-night scene, filled with jazz, rock, and trolling singles.

Most activity focuses on Vieux Nice. Rue de la Préfecture and Place du Palais are ground zero for bar life, though Place Rossetti and Rue Droite are also good targets. **Distilleries Ideales** is a good place to start or end your evening, with a lively international crowd, a *Pirates of the Caribbean* interior, and a *Cheers* vibe (15 beers on tap, where Rue de la Poissonnerie and Rue Barillerie meet, happy hour 18:00-21:00). **Wayne's Bar** is a happening spot for the younger, English-speaking backpacker crowd (15 Rue Préfecture; see map on page 312 for both bar locations). Along the Promenade des Anglais, the plush bar at **Hôtel Negresco** is fancy-cigar old English.

Sleeping in Nice

Don't look for charm in Nice. I prefer to stay in the new town—a 10-minute walk from the old town—for modern, clean, and air-conditioned rooms. The rates listed here are for April through October. Prices generally drop considerably November through

March, but go sky-high during the Nice Carnival (two weeks in mid-late-Feb, www.nicecarnaval.com), the Cannes Film Festival (12 days in mid-May, www.festival-cannes.com), and Monaco's Grand Prix (late May, www.acm.mc). Between the film festival and the Grand Prix, the second half of May is slammed. Nice is also one of Europe's top convention cities, and June is convention month here. For parking, ask your hotelier, or see "Arrival in Nice—By Car" on page 289.

I've divided my sleeping recommendations into three areas: city center, Old Nice, and near the Promenade des Anglais. Those in the city center are between the train station and Place Masséna (easy access to the train station and Vieux Nice via the tram, 20-minute walk to Promenade des Anglais). Those in Vieux Nice are between Place Masséna and the sea (east of the parkway, good access to the sea at Quai des Etats-Unis). And those near the Promenade des Anglais are between Boulevard Victor Hugo and the sea (a classier and quieter area, offering better access to the sea but longer walks to the train station and Vieux Nice). Before reserving, check hotel websites for deals (more common at larger hotels). Book directly with the hotel to get any special discounts for Rick Steves readers.

IN THE CITY CENTER

The train station area offers Nice's cheapest sleeps, but the neighborhood can feel seedy after dark. The cheapest places are older, well-worn, and come with some street noise. Places closer to Avenue Jean Médecin are more expensive and in a more comfortable area.

$$ Hôtel Durante*** feels Mediterranean—a happy, orange building with rooms wrapped around a flowery courtyard. All but two of its quiet rooms overlook the well-maintained patio. The rooms are good enough (mostly modern decor), the price is right enough, and the parking is free—book well ahead (Sb-€85-115, Db-€100-130, Tb-€155-185, Qb-€190-220, breakfast-€10, 16 Avenue Durante, tel. 04 93 88 84 40, www.hotel-durante.com, info@hotel-durante.com).

$$ Hôtel Lafayette***, located a block behind the Galeries Lafayette department store, is a modest, homey place with 17 mostly spacious and good-value rooms (some with thin walls, some traffic noise, all one floor up from the street). It's family-run by Kiril and George (standard Db-€105-130, spacious Db-€120-150, Tb-€130-180, preferential direct booking rates for Rick Steves readers, breakfast-€12, no elevator, 32 Rue de l'Hôtel des Postes—see map on page 312, tel. 04 93 85 17 84, www.hotellafayettenice.com, info@hotellafayettenice.com).

$$ Hôtel St. Georges**, five blocks from the station toward

Sleep Code

Abbreviations   **(€1=about $1.10, country code: 33)**
S=Single, **D**=Double/Twin, **T**=Triple, **Q**=Quad, **b**=bathroom, *=French hotel rating (0-5 stars)
Price Rankings
 $$$ **Higher Priced**—Most rooms €200 or more
  $$ **Moderately Priced**—Most rooms €100-200
   $ **Lower Priced**—Most rooms €100 or less
Unless otherwise noted, credit cards are accepted, English is spoken, elevators and air-conditioning are available, and free Wi-Fi and/or a guest computer is generally provided. Prices change; verify current rates online or by email. For the best prices, always book directly with the hotel.

---

the sea, offers a good location, a backyard patio, and friendly Houssein at the reception. Rooms are just adequate but fairly priced; check website for deals (Sb-€100, Db-€100-130, Tb with 3 beds-€160, extra bed-€20, breakfast-€9, limited parking—book ahead, 7 Avenue Georges Clemenceau, tel. 04 93 88 79 21, www.hotelsaintgeorges.fr, contact@hotelsaintgeorges.fr).

$$ Hôtel Vendôme*** gives you a whiff of the belle époque, with pink pastels, high ceilings, and grand staircases in a mansion set off the street. The modern rooms come in all sizes; many have balconies (Db-€140-185, Tb-€180-210, check website for deals, breakfast-€15, limited parking for €15/day—book ahead, 26 Rue Pastorelli at the corner of Rue Alberti, tel. 04 93 62 00 77, www.hotel-vendome-nice.com, contact@vendome-hotel-nice.com).

$$ Hôtel Ibis Nice Centre Gare***, 100 yards to the right as you leave the station, provides a secure refuge in this seedy area. It's big (200 rooms), modern, and a decent value with well-configured rooms, a refreshing pool, and €10 overnight parking (Db-€90-€135, bigger Db-€110-155, breakfast-€10, bar, café, 14 Avenue Thiers, tel. 04 93 88 85 85, www.ibishotel.com, h1396@accor.com).

$ Hôtel Belle Meunière*, in an old mansion built for Napoleon III's mistress, attracts budget-minded travelers of all ages with cheap beds and private rooms a block below the train station. Creaky but well-kept, the place has adequate rooms, thin mattresses, and charismatic Mademoiselle Marie-Pierre presiding with her perfect English (bunk in 4-bed dorm-€28 with private bath, less with shared bath; Db-€60-86, Tb-€86-100, Qb-€118-135, breakfast-€6 or free if you book direct, no air-con, no elevator, laundry service, limited parking-€9/day, 21 Avenue Durante, tel. 04 93 88 66 15, www.bellemeuniere.com, hotel.belle.meuniere@cegetel.net).

$ B&B Nice Home Sweet Home is a good budget value.

Nice Hotels

NICE

1 Hôtel Durante
2 Hôtel St. Georges
3 Hôtel Vendôme
4 Hôtel Ibis Nice Centre Gare
5 Hôtel Belle Meunière
6 B&B Nice Home Sweet Home
7 Auberge de Jeunesse les Camélias
8 Hôtel Negresco
9 Hôtel West End
10 Hôtels Splendid & Gounod
11 Hôtel Villa Victoria
12 Hôtel Massenet
13 Hôtel les Cigales
14 Hôtel la Villa & Le Grimaldi
15 Hôtel Victor Hugo
16 To Chemins de Fer Station
17 SNCF Boutique

Genevieve (a.k.a. Jennifer) Levert rents out four large rooms and one small single in her home. Her rooms (only one of which has a private bath) are simply decorated, with high ceilings, big windows, and space to spread out (S-€35-44, D-€61-75, Db-€65-78, Tb-€75-85, Q-€80-110, includes breakfast, elevator, one floor up, washer/dryer-€6, kitchen access, 35 Rue Rossini at intersection with Rue Auber, mobile 06 50 83 25 85, www.nicehomesweethome.com, glevert@free.fr).

Hostels: **$ Auberge de Jeunesse les Camélias** is a fun, laid-back hostel with a handy location, modern facilities, and a lively evening atmosphere. Rooms accommodate four to eight people of all ages in bunk beds (136 beds in all) and come with showers and sinks—WCs are down the hall (€28/bed, one-time €11 extra charge without hostel membership, includes breakfast, rooms closed 11:00-15:00 but can leave bags, laundry, kitchen, safes, bar, 3 Rue Spitalieri, tel. 04 93 62 15 54, www.hihostels.com, accueil.nice@hifrance.org).

$ Villa Saint Exupéry Beach is a hostel-hotel in the center of Nice with a young and friendly vibe, a fun bar, and *beaucoup* services including laundry, yoga classes, and scuba diving (€40/person in dorm bunk, S-€50-70, Db-€100-120, Tb-€120-160, big breakfast-€4, no curfew, 6 Rue Sacha Guitry—see map on page 312, tel. 04 93 16 13 45, www.villahostels.com, beach@villahostels.com).

IN OR NEAR VIEUX NICE

These Vieux Nice hotels are either on the sea or within an easy walk of it. For locations, see the map on page 312.

$$$ Hôtel la Perouse****, built into the rock of Castle Hill at the east end of the bay, is a fine splurge. This refuge-hotel is top-to-bottom flawless in every detail—from its elegant rooms (satin curtains, velour headboards) and attentive staff to its rooftop terrace with Jacuzzi, sleek pool, and lovely garden restaurant (€40 *menus*). Sleep here to be spoiled and escape the big city (garden-view Db-€300-400, seaview Db-€420-580, good family options and Web deals, 11 Quai Rauba Capeu, tel. 04 93 62 34 63, www.hotel-la-perouse.com, lp@hotel-la-perouse.com).

$$$ Hôtel Suisse****, below Castle Hill, has Nice's best sea and city views for the money, and is surprisingly quiet given the busy street below. Rooms are comfortable and the decor is tasteful. Sleep elsewhere if you don't land a view—I've listed prices only for view rooms, most of which have balconies (Db-€170-340, breakfast-€18, book in advance for better rates, 15 Quai Rauba Capeu, tel. 04 92 17 39 00, www.hotels-ocre-azur.com, hotel.suisse@hotels-ocre-azur.com).

$$ Hôtel Albert 1er*** is a fair deal in a great location on Albert I Park, two blocks from the beach and Place Masséna. The staff is formal and rooms are well-appointed, with heavy brown tones. Some have views of the bay, others overlook the park (standard Db-€169-209, sea- or park-view Db-€179-259, Tb-€189-309, breakfast-€12, 4 Avenue des Phocéens, tel. 04 93 85 74 01, www. hotelalbert-1er.com, info@hotel-albert1er.com).

$$ Hôtel Mercure Marché aux Fleurs** is ideally situated near the sea and Cours Saleya. Rooms are tastefully designed and prices can be reasonable—check their website for deals (standard Db-€180, superior Db-€225-260 and worth the extra euros, smaller seaview room-€50 extra, 91 Quai des Etats-Unis, tel. 04 93 85 74 19, www.hotelmercure.com, h0962@accor.com).

$$ Hôtel de la Mer** is an intimate, 12-room place with an enviable position overlooking Place Masséna, just steps from Vieux Nice. Rooms are modern and comfortable, and the non-French owners have a laissez faire style (Db-€110-€140, Tb-€160, breakfast-€8, 4 Place Masséna, tel. 04 93 92 09 10, www. hoteldelamernice.com, contact@hoteldelamernice.com).

NEAR THE PROMENADE DES ANGLAIS

These hotels are close to the beach (and mostly far from Vieux Nice). The Negresco and West End are big, vintage Nice hotels that open onto the sea from the heart of the Promenade des Anglais.

$$$ Hôtel Negresco*** owns Nice's most prestigious address on the Promenade des Anglais and knows it. Still, it's the kind of place that if you were to splurge just once in your life... Rooms are opulent (see page 323 for more description), tips are expected, and it seems the women staying here have cosmetically augmented lips (viewless Db-€380-560, seaview Db-€450-700, view suite-€890-2,900; Old World bar, 37 Promenade des Anglais, tel. 04 93 16 64 00, www.hotel-negresco-nice.com, reservations@ hotel-negresco.com).

$$$ Hôtel West End** opens onto the Promenade des Anglais with formal service and decor, classy public spaces, and high prices (viewless Db-€300, seaview Db-€350, check website for deals, 31 Promenade des Anglais, tel. 04 92 14 44 00, www.hotel-westend.com, reservation@westendnice.com).

$$$ Hôtel Splendid** is a worthwhile splurge if you miss your Marriott. The panoramic rooftop pool, bar/restaurant, and breakfast room almost justify the cost...but throw in plush rooms, a free gym, and spa services, and you're as good as at home (Db-€250, deluxe Db with terrace-€290, suites-€410, breakfast-€20, better prices available on website, parking-€25/day, 50 Boulevard Victor Hugo, tel. 04 93 16 41 00, www.splendid-nice.com, info@ splendid-nice.com).

$$$ Hôtel Villa Victoria** is a fine place managed by cheery Marlena, who welcomes travelers into her spotless, classy old building with an open, attractive lobby overlooking a sprawl-ing garden-courtyard. Rooms are comfortable and well-kept, with space to stretch out (streetside Db-€170-200, gardenside Db-€175-225, Tb-€190-240, suites-€210, breakfast-€15, parking-€18/day, 33 Boulevard Victor Hugo, tel. 04 93 88 39 60, www.villa-victoria.com, contact@villa-victoria.com).

$$ Hôtel Massenet* is a reasonable, central value tucked away a block off the Promenade des Anglais in a pedestrian zone. It has 29 comfortable and mostly spacious rooms at fair rates—considering the shag carpet (small Db-€110, standard Db-€150-180, larger Db with terrace-€195, breakfast-€10, parking-€15/day, 11 Rue Massenet, tel. 04 93 87 11 31, www.hotelmassenet.com, hotelmassenet@wanadoo.fr).

$$ Hôtel les Cigales*, a few blocks from the Promenade des Anglais, is a little pastel place with 19 sharp rooms and a nifty upstairs terrace, all well-managed by friendly Stephane, Veronique, and Elaine (standard Db-€110-160, Tb-€130-180, discount for Rick Steves readers—ask, look for deals on their website, 16 Rue Dalpozzo, tel. 04 97 03 10 70, www.hotel-lescigales.com, info@hotel-lescigales.com).

$$ Hôtel la Villa* is a classy, well-run hotel with 47 rooms, contemporary decor in its light-filled public spaces, and a small front terrace (standard Db-€100-160, larger Db-€200, good breakfast-€12, 19 bis Boulevard Victor Hugo, tel. 04 93 87 15 00, www.hotels-la-villa.com, contact@hotel-villa-nice-centre.com.)

$$ Le Grimaldi**, an Old World place with a comfortable lobby, rents 48 spacious rooms with high ceilings and traditional decor (standard Db-€130-160, larger Db-€180-200, big break-fast-€15, a few suites and connecting rooms ideal for families, 15 Rue Grimaldi, tel. 04 93 16 00 24, www.le-grimaldi.com, info@le-grimaldi.com).

$$ Hôtel Gounod* is behind Hôtel Splendid. Because the two share the same owners, Gounod's guests are allowed free ac-cess to Splendid's pool, Jacuzzi, and other amenities. Most rooms are comfortable and quiet, with high ceilings but tired bathrooms (Db-€140-190, palatial 4-person suites-€290, breakfast-€14, park-ing-€18/day, 3 Rue Gounod, tel. 04 93 16 42 00, www.gounod-nice.com, info@gounod-nice.com).

$$ Hôtel Victor Hugo delivers simple, good value in a fine turn-of-the-century building a short walk from the Promenade des Anglais. All seven rooms come with kitchenettes (Db-€100-150, includes breakfast, 10 percent discount for Rick Steves readers who book direct, 59 Boulevard Victor Hugo, tel. 04 93 88 12 39, www.hotel-victor-hugo-nice.com).

Vieux Nice Hotels & Restaurants

NICE

1 Hôtel Lafayette
2 Villa Saint Exupéry Beach Hostel
3 Hôtel la Perouse & Hôtel Suisse
4 Hôtel Albert 1er
5 Hôtel Mercure Marché aux Fleurs
6 Hôtel de la Mer
7 Le Safari Restaurant
8 Pizzeria Rossopomodoro

9 L'Acchiardo Restaurant
10 Chez Palmyre Restaurant
11 Le Bistrot du Fromager
12 Bistrot D'Antoine
13 La Merenda Restaurant
14 Lou Pilha Leva Restaurant
15 Oliviera Shop/Restaurant
16 Restaurant Castel

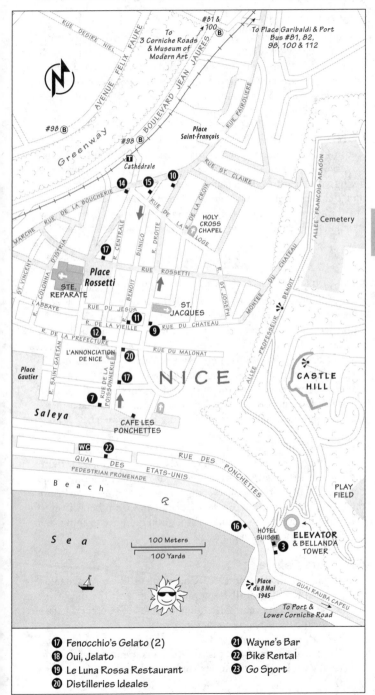

NICE

NEAR THE AIRPORT

Several airport hotels offer a handy and cheap port-in-the-storm for those with early flights or who are just stopping in for a single night: **Hôtels Campanile** (www.campanile.fr) and **Nouvel** (www.novotel.com) are closest, and **Hôtel Ibis Budget Nice Aéroport** (www.ibis.com) is a few minutes away. Free shuttles connect these hotels with both airport terminals.

LONGER-STAY RENTALS

Renting an apartment, house, villa, or *gîte* can be a cost-effective way to explore the Côte d'Azur. Rentals are typically by the week, giving you time to take advantage of day-trip possibilities. **Riviera Pebbles** offers a wide range of rental apartments throughout the Riviera and gets good reviews from happy clients (www.rivierapebbles.com). See page 486 for more on longer-stay rentals.

Eating in Nice

Historically, Nice is not quite France. You'll find lots of regional dishes and lots of Italian influence mixing in with classic French cuisine. As you're in a resort, your priorities should probably be ambience and fun, rather than high cuisine. For the most energy and variety, I'd eat in Vieux Nice. If Old Nice is too far, I've listed good places handier to your hotel. Promenade des Anglais is ideal for picnic dinners on warm, languid evenings or a meal at a beach-side restaurant. For a more romantic (and expensive) meal, head for nearby Villefranche-sur-Mer (see page 356). Avoid the fun-to-peruse but terribly touristy eateries lining Rue Masséna.

IN VIEUX NICE

Nice's dinner scene converges on Cours Saleya, which is entertaining enough in itself to make the generally mediocre food a good deal. It's a fun, festive spot to compare tans and mussels. Most of my recommendations are on side lanes inland from here. Even if you're eating elsewhere, wander through here in the evening. For locations, see the map on page 312.

On Cours Saleya

While local foodies would avoid Cours Saleya like a McDonalds, the energy of wall-to-wall restaurants taking over the old town's market square each evening is enticing. Here are two good bets—one for local cuisine and the other for pizza.

Le Safari is a fair option for Niçois cuisine and outdoor dining. The place, convivial and rustic with a mix of modern art inside, is packed with locals and tourists, and staffed with hurried waiters

(€18-30 *plats,* open daily, 1 Cours Saleya, tel. 04 93 80 18 44, www. restaurantsafari.fr).

Pizzeria Rossopomodoro is a fun little place where hard-working Armando serves excellent Neapolitan-style pizzas either inside or on the square (€13-15, 26 Cours Saleya, tel. 04 93 80 02 99).

Characteristic Places in the Old Town

L'Acchiardo is a homey eatery that mixes loyal clientele with hungry tourists. As soon as you sit down you know this is a treat. Its simple, hearty Niçois cuisine is served by Monsieur Acchiardo and his good-looking sons. The small plaque under the menu outside says the restaurant has been run by father and son since 1927 (€9 starters, €16 *plats,* €7 desserts, closed Sat-Sun, indoor seating only, 38 Rue Droite, tel. 04 93 85 51 16).

Chez Palmyre, your best budget bet in the old town, is tiny and popular, so book ahead. The ambience is rustic and fun, with people squeezed onto shared tables to enjoy the home-style cooking. Everyone eats the three-course, €17 *menu,* which changes every two weeks (closed Sun, cash only, 5 Rue Droite, tel. 04 93 85 72 32).

Bistrot du Fromager's owner, Hugo, is crazy about cheese and wine. Come here to escape the heat and dine in cozy, cool, vaulted cellars surrounded by shelves of wine. All dishes use cheese as their base ingredient, although you'll also find pasta, ham, and salmon (with cheese, of course). This is a good choice for vegetarians (€10-15 starters, €15-22 *plats,* €6 desserts, closed Sun for dinner, just off Place du Jésus at 29 Rue Benoît Bunico, tel. 04 93 13 07 83).

Bistrot D'Antoine has street appeal. It's a warm, popular, vine-draped option whose menu emphasizes Niçois cuisine and good grilled selections. The food is delicious and the prices are reasonable. Call a day ahead to reserve a table—the upstairs room is quieter (€10 starters, €17 *plats,* €7 desserts, closed Sun-Mon, 27 Rue de la Préfecture, tel. 04 93 85 29 57).

La Merenda is a shoebox where you'll sit on small stools and dine on simple, home-style dishes in a communal environment. The menu changes with the season, but the hardworking owner, Dominique, does not. This place fills fast, so arrive early, or better yet, drop by during the day to reserve—they have two seatings at 19:00 and 21:00 (€10 starters, €14 *plats,* €6 desserts, closed Sat-Sun, cash only, 4 Rue Raoul Bosio, no telephone, www.lamerenda. net).

Lou Pilha Leva delivers fun and cheap lunch or dinner options with Niçois specialties and always-busy, outdoor-only, picnic-table dining (daily, located where Rue de la Loge and Rue Centrale meet).

Oliviera venerates the French olive. This shop/restaurant serves both oil tastings and a menu of dishes paired with specific oils (like a wine pairing). Owner Nadim speaks excellent English, knows all his producers, and provides "Olive Oil 101" explanations with his tastings (best if you buy something afterward or have a meal). You'll learn how passionate he is about his products, and once you've had a taste, you'll want to stay and eat (allow €40 with wine, €16-26 main dishes, Tue-Sat 10:00-22:00, closed Sun-Mon, indoor seating only, 8 bis Rue du Collet, tel. 04 93 13 06 45).

Dining on the Beach

Restaurant Castel is a fine eat-on-the-beach option, thanks to its location at the very east end of Nice, under Castle Hill. The city vanishes as you step down to the beach. The food is creative and nicely presented and the tables feel elegant, even at the edge of the sand. Arrive for the sunset and you'll have an unforgettable meal (€19 salads and pastas, €20-25 daily plates, open for dinner mid-May-Aug, lunch April-Sept, 8 Quai des Etats-Unis, tel. 04 93 85 22 66, www.castelplage.com). Sunbathers can rent beach chairs and have drinks and meals served literally on the beach (lounge chairs €16/half-day, €19/day).

And for Dessert...

Gelato lovers should save room for the tempting ice-cream stands in Vieux Nice (open daily until late). **Fenocchio** is the city's favorite, with mouthwatering displays of dozens of flavors ranging from lavender to avocado (two locations: 2 Place Rossetti and 6 Rue de la Poissonnerie). Gelato connoisseurs should head for **Oui, Jelato,** where the quality is the priority rather than the selection (5 Rue de la Préfecture, on the Place du Palais).

IN THE CITY CENTER
Near Nice Etoile

For a more contemporary, urban slice of France, try one of these spots around the Nice Etoile shopping mall.

On Rue Biscarra: An appealing lineup of bistros overflowing with outdoor tables stretches along the broad sidewalk on Rue Biscarra (just east of Avenue Jean Médecin behind Nice Etoile, all closed Sun). Come here to dine with area residents away from the tourists. **Le 20 sur Vin** is a neighborhood favorite with a cozy, wine-bar-meets-café ambience. It offers good wines and tasty bistro fare (tel. 04 93 92 93 20).

Rolancy's Restaurant & Bistrot des Viviers attract those looking for formal service and authentic Niçois cuisine with a big emphasis on fish. This classy splurge offers two intimate yet distinct settings: a soft, formal restaurant (*menus* from €50, €25-26 *plats,*

Nice Restaurants

1 Rue Biscarra Eateries
2 Rolancy's Restaurant & Bistrot des Viviers
3 L'Ovale Restaurant
4 Le Luna Rossa Restaurant
5 La Maison de Marie Rest.
6 Voyageur Nissart Rest.
7 Zen Japanese Restaurant
8 Place Grimaldi Eateries
9 Monoprix Grocery Store

€45 bouillabaisse), and a cozy bistro (similar prices) with some out-door seating (closed Sun, 5-minute walk west of Avenue Jean Mé-decin at 22 Rue Alphonse Karr, tel. 04 93 16 00 48).

L'Ovale takes its name from the shape of a rugby ball. Owner Jacqueline brings a welcoming, down-to-earth feel to this quality café-bistro. The menu features cuisine from southwestern France (rich and meaty). Dine inside on big *plats* for €12-17; consider the *cassoulet* (€17), the hearty *salade de manchons* with duck and walnuts (€14), or the €18 three-course *menu* (daily, 29 Rue Pastorelli, tel. 04 93 80 31 65).

Le Luna Rossa is a small neighborhood place serving deli-cious French-Italian dishes. Owner Christine welcomes diners with attentive service and reasonable prices. Dine inside (classy tables) or outside on a sidewalk terrace (€10 starters, €14-27 *plats*, closed Sun-Mon, just north of parkway at 3 Rue Chauvain—see map on page 314, tel. 04 93 85 55 66).

La Maison de Marie is a surprisingly high-quality refuge off Nice's touristy restaurant row—Rue Masséna. The interior tables are as appealing as those in the courtyard, but expect some smok-ers outside. The €24 *menu* is a good value (€12-18 starters, €20-30 *plats,* open daily, 5 Rue Masséna, tel. 04 93 82 15 93).

Near the Train Station

Both of these restaurants, a block below the train station, provide good indoor and outdoor seating as well as excellent value.

Voyageur Nissart has blended good-value cuisine with friendly service since 1908. Kind owner Max is a great host, and the quality of his food makes his place both very popular and a good choice for travelers on a budget (book ahead, leave a message in English). Try anything *à la niçoise,* including the fine €8 *salade niçoise* (€17 three-course *menus,* good *plats* from €11, inexpensive wines, closed Mon, 19 Rue d'Alsace-Lorraine, tel. 04 93 82 19 60).

Zen Japanese Restaurant provides a break from French cui-sine. Interior seating is arranged around the chef's stove, and the tasty specialties draw a strong following (€16 three-course *menu,* €8-15 sushi, open daily, 27 Rue d'Angleterre, tel. 04 93 82 41 20).

ON PLACE GRIMALDI

This square near the Promenade des Anglais nurtures a lineup of locals-only restaurants with good indoor and outdoor seating along a broad sidewalk under tall, leafy sycamore trees. **Crêperie Bret-onne** is the place to eat here and the only *crêperie* I list in Nice. Dine on the broad terrace or inside with jovial service and jukebox-meets-gramophone ambience. Their top-end, house-special crêpes are creative and enticing (delicious €12-14 dinner crêpes, split a salad to start—try the goat cheese salad with honey, closed Sun, tel. 04 93 82 28 47).

Nice Connections

BY TRAIN

For a comparison of train and bus connections from Nice to nearby coastal towns, see the "Public Transportation in the French Riviera" sidebar on page 282.

Most long-distance train connections to other French cities require a change in Marseille. The Grande Ligne train to Bordeaux (serving Antibes, Cannes, Toulon, and Marseille—and connecting from there to Arles, Nîmes, and Carcassonne) requires a reservation.

From Nice by Train to: Cannes (2/hour, 30 minutes), **Antibes** (2/hour, 20 minutes), **Villefranche-sur-Mer** (2/hour, 10 minutes), **Eze-le-Village** (2/hour, 15 minutes to Eze-Bord-de-Mer, then bus #83 to Eze, 8/day, 15 minutes), **Monaco** (2/hour, 20 minutes), **Menton** (2/hour, 25 minutes), **Grasse** (15/day, 1 hour, better by bus), **Marseille** (18/day, 2.5 hours), **Cassis** (hourly, 3 hours, transfer in Toulon or Marseille), **Arles** (11/day, 4 hours, most require transfer in Marseille or Avignon), **Avignon** (10/day, most by TGV, 4 hours, many require transfer in Marseille), **Paris'** Gare de Lyon (hourly, 6 hours, may require change; 11-hour night train goes to Paris' Gare d'Austerlitz), **Aix-en-Provence** TGV Station (10/day, 2-3 hours, usually changes in Marseille), **Chamonix** (4/day, 10 hours, many change in St-Gervais and Lyon), **Beaune** (7/day, 7 hours, 1-2 transfers), **Florence** (6/day, 8 hours, 1-3 transfers), **Milan** (7/day, 5 hours, all with transfers), **Venice** (5/day, 9 hours, all with transfers), **Barcelona** (1/day via Montpellier, 10 hours, more with multiple changes).

BY BUS

Most one-way rides on regional buses (except express airport buses) cost €1.50—regardless of length. Tickets are good for up to 74 minutes of travel in one direction, including transfers.

From Nice by Bus to: Cannes (#200, 4/hour Mon-Sat, 2/hour Sun, 2 hours), **Antibes** (#200, 4/hour Mon-Sat, 2/hour Sun, 1.5 hours), **Villefranche-sur-Mer** (#100, 3-4/hour, 20 minutes; or #81, 2-3/hour, 20 minutes), **St-Jean-Cap-Ferrat** (#81, 2-3/hour, 30 minutes), **Eze-le-Village** (#82 or #112, 16/day Mon-Sat, 8/day Sun, 40 minutes), **La Turbie** (#T66, 7/day, 45 minutes, Pont St. Michel tram stop; also #116, 6/day, 45 minutes, Vauban tram stop), **Monaco** (#100, 3-4/hour, 45 minutes), **Menton** (#100, 3-4/hour, 1.5 hours), **St-Paul-de-Vence** (#400, 2/hour, 45 minutes), **Vence** (#400, 2/hour, 50 minutes), **Grasse** (#500, 2/hour, 1 hour).

BY PLANE

Nice's easy-to-navigate airport (Aéroport de Nice Côte d'Azur, airport code: NCE) is literally on the Mediterranean—with landfill runways, a 30-minute drive west of the city center. Planes leave roughly hourly for Paris (one-hour flight, about the same price as a train ticket, check www.easyjet.com for the cheapest flights to Paris' Orly airport). The two terminals are connected by shuttle buses *(navettes)*. Both terminals have TIs, banks, ATMs, and buses to Nice (tel. 04 89 88 98 28, www.nice.aeroport.fr).

Getting from the Airport to the City Center

By Taxi: A taxi into the center is expensive considering the short distance (figure €35 to Nice hotels, €60 to Villefranche-sur-Mer, €70 to Antibes, small fee for bags). Nice's airport taxis are notorious for overcharging. Before riding, confirm that your fare into town is roughly €35 (or €40 at night or on Sun). Don't pay much more. It's always a good idea to ask for a receipt *(reçu)*.

By Airport Shuttle: These work better for trips from your hotel to the airport, since they require you to book a precise pickup time in advance—even though you can't ever know exactly when your flight will actually arrive. Shuttle vans offer a fixed price (figure €30 for one person, and only a little more for additional people). Your hotel can arrange this. Try **Nice Airport Shuttle** (1-2 people-€32, additional person-€14, mobile 06 60 33 20 54, www.nice-airport-shuttle.com) or **Med-Tour** (tel. 04 93 82 92 58, mobile 06 73 82 04 10, www.med-tour.com).

By Bus: Two bus lines connect the airport with the city center, offering good alternatives to high-priced taxis. **Bus #99** (airport express) runs to Nice's main train station (€6, 2/hour, 8:00-21:00, 30 minutes, drops you within a 10-minute walk of many recommended hotels). To take this bus *to* the airport, catch it right in front of the train station (departs on the half-hour). If your hotel is within walking distance of the station, #99 is your best budget bet.

Bus #98 runs along Promenade des Anglais and along the edge of Vieux Nice (€6, 3/hour, from the airport 6:00-23:00, to the airport until 21:00, 30 minutes, see map on page 312 for stops).

For all buses, buy tickets from the driver. To reach the bus information office and stops at Terminal 1, turn left after passing customs and exit the doors at the far end. Buses serving Terminal 2 stop across the street from the airport exit (information kiosk and ticket sales to the right as you exit).

Getting from the Airport to Nearby Destinations

To get to **Villefranche-sur-Mer** from the airport, take bus #98 (described above) to Place Garibaldi. From there, use the same ticket to transfer to bus #81 or #100 (see "Nice Connections—By

Bus," earlier, for bus frequencies and the map on page 330 for stop locations; note that you may need to walk to the port to catch east-bound buses in 2016 due to work on the tram system).

To reach **Antibes,** take bus #250 from either terminal (about 2/hour, 40 minutes, €10). For **Cannes,** take bus #210 from either terminal (1-2/hour, 50 minutes on freeway, €20). Express bus #110 runs from the airport directly to **Monaco** (2/hour, 50 minutes, €20).

BY CRUISE SHIP

Nice's port is at the eastern edge of the town center, below Castle Hill; the main promenade and old town are on the other side of the

hill. Cruise ships dock at either side of the mouth of this port: Terminal 1 to the east or Terminal 2 to the west.

NICE

Getting into the City Center: To reach Vieux Nice or the tram, head to Place Garibaldi by walking or riding the shuttle bus to the top of the port, then angling up Rue Cassini to the square (20-minute walk from either cruise terminal). From here it's a short **walk** to Vieux Nice or to the tram stop. You can ride the **tram** to Place Masséna for the start of my Old Nice Walk or to catch a bus to the Chagall or Matisse museums (#15 or #22).

If arriving at Terminal 2 and heading to Vieux Nice, you can skip the walk to Place Garibaldi and stroll directly there by heading around the base of the castle-topped hill, with the sea on your left (10-15 minutes).

Other options to get into town include a **taxi** from the terminals (about €20 to points within Nice) or the **hop-on, hop-off bus,** which has a stop at the top of the port (see page 295).

Getting to Nearby Destinations: To visit Villefranche-sur-Mer or Monaco, it's best to take **bus #100** (the train is faster, but the bus stop is much closer to Nice's port). The bus stops along the top of the port, near the right end of Place de l'Ile de Beauté (see map on page 290).

To take the **train** to Villefranche-sur-Mer, Monaco, Antibes, Cannes, or elsewhere, hop on the tram (stop near Place Garibaldi, described earlier), then ride to the Gare Thiers stop and walk one long block to the main train station. For bus and train connections to nearby destinations, see page 319.

Taxis at the terminals charge about €40 one-way to Villefranche-sur-Mer, or €95 one-way to Monaco.

PROMENADE DES ANGLAIS WALK

Welcome to the Riviera. There's something for everyone along this four-mile-long promenade. Stroll like the belle-époque English aristocrats for whom the promenade was paved. Watch Europeans at play, admire the azure Mediterranean, anchor yourself on a blue seat, and prop your feet up on the made-to-order guardrail. Later, you can come back to join the evening parade of tans along the promenade.

The broad sidewalks of the Promenade des Anglais ("Walkway of the English") were financed by upper-crust English tour-

ists who wanted a secure and comfortable place to stroll and admire the view. The Brits originally came to Nice seeking relief from tuberculosis; both the dry climate and the salt air helped ease their suffering. It was an era when tanned bodies were frowned upon (aristocrats didn't want to resemble lower-class laborers who had to work outside). The walk was paved in marble in 1822 so the aristocrats wouldn't have to dirty their shoes or smell the fishy gravel. Visitors wouldn't swim in the Mediterranean for another hundred years, when the region took off as a tourist destination.

This leisurely, level walk is a straight line along this much-strolled beachfront. It begins near the landmark Hôtel Negresco and ends just before Castle Hill. While this one-mile walk is enjoyable at any time, the first half makes a great pre- or post-dinner stroll (perhaps with a dinner on the beach). If planning to extend this stroll to Castle Hill, it's ideal to time things so you wind up on top of the hill at sunset. Allow one hour at a promenade pace to reach the elevator up to Castle Hill.

The Walk Begins

• *Start at the pink-domed...*

❶ Hôtel Negresco

Nice's finest hotel is also a historic monument, offering up the city's most expensive beds and a museum-like interior. While the hotel is off-limits to nonguests, the doorman explained to me that shoppers and drinkers are "guests" as much as people actually sleeping there. So, tuck in your shirt, stand tall, appear confident, and march in. If someone questions you, say you're going in for a drink or to shop (a string of clothing and jewelry shops is inside), and you're legit.

The huge ballroom (walk straight until you see the big chandelier) is the **Salon Royal.** The chandelier hanging from its Eiffel-built dome is made of 16,000 pieces of crystal. It was built in France for the Russian czar's Moscow palace...but thanks to the Bolshevik Revolution in 1917, he couldn't take delivery. Bronze portrait busts of Czar Alexander III and his wife, Maria Feodorovna—who returned to her native Denmark after the revolution—are to the right, facing the shops. Circle the interior and then the perimeter to enjoy both historic and modern art. Fine portraits include Emperor Napoleon III and wife Empress Eugénie (who acquired Nice for France from Italy in 1860), and Jeanne Augier (who owns the hotel). She's quite elderly now, lives up in the cupola, and has willed the Negresco to organizations that care for orphans and stray animals.

If the **Le Relais bar** door is open (after noon), wander up the marble steps for a look. Farther along, in the little shopping lane, nip into the toilets for either an early 20th-century powder room or a Battle of Waterloo experience. The chairs with the high, scooped backs were typical of the age (cones of silence for an afternoon nap sitting up). The hotel's **Chantecler restaurant** is one of the Riviera's best (allow €100 per person before drinks).

On your way out, pop into the **Salon Versailles** (right of entry lobby as you leave), with a grand fireplace and France's Sun King, Louis XIV, on the wall (English descriptions explain the room).

If you wonder why such a grand hotel has such an understated

Promenade des Anglais Walk

1 Hôtel Negresco
2 Villa Masséna (Museum)
3 Bay of Angels Stop
4 Palais de la Méditerranée
5 Albert I Park
6 Steel Girders Sculpture
7 Metal Winch

entry, it's because today's front door was originally the back door. In the 19th century, elegant people stayed out of the sun, and any posh hotel that cared about its clientele would design its entry on the shady north side. If you walk around to the back you'll see a grand but unused front door.

• *Across the street from the Hôtel Negresco is...*

❷ Villa Masséna

When Nice became part of France, France invested heavily in what it expected to be the country's new high society retreat—an elite resort akin to Russia's Sochi. The government built this fine palace for the military hero of the Napoleonic age, Jean-Andre Masséna and his family. Take a moment to stroll around the lovely garden (free, open daily 10:00-18:00). The Masséna Museum inside (described on page 302) offers an interesting look at belle-époque Nice.

• *From Villa Masséna, head for the beach and begin your Promenade des Anglais stroll. But first, grab a blue chair and gaze out to the...*

❸ Bay of Angels (Baie des Anges)

Face the water. The body of Nice's patron saint, Réparate, was supposedly escorted into this bay by angels in the fourth century. To your right is where you might have been escorted into France—Nice's airport, built on a massive landfill. The tip of land beyond the runway is Cap d'Antibes. Until 1860, Antibes and Nice were in different countries—Antibes was French, but Nice was a protectorate of the Italian kingdom of Savoy-Piedmont, a.k.a. the Kingdom of Sardinia. During that period, the Var River—just west of Nice—was the geographic border between these two peoples (and to this day the river functions as a kind of cultural border). In 1850 the people here spoke Italian and ate pasta. As Italy was uniting, the region was given a choice: Join the new country of Italy or join France (which was enjoying prosperous times under the rule of Napoleon III). The vast majority voted in 1860 to go French...and *voilà!* (While that was the official story, in reality the Italian king needed France's support in helping Italian regions controlled by Austria break away to join the emerging union of Italian states. Italy's price for France's support against Austria: the city and region of Nice.)

The lower green hill to your left is Castle Hill. Farther left lie Villefranche-sur-Mer and Cap Ferrat (marked by the tower at land's end, and home to lots of millionaires), then Monaco (which you can't see, with more millionaires), then Italy. Behind you are the foothills of the Alps, which trap threatening clouds, ensuring that the Côte d'Azur enjoys sunshine more than 300 days each year. While half a million people live here, pollution is carefully treated—the water is routinely tested and is very clean. But with climate change, the warmer water is attracting jellyfish in the summer, making swimming a stinging memory.

• *With the sea on your right, begin strolling.*

The Promenade

Nearby sit two fine belle-époque establishments: the West End and Westminster hotels, both boasting English names to help those

original guests feel at home (the West End is now part of the Best Western group...to help American guests feel at home). These hotels symbolize Nice's arrival as a tourist mecca in the 19th century, when the combination of leisure time and a stable economy allowed visitors to find the sun even in winter.

As you walk, be careful to avoid the green bike lane. The promenade you're walking on was originally much narrower. It's been widened over the years to keep up with tourist demand, including increased bicycle use.

You'll pass a number of separate rocky beaches. In spite of the lack of sand, they're still a popular draw. France has a strong ethic

of public access when it comes to its beaches. In response to a greedy development project in the 1970s designed to privatize a stretch of coastline, a law was passed in 1980 guaranteeing the public free access to beaches like these. All along the Riviera you'll find public beaches (and public showers).

You can go local and rent gear—about €15 for a *chaise longue* (long chair) and a *transat* (mattress), €5 for an umbrella, and €4 for a towel. You'll also pass several beach restaurants. Some of these eateries serve breakfast, all serve lunch, some do dinner, and a few have beachy bars...tailor-made for a break from this walk. (Plage Beau Rivage, farther along on Quai des Etats-Unis, is cool for a drink.)

Even a hundred years ago, there was sufficient tourism in Nice to justify building its first casino (a leisure activity imported from Venice). Part of an elegant casino, La Jetée Promenade stood on those white-covered pilings (with flags flapping) just offshore, until the Germans destroyed it during World War II. When La Jetée was thriving, it took gamblers two full days to get to the Riviera by train from Paris.

Although La Jetée Promenade is gone, you can still see the striking 1927 Art Nouveau facade of the ❹ **Palais de la Méditerranée**, a grand casino, hotel, and theater. It became one of the grandest casinos in Europe, and today it is one of France's most exclusive hotels, though the casino feels cheap and cheesy.

The unappealing Casino Ruhl (with the most detested facade on the strip) disfigures the next block. Anyone can drop in for some one-armed-bandit fun, but to play the tables at night you'll need to dress up and bring your passport.

❺ **Albert I Park** is named for the Belgian king who enjoyed wintering here—these were his private gardens. While the English came first, the Belgians and Russians were also big fans of 19th-century Nice. That tall statue at the edge of the park commemorates the 100-year anniversary of Nice's union with France. The happy statue features two beloved women embracing the idea of union (Marianne—Ms. Liberty, Equality, and Brotherhood, and the symbol of the Republic of France—and Catherine Ségurane, a 16th-century heroine who helped Nice against the Saracen pirates).

The park is a long, winding greenbelt called the Promenade du Paillon. The Paillon River flows under the park on its way to the sea. This is the historical divide between old Nice and the new town. Continue along, past the vintage belle-époque carousel. You're now on Quai des Etats-Unis ("Quay of the United States"). This name was given as a tip-of-the-cap to the Americans for finally entering World War I in 1917. Check out the laid-back couches at the Plage Beau Rivage lounge. The big, blue chair statue celebrates the inviting symbol of this venerable walk and kicks off what I consider the best stretch of beach—quieter and with less traffic.

The tall, rusted ❻ **steel girders** reaching for the sky were erected in 2010 to celebrate the 150th anniversary of Nice's union with France. (The seven beams represent the seven valleys of the Nice region.) Done by the same artist who created the popular Arc of the Riviera sculpture in the parkway near Place Masséna, this "art" infuriates many locals as an ugly waste of money. But I know how to make it easier to appreciate the erection every local loves to hate: Stand directly under it, look straight up, and spin 720 degrees. Then look across the way to marvel at the 18th-century facades that line the Esplanade Georges Pompidou. Then find the one that is entirely fake-painted on a flat stucco surface. Then, look down and notice the buried uplighting—a French forte. And then, give it another 720 degrees of spin and try to walk on.

At the first palm tree, ladies enjoy looking left (at the delightful back side of Apollo, a couple of blocks away), and men head to the right for a view of the beach action. Topless bathing is now out of fashion. Locals say that the awareness of skin cancer and the proliferation of North African and tourist looky-loos have made it less appealing. Some say the only people still bathing topless are older ladies who remember fondly the liberation of 1968...and tourists.

The elegant back side of Nice's opera house faces the sea. In front of it, a tiny bronze Statue of Liberty reminds all that this stretch of seafront promenade is named for the USA.

The long, low building lining the walk on the left once served the city's fishermen. Behind its gates bustles the Cours Saleya Market—long the heart and soul of old Nice.

Ahead, on the right, find the three-foot-tall white ❼ **metal winch.** It's a reminder that long before tourism and long before Nice dredged its harbor, hard-working fishing boats rather than vacationing tourists lined the beach. The boats were hauled in through the surf by winches like this and tied to the iron rings on either side.

• *Your walk is over. From here you have several great options: Continue 10 minutes along the coast to the **port,** around the foot of Castle Hill (fine views of the entire promenade and a monumental war memorial carved into the hillside); hike or ride the elevator up to **Castle Hill** (catch the elevator next to Hôtel Suisse—free, daily 10:00–19:00, until 20:00 in summer, see listing for Castle Hill on page 304); head into the **old town** (you can follow my "Old Nice Walk"); or grab a blue chair or piece of **beach** and just be on vacation—Riviera style.*

OLD NICE WALK

This self-guided walk through Nice's old town, from Place Masséna to Place Rossetti, gives you a helpful introduction to the city's bicultural heritage and its most interesting neighborhoods. Allow about an hour at a leisurely pace for this level walk. It's best done in the morning (while the outdoor market thrives), and preferably not on a Sunday, when things are quiet. This ramble is also a joy at night, when fountains glow and pedestrians control the streets.

The Walk Begins

• *Start where Avenue Jean Médecin hits the people-friendly Place Masséna—the successful result of a long, expensive city upgrade and the new center of Nice.*

Place Masséna

The grand Place Masséna is Nice's drawing room, where old meets new, and where the tramway bends between Vieux (Old) Nice and

the train station. The square's black-and-white pavement feels like an elegant outdoor ballroom, with the sleek tram waltzing across its dance floor. While once congested with cars, the square today is frequented only by these trams, which swoosh silently by every couple of minutes. The men on pedestals sitting high above are modern-art additions that arrived with the tram. For a mood-altering experience, return after dark and watch the illuminated figures float yoga-like above. Place Masséna is at its sophisticated best after the sun goes down.

This vast square dates from 1848 and pays tribute to Jean-

Old Nice Walk

OLD NICE WALK

To Train Station

R. G. DELOYE

RUE BLACAS

RUE L'HOTEL DES POSTES

RUE ALBERTI

RUE DU LYCÉE

AVE. JEAN MÉDECIN

R. S. GUITRY

GIOFFREDO

RUE GUBERNATIS

GALERIES LAFAYETTE

T Masséna

B #15, #17 & #22

RUE CHAUVAIN

PASSAGE GIOFFREDO

RUE

GIOFFREDO

#98 B

FÉLIX FAURE

AVENUE

Vert

JEAN JAURES

#98 B

DESCENTE CROTTI

WALK BEGINS

FOUNTAINS

BOULEVARD

T Opéra

RUE DE

Place Masséna

1

V I E U X

RUE DE LOPÈS

Coulée

R. DESBOUTIN

RUE L'HOTEL DE VILLE

ALEXANDRE MARI

R. RAOUL BOSIO

P

Place du Palais

ST. FRANCOIS-DE-PAULE

PATISSERIE AUER

POST

RUE ST. FRANCOIS

2

DE PAULE

Cours

B #98

R. VANLOO

MOLINARD PERFUME MUSEUM

P

RUE ROBINS

OPERA

CITE DU

QUAI DES ETATS-UNIS

QUAI DES ETATS-UNIS

PEDESTRIAN PROMENADE

To Promenade des Anglais

Beach

M e d i t e r r a n e a n

" B a y   o f   A n g e l s "

1 Place Masséna
2 Rue St. François de Paule
3 Cours Saleya
4 Rue de la Poissonnerie
5 Rue Droite
6 Place Rossetti

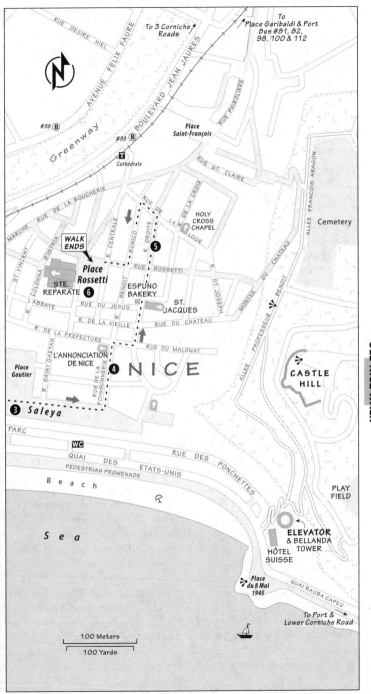

N

RUE DESIRE NIEL

AVENUE FELIX FAURE

BOULEVARD JEAN JAURÈS

To 3 Corniche Roads

To Place Garibaldi & Port
Bus #81, 82, 98, 100 & 112

RUE PAIROLIÈRE

#98 B

Greenway

#98 B

Place Saint-François

T Cathédrale

RUE ST. CLAIRE

ALLÉE FRANCOIS ARAGON

Cemetery

RUE DE LA BOUCHERIE

RUE DE LA CROIX

RUE DE LA LOGE

HOLY CROSS CHAPEL

RUE DROITE

BUNICO

R. CENTRALE

WALK ENDS

⑤

MARCHÉ

ST. VINCENT

COLONNA D'ISTRIA

Place Rossetti

STE. REPARATE ⑥

RUE ROSSETTI

R. BENOIT

RUE DU JÉSUS

ESPUNO BAKERY

ST. JACQUES

ST. JOSEPH

MONTÉE DU CHÂTEAU

BENOIT

ALLÉE PROFESSEUR

L'ABBAYE

RUE DE LA VIEILLE

RUE DU CHÂTEAU

R. DE LA PREFECTURE

RUE DU MALONAT

N I C E

K. SAINT GAÉTAN

Place Gautier

L'ANNONCIATION DE NICE ④

RUE DE LA POISSONNERIE

CASTLE HILL

③ *Saleya*

PARC

WC

QUAI DES ETATS-UNIS

RUE DES PONCHETTES

PEDESTRIAN PROMENADE

B e a c h

PLAY FIELD

ELEVATOR & BELLANDA TOWER

HÔTEL SUISSE

S e a

Place du 8 Mai 1945

QUAI RAUBA CAPEU

To Port & Lower Corniche Road

100 Meters

100 Yards

OLD NICE WALK

André Masséna, a French military leader during the Revolutionary and Napoleonic wars. Not just another pretty face in a long lineup of French military heroes, he's considered among the greatest commanders in history—anywhere, anytime. Napoleon called him "the greatest name of my military Empire." No wonder this city is proud of him.

Under the pavement, Nice's historic river, the Paillon, is flowing to the sea. For centuries this river was Nice's natural defense to the north and west (the sea protected the south, and Castle Hill defended the east). A fortified wall once ran along the river's length to the sea. It's been covered since the late 1800s.

Standing in the center of the square, face the sea and start a clockwise spin tour: The towering **modern swoosh sculpture** in the park is meant to represent the "curve of the French Riviera"— the arc of the bay. To the right stretches modern Nice, born with the arrival of tourism in the 1800s. **Avenue Jean Médecin,** Nice's main street, cuts from here through the new town to the train station. In the distance you can see the tracks, the freeway, and the Alps beyond that. Once crammed with cars, buses, and delivery vehicles tangling with pedestrians, Avenue Jean Médecin was turned into a walking and cycling nirvana in 2007. I used to avoid this street. Now I can't get enough of it. Businesses along it flourish in the welcoming environment of generous sidewalks and no traffic.

Appreciate the city's Italian heritage—it feels as much like Venice as Paris. The portico flanking Avenue Jean Médecin is Italian, not French. The rich colors of the buildings reflect the taste of previous Italian rulers.

Turn to your right and look east to see Nice's ongoing effort to "put the human element into the heart of the town." The unsightly bus station and parking structures were demolished and the green parkway—**La Coulée Verte**—now stretches from the sea to Place Masséna and on to the Museum of Modern Art. Forming a key spine for biking and walking, this ambitious 30-acre project is another example of Nice's determination to make its urban center more livable. Notice the fountain—its surprise geysers delight children by day and its fine lighting enhances romance at night. Beyond the fountain stands a bronze statue of the square's namesake, Masséna. And the hills beyond that separate Nice from Villefranche-sur-Mer.

Turn further to the right to see the old town, with its jumbled and characteristic facades below Castle Hill. The **statue of Apollo** holds a beach towel as if to say, "It's beer o'clock, let's go."

• *Walk past Apollo with the beach towel into the old town. After a block down Rue de l'Opéra, turn left onto Rue St. François de Paule (or you can detour right one block to the **Molinard** perfume shop at #20, which* *has a free one-room museum and offers create-your-own-perfume sessions for a price; see www.molinard.com).*

Rue St. François de Paule

This colorful street leads into the heart of Vieux Nice. On the left is the Hôtel de Ville (City Hall). Peer into the **Alziari olive oil shop** (at #14 on the right). Dating from 1868, the shop produces top-quality stone-ground olive oil. The proud and charming owner, Gilles Piot, claims that stone wheels create less acidity, since metal grinding builds up heat (see photo in back over the door). Locals fill their own containers from the huge vats.

La Couqueto (at #8) is a colorful shop filled with Provençal handicrafts, including lovely folk characters *(santons)*.

Across the street is Nice's grand **opera house.** Imagine this opulent jewel back in the 19th century, buried deep in the old town of Nice. With all the fancy big-city folks wintering here, this rough-edged town needed some high-class entertainment. And Victorians needed an alternative to those "devilish" gambling houses. (Queen Victoria, so disgusted by casinos, would actually close the drapes on her train window when passing Monte Carlo.) The four statues on top represent theater, dance, music, and party poopers.

On the left (at #7), **Pâtisserie Auer's** grand old storefront would love to tempt you with chocolates and candied fruits. It's changed little over the centuries. The writing on the window says, "Since 1820 from father to son." The gold royal shields on the back wall remind shoppers that Queen Victoria indulged her sweet tooth here.

• *Continue on, sifting your way through a cluttered block of tacky souvenir shops to the big market square.*

Cours Saleya

Named for its broad exposure to the sun *(soleil),* Cours Saleya (koor sah-lay-yuh)—a commotion of color, sights, smells, and people—

has been Nice's main market square since the Middle Ages (flower market all day Tue-Sun, produce market Tue-Sun until 13:00, antiques on Mon). While you're greeted by the ugly mouth of an underground parking lot, much of this square itself was a parking lot until 1980, when the mayor of Nice had this solution dug.

The first section is devoted to the Riviera's largest flower market. In operation since the 19th century, this market offers plants and flowers that grow effortlessly and ubiquitously in this climate, including the local favorites: carnations, roses, and jasmine. Locals know the season by what's on sale (mimosas in February, violets in March, and so on). Until the recent rise in imported flowers, this region supplied all of France with flowers. Still, fresh flowers are cheap here, the best value in this notoriously expensive city. The Riviera's three big industries are tourism, flowers, and perfume (made from these flowers...take a whiff).

The boisterous produce section trumpets the season with mushrooms, strawberries, white asparagus, zucchini flowers, and more—whatever's fresh gets top billing. What's in season today?

The market opens up at Place Pierre Gautier. It's also called Plassa dóu Gouvernou—you'll see bilingual street signs here that include the old Niçois language, an Italian dialect. This is where farmers set up stalls to sell their produce and herbs directly. For a **rooftop view** over the market, climb the steps by Le Grand Bleu restaurant (you may have to step over the trash sacks, but it's allowed).

Look up to the **hill** that dominates to the east. The city of Nice was first settled up there by Greeks (circa 400 B.C.). In the Middle Ages, a massive castle stood there with soldiers at the ready. Over time, the city grew down to where you are now. With the river guarding one side and the sea the other, this mountain fortress seemed strong—until Louis XIV leveled it in 1706. Nice's medieval seawall ran along the line of two-story buildings where you're standing.

Now, look across Place Pierre Gautier to the large "palace." The **Ducal Palace** was where the kings of Sardinia, the city's Italian rulers until 1860, resided when in Nice. (For centuries, Nice was under the rule of the Italian capital of Torino.) Today, the palace is the local police headquarters. The land upon which the Cours Saleya sits was once the duke's gardens and didn't become a market until Nice's union with France.

• *Continue down Cours Saleya. The fine golden building that seals the end of the square is where Henri Matisse spent 17 years. I imagine he was inspired by his view. The* **Café les Ponchettes** *is perfectly positioned for you to enjoy the view too if you want a coffee break. At the café, turn onto...*

Rue de la Poissonnerie

Look up at the first floor of the first building on your right. **Adam and Eve** are squaring off, each holding a zucchini-like gourd. This scene represents the annual rapprochement in Nice to make up for the sins of a too-much-fun Carnival (Mardi Gras, the pre-Lenten festival). Residents of Nice have partied hard during Carnival for more than 700 years. The **spice shop** below offers a fine selection of regional herbs.

As you continue down the street, look above the doors. The iron grills (like the one above #6) allow air to enter the buildings but keep out uninvited guests. You'll see lots of these open grills in Vieux Nice. They were part of a clever system that sucked in cool air from the sea, circulating it through homes and blowing it out through vents in the roof.

A few steps ahead, check out the small **Baroque church** (Notre-Dame de l'Annonciation) dedicated to Ste. Rita, the patron saint of desperate causes and desperate people. She holds a special place in locals' hearts, making this the most popular church in Nice. Drop in for a peek at the dazzling Baroque. Inside, the first chapel on the right is dedicated to St. Erasmus, protector of mariners.

• *Turn right on the next street, where you'll pass Vieux Nice's most happening bar (Distilleries Ideales), with a Pirates of the Caribbean-style interior. Pause at the next corner and simply study the classic Old Nice scene. Now turn left on Rue Droite and enter an area that feels like Little Naples.*

Rue Droite

In the Middle Ages, this straight, skinny street provided the most direct route from river to sea within the old walled town. Pass the recommended restaurant L'Acchiardo. Notice stepped lanes leading uphill to the castle. Stop at **Espuno bakery** (at Place du Jésus) and say *"Bonjour,* what's cooking?" to Natalie from England and her husband Fabrice, who's from here. Notice the firewood stacked behind the oven. Try the house specialty, *tourte aux blettes*—a tart stuffed with Swiss chard, apples, pine nuts, and raisins.

Pop into the Jesuit **Eglise St-Jacques** (also called Eglise du Gésu) for an explosion of Baroque exuberance hidden behind that plain facade. At the wooden pulpit, notice the crucifix held by a sculpted arm. This clever support allowed the priest to focus on his sermon while reminding the congregation that Christ died for their sins.

The balconies of the large mansion on the left mark the **Palais Lascaris** (c. 1647), home of one of Nice's most prestigious families. Today it is a museum with an impressive collection of antique musical instruments—harps, guitars, violins, and violas (good English explanations)—along with elaborate tapestries and a few well-furnished rooms. The palace has four levels: The ground floor was used for storage, the first floor was devoted to reception rooms (and musical events), the owners lived a floor above that, and the servants lived at the top. Look up and make faces back at the guys under the balconies.

• *Turn left on the Rue de la Loge, then left again on Rue Benoît Bunico.*

In the 18th century, Rue Benoît served as a **ghetto** for Nice's

Jews. At sunset, gates would seal the street at either end, locking people in until daylight. To identify Jews as non-Christians, the men were forced to wear yellow stars and the women wore yellow scarves. The white columns across from #19 mark what was the synagogue until 1848, when revolution ended the notion of ghettos in France.

• *Around the corner and downhill on Rue Benoît Bunico find...*

Place Rossetti

The most Italian of Nice's piazzas, Place Rossetti comes alive after dark—in part because of the **Fenocchio gelato shop,** popular for its many innovative flavors.

Check out the **Cathedral of St. Réparate**—an unassuming building for a big city cathedral. It was relocated here in the 1500s, when Castle Hill was temporarily converted to military use only. The name comes from Nice's patron saint, a teenage virgin named Réparate, whose martyred body floated to Nice in the fourth century accompanied by angels (remember the Bay of Angels?). The interior of the cathedral gushes Baroque, a response to the challenge of the Protestant Reformation in the 16th century. With the Catholic Church's Counter-Reformation, the theatrical energy of churches was cranked up with re-energized, high-powered saints and eye-popping decor.

• *This is the end of our walk. From here you can hike up* **Castle Hill** *(from Place Rossetti, take Rue Rossetti uphill; see Castle Hill listing on page 304). Or you can have an ice cream and browse the colorful lanes of Old Nice. Or you can grab Apollo and hit the beach.*

OLD NICE WALK

CHAGALL MUSEUM TOUR

Musée Chagall

Even if you don't get modern art, this museum—with the world's largest collection of Marc Chagall's work in captivity—is a delight. After World War II, Chagall returned from the United States to settle in Vence, not far from Nice. Between 1954 and 1967 he painted a cycle of 17 large murals designed for, and donated to, this museum. These paintings, inspired by the biblical books of Genesis, Exodus, and the Song of Songs, make up the "nave," or core, of what Chagall called the "House of Brotherhood." Combining his Russian and Jewish heritage with the Christian message, he hoped this would be a place where people of all faiths could come together and celebrate love.

Orientation

Cost: €8, €1-2 more during frequent special exhibits.

Hours: May-Oct Wed-Mon 10:00-18:00, Nov-April Wed-Mon 10:00-17:00, closed Tue year-round.

Getting There: The museum is located on Avenue Docteur Ménard. **Taxis** to and from the city center cost €12. **Buses** connect the museum with downtown Nice and the train station. From downtown, catch bus #15 (6/hour, 10 minutes) from the east end of the Galeries Lafayette department store, near the Masséna tram stop, on Rue Sacha Guitry (see map on page 290); on Sunday catch #22 from the same stop. From the train station, take bus #17. Exit the bus at the stop called Musée Chagall on Boulevard de Cimiez.

Information: Tel. 04 93 53 87 20, http://en.musees-nationaux-alpesmaritimes.fr.

Tours: Although Chagall would suggest that you explore his art without guidance, the included audioguide is very helpful, giving you detailed explanations of his works.

Informational Film on Chagall: A wonderful film (52 minutes) plays at the top of each hour in the auditorium (alternately in French and English—English version often at 10:00, 12:00, 14:00, and 16:00). See the schedule at the entry. Even the French version offers a fascinating look at old clips of the master and a chance to see the creative energy and charisma in his eyes.

Length of This Tour: About one hour.

Baggage Check: Daypacks must be checked.

Photography: Allowed without flash.

Cuisine Art: An idyllic café (€12 salads and *plats*) awaits in the corner of the garden.

The Tour Begins

This small museum consists of six rooms: two rooms (the main hall and Song of Songs room) with the 17 murals, two rooms for special exhibits, an auditorium with stained-glass windows, and a mosaic-lined pond (viewed from inside). In the main hall you'll find the core of the collection (Genesis and Exodus scenes). The adjacent octagonal Song of Songs room houses five more paintings.

• *Buy your ticket, pass through the garden, and enter the museum at the baggage-check counter. Pick up your included audioguide and step into the main hall.*

Main Hall: Old Testament Scenes

Each painting is a lighter-than-air collage of images that draws from Chagall's Russian folk-village youth, his Jewish heritage, biblical themes, and his feeling that he existed somewhere between heaven and earth. He believed that the Bible was a synonym for nature, and that both color and biblical themes were key for understanding God's love for his creation. Chagall's brilliant blues and reds celebrate nature, as do his spiritual and folk themes. Notice the focus on couples. To Chagall, humans loving each other mirrored God's love of creation.

The paintings are described below in the order you should see them, going counterclockwise around the room.

Abraham and the Three Angels

In the heat of the day, Abraham looked up and saw three men. He said, "Let a little food and water be brought, so you can be refreshed..." (Genesis 18:1-5)

Abraham refreshes God's angels on this red-hot day and, in return, they promise Abraham a son (in the bubble, at right), thus making him the father of the future Israelite nation.

The Sacrifice of Isaac

Abraham bound his son Isaac and laid him on the altar. Then he took the knife to slay his son. But the angel of the Lord called out to him from heaven, "Abraham!" (Genesis 22:9-11)

Tested by God, Abraham prepares to kill his only son, but the angel stops him in time. Notice that Isaac is posed exactly as Adam is in *The Creation* (described next). Abraham's sacrifice echoes three others: the sacrifice all men must make (Adam, the everyman), the sacrifice of atonement (the goat tied to a tree at left), and even God's sacrifice of his own son (Christ carrying the cross, upper right).

CHAGALL MUSEUM

Chagall's Style

Chagall uses a deceptively simple, almost childlike style to paint a world that's hidden to the eye—the magical, mystical world below the surface. Here are some of the characteristics of his paintings:

- **Deep, radiant colors,** inspired by Expressionism and Fauvism (an art movement pioneered by Matisse and other French painters).
- **Personal imagery,** particularly from his childhood in Russia—smiling barnyard animals, fiddlers on the roof, flower bouquets, huts, and blissful sweethearts.
- **A Hasidic Jewish perspective,** the idea that God is everywhere, appearing in everyday things like nature, animals, and humdrum activities.
- **A fragmented Cubist style,** multifaceted and multidimensional, a perfect style to mirror the complexity of God's creation.
- **Overlapping images,** like double-exposure photography, with faint imagery that bleeds through, suggesting there's more to life under the surface.
- **Stained-glass-esque technique** of dark, deep, earthy, "potent" colors, and simplified, iconic, symbolic figures.
- **Gravity-defying compositions,** with lovers, animals, and angels twirling blissfully in midair.
- **Happy (not tragic) mood** depicting a world of personal joy, despite the violence and turmoil of world wars and revolution.
- **Childlike simplicity,** drawn with simple, heavy outlines, filled in with Crayola colors that often spill over the lines. Major characters in a scene are bigger than the lesser characters. The grinning barnyard animals, the bright colors, the magical events presented as literal truth...Was Chagall a lightweight? Or a lighter-than-air-weight?

The Creation

God said, "Let us make man in our image, in our likeness..." (Genesis 1:26)

A pure-white angel descends through the blue sky and carries a still-sleeping Adam from radiant red-yellow heaven to earth. Heaven is a whirling dervish of activity, spinning out all the events of future history, from the tablets of the Ten Commandments to the Crucifixion—an overture of many images that we'll see in later paintings. (Though not a Christian, Chagall saw the Crucifixion as a universal symbol of man's suffering.)

Moses Receives the Ten Commandments

The Lord gave him the two tablets of the Law, the tablets of stone inscribed by the finger of God... (Exodus 31:18)

An astonished Moses stretches toward heaven, where God reaches out from a cloud to hand him the Ten Commandments.

While Moses tilts one way, Mount Sinai slants the other, leading our eye up to the left, where a golden calf is being worshipped by the wayward Children of Israel. But down to the right, Aaron and the menorah assure us that Moses will set things right. In this radiant final panel, the Jewish tradition—after a long struggle—is finally established.

• *Skip around the corner to...*

Driven from Paradise

So God banished him from the Garden of Eden...and placed cherubim and a flaming sword to guard the way... (Genesis 3:23-24)

An angel drives them out with a fire hose of blue (there's Adam still cradling his flaming-red *coq*), while a sparkling yellow, flower-filled tree stands like a wall preventing them from ever returning. Deep in the green colors, the painting offers us glimpses of the future—Eve giving birth (lower-right corner) and the yellow sacrificial goat of atonement (top right).

Paradise

God put him in the Garden of Eden...and said, "You must not eat from the tree of the knowledge of good and evil..." (Genesis 2:15-17)

Paradise is a rich, earth-as-seen-from-space pool of blue, green, and white. On the left, amoebic, still-evolving animals float around Adam (celibately practicing yoga) and Eve (with lusty-red hair). On the right, an angel guards the tempting tree, but Eve offers an apple and Adam reaches around to sample the forbidden fruit while the snake gawks knowingly.

The Rainbow

God said, "I have set my rainbow in the clouds as a sign of the covenant between me and the earth." (Genesis 9:13)

A flaming angel sets the rainbow in the sky, while Noah rests beneath it and his family offers a sacrifice of thanks. The pure-white rainbow's missing colors are found radiating from the features of the survivors.

Marc Chagall (1887-1985)

1887-1910: Russia
Chagall is born in the small town of Vitebsk, Belarus. He's the oldest of nine children in a traditional Russian Hasidic Jewish family.

He studies realistic art in his hometown. In St. Petersburg, he is first exposed to the Modernist work of Paul Cézanne and the Fauves.

1910-1914: Paris
A patron finances a four-year stay in Paris. Chagall hobnobs with the avant-garde and learns technique from the Cubists, but he never abandons painting recognizable figures or his own personal fantasies. (Some say his relative poverty forced him to paint over used canvases, which gave him the idea of overlapping images that bleed through. Hmm.)

1914-1922: Russia
Returning to his hometown, Chagall marries Bella Rosenfeld (1915), whose love will inspire him for decades. He paints happy scenes despite the turmoil of wars and the Communist Revolution. Moving to Moscow (1920), he paints his first large-scale works, sets for the New Jewish Theater. These would inspire many of his later large-scale works.

CHAGALL MUSEUM

Jacob's Ladder
He had a dream in which he saw a ladder resting on the earth with its top reaching to heaven, and the angels of God were ascending and descending on it... (Genesis 28:12)

In the left half, Jacob (Abraham's grandson, in red) slumps asleep and dreams of a ladder between heaven and earth. On the right, a lofty angel with a menorah represents how heaven and earth are bridged by the rituals of the Jewish tradition.

Jacob Wrestles with an Angel
So Jacob wrestled with him till daybreak. Jacob said, "I will not let you go unless you bless me..." (Genesis 32: 24, 26)

Jacob holds on while the angel blesses him with descendants (the Children of Israel) and sends out rays from his hands. On the right are scenes from Jacob's life, including his son Joseph being stripped of his bright-red coat and sold into slavery by his brothers.

Noah's Ark
Then he sent out a dove to see if the water had receded... (Genesis 8:8)

Adam and Eve's descendants have become so wicked that God destroys the earth with a flood, engulfing the sad crowd on the

1923-1941: France and Palestine

Chagall returns to France. In 1931 he travels to Palestine, where the bright sun and his Jewish roots inspire a series of gouaches (opaque watercolor paintings). These gouaches would later inspire 105 etchings to illustrate the Bible (1931-1952), which would eventually influence the 17 large canvases of biblical scenes in the Chagall Museum (1954-1967).

1941-1947: United States/World War II

Fearing persecution for his Jewish faith, Chagall emigrates to New York, where he spends the war years. The Crucifixion starts to appear in his paintings—not as a Christian symbol, but as a representation of the violence mankind perpetrates on itself. In 1947 his beloved Bella dies, and he stops painting for months.

1947-1985: South of France

After the war, Chagall returns to France, eventually settling in St-Paul-de-Vence. In 1952 he remarries. His new love, Valentina Brodsky, plus the southern sunshine, brings Chagall a revived creativity—he is extremely prolific for the rest of his life. He experiments with new techniques and media—ceramics, sculpture, book illustrations, tapestry, and mosaic. In 1956 he's commissioned for his first stained-glass project. Eventually he does windows for cathedrals in Metz and Reims, and a synagogue in Jerusalem (1960). The Chagall Museum opens in 1973.

right. Only righteous Noah (center), his family (lower right), and the animals (including our yellow goat) are spared inside an ark. Here Noah opens the ark's window and sends out a dove to test the waters.

Moses Brings Water from the Rock

The Lord said, "Strike the rock, and water will come out of it for the people to drink..." (Exodus 17:5-6)

In the brown desert, Moses nourishes his thirsty people with water miraculously spouting from a rock. From the (red-yellow) divine source, it rains down actual (blue) water, but also a gush of spiritual yellow light.

Moses and the Burning Bush

The angel of the Lord appeared to him in flames of fire from within a bush... (Exodus 3:2)

Horned Moses—Chagall depicts him according to a medieval tradition—kneels awestruck before the burning bush, the event that calls him to God's service. On the left, we see Moses after the call, his face radiant, leading the Israelites out of captivity across the Red Sea, while Pharaoh's men drown (lower half of Moses' robe). The Ten Commandments loom ahead.

• *Return to* Moses Receives the Ten Commandments, *then walk past a window into a room with five red paintings.*

SONG OF SONGS

Chagall wrote, "I've been fascinated by the Bible ever since my earliest childhood. I have always thought of it as the most extraordinary source of poetic inspiration imaginable. As far as I am concerned, perfection in art and in life has its source in the Bible, and exercises in the mechanics of the merely rational are fruitless. In art as well as in life, anything is possible, provided there is love."

The paintings in this room were inspired by the Old Testament Song of Songs. Chagall cherished verses such as: *I sleep, but my heart is awake* (5:2). *Until the* *day breaks and the shadows flee, turn, my lover, and be like a gazelle or like a young stag on the rugged hills* (2:17). *Your stature is like that of the palm, and your breasts like clusters of fruit* (7:7). Chagall, who dedicated this room to his wife Valentina (Vava), saw divine love and physical love as a natural mix.

Chagall enjoyed the love of two women in his long life—his first wife, Bella, then Valentina, who gave him a second wind as he was painting these late works. Chagall was one of the few "serious" 20th-century artists to portray unabashed love. Where the Bible uses the metaphor of earthly, physical, sexual love to describe God's love for humans, Chagall uses unearthly colors and a mystical ambience to celebrate human love. These red-toned canvases are hard to interpret on a literal level, but they capture the rosy spirit of a man in love with life.

• *Head back toward the entry and turn left at* The Sacrifice of Isaac *to find...*

THE POND

The great mosaic (which no longer reflects in the filthy reflecting pond) evokes the prophet Elijah in his chariot of fire (from the Second Book of Kings)—with Chagall's addition of the 12 signs of the zodiac, which he used to symbolize Time.

• *Return to the main hall, veer left, and exit the hall to the right. Pass through the exhibition room with temporary displays. At the end, you'll find...*

THE AUDITORIUM

This room, where the Chagall documentary film shows (see page 337), is worth a peaceful moment to enjoy three Chagall stained-glass windows depicting the seven days of creation (right to left): the creation of light, elements, and planets (a visual big bang that's four "days" wide); the creation of animals, plants, man and woman, and the ordering of the solar system (two "days" wide, complete with fish and birds still figuring out where they belong); and the day of rest (the narrowest—only one "day" wide, imagine angels singing to the glory of God).

• *Our tour is over. From here, you can return to downtown Nice or the train station area, or go to the Matisse Museum. **Taxis** usually wait in front of the museum. For the **bus** back to downtown Nice, turn right out of the museum, then make another right down Boulevard de Cimiez, and ride bus #15 or #22 heading downhill. To continue on to the Matisse Museum, catch #15 or #22 using the uphill stop located across the street.*

*To **walk** to the train station area from the museum (20 minutes), turn left out of the museum grounds on Avenue Docteur Ménard, and follow the street to the left at the first intersection, continuing to hug the museum grounds. Where the street curves right (by #32), take the ramps and staircases down on your left, turn left at the bottom, cross under the freeway and the train tracks, then turn right on Boulevard Raimbaldi.*

EAST OF NICE

Villefranche-sur-Mer • The Three Corniches • Cap Ferrat • Eze-le-Village

Between Nice and Monaco lies the Riviera's richest stretch of real estate, paved with famously scenic roads (called the Three Corniches) and dotted with cliff-hanging villages, million-dollar vistas, and sea-splashed walking trails connecting beach towns. Fifteen minutes east of Nice, little Villefranche-sur-Mer stares across the bay to woodsy and exclusive Cap Ferrat. The eagle's-nest Eze-le-Village and the Corniche-topping Le Trophée des Alpes survey the scene from high above.

Villefranche-sur-Mer

In the glitzy world of the Riviera, Villefranche-sur-Mer offers travelers an easygoing slice of small-town Mediterranean life. From here, convenient day trips allow you to gamble in Monaco, saunter the Promenade des Anglais in Nice, or enjoy views from Eze-le-Village and the Grande Corniche.

Villefranche-sur-Mer feels more Italian than French, with pastel-orange buildings; steep, narrow lanes spilling into the sea; and pasta on menus. Luxury yachts glisten in the bay. Cruise ships make regular calls to Villefranche-sur-Mer's deep harbor, creating periodic rush hours of frenetic shoppers and bucket-listers. Sand-pebble beaches, a handful of interesting sights, and quick access to Cap Ferrat keep other visitors just busy enough.

Originally a Roman port, Villefranche-sur-Mer was over-

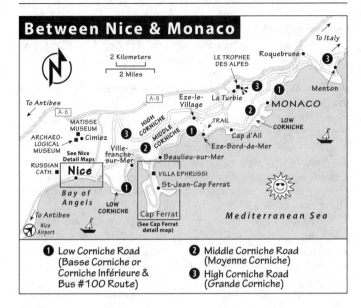

Between Nice & Monaco

● Low Corniche Road
(Basse Corniche or
Corniche Inférieure &
Bus #100 Route)

● Middle Corniche Road
(Moyenne Corniche)

● High Corniche Road
(Grande Corniche)

taken by fifth-century barbarians. Villagers fled into the hills, where they stayed and farmed their olives. In 1295 the Duke of Provence—like many in coastal Europe—needed to stand up to the Saracen Turks. He asked the olive farmers to move from the hills down to the water and establish a front line against the invaders, thus denying the enemy a base from which to attack Nice. In return for tax-free status, they stopped farming, took up fishing, and established a *Ville-* (town) *franche* (without taxes). Since there were many such towns, this one was specifically "Tax-free town on the sea" *(sur Mer)*. In about 1560, the Duke of Savoy built an immense, sprawling citadel in the town. And today, while the town has an international following, two-thirds of its 8,000 people call it their primary residence. That makes Villefranche-sur-Mer feel more like a real community than neighboring Riviera towns.

Orientation to Villefranche-sur-Mer

TOURIST INFORMATION

There are two TIs. The main one is off the road that runs between Nice and Monaco, located in a park (Jardin François Binon) below the Nice/Monaco bus stop, labeled *Octroi* (mid-June-mid-Sept daily 9:00-18:00; mid-Sept-mid-June Mon-Sat 9:00-12:00 & 14:00-17:00, closed Sun; tel. 04 93 01 73 68, www.villefranche-sur-mer.com). A smaller TI is at the port, where cruise-ship passengers disembark (mid-May-mid-Sept Fri-Wed 10:00-17:00, closed Thu and off-season). Pick up regional bus schedules and information on

EAST OF NICE

seasonal sightseeing boat rides. The TI has an excellent brochure-map showing seaside walks around neighboring Cap Ferrat and information on the Villa Ephrussi de Rothschild's gardens.

ARRIVAL IN VILLEFRANCHE-SUR-MER

By Bus: Get off at the Octroi stop. To reach the old town, walk downhill past the TI along Avenue Général de Gaulle, take the first stairway on the left, then make a right at the street's end.

By Train: Not all trains stop in Villefranche-sur-Mer (you may need to transfer to a local train in Nice or Monaco). Ville-franche-sur-Mer's train station is just above the beach, a short stroll from the old town and most of my recommended hotels. Taxis from the station to my recommended hotels cost about €10.

By Car: From Nice's port, follow signs for *Menton, Monaco,* and *Basse Corniche.* In Villefranche-sur-Mer, turn right at the TI (first signal after Hôtel la Flore) for parking and hotels. For a quick visit to the TI, park at the pay lot just below the TI (€1/hour) or at Parking Wilson (pay lot on the water, €2/hour). Some hotels have their own parking. All public parking is paid except during 12:00-14:00 and 19:00-9:00.

By Plane: Allow an hour from Nice's airport to Villefranche-sur-Mer (for details on this connection, see page 320).

By Cruise Ship: For information on arrival by cruise ship, see page 358.

HELPFUL HINTS

Market Day: A fun bric-a-brac market enlivens Villefranche-sur-Mer on Sundays (on Place Amélie Pollonnais by Hôtel Welcome, and in Jardin François Binon by the TI). On Saturday and Wednesday mornings, a small food market sets up in Jardin François Binon. A small trinket market springs to action on Place Amélie Pollonnais whenever cruise ships grace the harbor.

Wi-Fi: The city provides free Wi-Fi at the port. On Place du Marché, both **Chez Net** and **L'X Café** have Wi-Fi and let you enjoy a late-night drink while surfing the Internet.

Laundry: There's a self-serve launderette just below the main road on Avenue Sadi Carnot (daily 7:00-20:00, opposite 6 Avenue Sadi Carnot).

Electric Bike Rental: The adventurous can try **Eco-Loc** electric bikes as an alternative to taking the bus to Cap Ferrat, Eze-le-Village, or even Nice. You get about 25 miles on a fully charged battery (after that you're pedaling; €20/half-day, €30/day, early April-Sept daily 9:00-17:00, deposit and ID required, try to make reservations 24 hours in advance; helmets, locks, baskets, and child seats available; pick up bike

across from small TI at the port, mobile 06 66 92 72 41, www.
ecoloc06.fr).

Tourist Train: Skip the useless white *petit train*, which goes nowhere interesting.

Spectator Sports: Lively *boules* action takes place each evening just
below the TI and the huge soccer field (see page 39).

GETTING AROUND VILLEFRANCHE-SUR-MER

By Bus: Little **minibus #80** saves you the sweat of walking uphill,
but it runs only about once per hour from the old port to the top
of the hill, stopping at Place Amélie Pollonnais, Hôtel la Fiancée
du Pirate, and the Col de Villefranche stop (for buses to Eze-le-
Village), before going to the outlying suburban Nice Riquier train
station (€1.50, runs daily 7:00-19:00, see map on page 350 for stop
locations, schedule posted at stops and available at TI). Many buses
serve Villefranche from other Riviera towns (see page 350).

By Taxi: General taxi tel. 04 93 55 55 55. Beware of taxi drivers who overcharge. The five-minute trip from the waterfront up to
the main street level (to bus stops on the Low Corniche or to the
train station) should be about €10. The normal weekday, daytime
rates to outside destinations should be about: €25 (to Cap Ferrat),
€40 (to central Nice or Eze-le-Village), €60 (to airport or Monaco).
For a reliable taxi in Villefranche-sur-Mer, call or email **Didier**
(mobile 06 15 15 39 15, taxididier.villefranchesurmer@orange.fr).

Villefranche-sur-Mer Town Walk

For tourists, Villefranche is a tiny, easy-to-cover town that snug-
gles around its harbor under its citadel. This quick self-guided walk
laces together everything of importance, starting at the waterfront
near where cruise-ship tenders land and finishing at the citadel.

• *If arriving by bus or train, you'll walk five minutes to the starting
point. Go to the end of the little pier directly in front of Hôtel Welcome,
where we'll start with a spin tour (spin to the right) to get oriented.*

The Harbor: Look out to sea. Cap Ferrat, across the bay, is
a landscaped paradise where the 1 percent of the 1 percent com-

pete for the best view. The Rothschild's pink mansion, Villa Ephrussi
(slightly left of center, hugging the
top) is the most worthwhile sight to
visit in the area. To its right, in the
saddle of the hill, the next home,
with the big red-tiled roof, belongs to
Paul Allen. Geologically, Cap Ferrat
is the southern tip of the Alps. The

Villefranche-sur-Mer

To 3

BLVD. DE LA CORNE D'OR

To Eze-Le-Village
& Monaco

BLVD. LAZARE SETTIMELLI

AVE. DE LA BARMASSA

100 Meters
100 Yards

AVE. DE LA BARMASSA

RUE VICTOIRE

AVE. DE GENERAL LECLERC

AVE. ALBERT 1ER

ST. MICHAEL'S

R. DU
AVE.

POST

AVE. SADI CARNOT

12

M. JOFFRE

VERDUN

16
B

T

AVE. DE SAINTE-ESTEVE

B 15

i

P

AVE. FOCH

Jardin
Binon

PLAY
AREA

ALLEE DU DUVAL

RUE DE LA CITADELLE

BLVD. PRINCESSE GRACE DE MONACO

AVE. DE LA MALMAISON

AVENUE DE GAULLE

Jardins
de Narvik

AVENUE DE GAULLE

EAST OF NICE

2

4

PLAY
AREA

QUAI DE LA CORDERIE

Port de la
Darse

To Mont-Alban
Fort & Nice

TRAIN STATION

BLVD. NAPOLEON III

To Eze-Bord-de-Mer & Monaco via Low Corniche Road

To ⑩

PROMENADE DES MARINIERES

Beach

To Cap Ferrat on foot

AVE. FERNAND MARTIN

AVE. ALBERT 1ER

GALLIENI

AVE. GEORGES CLEMENCEAU

CHEMIN DE LA FOUAN

QUAI COURBET

RUE VOLTI

RUE BARON DE BRES

Place du Conseil

RUE DU POILU

RUE OBSCURE

R. DE L'EGLISE

OLD

TOWN

VALLON

SADI CARNOT

M. JOFFRE

AVE. SADI CARNOT

Place Amélie Pollonnais

CHAPEL OF ST. PIERRE

GARE MARITIME (CRUISE TENDER DOCK)

ⓑ #80

ATM

ⓟ

CITADEL

SCENIC WALKWAY

M e d i t e r r a n e a n

S e a

① Hôtel Welcome
② Hôtel La Flore
③ To Hôtel la Fiancée du Pirate
④ Hôtel de la Darse & La Trinquette Restaurant
⑤ Les Palmiers & Cosmo Brasserie
⑥ La Grignotière Restaurant
⑦ L'Aparté & Casino Grocery
⑧ La Serre Restaurant
⑨ La Mère Germaine Restaurant
⑩ To Restaurant de la Plage de Passable & Hôtel Patricia
⑪ Internet Access
⑫ Launderette
⑬ Boat Rides & Electric Bike Rental
⑭ Dark Pelican Motor Boat Rental
⑮ Octroi Bus Stop (from Nice; to Monaco & Cap Ferrat)
⑯ Octroi Bus Stop (to Nice; from Monaco & Cap Ferrat)

EAST OF NICE

range emerges from the sea here and arcs all across Europe, over 700 miles, to Vienna.

Today, ships bring not pirates but tourists. The bay here is generally filled with beautiful yachts. (In the evenings, you might see well-coiffed captains being ferried in by dutiful mates to pick up statuesque call girls.) Local guides keep a list of the world's 100 biggest yachts and talk about some of them as if they're part of the neighborhood.

At 2,000 feet, this is the deepest natural harbor on the Riviera and was the region's most important port until Nice built its own in the 18th century. Greek, Roman, and American ships appreciated the setting, as do cruise ships today. The biggest cruise ships drop their hooks here rather than in Nice or Monaco. The tiny jetty is the landing point for the cruise-ship tenders that come ashore each morning in season.

Up on the hill, the 16th-century citadel (where this walk ends) is marked by flags. The yellow fisherman's chapel (with the little-toe bell tower) has an interior painted by Jean Cocteau. Hôtel Welcome offers the balconies of dreams. Up the lane is the baroque facade of St. Michael's Church. The promenade, lined by fancy fish restaurants, leads to the town beach. Fifty yards above the beach stands the train station and above that, supported by arches, is the Low Corniche road, which leads to Monaco. Until that road was built in the 1860s, those hills were free of any development all the way to Monaco. The big yellow building beyond is rentable for €300,000 a month (as Madonna did for a recent birthday).

• *Walk left 30 yards past the last couple of fishing boats surviving from the town's once important fishing community to a small bronze bust of Jean Cocteau, the artist who said, "When I look at Villefranche, I see my youth." Step up to the little chapel he painted.*

Chapel of St. Pierre (Chapelle Cocteau): This chapel is the town's cultural highlight. Cocteau, who decorated the place, was a Parisian transplant who adored little Villefranche-sur-Mer and whose career was distinguished by his work as an artist, poet, novelist, playwright, and filmmaker. Influenced by his pals Marcel Proust, André Gide, Edith Piaf, and Pablo Picasso, Cocteau was a leader among 20th-century avant-garde intellectuals. At the door, Marie-France—who is passionate about Cocteau's art—collects a €3 donation for a fishermen's charity. She then sets you free to enjoy the chapel's small but intriguing interior. She's happy to give explanations if you ask (open Wed-Mon 10:00-12:00 & 15:00-19:00, usually closed Tue, hours vary with cruise-ship traffic and season).

In 1955 Cocteau tattooed the barrel-vaulted chapel with heavy black lines and pastels. Each of Cocteau's Surrealist works—the Roma (Gypsies) of Stes-Maries-de-la-Mer who dance and sing to honor the Virgin, girls wearing traditional outfits, and three scenes

EAST OF NICE

from the life of St. Peter—is explained in English. Is that Ville-franche-sur-Mer's citadel in the scene above the altar?

• *From the chapel, stroll the harbor promenade 100 yards past romantic harborside tables.* **Restaurant La Mère Germaine** *is named for Mother Germaine, who famously took care of US Navy troops in World War II (step inside to see sketches and old photos on the wall). Just past the restaurant, a lane (signed* Vieille Ville*) leads up into the old town. Walk a few steps until you reach a long tunnel-like street.*

Rue Obscure, the Old Town, and St. Michael's Church: Here, under these 13th-century vaults, you're in another age. Before the long stepped lane (which we'll climb later), turn right and walk to the end of Rue Obscure (which means "dark street"). At the end, wind up to the sunlight past a tiny fountain at Place du Conseil, and a few steps beyond that to a viewpoint overlooking the beach. Then stroll back past the fountain and gently downhill. At Place des Deux Canons, turn right and climb the stepped lanes, and then take your first left at a restaurant to St. Michael's Church, facing a delightful square (Place de l'Eglise) with a single magnolia tree. The church features an 18th-century organ, a particularly engaging crucifix at the high altar, and (to the left) a fine statue of a recumbent Christ—carved, they say, from a fig tree by a galley slave in the 1600s.

• *Leaving St. Michael's, go downhill halfway to the water, where you hit the main commercial street. Go right on Rue du Poilu to Place de la République. (Browse real-estate windows if you'd like to move here.) Head through the square and angle left, up the hill to the...*

Citadel: The town's mammoth castle was built in the 1500s by the Duke of Savoy to defend against the French. When the region joined France in 1860, the castle became just a barracks. Since the 20th century, it's housed the police station, City Hall, a summer outdoor theater, and art galleries. The single fortified entry—originally a drawbridge over a dry moat (a.k.a. kill zone)—still leads into this huge complex.

The exterior walls slope thickly at the base, indicating that they were built in the "Age of Black Powder"—the 16th century—when the advent of gunpowder made thicker, cannonball-deflecting walls a necessity for any effective fortification. The bastions are designed for smarter crossfire during an attack. The inside feels vast and empty. If you wander around, you'll find a memorial garden for victims of World War II, five free and empty museums and galleries, a garden in the bastion, and the City Hall (which offers a free WC, as all City Halls in France are required to by law).

• *And that concludes our introductory walk.*

EAST OF NICE

Activities in Villefranche-sur-Mer

Boat Rides (Promenades en Mer)

To view this beautiful coastline from the sea, consider taking a quick sightseeing cruise (€12 for a one-hour trip around Cap Ferrat, €20 for a two-hour cruise as far as Monaco, departures at 15:00 from the harbor across from Hôtel Welcome, June-Sept Wed and Sat, also Thu in July-Aug, no trips Oct-May, reservations a must, tel. 04 93 76 65 65, www.amv-sirenes.com). Or, to be your own skipper, rent a **motor boat** through Dark Pelican (€100/half-day, €170/day, deposit required, on the harbor at the Gare Maritime, tel. 04 93 01 76 54, www.darkpelican.com).

Seafront Walks

A seaside walkway originally used by customs agents to patrol the harbor leads under the citadel and connects the old town with the workaday harbor (Port de la Darse). At the port you'll find a few cafés, France's Institute of Oceanography (an outpost for the University of Paris oceanographic studies), and an 18th-century dry dock. This scenic walk turns downright romantic after dark. You can also wander the other direction along Villefranche-sur-Mer's waterfront and continue beyond the train station for postcard-perfect views back to Villefranche-sur-Mer (ideal in the morning—go before breakfast). You can even extend your walk to Cap Ferrat (see "Getting to Cap Ferrat" on page 361).

Hike to Mont-Alban Fort

This fort, with a remarkable setting on the high ridge that separates Nice and Villefranche-sur-Mer, is a good destination for hikers (also accessible by car; info at TI). From the TI, walk on the main road toward Nice about 200 yards past Hôtel Versailles. Look for wooden trail signs labeled *Escalier de Verre* and climb about 45 minutes as the trail makes long switchbacks through the woods up to the ridge. Find your way to Mont-Alban Fort (interior closed to tourists) and its view terrace. (To visit without having to hike or for an easier return, bus #30 from Nice and bus #80 from Villefranche-sur-Mer's port stop a few blocks from the fort.)

Sleeping in Villefranche-sur-Mer

You have a handful of good hotels to choose from in Villefranche-sur-Mer. The ones I list have sea views from at least half of their rooms—well worth paying extra for.

$$$ Hôtel Welcome** has the best location in Villefranche-sur-Mer, and charges for it. Anchored seaside in the old town, with all of its 35 comfortable, balconied rooms overlooking the harbor and a lounge/wine bar that opens to the water, this place always

Sleep Code

Abbreviations   **(€1=about $1.10, country code: 33)**
S=Single, **D**=Double/Twin, **T**=Triple, **Q**=Quad, **b**=bathroom,
*=French hotel rating (0-5 stars)
Price Rankings
  $$$ **Higher Priced**—Most rooms €160 or more
    $$ **Moderately Priced**—Most rooms €100-160
      $ **Lower Priced**—Most rooms €100 or less
Unless otherwise noted, credit cards are accepted, elevators
and air-conditioning are available, free Wi-Fi and/or a guest
computer is generally provided, and English is spoken. Prices
change; verify current rates online or by email. For the best
prices, always book directly with the hotel.

lowers my pulse (standard Db-€250-300, bigger Db-€365-420,
suites-€550 and up, breakfast-€18, parking garage-€45/day—
must reserve, 3 Quai Amiral Courbet, tel. 04 93 76 27 62, www.
welcomehotel.com, resa@welcomehotel.com).

$$ Hôtel La Flore*** is a fine value if your idea of sightsee-
ing is to enjoy the view from your spacious bedroom deck. It's a
15-minute uphill hike from the old town, but the parking is free,
and the bus stops for Nice and Monaco are close by (Db with no
view-€120, Db with view and deck-€170, larger Db with even bet-
ter view and bigger deck-€230, Qb loft with huge terrace-€240,
breakfast-€14, on main road at 5 Boulevard Princesse Grace de
Monaco; tel. 04 93 76 30 30, www.hotel-la-flore.fr, infos@hotel-
la-flore.fr).

$$ Hôtel la Fiancée du Pirate*** is a family-friendly refuge
high above Villefranche-sur-Mer on the Middle Corniche with
no street appeal (best for drivers, although it is on bus lines #80,
#82, and #112 to Eze-le-Village and Nice). Inside, Eric and Lau-
rence offer 15 bright, tasteful, and comfortable rooms, a large pool,
a nice garden, and a view lounge area. The big breakfast features
homemade crêpes (Db-€140-165, Tb-€160-200, Qb-€210-260,
breakfast-€12, laundry service, free parking, 8 Boulevard de la
Corne d'Or, Moyenne Corniche/N-7, tel. 04 93 76 67 40, www.
fianceedupirate.com, info@fianceedupirate.com).

$ Hôtel de la Darse** is a shy little hotel burrowed in the
shadow of its highbrow neighbors and the only budget option in
Villefranche. It's less central—figure 10 scenic minutes of level
walking to the harbor and a steep 15-minute walk up to the main
road (hourly minibus #80 stops in front). Seaview rooms are easily
worth the extra euros (seaview Db-€90-103, no view Db-€70-88,
breakfast-€10, tel. 04 93 01 72 54, www.hoteldeladarse.com, info@
hoteldeladarse.com). From the TI, walk or drive down Avenue

Général de Gaulle (walkers should turn left on Allée du Colonel Duval into the Jardins de Narvik and follow steps to the bottom; for drivers, parking is usually available nearby).

Eating in Villefranche-sur-Mer

Comparison-shopping is half the fun of dining in Villefranche-sur-Mer. Make an event out of a predinner stroll through the old city. Check what looks good on the lively Place Amélie Pollonnais (next to Hôtel Welcome), where the whole village seems to converge at night; saunter past the string of pricey candlelit places lining the waterfront; and consider the smaller, less expensive eateries embedded in the old town. For dessert, consider popping into a *gelateria*, and then enjoy a floodlit, postdinner stroll along the sea.

La Grignotière, hiding in the back lanes, serves generous and tasty €21 *plats*. Gregarious Michel speaks English and runs the place with Brigitte. Their mixed-seafood grill is a smart order, as are the spaghetti and *gambas* (shrimp) and Michel's personal-recipe bouillabaisse (€23). Dining is inside, making this a good choice for cooler days (daily except closed Wed Nov-April, 3 Rue du Poilu, tel. 04 93 76 79 83).

L'Aparté is where locals go for fresh cuisine and a special experience. Book ahead, then order from the chalkboard. The focus is seafood, servings are generous, and the presentation is tops (€12 starters, €25 *plats*, €8 desserts, closed Mon, a few steps up from the port at 1 Rue Obscure, tel. 04 93 01 84 88,).

La Serre, nestled in the old town below St. Michael's Church, is a simple place with a hardworking owner. Sylvie serves well-priced dinners to a loyal local clientele. Choose from the many pizzas (named after US states and €10 or less), salads, and meats; or try the €17 three-course *menu* (open evenings only, cheap house wine, 16 Rue de May, tel. 04 93 76 79 91).

La Mère Germaine, right on the harbor, is the only place in town classy enough to lure a yachter ashore. It's dressy, with formal service and high prices. The name commemorates the current owner's grandmother, who fed hungry GIs during World War II. Try the bouillabaisse, served with panache (€77/person with 2-person minimum, €52 mini version for one, €45 *menu*, open daily, reserve harborfront table, 9 Quai de l'Amiral Courbet, tel. 04 93 01 71 39, www.meregermaine.com).

La Trinquette is a relaxed, low-key place away from the fray on the "other port," next to the recommended Hôtel de la Darse (a lovely 10-minute walk from the other recommended restaurants). The cuisine is good, and weekends bring a cool live-music scene (€8 starters, €12-20 *plats,* daily in summer, closed Wed off-season, 30 Avenue Général de Gaulle, tel. 04 93 16 92 48).

On Place Amélie Pollonnais: **Les Palimiers** and **Le Cosmo** each serves average brasserie fare on the town's appealing main square (daily).

Grocery Store: A handy **Casino** is a few blocks above Hôtel Welcome at 12 Rue du Poilu (Thu-Tue 7:30-12:30 & 15:30-19:00 except closed Sun afternoon and all day Wed).

Dinner Options for Drivers: If you have a car and are staying a few nights, take the short drive up to Eze-le-Village or, better still, La Turbie. If it's summer (June-Sept), the best option of all is to go across to one of Cap Ferrat's beach restaurants for a before-dinner drink or a dinner you won't soon forget.

Villefranche-sur-Mer Connections

For a comparison of connections by train and bus, see the "Public Transportation in the French Riviera" sidebar on page 282.

BY TRAIN
Trains are faster and run later than buses (until 24:00). It's a level, 10-minute walk from the port to the train station.

From Villefranche-sur-Mer by Train to: Monaco (2/hour, 10 minutes), **Nice** (2/hour, 10 minutes), **Antibes** (2/hour, 40 minutes), and **Eze-Bord-de-Mer** (2/hour, 5 minutes)—transfer to bus #83 for Eze-le-Village (see page 368).

BY BUS
All buses in this area cost €1.50 per ride (buy ticket from driver). Tickets are good for 74 minutes in one direction and for transfers. In Villefranche-sur-Mer, the most convenient stop is Octroi, just above the TI.

These are the key routes: **Bus #81** follows a circular route from Nice through Villefranche-sur-Mer, Beaulieu-sur-Mer, then to all Cap Ferrat stops, ending at the port in the village of St-Jean (2-3/hour, daily 6:35-20:15 from Nice, last return trip from St-Jean at 20:50). **Bus #100** runs along the coastal road between Nice, Monaco, and Menton (3-4/hour). The last bus leaves Nice for Villefranche-sur-Mer at about 19:45; the last bus from Villefranche-sur-Mer to Nice departs at about 20:30.

From Villefranche-sur-Mer by Bus to: St-Jean-Cap-Ferrat (#81, 20 minutes; for other transportation options, see "Getting to Cap Ferrat," later), **Beaulieu-sur-Mer** (#81 or #100, 10 minutes),

Public Transportation Between Nice & Monaco

FRANCE

ITALY

To Ventimiglia

····· Rail
----- Bus

Not to Scale

La Turbie

Menton

#166 & 116

Eze-le-Village

#11

#100

HIGH CORNICHE

#112

Monaco

MIDDLE CORNICHE

#65

#100

Cap d'Ail

#166 & 116

#82 & #112

#100

Eze-Bord-de-Mer

LOW CORNICHE

#81 & #100

RIVIERA

#80

Beaulieu-sur-Mer

Nice

#81 & #100

#81

Cap Ferrat

Villefranche-sur-Mer

Mediterranean Sea

Antibes

Monaco (#100, 25 minutes), Nice (#81 or #100, 20 minutes), and Eze-le-Village (#100 to Eze-Bord-de-Mer and transfer to #83; also #82 or #112 from Col de Villefranche stop).

BY CRUISE SHIP

Tenders deposit passengers at a slick terminal building (Gare Maritime) at the Port de la Santé, right in front of Villefranche-sur-Mer's old town.

Getting into Town: It's easy to **walk** to various points in Villefranche-sur-Mer. The town's charming, restaurant-lined square is a straight walk ahead from the terminal, the main road (with the main TI and bus stop) is a steep hike above, and the train station is a short stroll along the beach. **Minibus #80,** which departs from in front of the cruise terminal, saves you some hiking up to the main road and bus stop (see page 349).

Getting to Nearby Towns: To connect to other towns, choose between the **bus** or **train.** Leaving the terminal, you'll see directional sights pointing left, to *Town center/bus* (a 10- to 15-minute, steeply uphill walk to the Octroi bus stop with connections west to Nice or east to Monaco); and right, to *Gare SNCF/train station* (a 10-minute, level stroll with some stairs at the end). See train and bus connections above.

Taxis wait in front of the cruise terminal and charge exorbitant rates (minimum €15 charge to train station, though many will refuse such a short ride). For farther-flung trips, see the price estimates on page 349. For an all-day trip, you can try negotiating a flat fee (e.g., €300 for a 4-hour tour).

The Three Corniches

Nice, Villefranche-sur-Mer, and Monaco are linked by three coastal routes: the Low, Middle, and High Corniches. The roads are nicknamed after the decorative frieze that runs along the top of a building (cornice). Each Corniche (kor-neesh) offers sensational views and a different perspective. You can find the three routes from Nice by driving up Boulevard Jean Jaurès past Vieux Nice. For the Low Corniche, follow signs to N-98 *(Monaco par la Basse Corniche)*, which leads past Nice's port. Shortly after the turnoff to the Low Corniche, you'll see signs for N-7 *(Moyenne Corniche)* leading to the Middle Corniche. Signs for the High *(Grande)* Corniche appear a bit after that; follow D-2564 to *Col des 4 Chemins* and the *Grande Corniche.*

Low Corniche: The Basse Corniche (also called "Corniche Inférieure") strings ports, beaches, and seaside villages together for a traffic-filled ground-floor view. It was built in the 1860s (along with the train line) to bring people to the casino in Monte Carlo. When this Low Corniche was finished, many hill-town villagers descended to the shore and started the communities that now line the sea. Before 1860, the population of the coast between Villefranche-sur-Mer and Monte Carlo was zero. Think about that as you make the congested trip today.

Middle Corniche: The Moyenne Corniche is higher, quieter, and far more impressive. It runs through Eze-le-Village and provides breathtaking views over the Mediterranean, with several scenic pullouts.

High Corniche: Napoleon's crowning road-construction achievement, the Grande Corniche caps the cliffs with staggering views from almost 1,600 feet above the sea. Two thousand years ago, this was called the Via Aurelia, used by the Romans to conquer the West.

Villas: Driving from Villefranche-sur-Mer to Monaco, you'll come upon impressive villas. A particularly grand entry leads to "La Leopolda," the sprawling estate named for a previous owner, King Leopold II of Belgium in the 1930s (who owned the entire peninsula of Cap Ferrat in addition to this estate). Those driving up to the Middle Corniche from Villefranche-sur-Mer can look down on this yellow mansion and its lush garden, which fill an entire hilltop. The property was later owned by the Agnelli family (of Fiat fame and fortune), and then by the Safra family (Brazilian bankers). Its current value is a half-billion dollars.

The Best Route: For a ▲▲▲ route, **drivers** should take the Middle Corniche from Nice or Villefranche-sur-Mer to Eze-le-Village; from there, follow signs to the *Grande Corniche* and *La Turbie*, keeping an eye out for brilliant views back over Eze-le-Village, then finish by dropping down into Monaco. **Buses** travel each route; the higher the Corniche, the less frequent the buses. There are no buses between Eze-le-Village and La Turbie (45-minute walk), though buses do connect Nice and Monaco with La Turbie.

If traveling by bus, follow my self-guided bus tour to Monaco (at the end of this chapter), then consider returning to Nice or Villefranche-sur-Mer by bus via Eze-le-Village, or to Nice via La Turbie (see "Monaco Connections" on page 389).

The following villages and sights are listed from west to east, in the order you'll reach them, traveling from Villefranche-sur-Mer to Monaco.

Cap Ferrat

This exclusive peninsula, rated ▲▲, decorates Villefranche-sur-Mer's views. Cap Ferrat is a peaceful eddy off the busy Nice-Monaco route (Low Corniche). You could spend a leisurely day on this peninsula, wandering the sleepy port village of St-Jean-Cap-Ferrat (usually called "St-Jean"), touring the Villa Ephrussi de Rothschild mansion and gardens and the nearby Villa Kérylos, and walking on sections of the beautiful trails that follow the coast. If you owned a house here, some of the richest people on the planet would be your neighbors.

Tourist Information: The main TI is near the Villa Ephrussi (Mon-Fri 9:00-16:00, closed Sat-Sun, 59 Avenue Denis Séméria, bus #81 stops here at the *office du tourisme*). A smaller TI is in St-Jean (closed Sun, 5 Avenue Denis Séméria, tel. 04 93 76 08 90, office-tourisme@saintjeancapferrat.fr).

PLANNING YOUR TIME

Here's how I'd spend a day on the Cap: From Nice or Villefranche-sur-Mer, take the bus (#81) to the Villa Ephrussi de Rothschild stop (called Passable), then visit the villa. Walk 30 minutes, mostly downhill, to St-Jean for lunch (many options, including grocery shops for picnic supplies) and poke around the village. Consider the 45-minute walk on the Plage de la Paloma trail (ideal for picnics). After lunch, follow a beautiful 30-minute trail to the Villa Kérylos in Beaulieu-sur-Mer and tour that villa. Return to Villefranche-sur-Mer, Nice, or points beyond by train or bus. (If you have a car, skip the loop drive around the peninsula; there's nothing to see from the road except the walls in front of homes owned by people whose challenge in life is keeping the public out.)

You can add Eze-le-Village to this day if you skip the small town of St-Jean and walk directly from the Villa Ephrussi de Rothschild to the Villa Kérylos. To get to Eze-le-Village, take bus #100 (direction: *Monaco*) from the stop near the Villa Kérylos and get off at the Gare d'Eze stop, where you meet bus #83, which shuttles up and up to the village (one €1.50 ticket covers both buses, get the #83 schedule at a TI or check www.lignedazur.com).

Here's an **alternative plan** for the star-gazing, nature-loving beach bum: Visit Villa Ephrussi first thing, walk to St-Jean for lunch, hike six miles around the entirety of Cap Ferrat (2-3 hours), and enjoy the late afternoon on the beach at Plage de Passable. For sunset, have dinner there (at the recommended Restaurant de la Plage de Passable), and then hitch a shuttle boat ride back to Villefranche or catch the bus.

Warning: Late-afternoon buses back to Villefranche-sur-Mer or Nice along the Low Corniche can be jammed (worse on weekends), potentially leaving passengers stranded at stops for long periods. To avoid this, either take the train or board bus #81 on the Cap itself (before it gets crowded).

GETTING TO CAP FERRAT

From Nice or Villefranche-sur-Mer: Bus #81 runs to all Cap Ferrat stops (see "Villefranche-sur-Mer Connections," earlier). For the Villa Ephrussi de Rothschild, get off at the Passable stop (allow 30 minutes from Nice and 10 minutes from Villefranche-sur-Mer's Octroi stop). Schedules are posted at stops, or get one from a TI. The times listed for *Direction Le Port/Cap Ferrat* are when buses depart from Nice—allow about 10 minutes after that for Villefranche-sur-Mer. The return bus (direction: *Nice*) begins in St-Jean.

Cap Ferrat is quick by **car** (take the Low Corniche) or **taxi** (allow €25 one-way from Villefranche-sur-Mer, €50 from Nice).

You can also **walk** an hour from Villefranche-sur-Mer to Cap Ferrat: Go past the train station along the small beach lane, then climb the steps at the far end of the beach and walk parallel to the tracks on Avenue Louise Bordes. Continue straight past the mansions, and take the first right on Avenue de Grasseuil. You'll see signs to *Villa Ephrussi de Rothschild,* then to Cap Ferrat's port.

Sights on Cap Ferrat

▲VILLA EPHRUSSI DE ROTHSCHILD

In what seems like the ultimate in Riviera extravagance, Venice, Versailles, and the Côte d'Azur come together in the pastel-pink Villa Ephrussi. Rising above Cap Ferrat, this 1905 mansion has

Cap Ferrat

To Villefranche-sur-Mer & Nice

To Monaco & Eze-le-Village

TRAIN STATION

LOW CORNICHE

l'Ange Gardien Stop

Bus #100 (Nice-to-Monaco) Stops

Beaulieu-sur-Mer

VILLA KERYLOS

400 Meters

400 Yards

LOW CORNICHE

Hôtel Royal Riviera

Golfe de St-Hospice

AVE. DE GRASSEUIL

AVE. D. SÉMÉRIA

DURANDY

VILLA EPHRUSSI DE ROTHSCHILD

Plage de Passable

CHEMIN DU ROY

#81

#81

#81

ALBERTO 1

St-Jean-Cap-Ferrat

#81

Plage de la Paloma

BLVD GENERAL DE GAULLE

BLVD GÉNÉRAL DE GAULLE

AVE. BELLEVUE

CORNICHE

LIGHTHOUSE

Mediterranean Sea

EAST OF NICE

Hotels/Restaurants

1. Hôtel Brise Marine
2. Hôtel Oursin & Le St. Jean Pizzeria/Rest.
3. Hôtel Patricia
4. Restaurant de la Plage de Passable
5. Plage de la Paloma Restaurant
6. Restaurant La Cabane de l'Écailler
7. Capitaine Cook Restaurant

Trails

A. St-Jean to Beaulieu-sur-Mer (30 min)
B. Plage de la Paloma Loop (45 min)
C. Plage de Passable to St-Jean (2-3 hrs)
D. Walk to Villefranche-sur-Mer (1 hr)

views west to Villefranche-sur-Mer and east to Beaulieu-sur-Mer. From this perch you'll look down on other oligarchs, but not on Paul Allen. As you enter the grounds, look back and see the villa's neighbor—Paul Allen's mansion—on an equally prominent high point surrounded by a private forest.

Cost and Hours: Palace and gardens-€13, includes audioguide, €20 combo-ticket with Villa Kérylos; mid-Feb-Oct daily 10:00-18:00, July-Aug until 19:00; Nov-mid-Feb Mon-Fri 14:00-18:00, Sat-Sun 10:00-18:00; tel. 04 93 01 33 09, www.villa-ephrussi.com. Kids enjoy the free treasure-hunt booklet.

Getting There: With luck, drivers can find a free spot to park along the entry road just inside the gate. There's a small turnaround at the top. The nearest bus stop is Passable, just a few minutes after the bus turns onto Cap Ferrat (bus #81, 10-minute walk uphill to the villa). If returning to Nice or Villefranche-sur-Mer by bus, check the posted schedule, and keep in mind that you're only a minute from the time-point listed for Port le St-Jean.

Visiting the Villa: Pick up the audioguide and garden map as you enter, then start with the well-furnished belle époque **interior** (well-described by the audioguide). Upstairs, an 18-minute film (with English subtitles) explains the gardens and villa and gives you good background on the life of rich and eccentric Beatrice, Baroness de Rothschild, the French banking heiress who built and furnished the place. Don't miss the view over the gardens from the terrace.

As you stroll through the rooms, you'll pass royal furnishings and personal possessions, including the baroness's porcelain collection and her bathroom case for cruises. Her bedroom, sensibly, has views to the sea on both the port and starboard sides, and toward the bow, stretching like the prow of a vast cruise ship, is her garden. An appropriately classy **garden-tearoom** serves drinks and lunches with a view (€17 *plats*, 12:00-17:30).

The gorgeous **gardens** are why most come here (pick up the garden map when you get your audioguide). The literally shipshape gardens were inspired by Beatrice's many ocean-liner trips. She even dressed her small army of gardeners like sailors. Behind the mansion, stroll through the seven lush gardens re-created from locations all over the world and with maximum sea views. Don't miss the Jardin Exotique's wild cactus, the rose garden at the far end, and the view back to the house from the "Temple of Love" gazebo.

Walks from the Villa Ephrussi: It's a lovely 30-minute stroll, mostly downhill and east, from the Villa Ephrussi to the Villa Kérylos in Beaulieu-sur-Mer (described later) or to the port of St-Jean. To get to either, make a hard left at the stop sign below the Villa Ephrussi and follow signs along a small road toward the Hôtel Royal Riviera on Avenue Henri Honoré Sauvan (see Cap Ferrat

EAST OF NICE

map). When the road comes to a T, keep going straight, passing a green gate down a pedestrian path, which ends at a trail—go left to reach the Villa Kérylos, or head right to get to St-Jean (be careful to follow the path left at the Villa Sonja Rello). It's about 15 minutes to either destination once you join this path.

To get to Plage de Passable from the Villa Ephrussi, turn left along the main road just below the villa; after 50 yards you'll find signs leading down to the beach.

BEACHES
Plage de Passable
This pebbly little beach, located below the Villa Ephrussi, comes with great views of Villefranche-sur-Mer. It's a peaceful place, popular with families. One half is public (free, with snack bar, shower, and WC), and the other is run by a small restaurant (€22 includes changing locker, lounge chair, and shower; they have 260 "beds," but still reserve ahead in summer or on weekends as this is a prime spot, tel. 04 93 76 06 17). If you were ever to do the French Riviera rent-a-beach ritual, this would be the place.

To park near the beach (curbside or in a nearby lot), figure about €8/day. Bus #81 stops just above the beach.

For me, the best reason to come here is for dinner. Arrive before sunset, then watch as darkness descends and lights flicker over Villefranche-sur-Mer's heavenly setting. **Restaurant de la Plage de Passable** is your chance to dine on the beach with romance and class while enjoying terrific views and the sounds of children still at play (€12-16 starters, €18-30 *plats*, open daily late May-early Sept, always make a reservation, tel. 04 93 76 06 17, www.plage-de-passable.com).

Plage de la Paloma
This half-private, half-public beach is a 10-minute walk from St-Jean-Cap-Ferrat (described below). For €24 you get a lounge chair and the freedom to relax on the elegant side. Or enjoy the pebbly free beach (with shower and WC).

Plage de la Paloma Restaurant is inviting for dining on the beach, with sandwiches and salads for lunch and elegant dinners (€20 starters, €20-30 *plats*, daily from 12:00 and from 20:00, closed late Sept-mid-April, tel. 04 93 01 64 71, www.paloma-beach.com).

ST-JEAN-CAP-FERRAT
This quiet harbor town lies in Cap Ferrat's center, yet is off most tourist itineraries and feels overlooked. St-Jean houses yachts, boardwalks, views, and boutiques packaged in a "take your time, darling" atmosphere. It's a few miles off the busy Nice-to-Mona-

co road—convenient for drivers. A string of restaurants line the port, with just enough visitors to keep them in business. St-Jean is especially peaceful at night. Sit on a whale-tail bench, enjoy the giant clamshell flowerboxes, and work on your Cyrillic (as many signs come in Russian to cater to the needs of the town's wealthiest guests).

There's a small TI in the village center with limited hours (described earlier). The stop for the bus back to Villefranche-sur-Mer is a block above the port near Hôtel la Frégate (if you need a taxi, call 04 93 76 86 00). The hiking trail to Beaulieu-sur-Mer (with access to the Villa Ephrussi and Villefranche-sur-Mer for hard-core walkers) begins past the beach, to the left of the port as you look out to the water (details follow). If it's lunchtime, you'll find plenty of good options.

Eating in St-Jean: For picnics, the short pedestrian street in St-Jean has all you need (grocery store, bakery, charcuterie, and pizza to go), and you'll have no trouble finding portside or seaside seating. Plage de la Paloma, described earlier, is a 10-minute walk away.

Le St. Jean Pizzeria/Restaurant is central, easygoing, and cheap—on the square with a view and salads (€10 pizzas, closed Wed, Avenue Denis Séméria, tel. 04 93 76 04 75).

Restaurant La Cabane de l'Ecailler, right on the harbor, with fancy yachts for a view, is elegant and expensive but offers a fine €19 two-course lunch Monday through Friday (Nouveau Port de Plaisance, tel. 04 93 87 39 31).

Capitaine Cook is a sweet little eatery that takes its fish seriously yet seems to turn its back on the harbor. There's a patio out back (no view) and a cozy interior (good €30 *menu*, consider their bouillabaisse, closed Wed, a block uphill from the port toward Plage de la Paloma at 11 Avenue Jean Mermoz, tel. 04 93 76 02 66).

▲▲WALKS AROUND CAP FERRAT

The Cap is perfect for a walk; you'll find well-maintained foot trails covering most of its length. You have three easy, mostly level options of varying lengths. The TIs in Villefranche-sur-Mer and St-Jean have maps of Cap Ferrat with

EAST OF NICE

walking paths marked, or you can use the following itineraries with this book's map.

Between St-Jean and Beaulieu-sur-Mer (30 minutes)

A level walk takes you past sumptuous villas, great views, and fun swimming opportunities. From St-Jean's port, walk along the harbor and past the beach with the water on your right. Head up the steps to Promenade Maurice Rouvier and continue; before long you'll see smashing views of the whitewashed Villa Kérylos.

To get from Beaulieu-sur-Mer to St-Jean or the Villa Ephrussi, start at the Villa Kérylos (with the sea on your left), walk toward the Hôtel Royal Riviera, and find the trail. If going to St-Jean, stay left at the Villa Sonja Rello (about halfway down); if going to the Villa Ephrussi, look for signs leading uphill before Villa Aurora (walk up the path to Avenue Henri Honoré Sauvan, then keep going). If you're walking from St-Jean to the Villa Ephrussi, turn left off the trail about 50 yards after passing Villa Aurora.

Plage de la Paloma Loop Trail (45 minutes)

Just east of St-Jean's port, a scenic trail offers a terrific sampling of Cap Ferrat's beauty. From the port, walk or drive about a quarter-mile east (with the port on your left, passing Hôtel La Voile d'Or); parking is available at the port or on streets near Plage de la Paloma. You'll find the trailhead where the road comes to a T—look for a *Plage Paloma* sign pointing left, but don't walk left. Cross the small dirt park to start the trail, and do the walk counterclockwise. The trail is level and paved, yet uneven enough that good shoes are helpful. Plunk your picnic on one of the benches along the trail, or eat at the restaurant on Plage de la Paloma at the end of the walk (described earlier).

Plage de Passable Around the Cape to St-Jean (2-3 hours)

For a longer hike that circles the cape, follow the signs below the Villa Ephrussi marked *Plage Passable* (10 minutes downhill on foot from the villa, parking available near the trailhead). Walk down to the beach (you'll find a good café that's ideal for lunch), turn left, and cross the beach. Go along a paved road behind the apartment building, and after about 60 yards, take the steps down to the trail *(Sentier Littoral)*. It's about six miles (10 kilometers) around the cape. Near the end of the trail, you'll pass by the port of St-Jean, where you have three options: Take bus #81 back to Villefranche-sur-Mer, walk back to the Villa Ephrussi and Plage de Passable via the shorter inland route (by reversing the directions under "Walks from the Villa Ephrussi," earlier), or continue on to Beaulieu-sur-Mer and take a bus to Monaco or Nice.

Sleeping on Cap Ferrat

While St-Jean is the main town serving the notoriously wealthy community of Cap Ferrat, it has some affordable hotels.

$$$ Hôtel Brise Marine*, graced with gardens and a view terrace, is a peaceful retreat. Warmly run by Monsieur Maître-Henri, this aged mansion—with faded, Old World character—feels lost in time. Many of its spacious rooms come with fine views, and some have small balconies (view Db with balcony-€200, view Db without balcony-€175, breakfast-€15, minibar, secure parking-€15/day with reservation, between the port and Plage de la Paloma at 58 Avenue Jean Mermoz, tel. 04 93 76 04 36, www.hotel-brisemarine.com, info@hotel-brisemarine.com).

$ Hôtel Oursin* is central to the port, with 14 well-priced and well-appointed rooms all on one floor. Run by mother-and-son team Chantal and Aubrey, it's a humble place with white walls that feels more like a B&B than a hotel (small D with shower-€45, smaller Db without air-con-€75, bigger Db with air-con-€90-110, larger Db with air-con and port views-€125, €20 less Oct-April, 1 Avenue Denis Séméria, tel. 04 93 76 12 55, www.hoteloursin.com, reception@hoteloursin.com).

Between St-Jean and Villefranche-sur-Mer:** $ Hôtel Patricia sits across from Villefranche-sur-Mer, at the start of Cap Ferrat. It's a 20-minute walk to Villefranche or the Villa Ephrussi, and 10 minutes into Beaulieu-sur-Mer. Helpful owners Joelle and Franck provide 11 simple and homey rooms with eclectic decor (Db-€90-105, larger Db-€130, no elevator, no air-con, free parking, near l'Ange Gardien bus stop at 310 Avenue de l'Ange Gardien, tel. 04 93 01 06 70, www.hotel-patricia.riviera.fr, hotelpatricia@free.fr).

Villa Kérylos

The village of Beaulieu-sur-Mer, right on the Low Corniche road (just after Cap Ferrat), is busy with traffic. It's a good place to pick

up the hiking trail to St-Jean and to visit the unusual Villa Kérylos. In 1902, an eccentric millionaire modeled his mansion after a Greek villa from the island of Delos from about 200 B.C. No expense was spared in re-creating this Greek fantasy, from the floor mosaics to Carrara marble columns to exquisite wood furnishings. The rain-powered shower is fun, and the included audioguide will increase your Greek IQ. The ceramics workshop—open only high season and weekend afternoons—offers a chance to test your talents.

EAST OF NICE

Cost and Hours: €12, €20 combo-ticket with Villa Ephrussi de Rothschild; mid-Feb-Oct daily 10:00-18:00, July-Aug until 19:00; Nov-mid-Feb Mon-Fri 14:00-18:00, Sat-Sun 10:00-18:00; tel. 04 93 01 47 29, www.villa-kerylos.com.

Getting There: Drivers should park near the casino in Beaulieu-sur-Mer, not on the villa's access road. Monaco-Nice bus #100 drops you at the Eglise stop at the Hôtel Metropole in Beaulieu (5-minute walk to the Villa Kérylos), while bus #81 from Villefranche-sur-Mer and Nice stops at the villa's access road (for details on these buses, see page 357). Trains (2/hour, 10 minutes from Nice or Monaco) leave you a 10-minute walk away: Turn left out of the train station and left again down the main drag, then follow signs. The walking trail from Villa Kérylos to Cap Ferrat and the Villa Ephrussi de Rothschild begins on the other side of the bay, beneath Hôtel Royal Riviera.

Eze-le-Village

Capping a peak high above the sea, flowery and flawless Eze-le-Village (don't confuse it with the seafront town of Eze-Bord-de-Mer) is entirely consumed by tourism.
This *village d'art et de gastronomie* (as it calls itself) is home to perfume outlets, stylish boutiques, steep cobbled lanes, and magnificent views. Touristy as it is, its stony state of preservation and magnificent hilltop setting over the Mediterranean affords a fine memory. Day-tripping by bus to Eze-le-Village from Nice, Monaco, or Villefranche-

sur-Mer works well. While Eze-le-Village can be tranquil early and late, during the day it is mobbed by cruise-ship and tour-bus groups.

GETTING TO EZE-LE-VILLAGE

There are two Ezes: Eze-le-Village (the spectacular hill town on the Middle Corniche) and Eze-Bord-de-Mer (a modern beach resort far below the "village" of Eze).

From Nice and upper Villefranche-sur-Mer, buses #82 and #112 provide 16 buses per day to Eze-le-Village (8 on Sun, 20 minutes from Villefranche).

From Nice, Villefranche-sur-Mer, or Monaco, you can also take the train or the Nice-Monaco bus to Eze-Bord-de-Mer, getting off at the Gare d'Eze stop. From there, take the infrequent #83 shuttle bus straight up to Eze-le-Village (8/day, daily about 9:00-18:00, schedule posted at stop, 15 minutes).

To connect Eze-le-Village directly with Monte Carlo in Monaco, take bus #112 (6/day Mon-Sat, none on Sun, 20 minutes).

There are no buses between La Turbie (Le Trophée d'Auguste) and Eze-le-Village (45-minute walk along the road's shoulder).

A taxi between the two Ezes or from Eze-le-Village to La Turbie will run you about €25 (tel. 06 09 84 17 84).

Orientation to Eze-le-Village

Tourist Information: The helpful TI is adjacent to Eze-le-Village's main parking lot, just below the town's entry. Ask here for bus schedules. Call a week in advance to arrange a €10, one-hour English-language tour of the village and its gardens (TI open April-Oct daily 9:00-18:00, July-Aug until 19:00; Nov-March Mon-Sat 9:00-17:00, closed Sun; Place de Gaulle, tel. 04 93 41 26 00, www.eze-tourisme.com).

Helpful Hints: The stop for **buses** to Nice is across the road by the Avia gas station, and the stops for buses to Eze-Bord-de-Mer and Monaco are on the village side of the main road, near the Casino grocery. Public **WCs** are just behind the TI and in the village behind the church.

Eze-le-Village Walk

This self-guided walk gives you a quick orientation to the village.
• *From the TI and parking lot, hike uphill into the town. You'll come to an exclusive hotel gate and the start of a steep trail down to the beach, marked* Eze/Mer. *For a panoramic view and an ideal picnic perch, side-trip 80 steps down this path (for details, see "Hike to Eze-Bord-de-Mer," later). Continuing up into the village, find the steps immediately after the ritzy hotel gate and climb to...*

Place du Centenaire: In this square, a stone plaque in the flower bed (behind the candy stand) celebrates the 100th anniversary of the 1860 plebiscite, the time when all 133 Eze residents voted to leave the Italian Duchy of Savoy and join France. A town map here helps you get oriented.
• *Now pass through the once-formidable town gate and climb into the 14th-century village.*

As you walk, stop to read the information plaques (in English) and contemplate the change this village has witnessed in the last 90 years. Eze-le-Village was off any traveler's radar until well after World War II (running water was made available only in the 1930s), yet today hotel rooms outnumber local residents two to one (66 to 33).

• *Wandering the narrow lanes, follow signs to the...*

Château Eza: This was the winter getaway of the Swedish royal family from 1923 until 1953; today it's a hotel. The château's

tearoom (Salon de Thé), on a cliff overlooking the jagged Riviera and sea, offers you the most scenic coffee or beer break you'll ever enjoy—for a price. The sensational view terrace is also home to an expensive-but-excellent restaurant (€7 teas, €10 beers and glasses of wine, €64 lunch *menus,* allow €130 for seven-course degustation dinner, open daily, tel. 04 93 41 12 24).

• *Backtrack a bit and continue uphill (follow signs to* Jardin Exotique*). The lane ends at the hilltop castle ruins— now blanketed by the...*

Jardins d'Eze: You'll find this prickly festival of cactus and exotic plants suspended between the sea and sky at the top of Eze-le-Village. Since 1949, the ruins of an old château have been home to 400 different plants 1,300 feet above the sea (€6, daily, hours usually June-Sept 9:00-19:00, Oct-May until dusk, well-described in English, tel. 04 93 41 10 30). At the top, you'll be treated to a commanding 360-degree view, with a helpful *table d'orientation.* On a clear day (they say...) you can see Corsica. The castle was demolished by Louis XIV in 1706. Louis destroyed castles like this all over Europe (most notably along the Rhine), because he didn't want to risk having to do battle with their owners at some future date.

• *As you descend, drop by the...*

Eze Church: Though built during Napoleonic times, this church has an uncharacteristic Baroque fanciness—a reminder that 300 years of Savoy rule left the townsfolk with an Italian savoir faire and a sensibility for decor.

Sights in Eze-le-Village

Fragonard Perfume Factory

This factory, with its huge tour-bus parking lot, lies on the Middle Corniche, 100 yards below Eze-le-Village. Designed for tour groups, it cranks them through all day long. If you've never seen mass tourism in action, this place will open your eyes. (The gravel is littered with the color-coded stickers each tourist wears so that salespeople know which guide gets the kickback.) Drop in for an informative and free tour (2/hour, 15 minutes). You'll see how the perfume and scented soaps are made before being herded into the gift shop.

Cost and Hours: Daily 8:30-18:30; best Mon-Fri 9:00-11:00 & 14:00-15:30, when the "factory" actually has people working; tel. 04 93 41 05 05.

Nearby: For a more intimate (but unguided) look at perfume, cross the main road in Eze-le-Village to visit the **Gallimard** shop. Explore the small museum (no English) and let the lovely ladies show you their scents (daily 9:00-18:00, across from Eze parking lot). They can give you a short tour if you ask.

Hike to Eze-Bord-de-Mer

A steep trail leaves Eze-le-Village from the foot of the hill-town entry, near the fancy hotel gate (60 yards up from the main road), and descends 1,300 feet to the sea along a no-shade, all-view trail. The trail is easy to follow but uneven—allow 45 minutes (good walking shoes are essential; expect to be on all fours in certain sections). Once in Eze-Bord-de-Mer, you can catch a bus or train to all destinations between Nice and Monaco. While walking this trail in the late 1800s, Friedrich Nietzsche was moved to write his unconventionally spiritual novel, *Thus Spoke Zarathustra*.

Eating in Eze-le-Village

To enjoy Eze-le-Village in relative peace, visit at sunset and stay for dinner. There's a handy **Casino** grocery at the foot of the village by the bus stop (daily 8:00-19:30) and a sensational picnic spot at the beginning of the trail to Eze-Bord-de-Mer. **Le Cactus** serves crêpes, salads, and sandwiches at outdoor tables near the entry to the old town and inside their cozy, vaulted-ceiling dining room (daily, tel. 04 93 41 19 02). For a real splurge, dine at **Château Eza** (described earlier, on my "Eze-le-Village Walk").

Le Trophée des Alpes

High above Monaco, on the Grande Corniche in the overlooked village of La Turbie, lies the ancient Roman "Trophy of the Alps," one of this region's most evocative historical sights (with dramatic views over the entire country of Monaco as a bonus). Rising well above all other buildings, this massive monument, worth ▲, commemorates Augustus Caesar's conquest of the Alps and its 44 hostile tribes. It's exciting to think that, in a way, Le Trophée des Alpes (also called "Le Trophée d'Auguste" for the emperor who

EAST OF NICE

built it) celebrates a victory that kicked off the Pax Romana—joining Gaul and Germania, freeing up the main artery of the Roman Empire, and linking Spain and Italy.

GETTING THERE

By Car: Take the High Corniche to La Turbie, ideally from Eze-le-Village (La Turbie is 10 minutes east of, and above, Eze-le-Village), then look for signs to *Le Trophée d'Auguste.* Once in La Turbie, park in the lot in the center of town (Place Neuve, follow *Monaco* signs for a short block) and walk from there (go five minutes around the old village, with the village on your right); or drive to the site by turning right in front of La Régence Café. Those coming from farther afield can take the efficient A-8 to the La Turbie exit. To reach Eze-le-Village from La Turbie, follow signs to *Nice,* and then look for signs to *Eze-le-Village.*

By Bus: From Nice, you can get here on bus #T66 from the Pont St. Michel tram stop (7/day, 45 minutes) or bus #116 from the Vauban tram stop (6/day, 45 minutes). From Monaco, bus #11 connects to La Turbie (8/day Mon-Sat, 5/day Sun, 30 minutes). La Turbie's bus stop is near the post office (PTT) on Place Neuve.

On Foot: Eze-le-Village is a 45-minute roadside walk downhill from La Turbie (no buses). There's a bike lane for half of the trip, but the rest is along a fairly quiet road with no shoulder. Follow D-2564 from La Turbie to Eze-le-Village, and don't miss the turnoff for D-45. The views of Eze-le-Village are magnificent as you get close.

ORIENTATION TO LE TROPHEE DES ALPES

Cost and Hours: €6, Tue-Sun mid-May-mid-Sept 9:30-13:00 & 14:30-18:30, off-season 10:00-13:30 & 14:30-17:00, closed Mon year-round.

Tours and Information: The audioguide is €3. Tel. 04 93 41 20 84, www.la-turbie.monuments-nationaux.fr.

VISITING THE MONUMENT

You'll enter through a small park that offers grand views over Monaco and allows you to appreciate the remarkable setting selected by the Romans for this monument. Walk around and notice how the

Romans built a fine stone exterior, filled in with rubble and coarse concrete. Flanked by the vanquished in chains, the towering inscription (the longest such inscription surviving from ancient times) tells the story: It was erected "by the senate and the people to honor the emperor."

The structure served no military purpose when built, though it was fortified in the Middle Ages (like the Roman Arena in Arles) as a safe haven for villagers. When Louis XIV ordered the destruction of the area's fortresses in the early 18th century, he sadly included this one. The monument later became a quarry before being restored in the 1930s and 1940s with money from the Tuck family of New Hampshire.

The good little one-room **museum** shows a reconstruction and translation of the dramatic inscription, which lists all the feisty alpine tribes that put up such a fight.

NEAR THE MONUMENT: LA TURBIE

The sweet old village of La Turbie sees almost no tourists, but it has plenty of cafés and restaurants. To stroll the old village, walk behind the post office and find brick footpaths that lead through the peaceful back lanes of the village.

Eating in La Turbie: **Restaurant La Terrasse** is your best bet. It's welcoming and convivial, with tables under umbrellas and big views. If dining here for the sunset, book a view table. Friendly Helen and Jacques would love to introduce you to their specialty—steak tartare (€10 salads, €15 plats, daily for lunch and dinner, near the post office at the main parking lot, 17 Place Neuve, tel. 04 93 41 21 84).

Quickie Riviera Bus Tour

The Riviera from Nice to Monaco and on to Menton is so easy to tour by bus and train that those with a car should consider leaving it at their hotel. While the train laces together the charms of this dramatic stretch of Mediterranean coast as if on a scenic bracelet, the public bus affords a far better view of the crags, dreamy villas, and much-loved beaches that make it Europe's coast with the most.

PLANNING YOUR TIME

This tour works best if you ride the bus from Nice the entire route to Menton (1.5 hours), enjoy Menton, and then see Monaco and Villefranche-sur-Mer on the way back to Nice. Get an early start (and remember that Monte Carlo's casino is closed to visitors from 12:30-14:00 and the game rooms don't open until 14:00). Keep in mind that afternoon buses back to Nice are often crammed and agonizingly slow after Villefranche-sur-Mer—at these times, you can always take the train.

BUS TIPS

Bus #100 runs along the Low Corniche (3-4/hour; because of construction in Nice, you may have to board at the city's port—ask).

EAST OF NICE

One simple €1.50 ticket is good for 74 minutes, no matter how far you go (one-way only). Pay the driver as you get on.

Riding from Nice toward Monaco, grab a seat on the right. To beat the beach-goers, start before 9:00. If there's a long line, you could wait for the next bus to be assured of a view seat. Stops are announced on most buses. The last bus leaves Monaco for Nice at about 20:00.

Since bus fares are cheap, consider hopping on and off at great viewpoints (the next bus is always 15 or 20 minutes away). All stops have names (usually posted on the shelter or bus stop sign)—I'll identify the ones that matter along this route.

Some bus drivers on this line are in training for the Grand Prix of Monaco—hold on tight.

FROM NICE TO MONACO

This route along the Low Corniche was inaugurated with the opening of the Monte Carlo Casino in 1863. It was designed to provide easy and safe access from Nice (and the rest of France) to the gambling fun in Monaco. Here's what you'll see along the way:

In Nice: From the regular starting point (Promenade des Arts; but the bus might leave from the port, see "Bus Tips" above), the ride begins with a quick glimpse of Nice's snazzy Museum of Modern Art on the left before passing by Place Garibaldi (easy transfer to the tram on your way back), with its linden trees and statue of Giuseppe Garibaldi (the romantic revolutionary leader who led the war to unite Italy in the 1860s) at the center.

Nice Harbor: This harbor—dredged by 400 convicts—was finished in the mid-1800s. Before then, boats littered Nice's beaches. You'll see some yachts, an occasional cruise ship, and the daily ferry to Corsica. The one-hour boat tour along Cap Ferrat and Villefranche-sur-Mer leaves from the right side, about half-way down (see page 295). If you get off here on your return, it's a pleasant 30-minute walk around the distant point to or from the Promenade des Anglais and Nice's old town.

From Nice to Villefranche-sur-Mer: As you glide away from Nice, look back for views of the harbor, Castle Hill, and the sweeping Bay of Angels. Imagine the views from the homes below, and imagine 007 on his deck admiring a sunset (the soft, yellow, rounded tower straight ahead near the top of the hill was part of Sean Connery's property). Elton John's home is higher up the hill (and out of view). Imagine his neighbor, Tina Turner, dropping by.

You'll soon pass the now-closed Hôtel Maerterlinck, one of several luxury hotels to go belly-up in recent years (slated for condo-conversion). Next, you'll come to the yacht-studded bay of Villefranche-sur-Mer and the peninsula called Cap Ferrat—playground of the rich and famous, marked by its lighthouse on the point just across the bay. This bay is a rare natural harbor along the Riviera. Since it's deeper than Nice's, it hosts huge cruise ships, which drop anchor and tender passengers in.

Villefranche-sur-Mer: To see charming Villefranche-sur-Mer, get off at the stop labeled *Octroi.* After passing through Villefranche-sur-Mer, look for sensational views back over the town (best from the Madonne-Noire stop). Looking ahead, the Baroness Rothschild's pink Villa Ephrussi, with its red-tiled roof, breaks the horizon on Cap Ferrat's peninsula. Keep an eye out as the road arcs to the right—the Rolling Stones recorded 1972's *Exile on Main Street* in the basement of the Villa Nellcôte, the mansion below where you see the l'Ange Gardien stop.

Cap Ferrat: This peninsula is home to the Villa Ephrussi de Rothschild, the port town of St-Jean, and some lovely seaside paths. As you leave Cap Ferrat, remember that this road was built in the 1860s to bring customers to Monaco. Before then, there was nothing along this route—no one even lived here—all the way to Monaco.

Beaulieu-sur-Mer: To visit the Villa Kérylos or to take the seaside walk to St-Jean on Cap Ferrat, get off at the Eglise stop, in front of the Hôtel Metropole. Just

after the town of Beaulieu-sur-Mer, the cliffs create a microclimate and a zone nicknamed "Little Africa." (The bus stop is labeled *Petite Afrique.*) Exotic vegetation (including the only bananas on the Riviera) grows among private, elegant villas that made Beaulieu-sur-Mer *the* place to be in the 19th century.

Eze-Bord-de-Mer: A few minutes after leaving Beaulieu-sur-Mer, be ready for quickie views way up to the fortified town of Eze-le-Village. After passing through a rock arch, you'll swing around a big bend going left: Eze-le-Village crowns the ridge in front of you. To reach Eze-le-Village by bus, the #83 shuttle bus makes the climb from the Gare d'Eze stop in Eze-Bord-de-Mer—see page 368. To reach the village on foot (see description on page 371), find the ramp at the east end of Eze-Bord-de-Mer, to the left just before the tunnel.

Cap d'Ail: After passing through several tunnels, you emerge at Cap d'Ail. The huge, yellowish, hospital-like building below once thrived as a luxury hotel popular with the Russian aristocracy. Now it's a luxury condo. At the first stop in the village of Cap d'Ail (labeled *Cap d'Ail-Edmonds*), look above at the switchbacks halfway up the barren hillside. It was at the bend connecting these two switchbacks that Princess Grace Kelly (the American movie star who married into the royal family of Monaco) was killed in a car crash in 1982. You can get off here and walk a lovely beach trail that will take you to Monaco in roughly 30 minutes.

Monaco (three bus stops): Cap d'Ail borders Monaco—you're about to leave France. You'll pass by some junky development along this no-man's-land stretch. Eventually, to the right, just before the castle-topped hill (Monaco-Ville), is Monaco's Fontvieille district, featuring tall, modern apartments all built on land reclaimed from the Mediterranean. The first Monaco stop (Place d'Armes) is best for visiting the palace and other old-town sights in Monaco-Ville.

If you stay on the bus, you'll pass through the tunnel, then emerge to follow the road that Grand Prix racers speed along. In late May you'll see blue bleachers and barriers set up for the big race.

You'll pass the second Monaco stop (on the port, named Princesse Antoinette), then enjoy the harbor and city views as you climb to the last Monaco stop (Casino), near the TI. Get off here for the casino. For information on Monaco, see the next chapter. If you stay on the bus for a few more minutes, you'll be back in France, and in 15 more minutes you'll reach the end of the line, **Menton** (described in the following chapter).

Bonne route!

MONACO

Despite high prices, wall-to-wall daytime tourists, and a Disney-esque atmosphere, Monaco is a Riviera must. Monaco is on the go. Since 1929, cars have raced around the port and in front of the casino in one of the world's most famous auto races, the Grand Prix de Monaco. The modern breakwater—constructed elsewhere and towed in by sea—enables big cruise ships to dock here, and the district of Fontvieille, reclaimed from the sea, bristles with luxury high-rise condos. But don't look for anything too deep in this glittering tax haven. Many of its 36,000 residents live here because there's no income tax—there are only about 6,000 true Monegasques.

This minuscule principality (0.75 square mile) borders only France and the Mediterranean. The country has always been tiny, but it used to be…less tiny. In an 1860 plebiscite, Monaco lost two-thirds of its territory when the region of Menton voted to join France. To compensate, France suggested that Monaco build a fancy casino and promised to connect it to the world with a road (the Low Corniche) and a train line. This started a high-class tourist boom that has yet to let up.

Although "independent," Monaco is run as a piece of France. A French civil servant appointed by the French president—with

the blessing of Monaco's prince—serves as state minister and manages the place. Monaco's phone system, electricity, water, and so on, are all French.

The glamorous romance and marriage of the American actress Grace Kelly to Prince Rainier added to Monaco's fairy-tale mystique.

Princess Grace first came to Monaco to star in the 1955 Alfred Hitchcock movie *To Catch a Thief*, in which she was filmed racing along the Corniches. She married the prince in 1956 and adopted the country, but tragically, the much-loved princess died in 1982 after suffering a stroke while driving on one of those same scenic roads. She was just 52 years old.

The death of Prince Rainier in 2005 ended his 56-year-long enlightened reign. Today Monaco is ruled by Prince Albert Alexandre Louis Pierre, Marquis of Baux—son of Prince Rainier and Princess Grace. Prince Albert had long been considered Europe's most eligible bachelor—until he finally married on July 2, 2011, at age 53. His bride, known as Princess Charlene, is a South African commoner 20 years his junior.

A graduate of Amherst College, Albert is a bobsled enthusiast who raced in several Olympics, and an avid environmentalist who seems determined to clean up Monaco's tarnished tax-haven, money-laundering image. (Monaco is infamously known as a "sunny place for shady people.") Monaco is big business, and Prince Albert is its CEO. Its famous casino contributes only 5 percent of the state's revenue, whereas its 43 banks—which offer a hard-to-resist way to hide your money—are hugely profitable. The prince also makes money with a value-added tax (20 percent, the same as in France), plus real estate and corporate taxes.

Monaco is a special place: There are more people in Monaco's philharmonic orchestra (about 100) than in its army (about 80 guards). Yet the princedom is well-guarded, with police and cameras on every corner. (They say you could win a million dollars at the casino and walk to the train station in the wee hours without a worry.) Stamps are printed in small quantities and increase in value almost as soon as they're available. And collectors snapped up the rare Monaco versions of euro coins (with Prince Rainier's portrait) so quickly that many Monegasques have never even seen one.

Orientation to Monaco

The principality of Monaco has three tourist areas: Monaco-Ville, Monte Carlo, and La Condamine. **Monaco-Ville** fills the rock high above everything else and is referred to by locals as Le Rocher ("The Rock"). This is the oldest part of Monaco, home to the Prince's Palace and all the sights except the casino. **Monte Carlo** is the area around the casino. **La Condamine** is the port, which lies between Monaco-Ville and Monte Carlo. From here it's a

25-minute walk up to the Prince's Palace or to the casino, or three minutes by bus to either (see "Getting Around Monaco," later).

The surgical-strike plan for most travelers is to start at Monaco-Ville (where you'll spend the most time), wander down along the port area, and finish by gambling away whatever you have left in Monte Carlo (the casino's game rooms don't open until 14:00). You can walk the entire route in about 1.5 hours, or take three bus trips and do it in 15 minutes.

TOURIST INFORMATION

The main TI is at the top of the **park above the casino** (Mon-Sat 9:00-19:00, Sun 11:00-13:00, 2 Boulevard des Moulins, tel. 00-377/92 16 61 16 or 00-377/92 16 61 66, www.visitmonaco.com). Another TI is at the **train station** (Tue-Sat 9:00-18:00, also open Sun-Mon in July-Aug, closed 12:00-14:00 off-season). There's also a TI desk for Monaco in Terminal 1 of **Nice's airport.**

ARRIVAL IN MONACO

By Bus from Nice and Villefranche-sur-Mer: See my "Quickie Riviera Bus Tour" on page 373 to plan your route. Bus riders need to pay attention, since stops are not always announced. Cap d'Ail is the town before Monaco, so be on the lookout after that (the last stop before Monaco is called "Cimetière"). You'll enter Monaco through the modern cityscape of high-rises in the Fontvieille district. When you see the rocky outcrop of old Monaco, be ready to get off.

There are three stops in Monaco. Listed in order from Nice, they are *Place d'Armes* (at the base of Monaco-Ville), *Princesse Antoinette* (on the port), and *Monte Carlo-Casino* (near the casino and the TI on Boulevard des Moulins).

By Train from Nice: You know your train is in Monaco when you're in a long, modern underground station. The station is in the center of Monaco, a 15-minute walk to the casino or to the port, and about 25 minutes to the palace. The station has no baggage storage.

The TI, train-ticket windows, and WCs are up the escalator at the Italy end of the station. There are three exits from the train platform level (one at each end and one in the middle).

To reach Monaco-Ville and the palace, take the exit at the Nice end of the tracks (signed *Sortie Fontvieille/Le Rocher*), which leads through a long tunnel to the base of Monaco-Ville at Place d'Armes. From here, it's about a 15-minute hike up to the palace, or take the bus (#1 or #2).

To reach Monaco's port and the casino, take the middle exit, following *Sortie Port* signs down the steps and escalators, and then *Accès Port* signs until you pop out at the port, where you'll see the

Monaco

FRANCE

To
Menton

MIDDLE CORNICHE

To
Nice

MONEGHETTI

BLVD. PRINCESSE

T ACCESS TO TRAIN STATION

B BUS STOP

TRAIN
STATION
(UNDERGROUND)

M O N A

T

T

B #1 & 2
and #100 to Nice

BLVD. DU JARDIN EXOTIQUE

RUE GRIMALDI

R. PRIN. ANT.

BLVD. ALBERT I

LA CONDAMINE

Jardin
Exotique

BLVD. RAINIER III

RUE DE LA TURBIE

R. SUFFREN-REYMOND

1

2

R. PRINCESSE CAROLINE

T

Place d'Armes
(Local Buses)

B

LOW CORNICHE

B #100
to Nice

B #1 & #2

B #1 & #2

AVE. DE FONTVIELLE

B #100
from Nice

RAMPE
MAJOR

AVE. DE LA

PRINCE'S
PALACE

*Place du
Palais*

RUE DES REMPARTS

RUE BASSE

R. COMTE GASTARDI

3

To
Nice

AVE. ALBERT II

👣 *WALK
BEGINS*

R. EMILE DE LOTH

R. COL. BELL. DE CASTRO

4

■ POST

✝ CATHEDRAL

AVE. SAINT-

LOUIS II
SOCCER
STADIUM

*Port du
Fontvielle*

*Jardin
Botanique*

FONTVIEILLE

MONACO

BEAUSOLIEIL

BLVD. DES MOULINS

To Villa Sauber & Menton

BLVD. LARVOTTO

#112 to Eze-le-Village

#100 from Nice & #11 to La Turbie

Casino Gardens

AVE. SPEL

#1 & 2 and #100 to Nice

#1 & 2

CHARLOTTE

AMERICAN-STYLE CASINO

AVE. DE LA COSTA

Place du Casino

CASINO

CO

MONTE CARLO

AVE. D'OSTENDE

PALAIS DES CONGRES &

P "Le Casino"

Port

LOTSA YACHTS!

SHUTTLE BOAT

CRUISE TENDER DOCK

MONACO-VILLE

FORT ANTOINE

AVE. QUARANTINE

PORTE NEUVE

Place de la Visitation

P

Mediterranean Sea

RUE EMILE DE LOTH

#1 & #2

Petit Train Stop

MARTIN

P "Le Palais"

AQUARIUM

WALK ENDS

MONACO

300 Meters

300 Yards

1 Hôtel de France
2 Huit et Demi Rest.
3 Boulangerie
4 U Cavagnetu Rest.

stop for buses #1 and #2 across the busy street. From here it's a 20-minute walk to the casino (up Avenue d'Ostende to your left), or a short trip via buses #1 or #2.

To return to Nice by train after 20:30, when ticket windows close, buy your return tickets now or be sure to have about €4 in coins for the ticket machines.

By Car: Follow *Centre-Ville* signs into Monaco (warning: traffic can be a problem), then watch for the red-letter signs to parking garages at *Le Casino* (for Monte Carlo) or *Le Palais* (for Monaco-Ville). You'll pay about €10 for four hours.

By Cruise Ship: For information on arrival by cruise ship, see "Monaco Connections," near the end of this chapter.

HELPFUL HINTS

Combo-Ticket: If you plan to see both of Monaco's big sights (Prince's Palace and the Cousteau Aquarium), buy the €19 combo-ticket at the first sight you visit.

Changing of the Guard: This popular event takes place daily at 11:55 at the Prince's Palace. Arrive by 11:30 to get a good viewing spot.

Loop Trip by Bus or Train: From Nice you can get to Monaco by bus or train, then take a bus from Monaco to Eze-le-Village or La Turbie, and return to Nice from there by bus. For bus numbers, frequencies, and stop locations, see "Monaco Connections," near the end of this chapter.

Evening Events: Monaco's **Philharmonic Orchestra** (tel. 00-377/98 06 28 28, www.opmc.mc) and **Monte Carlo Ballet** (tel. 00-377/99 99 30 00, www.balletsdemontecarlo.com) offer performances at reasonable prices.

Passport Stamp: If you want an official memento of your visit, you can get your passport stamped at the main TI (listed earlier).

GETTING AROUND MONACO

By Local Bus: Buses #1 and #2 link all areas with frequent service (single ticket-€2, 6 tickets-€10, day pass-€5, pay driver or save a little and buy from curbside machines, 10/hour, fewer on Sun, buses run until 21:00). You can split a six-ride ticket with your travel partners. Bus tickets are good for a free transfer if used within 30 minutes.

For a **cheap and scenic loop ride** through Monaco, ride bus #2 from one end to the other and back (25 minutes each way). You need two tickets and have to get off the bus at the last stop and then get on again.

By Open Bus Tour: You can pay €21 for a hop-on, hop-off open-deck bus tour that makes 12 stops in Monaco, but I wouldn't.

If you want a scenic tour of the principality that includes its best views, take local bus #2 (listed earlier).

By Tourist Train: "Monaco Tour" trains are an efficient way to enjoy a blitz tour of Monaco. They begin at the aquarium and pass by the port, casino, and palace (€8, 2/hour, 40 minutes, recorded English commentary).

By Taxi: If you've lost all track of time at the casino, you can call the 24-hour taxi service (tel. 00-377/93 15 01 01)...provided you still have enough money to pay for the cab home.

Monaco-Ville Walk

All of Monaco's major sights (except the casino) are in Monaco-Ville, packed within a few cheerfully tidy blocks. This self-guided walk connects these sights in a tight little loop, starting from the palace square.

• *To get from anywhere in Monaco to the palace square (Monaco-Ville's sightseeing center and home of the palace), take bus #1 or #2 to the end of the line at Place de la Visitation. Turn right as you step off the bus and walk five minutes down Rue Emile de Loth. You'll pass the post office, a worthwhile stop for its collection of valuable Monegasque stamps (we'll go there later—to visit it now, see page 386).*

If you're walking up from the port or the Place d'Armes stop for bus #100, a well-marked lane leads directly to the palace.

Palace Square (Place du Palais)

This square is the best place to get oriented to Monaco. Facing the palace, go to the right and look out over the city (er...principal-

ity). This rock gave birth to the little pastel Hong Kong look-alike in 1215, and it's managed to remain an independent country for most of its nearly 800 years. Looking beyond the glitzy port, notice the faded green roof above and to the right: It belongs to the casino that put Monaco on the map in the 1800s. It was located away from Monaco-Ville because Prince Charles III (r. 1856-1889) wanted to shield his people from low-life gamblers.

The modern buildings just past the casino mark the eastern limit of Monaco. The famous Grand Prix runs along the port and then up the ramp to the casino (at top speeds of 180 mph). Italy is so close, you can almost smell the pesto. Just beyond the casino is France again (which flanks Monaco on both sides)—you could walk one-way from France to France, passing through Monaco in about 60 minutes.

The odd statue of a woman with a fishing net is dedicated to the glorious reign of **Prince Albert I** (1889-1922). The son of Charles III (who built the casino), Albert I was a true Renaissance Man. He had a Jacques Cousteau-like fascination with the sea (and built Monaco's famous aquarium) and was a determined pacifist who made many attempts to dissuade Germany's Kaiser Wilhelm II from becoming involved in World War I.

• *As you head toward the palace, you'll find a statue of a monk grasping a sword nearby.*

Meet **François Grimaldi,** a renegade Italian dressed as a monk, who captured Monaco in 1297 and began the dynasty that still rules the principality. Prince Albert is his great-great-great... grandson, which gives Monaco's royal family the distinction of being the longest-lasting dynasty in Europe.

• *Now walk to the...*

Prince's Palace (Palais Princier)

A medieval castle sat where the palace is today. Its strategic setting has had a lot to do with Monaco's ability to resist attackers. Today, Prince Albert and his wife live in the palace, while poor Princesses Stephanie and Caroline live down the street. The palace guards protect the prince 24/7 and still stage a **Changing of the Guard** ceremony with all the pageantry of an important nation (daily at 11:55, fun to watch but jam-packed, arrive by 11:30). Audioguide

tours take you through part of the prince's lavish palace in 30 minutes. The rooms are well-furnished and impressive, but interesting only if you haven't seen a château lately.

Cost and Hours: €8, includes audioguide, €19 combo-ticket also covers Cousteau Aquarium; hours vary but generally April-Oct daily 10:00-18:00, closed Nov-March, last entry 30 minutes before closing; tel. 00-377/93 25 18 31.

• *Head to the west end of the palace square. Below the cannonballs is the district known as...*

Fontvieille

Monaco's newest, reclaimed-from-the-sea area has seen much of Monaco's post-WWII growth (residential and commercial—notice the lushly planted building tops). Prince Rainier continued—some say, was obsessed with—Monaco's economic growth, creating landfills (topped with apartments, such as in Fontvieille), flashy ports, more beaches, a big sports stadium marked by tall arches, and a rail station. (An ambitious new landfill project is in the works and would add still more prime real estate to Monaco's portfolio.) Today, thanks to Prince Rainier's past efforts, tiny Monaco is a member of the United Nations. (If you have kids with you, check out the nifty play area just below.)

• *With your back to the palace, leave the square through the arch near the white flag (under one elegant police station—where the guards come from during the Changing of the Guard) and find the...*

Cathedral of Monaco (Cathédrale de Monaco)

The somber but beautifully lit cathedral, rebuilt in 1878, shows that Monaco cared for more than just its new casino. It's where centuries

of Grimaldis are buried, and where Princess Grace and Prince Rainier were married. Inside, circle slowly behind the altar (counterclockwise). The second tomb is that of Albert I, who did much to put Monaco on the world stage. The second-to-last tomb—inscribed *"Gratia Patricia, MCMLXXXII"*—is where Princess Grace was buried in 1982. Prince Rainier's tomb lies next to Princess Grace's (daily 8:30-19:15).

• *As you leave the cathedral, find the 1956 wedding photo of Princess Grace and Prince Rainier, then dip into the immaculately maintained **Jardin Botanique**, with more fine views. In the gardens, turn left. Eventually you'll find the impressive building housing the...*

Cousteau Aquarium (Musée Océanographique)

Prince Albert I built this cliff-hanging aquarium in 1910 as a monument to his enthusiasm for things from the sea. The aquarium, which Jacques Cousteau captained for 32 years, has 2,000 different specimens, representing 250 species. You'll find Mediterranean fish and colorful tropical species (all well-described in English). Rotating exhibits occupy the entry floor. Upstairs, the fancy Albert I Hall houses a museum that's filled with ship models, whale skeletons, oceanographic instruments and tools, and scenes of Albert and his beachcombers hard at work—but sadly, only scant English information is provided here. Don't miss the elevator to the rooftop terrace view café.

Cost and Hours: €14, kids-€7, €19 combo-ticket includes Prince's Palace; daily April-Sept 10:00-19:00, July-Aug until 19:30, Oct-March 10:00-18:00; down the steps from Monaco-Ville bus stop, at the opposite end of Monaco-Ville from the palace; tel. 00-377/93 15 36 00, www.oceano.mc.

• *The red-brick steps across from the aquarium lead up to stops for buses #1 and #2, both of which run to the port, the casino, and the train station. To walk back to the palace and through the old city, turn left at the top of the brick steps. If you're into stamps, walk down Rue Emile de Loth to find the **post office**, where philatelists and postcard writers with panache can buy—or just gaze in awe at—the impressive collection of Monegasque stamps (Mon-Fri 8:00-19:00, Sat 8:00-13:00, closed Sun).*

Sights in Monaco

Jardin Exotique

This cliffside municipal garden, located above Monaco-Ville, has eye-popping views from France to Italy. It's home to more than a thousand species of cacti (some giant) and other succulent plants, but worth the entry only for view-loving botanists (some posted English explanations provided). Your ticket includes entry to a skippable natural cave, an anthropological museum, and a view snack bar/café. You can get similar views over Monaco for free from behind the souvenir stand at the Jardin's bus stop; or, for even grander vistas, cross the street and hike toward La Turbie.

Cost and Hours: €7.20, daily 9:00-19:00, Oct-April until about dusk, take bus #2 from any stop in Monaco, tel. 00-377/93 15 29 80, www.jardin-exotique.com.

▲Monte Carlo Casino (Casino de Monte-Carlo)

Monte Carlo, which means "Charles' Hill" in Spanish, is named for the prince who presided over Monaco's 19th-century makeover.

In the mid-1800s, olive groves stood here. Then, with the construction of casino and spas, and easy road and train access, one of Europe's poorest countries was on the Grand Tour map—*the* place for the vacationing aristocracy to play. Today, Monaco has the world's highest per-capita income.

The Monte Carlo casino is intended to make you feel comfortable while losing your retirement nest egg. Charles Garnier designed the place (with an opera house inside) in 1878, in part to thank the prince for his financial help in completing Paris' Opéra Garnier (which the architect also designed). The central doors provide access to slot machines, private gaming rooms,

Le Grand Prix Automobile de Monaco

The Grand Prix de Monaco focuses the world's attention on this little country. The race started as an enthusiasts' car rally

by the Automobile Club of Monaco (and is still run by the same group, more than 80 years later). The first race, held in 1929, was won by a Bugatti at a screaming average speed of...48 mph (today's cars double that speed). To this day, drivers consider this one of the most important races on their circuits. The race takes place every year toward the end of May (www.acm.mc).

By Grand Prix standards, it's an unusual course, running through the streets of this tiny principality, sardined between mountains and sea. The hilly landscape means that the streets are narrow, with tight curves, steep climbs, and extremely short straightaways. Each lap is about two miles, beginning and ending at the port. Cars climb along the sea from the port, pass in front of the casino, race through the commercial district, and do a few dandy turns back to the port. The race lasts 78 laps, and whoever is still rolling at the end wins (most don't finish).

The Formula 1 cars look like overgrown toys that kids might pedal up and down their neighborhood street (if you're here a week or so before the race, feel free to browse the parking structure below Monaco-Ville, where many race cars are kept). Time trials to establish pole position begin three days before the race, which is always on a Sunday. More than 150,000 people attend the gala event; like the nearby film festival in Cannes, it's an excuse for yacht parties, restaurant splurges, and four-digit bar tabs at luxury hotels. During this event, hotel rates in Nice and beyond rocket up (even for budget places).

and the opera house. The private gaming rooms occupy the left wing of the building.

Cost and Hours: Hours and entry fees are shuffled regularly. Plan on €10 to enter at any hour, whether you gamble or not. Public areas are open daily 9:00-12:30 (no gambling). Guided tours may be available, or take an English brochure and tour on your own. From 14:00 to very late the gaming rooms are open to appropriately attired humans over 18 (bring your passport as proof). Tel. 00-377/92 16 20 00, www.montecarlocasinos.com.

Dress Code: Before 14:00, shorts are allowed in the atrium

MONACO

area, though you'll need decent attire to go any farther. After 14:00, shorts are off-limits everywhere, and tennis shoes are not permitted. Men should wear a jacket and slacks, and women should dress appropriately.

Visiting the Casino: Count the counts and Rolls-Royces in front of Hôtel de Paris (built at the same time, visitors allowed in the hotel, no shorts, www.montecarloresort.com), then strut inside the casino to the sumptuous **atrium.** This is the lobby for the 520-seat opera house (open Nov-April only for performances). A model of the opera house is at the far right side of the room, near the marble WCs.

The **first rooms** (Salle Renaissance, Salon de l'Europe, and Salle des Amériques) have European and English roulette, black-jack, craps, and slot machines. The more glamorous **private game rooms** (Salons Touzet, Salle Medecin, and Terrasse Salle Blanche) have those same games, plus Trente et Quarante, Ultimate Texas Hold 'Em poker, and Punto Banco—a version of baccarat.

The scene, flooded with camera-toting tourists during the day, is great at night—and downright James Bond-like in the private rooms. This is your chance to rub elbows with some high rollers.

The **park** behind the casino offers a peaceful **café** with a good view of the building's rear facade and of Monaco-Ville.

Take the Money and Run: The stop for buses returning to Nice and Villefranche-sur-Mer and for local buses #1 and #2 is on Avenue de la Costa, at the top of the park above the casino (at the small shopping mall). To reach the train station from the casino, take bus #1 or #2 from this stop, or walk about 15 minutes down Avenue d'Ostende toward the port, and follow signs to *Gare SNCF*.

Sleeping in Monaco

$$ Hôtel de France** is centrally located, comfortable, well run by friendly Sylvie, and reasonably priced—for Monaco (Sb-€115, Db-about €135, Tb-about €160, all rooms with showers, includes breakfast, air-con, near west exit from train station at 6 Rue de la Turbie, tel. 00-377/93 30 24 64, www.monte-carlo.mc/france, hoteldefrance@monaco.mc).

Eating in Monaco

On the Port: Several cafés serve basic, inexpensive fare (day and night) on the port. Troll the places that line the flowery and traffic-free Rue de la Princesse Caroline between Rue Grimaldi and the port. **Huit et Demi** is a reliable choice, with a white-tablecloth-meets-director's-chair ambience and good outdoor seating (€15 pizzas and pastas, €18-26 *plats,* closed Sun, 7 Rue de la Princesse Caroline, tel. 00-377/93 50 97 02).

In Monaco-Ville: You'll find massive *pan bagnat,* quiche, and sandwiches at the yellow-bannered **Boulangerie,** a block off Place du Palais (open daily until 21:00, 8 Rue Basse). Try a *barbajuan* (a spring roll-size beignet with wheat, rice, and Parmesan), the *tourta de bléa* (pastry stuffed with pine nuts, raisins, and white beets), or the focaccia sandwich (salted bread with herbs, mozzarella, basil, and tomatoes, all drenched in olive oil). For dessert, order the *fougasse monégasque* (a soft-bread pastry topped with sliced almonds and anise candies).

U Cavagnetu provides good-value food in Monaco-Ville. You'll dine cheaply on specialties from Monaco just a block from Albert's palace (€13 pizzas and pastas, €27 *menu,* daily, 14 Rue Comte Félix Gastaldi, tel. 00-377/97 98 20 40). Monaco-Ville has other pizzerias, *crêperies,* and sandwich stands, but the neighborhood is dead at night.

Monaco Connections

BY TRAIN

For a comparison of train and bus connections, see the "Public Transportation in the French Riviera" sidebar on page 282. Most trains heading west will stop in Villefranche-sur-Mer and Nice (ask). Note that the last train leaves Monaco for Villefranche-sur-Mer and Nice at about 23:30. If you plan to leave Monaco by a late train (after 20:30, when ticket windows close), buy your tickets in advance or bring enough coins for the machines.

From Monaco by Train to: Villefranche-sur-Mer, Nice, Antibes, or **Cannes** (2/hour).

BY BUS

Bus #100, which runs along the Low Corniche back to **Nice** (3-4/hour, 45 minutes), is often crowded. To have a better chance of securing a seat, board it at the stop near the TI on Avenue de la Costa (see map on page 380) rather than the stop near Place d'Armes. Bus #100 also stops near **Cap Ferrat** (20 minutes plus 20-minute walk or transfer to bus #81) and in **Villefranche-sur-Mer** (25 minutes). The last bus leaves Monaco for Nice at about 20:00. In the other direction bus #100 goes to **Menton** (40 minutes).

Bus #112, which goes along the scenic Middle Corniche to **Eze-le-Village** (6/day Mon-Sat, none on Sun, 20 minutes), departs Monaco from Place de la Crémaillère, one block above the main TI and casino park. Walk up Rue Iris with Barclays Bank to your left, curve right, and find the bus shelter across the street at the green Costa à la Crémaillère café (bus number not posted).

Bus #11 to **La Turbie** (8/day Mon-Sat, 5/day Sun, 30 minutes) stops just past the TI (same side of street).

Bus #110 express takes the freeway to **Nice Airport** (2/hour, 50 minutes, €20).

BY CRUISE SHIP

Cruise ships tender passengers to the end of Monaco's yacht harbor, a short walk from downtown. It's a long walk or a short bus ride to most sights in town. To reach other towns, such as Villefrance-sur-Mer or Nice, you can take public transportation. To summon a taxi (assuming none are waiting when you disembark), look for the gray taxi call box near the tender dock—just press the button and wait for your cab to arrive.

Getting into Town: To reach **Monaco-Ville,** which towers high over the cruise terminal, you can either hike steeply and scenically up to the top of the hill, or walk to Place d'Armes and hop on bus #1 or #2, which will take you up top sweat-free. It's a 10-minute, level walk to the bus stop from the port: Cross Boulevard Albert I, follow green *Gare S.N.C.F./Ferroviare* signs, and take the public elevator to Place d'Armes.

The ritzy skyscraper zone of **Monte Carlo** is across the harbor from the tender dock, about a 25-minute walk. You can also ride the little electric "bateau bus" shuttle boat across the mouth of the harbor (small fee). To reach the upper part of Monte Carlo—with the TI and handy bus stops (including for Eze-le-Village and La Turbie)—catch bus #1 or #2 at the top of the yacht harbor, along Boulevard Albert I.

Getting to Sights Beyond Monaco: Monaco is connected to most nearby sights by both train and bus. **Trains** run about twice hourly to Villefranche-sur-Mer (10 minutes), then on to Nice (20 minutes). The train station is about a 20-minute walk from the tender harbor—first walk to Place d'Armes (directions above), then follow Rue Grimaldi to find stairs and an elevator to the station.

Buses run regularly to nearby towns (see "By Bus," earlier, for bus stop locations and frequencies). If taking bus #112 to Eze-le-Village or bus #11 to La Turbie, first ride bus #1 or #2 to the TI and casino, then follow the directions above.

Menton

If you wish the Riviera were less glitzy and more like a place where humble locals take their families to lick ice cream and make sand castles, visit Menton (east of Monaco). Menton feels like a poor man's Nice. It's unrefined and unpretentious, with lower prices, fewer rentable umbrellas, and lots of Italians day-tripping in from just over the border (five miles away). There's not an American in sight.

Though a bit rough, the Menton beach is a joy. An inviting promenade lines the beach, and seaside cafés serve light meals and salads (much cheaper than in Nice). A snooze or stroll here is a fine Riviera experience. From the promenade, a pedestrian street leads through town. Small squares are alive with jazz bands playing crowd-pleasers under palm trees.

Stepping into the old town—which blankets a hill capped by a fascinating cemetery—you're immersed in a pastel-painted, yet dark and tangled Old World scene with (strangely) almost no commerce. A few elegant restaurants dig in at the base of the towering centuries-old apartment flats. The richly decorated Baroque St. Michael's Church (midway up the hill, Mon-Fri 10:00-12:00 & 15:00-17:15, closed to visitors Sat-Sun) is a reminder that, until 1860, Menton was a thriving part of the larger state of Monaco. Climbing past sun-grabbing flower boxes and people who don't get out much anymore, the steep stepped lanes finally deposit you at the ornate gate of a grand cemetery that fills the old castle walls. Explore the cemetery, which is the final resting place of many aristocratic Russians (buried here in the early 1900s) and offers breathtaking Mediterranean views.

Getting to Menton: While trains serve Menton regularly, the station is a 15-minute walk from the action. Buses are more convenient, as they drop visitors right on the beach promenade (#100, 3-4/hour, 1.5 hours from Nice, 40 minutes from Monaco). To return to Monaco or Nice, catch bus #100 on Avenue Thiers, just off Avenue de Verdun.

MONACO

ANTIBES, CANNES & ST-TROPEZ

The Riviera opens up west of Nice with bigger, sandier beaches and an overabundance of tasteless beachfront development. Ancient Antibes and superficial Cannes buck the slap-it-up high-rise trend, both with thriving centers busy with pedestrians and yachts. Glamorous St-Tropez, a scenic 1.5-hour drive from Antibes, marks the western edge of the French Riviera.

Antibes

Antibes has a down-to-earth, easygoing ambience. Its old town is a warren of narrow streets and red-tile roofs rising above the blue Med, protected by twin medieval towers and wrapped in extensive ramparts. Visitors making the short trip from Nice can browse Europe's biggest yacht harbor, snooze on a sandy beach, loiter through an enjoyable old town, and hike along a sea-swept trail. The town's cultural claim to fame, the Picasso Museum (closed on Mondays), shows off its appealing collection in a fine old building.

Though much smaller than Nice, Antibes has a history that dates back just as far. Both towns were founded by Greek traders in the fifth century B.C. To the Greeks, Antibes was "Antipolis"—the town *(polis)* opposite *(anti)* Nice. For the next several centuries, Antibes remained in the shadow of its neighbor. By the turn of the 20th century, the town was a military base—so the rich and famous partied elsewhere. But when the army checked out after World War I, Antibes was "discovered" and enjoyed a particularly roaring '20s—with the help of party animals like Rudolph Valentino and the rowdy (yet silent) Charlie Chaplin. Fun seekers even invented water-skiing right here in the 1920s.

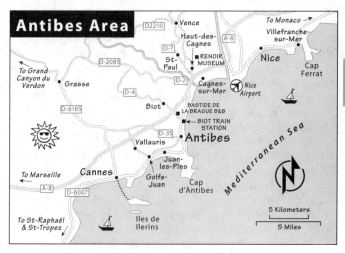

Orientation to Antibes

Antibes' old town lies between the port and Boulevard Albert I and Avenue Robert Soleau. Place Nationale is the old town's hub of

activity. Stroll above the sea between the old port and Place Albert I (where Boulevard Albert I meets the water). The best beaches lie just beyond Place Albert I, and the walk is beautiful. Good play areas for children are along this path and on Place des Martyrs de la Résistance (close to recommended Hôtel Relais du Postillon).

TOURIST INFORMATION
The TI is a few blocks from the train station at 42 Avenue Robert Soleau (July-Aug daily 9:00-19:00; Sept-June Mon-Fri 9:00-12:30 & 13:30-18:00, Sat 9:00-12:00 & 14:00-18:00, Sun 9:00-13:00; tel. 04 22 10 60 10, www.antibesjuanlespins.com). Free Wi-Fi is available here.

ARRIVAL IN ANTIBES
By Train: Bus #14 runs frequently from the train station to the *gare routière* (bus station; near several recommended hotels and the old town), and continues to the fine Plage de la Salis, with quick access to the Phare de la Garoupe trail (2/hour, none on Sun, bus stop 100 yards to right as you exit train station). **Taxis** usually wait in front of the station.

To **walk** to the port, the old town, and the Picasso Museum

(15 minutes), cross the street in front of the station, skirting left of the café, and follow Avenue de la Libération downhill as it bends left. At the end of the street, head right along the port. If you walk on the water's edge, you'll see the yachts get bigger as you go. To walk directly to the TI and recommended hotels in the old town, turn right out of the station and walk down Avenue Robert Soleau.

There's no baggage check at the station. The last train back to Nice leaves at about midnight.

By Bus: Regional buses (including airport bus #250) stop at the long bus platform behind the train station (called the *Pôle d'Echange*, bus info office). Take the pedestrian overpass from behind the train station. City buses use the bus station at the edge of the old town on Place Guynemer, a block below Place Général de Gaulle (info desk open Mon-Fri 7:30-19:00, Sat 8:30-12:00 & 14:30-17:30, closed Sun, www.envibus.fr).

By Car: Day-trippers follow signs to *Centre-Ville*, then *Port Vauban*. The easiest place to park is a convenient but pricey underground parking lot located outside the ramparts near the archway leading into the old town (€9/4 hours, €20/12 hours, see map on page 396). A free lot is available opposite Fort Carré (north of the port). It's a 15-minute walk to the old town from here; you can also catch bus #14. Street parking is free Monday through Saturday (12:00-14:00 & 19:00-8:00), and all day Sunday.

If you're sleeping here, follow *Centre-Ville* signs, then signs to your hotel. The most appealing hotels in Antibes are best by car, and Antibes works well for drivers—compared with Nice, parking is easy, traffic is minimal, and it's a convenient springboard for the Inland Riviera. Pay parking is available at Antibes' train station, so drivers can ditch their cars here and day-trip from Antibes by train.

HELPFUL HINTS

Markets: Antibes' old-time market hall (Marché Provençal) hosts a vibrant produce market (daily until 13:30, closed Mon Sept-May), and a lively antiques/flea market fills Place Nationale and Place Audiberti, next to the port (Thu and Sat 7:00-18:00). A clothing market winds through the streets around the post office on Rue Lacan (Thu 9:00-18:00).

English Bookstore: Antibes Books has a welcoming vibe and a good selection of new and used books, with many guide-books—including mine (Tue-Sat 10:00-19:00, Sun-Mon 11:00-18:00, 13 Rue Georges Clemenceau, tel. 04 93 34 74 11, www.antibesbooks.com).

Laundry: There's a launderette at 19 Avenue du Grand Cavalier (daily 8:00-20:45).

Taxi: For a taxi, call tel. 04 93 67 67 67.

Car Rental: The big-name agencies have offices in Antibes (all close Mon-Sat 12:00-14:00 and all day Sun). The most central are **Avis** (at the train station, tel. 04 93 34 65 15) and **Hertz** (across from the train station at 52 Avenue Robert Soleau, tel. 04 92 91 28 00).

Bike Rental: The TI has a list of places where you can rent bikes (including electric bikes). A bike path leads along the sea toward Nice, and bikes are a good way for nondrivers to reach the hikes described later in this chapter.

Boat Rental: You can motor your own seven-person yacht thanks to **Antibes Bateaux Services** (€100/half-day, at the small fish market on the port, mobile 06 15 75 44 36, www.antibes-bateaux.com).

GETTING AROUND ANTIBES

Antibes' buses (Envibus) cost €1 and are handiest for carless travelers wanting access to Cap d'Antibes. **Bus #14** links the train station, bus station, old town, and Plage de la Salis. It also takes you to Fort Carré, where free parking is available. **Bus #2** provides access to the best beaches, the path to La Phare de la Garoupe, and the Cap d'Antibes trail. It runs from the bus station down Boulevard Albert I (daily 7:00-19:00, every 40 minutes). Pick up a schedule at the bus station.

A **tourist train** offers 40-minute circuits around old Antibes, the port, the ramparts, and to Juan-les-Pins (€8, departs from pedestrian-only Rue de la République, mobile 06 15 77 67 47).

Antibes Walk

This 40-minute self-guided walk will help you get your bearings, and works well day or night.

• *Begin at the old port (Vieux Port) at the southern end of Avenue de Verdun. Stand at the port, across from the archway with the clock.*

Old Port: Locals claim that this is Europe's first and biggest pleasure-boat harbor, with 1,600 stalls. That star-shaped stone

structure crowning the opposite end of the port is **Fort Carré,** which protected Antibes from foreigners for more than 500 years.

The pathetic remains of a once-hearty **fishing fleet** are moored in front of you. The Mediterranean is pretty much fished out. Most of the seafood you'll eat here comes from fish farms or the Atlantic.

• *With the port on your left, pass the sorry fleet and duck under the arches to the shell-shaped...*

Antibes

1 Hôtel Pension le Mas Djoliba
2 To Hôtels la Jabotte & Beau-Site
3 To Bastide de la Brague
4 Hôtel la Place
5 Hôtel Relais du Postillon
6 Modern Hôtel
7 Chez Lulu
8 La Marmite Restaurant
9 L'Aubergine Restaurant
10 Le Broc en Bouche Restaurant
11 Le Vauban Restaurant
12 Le Brulot & Le Brulot Pasta and Pizza
13 L'Épicerie du Marché Grocery
14 Monoprix
15 Launderette
16 Avis Car Rental
17 Hertz Car Rental
18 Boat Rental

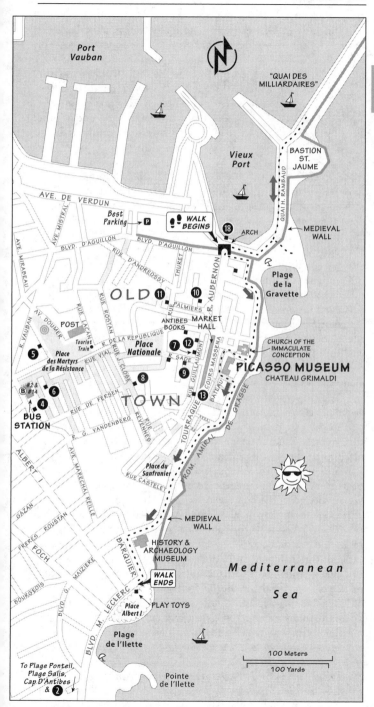

Plage de la Gravette: This normally quiet public beach is tucked right in the middle of old Antibes. Consider the scale of the ramparts that protected this town. Because Antibes was the last fort before the Italian border, the French king made sure the ramparts were top-notch. The twin towers crowning the old town are the church's bell tower and the tower topping Château Grimaldi (today's Picasso Museum). As you face the old town, forested Cap d'Antibes is the point of land in the distance to the left. Is anyone swimming? Locals don't swim much in July and August because of jellyfish—common now in warmer water. Throughout the Mediterranean, you'll see red flags warning of dangerous storms or tides. Many beaches now also have white flags with jellyfish symbols warning that swimming might be a stinging experience.

• *For a close-up look at the megayachts and a walk along the ramparts, follow this fun detour. Otherwise, skip ahead to the "Market Hall" stop.*

Antibes' Megayacht Harbor: For a glimpse at the epitome of conspicuous consumption, take a three-block detour to the right as you leave Plage de la Gravette. You'll walk along the harbor under the ramparts; enjoy the historic drawings and photos of the port along the wall.

You'll eventually reach a restricted area harboring massive yachts. Walk in and browse the line of huge pleasure craft stern-tied to the pier (which was built in the 1970s with financial aid from mostly Saudi Arabian yacht owners, who wanted a decent place to tie up). Locals call this the *Quai des Milliardaires* ("billionaire's dock"). The Union Jacks fluttering above most of the boats show that they're registered in the Cayman Islands (can you say tax dodge?). The crews you see keep these toys shipshape all year long—even though many of them are used for just a few days a year. Today, Antibes is the haunt of a large community of English, Irish, and Aussie boaters who help crew these giant yachts. (That explains the Irish pubs and English bookstores.)

Just outside the restricted area, climb up the rampart and make your way to the **modern white sculpture.** *Nomade*—a man of letters looking pensively out to sea—was created in 2010 by the Spaniard Jaume Plensa. You can sit in it and ponder how communication forms who we are and links all people.

• *Now let's backtrack to where we started and enter Antibes' old town through the arch under the clock. You can walk directly up the main street to get to our next stop, but here's a more scenic option: Passing through the gate, turn immediately left, walk along the wall and then up the stairs. At the terrace corner is another fine viewpoint. Turn right and walk straight through the arch at #14 and into Place du Revely, the most picturesque corner of the old town. Cross Place du Revely, turn right, and go downhill through another arch. Continue down the ramp and uphill straight into the old town and Antibes' market hall, Le Marché Provençal.*

Market Hall: Antibes' market hall bustles under a 19th-century canopy, with flowers, produce, Provençal products, and

beach accessories. The market wears many hats: produce until 13:30 (daily but closed Mon Sept-May), handicrafts most afternoons (Thu-Sun), and fun outdoor dining in the evenings, on Cours Masséna.

On the right (at the corner of Rue Sade), a pretty shop hides an atmospheric **absinthe bar** in its cellar. You're welcome to go through the shop (or enter via Rue Sade) and descend.

• Facing the front of the market, go left uphill on Rue Christian Chessel and find the pretty pastel...

Church of the Immaculate Conception: Built on the site of a Greek temple, this is worth a peek inside. A church has stood on this site since the 12th century. This one served as the area's cathedral until the mid-1200s. The stone bell tower standing in front of the church predates it by 600 years, when it was part of the city's defenses. Many of those heavy stones were pillaged from Antibes' Roman monuments.

• Looming above the church on prime real estate is the white-stone...

Château Grimaldi: This site was home to the acropolis of the Greek city of Antipolis and later a Roman fort. Later still, the château was the residence of the Grimaldi family (a branch of which still rules Monaco). Today it houses Antibes' Picasso Museum. Its proximity to the cathedral symbolized the sometimes too-cozy relationship between society's two dominant landowning classes: the Church and the nobility. (In 1789, the French Revolution changed all that.)

*• After visiting the **Picasso Museum** (see page 400), exit it to the left. Work your way through the warren of pretty lanes, then head out to the water, turn right along the ramparts, and find a sweeping sea view. As you walk, you'll pass a charming neighborhood (La Commune Libre du Safranier) on your right. The rampart walk leads to a viewpoint atop the History and Archaeology Museum.*

Viewpoint: From this perch you can enjoy a clear view of **Cap d'Antibes** (to the south), crowned by its lighthouse and studded with mansions (a proposed hike here is described later). The Cap was long the refuge of Antibes' rich and famous, and a favorite haunt of F. Scott Fitzgerald and Ernest Hemingway.

• *After taking a quick spin through the* **History and Archaeology Museum** *(see page 401), continue hugging the shore past Place Albert I until you see the views back to old Antibes. Benches and soft sand await (a few copies of famous artists' paintings of Antibes are placed on bronze displays along the beach walkway). You're on your own from here—energetic walkers can continue on the trail, which leads all the way to Cap d'Antibes (see page 404); others can return to old Antibes and wander around in its peaceful back lanes.*

Sights in Antibes

▲▲Picasso Museum (Musée Picasso)

Sitting serenely where the old town meets the sea, this compact three-floor museum offers a manageable collection of Picasso's paintings, sketches, and ceramics.

Picasso lived in this castle for four months in 1946, when he cranked out an amazing amount of art (most of the paintings you'll see are from this short but prolific stretch of his long and varied career). He was elated by the end of World War II, and his works show a celebration of color and a rediscovery of light after France's long nightmare of war. Picasso was also re-energized by his young and lovely companion, Françoise Gilot (with whom he would father two children). The resulting collection (donated by Picasso) put Antibes on the tourist map. For more on Picasso's life, see the sidebar on page 402.

Cost and Hours: €6; mid-June-mid-Sept Tue-Sun 10:00-18:00, July-Aug Wed and Fri until 20:00; mid-Sept-mid-June Tue-Sun 10:00-12:00 & 14:00-18:00, closed Mon year-round, tel. 04 92 90 54 20, www.antibes-juanlespins.com.

Visiting the Museum: After buying your ticket, go through the glass door. Before heading inside, pause in the **sculpture garden** to appreciate Picasso's working environment (and wonder why he spent only four months here).

The museum's interior is a calm place of white walls, soft arches, and ample natural light—a great space for exhibiting art. The **ground floor** houses temporary exhibits of other artists' work.

The museum's highlight is on the **top floor,** where you'll find the permanent collection of Picasso's works. Visitors are greeted by a large image of Picasso and a display of photographs of the artist at work and play during his time in Antibes. Times were tough in

1946. Artists had to improvise. Picasso experimented with materials and surfaces like industrial paint on recycled canvases, random pieces of plywood, and even concrete. Try not to analyze too much. He's happy and in the French Riviera. Remember: The war's over and he's in love—this is pure happiness.

Tour the floor clockwise, noticing the focus on sea creatures, tridents, and other marine themes (*oursin* is a sea urchin, *poulpe* is an octopus, and *poisson* is, well, fishy). *Nature morte* means still life, and you'll see many of these in this collection.

The first gallery room (up the small staircase to your left) houses several famous works, including the lively, frolicking, and big-breasted *La Joie de Vivre* painting (from 1946). This Greek bacchanal sums up the newfound freedom in a just-liberated France and sets the tone for the rest of the collection. You'll also see the colorless, three-paneled *Satyr, Faun and Centaur with Trident* and several ceramic creations.

As you tour the museum, you'll see both black-and-white and colorful ink sketches that challenge the imagination—these show off Picasso's skill as a cartoonist and caricaturist. Look also for the Basque fishermen and several Cubist-style nudes *(nus couchés)*, one painted on plywood.

Near the end, don't miss the wall devoted to his ceramic plates. In 1947, inspired by a visit to a ceramics factory in nearby Vallauris, Picasso discovered the joy of this medium. He was smitten by the texture of soft clay and devoted a great deal of time to exploring how to work with it—producing over 2,000 pieces in one year. In the same room, the wall-sized painting *Ulysses and the Sirens* screams action and anxiety. Lashed to the ship mast, Ulysses survives the temptation of the sirens.

History and Archaeology Museum (Musée d'Histoire et d'Archéologie)

More than 2,000 years ago, Antibes was the center of a thriving maritime culture. It was an important Roman city with aqueducts, theaters, baths, and so on. This museum—the only place to get a sense of the city's ancient roots—displays Greek, Roman, and Etruscan odds and ends in two simple halls (no English descriptions). Your visit starts at an 1894 model of Antibes and continues past displays of Roman coins, cups, plates, and scads of amphorae. The lanky lead pipe connected to a center box was used as a bilge pump; nearby is a good display of Roman anchors made of lead.

Cost and Hours: €3; mid-June-mid-Sept Tue-Sun 10:00-12:00 & 14:00-18:00, mid-Sept-mid-June Tue-Sun 10:00-13:00 & 14:00-17:00, closed Mon year-round; on the water between Picasso Museum and Place Albert I, tel. 04 92 90 54 37, www.antibes-juanlespins.com.

Pablo Picasso (1881-1973)

Pablo Picasso was the most famous and, for me, the greatest artist of the 20th century. Always exploring, he became the master of many styles (Cubism, Surrealism, Expressionism, and so on) and of many media (painting, sculpture, prints, ceramics, and assemblages). Still, he could make anything he touched look unmistakably like "a Picasso."

Born in Málaga, Spain, Picasso was the son of an art teacher. At a very young age, he quickly advanced beyond his teachers. Picasso's teenage works are stunningly realistic and capture the inner complexities of the people he painted. As a youth in Barcelona, he fell in with a bohemian crowd that mixed wine, women, and art.

In 1900, at age 19, Picasso started making trips to Paris. Four years later, he moved to the City of Light and absorbed the styles of many painters (especially Henri de Toulouse-Lautrec) while searching for his own artist's voice. His paintings of beggars and other social outcasts show the empathy of a man who was himself a poor, homesick foreigner. When his best friend, Spanish artist Carlos Casagemas, committed suicide, Picasso plunged into a **Blue Period** (1901-1904)—so called because the dominant color in these paintings matches their melancholy mood and subject matter (emaciated beggars, hard-eyed pimps, and so on).

In 1904, Picasso got a steady girlfriend (Fernande Olivier) and suddenly saw the world through rose-colored glasses—the **Rose Period.** He was further jolted out of his Blue Period by the "flat" look of the Fauves. Not satisfied with their take on 3-D, Picasso played with the "building blocks" of line and color to find new ways to reconstruct the real world on canvas.

At his studio in Montmartre, Picasso and his neighbor Georges Braque worked together, in poverty so dire they often didn't know where their next bottle of wine was coming from. And then, at the age of 25, Picasso reinvented painting. Fascinated by the primitive power of African and Iberian tribal masks, he sketched human faces with simple outlines and almond eyes. Intrigued by the body of his girlfriend, Fernande, he sketched it from every angle, then experimented with showing several different views on the same canvas. A hundred paintings and nine months later, Picasso gave birth to a monstrous canvas of five nude, fragmented prostitutes with masklike faces—*Les Demoiselles d'Avignon* (1907).

This bold new style was called **Cubism.** With Cubism, Picasso shattered the Old World and put it back together in a new way. The subjects are somewhat recognizable (with the help of the titles), but they're built with geometric shards (let's call them "cubes")—like viewing the world through a kaleidoscope of brown and gray. Cubism gives us several different angles of the subject at once—say, a woman seen from the front and side angles simultaneously, resulting in two eyes on the same side of the nose. This involves showing the traditional three dimensions, plus Einstein's new fourth dimension—the time it takes to walk around the subject to see other angles.

In 1918, Picasso married his first wife, Olga Kokhlova, with whom he had a son. He then traveled to Rome and entered a **Classical Period** (the 1920s) of more realistic, full-bodied women and children, inspired by the three-dimensional sturdiness of ancient statues. While he flirted with abstraction, throughout his life Picasso always kept a grip on "reality." His favorite subject was people. The anatomy might be jumbled, but it's all there.

Though he lived in France and Italy, Picasso remained a Spaniard at heart, incorporating Spanish motifs into his work. Unrepentantly macho, he loved bullfights, seeing them as a metaphor for the timeless human interaction between the genders. The horse—clad with blinders and pummeled by the bull—has nothing to do with the fight. To Picasso, the horse symbolizes the feminine, and the bull, the masculine. Spanish imagery—bulls, screaming horses, a Madonna—appears in Picasso's most famous work, *Guernica* (1937, on display in Madrid). The monumental canvas of a bombed village summed up the pain of Spain's brutal civil war (1936-1939) and foreshadowed the onslaught of World War II.

At war's end, Picasso left Paris, his wife, and all of his emotional baggage behind, finding fun in the sun in the **south of France.** Sun! Color! Water! Spacious skies! Freedom! Senior citizen Pablo Picasso was reborn, enjoying worldwide fame. He lived at first with the beautiful young painter Françoise Gilot, mother of two of his children, but soon replaced her with another young beauty, Jacqueline Roque, who became his second wife. Dressed in rolled-up white pants and a striped sailor's shirt, bursting with pent-up creativity, Picasso often cranked out a painting a day. Picasso's Riviera works set the tone for the rest of his life—sunny, lighthearted, childlike, experimenting in new media and using motifs of the sea, of Greek mythology (fauns, centaurs), and animals (birds, goats, and pregnant baboons). His simple drawing of doves became an international symbol of peace.

Picasso also made collages, built "statues" out of wood, wire, ceramics, papier-mâché, or whatever, and even turned everyday household objects into statues (like his famous bull's head made of a bicycle seat with handlebar horns). **Multimedia** works like these have become so standard today that we forget how revolutionary they were when Picasso invented them. His last works have the playfulness of someone much younger. As it is often said of Picasso, "When he was a child, he painted like a man. When he was old, he painted like a child."

Fort Carré

This impressively situated, mid-16th-century citadel, on the headland overlooking the harbor, protected Antibes from Nice (which until 1860 wasn't part of France). You can tour this unusual star-shaped fort (€3) for the fantastic views over Antibes, but there's little to see inside.

▲Beaches *(Plages)*

Good beaches stretch from the south end of Antibes toward Cap d'Antibes. They're busy but manageable in summer and on weekends, with cheap snack stands and good views of the old town. The closest beach to the old town is at the port (Plage de la Gravette), which seems calm in any season.

HIKES

I list two good hikes below. Where Boulevard Albert I meets the beach (at Place Albert I), you get a good view of Plage de la Salis and Cap d'Antibes. That tower on the hill is your destination for the first hike. The longer Cap d'Antibes hike begins on the next beach, just over that hill. The two hikes are easy to combine by bus, bike, or car.

▲▲Chapelle et Phare de la Garoupe Hike

The territorial views—best in the morning, skippable if it's hazy—from this viewpoint more than merit the 20-minute uphill climb from Plage de la Salis (a few blocks after Maupassant Apartments, where the road curves left, follow signs and the rough, cobbled Chemin du Calvaire up to lighthouse tower). An orientation table explains that you can see from Nice to Cannes and up to the Alps.

Getting There: Take bus #2 or bus #14 to the Plage de la Salis stop and find the trail a block ahead. By car or bike, follow signs for *Cap d'Antibes*, then look for *Chapelle et Phare de la Garoupe* signs.

▲▲Cap d'Antibes Hike (Sentier Touristique de Tirepoil)

Cap d'Antibes itself is filled with exclusive villas and mansions protected by high walls. Roads are just lanes, bounded on both sides by the high and greedy walls in this home of some of the most expensive real estate in France (and where "public" seems like a necessary evil). But all the money in the world can't buy you the beach in France, so a thin strip of rocky coastline forms a two-mile long, park-like zone with an extremely scenic, mostly paved but often rocky trail (Sentier Touristique de Tirepoil).

As you walk, you'll have fancy fences with security cameras on one side and dramatic sea views on the other. The public space is rarely more than 50 yards wide and often extremely rocky—impassible if not for the paved trail carved out of it for the delight of hikers.

At a fast clip you can walk the entire circle in just over an hour. Don't do the hike without the tourist map (available at hotels or the TI). While you can do it in either direction (or in partial segments), I'd do the entire loop counterclockwise like this:

From the La Fontaine bus stop (see "Getting There," below), walk five minutes down Avenue Mrs. L. D. Beaumont to the gate of the Villa Eilenroc. From here leave the road and enter a trail, skirting the villa on your left, and walk five more minutes to the rocky coastal trail. Now turn left and follow the trail for nearly an hour around Cap Gros. There's no way to get lost without jumping into the sea or scaling villa security walls. You return to civilization at a tiny resort (Plage de la Garoupe), with an expensive restaurant, a fine beach (both public and private), and a fun and inexpensive beachside bar/restaurant. From here it's a 10-minute walk uphill to your starting point and the bus stop. With a car (or bike), you could start and end at Plage de la Garoupe. For a shorter version, walk from Plage de la Garoupe to Cap Gros and back.

Getting There: Ride bus #2 from Antibes for about 15 minutes to the La Fontaine stop at Rond-Point A. Meiland (next to the recommended Hôtel Beau-Site). By car or bike, follow signs to *Cap d'Antibes*, then to *Plage de la Garoupe*, and park there. The trail begins at the far-right end of Plage de la Garoupe.

NEAR ANTIBES
Juan-les-Pins Town

The low-rise town of Juan-les-Pins, sprawling across the Cap d'Antibes isthmus from Antibes, is where the action is...after hours. It's a modern waterfront resort with good beaches, plenty of lively bars and restaurants, and a popular jazz festival in July. The town is also known for its clothing boutiques that stay open until midnight (people are too busy getting tanned to shop at normal hours). As locals say, "Party, sleep in, shop late, party more."

Getting There: Buses, trains, and even a tourist train (see "Getting Around Antibes" on page 395) make the 10-minute trip to and from Antibes constantly.

Marineland and Parc de la Mer

Parc de la Mer is a world of waterslides, miniature golf, exhibits, and more. Marineland anchors this sea-park extravaganza with French-language shows featuring dolphins, sea lions, and killer whales.

Cost and Hours: Marineland only-€40, kids-€32; with Aquasplash waterslide park-€56, kids-€44; daily 10:00-19:00, July-Aug until 23:00, closed in winter; tel. 04 93 33 49 49, www.marineland.fr.

Getting There: The park is walkable from the train station in nearby Biot (5 minutes from Antibes) and about 15 minutes from Antibes' bus station on buses #200 or #7. By car, the park is signed from RN-7, several miles from Antibes toward Nice.

Renoir Museum (Musée Renoir)

Halfway between Antibes and Nice, above Cagnes-sur-Mer, Pierre-Auguste Renoir found his Giverny. Here, the artist spent the last 12 years of his life (1907-1919) tending his gardens, painting, and even dabbling in sculpture (despite suffering from rheumatoid arthritis). His home was later converted into a small museum. Visitors to the museum get a personal look into Renoir's later years. You'll see his studio, wheelchair, and bedroom; take a stroll in his gardens; and enjoy several of his and other artists' paintings of people and places around Cagnes-sur-Mer. It's a pleasant place and enjoyable for his fans.

Cost and Hours: €4, Wed-Mon 10:00-12:00 & 14:00-18:00, Oct-April until 17:00, closed Tue year-round, Chemin des Collettes, tel. 04 93 20 61 07.

Getting There: It's complicated by public transport (and not worth the trouble for most), but manageable by car: Go to Cagnes-sur-Mer, then follow brown *Musée Renoir* signs.

Biot Village

The artsy pottery and glassblowing village of Biot is home to the Fernand Léger Museum as well as Parc de la Mer (listed earlier).

Getting There: Biot is easy to reach on bus #10 from Antibes' bus station (2/hour). The best parking is just above the town, allowing direct access to its pretty pedestrian street.

Sleep Code

Abbreviations   (€1=about $1.10, country code: 33)
S=Single, **D**=Double/Twin, **T**=Triple, **Q**=Quad, **b**=bathroom,
*=French hotel rating (0-5 stars)
Price Rankings
$$$ **Higher Priced**—Most rooms €140 or more
$$ **Moderately Priced**—Most rooms €100-140
$ **Lower Priced**—Most rooms €100 or less
Unless otherwise noted, credit cards are accepted, elevators
and air-conditioning are available, free Wi-Fi and/or a guest
computer is generally provided, and English is spoken. Prices
change; verify current rates online or by email. For the best
prices, always book directly with the hotel.

Sleeping in Antibes

Several sleepable options are available in the town center, but my
favorite Antibes hotels are farther out and most convenient for
drivers.

OUTSIDE THE TOWN CENTER

$$$ Hôtel Pension le Mas Djoliba* is a traditional manor house
with chirping birds and a flower-filled moat. While convenient for
drivers, it's workable for walkers (10-minute walk to Plage de la
Salis, 15 minutes to old Antibes). The bigger rooms are worth the
additional cost, and several rooms come with small decks (Db-
€145-190 depending on size, several good family rooms-€280,
breakfast-€14, no elevator but just three floors, *boules* court and
loaner balls; 29 Avenue de Provence—from Boulevard Albert I,
look for gray signs two blocks before the sea, turn right onto Boule-
vard Général Maizière, and follow signs; tel. 04 93 34 02 48, www.
hotel-djoliba.com, contact@hotel-djoliba.com, Delphine).

$$$ Hôtel la Jabotte is a cozy boutique hotel hidden along
an ignored alley a block from the famous beaches and a 15-minute
walk from the old town. Run with panache by Nathalie, the hotel's
rich colors and decor show a personal touch. The cozy rooms have
tight bathrooms and individual terraces facing a small, central garden where you'll get to know your neighbor (Db-€155, Db suite-
€200, Rick Steves readers get a free breakfast and a free parking
spot if available, 13 Avenue Max Maurey, take the third right after
passing Hôtel Josse, tel. 04 93 61 45 89, www.jabotte.com, info@
jabotte.com).

$$ Hôtel Beau-Site*, my only listing on Cap d'Antibes, is
a 10-minute drive from town. It's a terrific value if you want to
get away...but not *too* far away. (Without a car, you'll feel isolated.)

Helpful Nathalie and Francine welcome you with a pool, a comfy patio garden, and free, secure parking. Rooms are spacious and comfortable, and several have balconies (standard Db-€95, bigger Db-€120-180, junior suites-€240; extra bed-€25, breakfast extra, electric bikes available, 141 Boulevard Kennedy, tel. 04 93 61 53 43, www.hotelbeausite.net, info@hotelbeausite.net). The hotel is a 10-minute walk from Plage de la Garoupe on the Cap d'Antibes loop hike (described earlier).

$ **Bastide de la Brague** is an easygoing bed-and-breakfast hacienda up a dirt road a 10-minute drive east of Antibes. The fun-loving family (wife Isabelle, who speaks English, and hubby Franck) rent seven comfy rooms; several are ideal for families. For a down-home experience, ask about a home-cooked dinner (Db-€88-110, Tb/Qb-€117-135, includes breakfast, 10 percent less for Rick Steves readers who book directly with the hotel, 55 Avenue No. 6, tel. 04 93 65 73 78, www.labastidedelabrague.com, bastidebb06@gmail.com). From Antibes, follow *Nice par Bord de la Mer* signs, turn left toward Marineland, then right at the roundabout (toward Groules), then follow the green signs. Antibes bus #10 drops you five minutes away, and if arranged in advance, they can pick you up at the Biot train station.

IN THE TOWN CENTER

$$$ **Hôtel la Place***** is central, pricey, and cozy. It overlooks the ugly bus station with tastefully designed rooms and a comfy lounge (Db-€140-180, no elevator, 1 Avenue 24 Août, tel. 04 97 21 03 11, www.la-place-hotel.com, contact@la-place-hotel.com).

$ **Hôtel Relais du Postillon****, with cute rooms at good rates, is a mellow place above a peaceful café on a central square. There are a few cheap true singles and 13 tastefully decorated doubles, some with small balconies, and some with good terraces (Sb-€65-85, Db-€85-100, larger Db-€130-150, 8 Rue Championnet, tel. 04 93 34 20 77, www.relaisdupostillon.com, relais@relaisdupostillon.com).

$ **Modern Hôtel****, in the pedestrian zone behind the bus station, is suitable for budget-conscious travelers. The 17 standard-size rooms are simple and spick-and-span (Db-€75-85, breakfast-€7, 1 Rue Fourmillière, tel. 04 92 90 59 05, www.modernhotel06.com, modern-hotel@wanadoo.fr).

Eating in Antibes

Antibes is a fun place to dine out. With so many good options, all within a few blocks of each other, I'd take a walk and survey these places for yourself.

Antibes' market hall (Marché Provençal) is chockablock

with diners each evening after the market stalls close. The food can be good, prices are usually reasonable, and sucking snails under a classic 19th-century canopy can make for a great memory. If considering dinner here, remember that tourists generally eat early while the locals dine late.

Chez Lulu is a fun family dining adventure that seems out of place on the Riviera. Diners fork over €25, and owner Greg (who speaks good English) does the rest, dishing out charcuterie, salads, a main course, and desserts to be shared family style. Tables seat 6-10, and the setting is warm. It's a great way for anyone to meet others (book a day ahead or arrive early, opens at 19:00, closed Sun-Mon, tel. 04 89 89 08 92, 5 Rue Frédéric Isnard).

La Marmite is an unpretentious 10-table place where Patrick offers diners an honest budget value. The service is sweet and the seafood is a favorite (*menus* from €18, closed Mon off-season, no air-con, 20 Rue James Close, tel. 04 93 34 56 79).

At **L'Aubergine's**—an intimate and feminine-feeling little place— Jenny delivers fine cuisine at fair prices, including good vegetarian options (*menus* from €25, opens at 18:30, closed Wed, 7 Rue Sade, tel. 04 93 34 55 93).

Le Broc en Bouche is part cozy wine bar, part bistro, and part collector's shop (*tartines*, €20-30 *plats*, closed Tue-Wed, 8 Rue des Palmiers, tel. 04 93 34 75 60).

Le Vauban is a dressy place, popular with locals for a special event and its seafood (€36-46 *menus*, closed for lunch Mon and Wed, closed all day Tue, opposite 4 Rue Thuret, tel. 04 93 34 33 05, www.levauban.fr).

Le Brulot, an institution in Antibes, is known for its Provençal cuisine and meats cooked on an open fire. It's a small place, overflowing onto the street, with a few outside tables and a dining room below (*menus* from €23; big, splittable portions, closed Sun, 2 Rue Frédéric Isnard, tel. 04 93 34 17 76).

Le Brulot Pasta and Pizza serves good and hearty pizza (the €13 *printanière* is tasty) and big portions of pasta. This family-friendly place has indoors-only seating in a noisy and fun, air-conditioned cellar under stone arches (daily, dinners only, 3 Rue Frédéric Isnard, tel. 04 93 34 19 19).

Picnic on the Beach or Ramparts: Romantics on a shoestring can drop by the handy **L'Épicerie du Marché** (a little grocery store open daily until 23:00, up the hill from the market hall at 3 Cours Masséna) and assemble their own picnic dinner to enjoy on the beach or ramparts. There's also a

410 Rick Steves Provence & the French Riviera

ANTIBES, CANNES, ST-TROPEZ

Monoprix, located on Place Général de Gaulle (Mon-Sat 8:30-20:30, Sun 9:00-12:30).

Antibes Connections

For a comparison of train and bus connections, see the "Public Transportation in the French Riviera" sidebar on page 282.

From Antibes by Train: TGV and local trains serve Antibes' little station. Trains go to **Cannes** (2/hour, 15 minutes), **Nice** (2/hour, 20 minutes), **Grasse** (1/hour, 40 minutes), **Villefranche-sur-Mer** (2/hour, 40 minutes), **Monaco** (2/hour, 50 minutes), and **Marseille** (16/day, 2.5 hours).

By Bus: All the buses listed below serve the Pôle d'Echange bus stops behind the train station. Handy **bus #200** ties everything together, but runs at a snail's pace when traffic is bad (4/hour Mon-Sat, 2/hour Sun, any ride costs €1.50). This bus goes west to **Cannes** (35 minutes); and east to near **Biot** village (15 minutes—bus #10 is better, described on page 406), **Cagnes-sur-Mer** (25 minutes), and **Nice** (1.5 hours).

Bus #250 runs from behind Antibes' train station to **Nice Airport** (2/hour, 40 minutes, €10; cross over the tracks on the pedestrian bridge—it's the last shelter to the right).

Cannes

Cannes (pronounced "can"), famous for its May film festival, is the sister city of Beverly Hills. That says it all. When I asked at the TI for a list of museums and sights, they just smiled. Cannes—with big, exclusive hotels lining mostly private stretches of perfect, sandy beach—is for strolling, shopping, dreaming of meeting a movie star, and lounging on the seafront. Cannes has little that's unique to offer the traveler...except a mostly off-limits film festival and quick access to two undeveloped islands. You can buy an ice-cream cone at the train station and see everything before you've had your last lick. Money is what Cannes has always been about—wealthy people come here to make the scene, and there's always enough *scandale* to go around. The king of Saudi Arabia purchased a serious slice of waterfront just east of town and built his compound with no regard to local zoning regulations. Money talks on the Riviera...and always has.

Orientation to Cannes

Don't sleep or drive in Cannes. Day-trip here by train or bus. It's a breeze, as trains and buses run frequently along the Riviera, and they all stop in Cannes. There's baggage storage at the train station, and you can pick up a city map at the TI or the train information desk. Buses arrive next to the train station. If you must drive, store your car at the parking garage next to the train station.

Tourist Information: Cannes' glamorously quiet main TI is located in the Film Festival Hall at 1 Boulevard de la Croisette (daily July-Aug 9:00-20:00, Sept-June 10:00-19:00).

Cannes Walk

This self-guided cancan will take you to Cannes' sights in a level, one-hour walk at a movie-star pace.

• *From the train station, cross the street, veer left, and walk for five unglamorous minutes down Rue des Serbes to the beachfront. Cross the busy Boulevard de la Croisette and make your way past snack stands to the sea. Find the round lookout and get familiar with...*

The Lay of the Land: Cannes feels different from its neighbors to the east. You won't find the pastel oranges and pinks of Old Nice and Villefranche-sur-Mer. Cannes was never part of Italy—and its architecture and cuisine reminds me more of Paris than Nice.

Face the water. The land jutting into the sea on your left is actually two islands, St-Honorat and Ste-Marguerite. St-Honorat

has been the property of monks for over 500 years; today its abbey, vineyards, trails, and gardens can be visited by peace-seeking travelers. Ste-Marguerite, which you also can visit, is famous for the stone prison that housed the 17th-century Man in the Iron Mask (whose true identity remains unknown). For more on visiting these islands, see page 414.

Now look to your right. Those striking mountains sweeping down to the sea are the Massif de l'Esterel. Their red-rock outcrops oversee spectacular car and train routes (see page 415). Closer in, the hill with the medieval tower caps Cannes' old town (Le Suquet). This hilltop offers grand views and pretty lanes, but little else. Below the old town, the port welcomes yachts of all sizes... provided they're big.

Face inland. Close on the left, find the unexceptional, cream-colored building that's home to the famous film festival (we'll visit there soon). Back the other way, gaze up the boulevard. That classy

Handy Cannes and St-Tropez Phrases

Where is a movie star?	Où est une vedette?
I am a movie star.	Je suis une vedette.
I am rich and single.	Je suis riche et célibataire.
Are you rich and single?	Etes-vous riche et célibataire?
Are those real?	Ils sont des vrais?
How long is your yacht?	Quelle est la longeur de votre yacht?
How much did that cost?	Combien coûtait-il?
You can always dream...	On peut toujours rêver...

building with twin black-domed roofs is Hôtel Carlton, our eventual target and as far as we'll go together in that direction.

• *Continue with the sea on your right and stroll the...*

Promenade (La Croisette): You're walking along Boulevard de la Croisette—Cannes' famed two-mile-long promenade. First popular with kings who wintered here after Napoleon fell, the elite parade was later joined by British aristocracy. Today, Boulevard de la Croisette is fronted by some of the most expensive apartments and hotels in Europe. If it's lunchtime, you might try one of the beach cafés. **Plage le Goéland's** café has fair prices.

• *Stop when you get to...*

Hôtel Carlton: This is the most famous address on Boulevard de la Croisette (small Db-€1,500, more spacious Db-€7,000). Face

the beach. The iconic Cannes experience is to slip into a robe (ideally, monogrammed with your initials), out of your luxury hotel (preferably this one), and onto the beach or pier. While you may not be doing the "fancy hotel and monogrammed robe" ritual on this Cannes excursion, you can—for about €25—rent a chair and umbrella and pretend you're tanning for a red-carpet premiere. Cannes has a few token public beaches, but most beaches are private and run by hotels like the Carlton. You could save money by sunning among the common folk, but the real Cannes way to flee the rabble and paparazzi is to rent a spot on a private beach.

Cross over and wander into the hotel—you're welcome to browse (harder during the festival). Ask for a hotel brochure, verify room rates, check for availability. Can all these people really afford this? Imagine the scene here during the film festival (see anyone famous?). An affordable café (considering the cost of a room) lies just beyond the champagne lounge.

• *You can continue your stroll down La Croisette, but I'm doubling back to the cream-colored building that is Cannes'...*

Film Festival Hall: Cannes' film festival (Festival de Cannes), staged since 1946, completes the "Big Three" of Riviera

events (with Monaco's Grand Prix and Nice's Carnival). The hall where the festival takes place—a busy-but-nondescript convention center that also hosts the town TI—sits plump on the beach. You'll recognize the formal grand entryway (most likely without the famed red carpet). Find the famous (Hollywood-style) handprints in the sidewalk nearby. To get inside during the festival, you have to be a star (or a photographer—some 3,000 paparazzi attend the gala event, and most bring their own ladders to get above the crowds).

The festival originated in part as an anti-fascist response to Mussolini's Venice Film Festival. Cannes' first festival was due to open in 1939, on the very day Hitler invaded Poland. Because of World War II, the opening was delayed until 1946. Cannes' film festival is also famous as the first festival to give one vote per country on the jury (giving films from smaller countries a better chance).

Though generally off-limits to curious tourists, the festival is all that matters around here—and is worth a day trip to Cannes if you happen to be in the region when it's on. The town buzzes with megastar energy, press passes, and revealing dresses. Locals claim that it's the world's third-biggest media event, after the Olympics and the World Cup (soccer). The festival prize is the Palme d'Or (like the Oscar for Best Picture). The French press can't cover the event enough, and the average Jean in France follows it as Joe would the World Series in the States. In 2015, 19 films were reviewed by the "film jury." The presidents of the jury were Joel and Ethan Coen (a.k.a. the Coen brothers).

• *Around the other side of the festival hall is the port (Gare Maritime).*

The Port and Old Town (Le Suquet): The megayachts line up closest to the Film Festival Hall. After seeing these amazing boats, everything else looks like a dinghy. Boat service to St-Tropez and the nearby islands of St-Honorat and Ste-Marguerite depart from

Yachters' Itinerary

If you're visiting Cannes on your private yacht, here's a suggested itinerary:

1. Take in the Festival de Cannes and the accompanying social scene. Organize an evening party on your boat.
2. Motor over to Monte Carlo for the Grand Prix, scheduled—conveniently for yachters—just after the film festival.
3. On your way back west to St-Tropez, deconstruct events from the film festival and Grand Prix with Brigitte Bardot.
4. Drop down to Porto Chervo on Sardinia, one of the few places in the world where your yacht is "just average."
5. Head west to Ibiza and Marbella in Spain, where your friends are moored for the big party scene.

the far side of the port (at Quai Laubeuf; for boat info, see "Activities in Cannes," later).

Cannes' oldest neighborhood, Le Suquet, crowns the hill past the port. Locals refer to it as their Montmartre. Artsy and charming, it's a steep 15-minute walk above the port, with little of interest except the panoramic views from its ancient church, Notre-Dame-de-l'Espérance (Our Lady of Hope).

• *To find the views in Le Suquet, aim for its clock tower and pass the bus station at the northwest corner of the port, then make your way up cobbled Rue Saint-Antoine (next to the Café St. Antoine). Turn left on Place du Suquet, and then follow signs to* Traverse de la Tour *for the final leg.*

Cue music. Roll end credits. Our film is over. For further exploration, look for Cannes' "underbelly" between Le Suquet and the train station—narrow lanes with inexpensive cafés and shops that regular folks can afford.

Activities in Cannes

Shopping

Cannes is made for window-shopping (the best streets are between the station and the waterfront). For the trendiest boutiques, stroll down handsome Rue d'Antibes (parallel to the sea about three blocks inland). Rue Meynadier anchors a pedestrian zone with more affordable shops closer to the port. To bring home a real surprise, why not consider cosmetic surgery? Cannes is well known as *the* place on the Riviera to have your face (or other parts) realigned.

Boat Excursions to St-Honorat and Ste-Marguerite Islands

Boats ferry tourists 15 minutes from the Quai Laubeuf dock in Cannes' port to St-Honorat and Ste-Marguerite, twin islands just offshore (€14 round-trip, daily 9:00-18:00, 1-2/hour, www.trans-cote-azur.com, no ferry runs between the 2 islands). The islands offer a refreshing change from the town scene, with almost no development, good swimming, and peaceful walking paths. On Ste-Marguerite you can visit the castle (part of which is now a youth hostel) and cell where the mysterious Man in the Iron Mask was imprisoned (good little museum with decent English explanations featuring cargo from a sunken Roman vessel). On St-Honorat you can hike seafront trails and visit the abbey where monks still live and pray.

Cannes Connections

TGV and local trains serve Cannes' station. Buses stop next to the train station.

From Cannes by Train to: Antibes (2/hour, 15 minutes), **Nice** (2/hour, 30 minutes), **Grasse** (roughly hourly, 30 minutes), **Monaco** (2/hour, 70 minutes).

By Bus: Bus #200 heads east from Cannes along the Riviera (4/hour Mon-Sat, 2/hour Sun, €1.50 for any destination), stopping at **Antibes** (35 minutes) and **Nice** (2 hours). Trip duration depends on traffic. **Bus #210** runs from the train station express on the freeway to **Nice Airport** (1-2/hour, 50 minutes, €20).

By Boat: Trans Côte d'Azur runs boat excursions from Cannes to **St-Tropez** (€50 round-trip, 1 hour each way; July-Aug daily 1/day; June and Sept 1/day Tue, Thu, and Sat-Sun only; no service Oct-May; tel. 04 92 98 71 30, www.trans-cote-azur.com). This boat trip is popular—book a few days ahead from June to September.

By Cruise Ship: Ships tender passengers to the west side of Cannes' port. From here, it's an easy **walk** into town: Head inland, with the port on your right-hand side. Note that the tender dock is near the end of my Cannes Walk; if planning to follow it, you can either start the walk here and do it in reverse or stroll about 10 minutes around the port to the walk's starting point (see page 411). If heading to points beyond Cannes, it takes about 15 minutes to walk from the tender dock to the train station, where you can catch a train for Antibes, Nice, or Villefranche-sur-Mer.

St-Tropez

St-Tropez is a busy, charming, and traffic-free port town smothered with fashion boutiques, elegant restaurants, and luxury boats. If you came here for history or quaintness, you caught the wrong yacht. But if you have more money than you know what to do with, you're home. There are 5,700 year-round residents...and more than 100,000 visitors daily in the summer. If St-Tropez is on your must-visit list, hit it on your way to or from Provence—and skip it altogether in summer and on weekend afternoons.

As with lots of now-famous villages in southern France, St-Tropez was "found" by artists. Paul Signac brought several of his friends to St-Tropez in the late 1800s, giving the village its first whiff of popularity (get rid of the yachts filling the harbor, and the town would resemble what it looked like then). But it wasn't until Brigitte Bardot made the scene here in the 1956 film ...*And God Created Woman* that St-Tropez became synonymous with Riviera glamour. Since then, it's the first place that comes to mind when people think of the jet set luxuriating on Mediterranean beaches. For many, the French Riviera begins here and runs east to Menton, on the Italian border.

The village is the attraction here; the nearest big beach is miles away. Window-shopping, people-watching, tan maintenance, and savoring slow meals fill people's days, weeks, and, in some cases, lives. Here, people dress up, size up one another's yachts or cars, and troll for a partner. While the only models you'll see are in the shop windows, Brigitte Bardot still hangs out on a bench in front of the TI signing autographs (Thu 15:00-17:30, and if you believe that...).

Wander the harborfront, where fancy yachts moor stern-in, their carefully coiffed captains and first mates enjoying *pu-pus* for happy hour—they're seeing and being seen. Take time to stroll the back streets (the small lanes below La Citadelle are St-Tropez's most appealing) while nibbling a chocolate-and-Grand Marnier crêpe. Find the big Place des Lices (good cafés and local hangout), and look for some serious games of *pétanque (boules)*.

Orientation to St-Tropez

St-Tropez lies between its famous port and the hilltop Citadelle (with great views). The network of lanes between the port and Citadelle are strollable in a Carmel-by-the-Sea sort of way.

Tourist Information: The main TI is on the starboard side of the port (to the right as you face the sea), where Quai Suffren and Quai Jean Jaurès meet (daily 9:30-19:00, closes for lunch around 12:30-14:30, Nov-March until 18:00, tel. 08 92 68 48 28, www.ot-saint-tropez.com). Pick up their helpful walking tour brochure, ask about events in town, and get maps and bus information if you plan to hike along the coast.

Arrival in St-Tropez: Buses leave you a few minutes' walk to the port, near the parking lot—Parking du Vieux Port—on Avenue Général de Gaulle. **Boats** from St-Raphaël deposit you by the same lot. For bus and boat details, see "St-Tropez Connections," at the end of this chapter.

If arriving by **car,** prepare for traffic in any season—worse on weekends (forget driving on Sunday afternoons), always ugly during summer, and downright impossible between St-Tropez and Ste-Maxime on weekends. You can avoid this bottleneck by taking the autoroute to Le Luc and following the windy D-558 to St-Tropez from here (via La Garde-Freinet and Port Grimaud). The last few miles to St-Tropez are along a too-long, two-lane road with one way in, one way out, and too many people going exactly where you're going. There are two main parking lots: Parking des Lices (near recommended hotels) and Parking du Port (best for day-trippers).

Sights in St-Tropez

The TI's self-guided walking tour brochure offers a worthwhile tour of St-Tropez's highlights. Use their tour to connect the following sights.

The Port

The port has been a key player in St-Tropez's economy since the 18th century, when it saw a brisk trade in wine, cork, and lumber. St-Tropez's shipyards were famous for their three-mast ships, which could carry more than 1,000 barrels of wine. Today's port is famous for its big boats. There's something bizarre about the size of those boats, stern-tied tightly in such a small harbor.

While strolling around, you'll see busy deckhands (hustling before their captains arrive) and artists competing for room. The red-tabled **Le Sénéquier,** by the TI, is one of the town's most venerated cafés—and has long attracted celebrities, including the philosopher Jean-Paul Sartre. High-end cafés and restaurants line the

St-Tropez

Mediterranean Sea

JETTY

MOLE J. REVEILLE

MOLE D'ESTIENNE D'ORVES

Port

ROUND TOWER

MUSEUM DE LA ANNONCIADE

Nouveau Port

R. DU 11 NOV. 1918

Place Gramont

QUAI

RUE

R. MERMOZ

RUE H. SEILLON

RUE GEN. ALLARD

RUE

To St-Raphaël

WC

AVE. GEN. DEGAULLE

AVE. DU HUIT MAI 1945

BUS STATION

WC

BLVD. L.

To Port Grimaud, Ste. Maxime & Nice

AVE. GEN. LECLERC

1 Hôtel la Ponche
2 Hôtel Lou Cagnard
3 Hôtel le Colombier

port from here to the jetty—it doesn't seem to matter that you can't see the sea for the big yachts.

The bulky **Tour du Portalet** tower at the port's end has views across the bay to the town of Ste-Maxime and out to sea. A plaque honors the American, British, and French troops who liberated Provence on August 15, 1944. Climb the jetty for great views over the port.

Museum of the Annonciade (Musée de l'Annonciade)

Though generally ignored, this museum houses an enchanting collection of works from the Post-Impressionist and Fauvist artists who decorated St-Tropez before Brigitte. Almost all canvases feature St-Tropez sights and landscapes. You'll see colorful paintings by Paul Signac, Henri Matisse, Georges Braque, Pierre Bonnard, Maurice de Vlaminck, and more. Gaze out the windows and notice how the port has changed since they were here.

Cost and Hours: Small fee, daily 10:00-13:00 & 14:00-18:00 except closed Tue off-season, Place Grammont, tel. 04 94 17 84 10.

Coastal Hike

The scenic Sentier du Littoral path, originally patrolled by customs agents, runs past the 1558 Citadelle fortress (which houses a maritime museum, tel. 04 94 97 59 43) and continues for 12 miles along the coast. The trail is marked with yellow dashes on the pavement, walls, and trees. Leave St-Tropez along the road below the Citadelle, pass the Sailors' Cemetery, and you'll join the path before long.

Boat Excursions

Several companies offer mildly interesting tours of the surrounding coastline. You'll learn a smidgen about St-Tropez's history and a lot about the villas of the rich and famous (get details at the TI).

Boules

The vast *pétanque (boules)* court on Place des Lices is worth your attention. Have a drink at Le Café and take in the action. Study up on the sport (see page 39) and root for your hero.

Port Grimaud

Although more modern than St-Tropez, Port Grimaud (located a few miles toward Ste-Maxime) is no less attractive or upscale. This "Venice of Provence" was reclaimed from a murky lagoon about 40 years ago, and is now lined with four miles of canals, lovely homes, and moorage for thousands of yachts. It's a fascinating look at what clever minds can produce from a swamp. Park at the lot across from the town entry (TI next to the parking lot, www.grimaud-provence.com), and cross the barrier and bridge into a beautiful world of privilege. Climb the church bell tower for a good panorama view.

Sleeping in St-Tropez

If you're spending the night here, remember that high season in St-Tropez runs from June through September, and weekends are busy year-round. Hotels worth considering (in descending order of price and comfort) are: **Hôtel la Ponche****** (3 Rue des Remparts, tel. 04 94 97 02 53, www.laponche.com); **Hôtel Lou Cagnard**** (18 Avenue Paul Roussel, tel. 04 94 97 04 24, www.hotel-lou-cagnard.com); and **Hôtel le Colombier**** (Impasse des Conquêtes, tel. 04 94 97 05 31, lecolombierhotel.free.fr).

St-Tropez Connections

With no trains to St-Tropez, buses and boats are your only options.

By Bus: Bus #7601 serves St-Tropez from behind St-Raphaël's train station via Ste-Maxime to the east (almost hourly, 1.5 hours to **St-Raphaël**, 30 minutes to **Ste-Maxime**). Bus #7801 and #7802 run from **Toulon's** train station to the west (6/day, 2 hours). If you're arriving in St-Raphaël or Toulon by train, check the bus schedules to St-Tropez in advance at www.varlib.fr to be sure you will make the connection.

By Boat: Boats make the one-hour trip between St-Tropez and **St-Raphaël** twice daily (€15 one-way, €30 round-trip, departs St-Tropez at 10:30 and 17:15, departs St-Raphaël at 9:30 and 14:30, tel. 04 94 95 17 46, www.bateauxsaintraphael.com). Boats between St-Tropez and **Ste-Maxime** run about every hour (€7, 3/hour in summer, 15 minutes, tel. 04 94 49 29 39, www.bateauxverts.com). For boats connecting St-Tropez with Nice, see page 294; with Cannes, page 415.

INLAND RIVIERA

*St-Paul-de-Vence • Vence •
Grasse • Grand Canyon du Verdon*

For a verdant, rocky, fresh escape from the beaches, head inland and upward. Some of France's most perfectly perched hill towns and splendid scenery hang overlooked in this region that's more famous for beaches and bikinis. A short car or bus ride away from the Mediterranean reaps big rewards: lush forests, deep canyons, and swirling hilltop villages. A longer drive brings you to Europe's greatest canyon, the Grand Canyon du Verdon.

GETTING AROUND THE INLAND RIVIERA

By Car: Driving is the best way to tour this area, though summer and weekend traffic and parking challenges will test your patience. Consider renting a car for a day (for rental places, see pages 394 and 292). I describe the best route later.

By Bus: Buses get you to many of the places in this chapter. Vence, St-Paul-de-Vence, and Grasse are well-served by bus from Nice (about 2/hour), and Grasse has train service from Nice, Antibes, and Cannes. A few buses to Tourrettes-sur-Loup, Le Bar-sur-Loup, and Grasse leave from Vence daily except Sunday (7/day, 15 minutes to Tourrettes-sur-Loup, 35 minutes to Le Bar-sur-Loup; 4/day to Grasse, 50 minutes). Bus connections for the Gorges du Loup, the village of Gourdon, or the Gorges du Verdon are either too complicated or nonexistent.

With a Local Guide: Informative and enjoyable guide **Sylvie Di Cristo** can show you around her backyard (see page 281 for contact information).

Benôit and Corinne, owners of the recommended Frogs' House in St-Jeannet, are happy to organize cooking classes, wine tastings, hiking trips, and other excursions around their native area (see page 431).

Inland Riviera Driving Tour

This splendid self-guided loop drive connects St-Paul-de-Vence, Vence, Tourrettes-sur-Loup, and Grasse. Some of the villages can be linked by bus, but a car is essential to do the loop as described. Each stop is only minutes away from the next, but allow 45 minutes to drive from Nice or Antibes to the first stop, St-Paul-de-Vence. Start early to see St-Paul-de-Vence without the mobs (have breakfast at St-Paul-de-Vence's Café de la Place). If you won't be visiting the Gorges du Verdon (or if you care more about nature than art), take the beautiful long way around from Vence to Gourdon (described later, under "Alternate Route"), and skip Tourrettes-sur-Loup and the Gorges du Loup (you won't miss them, trust *moi*). Be prepared for twisty mountain roads and tailgating French drivers; they come with the territory. Note that most of the towns and sights on this drive are explained in detail later in this chapter.

FROM NICE TO GRASSE

From Nice, leave along the Promenade des Anglais and head toward Cannes and Antibes. Follow *Grasse* signs, then *Vence* and *St-Paul-de-Vence* signs. You'll pass the Renoir Museum in Cagnes-sur-Mer (see page 406). Continue following *St-Paul-de-Vence* signs into the village, and park as close to the center as you can. After sampling **St-Paul-de-Vence,** visit the **Fondation Maeght** just above the town (park at the museum for free, or walk 20 minutes up from St-Paul-de-Vence, following signs).

After completing your course in contemporary art, find artsy **Vence,** a few miles away, with many good lunch options. From

INLAND RIVIERA

Vence visit Matisse's famous **Chapel of the Rosary** (limited opening hours and sparse parking). The best views of Vence are a mile beyond the chapel, where there's a turnaround.

Next, head for slippery-sloped **Tourrettes-sur-Loup** (from Vence, follow D-2210)—or skip Tourrettes-sur-Loup and follow the "Alternate Route" described later. From Tourrettes-sur-Loup, continue along D-2210 (great views of Tourrettes-sur-Loup a quarter-mile after leaving, look for the bus stop *Chemin de la Gare*). Before long you'll see views of Le Bar-sur-Loup, clinging to its hillside in the distance. (Sugar addicts can detour quickly down to Pont-du-Loup and visit the small candied-fruit factory of **Confiseries Florian**).

Follow *Gourdon* and *Gorges du Loup* signs to the right along D-6 and climb into the teeth of a rocky canyon, the **Gorges du Loup.** It's a mostly second-gear road that winds between severe rock faces above a surging stream. (Buses cannot enter the Gorges du Loup, so nondrivers must continue on directly to Grasse.) Several miles into the gorge, you can visit the Cascades du Saut du Loup **waterfall,** which may have you thinking you've made a wrong turn into Hawaii (small fee, easy walk down).

The drive passes all too quickly to where the road hooks back, crossing Pont du Bramafen and up toward Gourdon on D-3. Climb above the canyon you just drove through and watch the world below miniaturize. At the top, the village of **Gourdon,** known as the "Eagle's Nest" (2,400 feet), waits for tourists with shops, good lunch options, and grand panoramas.

From Gourdon, slide downhill—passing stone quarries—toward **Grasse.** Enjoy sensational views down to (literally) over-

looked Le Bar-sur-Loup. Follow signs to *Grasse,* then *Centre-Ville,* and park at the first underground lot you come to. After mastering your scent in Grasse—the capital of perfume—return to your Riviera home base (allow 45 minutes to Nice or 30 minutes to Antibes via Cannes and the autoroute), or continue to the Gorges du Verdon.

ALTERNATE ROUTE

If you won't be visiting the Gorges du Verdon, consider this dilly of a detour (ideal if staying in Vence): Follow the route described above until Vence, then find D-2 just before the bridge that leads to St-Jeannet, and follow signs for *Col de Vence* (the Vence pass). This road rises beyond the tree line into a stones-only landscape to the pass in about 15 minutes. (For a 45-minute uphill hike to views

over Vence and the Riviera, pass the Château St-Martin, drive another kilometer, then look for the brown trailhead sign to *Baous des
Blancs*.) From the pass (3,000 feet), continue on D-2, trading rocky
slabs for lush forests, pastures, and vast canyons.

You'll soon pass the postcard-perfect village of Coursegoules
(worth a photo but not a detour), then follow signs to *Gréolières*. At
a roundabout just before Gréolières find D-3, which leads to Nice,
Gorges du Loup, and Gourdon. But first, continue a few minutes
past Gréolières to the pullout barely above the village, with stir-
ring views over the village and its ruined castle. Consider a coffee
break in Gréolières before backtracking to the roundabout, following signs to *Gourdon*. After visiting Gourdon, you can continue to
Grasse, or return to Nice or Antibes.

St-Paul-de-Vence

This most famous of Riviera hill towns is also the most-visited village in France. And it feels that way—like an overrun and over-
restored artist shopping-mall. Its attraction is understandable, as

every cobble and flower seems just so,
and the setting is postcard-perfect.
Avoid visiting between 11:00 and
18:00, particularly on weekends.
Beat the crowds by skipping breakfast at your hotel and eating it in
St-Paul-de-Vence, or come for dinner and experience the village at its
tranquil best.

Orientation to St-Paul-de-Vence

Tourist Information: The helpful TI, just through the gate into
the old city on Rue Grande, has maps with minimal explanations
of key buildings (daily 10:00-18:00, June-Sept until 19:00, closed
for lunch on weekends). The TI offers walking tours with English
translations, including tours focused on history, art, and *pétanque
(boules)*. Call or email in advance to reserve (€7, tel. 04 93 32 86
95, www.saint-pauldevence.com, serviceguide@saint-pauldevence.
com).

Arrival in St-Paul-de-Vence: Arrive early to park near the
village (cars are not allowed inside St-Paul). Bus #400 (connects
with Nice and Vence) stops on the main road, a short walk from
the village. If the traffic-free lane leading to the old city is jammed,

walk along the road that veers up and left just after Café de la Place, and enter the town through its side door.

Sights in St-Paul-de-Vence

The Old Town

St-Paul's old city has no essential sights, though its lovely cobbled lanes and peekaboo views delight most who come. You'll pass the vintage **Café de la Place** on entering the village—a classic place to have a coffee and croissant and watch as waves of tourists crash into the town (daily from 7:00, tel. 04 93 32 80 03). On the square, serious *boules* competitions take place all day long. Meander deep into St-Paul-de-Vence's quieter streets to find panoramic views. Visit Marc Chagall's grave in the cemetery at the opposite end of town (from the cemetery entrance, turn right, then left; it's the third gravestone). Walk up the stairs to the view platform and try to locate the hill town of Vence at the foot of an impressive mountain. Is the sea out there—somewhere?

▲Fondation Maeght

This inviting, pricey, and far-out private museum is situated a steep walk or short drive above St-Paul-de-Vence. Fondation Maeght (fohn-dah-shown mahg) offers an excellent introduction to modern Mediterranean art by gathering many of the Riviera's most famous artists under one roof. Sadly, there are no English explanations anywhere.

Cost and Hours: €15, €5 to take photos, daily July-Sept 10:00-19:00, Oct-June 10:00-18:00, tel. 04 93 32 81 63, www.fondation-maeght.com.

Getting There: The museum is a steep uphill-but-doable 20-minute walk from St-Paul-de-Vence and the bus stop. Signs indicate the way (parking is usually available at the upper lot). From the lower lot, signed *Parking Conseille*, a shortcut on a steep, dirt path through the trees leads directly to the green gate in front of the ticket booth.

Visiting the Museum: The founder, Aimé Maeght, long envisioned the perfect exhibition space for the artists he supported and

befriended as an art dealer. He purchased this arid hilltop, planted 35,000 plants, and hired an architect (José Luis Sert) with the same vision.

A sweeping lawn laced with amusing sculptures and bending pine trees greets visitors. On the right, a chapel designed by Georges Braque—in memory of the Maeghts' young son, who died of leukemia—features a moving purple stained-glass work over the altar. The unusual museum building is purposely low profile, to let its world-class modern-art collection take center stage. Works by Fernand Léger, Joan Miró, Alexander Calder, Georges Braque, and Marc Chagall are thoughtfully arranged in well-lit rooms. The backyard of the museum has views, a Gaudí-esque sculpture labyrinth by Miró, and a courtyard filled with the wispy works of Alberto Giacometti. The only permanent collection in the museum consists of the sculptures, though there's a good selection of paintings by the famous artists here year-round. For a review of modern art, see "The Riviera's Art Scene" on page 285. There's also a great gift shop and cafeteria.

Eating in St-Paul-de-Vence

Le Tilleul is the place to dine well in St-Paul, with inviting tables on a broad terrace or in the cozy interior (à la carte only, allow €50/person for three courses, open daily, tel. 04 93 32 80 36, www.restaurant-letilleul.com).

Book well ahead at **La Colombe d'Or**, a historic place where the menu hasn't changed in 50 years. Back when the town was teeming with artists, this restaurant served as their clubhouse. Walls are covered with paintings by Picasso, Miró, Braque, Chagall, and others, who were given free meals in exchange for their art. Dine inside by the fire to best feel its pulse (figure €60/person with wine, across from Café de la Place, closed Nov-Dec, tel. 04 93 32 80 02, www.la-colombe-dor.com; for reservations, email contact@la-colombe-dor.com).

Vence

Vence is a well-discovered yet appealing town set high above the Riviera. While growth has sprawled beyond Vence's old walls, and cars jam its roundabouts, the mountains are front and center and the breeze is fresh. Vence bubbles with workaday life and ample tourist activity in the day but is quiet at night, with fewer visitors and cooler temperatures than along the coast. Vence makes a handy base for travelers wanting the best of both worlds: a hill-town refuge near the sea. Some enjoy the Gorges du Verdon as a long day trip from Vence (see the route described on page 436).

Orientation to Vence

Tourist Information: Vence's fully loaded TI faces the main square at 8 Place du Grand Jardin, across from the merry-go-round. It offers free Wi-Fi, bus schedules, and a city map with a well-devised self-guided walking tour that incorporates informative wall plaques. Pick up the list of art galleries with helpful descriptions of the collections. Ask about their *pétanque* instructions with *boules* to rent and about guided walking tours in English (April-Oct Mon-Sat 9:00-19:00, Sun 10:00-18:00; Nov-March Mon-Sat 10:00-17:00, closed Sun; tel. 04 93 58 06 38, www.ville-vence.fr).

Arrival in Vence: Bus #94 or #400 (from Nice, Cagnes-sur-Mer, and St-Paul-de-Vence) drops you at the bus stop labeled *Halte Routière de l'Ara,* which is on a roundabout at Place Maréchal Juin. It's a 10-minute walk to the town center along Avenue Henri Isnard or Avenue de la Résistance. If arriving by **car,** follow signs to *cité historique* and park in the underground Parking Grand Jardin, across from the TI. Some hotels offer discounted rates for parking.

Helpful Hints: Market day in the *cité historique* (old town) is on Friday mornings on Place Clemenceau. A big all-day antiques market is on Place du Grand Jardin every Wednesday. If you miss market day, a Monoprix **supermarket** is on Avenue de la Résistance, across from the entrance to the Marie Antoinette parking lot (grocery store upstairs, Mon-Sat 8:30-20:00, Sun 9:00-13:00). For a **taxi,** call 04 93 58 11 14.

Sights in Vence

Explore the narrow lanes of the old town using the TI's worthwhile self-guided tour map. Connect the picturesque streets, enjoy a drink on a quiet square, inspect an art gallery, and find the small 11th-century cathedral with its colorful Chagall mosaic of Moses (for background, see the Chagall Museum Tour chapter). If you're here later in the day, enjoy the *boules* action across from the TI (rent a set from the TI and join in).

Château de Villeneuve

This 17th-century mansion, adjoining an imposing 12th-century watchtower, bills itself as "one of the Riviera's high temples of modern art," with a rotating collection. Check with the TI to see what's playing in the temple.

Cost and Hours: €8, Tue-Sun 11:00-18:00, closed Mon, tel. 04 93 58 15 78.

▲Chapel of the Rosary (Chapelle du Rosaire)

The chapel, a short drive or 20-minute walk from town, was designed by an elderly and ailing Henri Matisse as thanks to the Do-

INLAND RIVIERA

Vence

1. La Maison du Frêne
2. Auberge des Seigneurs
3. To Aux 3 Lits qui Chantent B&B & The Frogs' House
4. La Cassolette Restaurant
5. Les Agapes Restaurant
6. La Litote Restaurant
7. Bistro du Peyra
8. Monoprix Grocery

AVENUE HENRI ISNARD

← To ③,
Col de Vence via D-2
& Chapel of the Rosary

CHATEAU DE VILLENEUVE
MODERN ART
MUSEUM

RUE DU DR. BINET

WC

AVENUE DE LA RESISTANCE

PLACE DU GRAND JARDIN

← To
Place M. Juin (Bus Stop),
Tourettes-sur-Loup
via D-2210
& St. Paul via D-7

TOWER →

PORTE DU
PEYRA

Place du Grand Jardin

Marie Antoinette
P

Grand Jardin
P

WC

RUE DES ARCS

RUE MASSENA

RUE GAMBETTA

minican sister who had taken care of him (he was 81 when the chapel was completed—see the timeline of Matisse's life on page

300). While the chapel is the ultimate pilgrimage for his fans, the experience may underwhelm others. (Picasso thought it looked like a bathroom.)

Cost and Hours: €5; Mon, Wed, and Sat 14:00-17:30, Tue and Thu 10:00-11:30 & 14:00-17:30, Sun only open for Mass at 10:00 followed by tour of chapel, closed Fri and mid-Nov-mid-Dec; 466 Avenue Henri Matisse, tel. 04 93 58 03 26.

Getting There: It's a 20-minute walk from the TI. Turn right out of the TI and take your first right and then a

INLAND RIVIERA

quick left onto Avenue Henri Isnard, then continue all the way to the traffic circle. Turn right across the one-lane bridge on Avenue Henri Matisse, following signs to *St-Jeannet*.

Visiting the Chapel: The modest chapel holds a simple series of charcoal black-on-white tile sketches and uses three symbolic colors as accents: yellow (sunlight and the light of God), green (nature), and blue (the Mediterranean sky). Bright sunlight filters through the stained-glass windows and does a cheery dance across the sketches.

Your entry ticket includes a 20-minute tour from one of the kind nuns who speaks English. Photography is not al-

INLAND RIVIERA

Sleep Code

Abbreviations   (€1=about $1.10, country code: 33)
S=Single, **D**=Double/Twin, **T**=Triple, **Q**=Quad, **b**=bathroom,
*=French hotel rating (0-5 stars)
Price Rankings
$$$ Higher Priced—Most rooms €110 or more
$$ Moderately Priced—Most rooms €70-110
$ Lower Priced—Most rooms €70 or less
Unless otherwise noted, credit cards are accepted, English is
spoken, air-conditioning is available, and free Wi-Fi and/or a
guest computer is generally provided. Prices change; verify
current rates online or by email. For the best prices, always
book directly with the hotel.

lowed. Downstairs you'll find displays of the vestments Matisse
designed for the priests, his models of the chapel, and sketches.

Matisse was the master of leaving things out. Decide for yourself whether Matisse met the goal he set himself: "Creating a religious space in an enclosed area of reduced proportions and to give
it, solely by the play of colors and lines, the dimension of infinity."

Sleeping in Vence

Several of the places I list close their reception desks between 12:00
and 16:00. Make arrangements in advance if you plan to arrive
during this time.

$$$ La Maison du Frêne is a modern, art-packed B&B with
four sumptuous suites centrally located behind the TI. Energetic
and art-crazy Thierry and Guy make fine hosts (Db-€162-185, in-
cludes good breakfast, kids sleep free; next to the Château de Vil-
leneuve at 1 Place du Frêne—turn right out of the TI, then right
again, then left; tel. 04 93 24 37 83, www.lamaisondufrene.com,
contact@lamaisondufrene.com).

$$ Auberge des Seigneurs feels medieval. It's a central, funky,
dark-wooded place in a 17th-century building with six simple but
spacious rooms over a restaurant. Ring the bell if no one is present
(small Db in back-€90, Db-€95, breakfast-€12, Wi-Fi in lobby,
includes parking voucher, 1 Rue du Docteur Binet, tel. 04 93 58
04 24, www.auberge-seigneurs.com, sandrine.rodi@wanadoo.fr).

$$ Aux 3 Lits qui Chantent ("The Three Singing Beds")
works well for those arriving by bus or car. This cozy B&B has
simple yet comfortable rooms a few blocks from the city center (Sb-
€69, Db-€81-99, family rooms-€120-156, includes breakfast, Rue
Elise, tel. 04 93 32 67 03, www.aux3litsquichantent.com).

NEAR VENCE IN ST-JEANNET

To melt into the Inland Riviera's quiet side, drive 15 minutes from Vence to the remarkably situated, no-tourist-in-sight hill town of St-Jeannet. Views are endless and everywhere. It's so quiet, it's hard to believe that the beach is only 10 miles away.

At **$$ The Frogs' House,** Benôit and Corinne welcome travelers with a full menu of good rooms, cooking lessons, hikes in the area, and day trips. If you don't have wheels, they'll pick you up at the train station or airport. Rooms are small but sharp (Db-€79-93, Db with balcony-€107, family suite with private salon-€174, less in off-season, includes hearty breakfast, tel. 04 93 58 98 05, mobile 06 28 06 80 28, www.thefrogshouse.com, info@thefrogshouse.com). A parking lot is at the bottom of St-Jeannet, a few blocks from this small hotel.

Eating in Vence

Tempting outdoor eateries litter the old town. Lights embedded in the cobbles illuminate the way after dark.

La Cassolette, is an intimate place with reasonable prices and a romantic terrace across from the floodlit church (€32-35 *menus,* €15-22 *plats,* closed Tue-Wed except July-Aug, 10 Place Clemenceau, tel. 04 93 58 84 15, www.restaurant-lacassolette-vence.com).

At **Les Agapes,** Chef Jean-Philippe goes beyond the standard fare with lavish presentations, creative food combinations, and moderate (for the Riviera) prices. Try the *sphere chocolat* dessert to round out your meal (€28 *menu,* closed Mon and also Sun in off-season, 4 Place Clemenceau, tel. 04 93 58 50 64, www.les-agapes.net).

Nearby, **La Litote** is lauded by locals as a good value, with outdoor tables on a quiet, hidden square (€26-32 two- and three-course meals, closed Sun, 7 Rue de l'Evêché, tel. 04 93 24 27 82).

For less expensive, casual dining, head to Place du Peyra, where you'll find ample outdoor seating and early dinner service. At **Bistro du Peyra,** enjoy a relaxed dinner salad or pasta dish outdoors to the sound of the town's main fountain (€15-20 *plats,* daily April-Oct, off-season closed Wed-Thu at lunch, closed Jan-Feb, 13 Place du Peyra, tel. 04 93 58 67 63).

Between Vence and Grasse

The following sights are connected by the Inland Riviera driving tour (see page 422).

Tourrettes-sur-Loup

This unspoiled and picturesque town, hemmed in by forests, looks like it's ready to skid down its hill. Stroll the beautifully preserved, narrow medieval lanes. Known as the *Cité des Violettes*, the village produces more violets than anywhere else in France, most of which end up in perfume. In early March, this small village fills with almost 10,000 visitors (hard to imagine) for the annual Violet Festival.

Park in the lot at the village center near the **TI** (Mon-Sat 9:30-13:00 & 14:00-18:00, closed Sun, tel. 04 93 24 18 93, www.tourrettessurloup.com). Wednesday is **market day** (on Place de la Libération).

With your back to the TI, walk to the right and under the clock tower, and onto Grande Rue. Stroll in a counterclockwise direction, ending up back at the parking lot. Along the way you'll find a smattering of arts and crafts boutiques, though fewer than in the "Vence towns," and a handful of places to eat or take a break.

Tom's Ice Cream may entice you with its violet-flavored scoops or tasty coffee and free Wi-Fi (daily from 13:30, 25 Grand Rue, tel. 04 93 24 12 12). Wine lovers should head to **La Cave de Tourrettes,** a small wine bar serving salads and quiches, with a daily by-the-glass selection and a vast cellar. The mini balcony has a nice view (Tue-Sun for lunch, Thu-Sat for dinner, closed Mon, 8 Rue de la Bourgade, near the St. Grégoire Church on the parking lot, tel. 04 93 24 10 12).

More views of Tourrettes-sur-Loup await a minute away on the drive to Pont-du-Loup.

Confiseries Florian

The candied-fruit factory hides between trees down in Pont-du-Loup (though their big, bright sign is hard to miss). Ten-minute tours of their factory leave regularly, covering the candied-fruit process and explaining the use of flower petals (like violets and jasmine) in their products. Everything they make is fruit-filled—even their chocolate (with oranges). The tour ends with a tasting of the *confiture* in the dazzling gift shop.

Cost and Hours: Tours are free, daily 9:00-12:00 & 14:00-18:30, gift shop stays open during lunch in summer, tel. 04 93 59 32 91, www.confiserieflorian.com.

Gorges du Loup

The Inland Riviera is crawling with spectacular canyons only miles from the sea. Slotted between Grasse and Vence, the Gorges du Loup is the easiest gorge to reach and works in well with a day trip from the Nice area. You can drive about five miles right up into the canyon (on D-6), passing waterfalls and sheer rock walls, then return on the gorge's rooftop (on D-3) to the "Eagle's Nest" village of Gourdon for magnificent vistas and a complete change of scenery.

Gourdon

This 2,400-foot-high, cliff-topping hamlet features grassy picnic areas, a short lineup of tourist shops, and a few good lunch options. The village's most famous building is its château, which is best enjoyed from the outside. A well-marked trail (Chemin du Paradis) leads down the cliffs to Le Bar-sur-Loup (1 hour)—now *that's* steep. The far side of the village features fabulous vistas, a

tiny Romanesque church, and a nice option for lunch with a view.

Eating in Gourdon: **La Taverne Provençale** boasts a popular spread of outdoor tables overlooking the grandeur (€14-24 *plats,* €26 *menu,* July-Aug daily lunch and dinner, Sept-June lunch only, turn right at the end of the main drag to Place de l'Eglise, tel. 04 93 09 68 22).

Grasse

The historic and contemporary capital of perfume, Grasse offers a contrast to the dolled-up hill towns above the Riviera. Though famous for its pricey product, Grasse's urban center is an unpolished but intriguing collection of walking lanes, peekaboo squares, and vertical staircases. The place feels in need of a graffiti-facelift and a jobs program for its large immigrant population. For me, Grasse is refreshingly real. Its historic alliance with Genoa explains the Italian-esque look of the old city. Still, the only good reasons to visit Grasse are if you care about perfume, or if you're heading to or from the Gorges du Verdon.

Orientation to Grasse

All sights in Grasse cluster near the Cours Honoré Cresp, also referred to as Place du Cours.

Tourist Information: The TI is a 10-minute walk from the center, on Place de la Buanderie, where buses from Nice and Cannes stop (July-mid-Sept Mon-Sat 9:00-19:00, Sun 9:00-18:00, shorter hours off-season, tel. 04 93 36 66 66, www.grasse.fr). Pick up an English map with a simple, self-guided tour of the old city. If heading to the Gorges du Verdon, get specifics here.

Arrival in Grasse: Fifteen **trains** a day connect Grasse with Nice (1.25 hours), Antibes (40 minutes), and Cannes (30 minutes). A shuttle bus called FUNIX runs from the train station to the town center every 15 minutes (€1.50 round-trip, none on Sun). Ask for the Parfumerie Fragonard stop. Taxis usually wait at the station.

Buses from Cannes and Nice are better than trains, as they stop at the TI and cost only €1.50. To reach the town center from the TI, walk out to Avenue Thiers, turn left, and merge onto Boulevard du Jeu de Ballon. Nice and Cannes buses also stop, along with buses from other destinations, at the main bus stop at the *gare routière*, next to the train station. See "Arrival in Grasse," above, for directions from here to the old city.

Those arriving by **car** are often confounded by Grasse's size, hilly terrain, and inconsistent signage. Follow signs to *Centre-Ville* and park at Parking Honoré Cresp. From this parking garage, follow the *Sortie Parfumerie* directly to the Fragonard perfume tour.

Sights in Grasse

▲International Museum of Perfume
(Musée International de la Parfumerie, MIP)

This city museum is a magnificent tribute to perfume, providing a thorough examination of its history and production from ancient Greece to today. The museum is well-designed, with excellent English explanations, a good audioguide, and impressive multimedia exhibits that could keep a perfume fan busy for days. Start in the Sensorial Room, where you'll spend nine minutes getting mellow while preparing your senses for the visit. The three floors below teach you everything there is to know about perfume. Your visit ends with a cool display of perfume packages for every year since 1900 and a chance to sniff 32 key perfume ingredients. Allow at least an hour to see everything.

Cost and Hours: €4, €5 combo-ticket includes gardens (see below); May-Sept daily 10:00-19:00, Oct-April Wed-Mon 10:30-17:30, closed Tue; audioguide-€1, two blocks above Fragonard Perfume at 2 Rue Jeu de Ballon, tel. 04 97 05 58 00, www.museesdegrasse.com.

Perfume Gardens: You can visit the museum's gardens, Les Jardins du MIP, about five miles from Grasse. These gardens feature acres of important plants and flowers used in perfume produc-

Fragrant Grasse

Grasse has been at the center of the fragrance industry since the 1500s, when it was known for its scented leather gloves. The cultivation of aromatic plants around Grasse slowly evolved to produce ingredients for soaps and perfumes, and by the 1800s, Grasse was recognized as the center for perfume (thanks largely to its flower-friendly climate), making it a wealthy city.

It can take a ton of carefully picked petals (like jasmine)—that's about 10,000 flowers—to make about two pounds of essence. A damaged flower petal is bad news. Today, perfumes are made from as many as 500 different scents; most are imported to Grasse from countries around the world. The "blender" of these scents and the perfume mastermind is called the "nose" (who nose best). The five master "noses" who work here must study their profession longer than a doctor goes to med school (seven years). They have to show that they have the gift before entering "nose school" (in Versailles), and they cannot drink alcohol, ever.

Skip the outlying perfumeries with French-only tours. Only three factories out of forty open their doors to visitors, and only one is worth visiting: Fragonard Perfume in Grasse.

tion (€3, €5 combo-ticket with museum, includes videoguide; daily May-Sept 10:00-19:00, April and Oct 11:00-18:00, closed Nov-March; see website or ask at museum for location).

Fragonard Perfume Factory (Visite de l'Usine)

This functioning factory, located dead-center in Grasse, provides frequent, fragrant, informative 20-minute tours and an interesting "museum" to explore while you wait. Pick up the English brochure describing what's in the museum cases, then drop down to where the tour begins. On your tour you'll learn that the difference between perfume, eau de toilette, and cologne is only a matter of perfume percentages. You'll also learn how the product is made today, as well as how they used to do it (by pressing flowers in animal fat). The tour ends with a whiff in the elegant gift shop.

Cost and Hours: Free guided tour, daily 9:00-18:00, closes for lunch Nov-Jan, just off Cours Honoré Cresp at 20 Boulevard Fragonard, tel. 04 93 36 44 65, www.fragonard.com.

Museum of Provençal Costume and Jewelry (Musée Provençal du Costume et du Bijou)

This dimly lit, small museum displays traditional dresses and jewelry from the 18th and 19th centuries. Upon leaving, you'll be given a card that you can exchange for a free gift at a shop next door.

Cost and Hours: Free, daily 10:00-13:00 & 14:00-18:30,

closed Sun in winter, a block above the *parfumerie* on the pedestrian street at 2 Rue Jean Ossola, tel. 04 93 36 44 65, www.fragonard.com.

Fragonard Museum (Musée Fragonard)

This air-conditioned, free museum houses paintings by three of Grasse's most famous artists: Jean-Honoré Fragonard, Marguerite Gérard, and Jean-Baptiste Mallet. Ask for the English explanations at the welcome desk.

Cost and Hours: Free, daily 10:00-18:00, just a few doors down from the costume museum, 14 Rue Jean Ossola, tel. 04 93 36 02 07, www.fragonard.com.

Villa Jean-Honoré Fragonard

The home of the 18th-century Baroque painter of swirling big bodies (whose father started the smelly business) has a good collection of his paintings and reproductions (with an excellent English handout).

Cost and Hours: Free; June-Sept daily 10:00-18:00; Oct-May Wed-Mon 11:00-18:00, closed Tue and all of Nov; turn left out of Fragonard Perfume and walk downhill to 23 Boulevard Fragonard, tel. 04 93 36 52 98, www.museesdegrasse.com.

Old Grasse

Just above Fragonard Perfume, Rue Jean Ossola leads into the labyrinthine ancient streets that form an intriguing pedestrian area. To get a good taste of old Grasse, you can follow the TI's minimalist self-guided tour with your map (takes an hour at a brisk pace, read the posted information plaques as you go) or, better, wander at will and read the plaques when you see them.

Start by strolling up Rue Jean Ossola (just above Boulevard Fragonard), then turn right down Rue Gazan to find the Romanesque cathedral opposite an unusual WWI monument (it's worth peering into the cathedral to see its tree-trunk-like columns and austere decor). Find the view terrace behind the cathedral—can you see the sea? From here you can descend many steps to the Italian-esque Place de l'Evêché (fun cafés) and work your way back up. Or skip the steps and double back to Rue Jean Ossola, turn right, then make a left up bohemian Rue de l'Oratoire and pop out onto a terrific square, Place aux Aires (with more good eating options).

Grand Canyon du Verdon

Two hours north of Nice and three hours east of Avignon lies the Parc Naturel Régional du Verdon (a.k.a. Gorges du Verdon). This immense area of natural beauty is worth ▲▲▲...even to Arizonans.

For millions of years, this region was covered by the sea. Over
time, sediments and the remains
of marine animals were deposited
here, becoming thick layers of limestone as they were buried. Later,
plate tectonics uplifted the limestone and erosion exposed it, and
the Verdon River—with help from
Ice Age glaciers—carved out the
gorges and its side canyons. At their
deepest points, the gorges drop
2,200 feet to the river. At the bottom, the canyons narrow to as little
as 26 feet across, while at the top,
the canyon walls spread as far as 4,700 feet apart.

INLAND RIVIERA

The Verdon River is named for its turquoise-green hue. The
striking color comes from very fine particles of rock suspended in
the water, pulverized by glaciers high at the river's source. It's a sight
that has inspired visitors since Ligurian Celts ruled the region.

PLANNING YOUR TIME

The Grand Canyon du Verdon, Europe's greatest canyon, offers a
magnificent detour between the Riviera and Provence (figure seven
hours with modest canyon time between Nice and the Luberon
or Aix-en-Provence; see my self-guided driving tour of the Inland
Riviera on page 422). I prefer to stop and smell the canyon, over-
nighting en route (suggestions later in this chapter). You can reach
the canyon on a very long round-trip drive from the Nice area if you
leave early (easier if staying in Vence or Antibes). To do this, take
the most direct route to or from the canyon and make it a one-way
loop (from Nice take the route via Grasse, tour the canyon in the
westbound direction, leave the route just before the Lac de Ste-
Croix, and connect to the autoroute back to Nice near Draguignan;
details below). The canyon can be overrun with cars in summer and
on weekends, but is quiet any day in the off-season.

Here are some rough driving times: Riviera to Grasse—1 hour,
Grasse to Balcon de la Mescla—1.5 hours, Balcon de la Mescla to
Aiguines—1.5 hours with photo stops, Aiguines to Moustiers-Ste-
Marie—20 minutes, Moustiers-Ste-Marie to Manosque (en route
to Provence)—1.5 hours.

INLAND RIVIERA

Orientation to Grand Canyon du Verdon

The Parc Naturel Régional du Verdon, far more than just its famous canyon, is a vast area mixing alpine scenery with misty villages, meandering streams, and seas of gentle meadows. The canyon is the heart of the park, where colossal slabs of white and salmon-colored limestone plunge impossible distances to the snaking Verdon River far below. You need a car, ample time, and a lack of vertigo to enjoy this area. If traveling in summer or on holiday weekends, go really early or skip it. Fill your tank before leaving Grasse or Moustiers-Ste-Marie. Roads crawl along the length of the canyon on both sides (Rive Gauche and Rive Droite); the Rive Gauche works best for most, though both are spectacular.

The Grand Canyon du Verdon is located between the villages of Moustiers-Ste-Marie and Aiguines to the west and Castellane to the east. The most scenic driving segments are along the south side (Rive Gauche), between Aiguines and the Balcon de la Mescla, and the north side (Rive Droite), between Moustiers-Ste-Marie and the Point Sublime overlook. Thrill seekers head for the Castellane area, where the whitewater rafting, climbing, and serious hiking trails are best.

There are fewer pullouts and viewpoints than you'd expect, but picnickers will find some good choices for the perfect lunch stop.

Grand Canyon du Verdon Driving Tour

FROM THE RIVIERA TO PROVENCE

For drivers connecting the Riviera with Provence via the canyon, this self-guided drive along the Rive Gauche offers the most accessible and most scenic tour of the gorges. Coming from the Riviera, you'll drive the canyon from east to west. The basic route: Drive through Grasse and toward Castellane, then turn off to hit the canyon at the Balcon de la Mescla. After seeing the canyon's most scenic stretch, you can either split off (after Aiguines) to return to the Riviera, or continue through Moustiers-Ste-Marie and on to Provence. (For drivers coming *from* Provence, this tour can be done in reverse, west to east; see "Approaching from Provence," at the end of the tour.)

Cannes to Balcon de la Mescla: The most direct route from the Riviera follows D-6185, which starts near Cannes (A-8 autoroute from Nice to Cannes saves time) and passes through Grasse, changing to D-6085 and continuing north toward Digne and Castellane. You'll turn left off D-6085 well before Castellane, following signs to the *Gorges du Verdon* and *Draguignan* (an impressive medieval bridge stands just north of the road, about 3 kilometers before Comps-sur-Artuby, signed *La Souche*). Turn right onto D-71 at Comps-sur-Artuby, following signs to *Gorges du Verdon, Rive Gauche* (not *Rive Droite*). In a few minutes, you'll reach a pullout with a good view of the village of Trigance.

Driving along D-71, you'll soon find yourself upon the canyon rim at the Balcon de la Mescla. Stop at **Le Relais de Balcon** café, with a friendly shop that has a good selection of maps and books. The lookout on the lower side of the gift shop/café is best.

Along the Canyon, from Balcon de la Mescla to Aiguines: From here, follow the canyon lip for about 90 serpentine minutes (including ample stops). You'll drive at an escargot's pace, navigating hairpin turns along the Corniche Sublime while enjoying constant views of rocky masses and vanishing-point views up the canyon. Hikes into the canyon are too long and steep for most. Most travelers are better off walking along the main road for a bit or detouring down some of the short paths scattered alongside the road. There are small pullouts along the route that come without warning. Don't expect U.S. national park conditions—you won't see a ranger, signage is minimal, and the road rarely has a shoulder.

A little beyond the Balcon de la Mescla, you can amble across Europe's second highest bridge, the **Pont de l'Artuby,** and imagine working on its construction crew *(non, merci)*. There's a large parking lot at the far end of the bridge; get out and breathe here. About three kilometers past the bridge is a dirt pullout on the north side of the road. A 10-minute stroll along the path leads to sensational views of the canyon and acres of limestone to scramble over.

About halfway through the canyon is the recommended **Hôtel-Restaurant Grand Canyon du Verdon,** clinging to its cliff like a baby to its mother. This concrete, funky place looks slapped together, but the café terrace has tables with stupendous views (drinks, snacks, and meals available at fair prices). If your driver feels cheated about missing the views, make sure you stop here for a break.

Back along the main road, the **Col d'Illoire**—the last pass before leaving the canyon—provides sweeping views from the western portal. Park in the large pullout, where you'll find a few picnic tables scattered above and some good rock-scampering just below.

Aiguines: Just west of the canyon, the small village of Aiguines squats below waves of limestone and overlooks the long turquoise Lac de Ste-Croix. This unspoiled village has a handful of shops, recommended hotels, and cafés. It's an outdoorsy, popular-with-hikers place that most canyon visitors cruise right through. Detour onto the grounds of the 15th-century *château* for the view over Aiguines (with picnic benches and a fun play area for kids; *château* interior closed to the public). Aiguines' **TI** is on the main drag (July-Aug daily 8:30-18:00, Sept-June Mon-Fri 9:00-17:00, closed Sat-Sun; Allée des Tilleuls, tel. 04 94 70 21 64, www.aiguines.com).

For more views over Aiguines and the lake, stroll up one of the many staircases along the main drag to the small **Chapelle St. Pierre.** From here, you can walk up the small road five minutes to the campground café, with nice tables on its broad view terrace (ideal for a predinner drink or morning coffee).

Returning to the Riviera: If you're day-tripping from the Riviera rather than continuing to Provence, follow signs for *Aups* (D-957) as you leave Aiguines, then *Draguignan,* then *Nice* via A-8.

Aiguines to Moustiers-Ste-Marie: If you're continuing to Provençal destinations, head for Moustiers-Ste-Marie and continue the tour below.

Barely 50 years old, the man-made **Lac de Ste-Croix** is about six miles long and is the last stop for water flowing out of the Gorges du Verdon. For a fun lake/river experience, rent a canoe or a paddleboat at either side of the low bridge halfway between Moustiers and Aiguines (no motor boats are allowed). You can paddle under the bridge, then follow the aquamarine inlet upstream as far as 2.5 miles, tracing the river's route up the gorge on its final journey to the lake (€14/hour for paddleboat or canoe, figure 2 hours for a good trip).

Moustiers-Ste-Marie: Here's another pretty Provençal face lined with boutiques—though this one comes with an impressive setting straddling a small stream at the base of the limestone cliffs of the Gorges du Verdon. The town is slammed with tourists clamoring for the locally famous china. Parking is difficult, especially in high season. The **TI** is in the center, next to the church (daily 10:00-12:30 & 14:00-18:00, no midday break July-Aug, free Wi-Fi, Place de l'Eglise, tel. 04 92 74 67 84, www.moustiers. fr). The supermarket **8 à Huit** is at the bottom of the town near the parking lots, and a smaller outlet is in the town center near the TI.

You can escape some of the crowds by climbing 20 minutes on a steep, ankle-twisting path (262 steps) to the **Chapelle Notre-Dame de Beauvoir**—a simple chapel that has attracted pilgrims for centuries. A notebook in the chapel allows travelers to pen a request for a miracle for a loved one. For most, the chapel does not warrant the effort, though you'll get great views over the village by walking a short way up the path.

Moustiers-Ste-Marie to Provence: From here it's another 1.5 to 2 hours to most Provençal destinations. From Moustiers-Ste-Marie, head for Riez, then Gréoux-les-Bains. From Gréoux-les-Bains, follow signs for *Manosque*, then *Apt* for Luberon and Avignon; or use A-51 south to reach Aix-en-Provence, Lourmarin in the Luberon, Cassis, Marseille, or Arles.

APPROACHING FROM PROVENCE

Drivers coming from Provence can do the above tour from west to east (Moustiers-Ste-Marie to the Balcon de la Mescla).

All roads from Provence pass through Gréoux-les-Bains, an hour northeast of Aix-en-Provence. Those coming from Cassis, Aix-en-Provence, the southern Luberon, and Arles will find A-51 north the fastest path; those coming from the central Luberon and Avignon should take D-900 via Apt (turns into D-4100), then follow signs for *Manosque*. From Gréoux-les-Bains, follow signs to *Riez, Moustiers-Ste-Marie,* and *Aiguines* before entering the Grand Canyon du Verdon (Rive Gauche). Ignore the *Grand Canyon du Verdon* signs as you leave Moustiers-Ste-Marie—they lead to the

Rive Droite. Follow the *Aiguines* signs instead to make sure you are going to the Rive Gauche.

Leave the canyon after the Balcon de la Mescla. To get to Nice, follow signs for *Comps-sur-Artuby* (and *Draguignan* for a short distance), then *Grasse* and *Nice*. The fastest way from Grasse to Nice is via Cannes and A-8.

Sleeping and Eating near the Grand Canyon du Verdon

These places are listed in the order you'll reach them on the self-guided driving tour from east to west. Most hotels in this area want you to take half-pension, but it is rarely required outside of high season. Budget-minded travelers will find lots of places to picnic, but bring groceries with you as stores are scarce (grocery stores and bakeries are in Gréoux and Moustiers if coming from the west, but there's not much if coming from the east—stock up before you head out).

MIDWAY THROUGH THE CANYON

$$ Hôtel-Restaurant Grand Canyon du Verdon** is housed in a funky structure that must have been grandfathered in to own such an unbelievable location—2,500 feet high on the Corniche Sublime. The hotel rents 15 basic, alpine-modern rooms, half on the canyon side, many with decks (worth reserving ahead, no-view Db-€125 for 2 people with half-pension, view Db-€140 for 2 people with half-pension—worth the added cost; room only: view Db-€95, no-view Db-€85; open mid-April-mid-Oct, easy parking, tel. 04 94 76 91 31, www.hotel-canyon-verdon.com, hotel.gd.canyon.verdon@wanadoo.fr).

IN AIGUINES

$$ Hôtel du Vieux-Château**, which has been in business for 200 years, is Aiguines' most characteristic hotel. Run by Frédéric, the hotel's 10 snug rooms are red-tiled, spotless, and cool—literally, as there's little direct light (Db-€124-136 for 2 people with half-pension, Db room only-€68-80, more expensive on weekends, breakfast-€9-12, cozy restaurant open daily with simple, hearty fare and good soups, Place de la Fontaine, closed Nov-March, tel. 04 94 70 22 95, www.hotelvieuxchateau.fr, contact@hotelvieuxchateau.fr).

$$ Hôtel Altitude 823**, just below, offers more predictable comfort with less character but better views (Db-€120-150 for 2 people with half-pension, Db room with breakfast-€86-116, open March-Oct, no air-con, tel. 04 98 10 22 17, www.hotel-

altitude823-verdon.com, altitude823@laposte.net, helpful owners
Patrice and Rosélyne).

IN MOUSTIERS-STE-MARIE

$$ La Bonne Auberge** has pastel, no-frills rooms, and a nice
pool at the southern edge of the old town (Db-€144 for 2 people
with half-pension, Db room only-€65-90, extra bed-€20, ga-
rage-€6, open April-Oct, Route de Castellane, tel. 04 92 74 66
18, www.bonne-auberge-moustiers.com, contact@bonne-auberge-
moustiers.com).

$$ Le Mas du Loup is a good-value *chambre d'hôte*, a 10-min-
ute walk outside of town. Charming Julie welcomes guests to her
five-bedroom *bastide,* where all rooms come with private patios and
comfortable beds (Db-€72-88, extra bed-€20, cash only, includes
breakfast, free parking, tel. 04 92 74 65 61, mobile 06 71 71 81 36,
www.le-mas-du-loup.com, masduloup7@hotmail.fr).

$ Restaurant/Chambres Clerissy has four spacious and spot-
less rooms. It's good for families (Db-€49, Tb-€59, breakfast-€6,
cash only, Place du Chevalier de Blacas, in the village center across
from the left transept of the church, mobile 06 76 12 40 66, tel. 04
92 77 29 30).

Eating: There is no shortage of dining options in Moustiers-
Ste-Marie. The simple **Restaurant Clerissy** (whose rooms are listed earlier) offers inexpensive and simple meals (crêpes and pizza)
and appealing indoor and outdoor tables. **Côté Jardin** is a haven
of quiet a few steps south of the old town, with a pleasing garden
setting, great views, and good cuisine at fair prices (€25-38 *menus,*
closed Mon evening and all day Tue, tel. 04 92 74 68 91).

INLAND RIVIERA

TRAVELING WITH CHILDREN

With relatively few must-see museums, plenty of outdoor activities, and cooperative weather, Provence and the French Riviera are practically made for kids. This part of France has beaches, fun canoeing on safe rivers, good biking, Roman ruins to scramble over, abundant sunshine, and swimming pools everywhere. Teenagers love the seaside resorts (Cassis and Antibes are best) and enjoy the hustle and bustle of cities like Avignon, Arles, Aix-en-Provence, and Nice. Younger kids tend to prefer the rural areas, which offer more swimming pools, open spaces, and parks.

Trip Tips

PLAN AHEAD

Involve your kids in trip planning. Have them read about the places that you may include in your itinerary (even the hotels you're considering), and let them help with your decisions.

Hotel selection is critical. In my recommendations, I've identified hotels that seem particularly kid-friendly (pools, table tennis, grassy areas, easygoing owners, etc.). If you're staying for a week or more in one place, one great option is to rent a *gîte* (see "*Gîtes* and Apartments" on page 486).

Most hotels have some sort of crib you can use. Car-rental agencies usually rent car seats, though you must reserve one in advance. Bring your own drawing supplies and English-language picture books, as these supplies are pricey in France.

If traveling with older kids, you can help them keep in touch with friends at home with cheap texting plans and by email. Hotel guest computers and Wi-Fi hotspots are a godsend. Readily available Wi-Fi (at hotels, some cafés, and all Starbucks and McDonald's) makes bringing a mobile device worthwhile. Most parents

Parenting French-Style

Famous for their topless tanning, French women are equally comfortable with public breastfeeding of their babies: No need for shawls or "hooter hiders" here. Changing tables are nonexistent, so bring a roll-up changing mat and get comfortable changing your baby on your knees, on a bench, or wherever you find enough space.

French grandmothers take their role as community elders seriously and won't hesitate to recommend that you put more sunscreen on your child in the summer, or add a layer of clothing if it's breezy.

Rather than saying *bonjour* to French children, say *coucou* (coo-coo) if they are young and *salut* (sal-oo) if they are pre-teens or older.

For older kids, be aware that the drinking age is 16 for beer and wine and 18 for the hard stuff: Your waiter will assume that your teen will have wine with you at dinner. Teens are also welcome in most bars and lounges (there's no 21-and-older section).

CHILDREN

find it worth the peace of mind to buy a supplemental messaging plan for the whole family: Adults can stay connected to teenagers while allowing them maximum independence (see page 502).

EATING
Try these tips to keep your kids content throughout the day.
- Eat dinner early (19:00-19:30 at restaurants, earlier at cafés). Skip romantic eateries. Try relaxed cafés (or fast-food restaurants) where kids can move around without bothering others.
- Kid-friendly foods that are commonly available and easy to order include crêpes (available at many takeout stands), *croque monsieurs* (grilled ham and cheese sandwiches), and *tartines* (open-faced sandwiches). Plain pasta is available at many cafés and some bistros (ask for *pâtes nature*). For breakfast, try a *pain au chocolat* (chocolate-filled pastry) or dip your baguette in a *chocolat chaud* (hot chocolate). Fruit, cereals, and yogurt are usually available. Carry a baguette to snack on. In the south of France, pizza is omnipresent.
- If your kids love peanut butter, bring it from home (hard to find in France)...or help your kids acquire a taste for Nutella, the tasty hazelnut-chocolate spread available everywhere. Look for organic *(bio)* stores in cities, where you can find numerous nut butters and *Chocolade*, a less-sugary version of Nutella.
- Picnics work well. *Boulangeries* are good places to grab off-

Books and Films for Kids

Get your kids into the traveling spirit with books and movies about France, Provence, and the French Riviera. For longer drives, audio books can be fun for the whole family (if carefully chosen). I recommend Peter Mayle's *A Year in Provence*. (Also see "Books and Films," including some good choices for teenagers, on page 535.)

Anatole (Eve Titus, 1956). This Caldecott Honor Book introduces young readers to the great world of French food via a mouse who finds work in a cheese factory.

Anni's Diary of France, by Anni Axworthy. This fun, picture-filled book about a young girl's trip will inspire your little ones.

Camille and the Sunflowers (Laurence Anholt, 1994). In a tale based on a true story, the postman's son Camille befriends his town's new resident, Vincent van Gogh.

The Cat Who Walked Across France (Kate Banks, 2004). Beautiful illustrations accompany the marvelous journey of a cat through France—including a stop at Pont du Gard near Avignon.

Discovering Great Artists: Hands-On Art for Children in the Styles of the Great Masters (MaryAnn Kohl, 1997). Get to know your favorite artists, from the Renaissance to the present day, by learning their techniques through various art activities.

Getting to Know France and French (Nicola Wright, 1993). This illustrated guide is a fun crash course for younger travelers, featuring history, school life, food, festivals, and language.

hour snacks when restaurants aren't serving. (See page 488 for picnic tips.)

SIGHTSEEING

These tips will help your children—and you—have a better trip.

- Let kids help choose daily activities, lead you through sights, and so on.
- Lower your sightseeing ambitions. Plan longer stays at fewer stops—you won't regret it.
- Minimize hotel changes by planning three-day stays. Aim for hotels with restaurants, so older kids can go back to the room while you finish a pleasant dinner.
- Museum audioguides are great for older children. For younger children, hit the gift shop first so they can buy postcards and have a scavenger hunt to find the pictured artwork. When boredom sets in, try "I spy" games or have them count how many babies or dogs they can spot in all the paintings in the room.
- To make your trip fun for everyone in the family, mix heavy-

CHILDREN

Henri's Scissors (Jeanette Winter, 2013). This beautiful picture book illustrates how Matisse found new inspiration in paper cut-outs as he lay in bed near the end of his life.

How Would You Survive in the Middle Ages? (Fiona MacDonald, 1995). MacDonald makes history fun for kids and adults alike in this engaging guide to life in the Middle Ages.

The Lady and the Squire (Terry Jones, 2000). In this fun read by a former Monty Python member, the Duke of Lancaster's squire, Tom, makes a fantastical visit to 19th-century Avignon.

Madeline (Ludwig Bemelmans, 1939). Kids love the *Madeline* series, which follows the adventures of a Parisian girl and her boarding-school pals. A live-action 1998 film brings the stories to life.

Picasso and the Girl with a Ponytail (Laurence Anholt, 2002). This picture book relates the story of Sylvette, who models for Picasso and then eventually becomes a painter herself.

Ratatouille (2007). In this animated film named for the famous Provençal dish, a mouse becomes a chef at a fine French restaurant.

The Red Balloon (1956). A small boy chases his balloon through the streets of Paris in this classic of French cinema.

When Pigasso Met Mootisse (Nina Laden, 1998). A silly picture-book take on the tempestuous relationship between Picasso and Matisse, which ultimately ended in friendship.

duty sights with kids' activities, such as playing *mini-golfs* or *boules*, renting bikes or canoes, and riding the little tourist trains popular in many towns. Some kids also like audioguides, available at important sights in many cities.

- It's good to have a "what if" procedure in place in case something goes wrong. Give your kids your hotel's business card, your phone number (if you brought a mobile phone), and emergency taxi fare. Let them know to ask to use the phone at a hotel if they are lost. And if they have mobile phones, show them how to make calls in France (see page 502).

- For memories that will last long after the trip, keep a family journal. Pack a small diary and a glue stick. While relaxing at a café over a *citron-pressé* (lemonade), take turns writing about the day's events and include mementos such as ticket stubs from museums, postcards, or stalks of lavender.

- Let kids pick out some toys and books. The best and cheapest toy selections are usually in department stores, like Monoprix and Galeries Lafayette. Note that Legos are sometimes different in Europe than in the US, and the French have wonderful doll clothes with a much wider selection than typically found in the US. Kids like the French adventure comics Astérix and Tintin (both available in English, sold in bigger bookstores with English sections).

- If you're in France near Bastille Day, remember that fireworks stands pop up everywhere on the days leading up to July 14. Putting on their own fireworks show can be a highlight for teenagers.

Top Kids' Sights and Activities

ATTRACTIONS

These are listed in no particular order:

- Pont du Gard. An entire wing of the museum is dedicated to kids, who can also swim or take a canoe trip on the river nearby (see page 141).
- Cassis. Boat trip to the *calanques,* or the port and beaches for teenagers (see page 247).
- Monaco. Changing of the Guard in Monaco (see page 384) and Cousteau Aquarium (see page 385).
- Pedal boats on the Mediterranean (see page 249) and into the Gorges du Verdon (see page 440).
- Biking or in-line skating on the Promenade des Anglais in Nice (see page 292).
- Biking through vineyards to small villages, from Vaison-la-Romaine (see page 166).
- Les Baux's castle ruins, with medieval weaponry and great walls to climb (see page 77).
- Canoeing on the Ardèche River (see page 186), the Sorgue River (see page 196), or into the Gorges du Verdon (see page 439).
- Boat trips from Nice (see page 295), Villefranche-sur-Mer (see page 354), or St-Tropez (see page 419).
- Marineland near Antibes (see page 406).

Honorable mention goes to Arles' Ancient History Museum (see page 60), horseback riding and public beaches in the Camargue (see page 95), Roman arenas in Nîmes (see page 130) and Arles (see page 51), the beaches of Antibes (see page 404), and the narrow-gauge train ride from Nice (see page 305).

ACTIVITIES

Movies

It's fun to take kids to movies (even if not in English) just to see how theaters work elsewhere. Movies shown in their original language—usually with subtitles—are listed as *v.o.* at the box office. (One showing could be *v.o.* and the next could be dubbed in

French, labeled *v.f.;* be aware that *v.o.* movies are hard to find out-side major cities.) *Dessin animé* means "cartoon." While many live-action movies can be found in their original language with French subtitles, cartoons and kids' movies (intended for an audience that doesn't read so well yet) are almost always dubbed.

Swimming
I've listed swimming pools in many places—they're great for kids. But be warned: Public pools in France commonly require a small, Speedo-like bathing suit for boys and men (American-style swim trunks won't do)—though they usually have these little suits for sale or loan. At hotel pools, any type of swimsuit will do.

Rides
You'll find old-style merry-go-rounds in many cities, perfect for younger travelers (my daughter's goal was to ride a merry-go-round in every town...she came close). There are also little tourist trains in nearly every city.

Farms
Visits to local goat-cheese makers in early spring yield good kid rewards (look for *fromage fermier de chèvre* signs along the country roads). Goats are social animals and goat-cheese makers will usu-ally let your child hold or pet one. You can also pick up some superb fresh cheese for your picnic.

Boules
Consider buying a set of *boules* (a.k.a. *pétanque,* a form of outdoor bowling—for the rules, see sidebar on page 39). Play *boules* before dinner, side by side with real players on the village court. Get your *boules de pétanque* at sporting-goods stores or larger department stores. Since they're heavy, buy a set only if you'll be driving. The *boules* also make fun, if weighty, souvenirs, and are just as enjoy-able to play back at home. TIs in some towns, such as Vence, have *boules* to rent.

SHOPPING

Provence and the Riviera offer France's best shopping outside of Paris, with a great range of reasonably priced items ideal for souvenirs and gifts. And if approached thoughtfully, shopping in the south of France can be a culturally enlightening experience. There's no better way to mix serious shopping business with travel pleasure than at the weekly markets *(marchés)* in towns and villages throughout the region. These traditional market days offer far more than fresh produce and fish; in many cases, about half the market is devoted to durable goods (baskets, tablecloths, pottery, and fabrics)—*très* handy for gift-scavenging travelers. If you miss market day, most Provençal towns have more than enough small shops that sell local products—and more than enough kitschy souvenirs. (They're often selling the same items you can find more cheaply at weekly markets.) If you crave French fashion, the cities described in this book have unlimited boutique shopping for clothing.

In this chapter you'll find information on shopping for souvenirs, navigating market days, and browsing boutiques. For information on VAT refunds and customs regulations, see page 473. For a comparison of French to US clothing sizes, see the appendix.

WHAT TO BUY

Here's a shopping list of locally made goods in Provence and the Riviera. You'll find most of these items in tourist-oriented boutiques, though many of them can be had for less on market days. If you buy more expensive, nonperishable goods, most stores will work with you to send them home.

- **Jams** *(confiture)* containing lush and often exotic fruits, such as *fruits de passion* (passion fruit), *figues* (figs), and *pastèque* or *citre* (different types of watermelon).
- **Honey** *(miel)*, particularly lavender *(lavande)* or rosemary *(ro-*

marin). Stronger palates should try the chestnut *(châtaigne)* or even oak-flavored *(chêne)* honey.

- Tins of **tapenade** (olive paste) and all kinds of **olives:** black, green, and stuffed with garlic or anchovies.

- **Olive-wood products** such as utensils and bowls. Olives are not just for nibbling; in Provence, the entire tree is used.

- Canned **pâtés,** including the buttery, rich foie gras (its "home" is Périgord, but you'll also find it in the markets of Provence). Canned goose, duck, and pork pâté can be imported to the US, but not beef.

- Packets of **herbs** (including the famous *herbes de Provence*), **salt** from the Camargue (look for *Fleur de Sel* for the best, and use sparingly), and bottles or tins of **olive oil** from local trees (Nyons is France's olive capital, though Les Baux is rightly proud of its olives as well). Most of these items can be found in attractive packaging that can be saved and enjoyed long after the product itself is gone.

- Sweets, including the famous *nougat de Montélimar* (a rich, chewy confection made with nuts and honey and sometimes flavored with lavender or other fragrances), *calissons* (orange-and-almond-flavored candy, shaped like the nut and originally from Aix-en-Provence), and **chocolates** from the Provençal producer Puyricard.

- **Soaps and lotions,** particularly those "perfumed" with local plants such as lavender *(lavande),* rosemary *(romarin),* or linden *(tilleul).* You'll also find colorful **sachets** containing the same fragrances.

- Brightly colored **table linens.** Souleiado and Les Olivades are the most famous local manufacturers, but good-quality knockoffs can be found in most any market or store.

- **Cloth bags** with French designs for grocery shopping (these pack easily and cost pennies).

- Local **pottery** (*poterie;* faïence is hand-painted *poterie*). Terre Provence is a well-known (and pricey) brand, but many other producers offer excellent quality, usually for less. Serious potters can plan ahead to visit a pottery fair featuring the best of the regions' potters.

- *Santons,* the tiny, brightly adorned clay or wood Provençal figurines. Originally designed for traditional Christmas crèche scenes, today's *santons* ("little saints") represent all walks of life—from the local *boulanger* to the woman sewing bright Provençal cloth to the village doctor. The most famous *santon* makers are in Séguret and Aubagne. All *santon* makers belong to the *santon*-maker guild (think medieval stonecutters or woodworkers), and each *santon* is handmade and signed.

SHOPPING

MARKET DAY *(JOUR DU MARCHE)*

Market days are a big deal throughout France, and in no other region are they more celebrated than in Provence and the Riviera.

Markets have been a central feature of life in rural areas since the Middle Ages. No single event better symbolizes the French preoccupation with fresh products and their strong ties to the small farmer, than the weekly market. Many locals mark their calendars with the arrival of the new season's produce.

Provence is a Mediterranean melting pot, where Italy, Spain, and North Africa intersect with France to do business. Notice the ethnic mix of the vendors (and the products they sell). Spices from Morocco and Tunisia, fresh pasta from Italy, saffron from Spain, and tapenade from Provence compete for your attention at Provence's *marchés*.

There are two kinds of weekly open-air markets: *les marchés* and *les marchés brocantes*.

Les marchés are more general in scope, more common, and more colorful, featuring products from area farmers and artisans. These markets can offer a mind-boggling array of choices, from the perishable (produce, meats, cheeses, breads, and pastries) to the nonperishable (kitchen wares, inexpensive clothing, brightly colored linens, and pottery).

Les marchés brocantes specialize in quasi-antiques and flea-market bric-a-brac. *Brocantes* markets began in the Middle Ages, when middlemen would gather to set up small stalls and sell old, flea-infested clothes and the discarded possessions of the wealthy at bargain prices to eager peasants. Buyers were allowed to *rummage* through piles of aristocratic garbage.

Many *marchés* have good selections of produce and some *brocantes*. The best of all market worlds may rest in the town of Isle-sur-la-Sorgue, where, on Sunday mornings, a brilliant food *marché* tangles with an active flea market and a good selection of antiques.

I've listed days and locations for both market types throughout this book. Notice the signs as you enter towns indicating the *jours du marché* (essential information to any civilized soul, and a reminder not to park on the streets the night before—be on the lookout for *stationnement interdit* signs that mark "no parking" areas). Most *marchés* take place once a week in the town's main square; larger *marchés* spill into nearby streets.

Usually, the bigger the market, the greater the overall selection, particularly of nonperishable goods. Bigger towns (like Arles) may have two weekly markets, one a bit larger than the other, with more nonperishable goods; in other towns (including Isle-sur-la-Sorgue), the second weekly market simply may be a smaller version of the main market day. The biggest market days are usually on weekends, so that everyone can go. In the largest cities (such as Avignon and Nîmes), modern market halls have been established, with produce stands and meat counters selling fresh goods daily.

Market day is as important socially as it is commercially—it's a weekly chance for locals to resume friendships and get the current gossip. Here neighbors can catch up on Henri's barn renovation, see photos of Jacqueline's new grandchild, and relax over *un café*. Dogs are tethered to café tables while friends exchange kisses. Tether yourself to a table and observe: three cheek-kisses for good friends (left-right-left), a fourth for friends you haven't seen in a while. (The appropriate number of kisses varies by region—Paris, Lyon, and Provence have different standards.)

Markets begin at about 8:00, with setup commencing in the predawn hours (for some, a reason not to stay in a main-square hotel the night before market day). They usually end by 13:00. Most perishable items are sold directly from the producers—no middlemen, no credit cards, just really fresh produce (*du pays* means "grown locally"). Sometimes you'll meet a widow selling a dozen eggs, two rabbits, and a wad of herbs tied with string. But most vendors follow a weekly circuit of markets they feel works best for them, showing up in the same spot every week, year in and year out. At a favorite market, my family has done business with the same olive vendor and "cookie man" for 20 years.

It's bad form to be in a hurry on market day. Allow the crowd to set your pace. Observe the interaction between vendor and client. Notice the joy they can find in chatting each other up. Wares are displayed with pride. Generally the rule is "don't touch"—instead, point and let them serve you. If self-serve is the norm, the seller will hand you a bag. Remember, they use metric weight. Ask for *un kilo* (about 2 pounds), *un demi-kilo* (about 1 pound—also called *une livre*), or *un quart-kilo* (pronounced "car-kilo," about half a pound). Many vendors speak enough English to assist you in your selection. Your total price will be hand-tallied on small scraps of paper and given to you. Vendors are normally honest. If you're struggling to find the correct change, just hold out your hand and they will take only what is needed. (Still, you're wise to double-check the amount you just paid for that olive tree.)

At the root of a good market experience is a sturdy shopping basket or bag. Find the vendor selling baskets and other wicker items and go local (*osier* is the French name for wicker, *cade* is the Provençal name—from the basket-making Luberon village of Cadenet); you can also find plastic and nylon versions. Most baskets

Key Shopping Phrases

English	French
Just looking.	*Je regarde.* (zhuh ruh-gard)
How much is it?	*Combien?* (koh<u>n</u>-bee-a<u>n</u>)
Too big/small/expensive	*Trop grand/petit/cher* (troh grah<u>n</u>/puh-tee/shehr)
May I try it on?	*Je peux l'essayer?* (zhuh puh lay-say-yay)
Can I see more?	*Je peux en voir d'autres?* (zhuh puh lay-say-yay)
I'd like this.	*Je voudrais ça.* (zhuh voo-dray sah)
On sale	*Solde* (sohld)
Discounted price	*Prix réduit* (pree ray-dwee)
Big discounts	*Prix choc* (pree shohk)

are inexpensive, make for fun and colorful souvenirs, and can come in handy for holding odd-shaped or breakable carry-ons on the plane trip home. With basket in hand, shop for your heaviest items first. (You don't want to put a kilo of fresh apples on top of the bread you bought for your picnic.)

Markets change seasonally. In April and May, look for asparagus (green, purple, or the prized white—after being cooked, these are dipped in vinegar or homemade mayonnaise and eaten by hand). In late spring, shop for strawberries, including the best: *fraises des bois* (wild strawberries). Almost equally prized are the strawberries called *gariguettes* and *maras des bois*. Soon after, you'll see cherries and other stone fruits, plus the famously sweet Cavaillon melons (resembling tiny cantaloupes, often served cut in half with a spoonful or two of the sweet Rhône white wine Beaumes de Venise). Don't worry if these are split open—the abundance of sugar and sunshine are the cause, and the *fendus* are considered the sweetest. In late June and early September, watch for figs *(figues)*. From July through September, essential vegetables for the Provençal dish ratatouille—including eggplant, tomatoes, zucchinis, and peppers—come straight from the open fields. In the fall you'll see stands selling game birds, other beasts of the hunt, and a glorious array of wild mushrooms.

After November and throughout the winter, look for little (or big, depending on your wallet size) black truffles. Truffles preserved and sealed in jars can safely be brought back to the United States. The Luberon is one of Provence's largest truffle-producing areas. The town of Carpentras hosts a truffles-only market on Friday mornings in winter. Listen carefully and you might hear the Provençal language being spoken between some vendors and buyers. Richerenches, Northern Provence's truffle capital, holds its own winter truffle market; during its annual truffle-themed Mass, many parishioners give a truffle as a small offering, instead of money. *Vive la France.*

For more immediate consumption, look for local cheeses (cow, called *vache;* sheep or ewe, called *brebis;* or the Provençal favorite: goat cheese, or chèvre, named *picodons*). Cheeses range from very fresh (aged one day) to aged for weeks. The older the cheese, the more dried and shrunken. Some may even be speckled with edible mold. Cheeses come in many shapes (round, logs, pyramids) and various sizes (from single-bite mouthfuls to wheels that will feed you for several meals). Some are sprinkled with herbs or spices. Others are more adorned, such as those rolled in ash *(à la cendre)* or wrapped in leaves *(banon)*. Watch for the locally produced *banon de banon,* a goat cheese soaked in *eau-de-vie* (the highly alcoholic "water of life"), then wrapped in chestnut leaves and tied with string—*ooh la la.*

Next, move on to the sausages (many also rolled in herbs or spices). Samples are usually free—try the *sanglier* (boar). Be on the lookout for locally produced wines or ciders (free tastings are standard) and find samples of foie gras (available in take-it-home tins), good with the sweet white wine of Beaumes de Venise. These items make perfect picnic fare when teamed with a crusty baguette.

Throughout Provence you'll see vendors selling paella made *sur place* (on the spot) in huge traditional round pans. Paella varies by area and chef, but most recipes include the traditional ingredients of fresh shellfish, chicken, and sausages mixed into saffron-infused rice. And throughout France you'll see vans selling sizzling, spit-roasted chicken (perfectly bagged for carrying-out) or pizza (made to your liking on the spot). *Bon appétit!*

CLOTHING BOUTIQUES

Those preferring fashion over food will be happy to learn that they don't have to go to Paris to enjoy the latest trends. The stylish boutiques lining the shopping streets of Avignon, Nîmes, Aix-en-Provence, St. Rémy, Uzès, Nice, and the ultra-trendy Juan-les-Pins offer more than sufficient selection and style for the fashion-conscious. Still, they play by a different set of rules in France, and the better knowledge you have of the rules, the better player you'll be. While many shopkeepers speak some English, an effort to speak even a minimum of French earns better service. These tips should get you off on the right track:

- In small stores, always say, *"Bonjour, Madame* or *Mademoiselle* or *Monsieur"* when entering. And remember to say *"Au revoir, Madame/Mademoiselle/Monsieur"* when leaving.

- The customer is not always right; in fact, some clerks figure they're doing you a favor by waiting on you.
- Except in department stores, it's not normal for the customer to handle clothing. Ask first before you pick up an item: *"Je peux?"* (zhuh puh), meaning, "Can I?"
- By law the price of items in a window display must be visible, often written on a slip of paper set on the floor or framed on the wall. This gives you an idea of how expensive or affordable the shop is.
- For clothing-size comparisons between the US and France, see the appendix.
- Forget returns (and don't count on exchanges).
- Observe French shoppers, then imitate them.
- Saturday afternoons are *très* busy and not for the faint of heart.
- Stores are closed on Sunday and usually on Monday mornings.
- Don't feel obliged to buy. If a shopkeeper offers assistance, just say, *"Je regarde, merci,"* meaning, "Just looking, thanks."
- For information on VAT refunds and customs regulations, see page 473.

SHOPPING

FRANCE: PAST AND PRESENT

FRENCH HISTORY IN AN ESCARGOT SHELL

About the time of Christ, Romans "Latinized" the land of the Gauls. With the fifth-century A.D. fall of Rome, the barbarian Franks and Burgundians invaded. Today's France evolved from this unique mix of Latin and Celtic cultures.

While France wallowed with the rest of Europe in medieval darkness, it got a head start in its development as a nation-state. In 507, Clovis, the king of the Franks, established Paris as the capital of his Christian Merovingian dynasty. Clovis and the Franks would eventually become Louis and the French. The Frankish military leader Charles Martel stopped the spread of Islam by beating the Spanish Moors at the Battle of Poitiers in 732. And Charlemagne, the most important of the "Dark Age" Frankish kings, was crowned Holy Roman Emperor by the pope in 800. Charles the Great presided over the "Carolingian Renaissance" and effectively ruled an empire that was vast for its time.

The Treaty of Verdun (843), which divided Charlemagne's empire among his grandsons, marks what could be considered the birth of Europe. For the first time, a treaty was signed in vernacular languages (French and German), rather than in Latin. This split established a Franco-Germanic divide and heralded an age of fragmentation. While petty princes took the reigns, the Frankish king ruled only Ile de France, a small region around Paris.

Vikings, or Norsemen, settled in what became Normandy. Later, in 1066, these "Normans" invaded England. The Norman king, William the Conqueror, consolidated his English domain, accelerating the formation of modern England. But his rule also muddied the political waters between England and France, kicking off a centuries-long struggle between the two nations.

In the 12th century, Eleanor of Aquitaine (a separate country

Typical Church Architecture

History comes to life when you visit a centuries-old church. Even if you wouldn't know your apse from a hole in the ground, learning a few simple terms will enrich your experience. Note that not every church has every feature, and a "cathedral" isn't a type of church architecture, but rather a designation for a church that's a governing center for a local bishop.

Aisles: The long, generally low-ceilinged arcades that flank the nave.

Altar: The raised area with a ceremonial table (often adorned with candles or a crucifix), where the priest prepares and serves the bread and wine for Communion.

Apse: The space beyond the altar, generally bordered with small chapels.

Barrel Vault: A continuous round-arched ceiling that resembles an extended upside-down U.

Choir: A cozy area, often screened off, located within the church nave and near the high altar where services are sung in a more intimate setting.

Cloister: Covered hallways bordering a (usually square-shaped) open-air courtyard, traditionally where monks and nuns got fresh air.

Facade: The exterior surface of the church's main (west) entrance, usually highly decorated.

Groin Vault: An arched ceiling formed where two equal barrel vaults meet at right angles. Less common usage: term for a medieval jock strap.

Narthex: The area (portico or foyer) between the main entry and the nave.

Nave: The long, central section of the church (running west to east, from the entrance to the altar) where the congregation sits or stands through the service.

Transept: In a traditional cross-shaped floor plan, the transept is one of the two parts forming the "arms" of the cross. The transepts run north-south, perpendicularly crossing the east-west nave.

West Portal: The main entry to the church (on the west end, opposite the main altar).

in southwest France) married Louis VII, king of France, bringing Aquitaine under French rule. They divorced, and she married Henry of Normandy, soon to be Henry II of England. This marital union gave England control of a huge swath of land, from the English Channel to the Pyrenees. For 300 years France and England would struggle for control of Aquitaine. Any enemy of the French king would find a natural ally in the English king.

In 1328, the French king Charles IV died without a son. The English king (Edward III), Charles IV's nephew, was interested in the throne, but the French resisted. This quandary pitted France, the biggest and richest country in Europe, against England, which had the largest army. They fought from 1337 to 1453 in what was modestly called the Hundred Years' War.

Regional powers from within France actually sided with England. Burgundy took Paris, captured the royal family, and recognized the English king as heir to the French throne. England controlled France from the Loire north, and things looked bleak for the French king.

Enter Joan of Arc, a 16-year-old peasant girl driven by religious voices. France's national heroine left home to support Charles VII, the dauphin (boy prince, heir to the throne but too young to rule). Joan rallied the French, ultimately inspiring them to throw out the English. In 1430 Joan was captured by the Burgundians, who sold her to the English, who convicted her of heresy and burned her at the stake in Rouen. But the inspiration of Joan of Arc lived on, and by 1453 English holdings on the Continent had dwindled to the port of Calais.

By 1500 a strong, centralized France had emerged, with borders similar to those of today. Its kings (from the Renaissance François I through the Henrys and all those Louises) were model divine monarchs, setting the standard for absolute rule in Europe.

Outrage over the power plays and spending sprees of the kings—coupled with the modern thinking of the Enlightenment (whose leaders were the French *philosophes*)—led to the French Revolution (1789). In France it was the end of the *ancien régime,* as well as its notion that some are born to rule, while others are born to be ruled.

The excesses of the Revolution in turn led to the rise of Napoleon, who ruled the French empire as a dictator. Eventually, *his* excesses ushered him into a South Atlantic exile, and after another half-century of monarchy and empire, the French settled on a compromise role for their leader. The modern French "king" is ruled by a constitution. Rather than dress in leotards and powdered wigs, the president goes to work in a suit and carries a briefcase.

The 20th century spelled the end of France's reign as a military and political superpower. Devastating wars with Germany in 1870,

Top French Notables in History

Madame and Monsieur Cro-Magnon: Prehistoric hunter-gatherers who moved to France (c. 30,000 B.C.), painted cave walls at Lascaux and Font-de-Gaume, and eventually settled down as farmers (c. 10,000 B.C.).

Vercingétorix (72-46 B.C.): This long-haired warrior rallied the Gauls against Julius Caesar's invading Roman legions (52 B.C.). Defeated by Caesar, France fell under Roman domination, resulting in 500 years of peace and prosperity. During that time, the Romans established cities, built roads, taught in Latin, and converted people to Christianity.

Charlemagne (742-814): For Christmas in 800, the pope gave King Charlemagne the title of Emperor, thus uniting much of Europe under the leadership of the Franks ("France"). Charlemagne stabilized France amid centuries of barbarian invasions. After his death, the empire was split, carving the outlines of modern France and Germany.

Eleanor of Aquitaine (c. 1122-1204): The beautiful, sophisticated ex-wife of the King of France married the King of England, creating an uneasy union between the two countries. During her lifetime, French culture was spread across Europe by roving troubadours, theological scholars, and skilled architects pioneering "the French style"—a.k.a. Gothic.

Joan of Arc (1412-1431): When France and England fought the Hundred Years' War to settle who would rule (1337-1453), teenager Joan of Arc—guided by voices in her head—rallied the French troops. Though Joan was captured and burned as a heretic, the French eventually drove England out of their country for good, establishing the current borders. Over the centuries, the church upgraded Joan's status from heretic to saint (canonized in 1920).

François I (1494-1547): This Renaissance king ruled a united, modern nation, making it a cultural center that hosted the Italian Leonardo da Vinci. François set the tone for future absolute monarchs, punctuating his commands with the phrase, "For such is our pleasure."

Louis XIV (1638-1715): Charismatic and cunning, the "Sun King" ruled Europe's richest, most populous, most powerful nation-state. Every educated European spoke French, dressed in Louis-style leotards and powdered wigs, and built Versailles-like palaces. Though Louis ruled as an absolute monarch (distracting the nobility with courtly games), his reign also fostered the arts and philosophy, sowing the seeds of democracy and revolution.

Marie Antoinette (1755-1793): As the Austrian-born wife of Louis XVI, she came to symbolize (probably unfairly) the decadence of France's ruling class. When the Revolution broke out (1789), she was arrested, imprisoned, and executed—one of thousands who were guillotined on Paris' Place de la Concorde as an enemy of the people.

Napoleon Bonaparte (1769-1821): This daring young military man became a hero during the Revolution, fighting Europe's royalty. He went on to conquer much of the Continent, become leader of France, and, eventually, rule as a dictator with the title of Emperor. In 1815 an allied Europe defeated and exiled Napoleon, reinstating the French monarchy—though future kings and emperors (including Napoleon's nephew, who ruled as Napoleon III) were somewhat subject to democratic constraints.

Claude Monet (1840-1926): Monet's Impressionist paintings captured the soft-focus beauty of the belle époque—middle-class men and women enjoying drinks in cafés, walks in gardens, and picnics along the Seine. At the turn of the 20th century, French culture reigned supreme while its economic and political clout was fading, soon to be shattered by the violence of World War I.

Charles de Gaulle (1890-1970): A career military man, de Gaulle helped France survive occupation by Nazi Germany during World War II with his rousing radio broadcasts and unbending faith in his countrymen. He left politics in the postwar period, but after France's divisive wars in Vietnam and Algeria, he came to the rescue, becoming president of the Fifth Republic in 1959. De Gaulle shocked supporters and allies by granting Algeria its independence, blocking Britain's entry into the Common Market, and withdrawing from the military wing of NATO. Turbulent student riots in the late 1960s eventually led to his resignation in 1969.

Contemporary French: Which recent French people will history remember? President François Mitterrand (1916-1996), the driving force behind Paris' La Grande Arche and Opéra Bastille? Marcel Marceau (1923-2007), white-faced mime? Chef Paul Bocuse (b. 1926), inventor of nouvelle cuisine? Brigitte Bardot (b. 1934), film actress, crusader for animal rights, and popularizer of the bikini? Yves Saint Laurent (1936-2008), one of the world's greatest fashion designers? Jean-Marie Le Pen (b. 1928), founder of the far-right National Front party, with staunch anti-immigration policies? Bernard Kouchner (b. 1939), co-founder of Doctors Without Borders and minister of foreign affairs under President Nicolas Sarkozy? Zinédine Zidane (b. 1972), France's greatest ever soccer player, whose Algerian roots helped raise the status of Arabs in France? Or Dominique Strauss-Kahn (b. 1949), disgraced International Monetary Fund chief? (I hope not.)

1914, and 1940—and the loss of her colonial holdings—left France with not quite enough land, people, or production to be a top player on a global scale. But the 21st century may see France rise again: Paris is a cultural capital of Europe, and France—under the EU banner—is a key player in unifying Europe as a single economic power. And when Europe becomes a superpower, Paris may yet be its capital.

CONTEMPORARY POLITICS IN FRANCE

Today, the main political issue in France is—like everywhere—the economy. Initially, France weathered the 2008 downturn better than the US, because it was less invested in risky home loans and the volatile stock market. But now France, along with the rest of Europe, has been struggling. French unemployment remains high (over 10 percent) and growth has flatlined. France has not balanced its books since 1974, and public spending, at 56 percent of GDP, chews up a bigger chunk of output than in any other eurozone country. Abroad, the entire eurozone has been dragged down by countries heavily in debt—Greece, Spain, Portugal, Italy, and Ireland. The challenge for French leadership is to address its economic problems while maintaining the high level of social services that the French people expect from their government.

France has its economic strengths: a well-educated workforce, an especially robust services sector and high-end manufacturing industry, and more firms big enough to rank in the global Fortune 500 than any other European country. Ironically, while France's economy may be one of the world's largest, the French remain skeptical about the virtues of capitalism and the work ethic. Globalization conflicts in a fundamental way with French virtues—many fear losing what makes their society unique in the quest for a bland, globalized world. Business conversation is generally avoided, as it implies a fascination with money that the French find vulgar. (It's considered gauche even to ask what someone does for a living.) In France, CEOs are not glorified as celebrities—chefs are.

The French believe that the economy should support social good, not vice versa. This has produced a cradle-to-grave social security system of which the French are proud. France's poverty rate is half of that in the US, proof to the French that they are on the right track. On the other hand, if you're considering starting a business in France, think again—taxes are formidable (figure a total small-business tax rate of around 66 percent—and likely to increase). French voters are notorious for their belief in the free market's heartless cruelty, and they tend to see globalization as a threat rather than a potential benefit. France is routinely plagued with strikes, demonstrations, and slowdowns as workers try to preserve their hard-earned rights in the face of a competitive global economy.

France is part of the 28-member European Union, a kind of "United States of Europe" that has successfully dissolved borders and implemented a common currency, the euro. France's governments have been decidedly pro-EU. But many French are Euroskeptics, afraid that EU meddling threatens their job security and social benefits.

The French political scene is complex and fascinating. France is governed by a president (currently François Hollande), elected by popular vote every five years. The president then selects the prime minister, who in turn chooses the cabinet ministers. Collectively, this executive branch is known as the *gouvernement*. The parliament consists of a Senate (348 seats) and the 577-seat Assemblée Nationale.

In France, compromise and coalition-building are essential to keeping power. Unlike America's two-party system, France has a half-dozen major political parties, plus more on the fringes. A simple majority is rare. Even the biggest parties rarely get more than a third of the votes. Since the parliament can force the *gouvernement* to resign at any time, it's essential that the *gouvernement* work with them.

For a snapshot of the current political landscape, look no further than the 2012 elections that brought François Hollande to power. He faced incumbent president Nicolas Sarkozy of the center-right Popular Movement Union (UMP)—the man who had cut taxes, reduced the size of government, limited the power of unions, cut workers' benefits, and (most controversially) raised the retirement age from 60 to 62.

Hollande's Socialist Party (PS) was just one of Sarkozy's challengers. There was the radical Left Front Party (which includes the once-powerful Communists) and the environmental Green Party (Les Verts). On the far-right was the National Front party (FN), led by Marine Le Pen. She called for expulsion of ethnic minorities, restoration of the French franc as the standard currency, secession from the EU, and broader police powers.

After several months and one TV debate (yes, the French election season is that short), Hollande emerged victorious. And just one month later, his Socialist Party captured more than half of the 577 seats of the Assemblée Nationale. Nevertheless, Hollande has to work closely with legislators, including a strong minority from opposing parties.

François Hollande is politically moderate and personally modest, even boring. Raised in a suburban Parisian middle-class home, he rose quietly through the ranks: assemblyman from a nondescript *département*, small-town mayor, secretary of the Socialist Party.

Trouble in Paradise: Population Growth in Southern France

Life is not as perfect as it may appear amid the breezy, sun-kissed beaches, cities, and villages of Provence and the French Riviera. The south of France has become a bouillabaisse of people in search of their Provençal paradise. While some say the influx into this region has invigorated the culture, many residents are feeling growing pains. Two major trends are fueling the population boom in the south: northern Europeans looking for their place in the sun, and North African immigrants looking for a better life in a new country. These trends are converging in southern France.

Cheap flights and lightning-fast train service have enabled northern Europeans to experience the south of France as a weekend getaway...and a growing number are choosing to stay. Thanks to its sunny climate, relatively inexpensive homes (if you're from northern Europe), and plentiful transportation options, this region is an understandably big draw. Unfortunately, as wealthy northerners pick off local homes and inflate prices, the average Jean is losing out.

Immigration, particularly from North Africa, is another cause of the population boom. With the historic loss of able-bodied men from World Wars I and II, and native-French birth rates unable to replace those losses, France looked across the Mediterranean to its old colonies for cheap sources of manual labor. When these workers came, they brought their families, who stayed in France and had families of their own (sound familiar?). Today, France has Europe's second-largest Muslim population—only Russia's is greater.

Five million North Africans legally reside in France—and many more live here illegally. Around 100,000 illegal immigrants arrive in France each year, about half of whom are North African. Most live in the south (more than a quarter of Marseille's population is North African). This concentration of immigrants among a very Catholic French population (Muslims outnumber Protestants 2 to 1), combined with high unemployment (nearly 20 percent compared to a national average of around 10 percent), has led to the rise of racist politics. This anti-immigrant movement has been spearheaded by the National Front party, which wants to keep "France for the French." Its founder, Jean-Marie Le Pen, has referred to the growing numbers of North Africans in France as "the silent invasion." The National Front generally receives about 20 percent of this region's vote in national elections.

PAST AND PRESENT

He's never before held a major elected office. Though Hollande is a "Socialist" (a word that spooks Rush Limbaugh), he's in the mainstream of the European political spectrum.

Hollande moved into the Elysée Palace (the French White House) with his "Première Dame" (or first lady), Valérie Trierweiler. Trierweiler is a well-known journalist who writes for the magazine *Paris Match* (the French counterpart to *Time*). She was the first unwed first lady to occupy the Elysée Palace. But in January 2014, it was revealed that Hollande was cheating on her (his personal guards drove him on a Vespa to his lover's apartment in the wee hours), which brought the relationship to an end. *Oh-la-la*—imagine this drama in the States. Reaction in France has been predictably understated, as one's personal business is, after all, personal.

But Hollande faces challenges beyond his home life. On the sluggish economy, he favors government expansion and stimulus rather than austerity: hiring thousands of teachers, building hundreds of thousands of homes, and taxing all income above a million euros at 75 percent. Abroad, he's run into trouble working with Germany to shore up weaker members of the eurozone. And he's had to abandon his promise to return the retirement age—at least for some workers—to 60. Hollande's *lune de miel* (honeymoon) has clearly passed—liberals and conservatives alike are furious over his economic policies. In the spring of 2015 his approval rating was below 20 percent.

In recent years the French political scene has become as polarized as in the United States, although the attack on the satirical magazine *Charlie Hebdo* in January 2015 brought some unity, if only for a short period. This attack shocked a nation unaccustomed to terrorism on its soil. The government's challenge: to respond with sufficient intensity to deter would-be terrorists without infringing on the rights of its Muslim population.

Another ongoing issue that French leaders must work together to address is immigration, which is shifting the country's ethnic and cultural makeup in ways that challenge French society. Ten percent of France's population is of North African descent, mainly immigrants from former colonies. The increased number of Muslims raises cultural questions in this heavily Catholic society that institutes official state secularism. The French have (quite controversially) made it illegal for women to wear a full, face-covering veil *(niqāb)* in public. They continue to debate whether banning the veil enforces democracy—or squelches diversity.

Finally, a prominent Socialist whom Hollande must contend with is Ségolène Royal. She lost to Sarkozy in the 2007 presidential election, and lost to Hollande in the 2011 primary. In 2014, she was appointed France's Minister of Ecology. As it happens, Royal and Hollande know each other well: They met in college,

lived together for 30 years, and raised four children before splitting up in 2007. They never married. French politics makes strange
bedfellows. But that's personal...

For more about French history, consider Europe 101: History and
Art for the Traveler *by Rick Steves and Gene Openshaw, available at
www.ricksteves.com.*

PRACTICALITIES

This chapter covers the practical skills of European travel: how to get tourist information, pay for things, sightsee efficiently, find good-value accommodations, eat affordably but well, use technology wisely, and get between destinations smoothly. To study ahead and round out your knowledge, check out "Resources."

Tourist Information

The French national tourist office is a wealth of information. **Before your trip,** scan their website—us.rendezvousenfrance.com. It has particularly good resources for special-interest travel and plenty of free-to-download brochures.

In France, a good first stop is generally the tourist information office (abbreviated **TI** in this book). Be aware that TIs are in business to help you enjoy spending money in their town. (Once upon a time, they were actually information services, but today some have become ad agencies masquerading as TIs.) While this corrupts much of their advice—and you can get plenty of information online—I still make a point to swing by the local TI upon arrival in a new town.

Even if they are overly commercial, TIs continue to be good places to confirm opening times, pick up a city map, and get information on public transit (including bus and train schedules), walking tours, special events, and nightlife. Prepare a list of questions and a proposed plan to double-check. Many TIs have information on the entire country or at least the region, so try to pick up maps for destinations you'll be visiting later in your trip. If you're arriving in town after the TI closes, call ahead or pick up a map in a neighboring town.

The French call TIs by different names: *Office de Tourisme* and *Bureau de Tourisme* are used in cities; *Syndicat d'Initiative* and *Information Touristique* are used in small towns. Also look for *Accueil* signs in airports and at popular sights. These information booths are staffed with seasonal helpers who provide tourists with limited, though generally sufficient, information. Smaller TIs are often closed from 12:00 to 14:00 and on Sundays.

Some TIs offer a room-booking service for a fee, though they're unable to give hard opinions on the relative value of one place over another. It's best to go direct with the listings in this book. But in a pinch, you could use the TI (or consult an online booking site, which can provide a broader range of options).

Travel Tips

Emergency and Medical Help: In France, dial 112 for any emergency. For English-speaking police, call 17. To summon an ambulance, call 15. If you get sick, do as the locals do and go to a pharmacist for advice. Or ask at your hotel for help—they'll know the nearest medical and emergency services.

Theft or Loss: To replace a passport, you'll need to go in person to an embassy or consulate (see page 533). If your credit and debit cards disappear, cancel and replace them (see "Damage Control for Lost Cards" on page 472). File a police report, either on the spot or within a day or two; you'll need it to submit an insurance claim for lost or stolen rail passes or travel gear, and it can help with replacing your passport or credit and debit cards. For more information, see www.ricksteves.com/help. To minimize the effects of loss, back up your digital photos and other files frequently.

Time Zones: France, like most of continental Europe, is generally six/nine hours ahead of the East/West Coasts of the US. The exceptions are the beginning and end of Daylight Saving Time: Europe "springs forward" the last Sunday in March (two weeks after most of North America), and "falls back" the last Sunday in

October (one week before North America). For a handy online time converter, see www.timeanddate.com/worldclock.

Business Hours: You'll find much of rural France closed weekdays from noon to 14:00 (lunch is sacred). On Sunday, most businesses are closed (family is sacred), though some small shops such as *boulangeries* (bakeries) are open until noon, special events and weekly markets pop up, and museums are open all day (but public transportation options are scant). On Mondays, some businesses are closed until 14:00 and possibly all day. Smaller towns are often quiet and downright boring on Sundays and Mondays, unless it's market day. Saturdays are virtually weekdays, with earlier closing hours at some shops. Banks are generally open on Saturday and closed on Sunday and possibly Monday. Friday and Saturday evenings are lively; Sunday evenings are quiet.

Watt's Up? Europe's electrical system is 220 volts, instead of North America's 110 volts. Most newer electronics (such as laptops, battery chargers, and hair dryers) convert automatically, so you won't need a converter, but you will need an adapter plug with two round prongs, sold inexpensively at travel stores in the US. Avoid bringing older appliances that don't automatically convert voltage; instead, buy a cheap replacement in Europe. You can buy low-cost hair dryers and other small appliances at Darty and Monoprix stores, which you'll find in major cities (ask your hotelier for the closest branch).

Discounts: Discounts aren't always listed in this book. However, many sights offer discounts for youths (usually up to age 18), students (with proper identification cards, www.isic.org), families, and groups of 10 or more. Always ask, and have your passport available at sights for proof. Seniors (age 60 and over) may get the odd discount, though these are often limited to citizens of the European Union (EU). To inquire about a senior discount, ask, *"Réduction troisième âge?"* (ray-dewk-see-ohn trwah-zee-ehm ahzh).

Online Translation Tips: You can use Google's Chrome browser (available free at www.google.com/chrome) to instantly translate websites. With one click, the page appears in (very rough) English translation. You can also paste the URL of the site into the translation window at www.google.com/translate. The Google Translate app converts spoken English into most European languages (and vice versa) and can also translate text it "reads" with your mobile device's camera.

Money

This section offers advice on how to pay for purchases on your trip (including getting cash from ATMs and paying with plastic), dealing with lost or stolen cards, VAT (sales tax) refunds, and tipping.

Exchange Rate

1 euro (€) = about $1.10

To convert prices in euros to dollars, add about 10 percent: €20=about $22, €50=about $55. (Check www.oanda.com for the latest exchange rates.) Just like the dollar, one euro (€) is broken down into 100 cents. You'll find coins ranging from €0.01 to €2, and bills from €5 to €500 (bills over €50 are rarely used).

WHAT TO BRING

Bring both a credit card and a debit card. You'll use the debit card at cash machines (ATMs) to withdraw local cash for most purchases, and the credit card to pay for larger items. Some travelers carry a third card, in case one gets demagnetized or eaten by a temperamental machine. For an emergency reserve, consider bringing €200 in hard cash in €20-50 bills (bring euros, as dollars can be hard to change in France).

CASH

Cash is just as desirable in Europe as it is at home. Small businesses (B&Bs, mom-and-pop cafés, shops, etc.) prefer that you pay your bills with cash. Some vendors will charge you extra for using a credit card, some won't accept foreign credit cards, and some won't take any credit cards at all. Cash is the best—and sometimes only—way to pay for cheap food, bus fare, taxis, and local guides.

Throughout Europe, ATMs are the standard way for travelers to get cash. They work just like they do at home. To withdraw money from an ATM (known as a *distributeur;* dee-stree-bew-tur), you'll need a debit card (ideally with a Visa or MasterCard logo for maximum usability), plus a PIN code (numeric and four digits). For increased security, shield the keypad when entering your PIN code, and don't use an ATM if anything on the front of the machine looks loose or damaged (a sign that someone may have attached a "skimming" device to capture account information). Try to withdraw large sums of money to reduce the number of per-transaction bank fees you'll pay.

When possible, use ATMs located outside banks—a thief is less likely to target a cash machine near surveillance cameras, and if your card is munched by a machine, you can go inside for help. Stay away from "independent" ATMs such as Travelex, Euronet, YourCash, Cardpoint, and Cashzone, which charge huge commissions, have terrible exchange rates, and may try to trick users with "dynamic currency conversion" (described at the end of "Credit and

Debit Cards," next). Although you can use a credit card to withdraw cash at an ATM, this comes with high bank fees and only makes sense in an emergency.

While traveling, if you want to monitor your accounts online to detect any unauthorized transactions, be sure to use a secure connection (see page 507).

Pickpockets target tourists. To safeguard your cash, wear a money belt—a pouch with a strap that you buckle around your waist like a belt and tuck under your clothes. Keep your cash, credit cards, and passport secure in your money belt, and carry only a day's spending money in your front pocket.

CREDIT AND DEBIT CARDS

For purchases, Visa and MasterCard are more commonly accepted than American Express. Just like at home, credit or debit cards work easily at larger hotels, restaurants, and shops. I typically use my debit card to withdraw cash to pay for most purchases. I use my credit card sparingly: to book hotel reservations, to buy advance tickets for events or sights, to cover major expenses (such as car rentals or plane tickets), and to pay for things online or near the end of my trip (to avoid another visit to the ATM). While you could instead use a debit card for these purchases, a credit card offers a greater degree of fraud protection.

Ask Your Credit- or Debit-Card Company: Before your trip, contact the company that issued your debit or credit cards.

• Confirm that your **card will work overseas,** and alert them that you'll be using it in Europe; otherwise, they may deny transactions if they perceive unusual spending patterns.

• Ask for the specifics on transaction **fees.** When you use your credit or debit card—either for purchases or ATM withdrawals—you'll typically be charged additional "international transaction" fees of up to 3 percent (1 percent is normal) plus $5 per transaction. Some banks have agreements with European partners that help save on fees (for example, Bank of America customers don't have to pay the transaction fee when using French Paribas-BNP ATMs). If your card's fees seem high, consider getting a different card just for your trip: Capital One (www.capitalone.com) and most credit unions have low-to-no international fees.

• Verify your daily ATM **withdrawal limit,** and if necessary, ask your bank to adjust it. I prefer a high limit that allows me to take out more cash at each ATM stop and save on bank fees; some travelers prefer to set a lower limit in case their card is stolen. Note that foreign banks also set maximum withdrawal amounts for their ATMs.

• Get your bank's emergency **phone number** in the US (but

not its 800 number, which isn't accessible from overseas) to call collect if you have a problem.

• Ask for your credit card's **PIN** in case you need to make an emergency cash withdrawal or you encounter Europe's chip-and-PIN system; the bank won't tell you your PIN over the phone, so allow time for it to be mailed to you.

Magnetic-Stripe versus Chip-and-PIN Credit Cards: Europeans use chip-and-PIN credit cards that are embedded with an electronic security chip and require a four-digit PIN. Your American-style card (with just the old-fashioned magnetic stripe) will work fine in most places. But it probably won't work at unattended payment machines, such as those at train and subway stations, toll plazas, parking garages, bike-rental kiosks, and gas pumps. If you have problems, try entering your card's PIN, look for a machine that takes cash, or find a clerk who can process the transaction manually.

Major US banks are beginning to offer credit cards with chips. Many of these are not true chip-and-PIN cards, but instead are "chip-and-signature" cards, for which your signature verifies your identity. These cards should work for live transactions and at some payment machines, but won't work for offline transactions such as at unattended gas pumps. If you're concerned, ask if your bank offers a true chip-and-PIN card. Andrews Federal Credit Union (www.andrewsfcu.org) and the State Department Federal Credit Union (www.sdfcu.org) offer these cards and are open to all US residents.

No matter what kind of card you have, it pays to carry euros; remember that you can always use an ATM to withdraw cash with your magnetic-stripe debit card.

Dynamic Currency Conversion: If merchants, hoteliers, or ATMs offer to convert your purchase price into dollars (called dynamic currency conversion, or DCC), refuse this "service." You'll pay even more in fees for the expensive convenience of seeing your charge in dollars.

Damage Control for Lost Cards

If you lose your credit, debit, or ATM card, you can stop people from using your card by reporting the loss immediately to the respective global customer-assistance centers. Call these 24-hour US numbers collect: Visa (tel. 303/967-1096), MasterCard (tel. 636/722-7111), and American Express (tel. 336/393-1111). In France, to make a collect call to the US, dial 08 00 90 06 24, then say "operator" for an English-speaking operator. European toll-free numbers (listed by country) can be found at the websites for Visa and MasterCard. For another option (with the same results), you can call these toll-free numbers in France: Visa (tel. 08 00 90 11

79) and MasterCard (tel. 08 00 90 13 87). American Express has a Paris office, but the call isn't free (tel. 01 47 77 70 00, greeting is in French, dial 1 to speak with someone in English).

Try to have this information ready: full card number, whether you are the primary or secondary cardholder, the cardholder's name exactly as printed on the card, billing address, home phone number, circumstances of the loss or theft, and identification verification (your birth date, your mother's maiden name, or your Social Security number—memorize this, don't carry a copy). If you are the secondary cardholder, you'll also need to provide the primary cardholder's identification-verification details. You can generally receive a temporary card within two or three business days in Europe (see www.ricksteves.com/help for more).

If you report your loss within two days, you typically won't be responsible for any unauthorized transactions on your account, although many banks charge a liability fee of $50.

TIPPING

Tipping *(donner un pourboire)* in France isn't as automatic and generous as it is in the US. For special service, tips are appreciated, but not expected. As in the US, the proper amount depends on your resources, tipping philosophy, and the circumstances, but some general guidelines apply.

Restaurants: At cafés and restaurants, a service charge is included in the price of what you order, and it's unnecessary to tip extra, though you can for superb service. For details on tipping in restaurants, see page 492.

Taxis: For a typical ride, round up your fare a bit (for instance, if the fare is €13, pay €14). If the cabbie hauls your bags and zips you to the airport to help you catch your flight, you might want to toss in a little more. But if you feel like you're being driven in circles or otherwise ripped off, skip the tip.

Services: In general, if someone in the service industry does a super job for you, a small tip of a euro or two is appropriate...but not required. If you're not sure whether (or how much) to tip for a service, ask a local for advice.

GETTING A VAT REFUND

Wrapped into the purchase price of your French souvenirs is a Value-Added Tax (VAT) of about 20 percent. You're entitled to get most of that tax back if you purchase more than €175 (about $195) worth of goods at a store that participates in the VAT-refund scheme. Typically, you must ring up the minimum at a single retailer—you can't add up your purchases from various shops to reach the required amount.

Getting your refund is straightforward and, if you buy a substantial amount of souvenirs, well worth the hassle. If you're lucky, the merchant will subtract the tax when you make your purchase. (This is more likely to occur if the store ships the goods to your home.) Otherwise, you'll need to:

Get the paperwork. Have the merchant completely fill out the necessary refund document, called a *bordereau de détaxe*. You'll have to present your passport. Get the paperwork done before you leave the store to ensure you'll have everything you need (including your original sales receipt).

Get your stamp at the border or airport. Process your VAT document at your last stop in the European Union (such as at the airport) with the customs agent who deals with VAT refunds. Arrive an additional hour before you need to check in for your flight to allow time to find the local customs office—and to stand in line. It's best to keep your purchases in your carry-on. If they're too large or dangerous to carry on (such as knives), pack them in your checked bags and alert the check-in agent. You'll be sent (with your tagged bag) to a customs desk outside security; someone will examine your bag, stamp your paperwork, and put your bag on the belt. You're not supposed to use your purchased goods before you leave. If you show up at customs wearing your chic new shoes, officials might look the other way—or deny you a refund.

Collect your refund. You'll need to return your stamped document to the retailer or its representative. Many merchants work with a service, such as Global Blue or Premier Tax Free, that has offices at major airports, ports, or border crossings (either before or after security, probably strategically located near a duty-free shop). At Charles de Gaulle, you'll find them at the check-in area (or ask for help at an orange ADP info desk). These services, which extract a 4 percent fee, can refund your money immediately in cash or credit your card (within two billing cycles). If the retailer handles VAT refunds directly, it's up to you to contact the merchant for your refund. You can mail the documents from home, or more quickly, from your point of departure (using an envelope you've prepared in advance or one that's been provided by the merchant). You'll then have to wait—it can take months.

CUSTOMS FOR AMERICAN SHOPPERS

You are allowed to take home $800 worth of items per person duty-free, once every 31 days. You can take home many processed and packaged foods: vacuum-packed cheeses, dried herbs, jams, baked goods, candy, chocolate, oil, vinegar, mustard, and honey. Fresh fruits and vegetables and most meats are not allowed, with exceptions for some canned items. As for alcohol, you can bring in one liter duty-free (it can be packed securely in your checked luggage, along with any other liquid-containing items).

To bring alcohol (or liquid-packed foods) in your carry-on bag on your flight home, buy it at a duty-free shop at the airport. You'll increase your odds of getting it onto a connecting flight if it's packaged in a "STEB"—a secure, tamper-evident bag. But stay away from liquids in opaque, ceramic, or metallic containers, which usually cannot be successfully screened (STEB or no STEB).

For details on allowable goods, customs rules, and duty rates, visit help.cbp.gov.

Sightseeing

Sightseeing can be hard work. Use these tips to make your visits to Provence and the Riviera's finest sights meaningful, fun, efficient, and painless.

PLAN AHEAD

Set up an itinerary that allows you to fit in all your must-see sights. For a one-stop look at opening hours in the bigger cities, see the "At a Glance" sidebars for Arles, Avignon, Marseille, Nice, and Monaco. Most sights keep stable hours, but you can easily confirm the latest by checking with the TI or visiting museum websites.

Don't put off visiting a must-see sight—you never know when a place will close unexpectedly for a holiday, strike, or restoration. Many museums are closed or have reduced hours at least a few days a year, especially on holidays such as Christmas, New Year's, and Labor Day (May 1). A list of holidays is on page 534; check online for possible museum closures during your trip. In summer, some sights may stay open late. Off-season, many museums have shorter hours.

Going at the right time helps avoid crowds. This book offers tips on the best times to see specific sights. Try visiting these busy villages and sights on weekdays, and arrive early or late in the day: Les Baux, Pont du Gard, Séguret, Roussillon, Fontaine de Vaucluse, Nice's Chagall and Antibes' Picasso museums, St-Paul-de-Vence, Eze-le-Village, and St-Tropez.

Evening visits are usually peaceful, with fewer crowds. Keep in mind that French monuments and cities (and some villages) are beautifully lit at night, making evening walks a joy.

Study up. To get the most out of the self-guided tours and sight descriptions in this book, read them before you visit.

AT SIGHTS

Here's what you can typically expect:

Entering: Several cities offer sightseeing passes that can be worthwhile values. Be warned that you may not be allowed to enter if you arrive 30 to 60 minutes before closing time. And guards start ushering people out well before the actual closing time, so don't save the best for last.

Some important sights have a security check, where you must open your bag or send it through a metal detector. Some sights require you to check daypacks and coats. (If you'd rather not check your daypack, try carrying it tucked under your arm like a purse as you enter.) If you check a bag, the attendant may ask you if it contains anything of value—such as a camera, phone, money, passport—since these usually cannot be checked.

At churches—which often offer interesting art (usually free) and a cool, welcome seat—a modest dress code (no bare shoulders or shorts) is encouraged though rarely enforced

Photography: If the museum's photo policy isn't clearly posted, ask a guard. Generally, taking photos without a flash or tripod is allowed. Some sights ban photos altogether.

Temporary Exhibits: Museums may show special exhibits in addition to their permanent collection. Some exhibits are included in the entry price, while others come at an extra cost (which you may have to pay even if you don't want to see the exhibit).

Expect Changes: Artwork can be on tour, on loan, out sick, or shifted at the whim of the curator. Pick up a floor plan as you enter, and ask museum staff if you can't find a particular item. Say the title or artist's name, or point to the photograph in this book and ask for its location by saying, *"Où est?"* (oo ay).

Audioguides and Apps: Many sights rent audioguides, which generally offer worthwhile recorded descriptions in English. If you bring your own earbuds, you can enjoy better sound and avoid holding the device to your ear. To save money, bring a Y-jack and share one audioguide with your travel partner. Increasingly, museums and sights offer apps—often free—that you can download to your mobile device (check their websites).

Services: Important sights may have an on-site café or cafeteria (usually a handy place to rejuvenate during a long visit). The WCs at sights are free and generally clean.

Before Leaving: At the gift shop, scan the postcard rack or thumb through a guidebook to be sure that you haven't overlooked something that you'd like to see.

Every sight or museum offers more than what is covered in this book. Use the information in this book as an introduction—not the final word.

Sleeping

Accommodations in Provence and the Riviera are a good value and generally easy to find. Choose from one- to five-star hotels (two and three stars are my mainstays), bed-and-breakfasts (*chambres d'hôtes,* usually cheaper than hotels), hostels, campgrounds, and even homes (*gîtes,* rented by the week).

I favor hotels and restaurants that are handy to your sightseeing activities. Rather than list hotels scattered throughout a city, I choose hotels in my favorite neighborhoods. My recommendations run the gamut, from dorm beds to fancy rooms with all of the comforts.

A major feature of the Sleeping sections of this book is my extensive and opinionated listing of good-value rooms. I like places

that are clean, central, relatively quiet at night, reasonably priced, friendly, small enough to have a hands-on owner and stable staff, and run with a respect for French traditions. (In France, for me, five out of these seven criteria means it's a keeper.) I'm more impressed by a convenient location and a fun-loving philosophy than flat-screen TVs and a pricey laundry service.

Book your accommodations well in advance, especially if you want to stay at one of my top listings or if you'll be traveling during busy times. Wherever you're staying, be ready for crowds during these holiday periods: Easter weekend; Labor Day; Ascension weekend; Pentecost weekend; Bastille Day and the week during which it falls; and the winter holidays (mid-Dec-early Jan).

See page 534 for a list of major holidays and festivals in France; for tips on making reservations, see page 484.

Some people make reservations as they travel, calling hotels and *chambres d'hôtes* a few days to a week before their arrival. If you'd rather travel without any reservations at all, you'll have greater success snaring rooms if you arrive at your destination early in the day. If you anticipate crowds (weekends are worst) on the day you want to check in, call hotels at about 9:00 or 10:00, when the receptionist knows who'll be checking out and which rooms will be available. If you encounter a language barrier, ask the fluent receptionist at your current hotel to call for you.

RATES AND DEALS

I've described my recommended accommodations using a Sleep Code (see sidebar). The prices I list are for one-night stays in peak season, do not include breakfast (unless noted), and assume you're booking directly with the hotel, not through an online hotel-book-

PRACTICALITIES

ing engine or TI. Booking services extract a commission from the hotel, which logically closes the door on special deals. Book direct.

If I give a single rate for a room, it applies to high season (figure Easter to October); if I give a range, the lower rates are likely available only in winter. Hotels in France must charge a daily tax *(taxe du séjour)* of about €1-2 per person per day. Some hotels include it in the listed prices, but most add it to your bill.

My recommended hotels each have a website (often with a built-in booking form) and an email address; you can expect a response in English within a day (and often sooner). You'll almost always find the lowest rates through a hotel's own website.

It's smart to email several hotels to ask for their best price. Comparison-shop and make your choice. This is especially helpful when dealing with the larger hotels that use "dynamic pricing," a computer-generated system that predicts the demand for particular days and sets prices accordingly: High-demand days can be more than double the price of low-demand days. This makes it impossible for a guidebook to list anything more accurate than a wide range of prices. I regret this trend. While you can assume that hotels listed in this book are good, it's difficult to say which ones are the better value unless you email to confirm the price.

As you look over the listings, you'll notice that some accommodations promise special prices to Rick Steves readers. To get these rates, you must book direct (that is, not through a booking site like TripAdvisor or Booking.com), mention this book when you reserve, and then show the book upon arrival. Rick Steves discounts apply to readers with ebooks as well as printed books. Because I trust hotels to honor this, please let me know if you don't receive a listed discount. Note, though, that discounts understandably may not be applied to promotional rates.

In general, prices can soften if you stay at least three nights or mention this book. You can also try asking for a cheaper room or a discount.

TYPES OF ACCOMMODATIONS
Hotels

In this book, the price for a double room will normally range from

€40 (very simple; toilet and shower down the hall) to €400-plus (grand lobbies, maximum plumbing, and the works), with most clustering around €80-110 (with private bathrooms).

The French have a simple hotel rating system based on amenities and rated by stars (indicated in this book by asterisks, from * through *****). One star is modest, two has most of the comforts, and three is generally a

Sleep Code

(€1 = about $1.10, country code: 33)

Price Rankings

To help you easily sort through my listings, I've divided the accommodations into three categories, based on the highest price for a basic double room with bath during high season:

$$$ **Higher Priced**
 $$ **Moderately Priced**
  $ **Lower Priced**

I always rate hostels as $, whether or not they have double rooms, because they have the cheapest beds in town.

Prices can change without notice; verify the hotel's current rates online or by email. For the best prices, always book directly with the hotel.

Abbreviations

To pack maximum information in minimum space, I use the following code to describe the accommodations in this book. Prices listed are per room, not per person. When a price range is given for a type of room (such as a double room listing for €100-130), it means the price fluctuates with the season, size of room, or length of stay; expect to pay the upper end for peak-season stays.

 S = Single room (or price for one person in a double)
 D = Double or twin room
 T = Triple (generally a double bed with a single)
 Q = Quad (usually two double beds; adding an extra child's bed to a T is usually cheaper)
 b = Private bathroom with toilet and shower or tub
 * = French hotel rating system, ranging from zero to five stars

According to this code, a couple staying at a "Db-€100" hotel would pay a total of €100 (about $110) for a double room with a private bathroom. Unless otherwise noted, breakfast is not included, hotel staff speak basic English, and credit cards are accepted. There's almost always Wi-Fi and/or a guest computer available, and it's generally free.

PRACTICALITIES

two-star with a fancier lobby and more elaborately designed rooms. Four-star places give marginally more comfort than those with three. Five stars probably offer more luxury than you'll have time to appreciate. Two- and three-star hotels are required to have an English-speaking staff, though nearly all hotels I recommend have someone who speaks English.

The number of stars does not always reflect room size or guarantee quality. One- and two-star hotels are less expensive, but some three-star (and even a few four-star hotels) offer good value, justifying the extra cost. Unclassified hotels (no stars) can be bargains or depressing dumps.

Within each hotel, prices vary depending on the size of room, whether it has a tub or shower, and the bed type (tubs and twins cost more than showers and double beds). If you have a preference, ask for it. Hotels often have more rooms with tubs (which the French prefer) and are inclined to give you one by default. You can save as much as €20 per night by finding the rare room without a private shower or toilet.

Most French hotels now have queen-size beds—to confirm, ask, *"Avez-vous des lits de cent-soixante?"* (ah-vay-voo day lee duh sahn-swah-sahnt). Some hotels push two twins together under king-size sheets and blankets to make *le king* size. If you'll take either twins or a double, ask for a generic *une chambre pour deux* (room for two) to avoid being needlessly turned away. Many hotels have a few family-friendly rooms that open up to each other *(chambres communiquantes)*.

Extra pillows and blankets are often in the closet or available on request. To get a pillow, ask for *"Un oreiller, s'il vous plaît"* (uhn oh-ray-yay, see voo play).

Hotel elevators, while becoming more common, are often very small—pack light, or you may need to take your bags up one at a time.

Hotel lobbies, halls, and breakfast rooms are off-limits to smokers, though they can light up in their rooms. Still, I seldom smell any smoke in my rooms. Some hotels have nonsmoking rooms or floors—ask.

Most hotels offer some kind of breakfast (see page 487), but it's rarely included in the room rates—pay attention when comparing rates between hotels. The price of breakfast correlates with the price of the room: The more expensive the room, the more expensive the breakfast. This per-person charge rises with the number of stars the hotel has and can add up, particularly for families. While hotels hope you'll buy their breakfast, it's optional unless otherwise noted; to save money, head to a bakery or café instead.

Some hoteliers, especially in resort towns, strongly encourage their peak-season guests to take *demi-pension* (half-pension)—that is, breakfast and either lunch or dinner at the hotel. By law, they can't require you to take half-pension unless you are staying three or more nights, but, in practice, some do during summer. And though the food is usually good, it limits your ability to shop around. I've indicated where I think *demi-pension* is a good value.

Hoteliers uniformly detest it when people bring food into bedrooms. Dinner picnics are particularly frowned upon: Hoteliers worry about cleanliness, smells, and attracting insects. Be tidy and considerate.

French Hotel-Room Lingo

Study the price list on the hotel's website or posted at the desk, so you know your options. Receptionists often don't mention the cheaper rooms—they assume you want a private bathroom or a bigger room. Here are the types of rooms and beds:

French	English
une chambre avec douche et WC (ewn shahm-bruh ah-vehk doosh ay vay-say)	room with private shower and toilet
une chambre avec bain et WC (ewn shahm-bruh ah-vehk ban ay vay-say)	room with private bathtub and toilet
une chambre avec cabinet de toilette (ewn shahm-bruh ah-vehk kah-bee-nay duh twah-leht)	room with a toilet (shower down the hall)
une chambre sans douche ni WC (ewn shahm-bruh sahn doosh nee vay-say)	room without a private shower or toilet
chambres communiquantes (shahm-bruh koh-mew-nee-kahnt)	connecting rooms (ideal for families)
une chambre simple, un single (ewn shahm-bruh san-pluh, uhn san-guhl)	a true single room
un grand lit (uhn grahn lee)	double bed (55 in. wide)
deux petits lits (duh puh-tee lee)	twin beds (30-36 in. wide)
un lit de cent-soixante (uhn lee duh sahn-swah-sahnt)	queen-size bed (63 in. wide)
un king size (uhn "king size")	king-size bed (usually two twins pushed together)
un lit pliant (uhn lee plee-ahn)	folding bed
un bérceau (uhn behr-soh)	baby crib
un lit d'enfant (uhn lee dahn-fahn)	child's bed

PRACTICALITIES

If you're arriving in the morning, your room probably won't be ready. Drop your bag safely at the hotel and dive right into sightseeing.

Hoteliers can be a great help and source of advice. Most know their city well, and can assist you with everything from public transit and airport connections to calling an English-speaking doctor, or finding a good restaurant, Wi-Fi hotspot (*point Wi-Fi,* pwan wee-fee), or self-service launderette (*laverie automatique,* lah-vay-ree oh-to-mah-teek).

Keep Cool

If you're visiting southern France in the summer, booking an air-conditioned room is the way to go. Most French air conditioners are operated with a control stick (like a TV remote; the hotel may require a deposit). You'll likely see these symbols and features: fan icon (click to toggle through wind power, from light to gale); louver icon (steady airflow or waves); snowflake and sunshine icons (cold air or heat); clock ("O" setting: run X hours before turning off; "I" setting: wait X hours to start); and the temperature control (21 or 22 degrees Celsius is comfortable; also see the thermometer diagram on page 539). When you leave your room for the day, turning off the air-conditioning is good form.

Even at the best places, mechanical breakdowns occur: Air-conditioning malfunctions, sinks leak, hot water turns cold, and toilets gurgle and smell. Report your concerns clearly and calmly at the front desk. For more complicated problems, don't expect instant results.

To guard against theft in your room, keep valuables out of sight. Some rooms come with a safe, and other hotels have safes at the front desk. I've never bothered using one.

Checkout can pose problems if surprise charges pop up on your bill. If you settle your bill the afternoon before you leave, you'll have time to discuss and address any points of contention (before 19:00, when the night shift usually arrives). Some hoteliers will ask you to sign their *Livre d'Or* (literally "Golden Book," for client comments). They take this seriously and enjoy reading your remarks.

Above all, keep a positive attitude. Remember, you're on vacation. If your hotel is a disappointment, spend more time out enjoying the place you came to see.

Modern Hotel Chains: France is littered with ultramodern hotels, providing drivers with low-stress accommodations, often located on cheap land just outside town (though you'll find some in city centers as well). The clean and inexpensive Ibis Budget chain (about €40-55/room for up to three people), the more attractive and spacious standard Ibis hotels (€80-110 for a double), and the cushier Mercure and Novotel hotels (€130-250 for a double) are all run by the same company, Accor (www.accorhotels.com). Though hardly quaint, these can be a good value (look for deals on their websites), particularly when they're centrally located; I list many in this book. Other chains to consider are Kyriad, with moderate prices and good quality (www.kyriad.com) and the familiar-

The Good and Bad of Online Reviews

User-generated travel review websites—such as TripAdvisor, Booking.com, and Yelp—have quickly become a huge player in the travel industry. These sites give you access to actual reports—good and bad—from travelers who have experienced the hotel, restaurant, tour, or attraction.

My hotelier friends in Europe are in awe of these sites' influence. Small hoteliers who want to stay in business have no choice but to work with review sites—which often charge fees for good placement or photos, and tack on commissions if users book through the site instead of directly with the hotel.

While these sites work hard to weed out bogus users, my hunch is that a significant percentage of reviews are posted by friends or enemies of the business being reviewed. I've even seen hotels "bribe" guests (for example, offer a free breakfast) in exchange for a positive review. Also, review sites aren't curated and can become an echo chamber, with one or two flashy businesses camped out atop the ratings, while better, more affordable, and more authentic alternatives sit ignored farther down the list. (For example, I find review sites' restaurant recommendations skew to very touristy, obvious options.) And you can't always give credence to the negative reviews: Different people have different expectations.

Remember that a user-generated review is based on the experience of one person. That person likely stayed at one hotel and ate at a few restaurants, and doesn't have much of a basis for comparison. A guidebook is the work of a trained researcher who has exhaustively visited many alternatives to assess their relative value. I recently checked out some top-rated TripAdvisor listings in various towns; when stacked up against their competitors, some are gems, while just as many are duds.

Both types of information have their place, and in many ways, they're complementary. If a hotel or restaurant is well-reviewed in a guidebook or two, and also gets good ratings on one of these sites, it's likely a winner.

to-Americans Best Western (www.bestwestern.com). Château and Hotels Collection has more cushy digs (www.chateauxhotels.com).

Bed & Breakfasts

B&Bs (*Chambres d'hôte*, abbreviated "CH") generally are found in smaller towns and rural areas. They're usually family-run and a great deal, offering double the cultural intimacy for less than most hotel rooms. While you may lose some hotel conveniences—such as lounges, in-room phones, daily bed-sheet changes, and credit-card payments—I happily make the trade-off for the personal touch and lower rates. It's always OK to ask to see the room be-

Making Hotel Reservations

Reserve your rooms several months in advance—or as soon as you've pinned down your travel dates. Note that some national holidays merit your making reservations far in advance (see page 534).

Requesting a Reservation: It's easiest to book your room through the hotel's website. (For the best rates, always use the hotel's official site and not a booking agency's site.) If there's no reservation form, or for complicated requests, send an email (see below for a sample request). Most recommended hotels take reservations in English.

The hotelier wants to know:
- the number and type of rooms you need
- the number of nights you'll stay
- your date of arrival (use the European style for writing dates: day/month/year)
- your date of departure
- any special needs (such as bathroom in the room or down the hall, cheapest room, twin beds vs. double bed)

Mention any discounts—for Rick Steves readers or otherwise—when you make the reservation.

Confirming a Reservation: Most places will request a credit-card number to hold your room. If they don't have a secure online reservation form—look for the *https*—you can email it (I do), but it's safer to share that confidential info via a phone call or two emails (splitting your number between them)

Canceling a Reservation: If you must cancel, it's courteous—and smart—to do so with as much notice as possible, especially

fore you commit. And though some CHs post small *Chambres* or *Chambres d'hôte* signs in their front windows, many are found only through the local tourist office.

I recommend reliable CHs that offer a good value and/or unique experience (such as CHs in renovated mills, châteaux, and wine *domaines*). While *chambres d'hôte* have their own star-rating system, it doesn't correspond to the hotels' rating system. So, to avoid confusion, I haven't listed these stars for CHs. But virtually all of my recommended CHs have private in-room bathrooms and Wi-Fi, and some have common rooms with refrigerators. Doubles generally cost €60-80; fancier places are about €100-120. Breakfast is usually included—ask. *Tables d'hôte* are CHs that offer an optional, reasonably priced, home-cooked dinner (usually a fine value, must be requested in advance). And though your hosts may not speak English, they will almost always be enthusiastic and pleasant.

From:	rick@ricksteves.com
Sent:	Today
To:	info@hotelcentral.com
Subject:	Reservation request for 19-22 July

Dear Hotel Central,

I would like to reserve a room for 2 people for 3 nights, arriving 19 July and departing 22 July. If possible, I would like a quiet room with a double bed and private bathroom inside the room.

Please let me know if you have a room available and the price.

Thank you!
Rick Steves

for smaller family-run places (which describes most of the hotels I list). Be warned that cancellation policies can be strict; read the fine print or ask about these before you book. Internet deals may require prepayment, with no refunds for cancellations.

Reconfirming a Reservation: Always call or email to reconfirm your room reservation a few days in advance. For B&Bs or very small hotels, I call again on my day of arrival to tell my host what time I expect to get there (especially important if arriving late—after 17:00).

Phoning: For tips on calling hotels overseas, see page 502.

Hostels

A hostel *(auberge de jeunesse)* provides cheap beds where you sleep alongside strangers for about €23-35 per night. Travelers of any age are welcome if they don't mind dorm-style accommodations and meeting other travelers. Most hostels offer kitchen facilities, guest computers, Wi-Fi, and a self-service laundry. Nowadays, concerned about bedbugs, hostels are likely to provide all bedding, including sheets. Family and private rooms may be available on request.

Independent hostels tend to be easygoing, colorful, and informal (no membership required); www.hostelworld.com is the standard way backpackers search and book hostels, but also try www.hostelz.com and www.hostels.com.

Official hostels are part of Hostelling International (HI) and share an online booking site (www.hihostels.com). HI hostels typically require that you either have a membership card or pay extra per night.

PRACTICALITIES

Camping

In Europe, camping is more of a social than an environmental experience. It's a great way for American travelers to make European friends. Camping costs about €22 per campsite per night, and almost every destination recommended in this book has a campground within a reasonable walk or bus ride from the town center and train station. A tent, pillow, and sleeping bag are all you need. Many campgrounds have small grocery stores and washing machines, and some even come with cafés and miniature golf. Local TIs have camping information. You'll find more detailed information in the annually updated *Michelin Camping France,* available in the United States and at most French bookstores.

Private Rooms, *Gîtes,* and Apartments

Renting an apartment, house, or villa can be a fun and cost-effective way to go local. Websites such as Booking.com, Airbnb, VRBO, and FlipKey let you browse properties and correspond directly with European property owners or managers. Airbnb and Roomorama also list rooms in private homes. Beds range from air-mattress-in-living-room basic to plush-B&B-suite posh. If you want a place to sleep that's free, Couchsurfing.org is a vagabond's alternative to Airbnb. It lists millions of outgoing members, who host fellow "surfers" in their homes.

Throughout France you can find reasonably priced rental homes, and nowhere are there more options than in Provence and the Riviera. Because this region is so small, you could rent one home in Provence and one in the Riviera, and day-trip to most of the sights described in this book.

Gîtes: These countryside homes (pronounced "zheet") are usually urbanites' second homes, rentable by the week, from Saturday to Saturday. The objective of the *gîte* program was to save characteristic rural homes from abandonment and to make it easy and affordable for families to enjoy the French countryside. The government offers subsidies to renovate such homes, then coordinates rentals to make it financially feasible for the owner. Today, France has more than 9,000 *gîtes.* One of your co-authors restored a farmhouse a few hours north of Provence, and even though he and his wife are American, they received the same assistance that French owners get.

Gîtes are best for drivers (they're usually rural, with little public-transport access) and ideal for families and small groups (since they can sleep many for the same price). Homes range in comfort from simple cottages and farmhouses to restored châteaux. Most have at least two bedrooms, a kitchen, a living room, and a bathroom or two. Sheets or linens may be included or provided for a bit extra. Like hotels, all *gîtes* are rated for comfort from one to four *épis* (ears of corn). Two or three *épis* generally indicate sufficient quality, but I'd lean toward three for more comfort. Prices generally range from €500 to €1,500 per week, depending on house size and amenities such as pools. Some owners may not speak English, so be prepared for doing business in French. For more information on *gîtes* in Provence, visit www.gites-de-france.com (with the most rentals), www.gite.com, or www.provence-guide.com.

Apartments: Less common than *gîtes*, apartments are available in cities and in towns along the Riviera (one-week minimum rentals). Avignon, Aix-en-Provence, Nice, and other Riviera towns have the biggest selection. It's usually more expensive to stay in an apartment than in a *gîte*.

You'll find homes and apartments for rent through TIs and online. To find a place, try the resources listed earlier, or one of these: **France Homestyle,** run by Claudette, a service-oriented French woman from Seattle who handpicks every home and apartment she lists (US tel. 206/325-0132, www.francehomestyle.com, info@francehomestyle.com), or **Ville et Village,** which has a bigger selection of higher-end places (US tel. 510/559-8080, www.villeetvillage.com).

Eating

The French eat long and well—nowhere more so than in the south. Relaxed and tree-shaded lunches with a chilled rosé, three-hour dinners, and endless hours of sitting in outdoor cafés are the norm. Here, celebrated restaurateurs are as famous as great athletes, and mamas hope their babies will grow up to be great chefs. Cafés, cuisine, and wines should become a highlight of any French adventure: It's sightseeing for your palate. Even if the rest of you is sleeping in a cheap hotel, let your taste buds travel first-class in France. (They can go coach in Britain.)

You can eat well without going broke—but choose carefully: You're just as likely to blow a small fortune on a mediocre meal as you are to dine wonderfully for €20. Read the information that follows, consider my restaurant suggestions in this book, and you'll do fine. When restaurant-hunting on your own, choose a spot filled with locals, not the place with the big neon signs boasting, "We Speak English and Accept Credit Cards." Venturing even a block or two off the main drag can lead to higher-quality food for less than half the price of the tourist-oriented places. Locals eat better at lower-rent locales.

BREAKFAST
Most hotels offer an optional breakfast, which is usually pleasant and convenient, for about €8-15. A few hotels serve a classic

continental breakfast, called *petit déjeuner* (puh-tee day-zhuh-nay). Traditionally, this consisted of a café au lait, hot chocolate, or tea; a roll with butter and marmalade; and a croissant. But these days most hotels put out a buffet breakfast (cereal, yogurt, fruit, cheese, croissants, juice, and hard-boiled eggs).

If all you want is coffee or tea and a croissant, the corner café offers more atmosphere and is less expensive (though you get more coffee at your hotel). Go local at the café and ask for *une tartine* (oon tart-een), a baguette slathered with butter or jam. If you crave eggs for breakfast, drop into a café and order *une omelette* or *œufs sur le plat* (fried eggs). Some cafés and bakeries offer worthwhile breakfast deals with juice, croissant, and coffee or tea for about €5 (for more on coffee and tea drinks, see page 500).

To keep it cheap, pick up some fruit at a grocery store and pastries at your favorite *boulangerie* and have a picnic breakfast, then savor your coffee at a café bar *(comptoir)* while standing, like the French do. As a less atmospheric alternative, some fast-food places offer cheap breakfasts.

PICNIC DINING AND FOOD TO GO

Whether going all out on a perfect French picnic or simply grabbing a sandwich to eat on an atmospheric square, dining with the village or city as your backdrop can be one of your most memorable meals.

Picnics

Great for lunch or dinner, French picnics can be first-class affairs and adventures in high cuisine. Be daring. Try the smelly cheeses, ugly pâtés, sissy quiches, and minuscule yogurts. Shopkeepers are accustomed to selling small quantities of produce. Get a succulent salad-to-go, and ask for a plastic fork. If you need a knife or corkscrew, borrow one from your hotelier (but don't picnic in your room, as French hoteliers uniformly detest this). Though drinking wine in public places is taboo in the US, it's *pas de problème* in France.

Assembling a Picnic: Visit several small stores to put together a complete meal. Shop early, as many shops close from 12:00 or 13:00 to 15:00 for their lunch break. Say *"Bonjour"* as you enter, then point to what you want and say, *"S'il vous plaît."* For other terminology you might need while shopping, see the sidebar on page 489.

At the *boulangerie* (bakery), buy some bread. A baguette usually does the trick, or choose from the many loaves of bread on display: *pain aux céréales* (whole grain with seeds), *pain de campagne* (country bread, made with unbleached bread flour), *pain complet*

Picnic Vocabulary

English	French
please	*s'il vous plaît* (see voo play)
a plastic fork	*une fourchette en plastique* (oon foor-sheht ahn plah-steek)
a small box	*une barquette* (oon bar-keht)
a knife	*un couteau* (uhn koo-toh)
corkscrew	*tire-bouchon* (teer-boo-shohn)
sliced	*tranche* (trahn-shay)
a slice	*une tranche* (oon trahnsh)
a small slice	*une petite tranche* (oon puh-teet trahnsh)
more	*plus* (plew)
less	*moins* (mwah)
It's just right.	*C'est bon.* (say bohn)
That'll be all.	*C'est tout.* (say too)
Thank you.	*Merci.* (mehr-see)

(wheat bread), or *pain de seigle* (rye bread). To ask for it sliced, say "*Tranché, s'il vous plaît.*"

At the ***pâtisserie*** (pastry shop, which is often the same place you bought the bread), choose a dessert that's easy to eat with your hands. My favorites are *éclairs* (*chocolat* or *café* flavored), individual fruit *tartes* (*framboise* is raspberry, *fraise* is strawberry, *citron* is lemon), and *macarons* (made of flavored cream sandwiched between two meringues, not coconut cookies like in the US).

At the ***crémerie*** or ***fromagerie*** (cheese shop), choose a sampling of cheeses. I usually get one hard cheese (like Comté, Cantal, or Beaufort), one soft cow's milk cheese (like Brie or Camembert), one goat's milk cheese (anything that says chèvre), and one blue cheese (Roquefort or Bleu d'Auvergne). Goat cheese usually comes in individual portions. For all other large cheeses, point to the cheese you want and ask for *une petite tranche* (a small slice). The shopkeeper will place a knife on the cheese indicating the size of the slice they are about to cut, then look at you for approval. If

you'd like more, say, "*Plus.*" If you'd like less, say, "*Moins.*" If it's just right, say, "*C'est bon!*"

At the **charcuterie** or **traiteur** (for deli items, prepared salads, meats, and pâtés), I like a slice of *pâté de campagne* (country pâté made of pork) and *saucissons sec* (dried sausages, some with pepper crust or garlic—you can ask to have it sliced thin like salami). I get a fresh salad, too. Typical options are *carottes râpées* (shredded carrots in a tangy vinaigrette), *salade de betteraves* (beets in vinaigrette), and *céleri rémoulade* (celery root with a mayonnaise sauce). The food comes in takeout boxes, and they may supply a plastic fork.

At a ***cave à vin*** you can buy chilled wines that the merchant is usually happy to open and re-cork for you.

At a ***supermarché, épicerie,*** or ***magasin d'alimentation*** (small grocery store or minimart), you'll find plastic cutlery and glasses, paper plates, napkins, drinks, chips, and a display of produce. Local *supermarchés* are less colorful than smaller stores, but cheaper, more efficient, and offer adequate quality. Department stores often have supermarkets in the basement. On the outskirts of cities, you'll find the monster *hypermarchés*. Drop in for a glimpse of hyper-France in action.

Another option is to visit open-air markets *(marchés),* which are fun and photogenic, but shut down around 13:00 (many are listed in this book; local TIs have complete lists). There's more information about these wonderful Provençal experiences in the Shopping chapter (see "Market Day" on page 452).

To-Go Food

Throughout Provence and the Riviera you'll find plenty of to-go options at *crêperies,* bakeries, and small stands. Baguette sandwiches, quiches, and pizza-like items are tasty, filling, and budget-friendly (about €4-5).

Sandwiches: Anything served *à la provençale* has marinated peppers, tomatoes, and eggplant. A sandwich *à la italienne* is a grilled *panini*. Here are some common sandwiches:

Fromage (froh-mahzh): Cheese (white on beige).

Jambon beurre (zhahn-bohn bur): Ham and butter (boring for most but a French classic).

Jambon crudités (zhahn-bohn krew-dee-tay): Ham with tomatoes, lettuce, cucumbers, and mayonnaise.

Pain salé (pan sah-lay) or ***fougasse*** (foo-gahs): Bread rolled up with salty bits of bacon, cheese, or olives.

Poulet crudités (poo-lay krew-dee-tay): Chicken with tomatoes, lettuce, maybe cucumbers, and always mayonnaise.

Saucisson beurre (saw-see-sohn bur): Thinly sliced sausage and butter.

Thon crudités (tohn krew-dee-tay): Tuna with tomatoes, lettuce, and maybe cucumbers, but definitely mayonnaise.

Quiche: Typical quiches you'll see at shops and bakeries are *lorraine* (ham and cheese), *fromage* (cheese only), *aux oignons* (with onions), *aux poireaux* (with leeks—my favorite), *aux champignons* (with mushrooms), *au saumon* (salmon), or *au thon* (tuna).

Crêpes: The quintessentially French thin pancake called a crêpe (rhymes with "step," not "grape") is filling, usually inexpensive, and generally quick. Simply place your order at the *crêperie* window or kiosk, and watch the chef in action. But don't be surprised if they don't make a wrapper for you from scratch; at some *crêperies,* they might premake a stack of wrappers and reheat them when they fill your order.

Crêpes generally are *sucrée* (sweet) or *salée* (savory). Technically, a savory crêpe should be made with a heartier buckwheat batter, and is called a galette. However, many cheap and lazy *crêperies* use the same sweet batter *(de froment)* for both their sweet-topped and savory-topped crêpes. A *socca* is a chickpea crêpe.

Standard crêpe toppings include cheese *(fromage;* usually Swiss-style Gruyère or Emmental), ham *(jambon),* egg *(oeuf),* mushrooms *(champignons),* chocolate, Nutella, jam *(confiture),* whipped cream *(chantilly),* apple jam *(compote de pommes),* chestnut cream *(crème de marrons),* and Grand Marnier.

RESTAURANT AND CAFE DINING

To get the most out of dining out in France, slow down. Allow enough time, engage the waiter, show you care about food, and enjoy the experience as much as the food itself.

French waiters probably won't overwhelm you with friendliness. As their tip is already included in the bill (see "Tipping," later), there's less schmoozing than we're used to at home. Notice how hard they work. They almost never stop. Cozying up to clients (French or foreign) is probably the last thing on their minds. They're often stuck with client overload, too, because the French rarely hire part-time employees, even to help with peak times. To get a waiter's attention, try to make meaningful eye contact, which is a signal that you need something. If this doesn't work, raise your hand and simply say, *"S'il vous plaît"* (see voo play)—"please."

This phrase should also work when you want to ask for the check. In French eateries, a waiter will rarely bring you the check unless you request it. For a French person, having the bill dropped off before asking for it is akin to being kicked out—*très gauche.* But busy travelers are often ready for the check sooner rather than later. If you're in a hurry, ask for the bill when your server comes to clear your plates or checks in to see if you want dessert or coffee. To request your bill, say, *"L'addition, s'il vous plaît."* If you don't ask now, the wait staff may become scarce as they leave you to digest in peace. (For a list of other restaurant survival phrases, see page 543.)

Note that all café and restaurant interiors are smoke-free. Today the only smokers you'll find are at outside tables, which—unfortunately—may be exactly where you want to sit.

For a list of common French dishes that you'll see on menus, see page 495. For specific suggestions on what to sample here in the south, see my cuisine suggestions in the introductions to Provence (page 31) and the Riviera (page 286). For details on ordering drinks, see page 499.

Tipping: At cafés and restaurants, a 12-15 percent service charge is always included in the price of what you order (*service compris* or *prix net*), but you won't see it listed on your bill. Unlike in the US, France pays servers a decent wage. Because of this, most locals never tip. If you feel the service was exceptional, tip up to 5 percent extra. If you want the waiter to keep the change when you pay, say *"C'est bon"* (say bohn), meaning "It's good." If you are using a credit card, leave your tip in cash—credit-card receipts don't even have space to add a tip. Never feel guilty if you don't leave a tip.

Cafés and Brasseries

French cafés and brasseries provide user-friendly meals and a relief from sightseeing overload. They're not necessarily cheaper than many restaurants and bistros, and famous cafés on popular squares can be pricey affairs. Their key advantage is flexibility: They offer long serving hours, and you're welcome to order just a salad, a sandwich, or a bowl of soup, even for dinner. It's also fine to split starters and desserts, though not main courses.

Cafés and brasseries usually open by 7:00, but closing hours vary. Unlike restaurants, which open only for dinner and sometimes for lunch, some cafés and all brasseries serve food throughout the day (usually with a limited menu), making them the best option for a late lunch or an early dinner. Note that many cafés in smaller towns close their kitchens from about 14:00 until 18:00.

Check the price list first, which by law must be posted prominently (if you don't see one, go elsewhere). There are two sets of prices: You'll pay more for the same drink if you're seated at a table *(salle)* than if you're seated or standing at the bar or counter *(comptoir)*. (For tips on ordering coffee and tea, see page 500.)

At a café or a brasserie, if the table is not set, it's fine to seat yourself and just have a drink. However, if it's set with a placemat and cutlery, you should ask to be seated and plan to order a meal. If you're unsure, ask the server before sitting down.

Ordering: A salad, crêpe, quiche, or omelet is a fairly cheap way to fill up. Each can be made with various extras such as ham, cheese, mushrooms, and so on. Omelets come lonely on a plate with a basket of bread.

Vegetarians, Allergies, and Other Dietary Restrictions

Many French people think "vegetarian" means "no red meat" or "not much meat." If you're a strict vegetarian, be specific: Tell your server what you don't eat—and it can be helpful to clarify what you do eat. Write it out on a card and keep it handy.

But be reasonable. Think of your meal (as the French do) as if it's a finely crafted creation by a trained artist. The chef knows what goes well together, and substitutions are considered an insult to his training. Picky eaters should try their best to just take it or leave it.

However, French restaurants are willing to accommodate genuine dietary restrictions and other special concerns, or at least point you to an appropriate choice on the menu. These phrases might help:

French	English
Je suis végétarien/végétarienne. (zhuh swee vay-zhay-tah-ree-an/ vay-zhay-tah-ree-ehn)	I am vegetarian.
Je ne peux pas manger de _____. (zhuh nuh puh pah mahn-zhay duh _____)	I cannot eat _____.
Je suis allergique à _____. (zhuh sweez ah-lehr-zheek ah _____)	I am allergic to _____.
Pas de_____. (pah duh _____).	No _____.

Sandwiches, generally served day and night, are inexpensive, but most are very plain (*boulangeries* serve better ones). To get more than a piece of ham (*jambon*) on a baguette, order a *sandwich jambon crudités,* which means it's garnished with veggies. Popular sandwiches are the *croque monsieur* (grilled ham-and-cheese) and *croque madame* (*monsieur* with a fried egg on top).

Salads are typically large and often can be ordered with warm ingredients mixed in, such as melted goat cheese, fried gizzards, or roasted potatoes. One salad is perfect for lunch or a light dinner. See page 496 for a list of classic salads.

The daily special—*plat du jour* (plah dew zhoor), or just *plat*— is your fast, hearty, and garnished hot plate for about €12-20. At most cafés, feel free to order only *entrées* (which in French means the starter course); many people find these lighter and more interesting than a main course. A vegetarian can enjoy a tasty, filling meal by ordering two *entrées* (for more on navigating France with dietary restrictions, see sidebar on this page).

Regardless of what you order, bread is free but almost never comes with butter; to get more bread, just hold up your basket and ask, *"Encore, s'il vous plaît?"*

Restaurants

Choose restaurants filled with locals. Consider my suggestions and your hotelier's opinion, but trust your instincts. If a restaurant doesn't post its prices outside, move along. Refer to my restaurant recommendations to get a sense of what a reasonable meal should cost.

Restaurants in the south open for dinner at 19:00 (cafés open earlier), and are most crowded about 20:30 (the early bird gets the table). Last seating is usually about 21:00 (22:00 in cities and on the French Riviera).

Tune into the quiet, relaxed pace of French dining. The French don't do dinner and a movie on date nights; they just do dinner. The table is yours for the night. Notice how quietly French diners speak in restaurants and how this improves your overall experience. Out of consideration for others, speak as softly as the locals.

If a restaurant serves lunch, it generally begins at 12:00 and goes until 14:00, with last orders taken at about 13:30. If you're hungry when restaurants are closed (late afternoon), go to a *boulangerie,* brasserie, or café (see previous section). Remember that even the fanciest places usually have affordable lunch *menus* (often called *formules* or *plat de midi*), allowing you to sample the same gourmet cooking for generally about half the cost of dinner.

Ordering: In French restaurants, you can choose something off the menu (called the *carte*), or you can order a multicourse, fixed-price meal (confusingly, called a *menu*). Or, if offered, you can get one of the special dishes of the day *(plat du jour)*. If you ask for *un menu* (instead of *la carte*), you'll get a fixed-price meal.

You'll have the best selection if you order à la carte (from what we would call the menu). I enjoy going à la carte especially when traveling with others and eating family style (waiters are happy to accommodate this approach and will bring small extra plates). It's traditional to order an *entrée* (a starter—not a main dish) and a *plat principal* (main course). The *plats* are generally more meat-based, while the *entrées* usually include veggies. Multiple course meals, while time-consuming (a positive thing in France), create the appropriate balance of veggies to meat. Elaborate meals may also have *entremets*—tiny dishes served between courses. Wherever you dine, consider the waiter's recommendations and anything *de la maison* (of the house), as long as it's not an organ meat (tripe, *rognons,* or andouillette).

Two people can split an *entrée* or a big salad (since small-size dinner salads are usually not offered á la carte) and then each get a *plat principal.* At restaurants, it's considered inappropriate for two diners to share one main course. If all you want is a salad or soup, go to a café or brasserie.

Fixed-price *menus,* which usually include two or three courses, are generally a good value and will help you pace your meal like the locals. With a three-course *menu* you'll choose a starter of soup, appetizer, or salad; select from three or four main courses with vegetables; and then finish up with a cheese course and/or a choice of desserts. It sounds like a lot of food, but portions are smaller in France, and what we cram onto one large plate they spread out over several courses. Wine and other drinks are extra, and certain premium items add a few euros to the price, clearly noted on the menu (*supplément* or *sup.*). Most restaurants offer less expensive and less filling two-course *menus,* sometimes called *formules,* featuring an *entrée et plat,* or *plat et dessert.* Some restaurants (and cafés) offer great-value lunch *menus,* and many restaurants have a reasonable *menu–enfant* (kid's meal).

In the south, I usually order *une entrée* and *un plat* from *la carte* (often as a two-course *menu* or *formule*), then find an ice-cream or crêpe stand and take a dessert stroll. If that sounds like too much, just order *un plat* (but don't skip the dessert stroll!).

FRENCH CUISINE

General styles of French cooking include *haute cuisine* (classic, elaborately prepared, multicourse meals); *cuisine bourgeoise* (the finest-quality home cooking); *cuisine des provinces* (traditional dishes of specific regions); and *nouvelle cuisine* (a focus on smaller portions and closer attention to the texture and color of the ingredients). Sauces are a huge part of French cooking. In the early 20th century, the legendary French chef Auguste Escoffier identified five French "mother sauces" from which all others are derived: *béchamel* (milk-based white sauce), *espagnole* (veal-based brown sauce), *velouté* (stock-based white sauce), *hollandaise* (egg yolk-based white sauce), and *tomate* (tomato-based red sauce).

The following list of items should help you navigate a typical French menu. Galloping gourmets should bring a menu translator. The most complete (and priciest) menu reader around is *A to Z of French Food* by G. de Temmerman. The *Marling Menu-Master* is also good. The *Rick Steves' French Phrase Book & Dictionary,* with a menu decoder, works well for most travelers. For specifics on specialties in Provence and the Riviera, see pages 31 and 286.

PRACTICALITIES

First Course *(Entrée)*

Crudités: A mix of raw and lightly cooked fresh vegetables, usually including grated carrots, celery root, tomatoes, and beets, often with a hefty dose of vinaigrette dressing. If you want the dressing on the side, say, *"La sauce à côté, s'il vous plaît"* (lah sohs ah koh-tay, see voo play).

Escargots: Snails cooked in parsley-garlic butter. You don't even have to like the snail itself. Just dipping your bread in garlic butter is more than satisfying. Prepared a variety of ways, the classic is *à la bourguignonne* (served in their shells).

Foie gras: Rich and buttery in consistency—and hefty in price—this pâté is made from the swollen livers of force-fed geese (or ducks, in *foie gras de canard)*. Spread it on bread, and never add mustard. For a real French experience, try this dish with some sweet white wine (often offered by the glass for an additional cost).

Huîtres: Oysters, served raw any month, are particularly popular at Christmas and on New Year's Eve, when every café seems to have overflowing baskets in their window.

Œuf mayo: A simple hard-boiled egg topped with a dollop of flavorful mayonnaise.

Pâtés **and** *terrines:* Slowly cooked ground meat (usually pork, though game, poultry liver, and rabbit are also common) that is highly seasoned and served in slices with mustard and *cornichons* (little pickles). Pâtés are smoother than the similarly prepared but chunkier *terrines.*

Soupe à l'oignon: Hot, salty, filling French onion soup is a beef broth served with a baked cheese-and-bread crust over the top.

Salads *(Salades)*

With the exception of a *salade mixte* (simple green salad, often difficult to find), the French get creative with their *salades*. Here are some classics:

Salade au chèvre chaud: This mixed green salad is topped with warm goat cheese on small pieces of toast.

Salade aux gésiers: Though it may not sound appetizing, this salad with chicken gizzards (and often slices of duck) is worth a try.

Salade composée: "Composed" of any number of ingredients, this salad might have *lardons* (bacon), Comté (a Swiss-style cheese), Roquefort (blue cheese), *œuf* (egg), *noix* (walnuts), and *jambon* (ham, generally thinly sliced).

Salade niçoise: A specialty from Nice, this tasty salad usually includes greens topped with green beans, boiled potatoes, tomatoes, anchovies, olives, hard-boiled eggs, and lots of tuna.

Salade paysanne: You'll usually find potatoes *(pommes de terre)*, walnuts *(noix)*, tomatoes, ham, and egg in this salad.

Main Course *(Plat Principal)*

Duck, lamb, and rabbit are popular in France, and each is prepared in a variety of ways. You'll also encounter various stew-like dishes that vary by region. The most common regional specialties are described here.

Bœuf bourguignon: A Burgundian specialty, this classy beef stew is cooked slowly in red wine, then served with onions, potatoes, and mushrooms.

Confit de canard: A favorite from the southwest Dordogne region is duck that has been preserved in its own fat, then cooked in its fat, and often served with potatoes (cooked in the same fat). Not for dieters. (Note that *magret de canard* is sliced duck breast and very different in taste.)

Coq au vin: This Burgundian dish is rooster marinated ever so slowly in red wine, then cooked until it melts in your mouth. It's served (often family-style) with vegetables.

Daube: Generally made with beef, but sometimes lamb, this is a long and slowly simmered dish, typically paired with noodles or other pasta.

Escalope normande: This specialty of Normandy features turkey or veal in a cream sauce.

Gigot d'agneau: A specialty of Provence, this is a leg of lamb often grilled and served with white beans. The best lamb is *pré salé*, which means the lamb has been raised in salt-marsh lands (like at Mont St-Michel).

Poulet rôti: Roasted chicken on the bone—French comfort food.

Saumon and **truite:** You'll see salmon dishes served in various styles. The salmon usually comes from the North Sea and is always served with sauce, most commonly a sorrel *(oseille)* sauce. Trout *(truite)* is also fairly routine on menus.

Steak: Referred to as *pavé* (thick hunk of prime steak), *bavette* (skirt steak), *faux filet* (sirloin), or *entrecôte* (rib steak), French steak is usually thinner and tougher than American steak and is always served with sauces (*au poivre* is a pepper sauce, *une sauce roquefort* is a blue-cheese sauce). Because steak is usually better in North America, I generally avoid it in France (unless the sauce sounds good). You will also see *steak haché*, which is a lean, gourmet hamburger patty served *sans* bun. When it's served as *steak haché à cheval*, it comes with a fried egg on top.

By American standards, the French undercook meats: Their version of rare, *saignant* (seh-nyahn), means "bloody" and is close to raw. What they consider medium, *à point* (ah pwan), is what an American would call rare. Their term for well-done, or *bien cuit* (bee-yehn kwee), would translate as medium for Americans.

Steak tartare: This wonderfully French dish is for adventurous types only. It's very lean, raw hamburger served with savory seasonings (usually Tabasco, capers, raw onions, salt, and pepper on the side) and topped with a raw egg yolk. This is not hamburger as we know it, but freshly ground beef.

Cheese Course *(Le Fromage)*

In France the cheese course is served just before (or instead of) dessert. It not only helps with digestion, it gives you a great opportunity to sample the tasty regional cheeses—and time to finish up your wine. Between cow, goat, and sheep cheeses, there are more than 400 different ones to try in France. Some restaurants will offer a cheese platter, from which you select a few different kinds. A good platter has at least four cheeses: a hard cheese (such as Cantal), a flowery cheese (such as Brie or Camembert), a blue or Roquefort cheese, and a goat cheese.

If you'd like to sample several types of cheese from the cheese plate, say, *"Un assortiment, s'il vous plaît"* (uhn ah-sor-tee-mahn, see voo play). You'll either be served a selection of several cheeses or choose from a large selection offered on a cheese tray or cart. If you serve yourself from the cheese tray, observe French etiquette and keep the shape of the cheese. It's best to politely shave off a slice from the side or cut small wedges.

A glass of good red wine complements your cheese course in a heavenly way.

Dessert *(Le Dessert)*

If you order espresso, it will always come after dessert. To have coffee with dessert, ask for *"café avec le dessert"* (kah-fay ah-vehk luh day-sayr). See the list of coffee terms on page 500. Here are the types of treats you'll see:

Baba au rhum: Pound cake drenched in rum, served with whipped cream.

Café gourmand: An assortment of small desserts selected by the restaurant—a great way to sample several desserts and learn your favorite.

Crème brûlée: A rich, creamy, dense, caramelized custard.

Crème caramel: Flan in a caramel sauce.

Fondant au chocolat: A molten chocolate cake with a runny (not totally cooked) center. Also known as *moelleux* (meh-leh) *au chocolat*.

Fromage blanc: A light dessert similar to plain yogurt (yet different), served with sugar or herbs.

Glace: Ice cream—typically vanilla, chocolate, or strawberry.

Ile flottante: A light dessert consisting of islands of meringue floating on a pond of custard sauce.

Mousse au chocolat: Chocolate mousse.

Profiteroles: Cream puffs filled with vanilla ice cream, smothered
in warm chocolate sauce.

Riz au lait: Rice pudding.

Sorbets: Light, flavorful, and fruity ices, sometimes laced with
brandy.

Tartes: Narrow strips of fresh fruit, baked in a crust and served in
thin slices (without ice cream).

Tarte tatin: Apple pie like grandma never made, with caramelized
apples, cooked upside down, but served upright.

BEVERAGES

In stores, unrefrigerated soft drinks, bottled water, and beer are
one-third the price of cold drinks. Bottled water and boxed fruit
juice are the cheapest drinks. Avoid buying drinks to-go at street-
side stands; you'll pay far less in a shop.

In bars and at eateries, be clear when ordering drinks—you
can easily pay €9 for an oversized Coke and €14 for a supersized
beer at some cafés. When you order a drink, state the size in cen-
tiliters (don't say "small," "medium," or "large," because the waiter
might bring a bigger drink than you want). For something small,
ask for 25 *centilitres* (vant-sank sahn-tee-lee-truh; about 8 ounces);
for a medium drink, order 33 cl (trahnte-twah; about 12 ounces—a
normal can of soda); a large is 50 cl (san-kahnt; about 16 ounces);
and a super-size is one liter (lee-truh; about a quart—which is more
than I would ever order in France). The ice cubes melted after the
last Yankee tour group left.

Water, Juice, and Soft Drinks

The French are willing to pay for bottled water with their meal
(*eau minérale;* oh mee-nay-rahl) because they prefer the taste over
tap water. Badoit is my favorite carbonated water (*l'eau gazeuse;* loh
gah-zuhz). To get a free pitcher of tap water, ask for *une carafe d'eau*
(oon kah-rahf doh). Otherwise, you may unwittingly buy bottled
water.

In France *limonade* (lee-moh-nahd) is Sprite or 7-Up. For a
fun, bright, nonalcoholic drink of 7-Up with mint syrup, order *un
diabolo menthe* (uhn dee-ah-boh-loh mahnt). For 7-Up with fruit
syrup, order *un diabolo grenadine* (think Shirley Temple). Kids love
the local orange drink, Orangina, a carbonated orange juice with

pulp (though it can be pricey). They also like *sirop à l'eau* (see-roh ah loh), flavored syrup mixed with bottled water.

For keeping hydrated on the go, hang on to the half-liter mineral-water bottles (sold everywhere for about €1) and refill. Buy juice in cheap liter boxes, then drink some and store the extra in your water bottle. Of course, water quenches your thirst better and cheaper than anything you'll find in a store or café. I drink tap water throughout France, filling up my bottle in hotel rooms.

Coffee and Tea

The French define various types of espresso drinks by how much milk is added. To the French, milk is a delicate form of nutrition: You need it in the morning, but as the day goes on, too much can upset your digestion. Therefore, the amount of milk that's added to coffee decreases as the day goes on. A *café au lait* is exclusively for breakfast time, and a *café crème* is appropriate through midday. You're welcome to order a milkier coffee drink later in the day, but don't be surprised if you get a funny look.

Provence is known for its herbal and fruit teas. Look for *tilleul* (linden), *verveine* (verbena), or interesting blends such as *poire-vanille* (pear-vanilla).

By law, a waiter must give you a glass of tap water with your coffee or tea if you request it; ask for *"un verre d'eau, s'il vous plaît"* (uhn vayr doh, see voo play).

Here are some common coffee and tea drinks:

Café (kah-fay): Shot of espresso

Café allongé, a.k.a. *café longue* (kah-fay ah-lohn-zhay; kah-fay lohn): Espresso topped up with hot water—like an Americano

Noisette (nwah-zeht): Espresso with a dollop of milk (best value for adding milk to your coffee)

Café au lait (kah-fay oh lay): Espresso mixed with lots of warm milk (used mostly for coffee made at home; in a café, order *café crème*)

Café crème (kah-fay krehm): Espresso with a sizable pour of steamed milk (closest thing you'll get to an American-style latte)

Grand crème (grahn krehm): Double shot of espresso with a bit more steamed milk (and often twice the price)

Décafféiné (day-kah-fee-nay): Decaf—available for any of the above

Thé nature (tay nah-tour): Plain tea

Thé au lait (tay oh lay): Tea with milk

Thé citron (tay see-trohn): Tea with lemon

Infusion (an-few-see-yohn): Herbal tea

Alcoholic Beverages

Be aware that the legal drinking age is 16 for beer and wine and 18 for the hard stuff—at restaurants it's *normale* for wine to be served with dinner to teens.

Wine: Wines are often listed in a separate *carte des vins*. House wine at the bar is generally cheap and good (about €3-6/glass). At a restaurant, a bottle or carafe of house wine costs €8-18. To order inexpensive wine at a restaurant, ask for table wine in a pitcher (only available when seated and when ordering food), rather than a bottle. Finer restaurants usually offer only bottles of wine. For specifics on Provençal wines, see page 34.

Here are some important wine terms:

Vin du pays (van duh pay): Table wine
Verre de vin rouge (vehr duh van roozh): Glass of red wine
Verre de vin blanc (vehr duh van blahn): Glass of white wine
Pichet (pee-shay): Pitcher
Demi-pichet (duh-mee pee-shay): Half-carafe
Quart (kar): Quarter-carafe (ideal for one)

Beer: Local *bière* (bee-ehr) costs about €5 at a restaurant and is cheaper on tap (*une pression;* oon pres-yohn) than in the bottle (*bouteille;* boo-teh-ee). France's better beers are Alsatian; try Kronenbourg or the heavier Pelfort (one of your author's favorites). *Une panaché* (oon pah-nah-shay) is a tasty French shandy (beer and lemon soda). *Un Monaco* is a red drink made with beer, grenadine, and lemonade.

Aperitifs and Digestifs: For a refreshing before-dinner drink, order a *kir* (pronounced "keer")—a thumb's level of *crème de cassis* (black currant liqueur) topped with white wine. In Provence, try sweet wines such as Muscat de Beaumes de Venise or Rasteau (Vin Doux Naturel). Both should be served chilled (from the fridge, never with ice cubes) and are enjoyable before dinner or with certain desserts; they're terrific with foie gras, melons, peaches, or Roquefort cheese. Look also for sparkling wines, usually inexpensive versions of the pricey Champagne.

If you like brandy, try a *marc* (regional brandy, e.g., *marc de Bourgogne*) or an Armagnac, cognac's cheaper twin brother. *Pastis*, the standard southern France aperitif, is a sweet anise (licorice) drink that comes on the rocks with a glass of water. Cut it to taste with lots of water.

Staying Connected

Staying connected in Europe gets easier and cheaper every year. The simplest solution is to bring your own device—mobile phone, tablet, or laptop—and use it just as you would at home (following the tips below, such as connecting to free Wi-Fi whenever possi-

How to Dial

Many Americans are intimidated by dialing European phone numbers. You needn't be. It's simple, once you break the code.

Dialing Rules

Here are the rules for dialing, along with examples of how to call one of my recommended hotels in Nice (tel. 04 97 03 10 70).

Dialing Internationally to France

Whether you're phoning from a US landline, your own mobile phone, a Skype account, or a number in another European country (e.g., Spain to France), you're making an international call. Here's how to do it:

1. Dial the **international access code** (011 if calling from a US or Canadian phone; 00 if calling from any European phone number outside of France). If dialing from a mobile phone, you can enter a + in place of the international access code (press and hold the 0 key).
2. Dial the **country code** (33 for France).
3. Dial the **phone number** (drop the initial 0).

Examples:
- To call the Nice hotel from a **US or Canadian phone,** dial 011, then 33, then 4 97 03 10 70.
- To call from **any European phone number** (outside of France), dial 00, then 33, then 4 97 03 10 70.
- To call from any **mobile phone** (except a French one), dial +, then 33, then 4 97 03 10 70.

Dialing Within France

If calling from a French mobile phone or landline (such as a hotel-room phone), simply dial the phone number, including the initial 0.

---

ble). Another option is to buy a European SIM card for your mobile phone—either your US phone or one you buy in Europe. Or you can travel without a mobile device and use European landlines and computers to connect. Each of these options is described below, and you'll find even more details at www.ricksteves.com/phoning.

USING YOUR OWN MOBILE DEVICE IN EUROPE

Without an international plan, typical rates from major service providers (AT&T, Verizon, etc.) for using your device abroad are about $1.50/minute for voice calls, 50 cents to send text messages, 5 cents to receive them, and $20 to download one megabyte of data. But at these rates, costs can add up quickly. Here are some budget tips and options.

Use free Wi-Fi whenever possible. Unless you have an unlimited-data plan, you're best off saving most of your online tasks

Example: To call my recommended Nice hotel, dial 04 97 03 10 70 (whether you're calling it from across the street or across the country).

Calling from any European Country to the US

To call the US or Canada from Europe (either from a mobile phone or landline), dial 00 (Europe's international access code), 1 (US/Canada country code), and the phone number, including area code. If calling from a mobile phone, you can enter a + instead of 00.

Example: To call my office in Edmonds, Washington, from anywhere in Europe, I dial 00-1-425-771-8303; or, from a mobile phone, +-1-425-771-8303.

More Dialing Tips

French Phone Prefixes: French phone numbers have prefixes that vary by region or type of call. For instance, all landlines in Provence and the Riviera begin with 04. Any number beginning with 06 or 07 is a mobile phone, and costs more to dial.

Toll and Toll-Free Calls: France's toll-free numbers start with 0800 and are called *numéro vert* (green number). You can dial these for free from any French phone, but you can't call France's toll-free numbers from America, nor can you count on reaching US toll-free numbers from France. Any 08 number that does not have a 00 directly following is a toll call (generally €0.10-0.50/minute; cost announced in French; you can hang up before being billed).

More Resources: The "Phoning Cheat Sheet" on page 505 shows how to dial per country, or you can check www.countrycallingcodes.com or www.howtocallabroad.com.

for Wi-Fi (pronounced *wee-fee* in French). You can access the Internet, send texts, and even make voice calls over Wi-Fi.

Many cafés (including Starbucks and McDonald's) have hotspots for customers; look for signs offering it and ask for the Wi-Fi password when you buy something. You'll also often find Wi-Fi at TIs, city squares, major museums, public-transit hubs, airports, aboard trains and buses, and at some autoroute (highway) rest stops.

Sign up for an international plan. Most providers offer a global calling plan that cuts the per-minute cost of phone calls and texts, and a flat-fee data plan that includes a certain amount of megabytes. Your normal plan may already include international coverage (T-Mobile's does).

Before your trip, call your provider or check online to confirm that your phone will work in Europe, and research your provider's international rates. A day or two before you leave, activate the plan by calling your provider or logging on to your mobile phone account. Remember to cancel your plan (if necessary) when your trip's over.

Minimize the use of your cellular network. When you can't find Wi-Fi, you can use your cellular network—convenient but slower and potentially expensive—to connect to the Internet, text, or make voice calls. When you're done, avoid further charges by manually switching off "data roaming" or "cellular data" (in your device's Settings menu; if you don't know how to switch it off, ask your service provider or Google it). Another way to make sure you're not accidentally using data roaming is to put your device in "airplane" or "flight" mode (which also disables phone calls and texts, as well as data), and then turn on Wi-Fi as needed.

Don't use your cellular network for bandwidth-gobbling tasks, such as Skyping, downloading apps, and watching YouTube—save these for when you're on Wi-Fi. Using a navigation app such as Google Maps can take lots of data, so use this sparingly.

Limit automatic updates. By default, your device is constantly checking for a data connection and updating apps. It's smart to disable these features so they'll only update when you're on Wi-Fi, and to change your device's email settings from "auto-retrieve" to "manual" (or from "push" to "fetch").

It's also a good idea to keep track of your data usage. On your device's menu, look for "cellular data usage" or "mobile data" and reset the counter at the start of your trip.

Use Skype or other calling/messaging apps for cheaper calls and texts. Certain apps let you make voice or video calls or send texts over the Internet for free or cheap. If you're bringing a tablet or laptop, you can also use them for voice calls and texts. All you have to do is log on to a Wi-Fi network, then contact any of your friends or family members who are also online and signed into the same service. You can make voice and video calls using Skype, Viber, FaceTime, and Google+ Hangouts. If the connection is bad, try making an audio-only call.

You can also make voice calls from your device to telephones worldwide for just a few cents per minute using Skype, Viber, or Hangouts if you prebuy credit.

To text for free over Wi-Fi, try apps like Google+ Hangouts, What's App, Viber, and Facebook Messenger. Apple's iMessage connects with other Apple users, but make sure you're on Wi-Fi to avoid data charges.

Phoning Cheat Sheet

Just smile and dial, using these rules.

Calling a European number
- **From a mobile phone** (whether you're in the US or in Europe):
  Dial + (press and hold 0), then country code and number*
- **From a US/Canadian number:** Dial 011, then country code and number*
- **From a different European country** (e.g., German number to French number): Dial 00, then country code and number*
- **Within the same European country** (e.g., German number to another German number): Dial the number as printed, including initial 0 if there is one

Drop initial 0 (if present) from phone number in all countries except Italy

Calling the US or Canada from Europe
Dial 00, then 1 (country code for US/Canada), then area code and number; on mobile phones, enter + in place of 00

Country	Country Code	Country	Country Code
Austria	43	Italy	39 [2]
Belgium	32	Latvia	371
Bosnia-Herzegovina	387	Montenegro	382
Croatia	385	Morocco	212
Czech Republic	420	Netherlands	31
Denmark	45	Norway	47
Estonia	372	Poland	48
Finland	358	Portugal	351
France	33	Russia	7 [3]
Germany	49	Slovakia	421
Gibraltar	350	Slovenia	386
Great Britain & N. Ireland	44	Spain	34
Greece	30	Sweden	46
Hungary	36 [1]	Switzerland	41
Ireland	353	Turkey	90

[1] For long-distance calls within Hungary, dial 06, then the area code and number.
[2] When making international calls to Italy, do not drop the initial 0 from the phone number.
[3] For long-distance calls within Russia, dial 8, then the area code and number. To call the US or Canada from Russia, dial 8, then 10, then 1, then the area code and number.

USING A EUROPEAN SIM CARD IN A MOBILE PHONE

This option works well for those who want to make a lot of voice calls at cheap local rates. Either buy a phone in Europe (as little as $40 from mobile-phone shops anywhere), or bring an "unlocked" US phone (check with your carrier about unlocking it). With an unlocked phone, you can replace the original SIM card (the microchip that stores info about the phone) with one that will work with a European provider.

In Europe, buy a European SIM card. Inserted into your phone, this card gives you a European phone number—and European rates. SIM cards are sold at mobile-phone shops, department-store electronics counters, some newsstands, and even at vending machines. Costing about $5-10, they usually include about that much prepaid calling credit, with no contract and no commitment. You can still use your phone's Wi-Fi function to get online. To get a SIM card that also includes data costs (including roaming), figure on paying $15-30 for one month of data within the country you bought it. This can be cheaper than data roaming through your home provider. To get the best rates, buy a new SIM card whenever you arrive in a new country.

I like to buy SIM cards at a mobile-phone shop where there's a clerk to help explain the options and brands. Certain brands—including Lebara and Lycamobile, both of which operate in multiple European countries—are reliable and economical. Ask the clerk to help you insert your SIM card, set it up, and show you how to use it. In some countries you'll be required to register the SIM card with your passport as an antiterrorism measure (which may mean you can't use the phone for the first hour or two).

When you run out of credit, you can top it up at newsstands, tobacco shops, mobile-phone stores, or many other businesses (look for your SIM card's logo in the window), or online.

USING LANDLINES AND COMPUTERS IN EUROPE

It's easy to travel in Europe without a mobile device. You can check email or browse websites using public computers and Internet cafés, and make calls from your hotel room.

Phones in your **hotel room** can be inexpensive for local calls and calls made with cheap international phone cards *(carte international)*, sold at many newsstands, street kiosks, tobacco shops, and train stations. You'll either get a prepaid card with a toll-free number and a scratch-to-reveal PIN code, or a code printed on a receipt; to make a call, dial the free (usually 4-digit) access number. If that doesn't work, dial the toll-free number, follow the prompts, enter the code, then dial your number.

Most hotels charge a fee for placing local and "toll-free" calls,

PRACTICALITIES

Tips on Internet Security

Using the Internet while traveling brings added security risks, whether you're accessing it with your own device or at a public terminal using a shared network.

First, make sure that your device is running the latest version of its operating system and security software. Next, ensure that your device is password- or passcode-protected so thieves can't access your information if your device is stolen. For extra security, set passwords on apps that access key info (such as email or Facebook).

On the road, use only legitimate Wi-Fi hotspots. Ask the hotel or café staff for the specific name of their Wi-Fi network, and make sure you log on to that exact one. Hackers sometimes create a bogus hotspot with a similar or vague name (such as "Hotel Europa Free Wi-Fi"). The best Wi-Fi networks require entering a password.

Be especially cautious when checking your online banking, credit-card statements, or other personal-finance accounts. Internet security experts advise against accessing these sites while traveling. Even if you're using your own mobile device at a password-protected hotspot, any hacker who's logged on to the same network may be able to see what you're doing. If you do need to log on to a banking website, use a hard-wired connection (such as an Ethernet cable in your hotel room) or a cellular network, which is safer than Wi-Fi.

Never share your credit-card number (or any other sensitive information) online unless you know that the site is secure. A secure site displays a little padlock icon, and the URL begins with *https* (instead of the usual *http*).

as well as long-distance or international calls—ask for the rates before you dial. Since you're never charged for receiving calls, it's better to have someone from the US call you in your room.

It's always possible to find **public computers:** at your hotel (many have one in their lobby for guests to use), or at an Internet café or library (ask your hotelier or the TI for the nearest location). If typing on a European keyboard, use the "Alt Gr" key to the right of the space bar to insert the extra symbol that appears on some keys. To type an @ symbol on French keyboards, press the "Alt Gr" and "à/0" key. If you can't locate a special character, simply copy it from a Web page and paste it into your email message.

MAIL

You can mail one package per day to yourself worth up to $200 duty-free from Europe to the US (mark it "personal purchases").

If you're sending a gift to someone, mark it "unsolicited gift." For details, visit www.cbp.gov and search for "Know Before You Go."

The French postal service works fine, but for quick transatlantic delivery (in either direction), consider services such as DHL (www.dhl.com). French post offices are referred to as *La Poste* or sometimes the old-fashioned PTT, for "Post, Telegraph, and Telephone." Hours vary, though most are open weekdays 8:00-19:00 and Saturday morning 8:00-12:00. Stamps and phone cards are also sold at *tabacs*. It costs about €1 to mail a postcard to the US. One convenient, if expensive, way to send packages home is to use the post office's Colissimo XL postage-paid mailing box. It costs €50-90 to ship boxes weighing 5-7 kilos (about 11-15 pounds).

Transportation

If you're debating between using public transportation, renting a car, or flying between destinations in Europe, consider these factors: Cars are best for three or more traveling together (especially families with small kids), those packing heavy, and those delving into the countryside. Trains and buses are best for solo travelers, blitz tourists, city-to-city travelers, and those who don't want to drive. Intra-European flights are an option to cover long distances, though the best deals are often at secondary airports. While a car gives you more freedom, trains and buses zip you effortlessly and scenically from city to city, usually dropping you in the center—often near a TI. For more detailed information on transportation throughout Europe, including trains, flying, renting a car, and driving, see www.ricksteves.com/transportation.

If you plan to focus on Arles, Avignon, Aix-en-Provence, and seaside destinations along the Riviera, go by train. Stations are centrally located in each city, which makes hotel-hunting and sightseeing easy. Buses and taxis pick up where trains leave off. While bus service can be sparse, taxis are generally available and reasonable. If relying on public transportation, visit fewer destinations, or hire one of the excellent minivan tour guides I recommend (see "Tours in Provence" on page 26).

I've included two sample itineraries—by car and by public transportation—to help you explore Provence and the French Riviera smoothly; you'll find these in the Introduction.

TRAINS

France's SNCF rail system (short for Société Nationale Chemins de Fer) sets the pace in Europe. Its super TGV (tay zhay vay; *Train à Grande Vitesse*) system has inspired bullet trains throughout the world. The TGV, which requires a reservation, runs at 170-220 mph. Its rails are fused into one long, continuous track for a faster

French Train Terms and Abbreviations

SNCF (Société Nationale Chemins de Fer): This is the Amtrak of France, operating all national train lines that link cities and towns.

TGV *(Train à Grande Vitesse):* SNCF's network of high-speed trains (twice as fast as regular trains) that connect major cities in France. These trains always require a reservation.

Intercité: These trains are the next best to the TGV in terms of speed and comfort.

TER (Transport Express Régional): These trains serve smaller stops within a region. For example, you'll find trains called TER Provence (Provence-only trains) and TER de Bourgogne (trains operating only in Burgundy).

and smoother ride. The TGV has changed commuting patterns throughout France by putting most of the country within day-trip distance of Paris.

TGV trains serve these cities in Provence and the Riviera: Avignon, Arles (very few trains), Nîmes, Marseille, Orange, Aix-en-Provence, Antibes, Cannes, and Nice. Avignon and Aix-en-Provence have separate TGV stations on their outskirts (with bus connections into the town center)—note carefully which station your train serves (either "Centre-Ville" or "TGV"; if it's not specified, it's the central station).

Any staffed train station has schedule information, can make reservations, and can sell tickets for any destination. For more on train travel, see www.ricksteves.com/rail.

Schedules

Schedules change by season, weekday, and weekend. Verify train times shown in this book—online, check www.bahn.com (Germany's excellent all-Europe schedule site), or check locally at train stations. The French rail website is www.sncf.com; for online sales, go to http://en.voyages-sncf.com. If you'll be traveling on one or two long-distance trains without a rail pass, it's worth looking online, as advance-purchase discounts can be a great deal.

Bigger stations may have helpful information agents roaming the station and at *Accueil* offices or booths. Make use of their help; don't stand in a ticket line if all you need is a train schedule.

Rail Passes

Long-distance travelers may save money with a France Rail Pass, sold only outside Europe (through travel agents or Rick Steves' Europe). For roughly the cost of a full-fare Paris-Avignon-Paris ticket, the France Rail Pass offers three days of travel (within a month)

Coping with Strikes

Going on strike *(en grève)* is a popular pastime in this revolution-happy country. Because bargaining between management and employees is not standard procedure, workers strike to get attention. Trucks and tractors block main roads and autoroutes (they call it Opération Escargot—"Operation Snail's Pace"), baggage handlers bring airports to their knees, and museum workers make artwork off-limits to tourists. Métro and train personnel seem to strike every year—probably during your trip. What does the traveler do? You could *jeter l'éponge* (throw in the sponge) and go somewhere less strike-prone (Switzerland's nice), or learn to accept certain events as out of your control. Strikes in France generally last no longer than a day or two, and if you're aware of them, you can usually plan around them. Your hotelier will know the latest (or can find out). Make a habit of asking your hotel receptionist about strikes, or check www.americansinfrance.net (look under "Daily Life").

anywhere in France. You can add up to six more days, each for the cost of a two-hour ride. You can save money by getting the second-class instead of the first-class version, but first class gives you more options when reserving popular TGV routes. The saverpass version gives two or more people traveling together a 15 percent discount.

Each day of use allows you to take as many trips as you want on one calendar day (you could go from Paris to Beaune in Burgundy, enjoy wine tasting, then continue to Avignon, stay a few hours, and end in Nice—though I wouldn't recommend it). Buy second-class tickets in France for shorter trips, and save your valuable pass days for longer trips.

A **Global Pass** can work well throughout most of Europe, but it's a bad value for travel exclusively in France. A cheaper version, the **Select Pass,** allows you to tailor a pass to your trip, provided you're traveling in four adjacent countries directly connected by rail or ferry. For instance, with a four-country pass allowing 10 days of train travel within a two-month period (about $700 for a single adult in 2015), you could choose France-Switzerland-Italy-Greece or Ireland-France-Spain-Italy.

Note that France's TGV trains require advance seat reservations, which are limited for passholders. Reserving these fast trains at least several weeks in advance is recommended (for strategies, see "Reservations," later). For more detailed advice on figuring out the smartest rail pass options for your train trip, visit the Trains & Rail Passes section of my website at www.ricksteves.com/rail.

Rail Passes

Prices listed are for 2015 and are subject to change. For the latest prices, details, and train schedules (and easy online ordering), see www.ricksteves.com/rail.

"Saver" prices are per person for two or more people traveling together. "Youth" means under age 26. Up to two kids age 4-11 travel free with each adult. Additional kids pay the youth rate. Kids under age 4 travel free.

FRANCE PASS FLEXI
Seniors age 60 and up pay prices similar to Saver, even if traveling alone!

	1st Class Indiv.	2nd Class Indiv.	1st Class Saver	2nd Class Saver	1st Class Youth	2nd Class Youth
1 day in 1 month	$139	$113	$124	$100	$100	$85
2 days in 1 month	198	161	175	142	143	121
3 days in 1 month	260	211	231	187	187	160
4 days in 1 month	297	242	264	213	215	181
5 days in 1 month	334	272	296	241	240	206
6 days in 1 month	371	301	327	267	267	228
7 days in 1 month	406	328	359	290	295	253
8 days in 1 month	442	356	388	316	320	275
9 days in 1 month	478	382	423	339	346	298
15 days in 1 month	623	499	552	442	451	389

FRANCE PASS CONSECUTIVE
Seniors age 60 and up pay prices similar to Saver, even if traveling alone!

	1st Class Indiv.	2nd Class Indiv.	1st Class Saver	2nd Class Saver	1st Class Youth	2nd Class Youth
2 days consecutive	$158	$128	$140	$114	$114	$96
4 days consecutive	237	193	211	170	171	145
5 days consecutive	268	218	237	193	192	165
8 days consecutive	353	285	310	253	256	220
15 days consecutive	499	399	442	353	362	311

Map key:
Approximate point-to-point one-way second-class rail fares in US dollars. First class costs 50 percent more. Add up fares for your itinerary to see if a rail pass will save you money.

Public Transportation in Provence

To Lyon & Paris

N

Montélimar

Not to Scale

Nyons

Buis-les-Baronnies

Vaison-la-Romaine

P R O V E N C E

Orange

CÔTES DU RHÔNE

To Grenoble

Châteauneuf-du-Pape

Uzès

PONT DU GARD

Avignon

Isle-sur-la-Sorgue

Avignon TGV

Roussillon

Cavaillon

Apt

LUBERON

Nîmes

Tarascon

Lourmarin

To Montpellier, Carcassonne & Barcelona (Spain)

St-Rémy

Arles

Les Baux

Aix-en-Provence

To Nice

Aigues-Mortes

C A M A R G U E

Aix TGV

Petit Rhône

Toulon

Stes-Maries-de-la-Mer

Marseille

Cassis Stn.

Les Calanques

La Ciotat

Cassis

Mediterranean Sea

Legend:

- ············ Rail
- ══════ TGV High Speed Rail
- - - - - Bus
- ·············· Boat
- ✈ Airports (Not All Shown)

Note: In some cases regular train lines and TGV lines share the same track

Buying Tickets

Online: While there's no deadline to buy any train ticket, the fast, reserved TGV trains get booked up. Buy well ahead for any TGV you cannot afford to miss. Tickets go on sale 90 to 120 days in advance, with a wide range of prices on any one route. The cheapest tickets sell out early and reservations for rail-pass holders also go particularly fast.

To buy the cheapest advance-discount tickets (50 percent less than full fare), visit http://en.voyages-sncf.com, three to four months ahead of your travel date. (A pop-up window may ask you to choose between being sent to the Rail Europe website or stay-

Public Transportation on the French Riviera

Not to Scale

To Grenoble

Veynes-Dévoluy

ITALY

Ventimiglia

FRANCE

To Genoa & Cinque Terre

Château-Arnoux-St-Auban · Digne-les-Bains

Eze-le-Village   La Turbie

Menton

Eze-Bord-de-Mer   Monaco

Manosque-Gréoux

Cap d'Ail

Beaulieu

Tourrettes · Vence   Nice

Cap Ferrat

To Aix-en-Provence

Le Bar   St-Paul

Villefranche-sur-Mer

Biot

Vallauris   Antibes

Grasse   Juan-les-Pins

RIVIERA

Cannes

Cap d'Antibes

To Toulon, Marseille, Avignon & Paris

St-Raphaël

Note: In some cases regular train lines and TGV lines share the same track

To Toulon

St-Tropez

M e d i t e r r a n e a n

S e a

Rail
TGV High Speed Rail
Bus
Boat
Airports (Not All Shown)

ing on the SNCF page—click "Stay.") Next, choose "Train," then "TGV." Under "Book your train tickets," pick your travel dates, and choose "France" as your ticket collection country. The cheapest (nonrefundable) tickets are called "Prems"; be sure it also says "TGV" (avoid iDTGV trains—they're very cheap, but this SNCF subsidiary doesn't accept PayPal). Choose the eticket delivery option (which allows you to print at home), and pay with your PayPal account to avoid credit-card approval issues. These low-rate tickets may not be available from Rail Europe or other USA agents.

After the Prems rates are sold out, you can buy other fare types on the French site with a US credit card if it has been set up for the "Verified by Visa," "MasterCard SecureCode," or "American Express SafeKey" program. For a credit-card purchase, choose "USA" as your ticket collection country.

Otherwise, US customers can order through a US agency, such as at www.ricksteves.com/rail, which offers both etickets and home delivery, but may not have access to all of the cheapest rates; or Capitaine Train (www.capitainetrain.com), which sells the "Prems" fare and iDTGV tickets.

Travelers with smartphones have the opion of saving tickets and reservations directly to their phones (choose "m-ticket"). For more details, see http://en.voyages-sncf.com/en/mobile.

In France: You can buy train tickets in person at SNCF Boutiques or at any train station, either from a staffed ticket window or from a machine. You can buy tickets on the train for a €4-10 surcharge depending on the length of your trip, but you must find the conductor immediately upon boarding; otherwise it's a €35 minimum charge.

The ticket machines available at most stations are great time savers when other lines are long. But the machines probably won't accept your American credit card, so be prepared with euro coins. Some machines have English instructions, but for those that don't, here are the prompts. (Turn the dial or move the cursor to your choice, and press *"Validez"* to agree to each step.)

1. *Quelle est votre destination?* (What's your destination?)
2. *Billet Plein Tarif* (Full-fare ticket—yes for most.)
3. *1ère ou 2ème* (First or second class; normally second is fine.)
4. *Aller simple ou aller-retour?* (One-way or round-trip?)
5. *Prix en Euro* (The price should be shown if you get this far.)

Reservations

Reservations are required for any TGV train, *couchettes* (sleeping berths) on night trains, and some other trains where indicated in timetables. You can reserve any train at any station up to three days before your departure or through SNCF Boutiques. If you're buying a point-to-point ticket for a TGV train, you'll reserve your seat when you purchase your ticket.

Popular TGV routes usually fill up quickly, making it a challenge to get reservations (particularly for rail-pass holders, who are allocated a very limited number of seats). It's wise to book well ahead for any TGV, especially on the busy Paris-Avignon-Nice line. If the TGV trains you want are fully booked, ask about TER trains serving the same destination, as these don't require reservations.

Seat reservations cost anywhere from €3 to €26, depending on the kind of train they're for, where you buy them, and if you're using a rail pass. International trains—such as Eurostar, Thalys, Artesia, and international TGV—have different (higher) reservation price ranges.

Rail-pass holders can book TGV reservations at French stations up to three days before departure; reservations, if still available, can be booked anytime as etickets at www.raileurope.com (if lower-priced passholder reservations are sold out, try for the "Easy Access" rate). Given the difficulty of getting TGV reservations with a rail pass, make those reservations online before you leave

---

Train-Ticket French

Hello, sir/madam, do you speak English?
Bonjour, monsieur/madame, parlez-vous anglais?
bohn-zhoor, muhs-yur/mah-dahm, par-lay-voo ahn-glay

I would like a departure for Avignon, on 10 May, about 9:00, the most direct way possible.
Je voudrais un départ pour Avignon, pour le 10 Mai, vers 9:00, la plus direct possible.
zhuh voo-dray uhn day-par poor ah-veen-yohn, poor luh dees may, vehr nuhf ur, lah plew dee-rehk poh-see-bluh

---

home or consider buying separate, advance-discount tickets for key TGV trips (and exclude those legs from your rail pass).

If you're taking an overnight train and need a *couchette*, it can be booked in advance through a US agent (such as www.raileurope.com).

Reservations are generally unnecessary for non-TGV trains (verify ahead, as some Intercité trains require reservations, like the Nice-Bordeaux train), but they are advisable during busy times (for example, Friday and Sunday afternoons, Saturday mornings, weekday rush hours, and holiday weekends; see "Holidays and Festivals" on page 534)

Baggage Check

Baggage check *(Consigne* or *Espaces Bagages)* is available only at a handful of the biggest train stations (about €5-10 per bag depending on size), and is noted where available in this book (which can depend on current security concerns, so be prepared to keep your bag). For security reasons, all luggage is supposed to carry a tag with the traveler's first and last name and current address (though it's not enforced). This applies to hand luggage as well as bigger bags that are stowed. Free tags are available at train stations in France.

Train Tips
At the Station
- Arrive at the station with plenty of time before your departure to find your platform (platform numbers are posted about 15 minutes prior to departure), confirm connections, and so on. Remember that Avignon and Aix-en-Provence have separate TGV stations that are outside the town center.
- Small stations are minimally staffed; if there's no agent at the station, go directly to the tracks and look for the overhead sign that confirms your train stops at that track.

PRACTICALITIES

- Larger stations have platforms with monitors showing TGV layouts (numbered forward or backward) so you can figure out where your car (voiture) will stop on the long platform and where to board each car.

Validating Tickets, Reservations, and Rail Passes

- You're required to validate (composter, kohm-poh-stay) all train tickets and reservations before boarding any SNCF train. Look for a yellow machine near the platform or waiting area to stamp your ticket or reservation.
- If you have a rail pass, validate it at a ticket window before using it the first time (don't stamp it in the machine). If you're traveling with a pass and have a reservation for a certain trip, you must activate the reservation by stamping it.
- If you have a rail flexipass, write the date on your pass each day you travel (before or immediately after boarding your first train).

On the Train

- Before getting on a train, confirm that it's going where you think it is. For example, if you want to go to Antibes, ask the conductor or any local passenger, "À Antibes?" (ah ahn-teeb; meaning, "To Antibes?")
- Some longer trains split off cars en route. Make sure your train car is continuing to your destination by asking, for example, "Cette voiture va à Avignon?" (seht vwah-toor vah ah ah-veen-yohn; meaning, "This car goes to Avignon?")
- If a non-TGV train seat is reserved, it'll likely be labeled réservé, with the cities to and from which it is reserved.
- If you don't understand an announcement, ask your neighbor to explain: "Pardon madame/monsieur, qu'est-ce qui se passe?" (kehs kee suh pahs; meaning, "Excuse me, what's going on?").
- Verify with the conductor all of the transfers you must make: "Correspondance à?"; meaning, "Transfer to where?"
- To guard against theft, keep your bags in sight (directly overhead is ideal but not always possible—the early boarder gets the best storage space). If you must store them in the lower racks by the doors (available in most cars), pay attention at stops. Your bags are most vulnerable to theft before the train takes off and whenever it stops.
- Note your arrival time, so you'll be ready to get off.
- Use the train's free WCs before you get off (but not while the train is stopped in a station).

Low-Cost TGV Trains to Southern France

A TGV train called OUIGO (pronounced "we go") offers a direct connection from Disneyland Paris to select cities in southern

France at rock-bottom fares with no-frills service. The catch: These trains leave from the Marne-la-Vallée TGV station, an hour from Paris on RER-A. You can hang at Disneyland Paris before (or after) your trip south and connect with a direct TGV. You must print your own ticket ahead of time, arrive 30 minutes before departure, and activate your ticket. You can't use a rail pass, and you can only bring one carry-on-size bag plus one handbag for free (children's tickets allow you to bring a stroller). Larger or extra luggage is €5/bag if you pay when you buy your ticket. If you just show up without paying in advance, it's €20/bag on the train—yikes. There's no food service on the train (BYO), but children under age 12 pay only €5 for a seat. The website explains it all in easy-to-understand English (www.ouigo.com).

BUSES

Regional buses work well for many destinations not served by trains. Buses are almost always comfortable and air-conditioned.

A few bus lines are run by the SNCF rail system and are covered by your rail pass (show rail pass at station to get free bus ticket), but most bus lines are not covered. Bus stations *(gare routière)* are usually located next to train stations. Train stations usually have bus information where train-to-bus connections are important—and vice versa for bus companies.

Bus Tips

- Read the train tips described earlier, and use those that apply (check schedules in advance, arrive at the station early, confirm the destination before you board, find out if you need to transfer, etc.).
- The bus company websites I've listed in this book are usually in French only. Here are some key phrases you'll see: *horaires* (schedules), *en semaine* (Monday through Saturday), *dimanche* (Sunday), *jours fériés* (holidays), *année* (bus runs all year on the days listed), *vac* (runs only during summer vacations), *scol/scolaire* (runs only when school is in session), *ligne* (route or bus line), and *réseau* (network—usually all routes).
- Use TIs to help plan your trip and verify times (TIs have regional bus schedules).
- Be aware that service is sparse or even nonexistent on Sunday. Wednesday bus schedules often are different during the school year, because school is out this day (and regional buses generally operate the school service).
- Confirm a bus stop's location in advance (rural stops are often not signed) and be at bus stops at least five minutes early.

RENTING A CAR

If you're renting a car in France, bring your driver's license. Rental companies require you to be at least 21 years old and to have held your license for one year. Drivers under the age of 25 may incur a young-driver surcharge, and some rental companies do not rent to anyone 75 or older. If you're considered too young or old, look into leasing (covered later), which has less-stringent age restrictions.

Research car rentals before you go. It's cheaper to arrange car rentals from the US. Consider several companies to compare rates. Most of the major US rental agencies (including Avis, Budget, Enterprise, Hertz, and Thrifty) have offices throughout Europe. Also consider the two major Europe-based agencies, Europcar and Sixt, and the French agency, ADA (www.ada.fr). It can be cheaper to use a consolidator, such as Auto Europe/Kemwel (www.autoeurope.com) or Europe by Car (www.europebycar.com), which compares rates at several companies to get you the best deal—but because you're working with a middleman, it's especially important to ask in advance about add-on fees and restrictions.

Always read the fine print carefully for add-on charges—such as one-way drop-off fees, airport surcharges, or mandatory insurance policies—that aren't included in the "total price." You may need to query rental agents pointedly to find out your actual cost.

For the best deal, rent by the week with unlimited mileage. I normally rent the smallest, least-expensive model with a stick shift (generally cheaper than an automatic). Almost all rentals are manual. If you need an automatic, request one in advance; be aware that these cars are usually larger models. Roads and parking spaces are narrow in France, so you'll do yourself a favor by renting the smallest car that meets your needs.

Figure on paying roughly $230 for a one-week rental during busy seasons. Allow extra for supplemental insurance, fuel, tolls, and parking. For trips of three weeks or more, leasing can save you money on insurance and taxes.

Picking Up Your Car: Big companies have offices in most cities; ask whether they can pick you up at your hotel. Small local rental companies can be cheaper but aren't as flexible.

Compare pickup costs (downtown can be less expensive than the airport or train station) and explore drop-off options. Always check the hours of the location you choose: Many rental offices close from midday Saturday until Monday morning and, in smaller towns, at lunchtime—though at certain locations like rail stations, you can usually drop off a car after-hours (put keys in lockbox).

When selecting a location, don't trust the agency's description of "downtown" or "city center." In some cases, a "downtown" branch can be on the outskirts of the city—a long, costly taxi ride from the center. Before choosing, plug the addresses into a mapping website. You may find that the "train station" location is handier. But returning a car at a big-city train station or downtown agency can be tricky; get precise details on the car drop-off location and hours, and allow ample time to find it.

If you want a car for only a day or two (e.g., for the Côtes du Rhône wine route or Luberon villages), you'll likely find it easy to rent on the spot just about anywhere in France. In many cases, this is a worthwhile splurge. All you need is your American driver's license and a major credit card (figure €65-90/day; some include unlimited mileage, others give you 100 kilometers—about 60 miles—for free).

When you pick up the rental car, check it thoroughly and make sure any damage is noted on your rental agreement. Find out how your car's lights, turn signals, wipers, radio, and fuel cap function, and know what kind of fuel the car takes (diesel vs. unleaded). When you return the car, make sure the agent verifies its condition with you. Some drivers take pictures of the returned vehicle as proof of its condition.

Navigation Options

Paper Maps: Michelin maps are available throughout France at bookstores, newsstands, and gas stations (about €6 each, cheaper than in the US). The orange Michelin map #527 (1:275,000 scale) covers this book's destinations with good detail for drivers. Michelin map #332 is good for the Luberon and the Côtes du Rhône, and map #340 is best for the Bouches-du-Rhône (the southern area around Arles). Drivers going beyond Provence and the Riviera should consider the soft-cover Michelin France atlas (the entire country at 1:200,000, well-organized in a €20 book with an index and maps of major cities). Spend a few minutes learning the Michelin key to get the most sightseeing value out of these maps.

Digital Maps: For a digital navigator you can use the mapping app that's already on your cellular-connected device, or download a mapping app that's designed to be used offline. As an alternative, you could rent a GPS device with your rental car (or bring your own GPS device from home).

To use your mobile device for pulling up maps or routes on the fly, for turn-by-turn directions, or for traffic updates, you'll need to go online—so it's smart to get an international data plan (see page 503). But just using GPS to locate your position on a map doesn't require an Internet connection (and therefore doesn't require Wi-Fi or cellular data). This means that once you have the map in your phone, you can navigate with it all day long without incurring data-roaming charges.

Using Your Device's Mapping App: The mapping app you

use at home (such as Google Maps or Apple Maps) will work just as well for navigating Europe.

The most economical approach is to download information while you're on Wi-Fi (at your hotel, before setting out for the day). Google Maps' "save map to use offline" feature is useful for this, allowing you to view a map when you're offline (though you can't search for an address or get directions). Apple Maps doesn't offer a save-for-offline feature, though it does automatically cache (save) certain data. So if you bring up the maps you need or plan your route while on Wi-Fi in the morning, the Apple Maps app may end up caching those maps and not using data roaming much during the day.

No matter which app you use, view the maps in standard view (not satellite view) to limit data use. And consider bringing a car charger: Even offline, mapping services gobble up battery life.

Using an Offline Mapping App: A number of well-designed apps allow you much of the convenience of online maps without any costly data demands. City Maps 2Go is popular; OffMaps and Navfree also offer good, zoomable offline maps—similar to Google Maps—for much of Europe. You need to be online to download the app, but once that's done, the maps are accessible anywhere (note that you won't get turn-by-turn directions, which require a data connection).

Using GPS: Some drivers prefer using a dedicated GPS unit—not only to avoid using cellular data, but because a stand-alone GPS can be easier to operate (important if you're driving solo). The downside: It's expensive—around $10-30 per day. Your car's GPS unit may only come loaded with maps for its home country—if you need additional maps, ask. And make sure your device's language is set to English. If you have a portable GPS device at home, you can take that instead, but you'll need to buy and download European maps before your trip. This option is far less expensive than renting.

Car Insurance Options

When you rent a car, you are liable for a very high deductible, sometimes equal to the entire value of the car. Limit your financial risk with one of these options: Buy Collision Damage Waiver (CDW) coverage with a low or zero deductible from the car-rental company, get coverage through your credit card (free, if your card automatically includes zero-deductible coverage), or get collision insurance as part of a larger travel-insurance policy.

Basic **CDW** includes a very high deductible (typically $1,000–1,500). Though each rental company has its own variation, basic CDW costs $10–30 a day (figure roughly 30 percent extra) and reduces your liability, but does not eliminate it. When you reserve or pick up the car, you'll be offered the chance to "buy down" the basic deductible to zero (for an additional $10–30/day; this is sometimes called "super CDW" or "zero-deductible coverage").

If you opt for **credit-card coverage,** there's a catch. You'll technically have to decline all coverage offered by the car-rental company, which means they can place a hold on your card (which can be up to the full value of the car). In case of damage, it can be time-consuming to resolve the charges with your credit-card company. Before you decide on this option, quiz your credit-card company about how it works.

If you're already purchasing a **travel-insurance policy** for your trip, adding collision coverage is an option. For example, Travel Guard (www.travelguard.com) sells affordable renter's collision insurance as an add-on to its other policies; it's valid everywhere in Europe except the Republic of Ireland, and some Italian car-rental companies refuse to honor it, as it doesn't cover you in case of theft.

For more on car-rental insurance, see www.ricksteves.com/cdw.

Leasing

For trips of three weeks or more, consider leasing (which automatically includes zero-deductible collision and theft insurance). By technically buying and then selling back the car, you save lots of money on tax and insurance. Leasing provides you a brand-new car with unlimited mileage and a 24-hour emergency assistance program. You can lease for as little as 21 days to as long as five and a half months; Idea Merge may offer two-week leases. Car leases must be arranged from the US.

These reliable companies offer 21-day lease packages:

Auto France (Peugeot cars only, US tel. 800-572-9655, www.autofrance.net)

Europe by Car (Peugeot, Citroën, and Renault cars, US tel. 800-223-1516, www.ebctravel.com)

Idea Merge (ask about two-week leases; Volkswagen, Citroën, Renault, and Peugeot, US tel. 503-715-5810, www.ideamerge.com)

Kemwel (Peugeot cars only, US tel. 877-820-0668, www.kemwel.com)

RV and Campervan Rental

Even given the extra fuel costs, renting your own rolling hotel can be a great way to save money, especially if you're sticking mainly to rural areas. Keep in mind that RVs in France are much smaller than those you see at home. Companies to consider:

Van It (mobile 06 70 43 11 86, www.van-it.com)

Idea Merge (best resource for small RV rental, see listing above)

Origin (current-model Volkswagen vans fully equipped for

PRACTICALITIES

2-3 people, rates less than RVs, mobile 06 80 01 72 77, www. origin-campervans.com)

DRIVING

It's a pleasure to explore France by car, but you need to know the rules.

Road Rules: Seat belts are mandatory for all, and children under age 10 must be in the back seat (hefty fine if caught *sans* belt).

In city and town centers, traffic merging from the right (even from tiny side streets) may have the right-of-way *(priorité à droite)*. So even when you're driving on a major road, pay attention to cars merging from the right. In contrast, cars entering the many suburban roundabouts must yield *(cédez le passage)*.

Be aware of typical European road rules; for example, many countries require headlights to be turned on at all times (in France, they must be used whenever visibility is poor), and it's generally illegal to drive while using your mobile phone without a hands-free device. In Europe, you're not allowed to turn right on a red light, unless a sign or signal specifically authorizes it, and on expressways it's illegal to pass drivers on the right. U-turns are prohibited throughout France. Ask your car-rental company about these rules, or check the US State Department website (www.travel.state.gov, search for your country in the "Learn about your destination" box, then click on "Travel and Transportation").

Speed Limits: Because speed limits are by road type, they typically aren't posted, so it's best to memorize them:

- Two-lane D and N routes outside cities and towns: 90 km/hour
- Two-lane roads in villages: 50 km/hour (unless posted at 30 km/hour)
- Divided highways outside cities and towns: 110 km/hour
- Autoroutes: 130 km/hour (unless otherwise posted)

STOP AND LEARN THESE ROAD SIGNS

Sign	Description
50	Speed Limit (km/hr)
50	Speed Limit No Longer Applies
	No Passing
	End of No Passing Zone
SENS UNIQUE	One Way
	Intersection
	Main Road
	Expressway
!	Danger
	No Entry
	Cars Prohibited
	All Vehicles Prohibited
T	No Through Road
	Restrictions No Longer Apply
	Yield to Oncoming Traffic
	No Stopping
P	Parking
	No Parking
DOUANE	Customs
	Yield

If it's raining, subtract 10 km/hour on D and N routes and 20 km/hour on divided highways and autoroutes. Speed-limit signs have a red circle around a number; when you see that same number again in gray with a broken line diagonally across it, this means that limit no longer applies. Speed limits drop to 30-50 km/hour in villages (always posted and enforced).

Road speeds are monitored regularly with cameras—a mere two kilometers over the limit yields a pricey ticket. The good news is that signs warn drivers a few hundred yards before the camera and show the proper speed (see image on previous page). Look for a sign with a radar graphic that says *Pour votre sécurité, contrôles automatiques.* The French use these cameras not to make money but to slow down traffic—and it works.

Drinking and Driving: The French are serious about curbing drunk driving. All motorists, including those in rental cars, are required to have a self-test Breathalyzer on hand so they can tell if they're over the legal blood-alcohol limit (0.05mg/ml—which is lower than in the US—drinker beware). When you pick up your rental car, ask if it has a kit or where to get one.

Tire Pressure: In Europe, tire pressure is measured in *bars* of pressure. To convert to PSI (pounds per square inch) the formula is: *bar* × 14.5 = PSI (so 2 *bars* would be 2 × 14.5, or 29 PSI). To convert to *bar* pressures from PSI, the formula is: PSI × 0.07 = *bar* (so 30 PSI × 0.07 would be 2.1 *bar*). Your car's recommended tire pressure is usually found on a sticker mounted on the driver-side doorframe.

Pulling to the Side of the Road: All rental cars are equipped with a yellow safety vest and triangle. You must wear the vest and display the triangle whenever you pull over on the side of the road (say, to fix a flat tire). If you don't, you could be fined.

Fuel: Gas *(essence)* is expensive—about $8 per gallon. Diesel *(gazole)* costs less—about $7 per gallon. Know what type of fuel your car takes before you fill up. Gas is most expensive on autoroutes and cheapest at big supermarkets. Your US credit and debit cards without a security chip won't work at self-serve pumps—so you'll need to find gas stations with attendants, or get a chip-and-PIN card before your trip (see page 471). Most drivers will spend about $150 per week on gas to prowl the roads in Provence and the French Riviera.

Plan ahead for Sundays, as most gas stations in town are closed. I fill my tank every Saturday. If stuck, use an autoroute on Sunday, where the gas stations are always staffed.

Autoroutes and Tolls: Autoroute tolls are pricey, but the alternative to these super-"feeways" usually means being marooned in countryside traffic—especially near the Riviera. Autoroutes save

Driving in Provence & the French Riviera

To Paris 400m · 5.5h
To Lyon 120m · 1.5h

PROVENCE

Grignan
15m · .5h
Nyons
20m · .75h
Vallon Pont d'Arc (Ardèche Gorges)
30m · 1h
Vaison-la-Romaine
30m · 1h
Brantes
35m · 1.25h
Bollène
20m · .5h
20m · .5h
10m · .25h
15m · .5h
Mont Ventoux
20m · .5h
20m · .5h
20m · .5h
Orange
30m · .75h
35m · 1h
35m · 1.5h
Isle-sur-la-Sorgue
Uzès
PONT DU GARD
Avignon
70m · 2h
15m · .5h
10m · .5h
30m · .75h
15m · .5h
16m · .5h
Roussillon
Nîmes
30m · .75h
St-Rémy
70m · 1h
15m · .5h
Lourmarin
To Carcassonne 120m · 1.5h
20m · .5h
LES BAUX
55m · 1h
25m · .75h
65m · 1.5h
10m · .25h
Arles
55m · .75h
Aigues-Mortes
30m · .75h
30m · .5h
30m · .75h
50m · .75h
Aix
20m · .5h
Phare de la Gacholle
Marseille-Provence
20m · .5h
Stes-Maries-de-la-Mer
95m · 2h (to Cannes)
Mediterranean Sea
Marseille
20m · .5h
25m · .5h
m = miles
h = hours
20 Kilometers
20 Miles
Cassis
La Ciotat
Toulon
10m · .5h (via Route des Crêtes)

enough time, gas, and nausea to justify the cost. Mix high-speed "autorouting" with scenic country-road rambling.

You'll usually take a ticket when entering an autoroute and pay when you leave. Figure roughly €1 in tolls for every 15 kilometers driven on the autoroute (or about €15 for two hours). Cash is your best payment option (for more on paying at tollbooths, see the sidebar on page 528).

Autoroute gas stations are open even on Sundays and usually come with well-stocked minimarts, clean restrooms, sandwiches, maps, local products, cheap vending-machine coffee, and sometimes Wi-Fi. Many have small cafés or more elaborate cafeterias with reasonable prices. For more information, see www.autoroutes.fr.

Highways: Roads are classified into departmental (D), national (N), and autoroutes (A). D routes (usually yellow lines on maps) are often slower but the most scenic. N routes and important D routes (red lines) are the fastest after autoroutes (orange lines on

FRENCH RIVIERA

Note: Your times may vary based on traffic, construction, and road conditions.

maps). Green road signs are for national routes; blue are for auto-routes. Note that some key roads in France are undergoing letter designation and number changes (mostly N roads converting to D roads). If you're using an older map, the actual route name may differ from what's on your map. Navigate by destination rather than road name...or buy a new map. There are plenty of good facilities, gas stations (most closed Sun), and rest stops along most French roads.

Parking: Finding a parking place can be a headache in larger cities. Ask your hotelier for ideas, and pay to park at well-patrolled lots (blue *P* signs direct you to parking lots in French cities). Parking garages require that you take a ticket with you and pay at a machine (called a *caisse*) on your way back to the car. US credit cards won't work in these machines, but euro coins will (some accept bills too). If you don't have enough coins to pay the fee, find the garage's *accueil* office, where the attendant can help or direct you to a nearby

French Road Signs

Signs You Must Obey

Allumez vos feux	Turn on your lights
Cédez le Passage	Yield
Déviation	Detour
Doublage Interdit	No passing
Parking Interdit/ Stationnement Interdit	No parking
Priorité à Droite	Right-of-way is for cars coming from the right
Rappel	Remember to obey the sign
Vous n'avez pas la priorité	You don't have the right of way (when merging)

Signs for Your Information

Autres Directions	Other directions (follow when leaving a city)
Centre Commercial	Shopping center (not city center)
Centre-Ville	City center
Feux	Traffic signal
Horodateur	Ticket-vending machine for parking
Parc de Stationnement/ Parking	Parking lot
Route Barrée	Road blocked
Rue Piétonne	Pedestrian-only street
Sauf Riverains	Local access only
Sortie des Camions	Work truck exit
Suivre... (e.g., Pont du Gard, suivre Nîmes)	Follow... (e.g., for Pont du Gard, follow signs for Nîmes)
Toutes Directions	All directions (follow when leaving a city)

Signs Unique to Autoroutes

Aire	Rest stop with WCs, telephones, and sometimes gas stations
Bouchon	Traffic jam ahead
Fluide	No traffic ahead
Péage	Toll
Par Temps de Pluie	When raining (modifies speed limit signs)
Télépéage	Automated tollbooths

shop where you can change bills into coins. Overnight parking in garages (usually 19:00-8:00) is generally reasonable (priciest in Nice, Avignon, and Antibes).

Curbside metered parking also works (usually free 12:00-14:00 & 19:00-9:00, and all day and night in Aug). Look for a small machine selling time (called an *horodateur*, usually one per block), plug in a few coins (€1.50-2 buys about an hour, varies by city), push the button, get a receipt showing the amount of time you have, and display it inside your windshield. (Avoid spaces outlined in blue, as they require a special permit.) For cheap overnight parking until the next afternoon, buy three hours' worth of time after 19:00. This gets you until noon the next day, after which two more hours are usually free (12:00-14:00), so you're good until 14:00.

Theft: Theft is a problem, particularly in southern France. Thieves easily recognize rental cars and assume they are filled with a tourist's gear. Try to make your car look locally owned by hiding the "tourist-owned" rental-company decals and putting a French newspaper in your back window. Be sure all of your valuables are out of sight and locked in the trunk—or, even better, with you or in your room. And don't assume that just because you're parked on a main street that you'll be fine. Thieves work fast.

Driving Tips

- France is riddled with roundabouts—navigating them is an art. The key is to know your direction and be ready for your turnoff. If you miss it, take another lap (or two).
- At intersections and roundabouts, French road signs use the name of the next destination for directions—the highway number is usually missing. That next destination could be a major city, or it could be the next minor town up the road. It's a good idea to check your map ahead of time and get familiar with the names of towns and cities along your route—and even major cities on the same road beyond your destination.
- When navigating into cities, approach intersections cautiously, stow the map, and follow the signs to *Centre-Ville* (city center). From there, head to the TI *(Office de Tourisme)* or your hotel.
- When leaving or just passing through cities, follow the signs for *Toutes Directions* or *Autres Directions* (meaning "anywhere else") until you see a sign for your specific destination. Look also for *Suivre* signs telling you to follow *(suivre)* signs for the (usually more important) destination listed to continue toward your destination.
- Driving on any roads but autoroutes will take longer than you think, so allow plenty of time for slower traffic (tractors, trucks, and hard-to-decipher signs all deserve blame). First-

PRACTICALITIES

French Tollbooths

For American drivers, getting through the toll payment stations on France's autoroutes is mostly about knowing which lanes to avoid—and having cash on hand. Skip lanes marked with a lowercase "t"—they're reserved for cars using the automatic Télépéage payment system. A pictograph of a credit card (usually a blue sign) means credit or debit cards only: Your US card won't work unless you have a chip-and-PIN card (and even then it's iffy). Look instead for green arrows above the tollbooth and/or icons showing bills or coins, which indicate booths accepting cash (booths often allow more than one payment method). Slow down as you approach tollbooths to study your options, and pull off to the side if you aren't positive of the tollbooth to choose.

Exits are entirely automated (if you have a problem at the tollbooth, press the red button for help). Have smaller bills ready (payment machines won't accept €50 bills). Shorter autoroute sections have periodic tollbooths, where you can pay by dropping coins into a basket (change is given for bills, but keep a good supply of coins handy to avoid waiting for an attendant).

To figure out how much cash to have on hand for tolls for your route, use the planning tool at ViaMichelin.com.

timers should estimate how long they think a drive will take... then double it. I pretend that kilometers are miles (for distances) and base my time estimates accordingly.

- While locals are eating lunch (12:00-14:00), many sights (and gas stations) are closed, so you can make great time driving—but keep it slow when passing through villages.
- Be very careful when driving on smaller roads—many are narrow and flanked by little ditches that lure inattentive drivers. I've met several readers who "ditched" their cars (and had to be pulled out by local farmers).
- On autoroutes, keep to the right lanes to let fast drivers by, and be careful when merging into a left lane, as cars can be coming at high speeds.
- Motorcycles will scream between cars in traffic. Be ready—they expect you to make space so that they can pass.
- Keep a stash of coins handy for parking and small autoroute tolls.

BIKING

You'll find areas in Provence and the Riviera where public transportation is limited and bicycle touring might be a good idea. For many, biking is a romantic notion, and the novelty wears off after the first hill or headwind. Realistically evaluate your physical condition, be clear on the limitations bikes present, and consider an electric bike (available in most of the destinations I recommend). Start with an easy pedal, then decide how ambitious you feel. Most find that two hours on a narrow, hard seat is enough. I've listed bike-rental shops where appropriate (TIs can also guide you), and I've suggested a few of my favorite rides. For a good touring bike, figure about €14 for a half-day and €20 for a full day. You'll pay more for better equipment; generally the best is available through bike shops, not at train stations or other outlets. French cyclists often do not wear helmets, though most rental outfits have them (for a small fee).

FLIGHTS

The best comparison search engine for both international and intra-European flights is www.kayak.com. For inexpensive flights within Europe, try www.skyscanner.com or www. hipmunk.com; for inexpensive international flights, try www. vayama.com.

Flying to Europe: Start looking for international flights four to five months before your trip, especially for peak-season travel. Off-season tickets can be purchased a month or so in advance. Depending on your itinerary, it can be efficient to fly into one city and out of another. If your flight requires a connection in Europe, see our hints on navigating Europe's top hub airports at www. ricksteves.com/hub-airports.

Flying within Europe: If you're visiting one or more French cities on a longer European trip—or linking up far-flung French cities (such as Paris and Nice)—a flight can save both time and money. When comparing your options, factor in the time it takes to get to the airport and how early you'll need to arrive to check in.

Well-known cheapo airlines include easyJet (www.easyjet. com) and Ryanair (www.ryanair.com). Also check Air France for specials. But be aware of the potential drawbacks of flying with a discount airline: nonrefundable and nonchangeable tickets, minimal or nonexistent customer service, pricey and time-consuming treks to secondary airports, and stingy baggage allowances with steep overage fees. If you're traveling with lots of luggage, a cheap flight can quickly become a bad deal. To avoid unpleasant surprises, read the small print before you book. These days you can also fly within Europe on major airlines affordably—and without all the aggressive restrictions—for around $100 a flight.

Flying to the US and Canada: Because security is extra tight for flights to the US, be sure to give yourself plenty of time at the airport. It's also important to charge your electronic devices before you board because security checks may require you to turn them on (see www.tsa.gov for latest rules).

Resources

RESOURCES FROM RICK STEVES

Books: *Rick Steves Provence & the French Riviera* is one of many books in my series on European travel, which includes coun-

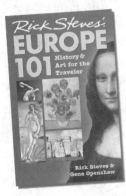

try guidebooks (including France), city guidebooks (Paris, Rome, Florence, London, etc.), Snapshot guides (excerpted chapters from my country guides), Pocket Guides (full-color little books on big cities), and my budget-travel skills handbook, *Rick Steves Europe Through the Back Door.* Most of my titles are available as ebooks. My phrase books—for French, Italian, German, Spanish, and Portuguese—are practical and budget-oriented. My other books include *Europe 101* (a crash course on art and history designed for travelers); *Mediterranean Cruise Ports* and *Northern European Cruise Ports* (how to make the most of your time in port); and *Travel as a Political Act* (a travelogue sprinkled with tips for bringing home a global perspective). A more complete list of my titles appears near the end of this book.

Video: My public television series, *Rick Steves' Europe,* covers Europe from top to bottom with over 100 half-hour episodes. To watch full episodes online for free, see www.ricksteves.com/tv. Or to raise your travel I.Q. with video versions of our popular classes (including my talks on travel skills, packing smart, European art for travelers, travel as a political act, and individual talks covering most European countries including France), see www.ricksteves.com/travel-talks.

Audio: My weekly public radio show, *Travel with Rick Steves,* features interviews with travel experts from around the world. A complete archive of 10 years of programs (over 400 in all) is available at www.ricksteves.com/radio. Most of this audio content is available for free through my **Rick Steves Audio Europe** app (see page 17).

Begin Your Trip at
www.RickSteves.com

My mobile-friendly **website** is *the* place to explore Europe. You'll find thousands of fun articles, videos, photos, and radio interviews organized by country; a wealth of money-saving tips for planning your dream trip; monthly travel news dispatches; my travel talks and travel blog; my latest guidebook updates (www.ricksteves.com/update); and my free Rick Steves Audio Europe app. You can also follow me on Facebook and Twitter.

Our **Travel Forum** is an immense, yet well-groomed collection of message boards, where our travel-savvy community answers questions and shares their personal travel experiences—and our well-traveled staff chimes in when they can be helpful (www.ricksteves.com/forums).

Our **online Travel Store** offers travel bags and accessories that I've designed specifically to help you travel smarter and lighter. These include my popular bags (rolling carry-on and backpack versions, which I helped design...and live out of four months a year), money belts, totes, toiletries kits, adapters, other accessories, and a wide selection of guidebooks and planning maps.

Choosing the right **rail pass** for your trip—amid hundreds of options—can drive you nutty. Our website will help you find the perfect fit for your itinerary and your budget: We offer easy, one-stop shopping for rail passes, seat reservations, and point-to-point tickets.

Want to travel with greater efficiency and less stress? We organize **tours** with more than three dozen itineraries and more than 800 departures reaching the best destinations in this book...and beyond. We offer a 13-day Loire to the South of France tour, 14-day Best of Eastern France tour, 7-day in-depth Paris city tour, 11-day Paris and the Heart of France tour (focusing on the best of the north), and 13-day My Way France tour. You'll enjoy great guides, a fun bunch of travel partners (with small groups of around 24 to 28 travelers), and plenty of room to spread out in a big, comfy bus when touring between towns. You'll find European adventures to fit every vacation length. For all the details, and to get our Tour Catalog and a free Rick Steves Tour Experience DVD (filmed on location during an actual tour), visit www.ricksteves.com or call us at 425/608-4217.

PRACTICALITIES

MAPS

The black-and-white maps in this book are concise and simple, designed to help you locate recommended places and get to local TIs, where you can pick up more in-depth maps of cities and regions (usually free). Better maps are sold at newsstands and bookstores. Before you buy a map, look at it to be sure it has the level of detail you want. Map apps for your smartphone or tablet are also handy. For more on recommended maps for drivers and using mapping apps and GPS devices, see "Navigation Options," earlier.

APPENDIX

Useful Contacts

Emergency Needs
Police: Tel. 17
Emergency Medical Assistance (called "SAMU"): Tel. 15
Collect Calls to the US: Dial 08 00 90 06 24, then say "operator" for an English-speaking operator.
Riviera Medical Services: Tel. 04 93 26 12 70, www.rivieramedical. com (has list of English-speaking physicians in the Riviera region and can help make an appointment or call an ambulance)

Embassies and Consulates
US Consulate in Nice: Tel. 04 93 88 89 55 (7 Avenue Gustave V, http://marseille.usconsulate.gov/nice.html; does *not* provide visa services—Paris is the nearest office for these services)
Canadian Consulate in Nice: Tel. 04 93 92 93 22 (2 Place Franklin). For emergency assistance, call collect to Canadian tel. 613/996-8885.
US Consulate in Marseille: Tel. 01 43 12 47 54; after business

hours call Paris office at tel. 01 43 12 22 22 (Place Varian Fry, http://marseille.usconsulate.gov)

US Consulate and Embassy in Paris: Tel. 01 43 12 22 22 (4 Avenue Gabriel, to the left as you face Hôtel Crillon, Mo: Concorde, http://france.usembassy.gov)

Canadian Consulate and Embassy in Paris: Tel. 01 44 43 29 02 (35 Avenue Montaigne, Mo: Franklin D. Roosevelt, www.amb-canada.fr). For 24/7 emergency assistance, call collect to Canadian tel. 613/996-8885.

Australian Consulate in Paris: Tel. 01 40 59 33 00 (4 Rue Jean Rey, Mo: Bir-Hakeim, www.france.embassy.gov.au)

Holidays and Festivals

This list includes selected festivals in the Provence and French Riviera region, plus national holidays observed throughout France. Many sights and banks close on national holidays—keep this in mind when planning your itinerary. Before planning a trip around a festival, verify its dates by checking the festival's website or the France TI (www.franceguide.com). Hotels get booked up on Easter weekend, Labor Day, Ascension Day, Pentecost, Bastille Day, and the winter holidays.

Jan 1	New Year's Day
Jan 6	Epiphany
Feb-March	Carnival-Mardi Gras, parades and fireworks, Nice (www.nicecarnaval.com)
March/April	Easter weekend (Good Friday-Easter Monday): March 25-28, 2016; April 14-17, 2017
March/April	Feria de Pâques (bullfights, coincides with Easter weekend), Arles
May	Cannes Film Festival, Cannes: May 11-22, 2016; May 10-20, 2017 (www.festival-cannes.com)
May	Ascension: May 5, 2016; May 25, 2017
May 1	Labor Day
May 8	V-E (Victory in Europe) Day
Late May	Monaco Grand Prix, auto race: May 26-29, 2016; May 25-28, 2017 (www.acm.mc)
May/June	Pentecost: May 15, 2016; June 4, 2017
June 21	Fête de la Musique, free concerts and dancing in the streets throughout France

Early July	International Music and Opera Festival, Aix-en-Provence (www.festival-aix.com)
July	Avignon Festival, theater, dance, and music, Avignon (www.festival-avignon.com)
July	Tour de France, national bicycle race culminating in Paris (www.letour.fr)
July 14	Bastille Day, fireworks, dancing, and revelry
Mid-July	"Jazz à Juan" International Jazz Festival, Antibes/Juan-les-Pins (www.jazzajuan.com)
Mid-July	Nice Jazz Festival, Nice (www.nicejazzfestival.fr)
Mid-July-early Aug	Chorégies d'Orange, music and opera performed in a Roman theater, Orange (www.choregies.fr)
July-Aug	International Fireworks Festival, Cannes (www.festival-pyrotechnique-cannes.com)
Aug 15	Assumption of Mary
Mid-Sept	Féria du Riz (bullfights), Arles
Nov 1	All Saints' Day
Nov 11	Armistice Day
Dec 25	Christmas Day
Dec 31	New Year's Eve

Recommended Books and Films

To learn more about France past and present, and specifically Provence and the French Riviera, check out a few of these books and films. To learn what's making news in France, you'll find *France 24 News* online at www.France24.com/en. See the Traveling with Kids chapter for recommendations for children.

Nonfiction

A to Z of French Food, a French to English Dictionary of Culinary Terms (G. de Temmerman, 1995). This is the most complete (and priciest) menu reader around—and it's beloved by foodies.

At Home in France (Ann Barry, 1996). An American author describes her visits to her country house.

The Course of French History (Pierre Goubert, 1988). Goubert provides a basic summary of French history.

A Distant Mirror (Barbara Tuchman, 1987). Respected historian Barbara Tuchman paints a portrait of 14th-century France.

French or Foe? (Polly Platt, 1994). This best seller, along with its follow-up, *Savoir-Flair!*, is an essential aid for interacting with the French and navigating the intricacies of their culture.

A Goose in Toulouse and other Culinary Adventures in France (Mort Rosenblum, 2000). This series of essays provides keen insights on rural France through its focus on cuisine.

La Seduction: How the French Play the Game of Life (Elaine Sciolino, 2011). Sciolino, former Paris bureau chief of the *New York Times*, gives travelers a fun, insightful, and tantalizing peek into how seduction is used in all aspects of French life—from small villages to the halls of national government.

Portraits of France (Robert Daley, 1991). Part memoir, part travelogue, this is a charming reminiscence of the writer's lifelong relationship with France, including marrying a French girl on his first trip there.

Postcards from France (Megan McNeill Libby, 1997). This perceptive account tells the adventures of an American exchange student adjusting to life in France.

The Road from the Past: Traveling Through History in France (Ina Caro, 1994). Caro's enjoyable travel essays take you on a chronological journey through France's historical sights.

Sixty Million Frenchmen Can't Be Wrong (Jean-Benoit Nadeau and Julie Barlow, 2003). This is a must-read for anyone serious about understanding French culture, contemporary politics, and what makes the French tick.

Travelers Tales: Paris and *Travelers' Tales: France* (edited by James O'Reilly, Larry Habegger, and Sean O'Reilly, 2002). Notable writers explore Parisian and French culture.

Two Towns in Provence (M. F. K. Fisher, 1964). Aix-en-Provence and Marseille are the subjects of these two stories by the celebrated American food writer. She also writes about her life in France in *Long Ago in France: The Years in Dijon* (1929).

A Year in Provence and *Toujours Provence* (Peter Mayle, 1989/1991). Mayle's memoirs include humorous anecdotes about restoring and living in a 200-year-old farmhouse in a remote area of the Lubéron.

The Yellow House: Van Gogh, Gauguin, and Nine Turbulent Weeks in Arles (Martin Gayford, 2006). This historical account vividly chronicles Van Gogh and Gauguin's tumultuous stay in Arles.

Fiction

The Fly-Truffler (Gustaf Sobin, 1999). After the death of his young wife, a Provençal man stays in touch with her spirit through intimate dream visions.

Hotel Pastis (Peter Mayle, 1993). Mayle, whose nonfiction books are recommended earlier, also writes fiction set in Provence, including this book and *A Good Year*.

Joy of Man's Desiring (Jean Giono, 1935). Giano captures the charm of rural France. (The author also wrote the Johnny Appleseed eco-fable set in Provence, *The Man Who Planted Trees*.)

Film and TV

The Chorus (2004). Filled with angelic choir music, this touching film tells the story of a schoolteacher and the boys he brings together.

Cyrano de Bergerac (1990). A homely, romantic poet woos his love with the help of another, better-looking man (look for scenes filmed at the Abbaye de Fontenay).

Dirty Rotten Scoundrels (1988). Steve Martin and Michael Caine star in this hilarious flick, filmed in and around Villefranche-sur-Mer.

French Kiss (1995). This romantic comedy includes scenes in the French countryside and Cannes, as well as Paris.

The Horseman on the Roof (1995). The beautiful Juliette Binoche seeks her missing husband in this romance-drama set in 1830's southern France.

Jean de Florette (1986). This marvelous tale of greed and intolerance follows a hunchback as he fights for the property he inherited in rural France. Its sequel, *Manon of the Spring* (1986), continues with his daughter's story.

My Father's Glory and *My Mother's Castle* (1991). These companion films, based on the memoirs of writer/filmmaker Marcel Pagnol, show his early life in Provence.

The Return of Martin Guerre (1982). A man returns to his village in southwestern France from the Hundred Years' War—but is he really who he claims to be?

Ronin (1998). Robert De Niro stars in this crime caper, which includes a car chase through Paris and scenes filmed in Nice, Villefranche-sur-Mer, and Arles.

To Catch a Thief (1955). Alfred Hitchcock's thriller showcases both the French Riviera and crackling performances by Grace Kelly and Cary Grant.

Conversions and Climate

NUMBERS AND STUMBLERS

- Europeans write a few of their numbers differently than we do. 1 = 1, 4 = 4, 7 = 7.
- In Europe, dates appear as day/month/year, so Christmas 2017 is 25/12/17.
- Commas are decimal points and decimals are commas. A dollar and a half is $1,50, one thousand is 1.000, and there are 5.280 feet in a mile.
- When counting with fingers, start with your thumb. If you hold up your first finger to request one item, you'll probably get two.
- What Americans call the second floor of a building is the first floor in Europe.
- On escalators and moving sidewalks, Europeans keep the left "lane" open for passing. Keep to the right.

METRIC CONVERSIONS

A kilogram is 2.2 pounds, and 1 liter is about a quart, or almost four to a gallon. A kilometer is six-tenths of a mile. I figure kilometers to miles by cutting them in half and adding back 10 percent of the original (120 km: 60 + 12=72 miles, 300 km: 150 + 30=180 miles).

1 foot = 0.3 meter	1 square yard = 0.8 square meter
1 yard = 0.9 meter	1 square mile = 2.6 square kilometers
1 mile = 1.6 kilometers	1 hectare = 2.47 acres
1 centimeter = 0.4 inch	1 ounce = 28 grams
1 meter = 39.4 inches	1 quart = 0.95 liter
1 kilometer = 0.62 mile	1 kilogram = 2.2 pounds
32°F = 0°C	

CLOTHING SIZES

When shopping for clothing, use these US-to-European comparisons as general guidelines (but note that no conversion is perfect).

- Women's dresses and blouses: Add 30
  (US size 10 = European size 40)
- Men's suits and jackets: Add 10
  (US size 40 regular = European size 50)
- Men's shirts: Multiply by 2 and add about 8
  (US size 15 collar = European size 38)
- Women's shoes: Add about 30
  (US size 8 = European size 38-39)
- Men's shoes: Add 32-34
  (US size 9 = European size 41; US size 11 = European size 45)

APPENDIX

NICE'S CLIMATE

First line, average daily high; second line, average daily low; third line, average days without rain. For more detailed weather statistics for destinations in this book (as well as the rest of the world), check www.wunderground.com.

J	F	M	A	M	J	J	A	S	O	N	D
50°	53°	59°	64°	71°	79°	84°	83°	77°	68°	58°	52°
35°	36°	41°	46°	52°	58°	63°	63°	58°	51°	43°	37°
23	22	24	23	23	26	29	26	24	23	21	21

FAHRENHEIT AND CELSIUS CONVERSION

Europe takes its temperature using the Celsius scale, while we opt for Fahrenheit. For a rough conversion from Celsius to Fahrenheit, double the number and add 30. For weather, remember that 28°C is 82°F—perfect. For health, 37°C is just right. At a launderette, 30°C is cold, 40°C is warm (usually the default setting), 60°C is hot, and 95°C is boiling.

For Weather   For Health

Packing Checklist

Whether you're traveling for five days or five weeks, you won't need more than this. Pack light to enjoy the sweet freedom of true mobility.

Clothing

- ❑ 5 shirts: long- & short-sleeve
- ❑ 2 pairs pants or skirt
- ❑ 1 pair shorts or capris
- ❑ 5 pairs underwear & socks
- ❑ 1 pair walking shoes
- ❑ Sweater or fleece top
- ❑ Rainproof jacket with hood
- ❑ Tie or scarf
- ❑ Swimsuit
- ❑ Sleepwear

Money

- ❑ Debit card
- ❑ Credit card(s)
- ❑ Hard cash ($20 bills)
- ❑ Money belt or neck wallet

Documents & Travel Info

- ❑ Passport
- ❑ Airline reservations
- ❑ Rail pass/train reservations
- ❑ Car-rental voucher
- ❑ Driver's license
- ❑ Student ID, hostel card, etc.
- ❑ Photocopies of all the above
- ❑ Hotel confirmations
- ❑ Insurance details
- ❑ Guidebooks & maps
- ❑ Notepad & pen
- ❑ Journal

Toiletries Kit

- ❑ Toiletries
- ❑ Medicines & vitamins
- ❑ First-aid kit
- ❑ Glasses/contacts/sunglasses (with prescriptions)
- ❑ Earplugs
- ❑ Packet of tissues (for WC)

Miscellaneous

- ❑ Daypack
- ❑ Sealable plastic baggies
- ❑ Laundry soap
- ❑ Spot remover
- ❑ Clothesline
- ❑ Sewing kit
- ❑ Travel alarm/watch

Electronics

- ❑ Smartphone or mobile phone
- ❑ Camera & related gear
- ❑ Tablet/ereader/media player
- ❑ Laptop & flash drive
- ❑ Earbuds or headphones
- ❑ Chargers
- ❑ Plug adapters

Optional Extras

- ❑ Flipflops or slippers
- ❑ Mini-umbrella or poncho
- ❑ Travel hairdryer
- ❑ Belt
- ❑ Hat (for sun or cold)
- ❑ Picnic supplies
- ❑ Water bottle
- ❑ Fold-up tote bag
- ❑ Small flashlight
- ❑ Small binoculars
- ❑ Insect repellent
- ❑ Small towel or washcloth
- ❑ Inflatable pillow
- ❑ Some duct tape (for repairs)
- ❑ Tiny lock
- ❑ Address list (to mail postcards)
- ❑ Postcards/photos from home
- ❑ Extra passport photos
- ❑ Good book

APPENDIX

Pronunciation Guide for Place Names

When using the phonetics: Try to nasalize the n sound (let the sound come through your nose). Note that the "ahn" combination uses the "ah" sound in "father," but the "an" combination uses the "a" sound in "sack." Pronounce the "ī" as the long "i" in "light." If your best attempt at pronunciation meets with a puzzled look, just point to the place name on the list.

Aigues-Mortes	ayg-mort
Aiguines	ayg-ween
Aix-en-Provence	ehks ahn proh-vahns
Antibes	ahn-teeb
Ardèche Gorges	ar-dehsh gorzh
Arles	arl
Avignon	ah-veen-yohn
Balazuc	bah-lah-zewk
Bedoin	buh-dwan
Biot	bee-oht
Bonnieux	bohn-yuh
Brantes	brahnt
Buis-les-Barronnies	bwee-lay-bah-roh-nee
Buoux	byoo
Cairanne	kay-rahn
Camargue	kah-marg
Cannes	kan
Cap Ferrat	kahp feh-rah
Cassis	kah-see
Cavaillon	kah-vī-yohn
Châteauneuf-du-Pape	shah-toh-nuhf-dew-pahp
Côte du Rhône	koht dew rohn
Crestet	kruh-stay
Eze-Bord-de-Mer	ehz-bor-duh-mehr
Eze-le-Village	ehz-luh-vee-lahzh
Gigondas	zhee-gohn-dahs
Gordes	gord
Gourdon	goor-dohn
Grasse	grahs
Grignan	green-yahn
Isle-sur-la-Sorgue	eel-sewr-lah-sorg
Joucas	zhoo-kahs
Juan-les-Pins	zhwahn-lay-pan
Le Trophée des Alpes	luh troh-fay dayz ahlp
La Turbie	lah tewr-bee

Pronunciation Guide for Place Names
(continued)

Lacoste	lah-kohst
Le Bar-sur-Loup	luh bar-sewr-loo
Les Baux	lay boh
Lourmarin	loor-mah-ran
Luberon	lew-buh-rohn
Marseille	mar-say
Ménerbes	may-nehrb
Menton	mahn-tohn
Monaco	moh-nah-koh
Monte Carlo	mohn-tay kar-loh
Mont Ventoux	mohn vahn-too
Moustier-Ste-Marie	moost-yay-sahnt-mah-ree
Nice	nees
Nîmes	neem
Nyons	nee-yohns
Oppède-le-Vieux	oh-pehd-luh-vee-uh
Orange	oh-rahnzh
Pont du Gard	pohn dew gar
Port Grimaud	por gree-moh
Provence	proh-vahns
Roussillon	roo-see-yohn
Saignon	sayn-yohn
Séguret	say-gew-ray
Ste-Jalles	san-zhahl
St-Jean	san-zhahn
St-Paul-de-Vence	san-pohl-duh-vahns
St-Rémy-de-Provence	san-ray-mee-duh-pro-vahns
St-Saturnin-lès-Apt	san-sah-tewr-nan-lehz-ahpt
St-Tropez	san-troh-pay
Stes-Maries-de-la-Mer	sahnt-mah-ree-duh-lah-mehr
Suzette	sew-zeht
Tourrettes-sur-Loup	too-reht-sewr-loo
Uzès	ew-zehs
Vaison-la-Romaine	vay-zohn lah roh-mehn
Vallauris	vah-loh-rees
Vence	vahns
Viens	vee-ahn
Villa Kérylos	vee-lah kay-ree-lohs
Villefranche-sur-Mer	veel-frahnsh-sewr-mehr

French Survival Phrases

When using the phonetics, try to nasalize the n sound.

English	French	Pronunciation
Good day.	Bonjour.	bohn-zhoor
Mrs. / Mr.	Madame / Monsieur	mah-dahm / muhs-yur
Do you speak English?	Parlez-vous anglais?	par-lay-voo ahn-glay
Yes. / No.	Oui. / Non.	wee / nohn
I understand.	Je comprends.	zhuh kohn-prahn
I don't understand.	Je ne comprends pas.	zhuh nuh kohn-prahn pah
Please.	S'il vous plaît.	see voo play
Thank you.	Merci.	mehr-see
I'm sorry.	Désolé.	day-zoh-lay
Excuse me.	Pardon.	par-dohn
(No) problem.	(Pas de) problème.	(pah duh) proh-blehm
It's good.	C'est bon.	say bohn
Goodbye.	Au revoir.	oh vwahr
one / two	un / deux	uhn / duh
three / four	trois / quatre	twah / kah-truh
five / six	cinq / six	sank / sees
seven / eight	sept / huit	seht / weet
nine / ten	neuf / dix	nuhf / dees
How much is it?	Combien?	kohn-bee-an
Write it?	Ecrivez?	ay-kree-vay
Is it free?	C'est gratuit?	say grah-twee
Included?	Inclus?	an-klew
Where can I buy / find...?	Où puis-je acheter / trouver...?	oo pwee-zhuh ah-shuh-tay / troo-vay
I'd like / We'd like...	Je voudrais / Nous voudrions...	zhuh voo-dray / noo voo-dree-ohn
...a room.	...une chambre.	ewn shahn-bruh
...a ticket to ___.	...un billet pour ___.	uhn bee-yay poor ___
Is it possible?	C'est possible?	say poh-see-bluh
Where is...?	Où est...?	oo ay
...the train station	...la gare	lah gar
...the bus station	...la gare routière	lah gar root-yehr
...tourist information	...l'office du tourisme	loh-fees dew too-reez-muh
Where are the toilets?	Où sont les toilettes?	oo sohn lay twah-leht
men	hommes	ohm
women	dames	dahm
left / right	à gauche / à droite	ah gohsh / ah dwaht
straight	tout droit	too dwah
When does this open / close?	Ça ouvre / ferme à quelle heure?	sah oo-vruh / fehrm ah kehl ur
At what time?	À quelle heure?	ah kehl ur
Just a moment.	Un moment.	uhn moh-mahn
now / soon / later	maintenant / bientôt / plus tard	man-tuh-nahn / bee-an-toh / plew tar
today / tomorrow	aujourd'hui / demain	oh-zhoor-dwee / duh-man

In a French Restaurant

English	French	Pronunciation
I'd like / We'd like...	Je voudrais / Nous voudrions...	zhuh voo-dray / noo voo-dree-ohn
...to reserve...	...réserver...	ray-zehr-vay
...a table for one / two.	...une table pour un / deux.	ewn tah-bluh poor uhn / duh
Is this seat free?	C'est libre?	say lee-bruh
The menu (in English), please.	La carte (en anglais), s'il vous plaît.	lah kart (ahn ahn-glay) see voo play
service (not) included	service (non) compris	sehr-vees (nohn) kohn-pree
to go	à emporter	ah ahn-por-tay
with / without	avec / sans	ah-vehk / sahn
and / or	et / ou	ay / oo
special of the day	plat du jour	plah dew zhoor
specialty of the house	spécialité de la maison	spay-see-ah-lee-tay duh lah may-zohn
appetizers	hors d'oeuvre	or duh-vruh
first course (soup, salad)	entrée	ahn-tray
main course (meat, fish)	plat principal	plah pran-see-pahl
bread	pain	pan
cheese	fromage	froh-mahzh
sandwich	sandwich	sahnd-weech
soup	soupe	soop
salad	salade	sah-lahd
meat	viande	vee-ahnd
chicken	poulet	poo-lay
fish	poisson	pwah-sohn
seafood	fruits de mer	frwee duh mehr
fruit	fruit	frwee
vegetables	légumes	lay-gewm
dessert	dessert	day-sehr
mineral water	eau minérale	oh mee-nay-rahl
tap water	l'eau du robinet	loh dew roh-bee-nay
milk	lait	lay
(orange) juice	jus (d'orange)	zhew (doh-rahnzh)
coffee / tea	café / thé	kah-fay / tay
wine	vin	van
red / white	rouge / blanc	roozh / blahn
glass / bottle	verre / bouteille	vehr / boo-tay
beer	bière	bee-ehr
Cheers!	Santé!	sahn-tay
More. / Another.	Plus. / Un autre.	plew / uhn oh-truh
The same.	La même chose.	lah mehm shohz
The bill, please.	L'addition, s'il vous plaît.	lah-dee-see-ohn see voo play
Do you accept credit cards?	Vous prenez les cartes?	voo pruh-nay lay kart
tip	pourboire	poor-bwahr
Delicious!	Délicieux!	day-lee-see-uh

For more user-friendly French phrases, check out *Rick Steves' French Phrase Book and Dictionary* or *Rick Steves' French, Italian & German Phrase Book.*

INDEX

INDEX

MAP INDEX

Explore Europe

At ricksteves.com you can browse through thousands of articles, videos, photos and radio interviews, plus find a wealth of money-saving travel tips for planning your dream trip. And with our mobile-friendly website, you can easily access all this great travel information anywhere you go.

TV Shows

Preview the places you'll visit by watching entire half-hour episodes of Rick Steves' Europe (choose from all 100 shows) on-demand, for free.

Radio Interviews

Enjoy ready access to
Rick's vast library of radio
interviews covering travel

tips and cultural insights
that relate specifically to
your Europe travel plans.

Travel Forums

Learn, ask, share! Our
online community of savvy
travelers is a great resource for first-time travelers to
Europe, as well as seasoned
pros. You'll find forums on
each country, plus travel
tips and restaurant/hotel
reviews. You can even ask
one of our well-traveled staff
to chime in with an opinion.

Travel News

Subscribe to our free Travel
News e-newsletter, and
get monthly updates from
Rick on what's
happening in
Europe.

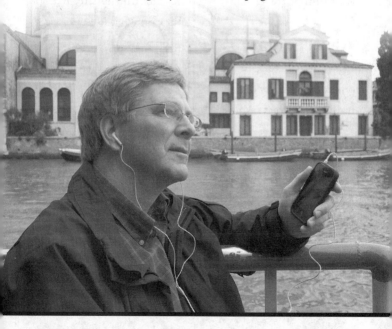

Gear up for your next adventure at ricksteves.com

Light Luggage

Pack light and right with Rick Steves' affordable, custom-designed rolling carry-on bags, backpacks, day packs and shoulder bags.

Accessories

From packing cubes to moneybelts and beyond, Rick has personally selected the travel goodies that will help your trip go smoother.

Experience maximum Europe

Save time and energy

This guidebook is your independent-travel toolkit. But for all it delivers, it's still up to you to devote the time and energy it takes to manage the preparation and logistics that are essential for a happy trip. If that's a hassle, there's a solution.

Rick Steves Tours

A Rick Steves tour takes you to Europe's most interesting places with great

with minimum stress

guides and small groups of 28 or less. We follow Rick's favorite itineraries, ride in comfy buses, stay in family-run hotels, and bring you intimately close to the Europe you've traveled so far to see. Most importantly, we take away the logistical headaches so you can focus on the fun.

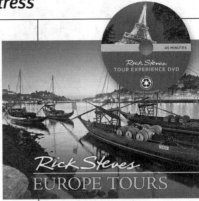

customers—along with us on 40 different itineraries, from Ireland to Italy to Istanbul. Is a Rick Steves tour the right fit for your travel dreams? Find out at ricksteves.com, where you can also get Rick's latest tour catalog and free Tour Experience DVD.

Join the fun

This year we'll take 18,000 free-spirited travelers— nearly half of them repeat

Europe is best experienced with happy travel partners. We hope you can join us.

See our itineraries at ricksteves.com

Rick Steves

EUROPE GUIDES

Best of Europe
Eastern Europe
Europe Through the Back Door
Mediterranean Cruise Ports
Northern European Cruise Ports

COUNTRY GUIDES

Croatia & Slovenia
England
France
Germany
Great Britain
Ireland
Italy
Portugal
Scandinavia
Spain
Switzerland

CITY & REGIONAL GUIDES

Amsterdam & the Netherlands
Belgium: Bruges, Brussels, Antwerp & Ghent
Barcelona
Budapest
Florence & Tuscany
Greece: Athens & the Peloponnese
Istanbul
London
Paris
Prague & the Czech Republic
Provence & the French Riviera
Rome
Venice
Vienna, Salzburg & Tirol

SNAPSHOT GUIDES

Basque Country: Spain & France
Berlin
Copenhagen & the Best of Denmark
Dublin
Dubrovnik
Hill Towns of Central Italy
Italy's Cinque Terre
Kraków, Warsaw & Gdansk
Lisbon
Loire Valley
Madrid & Toledo
Milan & the Italian Lakes District
Naples & the Amalfi Coast
Northern Ireland
Norway
Scotland
Sevilla, Granada & Southern Spain
St. Petersburg, Helsinki & Tallinn
Stockholm

POCKET GUIDES

Amsterdam
Athens
Barcelona
Florence
London
Munich & Salzburg
Paris
Rome
Venice
Vienna

Rick Steves guidebooks are published by Avalon Travel, a member of the Perseus Books Group

Maximize your travel skills with a good guidebook.

TRAVEL CULTURE

Europe 101
European Christmas
Postcards from Europe
Travel as a Political Act

eBOOKS

Nearly all Rick Steves guides are available as ebooks. Check with your favorite bookseller.

RICK STEVES' EUROPE DVDs

12 New Shows 2015–2016
Austria & the Alps
The Complete Collection 2000-2016
Eastern Europe
England & Wales
European Christmas
European Travel Skills & Specials
France
Germany, BeNeLux & More
Greece, Turkey & Portugal
The Holy Land: Israelis & Palestinians Today
Iran
Ireland & Scotland
Italy's Cities
Italy's Countryside
Scandinavia
Spain
Travel Extras

PHRASE BOOKS & DICTIONARIES

French
French, Italian & German
German
Italian
Portuguese
Spanish

PLANNING MAPS

Britain, Ireland & London
Europe
France & Paris
Germany, Austria & Switzerland
Ireland
Italy
Spain & Portugal

Photo © Patricia Feaster

RickSteves.com @RickSteves

Credits

RESEARCHERS
To help update this book, Rick and Steve relied on...

Tom Griffin

After growing up in Wisconsin, Tom first headed east—living in London, Paris, and Germany—before reversing direction to end up on the West Coast. A former newspaper reporter, magazine editor, and ESL teacher, he now researches and edits guidebooks for Rick Steves' Europe. He lives in Seattle with his wife Julie.

CONTRIBUTOR
Gene Openshaw

Gene has co-authored a dozen Rick Steves books, specializing in writing walks and tours of Europe's cities, museums, and cultural sights. He also contributes to Rick's public television series, produces tours for Rick Steves Audio Europe, and is a regular guest on Rick's public radio show. Outside of the travel world, Gene has co-authored *The Seattle Joke Book*. As a composer, Gene has written a full-length opera called *Matter* (soundtrack available on Amazon), a violin sonata, and dozens of songs. He lives near Seattle with his daughter, enjoys giving presentations on art and history, and roots for the Mariners in good times and bad.

ACKNOWLEDGMENTS
The co-authors would like to thank David Price, who lives in Avignon and is a fine source of information about key sights in Provence.

Avalon Travel
a member of the Perseus Books Group
1700 Fourth Street
Berkeley, CA 94710

ISBN 978-1-63121-197-3
ISSN 1546-2749

For the latest on Rick's lectures, guidebooks, tours, public radio show, and public television series, contact Rick Steves' Europe, Inc., 130 Fourth Avenue North, Edmonds, WA 98020, tel. 425/771-8303, www.ricksteves.com, rick@ricksteves.com.

Rick Steves' Europe
Special Publications Manager: Risa Laib
Managing Editor: Jennifer Madison Davis
Editors: Glenn Eriksen, Tom Griffin, Katherine Gustafson, Suzanne Kotz, Cathy Lu, John Pierce, Carrie Shepherd
Editorial & Production Assistant: Jessica Shaw
Editorial Intern: Chelsea Wing
Researcher: Tom Griffin
Contributor: Gene Openshaw
Maps & Graphics: David C. Hoerlein, Sandra Hundacker, Lauren Mills, Mary Rostad

Avalon Travel
Senior Editor and Series Manager: Madhu Prasher
Editor: Jamie Andrade
Associate Editor: Maggie Ryan
Copy Editor: Patrick Collins
Proofreader: Kelly Lydick
Indexer: Beatrice Wikander
Production & Typesetting: Rue Flaherty and Tabitha Lahr
Cover Design: Kimberly Glyder Design
Maps & Graphics: Kat Bennett, Mike Morgenfeld

Photo Credits
Front Cover: Stone arched gate to the medieval village of Lacoste with Mont Ventoux in the background © Danita Delimont/Getty Images
Title Page: Flowers © Dominic Arizona Bonuccelli
Front Matter Color: page viii, Côtes du Rhône Wine Loop © Steve Smith
Additional Photography: Dominic Arizona Bonuccelli, Rich Earl, Trish Feaster, Cameron Hewitt, David C. Hoerlein, Gene Openshaw, Paul Orcutt, Michael Potter, Steve Smith, Robyn Stencil, Rick Steves, Wikimedia Commons (PD-Art/PD-US), Dorian Yates (photos are used by permission and are the property of the original copyright owners).